A Frequency Dictionary of Japanese

A Frequency Dictionary of Japanese is an invaluable tool for all learners of Japanese, providing a list of the 5,000 most commonly used words in the language.

Based on combined corpora of over 107 million words—covering spoken and written, fiction and non-fiction registers—this dictionary provides the user with a detailed frequency-based list, as well as alphabetical and part-of-speech indexes.

All entries in the frequency list feature the English equivalent and a sample sentence with English translation. The dictionary also contains 25 thematically organized lists of frequently used words on a variety of topics such as food, weather, occupations and leisure. Numerous bar charts are also included to highlight the phonetic and spelling variants across register.

A Frequency Dictionary of Japanese enables students of all levels to maximize their study of Japanese vocabulary in an efficient and engaging way. It is also an excellent resource for teachers of the language.

Yukio Tono is Professor at the Graduate School of Global Studies, Tokyo University of Foreign Studies. **Makoto Yamazaki** is Associate Professor at the Department of Corpus Studies, the National Institute for Japanese Language and Linguistics. **Kikuo Maekawa** is Professor at the Department of Corpus Studies, the National Institute for Japanese Language and Linguistics.

Routledge Frequency Dictionaries

General Editors:
Paul Rayson, *Lancaster University, UK*
Mark Davies, *Brigham Young University, USA*

Editorial Board:
Michael Barlow, *University of Auckland, New Zealand*
Geoffrey Leech, *Lancaster University, UK*
Barbara Lewandowska-Tomaszczyk, *University of Lodz, Poland*
Josef Schmied, *Chemnitz University of Technology, Germany*
Andrew Wilson, *Lancaster University, UK*
Adam Kilgarriff, *Lexicography MasterClass Ltd and University of Sussex, UK*
Hongying Tao, *University of California at Los Angeles, USA*
Chris Tribble, *King's College London, UK*

Other books in the series:
A Frequency Dictionary of Arabic
A Frequency Dictionary of Mandarin Chinese
A Frequency Dictionary of Czech
A Frequency Dictionary of American English
A Frequency Dictionary of French
A Frequency Dictionary of German
A Frequency Dictionary of Portuguese
A Frequency Dictionary of Russian (forthcoming)
A Frequency Dictionary of Spanish

The Frequency Dictionaries are all available as data CDs. These CD versions are specifically designed for use by corpus and computational linguists. They provide the frequency corpus in a tab-delimited format allowing users the flexibility to process the material for their own research purposes.

A Frequency Dictionary of Japanese

Core vocabulary for learners

Yukio Tono, Makoto Yamazaki and Kikuo Maekawa

LONDON AND NEW YORK

First published 2013
by Routledge
2 Park Square, Milton Park, Abingdon, Oxon OX14 4RN

Simultaneously published in the USA and Canada
by Routledge
711 Third Avenue, New York, NY 10017

Routledge is an imprint of the Taylor & Francis Group, an informa business

© 2013 Yukio Tono, Makoto Yamazaki and Kikuo Maekawa

The right of Yukio Tono, Makoto Yamazaki and Kikuo Maekawa to be identified as authors of this work has been asserted by them in accordance with sections 77 and 78 of the Copyright, Designs and Patents Act 1988.

All rights reserved. No part of this book may be reprinted or reproduced or utilised in any form or by any electronic, mechanical, or other means, now known or hereafter invented, including photocopying and recording, or in any information storage or retrieval system, without permission in writing from the publishers.

Trademark notice: Product or corporate names may be trademarks or registered trademarks, and are used only for identification and explanation without intent to infringe.

British Library Cataloguing in Publication Data
A catalogue record for this book is available from the British Library

Library of Congress Cataloging in Publication Data
Tono, Yukio.
  A frequency dictionary of Japanese : core vocabulary for learners / Yukio Tono, Kikuo Maekawa and Makoto Yamazaki.
    p. cm. – (Routledge frequency dictionaries)
  Includes bibliographical references and index.
  1. Japanese language – Word frequency – Dictionaries. 2. Japanese language – Dictionaries.
  3. Japanese language – Textbooks for foreign speakers – English. I. Makawa, Kikuo. II. Yamazaki, Makato.
  III. Title.
  PL685.T593 2013
  495.6′321 – dc23

2012021445

ISBN: 978-0-415-61012-4 (hbk)
ISBN: 978-0-415-61013-1 (pbk)
ISBN: 978-0-415-60104-7 (CD)

Typeset in Parisine
by Graphicraft Limited, Hong Kong

Printed and bound in Great Britain by
TJ International Ltd, Padstow, Cornwall

Contents

Thematic vocabulary lists | **vi**

Series preface | **vii**

Acknowledgments | **ix**

Abbreviations | **x**

Introduction | **1**

References | **9**

Frequency index | **10**

Alphabetical index | **247**

Part of speech index | **302**

Word types (origins) | **357**

Thematic vocabulary lists

1 Animals | **20**
2 Body | **29**
3 Clothing | **38**
4 Colors | **47**
5 Countries | **55**
6 Emotions | **65**
7 Family | **77**
8 Food | **86**
9 Furniture | **96**
10 Greetings | **105**
11 House | **114**
12 Leisure | **123**
13 Occupations | **132**

14 Plants | **141**
15 School | **151**
16 Shops | **160**
17 Sports | **169**
18 Taste | **178**
19 Time | **188**
20 Transportation | **197**
21 Weather | **206**
22 Words including letters of the alphabet | **215**
23 *o-/go-* (Honorifics) | **224**
24 Honorific expressions | **233**
25 Numbers/numerals | **243**

Series preface

Frequency information has a central role to play in learning a language. Nation (1990) showed that the 4,000–5,000 most frequent words account for up to 95 per cent of a written text and the 1,000 most frequent words account for 85 per cent of speech. Although Nation's results were only for English, they do provide clear evidence that, when employing frequency as a general guide for vocabulary learning, it is possible to acquire a lexicon which will serve a learner well most of the time. There are two caveats to bear in mind here. First, counting words is not as straightforward as it might seem. Gardner (2007) highlights the problems that multiple word meanings, the presence of multiword items, and grouping words into families or lemmas present in counting and analysing words. Second, frequency data contained in frequency dictionaries should never act as the only information source to guide a learner. Frequency information is nonetheless a very good starting point, and one which may produce rapid benefits. It therefore seems rational to prioritise learning the words that you are likely to hear and read most often. That is the philosophy behind this series of dictionaries.

Lists of words and their frequencies have long been available for teachers and learners of language. For example, Thorndike (1921, 1932) and Thorndike and Lorge (1944) produced word frequency books with counts of word occurrences in texts used in the education of American children. Michael West's *General Service List of English Words* (1953) was primarily aimed at foreign learners of English. More recently, with the aid of efficient computer software and very large bodies of language data (called corpora), researchers have been able to provide more sophisticated frequency counts from both written text and transcribed speech. One important feature of the resulting frequencies presented in this series is that they are derived from recently collected language data. The earlier lists for English included samples from, for example, Austen's *Pride and Prejudice* and Defoe's *Robinson Crusoe*, thus they could no longer represent present-day language in any sense.

Frequency data derived from a large representative corpus of a language brings students closer to language as it is used in real life as opposed to textbook language (which often distorts the frequencies of features in a language, see Ljung, 1990). The information in these dictionaries is presented in a number of formats to allow users to access the data in different ways. So, for example, if you would prefer not to simply drill down through the word frequency list, but would rather focus on verbs for example, the part of speech index will allow you to focus on just the most frequent verbs. Given that verbs typically account for 20 per cent of all words in a language, this may be a good strategy. Also, a focus on function words may be equally rewarding—60 per cent of speech in English is composed of a mere 50 function words. The series also provides information of use to the language teacher. The idea that frequency information may have a role to play in syllabus design is not new (see, for example, Sinclair and Renouf, 1988). However, to date it has been difficult for those teaching languages other than English to use frequency information in syllabus design because of a lack of data.

Frequency information should not be studied to the exclusion of other contextual and situational knowledge about language use and we may even doubt the validity of frequency information derived from large corpora. It is interesting to note that Alderson (2007) found that corpus frequencies may not match a native speaker's intuition about estimates of word frequency and that a set of estimates of word frequencies collected from language experts varied widely. Thus corpus-derived frequencies are still the best current estimate of a word's importance that a learner will come across. Around the time of the construction of the first machine-readable corpora, Halliday (1971: 344) stated that "a rough indication of frequencies is often just what is needed". Our aim in this series is to provide as accurate as possible estimates of word frequencies.

Paul Rayson and Mark Davies
Lancaster and Provo, 2008

References

Alderson, J. C. (2007) "Judging the frequency of English words." *Applied Linguistics*, 28 (3): 383–409.

Gardner, D. (2007) "Validating the construct of Word in applied corpus-based vocabulary research: a critical survey." *Applied Linguistics*, 28, pp. 241–65.

Halliday, M. A. K. (1971) "Linguistic functions and literary style." In S. Chatman (ed.) *Style: A Symposium*. Oxford University Press, pp. 330–65.

Ljung, M. (1990) *A Study of TEFL Vocabulary*. Almqvist & Wiksell International, Stockholm.

Nation, I. S. P. (1990) *Teaching and Learning Vocabulary*. Heinle & Heinle, Boston.

Sinclair, J. M. and Renouf, A. (1988) "A lexical syllabus for language learning." In R. Carter and M. McCarthy (eds) *Vocabulary and Language Teaching*. Longman, London, pp. 140–58.

Thorndike, E. (1921) *Teacher's Word Book*. Columbia Teachers College, New York.

Thorndike, E. (1932) *A Teacher's Word Book of 20,000 Words*. Columbia University Press, New York.

Thorndike, E. and Lorge, I. (1944) *The Teacher's Word Book of 30,000 Words*. Columbia University Press, New York.

West, M. (1953) *A General Service List of English Words*. Longman, London.

Acknowledgments

We are first and foremost grateful to Paul Rayson and Mark Davies for their guidance and suggestions throughout the project. We thank Adam Kilgarriff for reviewing our draft proposal and giving us useful suggestions. We are especially indebted to Yukari Honda, a postgraduate student at Tokyo University of Foreign Studies, who has worked closely with the first author to organize the team of research assistants in writing the draft entries. Without her dedication, this work would not have been possible.

We are also indebted to a number of research assistants who helped with this project: Yukari Honda, Makiko Kobayashi, Kanako Maebo, Kimie Abo, Satomi Kurusu, Tomoyo Fujita, Atsuko Yamashita, and Fumiko Watanabe.

Special thanks to the National Institute for Japanese Language and Linguistics for the use of the Balanced Corpus of Contemporary Written Japanese (BCCWJ) and the Corpus of Spontaneous Japanese (CSJ). Thanks also go to the Japan Society for the Promotion of Science for their financial support.

Yukio Tono
Makoto Yamazaki
Kikuo Maekawa

Abbreviations

Part of speech		Example
adn.	adnominal	30 その sono *adn.* that
adv.	adverb	39 そう soo *adv.* so, such
aux.	auxiliary	50 せる seru *aux.* CAUSATIVE
conj.	conjunction	31 けれど keredo *conj.* though, although
cp.	compound	13 ている, てる te iru, te ru *cp.* CONTINUATION
i-adj.	*i*-adjective	47 無い nai *i-adj.* There is no . . . , no . . .
interj.	interjection	18 えー, ええ ee *interj.* eh?, what?; well, yes
n.	noun	17 事 koto *n.* thing
na-adj.	*na*-adjective	121 風 fuu *na-adj.* style, type, way, like
num.	numeral	1094 十 juu *num.* ten
p.	particle	11 も mo *p.* too, also
p. case	case particle	12 で de *p. case* in; at; from; by
p. conj.	conjunctive particle	8 て te *p. conj.* REASON
p. disc.	discourse particle	26 ね ne *p. disc.* isn't it?, don't you?
prefix	prefix	2301 御 o *prefix* POLITENESS
pron.	pronoun	40 何 nani *pron.* what; something; anything; nothing
suffix	suffix	1694 等 tou *suffix* and so on
v.	verb	19 言う iu, yuu *v.* say, speak, talk

Register		Example
BK	books	1 の no *p. case* of; in; at; for; by
		• 彼はこの大学の学生だ。— He is a student at this university. 47078 | 0.98 | BK
NM	newspapers & magazines	564 午後 gogo *n.* afternoon, p.m.
		• 午後、会議がある。— There is a meeting in the afternoon. 118 | 0.37 | NM
OF	official documents	106 ておる te oru *cp.* CONTINUATION (polite)
		• お返事をお待ちしております。— I look forward to hearing from you at your earliest convenience. 1017 | 0.63 | OF
SP	spoken	23 まー, まあ maa *interj.* Wow!, Oh my God!
		• まー、なんて素晴らしいんでしょう。— Wow! That's amazing! 6950 | 0.04 | SP
WB	web	14 です desu *aux.* COPULA (polite)
		• 彼は独身です。— He is single. 9828 | 0.83 | WB

Introduction

The value of a frequency dictionary of Japanese

A Frequency Dictionary of Japanese provides a list of core vocabulary for learners of Japanese as a second or foreign language. Like other volumes in the *Routledge Frequency Dictionary* series, it gives the most up-to-date, reliable frequency guidelines for common vocabulary in spoken and written Japanese, which helps learners of Japanese set practical goals for acquiring both productive and receptive knowledge of vocabulary. For teachers, it provides a valuable pedagogical tool with which to organize their teaching syllabus, prepare teaching materials, and assess their learners' vocabulary level and size.

Japanese is rather unique in its linguistic status. It is one of the very popular foreign languages that people want to learn. According to the 2006 Survey Report by the Japan Foundation, there are approximately 3 million students studying Japanese at 13,000 institutions in 130 countries. This does not include people learning Japanese via the TV or radio, so the potential number would be much larger. Despite such a huge demand, Japanese as a language has been very difficult to describe systematically. We use three different types of characters: two sets of Japanese syllabaries, *hiragana* and *katakana*, and a set of Chinese characters. The word spelled "Seiko" in English could be a person's name (聖子) if the final vowel "o" is short, or a word meaning *success* (成功), or the name of the famous watch brand in katakana (セイコー)! Also we have three sources of word origins: *wago* (native Japanese words), *kango* (words adopted from Chinese), and *gairaigo* (words adopted from Western languages). It is useful to know what types of words are important to learn. Therefore, a frequency dictionary like the present one will be a great resource for teachers and learners to find which words are used for which meanings in speech and writing.

The shortage of such good resources is partly due to the lack of good data. In Japan, we have very advanced technologies in natural language processing (NLP), but people have not shown any interest in the so-called "balanced corpus" until recently. Most NLP work has been carried out on a large body of newspaper texts, and is thus not suitable for educational purposes. There has been very little exchange of information between humanities and information sciences until the turn of the century. The advent of computers and corpus linguistics, however, has changed the whole picture recently, and the National Institute of Japanese Language and Linguistics (NINJAL) finally completed the Balanced Corpus of Contemporary Written Japanese, BCCWJ, in 2011. We therefore feel that it is quite timely to publish this title as part of the Routledge Frequency Dictionary series.

Contents of the dictionary

This frequency dictionary is designed to meet the needs of students and teachers of Japanese, as well as those who are interested in the computational processing of Japanese. The main index contains the 5,000 most common words in contemporary written and spoken Japanese, ranging from very basic core grammatical words such as the particles *ga* or *wa*, to more intermediate and advanced vocabulary. Each entry in the main index contains the word itself in Japanese orthography, a romanized headword, its part(s) of speech, an English equivalent, an example sentence in Japanese, an English translation of the illustrative example, and summary statistics about the usage of that word.

Aside from the main frequency listing, there are also indexes that sort the entries by Japanese alphabetical order (*gojuuon*), parts of speech, and different word types, "*wago* (native Japanese word)," "*kango* (Sino-Japanese word)," and "*gairaigo* (loan word)." The Japanese alphabetical order will be very helpful for students who, for example, come across Japanese words in reading and want to check how common the word is and whether it is worth learning. The part of speech indexes could be of benefit to understand how the grammar system of Japanese works or to learn by focusing selectively on particular parts of speech. The list of different word types will inform the readers of very important lexical characteristics of Japanese. Finally, there are a number of thematically related lists (foods, greetings, emotions, etc.) as well as honorific expressions, all of which should enhance the learning experience. The expectation, then, is that this dictionary will greatly help the efforts of a wide range of students and teachers who are involved in the acquisition and teaching of Japanese vocabulary.

Previous frequency dictionaries of Japanese

As far as the Japanese language is concerned, no frequency dictionary has been published on a commercial basis. This does not mean, however, that no statistical analysis has ever been conducted on the language. On the contrary, Japanese is one of the languages whose lexical characteristics have been most extensively examined using statistical methods.

A series of statistical word surveys have been conducted by the National Language Research Institute (NLRI) (which changed its English title to the National Institute of Japanese Language and Linguistics (NINJAL) in 2001), founded for the scientific study of the Japanese language in 1948. The NLRI lexical surveys covered various registers like newspapers (published in 1952, 1959 and 1970–73), magazines from different genres (1953, 1957, 1962, 1987, and 2005), school textbooks (1983–84, 1986–97) and TV programs (1995, 1997), and in these surveys, samples were randomly selected from rigidly defined statistical populations so that techniques of statistical inference could be applied to the data.

There is, however, an important drawback common to all the surveys: the lack of consistent definition of a "word" for sampling and analysis purposes. Since it is a so-called agglutinative language, it is difficult, if not impossible, to find a unitary definition of "word" for Japanese. For example, *kokuritsukokugokenkyuujo* (the Japanese title for the NLRI) could be analyzed in at least four different ways: as four words—*kokuritsu* (national), *kokugo* (national language), *kenkyuu* (research) and *jo* (institute); as three words—*kokuritsu*, *kokugo* and *kenkyuujo*; as two words—*kokuritsu* and *kokugokenkyuujo*; and as one word.

In the surveys mentioned above, different definitions of "word" were used according to the purposes of the surveys. As a result, it was virtually impossible to cross-compare the results obtained in different surveys. As will be explained in the following sections, recent corpora employ dual part of speech (POS) analyses to overcome this difficulty. Another drawback of the NLRI word surveys is that they lack control of the timeline as a sampling frame. Due to the different sampling frames in terms of years of publication, it was impossible to make a valid comparison between newspaper surveys and those of textbooks.

The last problem of the NLRI word surveys is the non-availability of the sampled data. Every time the NLRI conducted a survey, the results were published in the form of word frequency lists, but the data has never been publicly available outside the NLRI. This seriously constrained the development of corpus-based analysis of the Japanese language. The NLRI changed its data handling policy in the mid-1990s. Since then, a series of Japanese corpora have been compiled and released for public use. The two corpora used for the compilation of this frequency dictionary are recent products of NINJAL.

The Corpus

Two corpora are used as the resource for this frequency dictionary: the Corpus of Spontaneous Japanese (CSJ) and the Balanced Corpus of Contemporary Written Japanese (BCCWJ).

CSJ

The CSJ was compiled during the years 1999–2004 through the collaboration of NINJAL and NICT (National Institute for Informatics and Communications Technology) as a resource for the development of an automatic speech recognition system for spontaneous speech. The CSJ is a richly annotated corpus of 7.5 million words or 652 hours. In addition to the digitized speech and the transcriptions including various disfluency phenomena, the complete transcription texts are annotated with respect to the POS information and clause-type information. Moreover, segmental and prosodic annotations are provided for a subset of the CSJ called the CSJ-Core (including about half a million words or 44 hours).

The speech recorded in the CSJ is so-called common, or standard, Japanese, a variety shared widely by educated people and used in more or less public settings. Speakers who had clear dialectal features in their morphology or segmental phonology were excluded.

There are two main sources of spontaneous speech for the CSJ: Academic Presentation Speech (APS) and Simulated Public Speaking (SPS). APS are live recordings of academic presentations in nine different academic societies covering the fields of engineering, social sciences, and the humanities. SPS, on the other hand, are recordings of speeches by paid laypeople, of about 10–12 minutes, on everyday topics such as "the happiest/saddest memory of my life," "the town I live in," "commentaries on recent news," and so forth. SPS were presented in front of small audiences and in a relatively relaxed atmosphere. The age and sex of SPS speakers were balanced as much as possible.

As predicted, there is a difference in the word distribution between the APS and SPS samples. The lexical items of the APS include technical terms (mostly compounds) used in various fields of science and technology, and the speaking style is relatively formal. The lexical items of the SPS, on the other hand, include much more everyday expressions, and the speaking style is comparatively casual.

Table 1 Size of the CSJ

REGISTER	# SUW	# LUW
Academic Presentation Speech	3,279,364	2,654,823
Simulated Public Speaking	3,605,729	3,115,302
Miscellaneous	640,032	543,749
TOTAL	7,525,125	6,313,874

All samples in the CSJ were dually POS analyzed using two definitions of "word," namely, short unit word (SUW) and long unit word (LUW). In the case of *kokuritsukokugokenkyuujo* cited above, the four-word analysis corresponds to the SUW, and, the one-word analysis corresponds to the LUW. Table 2 shows the number of running SUWs and LUWs in the APS and SPS of the CSJ. The last register, entitled "miscellaneous," includes samples of dialogues (interviews on the content of the APS and SPS, task-oriented dialogues and free dialogues) and reading aloud of the transcriptions of the APS and/or the SPS previously spoken by the same speakers.

Table 2 Comparison of examples in the SUW and LUW POS analyses

GLOSS	SUW Lemma	SUW POS	LUW Lemma	LUW POS
binaural	両耳	Noun	両耳受聴	Noun
perception	受聴	Noun		
PLACE	に	Particle	によって	Particle
be based upon	拠る	Verb		
CONJUNCTION	て	Particle		
obtain	得る	Verb	得る	Verb
information	情報	Noun	情報	Noun
PLACE	に	Particle	に	Particle
TOPIC	は	Particle	は	Particle
power	パワー	Noun	パワースペクトル情報	Noun
spectrum	スペクトル	Noun		
information	情報	Noun		
and	と	Particle	と	Particle
binaural	両耳	Noun	両耳間位相差	Noun
between	間	Suffix		
phrase	位相	Noun		
difference	差	Noun		
NOMINATIVE	が	Particle	が	Particle
exist	ある	Verb	ある	Verb
POLITE	ます	Auxiliary	ます	Auxiliary

Note that LUW covers not only compound nouns and verbs but also compound particles. For example, *"niyotte* (by, because of)" is analyzed as a compound particle in the LUW analysis, but as three separate units in the SUW analysis; the case particle *ni* followed by the adverbial form of verb *yoru* (be based upon), which is followed by a conjunction particle *te*. Table 2 compares the SUW and LUW analyses of the same phrase taken from an APS sample:「両耳受聴によって得る情報にはパワースペクトル情報と両耳間位相差があります」 (the information obtained by binaural perception includes power-spectrum information and binaural phrase difference information). This phrase consists of 20 SUWs and 12 LUWs. Note that SUWs that are not part of larger compounds are analyzed as independent LUWs. See, for example, the last three lines of Table 2.

BCCWJ

The BCCWJ is the first balanced corpus of written Japanese, and was compiled during the years 2006–11 in the NINJAL. It consists of three main subcorpora: publication, library, and special-purpose. The publication subcorpus consists of texts randomly sampled from the populations of books, magazines, and newspapers published during the years 2001–5, whose total size is about 35 million words. The library subcorpus contains samples of books found in public libraries. The statistical population consists of the totality of books that are registered in more than 13 public libraries in Tokyo; the size of this population is almost equal to that of the books in the publication subcorpus – about 30 million words. Finally, the special-purpose subcorpus covers various registers that are indispensable for the language planning studies of the NINJAL, but not covered by the publication and library subcorpora. This subcorpus contains samples of texts in governmental white papers, school textbooks (covering elementary, junior and senior high schools), various reports issued by local governments for public relations purposes, bestselling books, texts on the Web (bulletin board *Yahoo! Chiebukuro* and *Yahoo! blog*), poetry, law, and the minutes of the National Diet. All these samples are randomly chosen from these populations. See Table 3 for more details.

Although the BCCWJ is designed as a corpus of contemporary Japanese, the timeline covered by the corpus is not necessarily narrow, and the length of the period differs depending on the register. Figure 1 shows the difference in temporal coverage of the 13 registers. Registers were labeled using the abbreviations shown in Table 3 below.

Table 3 Size of the BCCWJ

SUBCORPUS	REGISTER	# SAMPLE	# SUW	# LUW
Publication Subcorpus	Books (PB)	10,117	28,552,283	22,857,932
	Magazines (PM)	1,996	4,4444,492	3,480,831
	Newspapers (PN)	1,473	1,370,233	997,535
Library Subcorpus	Books (LB)	10,551	30,377,866	25,092,641
Special-Purpose Subcorpus	White papers (OW)	1,500	4,882,812	3,100,617
	Textbooks (OT)	412	928,448	746,170
	Local government reports (OP)	354	3,755,161	2,308,450
	Bestselling books (OB)	1,390	3,742,261	3,185,745
	Internet bulletin board texts (OC)	91,445	10,256,877	8,613,610
	Blog texts (OY)	52,680	10,194,143	8,285,554
	Poetry (OV)	252	225,273	202,425
	Law (OL)	346	1,079,146	706,313
	Minutes of National Diet (OM)	159	5,102,469	4,007,842
TOTAL		172,675	104,911,464	83,585,665

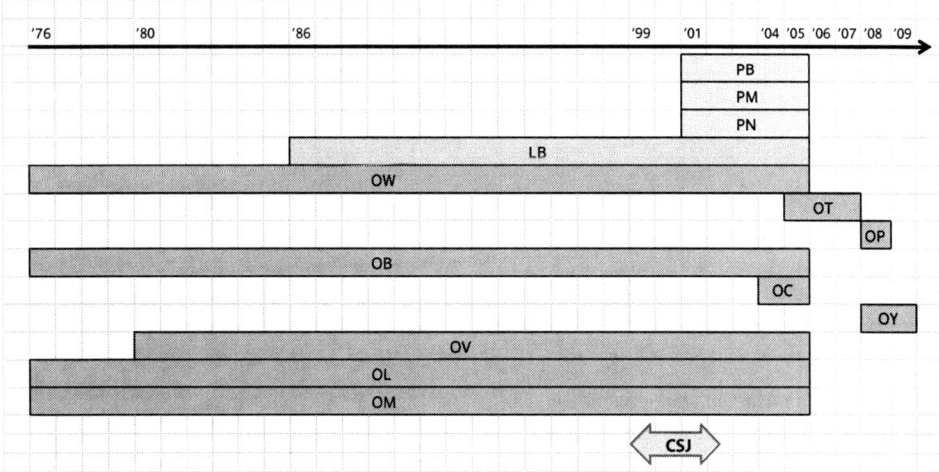

Figure 1 Temporal coverage of the BCCWJ registers

Target vocabulary identification and description

Corpus balance
Based on the CSJ and BCCWJ, a breakdown of the spoken and written components of the corpus was determined. The section of simulated public speaking (SPS) was used from the CSJ, because this was more closely related to natural spoken language used in daily situations. For the written section, the entire BCCWJ was used. As regards the unit of morphological analysis, LUW was used, which is comprised of a set of compounds as a word unit, e.g. "自動 | 車 (car)" or "飛行 | 機 (airplane)". Whilst short unit words are often used for normal morphological analysis, they cause serious problems in decomposing meaningful units into smaller morphemes, which is not often useful for teaching and learning purposes. The version of BCCWJ used for this dictionary was as of June 2011, and is slightly different in the total running words from the DVD version released in December 2011.

Lemmatisation
The headword as lemma was determined in the following way. First, each lemma was identified if base forms and their pronunciations, and parts of speech were all identical. Frequency counts are based on this notion of lemma. Then the following further adjustments were made. All the items that have the same base forms and pronunciations but different parts of speech were regarded as the same lemma. This is the same way that most Japanese dictionaries treat headwords. Thus, those words whose stems are nouns, such as "解決 (*kaiketsu*: solution)" but behave as verbs when *suru* is attached to the end, e.g. "解決する (*kaiketsu-suru*: solve)" were classified as the same lemmas. Variant forms such as the following were all grouped under the standard forms:

(i)   polite forms: *okangaeitadaku* for "*kangaeru* (think)"
(ii) potential forms: *yareru* for "*yaru* (do)"
(iii) forms with prefixes *o-* or *go-*: *okaasan* for "*kaasan* (mother)"
(iv) forms with suffixes *-san*, *-sama*, and *-chan*: *musume-san* for "*musume* (daughter)"

The words that appeared in the original frequency list but were considered inappropriate for the wordlist were deleted, e.g. archaic words, single letters of the English alphabet, specific company names (e.g. SONY), personal names (e.g. 信長), English words (e.g. アンド), too domain-specific terms, etc.

Frequency and dispersion
Word frequencies of the CSJ and BCCWJ were both normalized to per million words, and the average of the normalized frequencies for the two corpora with equal balance (50 percent each) was used for the

Table 4 Text registers

Register	BCCWJ-register (see Table 3 for abbreviations)
Books [BK]	LB/ PB/ OB/ OV
Web [WB]	OC/ OY
Official documents [OF]	OW/OL/OM/OT
Newspapers & magazines [NM]	PN/PM/OP
Spoken [SP]	SPS in CSJ

standard frequency index. In order to provide information on register variations, the five registers were defined based on the 13 subcorpora from BCCWJ and CSJ (see Table 4):

For all 5,000 entry words, log-likelihood values were calculated across the five registers above, and any words that were significantly high in log-likelihood values, e.g. within the top 50 in the list, were specified with a special register code, e.g. [+BK], showing the word's distribution across registers.

There are many dispersion measures available (see Gries 2008 for review), but in this book, Carroll's D2 were used. This will take the value ranging from 0 to 1, where 1 means that the word is most evenly distributed.

rank	lemma	form	pos	English	pmw	disp.
32	から	kara	p.case	from	4739.328	0.999
2130	引き継ぐ	hikitsugu	v.	continue	26.779	0.500
4293	落札者	rakusatsu-sha	n.	bidder	10.573	0.033

Developing associated information

Parts of speech were identified in the following procedures. First, a morphological analyzer called MeCab[1] with a dictionary called UniDic[2], specially developed for the BCCWJ project, were used for SUW analysis. These SUWs were then filtered by a tool called Comainu[3] and made into LUWs. The part-of-speech mapping list between SUWs and LUWs was applied to the output of Comainu. Glossing the terms was carried out manually. An effort was made to give the most representative meaning(s) among sometimes too many candidates for translation equivalents. Illustrative examples were again supplied manually, and an effort was made to make the context clear, self-contained, and reflecting the core meaning of the word, based on the available examples from the corpus data. Sometimes finding good English translations was difficult because the one-to-one translation equivalent for the Japanese headword does not always match the expressions used in the English translations of the Japanese examples. Every effort was made to match the two, but different expressions were sometimes used for natural translations of the illustrative examples.

Finally, we compiled the thematic lists using both automatic and manual techniques. While we worked on the creation of English translations, we annotated the list for thematic categories, such as food and weather. We also consulted the previous titles of the Frequency Dictionary series, because many of the thematic lists overlap across languages.

In conclusion, this dictionary is carefully tuned to the needs of learners and teachers of Japanese, fully exploiting the most advanced information from the newly developed Japanese corpora, BCCWJ and CSJ. We are confident that this dictionary will provide users with one of the most reliable resources for learning Japanese.

The main frequency index

The main index in this dictionary is a rank-ordered listing of the top 5,000 words (lemma) in Japanese, starting with the most frequent word and progressing through to the lowest one. The following information is given for each entry:

> rank frequency (1, 2, 3, . . .), lemma, romanized word, part of speech
> English gloss, illustrative example, English translation of the example
> normalised frequency, dispersion (0.00 – 1.00), (indication of register variation)

As a concrete example, let us look at the entry for the verb *omou*:

> **34 思う** *omou v* to think
> • 私はそう思いません。— I don't think so.
> 4599 | 0.88

This entry shows that word number 34 in our rank order list is the verb 思う. The romanized version of the entry is provided for recognition purposes. The English gloss "to think" is provided next. One illustrative example is shown, which shows the related negative forms of this verb with a polite form-ending, "思いません". An English translation for the example then appears. The last line of the entry shows the average normalised frequency (per million) based on the BCCWJ and CSJ (4,599 tokens), and the dispersion (0.88 in this case).

Here are some additional notes for the items appearing in the entries.

The part(s) of speech
More than two parts of speech can be found for some words in the corpus. Due to the space limitations, the two most frequent parts of speech were selected in this case. We tried to offer corresponding English glosses for each part of speech, but sometimes the information was omitted when the users are expected to figure out glosses on their own.

Besides general adjectival usage, *i*-adjectives and *na*-adjectives can also be used as adverbs, modifying verbs. This usage is a regular, additional feature of *i*- and *na*-adjectives, so we omitted this adverbial information from POS, with a few exceptions, for the sake of brevity.

The English gloss
The gloss is meant to be indicative only—it is not a complete listing of all possibilities. Some words are polysemous, and very difficult to describe in one line. These meanings are not included in the glosses since the main focus in this dictionary is frequency information from the corpus.

The Japanese illustrative examples
Illustrative examples were invented by examining corpus examples. Many examples show inflected forms of the entries, which might look slightly confusing for beginning-level learners of Japanese. However, we are aware that the selection of examples would become extremely difficult and unnatural if we stuck only to the base form of the entry. Thus, we aimed for the natural usage of the entry words in example sentences. In many cases, the subjects or proper names in the examples had to be replaced by general pronouns or popular places in Japan, which sometimes made the examples a bit awkward, but every effort was made to make them sound natural. If the entry has multiple parts of speech, an example was given only for the most common part of speech and usage. For the entries of numerals such as "三" or "七," examples were designed by using the entry items independently without other compounds, but sometimes compound expressions had to be used to make the examples more user-friendly.

The English translation of the examples
Whilst an attempt was made to project the register, style, and structure of the source example into its translation, an English translation sometimes involves the use of words which do not exactly match the English gloss. In many cases, we tried to avoid such mismatches, but there are some cases in which we gave up using the same English glosses in the translations of Japanese examples.

The statistical and register information
The last line of each entry has two numbers divided by a vertical bar. The first is the average of the normalized frequencies per million words, taken from BCCWJ and CSJ respectively. The second is the dispersion value. Some words also have a register code that specifies the word's distribution across registers. We provide only the positive value for the five registers: books, webs, official documents, newspapers and magazines, and spoken.

Thematic Vocabulary ("call-out boxes")

A number of thematically grouped words are provided in tables that are placed throughout the main frequency-based index. These include thematic lists related to the body, food, family, weather, professions, nationalities, colors, emotions, clothing, greetings, sports, and several other semantic domains. There are also lists with complicated, thus hard-to-master, phonetic and orthographic variants across spoken and written texts. Other tables give data on loan words, honorific expressions, and words with *o-* and *go-* prefixes.

Alphabetical and part of speech indexes

The Japanese alphabetical index gives a listing of all the entries in the frequency index, ordered by the

Japanese ordering of kana, called *gojuuon*. Each entry in this chapter includes: (1) the lemma, (2) the part of speech, (3) a basic English equivalent, and (4) the word's ranking in this dictionary.

The part of speech index lists the words from the frequency index, this time arranged by parts of speech. Each category lists the lemmas in decreasing order of frequency.

Word type index

The last section of the dictionary provides the frequency index words classified by their word types or origins. As mentioned previously, the Japanese language has three sources of word origins: *wago* (native Japanese words), *kango* (words adopted from Chinese), and *gairaigo* (words adopted from Western languages). In this section, the first 1,000 most frequent words are classified into the above three word categories, (1) *wago*, (2) *kango*, (3) *gairaigo*, as well as (4) *konseigo*, a blend of the three types, and (5) proper nouns, with the original ranking information.

Notes on romanization

Romanization of Japanese is largely based upon the so-called Hepburn system. Japanese syllables (or morae) サ, シ, ス, セ, ソ, タ, チ, ツ, テ, ト, ハ, ヒ, フ, ヘ, ホ, ザ, ジ, ズ, ゼ, and ゾ are romanized respectively as "sa", "shi", "su", "se", "so", "ta", "chi", "tsu", "te", "to", "ha", "hi", "fu", "he", "ho", "za", "ji", "zu", "ze", and "zo". So-called *youon* (palatalized syllables) like キャ, シャ, チャ, ニャ, ヒャ, ミャ, リャ, ギャ, ジャ, ビャ, and ピャ are represented as "kya", "sha", "cha", "nya", "hya", "mya", "rya", "gya", "ja", "bya", and "pya" respectively. Note also that ヤ, ユ, and ヨ are romanized as "ya", "yu", and "yo".

Sokuon (geminate) is represented by doubling the relevant consonant, as in *yappari* (やっぱり), *chotto* (ちょっと), *shikkari* (しっかり), and *beddo* (ベッド).

Romanization of *Hatsuon* (syllabic nasal) is slightly different from the genuine Hepburn system. It is consistently represented by a letter "n", as in *mikan* (ミカン), *konbanwa* (こんばんは), *kantan* (簡単 かんたん), and *manga* (マンガ). When there is a morphological boundary between a hatsuon and the following morphonem beginning with a vowel, an apostrophe is inserted after the hatsuon, as in *han'i* (範囲 はんい), *ren'ai* (恋愛 れんあい), and *han'ei* (反映 はんえい).

Another important deviation from the traditional Hepburn system is the representation of long vowels and vowel sequences. In this respect, the romanization adopted in this dictionary follows the convention of present-day Japanese orthography (*Gendai kanazukai*). The long vowels /a/, /i/, and /u/ are represented by doubling the vowels, as in *baai* (場合 ばあい), *sukaato* (スカート), *tanoshii* (楽しい), *takushii* (タクシー), *riyuu* (理由 りゆう), and *yuuzaa* (ユーザー).

The long vowel /e/ is represented either by "ei" or "ee", following the convention of *Gendai kanazukai*, as in *tokei* (時計), *meiwaku* (迷惑 めいわく), *keeki* (ケーキ), and *meeru* (メール). In the same vein, "ou" and "oo" are used to represent the long vowel /o/, as in *koukan* (交換 こうかん), *osou* (襲う おそう), *koohii* (コーヒー), and *soosu* (ソース).

Some loan words contain syllables that are not found in the syllable inventory of traditional Japanese. These include, for example, "ti" in *paatii* (パーティー), "di" in *merodii* (メロディー), and "fi" in *ofisu* (オフィス).

Segmentation of headwords

Headwords are generally romanized using spaces between SUWs, e.g. *te iru* (ている), *de wa nai* (ではない), *ni tsui te* (について), *shi yakusho* (市役所), *kousoku douro* (高速道路). This is to clearly indicate that these headwords are composed of more than one SUW. However, a hyphen is used for the following cases:

(i) if part of speech of the given SUW is either prefix or suffix, e.g. *watashi-tachi* (私達), *tukuri-kata* (作り方), *ik-kai* (一回) [Affixes are underlined.]

(ii) if a space separates geminate consonants, e.g. is-shuukan (一週間)

Notes

1 http://mecab.googlecode.com/svn/trunk/mecab/doc/index.html
2 http://www.tokuteicorpus.jp/dist/
3 http://slp.itc.nagoya-u.ac.jp/~kozawa/Comainu/

References

Carroll, J. B. (1970)
"An alternative to Juilland's usage coefficient for lexical frequencies and a proposal for a standard frequency index." *Computer Studies in the Humanities and Verbal Behavior*, 3(2): 61–65.

Gries, S. Th. (2008)
"Dispersions and adjusted frequencies in corpora." *International Journal of Corpus Linguistics* 13: 403–37.

National Language Research Institute (1952)
Goi-chousa: Gendai Shinbun Yougo no Ichirei. (Research on vocabulary used in modern newspaper articles).

National Language Research Institute (1953)
Fujin Zasshi no Yougo—Gendaigo no Goi Chousa. (Research on vocabulary in women's magazines).

National Language Research Institute (1957)
Sougou Zasshi no Yougo—Gendaigo no Goi Chousa. (Research on vocabulary in cultural reviews).

National Language Research Institute (1959)
Meiji Shoki no Shinbun no Yougo. (On the vocabulary in newspapers in the early years of the Meiji period).

National Language Research Institute (1962)
Gendai Zasshi 90-shu no Yougo Youji Daiichi Bunsatsu Goihyou. (Vocabulary and Chinese characters in 90 contemporary magazines. Vol.1: General descriptions and vocabulary frequency table).

National Language Research Institute (1970–3)
Denshikeisanki ni yoru Shinbun no Goi Chousa. (Computer studies on the vocabulary in modern newspapers).

National Language Research Institute (1983–4)
Koukou Kyoukasho no Goi Chousa I. (Studies on the vocabulary in senior high school textbooks, Vol. 1–2).

National Language Research Institute (1986–7)
Chuugakkou Kyoukasho no Goi Chousa I. (Studies on the vocabulary in junior high school textbooks. Vol. 1–2).

National Language Research Institute (1987)
Zasshi Yougo no Hensen. (Changes in the language of magazines).

National Language Research Institute (1995)
Terebi Housou no Goi Chousa I. (Vocabulary survey of television broadcasts I).

National Language Research Institute (1997)
Terebi Housou no Goi Chousa II. (Vocabulary survey of television broadcasts II).

National Institute of Japanese Language and Linguistics (2005)
Gendai Zasshi no Goi Chousa. (A survey of vocabulary in contemporary magazines).

Frequency index

> **rank, lemma**, romanization, *part of speech*, English gloss
> • illustrative example — English translation
> frequency | dispersion | register code

1 の no *p. case* of; in; at; for; by
• 彼はこの大学の学生だ。— He is a student at this university.
47078 | 0.98 | BK

2 に ni *p. case* at; on; in; to; for
• 私は大阪に住んでいます。— I live in Osaka.
32231 | 1.00 | BK

3 は wa *p.* TOPIC
• 好きなスポーツはテニスです。— My favorite sport is tennis.
31572 | 1.00 | BK

4 た ta *aux.* PAST
• 昨日、彼を見ましたか。— Did you see him yesterday?
31549 | 0.98 | BK

5 を o *p. case* ACCUSATIVE
• 彼は毎晩ビールを飲む。— He drinks beer every night.
29120 | 0.99 | BK

6 だ da *aux.* COPULA
• 僕は英語が苦手だ。— I'm not good at English.
27686 | 0.99 | BK

7 が ga *p. case* NOMINATIVE
• こちらが私の妻です。— This is my wife.
26904 | 1.00 | BK

8 て te *p. conj.* REASON
• お金がなくて、海外旅行できない。— I don't have money so I can't travel abroad.
22523 | 0.96

9 と to *p. case* and; or; with; if
• 彼とレストランへ行った。— I went to a restaurant with my boyfriend.
18509 | 1.00 | BK

10 ます masu *aux.* POLITE (after verb)
• 来週京都へ行きます。— I will go to Kyoto next week.
16855 | 0.95

11 も mo *p.* too, also
• 彼が行くなら、私も行きます。— If he is going, I will go too.
16147 | 0.97

12 で de *p. case* in; at; from; by
• 東京駅で彼女に会った。— I met her at Tokyo station.
14058 | 1.00 | BK

13 ている、てる te iru, teru *cp.* CONTINUATION
• 雨が降っている。— It's raining.
13555 | 0.99

14 です desu *aux.* COPULA (polite)
• 彼は独身です。— He is single.
9828 | 0.83 | WB

15 れる reru *aux.* PASSIVE
• 日本で使われている通貨は円です。— The currency used in Japan is yen.
9234 | 0.99 | BK

16 という、つう to iu, to yuu, tsuu *cp.* called, named
• 太郎という男の子を知っていますか。— Do you know a boy called Taro?
9073 | 0.80

17 事 koto *n.* thing
• 今年はいろいろな事があった。— All kinds of things happened this year.
8747 | 0.96

18 えー、ええ ee *interj.* eh?, what?; well, yes
• あの人は、えー、ちょっと名前が思い出せません。— That man is..., well I cannot remember his name.
• ええ、そうです。— Right.
8636 | 0.07 | SP

19 言う iu, yuu *v.* say, speak, talk
• はっきり言うと、あなたの言っていることは無意味です。— Frankly speaking, you are talking nonsense.
8549 | 0.91

20 のです、んです no desu, n desu *cp.* ASSERTION (polite)
• どうしたんですか。— What's the matter?
8439 | 0.71

21 あの、あのう、あのー ano, anoo *interj.* Excuse me; uh, eh, um, ah, er
• あの、ちょっとお聞きしたいんですが、バス乗り場はどこですか。— Excuse me, could you tell me where the bus stop is?
8431 | 0.00 | SP

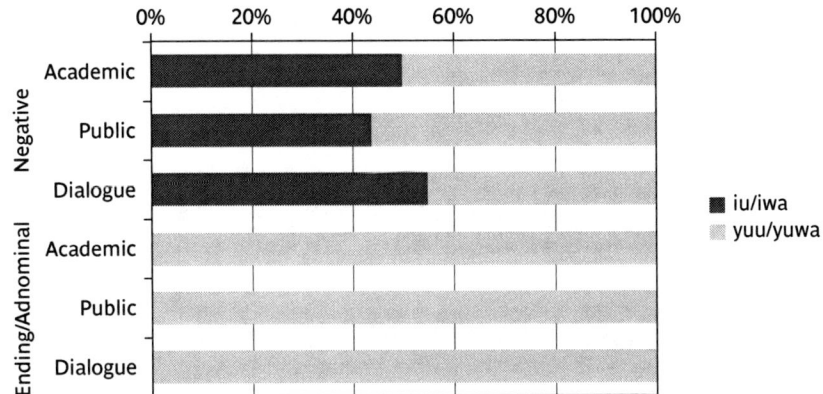

Variation of *iu* (say/speak/talk) and the conjugation: When the verb is in the negative form (*mizenkei*), it is often pronounced as *iwanai*. In its ending- and adnominal-forms, the verb is pronounced almost regularly as *yuu* as in *sou yuu hito*. All the analyses of pronunciation variants hereafter were based on the CSJ data.

22 する suru *v.* do; make
- 仕事をしなければなりません。— I have to do my work.
7644 | 0.99

23 まー, まあ maa *interj.* Wow!, Oh my God!
- まー、なんて素晴らしいんでしょう。— Wow! That's amazing!
6950 | 0.04 | SP

24 の no *p.* POSSESSIVE
- 彼が言ったのは本当だ。— What he said is true.
6883 | 0.95

25 ある aru *v.* be (existence), have (possession), happen, occur
- 彼の報告書は問題がある。— His report has some problems.
6496 | 0.98

26 ね ne *p. disc.* isn't it?, don't you?
- いい天気ですね。— It's a nice day, isn't it?
6282 | 0.70

27 ない nai *aux.* not
- 彼は朝ごはんを食べない。— He doesn't have breakfast.
6253 | 0.98

28 なる naru *v.* become, get; come to do, start to do; turn into
- 彼は金持ちになるでしょう。— He will become rich.
5977 | 0.99

29 か ka *p. disc.* QUESTION
- コーヒーか紅茶はいかがですか。— Would you like some coffee or tea?
5594 | 0.91

30 その sono *adn.* that
- そのカバンを取ってくれませんか。— Can you pass me that bag?
5546 | 0.95 | BK

31 けれど keredo *conj.* though, although
- このアパートはあまり良くないけれど安い。— This apartment is cheap, though it's not so nice.
5293 | 0.64

32 から kara *p. case* from
- ここからその店までは遠い。— The shop is a long way from here.
4740 | 1.00

33 よう you *aux.* INDUCEMENT
- 一緒にDVDを見よう。— Let's watch a DVD together.
4638 | 0.97 | BK

34 思う omou *v.* think, believe; feel; expect
- 私はそう思いません。— I don't think so.
4599 | 0.88

35 で de *conj.* so, then
- で、あの話はどうなりましたか？ — So what happened about the story you mentioned?
4412 | 0.15 | SP

36 か ka *p.* if; or
- 誰か来たようだ。— It seems that someone has come.
4308 | 0.94

37 が ga *p. conj.* ADVERSATIVE
- いい天気だが、風が冷たい。— It's a sunny day but the wind is chilly.
4168 | 0.96

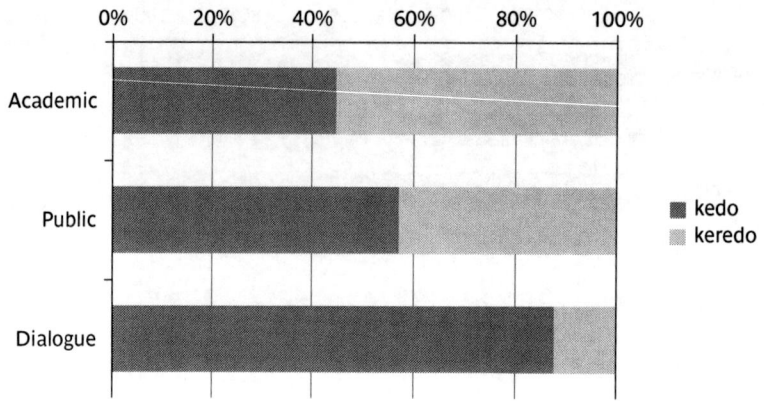

Variation of *keredo* (although): The casual variant *kedo* is the most frequent in dialogue. In academic presentation and public speaking, *kedo* and *keredo* are used more or less equally.

38 物 mono *n.* thing, object, stuff
- そんなに高い物は買えません。— I can't buy such expensive stuff.
3676 | 0.96

39 そう sou *adv.* so, such
- 私もそう思います。— I think so too.
3586 | 0.80

40 何 nani *pron.* what; something; anything; nothing
- 何を考えているんですか？— What are you thinking?
3497 | 0.76

41 と to *p. conj.* if, when; with
- お酒を飲みすぎると、眠くなってしまう。— Drinking too much makes me sleepy.
3458 | 0.97

42 私 watashi, watakushi, atashi *pron.* I
- 私は寿司が好きです。— I like sushi.
3404 | 0.90

43 てしまう te shimau *cp.* end up doing ...
- ダイエット中なのに、つい、甘いものを食べてしまう。— I'm on a diet, but I can't stop eating sweets.
3352 | 0.78

44 それ sore *pron.* that
- それは明子さんのカバンですか。— Is that Akiko's bag?
3278 | 0.91 | BK

45 とか to ka *p.* and; or
- ケーキとかチョコレートばかり食べるから、君は太るんだ。— You gain weight, because you always eat cake and chocolate.
3174 | 0.00 | SP

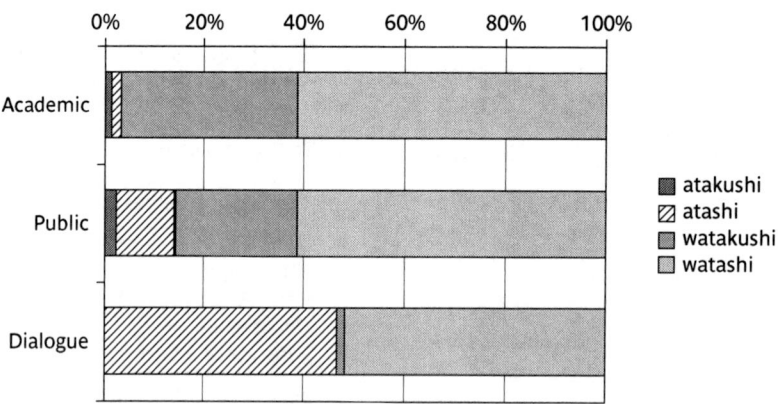

Variation of *watashi* (I): The most formal variant, *watakushi*, is used most frequently in academic presentations, and is rarely used in dialogue. The most casual variant, *atashi*, shows the opposite pattern.

46 この kono *adn.* this
- この本をもう読みましたか。— Have you read this book?
2974 | 0.97 | BK

47 無い nai *i-adj.* There is no ... , no ...
- 今、お金が無いんです。— I have no money now.
2953 | 0.96

48 行く iku, yuku *v.* go; come
- すぐ行きます。— I'm just coming.
2746 | 0.88

49 のだ、んだ no da, n da *cp.* ASSERTION
- 彼女は何も知らないのだ。— She doesn't know anything.
2708 | 0.94

50 せる seru *aux.* CAUSATIVE
- 子供にピアノを習わせたい。— I want my child to learn how to play the piano.
2702 | 0.87

51 これ kore *pron.* this
- これをください。(レストランや店で) — I will take this. (in a restaurant or shop)
2685 | 0.93

52 もう moo *adv.* already; soon; again
- もう寝ます。— I'll go to bed soon.
2630 | 0.66

53 である de aru *cp.* COPULA (formal)
- これが実験の結果である。— These are the results of the experiment.
2586 | 0.81 | BK

54 時 toki *n.* time
- 時が悲しみを癒してくれますよ。— Time will heal your sorrow.
2514 | 0.96

55 な na *p. disc.* PROHIBITION
- 動くな、手を挙げろ。— Don't move! Get your hands up!
2265 | 0.78

56 ず zu *aux.* NEGATION
- 彼は何も言わずに去ってしまった。— He left without saying anything.
2250 | 0.94

57 ので、んで no de, n de *p. conj.* as, because, since
- 娘はまだ小さいので手がかかります。— As my daughter is still very young, she needs to be looked after.
2181 | 0.00 | SP

58 人 hito *n.* person, people, human being
- その歌手は若い人に人気がある。— That singer is popular among young people.
2178 | 0.93

59 よ yo *p. disc.* ASSERTION, REMINDING (informal)
- また来るよ。— I will come again.
2134 | 0.88

60 こう koo *adv.* so, like this
- 粉と水を混ぜ、こうしてよくこねてください。— Mix flour and water together, and knead the dough like this.
2099 | 0.73

61 から kara *p. conj.* because, since
- 雨が降っているから、出かけるのはやめます。— I will not go out, because it's raining.
2028 | 0.96

62 ば ba *p. conj.* if
- 雨がふれば、試合は中止だ。— If it rains, the game will be cancelled.
1909 | 0.98

63 や ya *p.* and; or
- 結婚式に家族や友人を招待した。— We invited our family and friends to the wedding.
1881 | 0.93

64 来る kuru *v.* come
- ここに来てください。— Come here, please.
1876 | 0.92

65 その sono *interj.* uh, er, um, mm
- 「どうして授業を休んだの。」「それは、その....」 — "Why were you absent from the class?" "Uh, well ..."
1868 | 0.01 | SP

66 まで made *p.* to, till, until
- 休暇は明日から来週の水曜日までです。— My vacation is from tomorrow till next Wednesday.
1839 | 0.99

67 見る miru *v.* see; look at, watch; check
- 通りを渡る前に左右を見た。— I looked left and right before crossing the street.
1814 | 0.98

68 たり tari *p.* and
- 日曜日はよく部屋の掃除をしたり、本を読んだりする。— I usually clean up my room and read books on Sunday.
1793 | 0.84

69 今 ima *n.* now
- 今、何時ですか。— What time is it now?
1760 | 0.92

70 良い、いい yoi, ii *i-adj.* good
- 彼は良い人だ。— He is a good man.
1734 | 0.84

71 所 tokoro *n.* place, point; part; aspect
- 先週はいろいろな所に行った。— I went to many places last week.
1714 | 0.93

72 自分 jibun *n.* oneself
- 彼は九十歳だが何でも自分でできる。— He is ninety years old, yet he can do everything by himself.
1709 | 0.86

73 ん n *interj.* oh, mm, well
- ん、何かがおかしいな。— Hmm, something is wrong ...
1706 | 0.16 | SP

74 あー aa *interj.* er, uh, um, hmm, ah, oh
- 「入ってもいい。」「あー、ちょっと待って。」— "Can I come in?" "Uh. Just a minute."
1695 | 0.36

75 やはり、やっぱり yahari, yappari *adv.* as (one) expected, still
- 彼女はやはり遅れた。— She was late for the appointment, as expected.
1680 | 0.66

76 たい tai *aux.* want to, like to
- コーヒーが飲みたいな、ちょっと休もう。— I want to have a cup of coffee. Let's have a break.
1663 | 0.98

77 やる yaru *v.* do; make; give
- 今すぐやります。— I'll do that right now.
1644 | 0.88

78 中 naka *n.* inside, in; into
- 太郎は部屋の中に入った。— Taro came into the room.
1534 | 0.97 | BK

79 いる iru *v.* be, exist; stay
- 「どこにいるの。」「ここだよ。」— "Where are you?" "I'm here."
1499 | 0.89

80 できる dekiru *v.* be ready
- 夕食ができましたよ。— Dinner is ready.
1490 | 0.96

81 など nado *p.* and so on, etc.
- 警察官は私の名前や年齢などを尋ねた。— The policeman asked me my name, age, and so on.
1471 | 0.91

82 として to shi te *cp.* as
- 彼女は女優としてはものにならなかった。— As an actress, she did not succeed.
1453 | 0.95

83 後 ato *n.* after, later
- 後で電話します。— I'll call you later.
1448 | 0.84

84 また mata *adv.* additionally, moreover *conj.* again; too, and
- 彼女は医者であり、また、歌手でもある。— She is a doctor as well as a singer.
- また同じ間違いをしてしまった。— I made the same mistake again.
1433 | 0.95

85 ちょっと chotto *adv.* (just) a little, a bit
- 最近、ちょっと太ってしまった。— I gained a bit of weight recently.
1352 | 0.66

86 てくる te kuru *cp.* go and ...
- スーパーへ行ってきます。— I am going to the supermarket.
1351 | 0.98

87 だけ dake *p.* only, alone, merely
- チャンスは一回だけだ。— I have only one chance.
1329 | 0.98

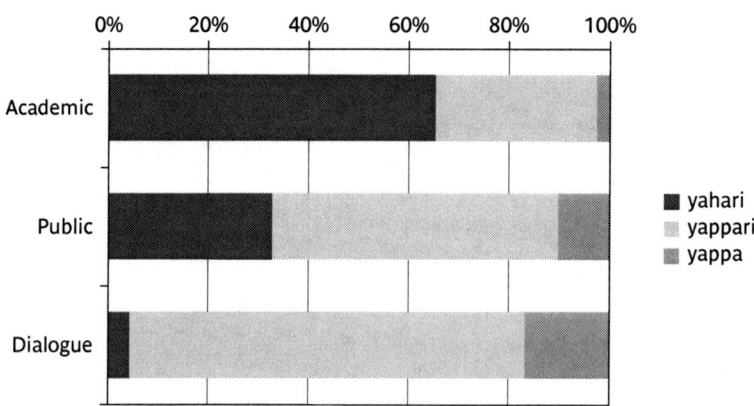

Variation of *yahari* (as expected/still): Casual *yappari* and formal *yahari* are used in all speech registers. *yappari* is more popular than *yahari* in dialogue. *yappa* is more casual than *yappari*.

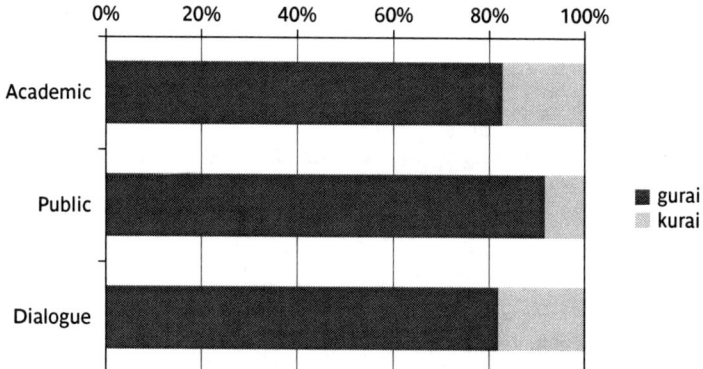

Variation of *kurai* (about/around): This suffix is often realized as *gurai* like *doregurai* (how much) in all speech registers.

88 くらい, ぐらい kurai, gurai *p.* about, around
- 彼女は二十歳ぐらいに見える。— She looks around twenty years old.
1318 | 0.79

89 ではない de wa nai *cp.* it is not the case that...
- 私は日本人ではない。— I'm not Japanese.
1304 | 0.96

90 えーと eeto *interj.* well, let me see
- えーと、会議は何時からだっけ。— Well, what time does the meeting start?
1303 | 0.01 | SP

91 方 hou *n.* direction, way; side
- この部屋は午後になると西の方から日が差す。— This room gets the sun in the afternoon from the west.
1301 | 0.95

92 ていく, てく te iku, teku *cp.* go and ...
- 明日の夕食会にはどんな服を着ていったらいいですか。— What kind of dress should I wear for the dinner tomorrow?
1245 | 0.92

93 訳 wake *n.* reason, cause
- 訳を話してください。— Tell me the reason.
1215 | 0.82

94 へ e *p. case* DESTINATION
- 明日、大阪へ行きます。— I will go to Osaka tomorrow.
1196 | 0.95 | BK

95 どう dou *adv.* how, what
- 彼をどう思いますか。— What do you think of him?
1173 | 0.96

96 し shi *p. conj.* and, besides
- 彼はハンサムだし背が高い。— He is handsome, and tall.
1167 | 0.88

97 本当 hontou *n.* truth, right
- それは本当かな。— I wonder if it is true.
1125 | 0.73

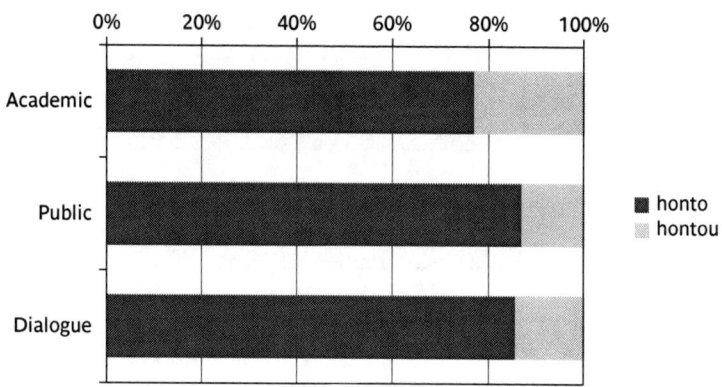

Variation of *hontou* (truth/right): The long vowel at the end of a word is often shortened to a short vowel. The shortening happens in all speech registers.

98 持つ motsu *v.* have, take, hold
- これを持ってくれませんか。— Can you hold this?
1106 | 0.97

99 出る deru *v.* go out, come out; attend
- 私は部屋から出た。— I went out of the room.
1093 | 0.95

100 ため tame *n.* for
- これは初心者のための本です。— This is a book for beginners.
1084 | 0.93

101 すごい sugoi *i-adj.* fantastic, wonderful; terrible
- 昨夜はすごい雨だった。— It was raining very hard last night.
1082 | 0.45

102 考える kangaeru *v.* think
- よく考えてから話しなさい。— Think it through before you speak.
1056 | 0.96

103 そこ soko *pron.* there; then
- 彼はよくそこでタバコを吸っている。— He often smokes there.
1045 | 0.89

104 う u *aux.* SOLICITATION
- さあ、行こう。— Let's go.
1038 | 0.00 | SP

105 分かる wakaru *v.* understand, see
- 彼女の言っていることはよく分からない。— I don't quite understand what she's saying.
1021 | 0.94

106 ておる te oru *cp.* CONTINUATION (polite)
- お返事をお待ちしております。— I look forward to hearing from you at your earliest convenience.
1017 | 0.63 | OF

107 について ni tsui te *cp.* about, concerning, as to
- 彼は太陽光発電について研究している。— He is doing research on solar power.
941 | 0.65

108 それで sore de *conj.* and then; so; that is why
- それで、彼は何と言ったの。— So, what did he say?
934 | 0.30 | SP

109 入る hairu *v.* enter, come in, go in
- どうぞお入りください。— Please come in.
913 | 0.94

110 作る tsukuru *v.* make, create, cook
- 彼女は朝食に目玉焼きを作った。— She cooked a fried egg for her breakfast.
847 | 0.97

111 てみる te miru *cp.* try …ing
- ちょっと味見してみますか。— Would you like to taste?
816 | 0.97

112 聞く、聴く kiku *v.* hear; listen; listen to, obey
- 彼女は母親の言うことを聞かなかった。— She didn't listen to her mother.
811 | 0.97

113 そして soshite *conj.* and, so
- 朝早く起きた。そして、散歩に出かけた。— I got up early in the morning, and went for a walk.
809 | 0.96

114 てくれる te kureru *cp.* [do something as a favor]
- 父が空港まで車で迎えに来てくれた。— My father came by car to the airport to pick me up.
806 | 0.89

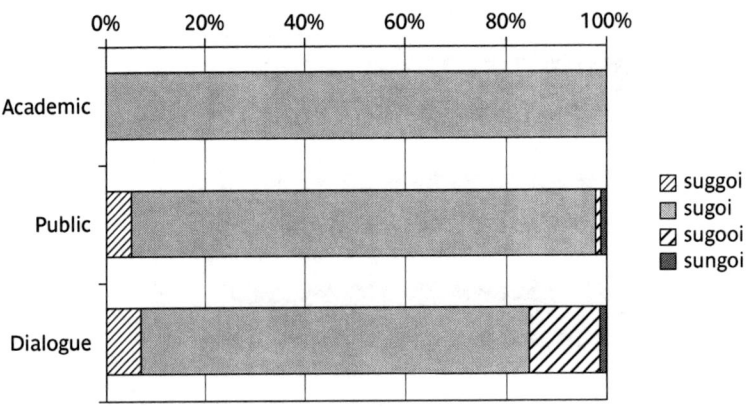

Variation of *sugoi* (fantastic): The adverb *sugoi* is emphasized in various ways.

115 場合 baai *n.* case, occasion
- 雨の場合、お祭りは中止です。— In case of rain, the festival will be cancelled.
801 | 0.95

116 話 hanashi *n.* story, talk
- 話があります。— I have something to tell you.
784 | 0.94

117 ながら nagara *p. conj.* with, over, while
- コーヒーでも飲みながら話しましょう。— Let's talk over a cup of coffee.
781 | 0.98 | BK

118 そんな sonna *adn.* that, such
- 彼がそんなことをするはずがない。— He can't do such a thing.
773 | 0.88

119 使う tsukau *v.* use, handle
- この鍋はミルクを温めるのに使っています。— I use this pan for warming milk.
771 | 0.95

120 日本 nihon, nippon *n.* Japan
- 来週、日本に帰国します。— I will go back to Japan next week.
770 | 0.98

121 風 fuu *na-adj.* style, type, way, like
- あんな風に踊れるようになりたい。— I wish that I could dance like that.
769 | 0.61 | OF

122 おー oo *interj.* Oh!, Wow!
- おー、これは立派な家だね。— Wow! This is a nice house.
757 | 0.24 | SP

123 前 mae *n.* forward; front; before
- 子供の前でそんな話はするべきではない。— We should not talk about things like that in front of children.
752 | 0.91

124 多い ooi *i-adj.* many, much, a lot of
- 今年は雨が多い。— There has been a lot of rain this year.
752 | 0.98

125 のではない、んではない no de wa nai, n de wa nai *cp.* it is not that ...
- あなただけが悪いのではない。— This is not only your fault.
726 | 0.89

126 よく yoku *adv.* good, well; often
- 私は彼をよく知っている。— I know him well.
717 | 0.90

127 一つ hito-tsu *n.* one
- オレンジを一つ食べた。— I ate an orange.
715 | 0.96

128 子供 kodomo *n.* child
- 私は子供が三人いる。— I have three children.
696 | 0.94

129 非常 hijou *na-adj.* very, extremely
- その国は非常に物価が高い。— Prices in that country are extremely high.
684 | 0.69

130 気 ki *n.* mind, heart
- 彼女は気が強い。— She is strong-minded.
681 | 0.88

131 ても te mo *p. conj.* even if
- どんなに食べても彼女は太らない。— No matter how much she eats, she never gains weight.
671 | 0.00 | SP

132 取る toru *v.* take, get; have; pass
- 塩をとってくれませんか。— Will you pass me the salt?
669 | 0.98

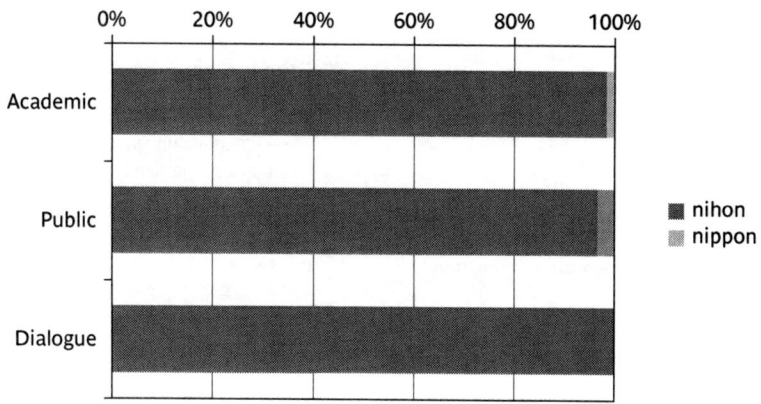

Nihon and *nippon* (Japan): *nihon* is by far more frequent than *nippon* in all speech registers.

133 うち uchi *n.* inside; of; before
- 寒いのでうちの中にいた。— I stayed home as it was cold outside.
655 | 0.97

134 知る shiru *v.* know
- 私は何も知りません。— I don't know anything about it.
645 | 0.94

135 より yori *p. case* than; from
- 東京より大阪のほうが好きです。— I like Osaka better than Tokyo.
643 | 0.99

136 それから sore kara *conj.* and then, after that, and
- 昨日は9時ごろ帰宅しました。それから、テレビを見ました。— I went home around nine, and then watched TV.
635 | 0.67

137 うー uu *interj.* Woo!, Oooh!
- うー、寒い。— Woo, it's cold.
625 | 0.22 | SP

138 感じ kanji *n.* feeling, impression; atmosphere
- 日本的な感じの部屋ですね。— This room has a Japanese atmosphere.
624 | 0.71

139 みたい mitai *na-adj.* like
- 明子ちゃんみたいにきれいな女の子は見たことがない。— I have never seen such a beautiful girl as Akiko.
604 | 0.74

140 でも de mo *conj.* but, however
- 結婚したい。でも、いい相手がいない。— I want to get married, but I can't find anyone.
597 | 0.80

141 ここ koko *pron.* here
- ここから彼の家まで一時間かかる。— It takes an hour from here to his house.
589 | 0.98

142 とても, とっても totemo, tottemo *adv.* very
- 今日はとても忙しかった。— I was very busy today.
585 | 0.72

143 いろいろ iroiro *adv., na-adj.* various
- その国立公園ではいろいろな動物が見られる。— You can see various animals in the national park.
584 | 0.85

144 一 ichi *num.* one
- 一からやる。— Start from scratch. (Start from the beginning.)
583 | 0.82

145 そう sou *n., na-adj.* be about to
- 彼女は今にも泣きそうだった。— She was almost crying.
581 | 0.86

146 行なう okonau *v.* do, carry out, hold
- 明日、会議が行う予定だ。— We will have a meeting tomorrow.
581 | 0.77

147 一番 ichiban *adv.* number one, first, most
- 昨日はこの冬で一番寒い日だった。— Yesterday was the coldest day of this winter.
581 | 0.83

148 二 ni *num.* two
- テストの成績がクラスで二番だった。— I got the second best score in my class in the examination.
574 | 0.78

149 同じ onaji *adn.* same
- 私たちは同じ飛行機で大阪まで行った。— We took the same flight to Osaka.
571 | 0.99

150 まず mazu *adv.* first; anyway
- まず、玉ねぎを炒め、次に肉を入れてください。— First, fry the onions, and then the meat.
569 | 0.90

151 必要 hitsuyou *na-adj.* necessary *n* necessity
- 必要な情報を集めている。— I am collecting the necessary information.
566 | 0.93

152 仕事(する) shigoto(suru) *n.* work, job *v.* work
- 彼は新しい仕事を探している。— He is looking for a new job.
562 | 0.91

153 余り amari *adv.* the rest *n.* (not) much
- うちの息子はあまり野菜が好きじゃない。— My son doesn't like vegetables very much.
561 | 0.86

154 によって ni yot-te *cp.* by, because of; depend on, depending on
- 価格は需要と供給のバランスによって決まる。— The price depends on the balance of supply and demand.
539 | 0.94 | BK

155 かもしれない ka mo shire nai *cp.* perhaps, maybe
- これは毒キノコかもしれない。— Maybe this is a poisonous mushroom.
538 | 0.89

156 僕 boku *pron.* I (used by male speakers)
- 僕はサッカーが好きだ。— I like football.
533 | 0.86 | BK

157 皆 mina, minna *n.* everyone; everything
- 皆、彼女の意見に賛成だ。— Everyone agrees with her opinion.
517 | 0.86

158 彼 kare *pron.* he
- 彼は私の兄です。— He is my elder brother.
516 | 0.78 | BK

159 方 kata *n.* person, man
- この方は山田さんです。— This is Mr. Yamada.
505 | 0.69

160 食べる taberu *v.* eat
- 彼女はよく食べる。— She eats a lot.
504 | 0.81

161 ほど hodo *p.* about; extent
- 一時間ほどで戻ります。— I'll be back in an hour or so.
504 | 0.95 | BK

162 しかし shikashi *conj.* but, however
- 彼はよく勉強した。しかし、試験に合格できなかった。— He studied hard, but he couldn't pass the exam.
490 | 0.92 | BK

163 書く kaku *v.* write
- 名前と住所を書くのを忘れずに。— Make sure you write your name and address.
488 | 0.96

164 入れる ireru *v.* put in; include
- カバンに財布を入れるのを忘れてしまった。— I forgot to put my wallet in my bag.
488 | 0.95

165 次 tsugi *n.* next, following, coming
- 次の日曜日、うちに来ませんか。— How about coming to our house next Sunday?
487 | 0.96

166 結構 kekkou *adv.* quite *na-adj.* good
- 東京の冬は結構寒い。— Winter in Tokyo is quite cold.
481 | 0.61

167 問題 mondai *n.* problem, question
- その問題をできるだけ早く解決したい。— I want to solve the problem as soon as possible.
477 | 0.85

168 例えば tatoeba *adv.* for example, such as
- この畑では野菜、例えばジャガイモやトマトを作っています。— Vegetables such as potatoes and tomatoes are grown in this field.
470 | 0.89

169 目, 眼 me *n.* eye
- 彼女は目が大きい。— She has big eyes.
467 | 0.89 | BK

170 頃 koro *n.* time, about, when
- 子供の頃、その町に住んでいた。— I lived in the town when I was a child.
467 | 0.82

171 上 ue *n.* top; above; up; on
- 机の上に本があります。— There is a book on the desk.
463 | 0.98

172 てくださる te kudasaru *cp.* [do something as a favor (honorific)]
- お手伝いしてくださるボランティアの方を募集しています。— We are looking for volunteers who could help us.
458 | 0.73 | WB

173 他 hoka *n.* other, another; else
- 他に質問はありませんか。— Do you have any other questions?
454 | 0.98

174 いつ itsu *pron.* when
- いつ日本へ来ますか。— When are you coming to Japan?
452 | 0.92

175 家 ie *n.* house, home
- 私はいつも夜8時ごろ家に帰る。— I always go home around eight o'clock.
444 | 0.90

176 付く tsuku *v.* stick; be stained with
- 服にインクのしみが付いた。— My clothes were stained with ink.
436 | 0.93

177 日, 陽 hi *n.* day; sun
- この部屋は日が良く当たって、とても暑くなる。— This room gets lots of sunlight and gets very hot.
436 | 0.99

178 出す dasu *v.* take out; pay; send
- その手紙は昨日出しました。— I sent the letter yesterday.
434 | 0.99

179 一人 hitori *n.* one person; alone
- 料金は一人五千円です。— The charge is five thousand yen per person.
434 | 0.94

180 人間 ningen *n.* human being, man
- 人間は神の前でみな平等だ。— All men are equal before God.
434 | 0.88 | BK

181 どこ doko *pron.* where
- どこへ行くんですか。— Where are you going?
430 | 0.94

182 ございます (<ござる) gozai masu *v.* [very polite form of "de aru"]
- ありがとうございます。— Thank you very much.
428 | 0.35 | OF

183 時間 jikan *n.* time
- もう行く時間だ。— It's time to go.
423 | 0.97

184 ただ tada *conj.* just *adv.* only, just, merely
- 彼女は美人だ。ただ、わがままだ。— She is beautiful, but selfish.
- ただ聞いてみただけです。— I just wanted to ask.
422 | 0.93

185 だから dakara *conj.* so, therefore, because
- 彼はハンサムで金持ちだ。だから、女性にもてる。— He is popular among women, because he is handsome and rich.
420 | 0.88

186 違う chigau *v.* be different; be wrong
- 彼の意見は私のと違う。— His opinion is different from mine.
416 | 0.94

187 受ける ukeru *v.* get, receive, take
- 私は大学から奨学金を受けている。— I receive a scholarship from the university.
416 | 0.95

188 言葉 kotoba *n.* word; language
- 外国での生活は言葉や習慣が違うので大変だ。— Living in a foreign country is difficult because of the different customs and language.
413 | 0.94 | BK

189 なんか nanka *p.* such as, like
- 彼なんかにできるはずがない。— Someone like him could never do it.
411 | 0.67

190 少し sukoshi *adv.* a little, a few
- 少し疲れました。— I'm a bit tired.
410 | 0.95

191 まま mama *adv.* as it is
- 眼鏡をかけたまま眠ってしまった。— I slept with my glasses on.
410 | 0.96

192 買う kau *v.* buy
- 彼は車を買った。— He bought a car.
409 | 0.81 | WB

193 まだ mada *n.* yet, still
- まだ雨が降っている。— It is still raining.
408 | 0.96

194 手 te *n.* hand
- 父の手は大きい。— My father has big hands.
407 | 0.91 | BK

195 話す hanasu *v.* talk, tell, speak
- 日本語が話せますか。— Can you speak Japanese?
404 | 0.87

196 好き suki *na-adj.* favorite, like, love
- 好きな食べ物は何ですか? — What is your favorite food?
403 | 0.79

197 返る kaeru *v.* return
- 私の本を返してくれませんか。— Can you return my book to me?
392 | 0.83

1 Animals

(frequency per million words)

犬 inu 182.125 dog	ネズミ nezumi 13.022 rat, mouse	ライオン raion 4.610 lion
猫 neko 108.284 cat	熊 kuma 12.481 bear	蟹 kani 4.080 crab
魚 sakana 98.845 fish	猿 saru 12.098 monkey	鯨 kujira 3.915 whale
馬 uma 70.521 horse	豚 buta 11.848 pig	チンパンジー chinpanjii 2.970 chimpanzee
鳥 tori 51.352 bird, poultry	蚊 ka 11.421 mosquito	山羊 yagi 2.086 goat
牛 ushi 21.848 cattle, cow, ox	羊 hitsuji 10.212 sheep	ゴリラ gorira 1.991 gorilla
ウサギ usagi 16.367 rabbit	亀 kame 9.497 turtle, tortoise	キリン kirin 1.604 giraffe
エビ ebi 14.089 prawn, shrimp	象 zou 9.288 elephant	トカゲ tokage 1.458 lizard
蛇 hebi 13.962 snake	貝 kai 8.511 shellfish, shell	ワニ wani 1.220 crocodile
鶏 niwatori 13.941 chicken (also baby bird)	雛 hina[1] 7.474 baby bird	水牛 suigyuu 0.770 water buffalo
ハムスター hamusutaa 13.841 hamster	キツネ kitsune 7.098 fox	シマウマ shimauma 0.293 zebra
カラス karasu 13.067 crow	カエル kaeru 6.829 frog	
	シカ shika 6.021 deer	
	虎 tora 5.748 tiger	

1 Also 9575 hiyoko.

198 てもらう te morau *cp.* [receive a favor]
- 知り合いに仕事を紹介してもらった。— My friend told me about the job.
389 | 0.95

199 掛ける kakeru *v.* hang; take; cost
- 壁に絵を掛けた。— I hung the picture on the wall.
388 | 0.98

200 終わる owaru *v.* end, finish
- 仕事が終わったら飲みに行きましょう。— Let's go out for a drink after work.
385 | 0.87

201 意味（する）imi(suru) *n.* meaning, sense *v.* mean
- それはどういう意味ですか。— What does it mean?
385 | 0.97

202 のである no de aru *cp.* ASSERTION (formal)
- 認めたくはないが、それが現実なのである。— It is difficult to accept, but it is a reality.
384 | 0.71 | BK

203 いろんな ironna *adn.* various
- そのパーティーではいろんな料理が出された。— All kinds of foods were served at the party.
384 | 0.61

204 付ける tsukeru *v.* put; attach; apply
- 私のパンにジャムを付けてくれますか。— Can you put some jam on my bread?
381 | 0.96

205 形 katachi *n.* form, shape, figure
- このリンゴは形が良い。— This apple has a nice shape.
380 | 0.91

206 かなり kanari *adv.* considerably, rather
- 今度の彼の作品は、前回のものとかなり違う。— His work this time is quite different from last time.
377 | 0.90

207 三 san *n.* three
- この春、彼は三回目の結婚をした。— He got married for the third time this spring.
375 | 0.81

208 最初 saisho *n.* first
- 最初は誰でも初心者だ。— Everyone is a beginner at first.
373 | 0.89

209 間 aida *n.* distance; period
- 彼女とは長い間会っていない。— I have not seen her for a long time.
372 | 0.97

210 感じる kanjiru *v.* feel
- 空腹を感じる。— I feel hungry.
368 | 0.95

211 しか shika *p.* only, just, no more than
- 砂糖は少ししか残っていない。— There is only a bit of sugar left.
366 | 0.90

212 かかる kakaru *v.* hang; take; cost
- 子どもを育てるのにはお金がかかる。— It costs a lot to raise children.
363 | 0.93

213 大きな ookina *adn.* big, large, great
- 大きな家に住みたい。— I want to live in a big house.
363 | 0.96

214 住む sumu *v.* live
- 私は東京に住んでいる。— I live in Tokyo.
362 | 0.75

215 最近 saikin *n.* recently, lately
- 私は最近忙しい。— I've been busy recently.
357 | 0.92

216 特に tokuni *adv.* especially, particularly
- コーヒーの中でも特に濃いコーヒーが好きです。— I like coffee, particularly strong ones.
355 | 0.95

217 誰 dare *pron.* who, whose, whom
- 誰を待っているんですか。— Who are you waiting for?
354 | 0.93

218 こんな konna *adn.* such, like that
- こんなことはもう二度としません。— I'll never do such a thing again.
349 | 0.92

219 友達 tomodachi *n.* friend
- 彼は私の友達です。— He is a friend of mine.
349 | 0.70

220 大きい ookii *i-adj.* big, large, great
- 大きい犬が吠えている。— A big dog is barking.
348 | 0.99

221 すぐ sugu *adv.* soon
- 彼はすぐ帰ってきますよ。— He will come back soon.
347 | 0.91

222 一緒 issho *n.* together, with
- 友達と一緒に買い物に行った。— I went shopping with my friends.
344 | 0.90

223 生活（する）seikatsu(suru) *n.* life *v.* live
- 日本の生活は慣れましたか。— Did you get used to living in Japan?
341 | 0.92

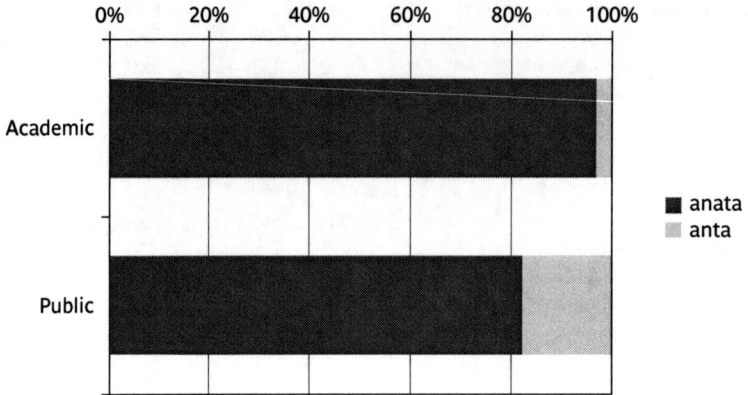

Anata and *anta* (you): the casual variant *anta* is used more frequently in public speaking than in academic presentation.

224 国 kuni *n.* country
- 私の国では雪が全く降らない。— It never snows in my country.
340 | 0.74

225 あげる ageru *v.* raise, lift
- 質問があれば手をあげてください。— Please raise your hand if you have a question.
340 | 0.98

226 あなた, あんた anata, anta *pron.* you
- あなたの協力が必要です。— I need your help.
336 | 0.86

227 現在 genzai *n.* present time, now
- 現在、気温は0度です。— The temperature is currently zero degrees.
335 | 0.97

228 高い takai *i-adj.* high, tall; expensive
- 彼は背が高い。— He is tall.
335 | 0.98

229 なんて nante *p.* [expresses belittlement]
- 彼女がタバコをやめたなんて信じられない。— I can't believe that she quit smoking.
333 | 0.85

230 悪い warui *i-adj.* bad
- 気分が悪い。— I feel sick.
329 | 0.89

231 気持ち kimochi *n.* feeling
- 風呂は気持ちがいい。— It feels good to take a bath.
328 | 0.92

232 乗る noru *v.* ride, get on, take
- 私は東京駅から電車に乗った。— I took a train from Tokyo station.
326 | 0.86

233 において ni oi te *cp.* at; in; on
- 日本において国際会議が開かれた。— An international conference was held in Japan.
325 | 0.43

234 見える mieru *v.* see, be seen
- ここから富士山が見える。— I can see Mt. Fuji from here.
324 | 0.93

235 変わる kawaru *v.* change
- 彼の考えは変わった。— His idea has changed.
323 | 0.99

236 べし beshi *aux.* must, should
- 結果は推して知るべし。— It should be easy to guess the results.
321 | 0.88

237 あるいは aruiwa *conj.* or; perhaps, probably, maybe
- 日本からアフリカへは、ヨーロッパ、あるいは中東経由で行ける。— One can go to Africa from Japan either via Europe or the Middle East.
319 | 0.72

238 大変 taihen *na-adj.* serious, terrible; hard, difficult
- 大きな家を掃除するのは大変だ。— It's hard work to clean a big house.
318 | 0.91

239 による ni yoru *cp.* be due to, be based on
- 父の病気は過労によるものだ。— My father's illness is from overwork.
317 | 0.72

240 会社 kaisha *n.* company, firm
- 父は貿易会社に勤めている。— My father works for a trading company.
317 | 0.92

241 ほとんど hotondo *adv.* almost, nearly
- ほとんどの人は彼の話を信じた。— Most people believed his story.
317 | 0.95

242 実際 jissai *n.* actually, in fact
- それは実際あったことです。— It actually happened.
315 | 0.95

243 先生 sensei *n.* teacher
- 先生に質問した。— I asked the teacher a question.
315 | 0.89

244 彼女 kanojo *pron.* she; girlfriend
- 彼女を両親に紹介した。— I introduced my girlfriend to my parents.
315 | 0.82 | BK

245 二人 futari *n.* two people
- この車には二人しか乗ることができない。— Only two people can ride in this car.
315 | 0.91

246 心 kokoro *n.* mind, heart; thought; feeling
- 心からあなたを愛している。— I love you with all my heart.
312 | 0.94

247 あの ano *adn.* that, those
- あの建物は博物館です。— That building is a museum.
311 | 0.91 | BK

248 らしい rashii *aux.* seem, look
- あの女はまだ生きているらしい。— It seems that that woman is still alive.
311 | 0.82

249 ある aru *adn.* one, a, some, a certain
- 私は去年、あるプロジェクトに関わった。— I joined a certain project last year.
310 | 0.94

250 金 kane *n.* money
- 金がすべてではない。— Money isn't everything.
310 | 0.93

251 顔 kao *n.* face
- 毎朝、顔を洗う。— I wash my face every morning.
310 | 0.83 | BK

252 ていただく te itadaku *cp.* [receive a favor (humble)]
- すみません、ちょっと教えていただけますか。— Excuse me, may I ask a question?
307 | 0.84

253 ずっと zutto *adv.* all the time, for a long time
- 今までずっとここにいたんですか。— Have you been here all the time?
304 | 0.80

254 さらに sarani *adv.* again, still more, moreover
- その会社はさらに成長するだろう。— The company is likely to grow further.
304 | 0.91

255 町, 街 machi *n.* town, city
- この町には高校がない。— This town does not have any high schools.
304 | 0.74

256 及び oyobi *conj.* and, as well as
- その会社は東京及び埼玉で事業を展開している。— The company operates in Tokyo and Saitama.
303 | 0.42 | OF

257 たくさん takusan *adv.* many, much
- たくさんの人達がパーティーに来ていた。— Many people came to the party.
301 | 0.89

258 いー ii *interj.* good, great
- いー、これ。— This is great.
300 | 0.01 | SP

259 大体 daitai *adv.* almost, nearly
- 仕事は大体終わった。— I've almost finished the work.
298 | 0.64

260 もちろん mochiron *adv.* of course, needless to say
- 喫煙が体に悪いことはもちろん知っています。— Of course I know that smoking is not good for one's health.
298 | 0.96

261 読む yomu *v.* read
- 毎朝、新聞を読む。— I read a newspaper every morning.
298 | 0.93

262 人たち hito-tachi *n.* people
- 若い人達に教えられた。— I learned from young people.
295 | 0.85

263 今日 kyou *n.* today
- 今日は金曜日です。— It's Friday today.
295 | 0.76 | WB

264 昔 mukashi *n.* ancient times, in the past, once
- 昔、ここに寺があった。— There used to be a temple here.
292 | 0.83

265 うん un *interj.* yes, yeah
- 「宿題やったの」「うん」— "Did you finish your homework?" "Yeah."
291 | 0.46

266 すべて subete *n.* everything, all
- これらの本は全て読みました。— I have read all these books.
290 | 0.98

267 教える oshieru *v.* teach, tell
- 私は英語を教えています。— I teach English.
290 | 0.65 | WB

268 子 ko *n.* child
- うちの子は5歳です。— My child is five years old.
287 | 0.90

269 ておく te oku *cp.* do something in advance, in preparation for something
- お客さんが来るので、部屋をきれいにしておいた。— I cleaned the room because I had a visitor.
287 | 0.99

270 に対して ni taishi te *cp.* to, toward; for; against
- 彼は誰に対しても優しい。— He is kind to everyone.
287 | 0.88

271 ばかり bakari *p.* only, just, almost
- 今朝、着いたばかりです。— I arrived here only this morning.
286 | 0.94

272 なぜ naze *adv.* why
- なぜ学校へ行かなかったの。— Why didn't you go to school?
283 | 0.95

273 水 mizu *n.* water
- グラスから水がこぼれた。— Water spilled from the glass.
282 | 0.97

274 当時 touji *n.* then, at that time
- 当時、日本の物価はもっと高かった。— The prices in Japan were higher then.
282 | 0.88

275 場所 basho *n.* place, spot, position
- ソファーを置く場所を変えましょう。— Let's change the position of the sofa.
280 | 0.92

276 置く oku *v.* put, place; leave
- 部屋に荷物を置いた。— I put my bag in the room.
280 | 0.99

277 楽しい tanoshii *i-adj.* pleasant, happy, enjoyable
- とても楽しかったです。— I had a very good time.
279 | 0.82

278 にとって ni tot-te *cp.* for
- 私にとって彼は大切な人です。— He is the significant other for me.
279 | 0.96

279 声 koe *n.* voice
- 彼は小さな声で話した。— He talked in a low voice.
275 | 0.90 | BK

280 普通 futsuu *na-adj.* normal, regular, ordinary, common
- 彼女は普通じゃない。— She is not normal.
275 | 0.82

281 残る nokoru *v.* remain, be left
- 仕事を終えるために一人でオフィスに残った。— I stayed in the office alone to finish the work.
273 | 0.91

282 最後 saigo *n.* last, end
- これが最後のチャンスだ。— This is the last chance.
272 | 0.95

283 車 kuruma *n.* car; wheel
- 彼女は車で買い物に出かけた。— She went shopping by car.
271 | 0.90

284 初めて hajimete *adv.* for the first time, first
- 彼と初めて会ったのは去年の夏です。— I met him last summer for the first time.
271 | 0.95

285 今度 kondo *n.* this time, next time
- 今度の日曜日、映画を見に行きませんか。— Would you like to go to see a movie next Sunday?
270 | 0.86

286 体 karada *n.* body
- 昨日フルマラソンに出たので体が痛い。— My body aches from running a marathon yesterday.
266 | 0.93

287 私達 watashi-tachi, watakushi-tachi *pron.* we
- 私達、結婚しました。— We got married.
264 | 0.92 | BK

288 強い tsuyoi *i-adj.* strong, powerful
- 彼は力が強い。— He is strong.
264 | 1.00

289 全く mattaku *adv.* entirely, completely; (not) at all
- 二人は兄弟だが、性格は全く違う。— They are brothers, but their characters are completely different.
263 | 0.96

290 呼ぶ yobu *v.* call
- タクシーを呼んでください。— Please call a taxi for me.
261 | 0.96 | BK

291 結局 kekkyoku *adv.* after all, in the end, finally
- よく考えたが、結局、新車は買わないことにした。— I decided not to buy a new car after all.
259 | 0.79

292 歩く aruku *v.* walk
- 祖母はゆっくり歩く。— My grandma walks slowly.
258 | 0.87

293 男 otoko *n.* man, male
- 彼は男の中の男だ。— He is a real man.
256 | 0.83 | BK

294 女性 josei *n.* woman, female
- 男性より女性のほうが長生きする。— Women live longer than men.
254 | 0.97

295 学校 gakkou *n.* school
- 私は歩いて学校へ通っている。— I go to school on foot.
253 | 0.93

296 生きる ikiru *v.* live
- 九十歳まで生きる人は多くない。— There are not many people who live up to ninety years old.
253 | 0.91

297 なかなか nakanaka *adv.* very, quite; (not) easily
- 彼はなかなかテニスが上手い。— He plays tennis quite well.
251 | 0.89

298 先 saki *n.* end, front
- その犬は尻尾の先が茶色い。— The end of the dog's tail is brown.
250 | 0.94

299 もっと motto *adv.* more
- もっといい方法があるはずだ。— There must be a better way.
249 | 0.96

300 ことができる koto ga dekiru *cp.* can, be able to
- この図書館は誰でも利用することができる。— Everybody can use this library.
246 | 0.81

301 テーマ teema *n.* theme, subject
- 論文のテーマは何ですか。— What is the theme of your thesis?
245 | 0.66

302 世界 sekai *n.* world
- これは世界で一番高いビルです。— This is the tallest building in the world.
245 | 0.99

303 状態 joutai *n.* state, conditions
- 患者は危険な状態だ。— The patient is in a critical condition.
244 | 0.97

304 と to *interj.* well, erm (abbreviation of "eeto")
- と、まあ、そんな感じです。— Erm, well, something like that.
243 | 0.19 | SP

305 もし moshi *adv.* if, in case
- もしお金があったら、海外旅行がしたい。— If I had enough money, I would travel abroad.
242 | 0.93

306 全然 zenzen *adv.* (not) at all; utterly, completely
- その新しいテレビドラマは全然面白くない。— The new TV drama series isn't interesting at all.
241 | 0.67

307 飲む nomu *v.* drink
- 昨日の夜は飲みすぎてしまった。— I drank too much alcohol last night.
241 | 0.85

308 新しい atarashii *i-adj.* new, fresh
- 新しいテレビを買った。— I bought a new TV.
240 | 1.00

309 の no *p. disc.* EMOTION/QUESTION
- どうして泣いてるの。— Why are you crying?
239 | 0.80

310 早い hayai *i-adj.* early, soon
- 諦めるのはまだ早い。— It's too early to give up.
236 | 0.96

311 会う au *v.* meet, see
- 昨日、友達と会った。— I met a friend of mine yesterday.
236 | 0.90

312 アメリカ amerika *n.* America
- アメリカは大きい。— America is big.
234 | 0.96

313 あれ are *pron.* that
- あれは誰の車ですか。— Whose car is that?
234 | 0.86

314 小さい chiisai *i-adj.* small, little, tiny
- このおもちゃは小さい子供向けです。— This toy is for small children.
233 | 0.92

315 相手 aite *n.* companion; partner
- 結婚したくても相手がいません。— I'd love to get married but can't find a partner.
232 | 0.91

316 母 haha *n.* mother
- 私の母は六十歳です。— My mother is sixty years old.
232 | 0.84

317 以上 ijou *n.* more than; mentioned above; since
- 七十歳以上の高齢者が毎年増加している。— The number of people over seventy years old is increasing every year.
232 | 0.87

318 関係 kankei *n.* relationship, connection
- 我が社は取引先とよい関係を築いている。— Our company has established a good business relationship with the client.
232 | 0.96

319 四 yon, shi *n.* four
- 日本では四という数字は不吉と考えられている。— The number four is considered unlucky in Japan.
231 | 0.81

320 たぶん tabun *adv.* probably, perhaps, maybe
- 彼女はたぶん来ないでしょう。— She probably won't come.
228 | 0.70

321 店 mise *n.* store, shop
- 通りにはおしゃれな店が並んでいる。— The streets are lined with fashionable shops.
228 | 0.84

322 どんな donna *adn.* what, what kind of
- 明子さんのご主人はどんな人ですか。— What is Akiko's husband like?
227 | 0.94

323 頭 atama *n.* head
- 彼は頭を掻いた。— He scratched his head.
227 | 0.90

324 電話(する) denwa(suru) *n.* (tele)phone, call *v.* (tele)phone, call
- 電話をお借りしてもいいですか。— Can I use your phone?
225 | 0.89

325 長い nagai *i-adj.* long
- 彼女は髪が長い。— Her hair is long.
224 | 0.97

326 ことになる koto ni naru *cp.* it happens that ..., it is decided that
- 来月、神戸へ転勤することになりました。— They've decided to move me to Kobe next month.
224 | 0.80

327 本 hon *n.* book
- 彼はよく本を読んでいる。— He often reads books.
223 | 0.90

328 どの dono *adn.* which, what
- どの人が田中さんですか。— Which is Mr. Tanaka?
222 | 0.94

329 こちら kochira *pron.* this place, here; this way; this
- こちらへ来てください。— Please come this way.
222 | 0.82

330 いわゆる iwayuru *adn.* what is called, what you call, so-called
- これがいわゆるスマートフォンです。— This is what is called a smartphone.
222 | 0.76

331 わ wa *p. disc.* EXCLAMATION
- まあ、きれいだわ。— How beautiful it is!
222 | 0.78 | BK

332 夜 yoru *n.* night, evening
- 昨日の夜、どこにいたんですか。— Where were you last night?
220 | 0.88

333 別 betsu *na-adj.* separate, different
- 恋愛と結婚は別だ。— A love affair and a marriage are two different things.
217 | 0.96

334 者 mono *n.* person, people
- 担当の者が戻りましたら、折り返しお電話いたします。— When the person in charge comes back, he will call you back.
217 | 0.67

335 タイトル taitoru *n.* title
- 論文のタイトルを考えている。— I'm thinking about the title of my thesis.
217 | 0.45

336 親 oya *n.* parent
- 親を悲しませるようなことはするべきではない。— You should not do things that make your parents sad.
216 | 0.90

337 名前 namae *n.* name
- 彼の名前が思い出せない。— I can't remember his name.
215 | 0.91

338 全部 zenbu *adv.* all, whole, entire
- 料理が多すぎて全部食べられなかった。— There was too much food, and I couldn't eat it all.
214 | 0.85

339 皆さん mina-san *n.* everybody, everyone
- 皆さん、こんばんは。— Good evening, everyone.
213 | 0.87 | WB

340 により *ni yori* *cp.* by; with; depending on
- 二十歳未満の若者の飲酒は、法律により禁止されています。— Drinking alcohol is illegal for people under twenty.
213 | 0.58

341 きれい *kirei* *na-adj.* beautiful, pretty; clean
- 彼の家はいつもきれいだ。— His house is always clean.
212 | 0.84

342 立つ *tatsu* *v.* stand
- 立ってください。— Please stand up.
212 | 0.97

343 毎日 *mainichi* *adv.* every day
- 毎日コーヒーを飲みます。— I drink coffee every day.
212 | 0.85

344 ために *tame ni* *cp.* for
- 健康のために野菜をたくさん食べています。— I eat a lot of vegetables for my health.
211 | 0.82

345 おいしい *oishii* *i-adj.* delicious, tasty
- おいしい料理を食べた。— I had a delicious meal.
210 | 0.75 | WB

346 または *mata wa* *conj.* or
- これに塩またはしょうゆを付けて食べてください。— Please eat this with some salt or soy sauce added.
210 | 0.75

347 家族 *kazoku* *n.* family
- クリスマスは毎年家族で過ごします。— I spend Christmas with my family every year.
209 | 0.93

348 に対する *ni taisuru* *cp.* to; for; against
- 政府に対する抗議デモが行われる。— A demonstration against the government will take place.
208 | 0.72

349 部分 *bubun* *n.* part, section
- 間違えた部分を修正してください。— Please correct the parts where you made errors.
207 | 0.98

350 一度 *ichi do* *n.* once
- 私は一度だけ沖縄へ行ったことがあります。— I have been to Okinawa only once.
207 | 0.95

351 結果 *kekka* *n.* result
- 調査の結果を報告します。— I'm going to report the results of the investigation.
205 | 0.96

352 じゃ *ja* *conj.* well, so, then
- じゃ、また明日。— So, see you tomorrow.
204 | 0.71

353 状況 *joukyou* *n.* state of affairs, situation
- 困難な状況の中で、救助活動が続けられている。— Rescue efforts are continuing in difficult circumstances.
203 | 0.87

354 時代 *jidai* *n.* time, era
- 内戦後、平和な時代になった。— After the civil war, peace has returned.
202 | 0.95

355 少ない *sukunai* *i-adj.* a little, a few
- 日本では年収が六百万円以上ある三十代の男性は少ない。— There are few men in their thirties in Japan who earn more than six million yen in a year.
201 | 1.00

356 他 *hoka* *n.* another, other
- その国は他の国に比べて資源が豊かだ。— The country is rich in natural resources in comparison to other countries.
201 | 0.83

357 うまい *umai* *i-adj.* delicious, tasty; good at
- この酒はうまい。— This sake is tasty.
- 彼は歌がうまい。— He is a good singer.
200 | 0.92

358 覚える *oboeru* *v.* learn, remember, memorize
- 酔っ払っていて、昨夜のことは何も覚えていない。— I don't remember anything about last night, because I got drunk.
200 | 0.84

359 東京 *toukyou* *n.* Tokyo
- 東京から大阪まで新幹線で約２時間半です。— It takes about two and a half hours from Tokyo to Osaka by bullet train.
200 | 0.95

360 てある *te aru* *cp.* [describes a state resulting from someone's action]
- このページに説明が書いてあります。— The explanation is written on this page.
200 | 0.96

361 続く *tsuzuku* *v.* continue, go on, last
- この不景気は数年間続いている。— The recession has continued for several years.
198 | 1.00

362 における *ni oke ru* *cp.* in
- 輸入牛肉が増えた結果、日本国内における小売価格が下がった。— As a result of the increase of imported beef, the retail price of beef in Japan went down.
197 | 0.47

363 俺 ore *pron.* I (used by male speakers)
- 彼は「俺について来い」と言った。— He said, "Follow me."
196 | 0.81 | BK

364 生まれる umareru *v.* be born
- 昨日、赤ちゃんが生まれた。— The baby was born yesterday.
196 | 0.95

365 父 chichi *n.* father
- 父はガンで亡くなった。— My father died of cancer.
194 | 0.83

366 確か tashika *na-adj., adv.* sure, certain, reliable *adv.* maybe, probably; if I remember rightly, it's my understanding that
- 彼の技術は確かだ。— His technique is reliable.
- 確か彼はここに来たことがあると思います。— If I remember rightly, he has been here before.
194 | 0.97

367 それぞれ sorezore *n.* each
- 人にはそれぞれ良い時と悪い時がある。— Each of us has ups and downs.
193 | 0.90

368 方法 houhou *n.* way, method
- いい方法を思いつきました。— I came up with a good method.
192 | 0.97

369 はず hazu *n.* ought to, should
- 彼女は今頃そこへ着いているはずだ。— She should have arrived there by now.
191 | 0.89

370 説明（する）setsumei(suru) *n.* explanation *v.* explain
- 詳しく説明してください。— Please explain it in detail.
191 | 0.98

371 なければいけない nakere ba ike nai *cp.* must, have to, need to
- もっと勉強しなければいけないと思った。— I thought that I must study more.
191 | 0.00 | SP

372 部屋 heya *n.* room
- 自分の部屋に戻った。— I went back to my room.
190 | 0.88

373 ちょうど choudo *adv.* just, exactly
- 彼は五時ちょうどにここへ来た。— He came here at five o'clock exactly.
190 | 0.74

374 当然 touzen *adv., n.* naturally, as a matter of course
- そう考えるのも当然だ。— It is natural for you to think so.
189 | 0.94

375 大学 daigaku *n.* university, college
- 私は地下鉄で大学へ通っている。— I go to university by subway.
189 | 0.88

376 ですから desu kara *conj.* so, therefore
- これは重要なことですから、覚えておいてください。— Please remember this, because it's very important.
188 | 0.68

377 実 jitsu *n.* truth, true, real
- 実を言うと、朝から何も食べていないんです。— To tell you the truth, I have not eaten anything since this morning.
187 | 0.77

378 朝 asa *n.* morning
- 彼女は朝から晩まで勉強している。— She is studying from morning till night.
187 | 0.83

379 どんどん dondon *adv.* rapidly, fast, soon
- 子供はどんどん大きくなる。— Children grow very quickly.
186 | 0.75

380 得る eru, uru *v.* get, obtain
- 多くの人の協力を得ることができた。— I got help from many people.
186 | 0.92

381 とにかく tonikaku *adv.* anyway, regardless
- とにかく、すぐに来てください。— Anyway, please come as soon as possible.
186 | 0.83

382 選ぶ erabu *v.* choose, select
- 彼女は結婚して主婦になる道を選んだ。— She chose to get married and be a housewife.
186 | 0.94

383 面白い omoshiroi *i-adj.* interesting; fun; funny
- 彼は面白い人です。— He is an interesting man.
186 | 0.84

384 戻る modoru *v.* return, go back
- 一時までに学校へ戻らなければならない。— I have to go back to school by 1 p.m.
185 | 0.90

385 勉強（する）benkyou(suru) *n.* study *v.* learn, study
- 彼は試験のために一生懸命勉強しています。— He is studying hard for the exam.
185 | 0.80

386 やめる yameru *v.* stop, give up
- 彼は煙草をやめた。— He gave up smoking.
183 | 0.91

387 下 shita *n.* under; below; down; low
- セーターの下にシャツを着ている。— I am wearing a shirt under my sweater.
183 | 0.99

388 始める hajimeru *v.* start, begin
- いつ日本語の勉強を始めたんですか。— When did you start studying Japanese?
182 | 0.96

389 まわり mawari *n.* circumference; surroundings, neighborhood, around
- この植物はその湖の周りに生えている。— That plant grows around the lake.
182 | 0.85

390 犬 inu *n.* dog
- 外で犬が吠えている。— A dog is barking outside.
182 | 0.79

391 必ず kanarazu *adv.* always, certainly, surely
- 彼は必ず成功するに違いない。— He must always succeed.
181 | 0.92

392 残す nokosu *v.* leave
- 留守番電話にメッセージを残した。— I left a message on the answering machine.
180 | 0.91

393 大事 daiji *na-adj.* important, serious
- 明日は大事な会議がある。— I have an important meeting tomorrow.
180 | 0.90

394 嬉しい ureshii *i-adj.* glad, happy
- 試験に合格して嬉しい。— I'm glad I passed the exam.
180 | 0.83

395 力 chikara *n.* power, strength
- 彼は力が強い。— He is strong.
180 | 0.98

396 遊ぶ asobu *v.* play
- コンピューターゲームで遊ぶのが好きだ。— I like to play computer games.
179 | 0.85

397 若い wakai *i-adj.* young
- その歌手は若い人に人気がある。— The singer is popular among young people.
179 | 0.92

398 理由 riyuu *n.* reason
- 彼女が独身でいるのには理由がある。— There is a reason why she chooses to remain single.
179 | 0.99

399 女 onna *n.* woman, female
- あの女の人は誰ですか。— Who is that woman?
179 | 0.82 | BK

400 簡単 kantan *na-adj.* easy
- インスタントラーメンを作るのは簡単だ。— It is easy to cook instant noodles.
178 | 0.96

401 始まる hajimaru *v.* start, begin
- 日本では新学期は四月に始まる。— The new school year starts in April in Japan.
178 | 0.97

402 死ぬ shinu *v.* die
- 人間はいつかは死ぬ。— All men must die.
176 | 0.86

2 Body

(frequency per million words)

目, 眼 **me** 467.309 **eye**
手 **te** 406.651 **hand**
顔 **kao** 309.511 **face**
頭 **atama** 226.889 **head**
足 **ashi** 167.325 **foot, leg**
口 **kuchi** 158.414 **mouth**
耳 **mimi** 85.091 **ear**
首 **kubi** 75.243 **neck, head (also firing, sacking (of an employee))**
胸 **mune** 72.392 **chest, heart**
肩 **kata** 58.469 **shoulder**
腰 **koshi** 54.982 **back, lower back, waist, hip**
腕 **ude** 53.929 **arm (also skill, ability)**

指 **yubi** 48.273 **finger**
腹 **hara** 42.044 **belly, stomach**
歯 **ha** 40.119 **tooth**
髪 **kami** 36.985 **hair**
鼻 **hana** 36.484 **nose**
背中 **senaka** 35.183 **back**
肌 **hada** 34.626 **skin**
骨 **hone** 34.407 **bone**
背 **se** 32.996 **back (also stature)**
膝 **hiza** 31.588 **knee, lap**
筋肉 **kinniku** 29.864 **muscle**
喉 **nodo** 26.585 **throat (also voice)**
唇 **kuchibiru** 26.490 **lip**
心臓 **shinzou** 21.016 **heart**
胃 **i** 19.729 **stomach, belly**

尻 **o-shiri** 18.831 **hips**
舌 **shita** 18.603 **tongue**
爪 **tsume** 17.709 **nail (also claw)**
毛 **ke** 17.503 **hair (also fur, wool)**
髪の毛 **kami no ke** 17.353 **hair**
皮膚 **hifu** 16.438 **skin**
顎 **ago** 15.310 **jaw, chin**
手のひら **tenohira** 14.759 **palm (of the hand)**
頬 **hoo** 14.198 **cheek**
脂肪 **shibou** 12.027 **fat**
肝臓 **kanzou** 11.046 **liver**
眉 **mayu** 10.304 **eyebrow**
肘 **hiji** 9.350 **elbow**

403 今回 konkai *n.* this time
- 今回、彼女は大統領に選ばれなかった。— This time, she wasn't elected as President.
176 | 0.92

404 に関する ni kansuru *cp.* be concerned with, be related to
- これは宗教に関する本です。— This is a book about religion.
175 | 0.55

405 人生 jinsei *n.* life
- 私は彼女に幸せな人生を送ってほしい。— I want her to have a happy life.
175 | 0.84

406 通り touri *n.* street; as
- 言われた通りにやりなさい。— Do as you are told.
174 | 0.88

407 内容 naiyou *n.* contents
- あなたが送る荷物の内容は何ですか。— What are the contents of the box you are sending?
174 | 0.89

408 テレビ terebi *n.* television, TV
- 今日は一日中テレビを見ていた。— I watched TV all day today.
174 | 0.87

409 経験(する) keiken(suru) *n.* experience *v.* experience
- 彼は仕事の経験がない。— He has no job experience.
173 | 0.95

410 木 ki *n.* wood; tree
- 公園に桜の木が植えられた。— Cherry trees were planted in the park.
173 | 0.77

411 点 ten *n.* point, score
- 不明な点があれば、私に聞いてください。— If you do not understand any points, please ask me.
172 | 0.77

412 自然 shizen *n.* nature *na-adj.* natural *adv.* naturally
- ここでは豊かな自然が守られている。— Rich nature is protected here.
172 | 0.96

413 音 oto *n.* sound, noise
- 車のエンジンの音が聞こえた。— I heard the sound of a car engine.
171 | 0.93

414 海 umi *n.* sea, ocean
- そのホテルの部屋は海に面している。— The hotel room faces the ocean.
171 | 0.91

415 一応 ichiou *adv.* at first glance; at least, just
- 必要かどうか分かりませんが、一応、その書類を持ってきてください。— I'm not sure if the papers are needed, but please take them, just in case.
170 | 0.68

416 与える ataeru *v.* give, present
- 私は彼女の両親に良い印象を与えようと努めた。— I tried to make a good impression on her parents.
170 | 0.95

417 利用(する) riyou(suru) *n.* use, utilization *v.* utilize
- 私は時々図書館を利用する。— I sometimes use the library.
169 | 0.93

418 働く hataraku *v.* work
- 兄は自動車工場で働いている。— My brother works at an automobile factory.
169 | 0.98

419 一杯 ippai *n., adv.* cup(ful), glass(ful), be full of, a lot of
- ワインを一杯飲んだ。— I took a glass of wine.
169 | 0.75

420 近く chikaku *n.* near, nearby
- いつも近くの店で買い物をする。— I always do the shopping at a nearby store.
169 | 0.84

421 つまり tsumari *adv.* in short, that is to say, after all
- つまり何が言いたいのですか。— In short, what is your point?
169 | 0.92 | BK

422 共 tomo *n.* with, together
- 妻と共に田舎で農業を始めた。— I took up farming with my wife in the countryside.
169 | 0.93

423 存在(する) sonzai(suru) *n.* existence *v.* exist
- 幽霊の存在を信じますか。— Do you believe in ghosts?
169 | 0.93 | BK

424 絶対 zettai *n., adv.* absolute, absolutely, whatever
- 明日の試合は絶対に勝たなければならない。— We must win the game tomorrow.
168 | 0.89

425 日本人 nihon-jin, nippon-jin *n.* Japanese (person)
- 日本人は勤勉だと思います。— I think that Japanese are diligent.
168 | 0.91

426 大切 taisetsu *na-adj.* important
- 継続的に努力することが大切だ。— It is important to make sustained efforts.
168 | 0.96

427 足 ashi *n.* foot; leg
- ハイヒールを履くと足が痛む。— My legs hurt when I wear high heels.
167 | 0.91

428 切る kiru *v.* cut
- 紙を半分に切ってください。— Please cut the paper in half.
167 | 0.94

429 走る hashiru *v.* run
- 駅まで走りましょう。間に合うかもしれません。— Let's run to the station. We might make it.
167 | 0.93

430 待つ matsu *v.* wait
- ちょっとお待ちください。— Wait a moment, please.
167 | 0.93

431 写真 shashin *n.* picture, photo
- 家族で写真を撮った。— I took a picture with my family.
163 | 0.88

432 子供たち kodomo-tachi *n.* children
- 公園で子供たちが遊んでいる。— Children are playing in the park.
162 | 0.91

433 だんだん dandan *adv.* gradually, more and more, less and less
- だんだん寒くなってきた。— It's getting colder and colder.
161 | 0.61

434 二つ futa-tsu *n.* two
- リンゴを二つ買った。— I bought two apples.
161 | 0.97

435 楽しむ tanoshimu *v.* enjoy, have a good time
- 休暇を楽しむつもりだ。— I will enjoy my holiday.
161 | 0.85

436 五 go *n.* five
- 五かける五は二十五。— Five times five equals twenty-five.
160 | 0.84

437 多く ooku *n.* many, most
- そこには毎年多くの観光客が訪れる。— Many tourists visit that place every year.
160 | 0.94

438 寝る neru *v.* sleep; lie down, go to bed
- 昨夜は十一時に寝た。— I went to bed at 11 p.m. last night.
159 | 0.81

439 英語 eigo *n.* English language
- 英語が話せますか。— Can you speak English?
159 | 0.77

440 決める kimeru *v.* decide, fix
- 待ち合わせの時間と場所を決めよう。— Let's fix the time and place to meet.
159 | 1.00

441 忘れる wasureru *v.* forget
- 忘れないでください。— Don't forget.
159 | 0.90

442 口 kuchi *n.* mouth
- 大きく口を開けてください。— Open your mouth, please.
158 | 0.86 | BK

443 送る okuru *v.* send; spend (time)
- 母に感謝の手紙を送る。— I will send my mother a letter of thanks.
157 | 0.93

444 姿 sugata *n.* figure, shape, appearance
- 最近彼の姿を見ない。— I have seen nothing of him lately.
157 | 0.93

445 なくなる nakunaru *v.* disappear; be gone
- 無駄遣いしていたので、すぐに貯金がなくなってしまった。— As I wasted money the savings quickly disappeared.
157 | 0.94

446 時期 jiki *n.* time, period, season
- この時期はいつも雪が降る。— It always snows at this time of the year.
156 | 0.98

447 逆 gyaku *n., na-adj.* contrary, opposite
- 予想とは逆の結果が出た。— The result was contrary to our expectations.
156 | 0.95

448 頑張る ganbaru *v.* do one's best
- 頑張ります。— I'll do my best.
156 | 0.77 | WB

449 示す shimesu *v.* show
- 大使はその大臣の提案に興味を示した。— The ambassador showed an interest in the minister's suggestion.
155 | 0.76

450 こそ koso *p.* EMPHATIC
- 今年こそ試験に合格したい。— I want to pass the exam this year for sure.
155 | 0.95

451 人々 hitobito *n.* people
- 不景気のため、多くの人々が職を失った。— Many people lost their jobs, because of the recession.
155 | 0.90 | BK

452 道 michi *n.* way, road
- 道を間違えてしまった。— I went the wrong way.
155 | 0.95

453 有名 yuumei *na-adj.* famous, well-known
- 彼はとても有名な作家です。— He is a very famous writer.
155 | 0.77

454 てもいい te mo ii *cp.* (I) don't mind if
- 電話をお借りしてもいいですか。— Do you mind if I use your phone?
154 | 0.90

455 思い omoi *n.* thought, mind, heart
- その子はさびしい思いをしていたに違いない。— The boy must have felt lonely.
154 | 0.94

456 しかも shikamo *conj.* moreover, besides
- その店の料理はおいしいし、しかも、安い。— The food at the restaurant is delicious; moreover, it is cheap.
154 | 0.98

457 難しい muzukashii, mutsukashii *i-adj.* difficult, hard
- その問題の解決は難しい。— The problem is difficult to solve.
153 | 0.99

458 彼ら kare-ra *pron.* they
- 彼らは会社の同僚です。— They are colleagues in my company.
153 | 0.79 | BK

459 山 yama *n.* mountain
- 週末は友達と山に登る。— I'm going to climb the mountain with my friends this weekend.
153 | 0.92

460 程度 teido *n.* degree, grade, level, limit
- そのテキストは中級程度の日本語学習者向けです。— The textbook was written for intermediate level learners of Japanese.
152 | 0.97

461 でない de nai *cp.* COPULA (NEGATIVE)
- その店には日本産でない製品がたくさんある。— There are many products in the shop which are not made in Japan.
152 | 0.97

462 願う negau *v.* wish, ask, pray
- お二人の幸せを願っております。— Best wishes for a happy life together.
152 | 0.82 | WB

463 すでに sudeni *adv.* already, before
- 電車は既に出た後だった。— The train had already gone.
151 | 0.95

464 昭和 shouwa *n.* Showa era
- 私は昭和の生まれです。— I was born in the Showa era.
151 | 0.55

465 向かう mukau *v.* face; go (toward, in the direction of)
- 私はこれから大阪へ向かいます。— I'm going to Osaka.
151 | 0.93

466 連れる tsureru *v.* take somebody, accompany
- 子供を公園へ連れて行った。— I took my children to the park.
150 | 0.82

467 変える kaeru *v.* change
- 話題を変えましょう。— Let's change the subject.
150 | 0.99

468 影響(する) eikyou(suru) *n.* influence *v.* affect, influence
- 彼の作品はピカソの影響を強く受けている。— His works are greatly influenced by Picasso.
149 | 0.92

469 病院 byouin *n.* hospital, clinic
- 具合が悪かったので病院へ行った。— I went to the hospital because I felt sick.
149 | 0.91

470 年 toshi *n.* year; age
- 彼女は年ほどには見えない。— She looks young for her age.
149 | 0.90

471 花 hana *n.* flower
- 公園に花が咲いている。— The flowers are in bloom in the park.
149 | 0.89

472 求める motomeru *v.* ask for, request, demand
- 私たちはその件について彼に説明を求めた。— We demanded an explanation of the matter from him.
149 | 0.88

473 情報 jouhou *n.* information
- 有益な情報を得た。— I got some useful information.
148 | 0.97

474 もらう morau *v.* get, have, receive
- 友達にすてきな絵をもらった。— My friend gave me a nice picture.
148 | 0.86

475 友人 yuujin *n.* friend
- 彼女は友人代表としてスピーチをした。— She made a speech on behalf of her friends.
148 | 0.81

476 だめ dame *na-adj.* useless, hopeless, impossible
- 私はお酒はだめなんです。— I can't drink alcohol.

148 | 0.88

477 経つ tatsu *v.* pass, go by
- 彼が死んでから十年経つ。— Ten years have passed since he died.

148 | 0.90

478 先程 sakihodo *n.* a short while ago
- 先程、田中様からお電話がありました。— Mr. Tanaka called you a little while ago.

148 | 0.68

479 一回 ikkai *n.* once
- 私は週に一回買い物に行きます。— I go shopping once a week.

147 | 0.80

480 十分 juubun *na-adj.* enough, sufficient *adv.* fully, sufficiently, adequately
- 留学するのに十分なお金を貯めた。— I saved enough money to study abroad.
- 彼は登山の危険性を十分理解している。— He fully understands the risks of mountain climbing.

147 | 0.90

481 小さな chiisana *adn.* small, little, tiny
- 彼女には小さな子供が二人いる。— She has two small children.

147 | 0.93

482 開く hiraku *v.* open; bloom; hold
- 会議は来週開かれる。— The meeting will be held next week.

146 | 0.94

483 無人島 mujin-tou *n.* uninhabited island
- あれは無人島です。— That is an uninhabited island.

146 | 0.07 | SP

484 続ける tsuzukeru *v.* continue, keep up, go on
- 彼女は結婚しても仕事を続けるつもりだ。— She will continue to work even after she gets married.

146 | 0.99

485 重要 juuyoo *na-adj.* important
- 彼は重要な役割を果たした。— He played an important role.

145 | 0.83

486 といった to it-ta *cp.* like, such as
- この地域ではリンゴやモモといった果物の栽培が盛んだ。— This area grows lots of fruit, such as apples and peaches.

145 | 0.95

487 当たる ataru *v.* hit, bump, touch; guess right, win
- ボールが頭に当たった。— The ball hit my head.

144 | 0.99

488 近い chikai *i-adj.* near, close
- その店はここから近い。— That shop is near here.

144 | 0.97

489 結婚(する) kekkon(suru) *n.* marriage *v.* marry, get married
- 彼女は来月結婚する。— She is going to get married next month.

144 | 0.91

490 認める mitomeru *v.* recognize, acknowledge, admit, approve, accept
- 父は私たちの結婚を認めなかった。— My father did not approve of our marriage.

144 | 0.84

491 これら kore-ra *pron.* these
- これらの製品は外国へ輸出されます。— These products will be exported to other countries.

143 | 0.74

492 歴史 rekishi *n.* history
- 歴史は繰り返す 。— History repeats itself.

143 | 0.92

493 増える fueru *v.* increase, gain
- 体重が3キロ増えた。— I have gained three kilograms.

143 | 0.99

494 音楽 ongaku *n.* music
- 私は音楽を聴くのが好きです。— I like to listen to music.

142 | 0.82

495 なければならない nakere ba nara nai *cp.* must
- 今日中にこのメールを出さなければならない。— I have to send this e-mail today.

142 | 0.62

496 外 soto *n.* outside
- 子供達が外で遊んでいる。— Children are playing outside.

142 | 0.93

497 進む susumu *v.* to go forward, make progress
- 計画は予定通り進んでいる。— The plan is progressing according to schedule.

142 | 0.97

498 起きる okiru *v.* get up; wake; happen
- 明日の朝、早く起きなければならい。— I have to get up early tomorrow morning.

141 | 0.97

499 嫌 iya, ya *n., na-adj.* unpleasant, disagreeable
- 嫌な匂いが服に染み付いた。— An unpleasant smell was ingrained in my clothes.

141 | 0.82

500 駅 eki *n.* station
- 次の駅で電車を降ります。— I get off the train at the next station.
139 | 0.73

501 いや iya *interj.* No
- 「私のせいだというんですか」「いや、そういうことではないんです」— "Are you saying this is my fault?" "No, that's not what I mean."
139 | 0.92

502 はい hai *interj.* yes; all right
- はい。わかりました。— Yes, I see.
139 | 0.81

503 映画 eiga *n.* movie
- 友達と映画を見た。— I saw the movie with a friend.
139 | 0.86

504 身 mi *n.* body, oneself; position
- 危険から身を守る。— You protect yourself from the danger.
139 | 0.91

505 客 kyaku *n.* guest, visitor; customer
- 店に客が一人もいない。— There are no customers in the store.
138 | 0.91

506 質問(する) shitsumon(suru) *n.* question *v.* question
- 質問があります。— I have a question.
138 | 0.72 | WB

507 含む fukumu *v.* contain, include
- みかんにはビタミンが含まれている。— Mandarin oranges contain vitamins.
138 | 0.84

508 地域 chiiki *n.* region, area
- 地域の住民はお互いに助け合った。— The residents of the area helped each other.
138 | 0.81

509 我が waga *adn.* my, our, one's
- 我が社は1900年に設立された。— Our company was established in 1900.
138 | 0.53

510 どうしても dou shi te mo *adv.* by all means, at any cost, no matter what, after all
- どうしても思い出せなかった。— I couldn't for the life of me remember it.
138 | 0.88

511 のに no ni *p. conj.* although, though; in order to
- 明日が試験なのに、彼女は遊んでいる。— Even though the exams are tomorrow, she is just lazing around.
137 | 0.00 | SP

512 娘 musume *n.* daughter
- 娘が二人います。— I have two daughters.
137 | 0.85

513 見せる miseru *v.* show
- そのカバンを見せてください。— Please show me that bag.
136 | 0.95

514 一日 ichi nichi *n.* a day, the day, one day
- 一日30分走っています。— I run half an hour a day.
136 | 0.94

515 今年 kotoshi *n.* this year
- 今年の夏は暑い。— It is hot this summer.
136 | 0.85

516 平成 heisei *n.* Heisei era
- 平成は1989年一月八日から始まった。— The Heisei era began on January 8, 1989.
136 | 0.59

517 図 zu *n.* drawing, figure, diagram
- 先生は図を書いて説明した。— The teacher drew and explained the figure.
135 | 0.63

518 紹介(する) shoukai(suru) *n.* introduction *v.* introduce
- 親に友達を紹介した。— I introduced my friend to my parents.
135 | 0.92

519 合わせる awaseru *v.* join, add up; adjust
- 彼らは手を合わせて祈った。— They joined their hands in prayer.
135 | 0.94

520 安い yasui *i-adj.* low, cheap
- 安い宿に泊まる。— I stay in cheap accommodation.
134 | 0.83 | WB

521 夢 yume *n.* dream
- 昨日、夢を見た。— I had a dream yesterday.
134 | 0.91

522 つらい tsurai *i-adj.* hard, difficult, painful
- 彼は仕事のストレスで辛い思いをしている。— He has a hard time with stress from work.
133 | 0.76

523 規定(する) kitei(suru) *n.* regulations, stipulations *v.* prescribe
- 条例によって規定されている。— It is prescribed by regulations.
133 | 0.27 | OF

524 どちら dochira *pron.* where; which; who
- 魚と肉とどちらが好きですか。— Which do you like, fish or meat?
133 | 0.92

525 中心 chuushin *n.* center
- ここは町の中心です。— This is the center of the town.
131 | 0.87

526 起こる okoru *v.* happen, occur, take place
- 近所で恐ろしい事件が起こった。— A terrible incident occurred in my neighborhood.
131 | 0.97

527 我々 wareware *pron.* we
- それは国民としての我々の義務だ。— It is our duty as citizens.
130 | 0.88

528 (お)母さん (o)-kaa-san *n.* mother, Mom
- お母さん、話があるのだけど。— Mom, I want to tell you something.
130 | 0.84

529 立てる tateru *v.* stand, set up, put up
- 山頂に国旗を立てた。— They put up the national flag at the top of mountain.
129 | 0.97

530 最も mottomo *adv.* most, extremely
- 富士山は日本で最も高い山だ。— Mt. Fuji is the highest mountain in Japan.
128 | 0.87

531 色 iro *n.* color
- 彼女はきれいな色のセーターを着ている。— She is wearing a sweater in a beautiful color.
128 | 0.94

532 探す sagasu *v.* look for, search for, seek
- アパートを探しています。— I am looking for an apartment.
127 | 0.90

533 ちゃんと chanto *adv.* exactly, regularly, properly
- ちゃんと手を洗いましたか。— Did you wash your hands properly?
127 | 0.86

534 興味 kyoumi *n.* interest
- 日本にずっと興味があった。— I always had an interest in Japan
127 | 0.85

535 三つ mit-tsu *n.* three
- オレンジが三つあります。— There are three oranges.
126 | 0.91

536 てほしい te hoshii *cp.* want/ask someone to do
- 私と結婚してほしい。— I want you to marry me.
126 | 0.96

537 いただく itadaku *v.* get, receive (humble)
- 読者から手紙を頂いた。— I received a letter from a reader.
126 | 0.93

538 売る uru *v.* sell
- 彼は古着をフリーマーケットで売った。— He sold his used clothes at flea markets.
126 | 0.87

539 変化(する) henka(suru) *n.* change *v.* change, vary
- 社会は常に変化している。— Society is constantly changing.
126 | 0.86

540 印象 inshou *n.* impression
- 日本の印象はいかがですか。— What are your impressions of Japan?
126 | 0.84

541 作品 sakuhin *n.* work, production
- この作家の作品は素晴らしい。— This writer's work is wonderful.
126 | 0.92

542 でございます de gozai masu *cp.* be (formal)
- 恐れ入りますが満室でございます。— I'm afraid all our rooms are fully booked.
125 | 0.00 | SP

543 参加(する) sanka(suru) *n.* participation *v.* take part in, participate
- 多くの人がその会議に参加した。— Many people took part in the conference.
125 | 0.91

544 夏 natsu *n.* summer
- 日本の夏は蒸し暑い。— Summer in Japan is humid.
125 | 0.90

545 よる yoru *v.* be due to
- 事故は彼の不注意によるものだった。— The accident was due to his carelessness.
124 | 0.76

546 理解(する) rikai(suru) *n.* understanding *v.* understand
- 何を言っているのか理解できない。— I don't understand what you are saying.
124 | 0.95

547 事件 jiken *n.* incident, event
- 恐ろしい事件が起きた。— A terrible incident occurred.
124 | 0.96

548 中国 chuugoku *n.* China
- 中国は長い歴史を持っている。— China has a long history.
123 | 0.99

549 ずつ... zutsu *p.* each, ... by ...
- 母親は子供にキャンディを一つずつあげた。— The mother gave her children candies, one each.
123 | 0.97

550 母親 hahaoya *n.* mother
- 子供が母親を探している。— A child is looking for his mother.
123 | 0.87

551 取り敢えず toriaezu *adv.* for the time being; at once
- とりあえずお知らせします。— I will let you know at once.
122 | 0.74 | WB

552 ところが tokoro ga *conj.* however
- ところが計画はうまくいかなかった。— However, the plan didn't turn out to be a success.
122 | 0.93

553 目的 mokuteki *n.* purpose
- 目的を持って人生を生きたい。— I want to live a life with purpose.
122 | 0.88

554 様々 samazama *na-adj.* various, all kinds of
- 様々なことに興味がある。— I am interested in all kinds of things.
122 | 0.91

555 答える kotaeru *v.* answer, respond
- 学生は質問に答えた。— A student answered the question.
121 | 0.94

556 過ごす sugosu *v.* spend, live
- 友人と楽しい時間を過ごす。— I have a good time with my friends.
121 | 0.86

557 上がる agaru *v.* go up, rise; end; get nervous
- 38度まで気温が上がった。— The temperature rose to 38 degrees.
121 | 0.98

558 一方 ippou *n.* one side *conj.* on the other hand
- 一方だけの話を聞くのは不公平だ。— It's unfair to hear only one side of the story.
120 | 0.84

559 病気 byouki *n.* sickness, illness
- 彼は病気になった。— He became sick.
120 | 0.94

560 心配（する）shinpai(suru) *na-adj.* anxious, worried *n.* anxiety, worry, care *v.* worry, be anxious
- 心配しなくていいよ。— You needn't worry.
120 | 0.95

561 それでも sore de mo *conj.* but, still
- それでも、彼女はあきらめなかった。— Still, she never gave up.
120 | 0.90

562 イメージ（する）imeeji(suru) *n.* image *v.* imagine, have an impression
- このデザインは春をイメージしている。— This design was created to give an impression of spring.
119 | 0.90

563 笑い warai *n.* laugh, laughter
- 笑いをこらえることができなかった。— I couldn't help laughing.
118 | 0.49 | WB

564 午後 gogo *n.* afternoon, p.m.
- 午後、会議がある。— There is a meeting in the afternoon.
118 | 0.37 | NM

565 後 go *n.* after, later, since
- その後、彼女には会っていない。— Since then, I have not seen her.
118 | 0.98

566 動く ugoku *v.* move; work (machine)
- 動くな。— Don't move!
117 | 0.96

567 主人 shujin *n.* shop owner; husband
- ご主人はいらっしゃいますか。— Is your husband at home?
117 | 0.79

568 加える kuwaeru *v.* add, include
- スプーン一杯の砂糖を加える。— Add a teaspoon of sugar.
117 | 0.91

569 困る komaru *v.* have difficulty, be in trouble
- 困ったことになった。— I'm in trouble.
116 | 0.94

570 取れる toreru *v.* come off; be removed
- コートのボタンが取れた。— The button came off my coat.
115 | 0.96

571 環境 kankyou *n.* environment
- 地球の環境を守らなければならない。— We have to protect the earth's environment.
114 | 0.94

572 対応（する）taiou(suru) *n.* correspondence, response *v.* respond to
- リーダーはあらゆる状況に対応すべきだ。— A leader should respond to every situation.
114 | 0.83

573 比べる kuraberu *v.* compare, contrast
- いろいろな店で値段を比べた。— I compared the prices at different shops.
114 | 0.82

574 高校 koukou *n.* high school
- 高校で英語を教えている。— She teaches English in high school.
114 | 0.75

575 食事（する） shokuji(suru) *n.* meal *v.* have a meal
- 母は食事の準備を始めた。— My mother started to prepare a meal.
114 | 0.93

576 引く hiku *v.* pull, draw, lead; subtract
- この紐を引くとベルが鳴る。— Pull this cord to ring the bell.
113 | 0.96

577 辺 hen *n.* region, area around
- この辺はアパートが多い。— There are a lot of apartment buildings around here.
113 | 0.79

578 要するに yousuru ni *conj.* in short, to sum up
- 要するに、計画は失敗だった。— In short, our plan failed.
113 | 0.68

579 離れる hanareru *v.* separate; leave; be away from
- 学校は街の中心から1キロ離れている。— The school is one kilometer away from the center of town.
112 | 0.94

580 火 hi *n.* fire
- 彼は火を消した。— He put out the fire.
112 | 0.86

581 実施（する） jisshi(suru) *n.* operation *v.* enforce, conduct
- その会社はダイエットについての調査を実施した。— The company has conducted a survey on diet.
112 | 0.52 | OF

582 今後 kongo *adv.* in the future, from now on
- 今後、国際化が進むだろう。— In the future, internationalization will continue.
112 | 0.79

583 社会 shakai *n.* society
- 社会のために働きたい。— I would like to work for society.
112 | 0.95

584 練習（する） renshuu(suru) *n.* practice, training *v.* practice, train
- 毎日、ピアノの練習をする。— I practice on the piano every day.
112 | 0.89

585 使用（する） shiyou(suru) *n.* use *v.* use
- エネルギーの使用を減らさねばならない。— We must reduce the use of energy.
112 | 0.94

586 越える koeru *v.* cross over, go over
- 彼らは山を越えて旅をした。— They traveled over the mountains.
112 | 0.94

587 図る hakaru *v.* attempt; plan; strive
- 事態の改善を図らなければならない。— We must attempt to remedy the situation.
111 | 0.40 | OF

588 企業 kigyou *n.* company, business
- 兄は日本企業で働いている。— My brother works at a Japanese company.
111 | 0.86

589 奴 yatsu *n.* guy, fellow
- 彼はおもしろい奴です。— He is an interesting guy.
111 | 0.83

590 はっきり hakkiri *adv.* clearly, certainly
- はっきり覚えています。— I remember it clearly.
111 | 0.97

591 怖い kowai *i-adj.* frightening, scary; terrified
- 蛇が怖い。— I'm scared of snakes.
111 | 0.81

592 例 rei *n.* example
- 例を挙げていただけますか。— Could you give me an example?
111 | 0.90

593 絵 e *n.* picture, painting
- 絵を描くことが好きです。— I like drawing pictures.
111 | 0.91

594 思い出す omoidasu *v.* remember
- 両親の言葉を思い出した。— I remembered the words of my parents.
110 | 0.87

595 に関して ni kanshi te *cp.* about, regarding, concerning
- その件に関して情報を得たい。— I would like to obtain information about the matter.
110 | 0.94

596 酒 sake *n.* alcohol, sake, rice wine
- 酒を飲むのをやめようと決めた。— I decided to give up drinking alcohol.
109 | 0.92

597 原因 gen'in *n.* cause
- 警察は事故の原因を調査した。— The police investigated the cause of the accident.
109 | 0.99

598 お前 omae *n.* you (colloquial)
- お前に関係ない。— It's none of your business!
109 | 0.83 | BK

599 守る mamoru *v.* protect, defend; keep, obey
- 彼女は約束を守った。— She kept her promise.
109 | 0.96

3 Clothing

(frequency per million words)

(服・靴) (Clothes, shoes)

服 fuku 44.047 clothes, dress, outfit
靴 kutsu 29.758 shoes
着物 kimono 28.467 kimono
洋服 youfuku 25.972 clothes, suit, dress
ボタン botan 24.901 button
ポケット poketto 17.478 pocket
コート kooto 16.109 coat (also court)
帽子 boushi 15.985 hat, cap
ベスト besuto 13.534 vest (also best)
スーツ suutsu 12.800 suit
衣装 ishou 12.372 costume
シャツ shatsu 12.366 shirt
Tシャツ tii shatsu 12.061 T-shirt
スカート sukaato 11.523 skirt
パンツ pantsu 10.779 pants, shorts, underpants
帯 obi 10.219 obi, belt
浴衣 yukata 10.189 yukata, cotton kimono
制服 seifuku 9.776 uniform
ズボン zubon 9.286 pants, trousers
ジャケット jaketto 8.491 jacket
下着 shitagi 8.344 underwear
ドレス doresu 8.279 dress
セーター seetaa 6.622 sweater

靴下 kutsushita 5.960 socks
ネクタイ nekutai 5.928 tie
上着 uwagi 5.765 jacket
手袋 tebukuro 5.740 gloves
ブーツ buutsu 5.685 boots
マフラー mafuraa 5.264 scarf
ワンピース wanpiisu 5.238 one-piece[1]
ブラウス burausu 3.748 blouse
スカーフ sukaafu 2.771 scarf
ハイヒール haihiiru 1.802 high heels
カーディガン kaadigan 1.507 cardigan
ソックス sokkusu 1.147 socks
運動靴 undou gutsu 0.936 sports shoes

(アクセサリー) (Accessories)

時計 tokei 22.236 watch (also clock)
眼鏡 megane 19.322 glasses, spectacles
バッグ baggu, bakku 16.658 bag
鞄 kaban 10.529 bag
アクセサリー akusesarii 7.308 accessory
ネックレス nekkuresu 5.278 necklace
ピアス piasu 4.550 earrings for pierced ears
ブレスレット buresuretto 1.733 bracelet
イヤリング iyaringu 1.453 earrings

1 Polysemous entry (could mean something other than clothes).

---

600 小学校 shou-gakkou *n.* elementary school, primary school
- 娘が小学校に入学した。— My daughter entered elementary school.
109 | 0.83

601 回る mawaru *v.* spin, turn, go around; go via
- 扇風機が回っていた。— The electric fan was spinning.
109 | 0.92

602 広い hiroi *i-adj.* wide, broad, large
- なんて広い居間なんでしょう。— What a large living room!
108 | 0.98

603 猫 neko *n.* cat
- 猫を飼っている。— We have a cat.
108 | 0.80

604 向こう mukou *n.* other side; over there
- 向こうを見て。— Look over there.
108 | 0.81

605 同時 douji *n.* simultaneous, at the same time
- 同時に二つのことはできない。— I can't do two things at the same time.
108 | 0.96

606 調べる shiraberu *v.* investigate; look up; examine; check
- 彼は辞書で単語を調べている。— He is looking up a word in the dictionary.
108 | 0.95

607 のぼる noboru *v.* go up, rise; reach
- 被災者の数は5000人に上った。— The number of victims rose to 5,000.
108 | 0.95

608 六 roku *num.* six
- 六足すと二十になる。— If you add six, that makes twenty.
108 | 0.87

609 のみ nomi *p.* only, merely
- 彼のみが知っている。— Only he knows.
107 | 0.93

610 向ける mukeru *v.* turn, point
- 父親は息子に目を向けた。— The father turned his eyes toward his son.
107 | 0.93

611 落ちる ochiru *v.* fall, drop
- 彼ははしごから落ちた。— He fell from a ladder.
107 | 0.91

612 だが da ga *conj.* but, however
- 彼女にメールした。だが、返信がなかった。— I sent her an e-mail, but she didn't reply.
106 | 0.57 | BK

613 決まる kimaru *v.* be decided
- それは会議で決まった。— It was decided at a meeting.
106 | 0.99

614 起こす okosu *v.* wake; raise; cause
- 不注意で事故を起こした。— My carelessness caused an accident.
106 | 0.97

615 場 ba *n.* field; place; occasion
- 作品を発表する場がほしい。— I want a place to present my work.
105 | 0.97

616 いずれ izure *adv.* anyway, sooner or later *pron.* either
- 真実はいずれわかるだろう。— The truth will come out anyway.
105 | 0.88

617 ホテル hoteru *n.* hotel
- 高級なホテルに泊まった。— We stayed at a high-class hotel.
105 | 0.87

618 対象 taishou *n.* object, target, subject
- 彼の研究の対象は何ですか。— What is the subject of his research?
105 | 0.62

619 打つ utsu *v.* hit, strike, beat
- 彼はバットでボールを打った。— He hit the ball with the bat.
105 | 0.94

620 以前 izen *n.* before, formerly
- 以前、ここに来たことがあります。— I have been here before.
105 | 0.88

621 夫 otto *n.* husband
- 夫と出かける。— I will go out with my husband.
105 | 0.93

622 確認(する) kakunin(suru) *n.* confirmation *v.* confirm
- 出発の時間を確認した。— I confirmed the departure time.
105 | 0.96

623 数 kazu *n.* number
- 観光客の数が増えている。— The number of tourists is increasing.
105 | 0.92

624 意見 iken *n.* opinion, idea
- 自分の意見を言う。— I express my opinion.
105 | 0.90

625 割と wari to *adv.* comparatively, rather
- 今日は割とあたたかい。— It's rather warm today.
105 | 0.36

626 大丈夫 daijoubu *na-adj.* safe, all right
- 大丈夫ですか。— Are you all right?
105 | 0.80

627 通う kayou *v.* attend, go to, commute
- 大学に通っている。— I am attending university.
105 | 0.85

628 申し上げる moushiageru *v.* tell, say (humble)
- 心からの感謝を申し上げます。— I'd like to express my heartfelt thanks.
104 | 0.42 | OF

629 可能性 kanou-sei *n.* possibility
- 問題が起きる可能性がある。— There is a possibility that problems will arise.
104 | 0.96

630 述べる noberu *v.* describe, say, state
- このことについて意見を述べたいと思います。— I would like to describe my observations about this.
104 | 0.86

631 是非 zehi *adv.* by all means, please; definitely, certainly
- 近いうちにぜひまたおいでください。— Do please come back again soon.
104 | 0.95

632 さえ sae *p.* even; besides; if only
- それは子供でさえわかる。— Even children can understand it.
104 | 0.89

633 三人 san-nin *n.* three people
- 兄弟が三人いる。— I have three brothers.
104 | 0.94

634 料理(する) ryouri(suru) *n.* cooking, dish *v.* cook
- 父は料理が上手だ。— My father is good at cooking.
103 | 0.86

635 一部 ichibu *n.* part
- 計画の一部を変更した。— We changed part of the plan.
103 | 0.91

636 きっと kitto *adv.* surely, certainly
- 彼女はきっと来ます。— She will certainly come.
103 | 0.85

637 どうして doushite *adv.* why
- どうして泣いているのですか。— Why are you crying?
103 | 0.92

638 歌う utau *v.* sing
- 歌うことが大好きです。— I love singing!
103 | 0.94

639 なお nao *adv.* more, still
- この国の産業はなお発展の余地がある。— There is still potential for developing industry in this country.
102 | 0.79

640 幾つ iku-tsu *n.* how many, how old
- リンゴはいくつありますか。— How many apples are there?
102 | 0.96

641 ぞ zo *p. disc.* EMPHASIS
- とうとう日本に来たぞ。— We're finally in Japan!
102 | 0.89

642 ほしい hoshii *i-adj.* want, desire
- 新しいパソコンがほしい。— I want a new computer.
102 | 0.82

643 新聞 shinbun *n.* newspaper
- 新聞を読む。— I read a newspaper.
101 | 0.89

644 気付く kizuku *v.* notice, become aware
- 彼が部屋を出て行ったことに気づかなかった。— I did not notice that he went out of the room.
101 | 0.89

645 歌 uta *n.* song
- 素敵な歌です。— It is a beautiful song.
101 | 0.94

646 開ける akeru *v.* open
- 彼女はドアを開けた。— She opened the door.
101 | 0.92

647 互い tagai *n.* each other
- 互いのことを良く知ろう。— Let's get to know each other well.
101 | 0.97

648 着る kiru *v.* put on, wear
- 彼女は着物を着ている。— She is wearing a kimono.
101 | 0.91

649 違い chigai *n.* difference
- AとBの違いを説明してください。— Could you explain the difference between A and B?
100 | 0.98

650 しっかり shikkari *adv.* hard, tight
- 電車のつり革にしっかりつかまった。— I held on tight to a strap on the train.
100 | 0.98

651 過ぎる sugiru *v.* pass, exceed
- 春が過ぎ、夏になった。— Spring passed, and it became summer.
100 | 0.93

652 記憶(する) kioku(suru) *n.* memory *v.* memorize
- それは古い過去の記憶だった。— It was an old memory of the past.
100 | 0.91

653 思い出 omoide *n.* memory, reminiscence
- 高校のときの良い思い出がある。— I have good memories of my high school days.
100 | 0.69

654 しばらく shibaraku *adv.* for a while, a minute, for a long time
- しばらく彼を待った。— I waited for him for a while.
100 | 0.89

655 基本的 kihon-teki *na-adj.* basic, fundamental
- 基本的な問題だ。— It is a basic problem.
100 | 0.94

656 四月 shi-gatsu *n.* April
- 日本は四月に入学式があります。— In Japan, the entrance ceremony is held in April.
100 | 0.74

657 君 kimi *n.* you
- 君の言うとおりにした。— I did what you told me to do.
100 | 0.74 | BK

658 笑う warau *v.* laugh; smile
- みな大声で笑った。— They laughed loudly.
99 | 0.84

659 いくら ikura *adv.* how much, however
- いくらですか。— How much is it?
99 | 0.95

660 魚 sakana *n.* fish
- 魚を焼く。— I grill a fish.
99 | 0.87

661 旅行(する) ryokou(suru) *n.* journey, travel *v.* travel
- 世界中を旅行したい。— I want to travel around the world.
98 | 0.73

662 父親 chichioya *n.* father
- 彼は父親に似ている。— He takes after his father.

98 | 0.85

663 どれ dore *pron.* which
- どれがいいですか。— Which one would you like?

98 | 0.96

664 見付ける mitsukeru *v.* find, look for
- 良い方法を見つけた。— I found a good method.

98 | 0.93

665 関わる kakawaru *v.* concern, affect, be involved
- 彼はその計画に関わっている。— He is involved in the project.

98 | 0.98

666 無理 muri *na-adj.* unreasonable, impossible; compulsory
- 全ての仕事を一人でするのは無理だ。— It's impossible to do all the work alone.

98 | 0.89

667 健康 kenkou *n.* health
- 健康に気をつけている。— I am careful of my health.

98 | 0.93

668 味 aji *n.* flavor, taste
- このスープは味が濃い。— This soup has a strong flavor.

98 | 0.87

669 深い fukai *i-adj.* deep
- 深い池だ。— It is a deep pond.

98 | 0.95

670 伝える tsutaeru *v.* tell; deliver; hand down
- 電話があったことを彼に伝えます。— I'll tell him you called.

97 | 0.96

671 自由 jiyuu *n.* freedom, liberty *na-adj.* free
- 自由に話していいです。— You can speak freely.

97 | 0.97

672 集まる atsumaru *v.* gather, crowd
- 人々は部屋に集まっている。— People are gathered in the room.

97 | 0.95

673 戦争 sensou *n.* war
- 戦争に反対する。— We are against war.

97 | 0.91

674 流れる nagareru *v.* flow, float, pass
- 利根川は関東平野を流れている。— The Tone River flows through the Kanto plain.

97 | 0.97

675 男性 dansei *n.* male, man
- この製品は二十代の男性を対象にしている。— The product is targeted at men in their twenties.

97 | 0.94

676 電車 densha *n.* train
- 電車に乗った。— I got on the train.

96 | 0.72

677 進める susumeru *v.* advance, move forward
- 彼は計画を進めた。— He went ahead with the plan.

96 | 0.70

678 含める fukumeru *v.* include, add
- 費用は食費を含めて5万円です。— It costs 50,000 yen including food.

96 | 0.89

679 致す itasu *v.* do (humble)
- どういたしましょうか。— How shall I do it?

96 | 0.33 | OF

680 着く tsuku *v.* arrive, reach
- 東京に着いた。— We arrived in Tokyo.

96 | 0.78

681 厳しい kibishii *i-adj.* strict, hard
- 彼は厳しい先生です。— He is a strict teacher.

96 | 0.98

682 女の子 onnanoko *n.* girl
- 公園で女の子が遊んでいる。— A girl is playing in the park.

96 | 0.85

683 パソコン pasokon *n.* personal computer
- 新しいパソコンを買いたい。— I want to buy a new personal computer.

96 | 0.86

684 おる oru *v.* be, exist (humble)
- 現在、オフィスにおります。— At the moment I am at my office.

96 | 0.93

685 活動(する) katsudou(suru) *n.* activity *v.* be active
- クラブでどんな活動をしていますか。— What sort of activities do you do in your club?

96 | 0.89

686 不安 fuan *n.* anxiety, concern *na-adj.* uneasy, insecure
- 世界経済への不安が高まっている。— The world economy is of increasing concern.

96 | 0.97

687 三十分 sanjup-pun, sanjip-pun *n.* thirty minutes
- 30分昼寝した。— I took a nap for thirty minutes.

95 | 0.34 | NM

688 限り kagiri *n.* limit
- 人にできることには限りがある。— There is a limit to what people can do.
95 | 0.97

689 いらっしゃる irassharu *v.* come, go (honorific); be (honorific)
- 高橋さんがいらっしゃいました。— Mr. Takahashi is here.
95 | 0.88

690 可能 kanou *na-adj.* possible
- それは可能ですか。— Is it possible?
95 | 0.94

691 可愛い kawaii *i-adj.* cute, nice, lovely
- 小さい子供は可愛いものだ。— Little children are cute.
94 | 0.76 | WB

692 際 sai *n.* when, in case of
- 京都に来た際にはぜひお電話ください。— Please give me a ring when you come to Kyoto.
94 | 0.96

693 途中 tochuu *n.* on the way; in the middle of
- 途中で友達に会った。— I met my friends on the way.
94 | 0.91

694 研究(する) kenkyuu(suru) *n.* research, study *v.* do research, study
- 彼の研究はユニークだ。— His study is unique.
94 | 0.84

695 様子 yousu *n.* state of affairs, situation; appearance
- そちらの様子はどうですか。— What's the situation like over there?
94 | 0.98

696 ものすごい monosugoi *i-adj.* terrible *adv.* terribly
- 今、ものすごく忙しい。— I'm terribly busy now.
94 | 0.70

697 合う au *v.* fit, suit, agree
- サイズが合うか試着した。— I tried it on for size.
94 | 0.95

698 済む sumu *v.* end, finish
- 仕事が済んだ。— I have finished my work.
94 | 0.95

699 通る touru *v.* pass, go along
- 駅の前をタクシーが通った。— The taxi passed in front of the station.
94 | 0.92

700 大人 otona *n.* adult
- 早く大人になりたい。— I want to grow up quickly.
94 | 0.89

701 期待(する) kitai(suru) *n.* expectation *v.* expect
- 良い結果を期待している。— We are expecting good results.
94 | 0.97

702 事実 jijitsu *n.* fact, actuality
- 事実は小説より奇なり。— Fact is stranger than fiction.
93 | 0.92

703 せい sei *n.* fault, cause for blame, because of
- 事故のせいで遅刻した。— I was late because of a traffic accident.
93 | 0.86

704 一年 ichi nen *n.* one year
- 一年が過ぎた。— One year has passed.
93 | 0.96

705 一体 ittai *n., adv.* how, what, why, who
- 一体どういうことですか。— What's all this about, then?
93 | 0.97

706 島 shima *n.* island
- 南の島へ行った。— I went to the southern islands.
93 | 0.76

707 描く egaku *v.* draw; describe
- 風景を描くのが好きだ。— I like to draw landscapes.
93 | 0.89

708 驚く odoroku *v.* be surprised
- そのニュースを聞いて驚いた。— I was surprised at the news.
93 | 0.89

709 動物 doubutsu *n.* animal
- 動物に食べ物を与えないでください。— Please don't feed the animals.
92 | 0.88

710 何度 nando *n.* how many times, how often
- この映画は何度も見た。— I have seen this movie many times.
92 | 0.92

711 元々 motomoto *adv.* from the first, originally
- 漢字はもともと絵から発達した。— Chinese characters developed originally from pictures.
92 | 0.93

712 素晴らしい subarashii *i-adj.* wonderful, marvelous
- 素晴らしいですね。— It's wonderful.
92 | 0.90

713 座る suwaru v. sit
- 彼は椅子に座った。— He sat on a chair.
92 | 0.88

714 定める sadameru v. provide; stipulate, decide
- その会社は経営方針を定めた。— The company decided on its business policy.
92 | 0.43 | OF

715 機会 kikai n. opportunity
- 機会を頂き、ありがとうございます。— Thank you for the opportunity.
92 | 0.98

716 楽しみ tanoshimi n. pleasure, enjoyment
- 私にとって写真を撮ることは楽しみです。— Taking pictures is a hobby for me.
92 | 0.83

717 考え kangae n. idea, thought
- 考えがあります。— I have an idea.
92 | 0.93

718 信じる shinjiru v. believe, trust
- 彼のことを信じている。— I trust him.
92 | 0.89

719 たまたま tamatama adv. accidentally, by chance
- 彼らはたまたまそこにいた。— They were there by chance.
91 | 0.70

720 古い furui i-adj. old
- 市は古い建物を取り壊した。— The city pulled down the old buildings.
91 | 0.95

721 さ sa p. disc. ATTRACT ATTENTION
- 実はさ、仕事を辞めたんだ。— Well, I've quit my job.
91 | 0.73

722 面 men n. side; page; surface
- 他の人の良い面を見る。— I see the good side of others.
91 | 0.85

723 三月 san gatsu n. March
- 三月は卒業の月だ。— March is graduation month in Japan.
91 | 0.74

724 ただし tadashi conj. but, however, though
- お金を貸してあげましょう。ただし、今回だけです。— I'll lend you money; however, just this once.
91 | 0.96

725 常 tsune n. way adv. always, usually
- 常にパスポートを携帯しなければならない。— You always have to carry your passport.
91 | 0.97

726 より yori adv. more, better
- より充実した人生を送りたい。— I want to live life more fully.
91 | 0.94

727 つもり tsumori n. intention
- 明日、買い物に行くつもりです。— Tomorrow, I intend to go shopping.
91 | 0.95

728 考え方 kangae-kata n. way of thinking, attitude
- 考え方が違う。— There are differences in ways of thinking.
91 | 0.84

729 ニュース nyuusu n. news
- テレビでニュースを聞いた。— I listened to the news on TV.
91 | 0.78

730 意識（する）ishiki(suru) n. consciousness, awareness v. be conscious
- 人々の意識が変わった。— People's awareness has changed.
91 | 0.98

731 元 moto n. beginning; original
- 元の原稿を見せてください。— Could you show me the original manuscript?
91 | 0.99

732 行動（する）koudou(suru) n. action, act v. act, behave
- 行動を行さなければいけない。— We must take action.
90 | 0.97

733 低い hikui i-adj. low, short
- この食事はカロリーが低い。— This meal is low in calories.
90 | 0.95

734 びっくり（する）bikkuri(suru) n. surprise v. be surprised, be amazed
- 彼から花束をもらってびっくりした。— I was surprised to receive a bouquet from him.
90 | 0.81

735 作り方 tsukuri-kata n. how to make
- 母がケーキの作り方を教えてくれた。— My mother taught me how to make cakes.
90 | 0.79

736 元気 genki n. health, vigor na-adj. lively, vigorous, well
- 元気な高齢者が増えた。— The number of healthy senior citizens has increased.
90 | 0.89

737 現われる arawareru v. appear, come into sight
- 歌手が舞台に現れた。— The singer appeared on stage.
90 | 0.92

738 聞こえる kikoeru *v.* hear; sound
- 友達が私を呼んでいるのが聞こえた。— I heard my friend calling me.
90 | 0.88

739 曲 kyoku *n.* piece (of music), song, tune
- 何の曲を弾いていますか。— What piece are you playing?
89 | 0.76 | WB

740 過去 kako *n.* past
- 過去を振り返るのはいやだ。— I hate looking back over the past.
89 | 1.00

741 やっと yatto *adv.* at last
- やっと試験が終わった。— At last the examinations were over.
88 | 0.84

742 思える omoeru *v.* it seems that
- 彼女は悩みがあるように思える。— It seems to me that she's got a problem.
88 | 0.90

743 明らか akiraka *na-adj.* clear, obvious
- 彼の死因は明らかではない。— The cause of his death is not clear.
88 | 0.89

744 つつ tsutsu *p. conj.* while doing; though
- 煙草は健康に悪いと知りつつ、吸い続けている。— I can't quit smoking, even knowing that it's bad for my health.
88 | 0.95

745 土地 tochi *n.* land, ground
- 彼はたくさんの土地を所有している。— He owns a lot of land.
88 | 0.89

746 振り返る furikaeru *v.* turn one's head, look back
- 時々、過去を振り返るべきだ。— Sometimes you should look back on the past.
87 | 0.84

747 初め hajime *n.* beginning
- 物語の初めは退屈だった。— The beginning of the story was boring.
87 | 0.86

748 評価(する) hyouka(suru) *n.* evaluation *v.* evaluate
- 教育では評価は重要だ。— Evaluation is crucial in teaching.
87 | 0.91

749 息子 musuko *n.* son
- 昨日、息子が生まれた。— My son was born yesterday.
87 | 0.86

750 限る kagiru *v.* limit, restrict
- 入場は100名に限られている。— Admission is limited to one hundred people.
86 | 0.96

751 似る niru *v.* look like, resemble
- 君はお父さんに似ている。— You look like your father.
86 | 0.91

752 悲しい kanashii *i-adj.* sad, unhappy
- なんと悲しい話だろう。— What a sad story!
86 | 0.72

753 雨 ame *n.* rain
- 雨が上がった。— The rain has stopped.
86 | 0.89

754 自分達 jibun-tachi *n.* themselves; ourselves
- 自分たちのことはすべて自分たちでする。— We do everything by ourselves.
86 | 0.91

755 詳しい kuwashii *i-adj.* detailed, know well, in detail
- 彼女は事情を詳しく説明した。— She explained the reasons in detail.
86 | 0.88

756 二十一世紀 nijuu is-seiki *n.* twenty-first century
- 21世紀は混沌としている。— The twenty-first century looks chaotic.
86 | 0.65

757 ひどい hidoi *i-adj.* cruel, serious, terrible
- ひどい頭痛がする。— I have a terrible headache.
86 | 0.91

758 昨日 kinou *n.* yesterday
- 昨日はとても忙しかった。— I was very busy yesterday.
86 | 0.54 | WB

759 下りる oriru *v.* go down; come down
- 階段を下りた。— I went down the stairs.
86 | 0.88

760 メール meeru *n.* e-mail
- メールをありがとうございます。— Thank you for your e-mail.
86 | 0.60 | WB

761 まあ maa *adv.* Oh!, well, now
- まあ、いいか。— Well, I guess it's OK.
86 | 0.68

762 喜ぶ yorokobu *v.* be glad, rejoice
- 私たちはニュースを聞いて喜んだ。— We were glad to hear the news.
86 | 0.92

763 便利 benri *n.* convenience *na-adj.* useful, convenient
- これは便利な道具だ。— This is a useful tool.
85 | 0.87

764 迎える mukaeru *v.* go to meet, invite, receive
- 私たちはお客さんを迎えた。— We welcomed visitors.
84 | 0.94

765 耳 mimi *n.* ear
- 彼は耳をかいた。— He scratched his ears.
85 | 0.90

766 表現(する) hyougen(suru) *n.* expression *v.* express
- このニュアンスを英語で表現できない。— These nuances cannot be expressed in English.
84 | 0.97

767 動き ugoki *n.* movement, action, motion
- 星の動きを観察するのが仕事です。— My job is to observe the motion of stars.
84 | 0.94

768 注意(する) chuui(suru) *n.* attention *v.* notice, be careful
- 風邪を引かないように気をつけて。— Be careful not to catch a cold.
84 | 0.97

769 では dewa *conj.* then, well
- では、明日、またお電話します。— Well, then, I'll call you back tomorrow.
84 | 0.96

770 てあげる te ageru *cp.* do something for somebody
- いいことを教えてあげる。— I'll tell you something good.
84 | 0.00 | SP

771 雰囲気 fun'iki *n.* atmosphere, ambience
- このレストランはいい雰囲気だ。— This restaurant has a nice atmosphere.
84 | 0.89

772 立場 tachiba *n.* position, standpoint, situation
- お互いの立場を尊重する。— We respect each other's positions.
84 | 0.90

773 基づく motozuku *v.* be based
- この話は私の経験に基づいている。— This talk is based on my own experiences.
84 | 0.53

774 間 ma *n.* time, interval; space
- 約束の時間まで少し間がある。— I have a little time before the appointment.
84 | 0.94

775 ことがある koto ga aru *cp.* have done; there are sometimes
- 北海道に行ったことがある。— I've been to Hokkaido.
84 | 0.82

776 痛い itai *i-adj.* painful, hurt
- どこが痛いですか。— Where does it hurt?
83 | 0.78

777 (お)父さん (o)-tou-san *n.* father
- お父さん、話があるんだけど。— Dad, I need to talk to you.
83 | 0.87

778 辺り atari *n.* area around
- いつもこの辺りを散歩している。— I always take a walk around here.
83 | 0.94

779 てやる te yaru *cp.* do something for somebody/something
- 彼女は孫にコートを買ってやった。— She bought a coat for her grandson.
83 | 0.96

780 将来 shourai *n.* future
- 彼は将来のことを考え始めた。— He began thinking about his future.
82 | 0.96

781 乗せる noseru *v.* take on, put on, pick up
- タクシーは駅で客を乗せた。— The taxi picked up a customer at the station.
82 | 0.94

782 自転車 jiten-sha *n.* bicycle
- ほとんどの学生は自転車で通学している。— Most students go to school by bike.
82 | 0.87

783 白い shiroi *i-adj.* white
- 彼女は白いセーターを着ていた。— She wore a white sweater.
82 | 0.91

784 川 kawa *n.* river, stream
- 日曜は川に釣りに行く。— I go fishing in the river on Sundays.
82 | 0.94

785 用いる mochiiru *v.* use, adopt
- この製品は最新の技術が用いられている。— A new technology is used for this product.
82 | 0.78

786 隣り tonari *n.* next door, next
- 隣の部屋から男の人が出てきた。— A man came out of the next room.
82 | 0.86

787 普段 fudan *n.* usually, ordinarily
- 普段から健康に気をつけている。— I always take care of my health.
81 | 0.87

788 法律 houritsu *n.* law
- 法律を守らなくてはならない。— We must obey the law.
81 | 0.48 | OF

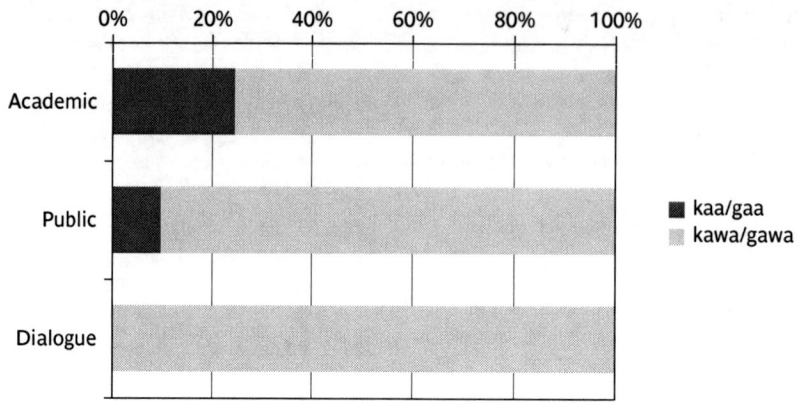

Variation of *kawa* (river): Variant without the intervocalic /w/ occurs in academic presentations and public speaking. Note that word-initial /k/ becomes voiced when it appears in the word-internal position of a compound like /kanda-gawa/ due to the effect of sequential-voicing.

789 妻 tsuma *n.* wife
- こちらは私の妻です。— This is my wife.
81 | 0.91

790 冬 fuyu *n.* winter
- 今年の冬は雪が少ない。— There hasn't been much snow this winter.
81 | 0.92

791 具体的 gutai-teki *na-adj.* specific, concrete
- 彼は具体的な例を挙げた。— He gave a concrete example.
81 | 0.82

792 もと moto *n.* under
- 料理長のもとで修行した。— I was trained under the master chef.
81 | 0.85

793 発生（する） hassei(suru) *n.* occurrence *v.* occur, happen
- 交通事故が発生した。— A traffic accident occurred.
81 | 0.86

794 繰り返す kurikaesu *v.* repeat, do over again
- 同じ失敗を繰り返すな。— Don't repeat the same mistakes.
81 | 0.97

795 泣く naku *v.* cry
- 男の子が大声で泣いている。— A boy is crying loudly.
81 | 0.88

796 七 nana *num.* seven
- 七は完全数です。— Seven is the perfect number.
81 | 0.86

797 手紙 tegami *n.* letter
- 手紙をポストに入れた。— I put a letter into the mailbox.
80 | 0.88

798 出かける dekakeru *v.* go out, leave
- 母は散歩に出かけました。— My mother has gone out for a walk.
80 | 0.90

799 努力（する） doryoku(suru) *n.* effort *v.* make an effort
- 彼の努力が報われた。— His effort was rewarded.
80 | 0.87

800 増加（する） zouka(suru) *n.* increase, gain *v.* increase, grow
- 会員は増加している。— The membership has increased.
80 | 0.44 | OF

801 判断（する） handan(suru) *n.* judgment *v.* judge
- 彼女は良い判断を下した。— She made a good judgment.
80 | 0.91

802 両親 ryoushin *n.* (both) parents
- 両親を尊敬している。— I respect my parents.
80 | 0.85

803 残念 zannen *na-adj.* disappointing, regrettable
- 私にとって残念な結果だった。— The result was disappointing for me.
79 | 0.93

804 おそらく osoraku *adv.* probably, likely
- おそらく彼はそのことを知らないのだろう。— He probably doesn't know about that.
79 | 0.95

4 Colors

(frequency per million words)

(i-adjective)
白い shiroi 82.295 white
赤い akai 46.253 red
黒い kuroi 44.745 black
青い aoi 32.368 blue (also pale; unripe)
黄色い kiiroi 13.818 yellow
茶色い chairoi 4.657 brown

(noun)
茶 cha 78.641 brown (also tea)[1]
緑 midori 57.430 green (also greenery)
黒 kuro 42.361 black
白 shiro 41.260 white (also innocence)
赤 aka 27.584 red
黄色 kiiro 15.512 yellow
ピンク pinku 12.791 pink
青 ao 12.015 blue
ブルー buruu 10.392 blue
緑色 midoriiro 9.734 green
茶色 chairo 7.394 brown
オレンジ orenji 7.150 orange[2]
灰色 haiiro 6.871 grey
紫 murasaki 6.096 purple
グレー gurei 5.111 grey
金色 kin'iro 4.429 gold
紫色 musarakiiro 3.967 purple
黄 ki 3.886 yellow
銀色 gin'iro 3.722 silver
紺 kon 3.102 navy blue
水色 mizuiro 2.527 light blue
紺色 kon'iro 1.563 navy blue
黄緑色 kimidori iro 0.739 yellow green
黄緑 kimidori 0.501 yellow green

(真〜)("ma-")
真っ赤 makka 16.050 bright red (also downright)
真っ白 masshiro 12.432 pure white
真っ暗 makkura 10.314 black (also pitch-dark)
真っ黒 makkuro 9.758 black
真っ青 massao 4.778 blue
真っ黄色 makkiiro 0.085 yellow

1 May include instances of "お茶 o-cha (tea)".
2 May include instances of "orange" as a fruit.

---

805 家庭 katei *n.* home, household, family
- 結婚したら温かい家庭を作りたい。— When I marry, I want to make a loving home.
79 | 0.97

806 軽い karui *i-adj.* light, slight
- この荷物は軽い。— This baggage is light.
79 | 0.94

807 払う harau *v.* pay; sweep away
- 私が払います。— I will pay the bill.
79 | 0.95

808 つながる tsunagaru *v.* be connected, be related
- これらの島々は橋でつながっている。— These islands are connected by a bridge.
79 | 0.99

809 船 fune *n.* ship, boat
- 彼は船で沖縄に行った。— He went to Okinawa by ship.
79 | 0.84

810 九月 ku gatsu *n.* September
- 九月は残暑が厳しい。— The late summer heat is severe in September.
79 | 0.70

811 きっかけ kikkake *n.* opportunity, motive
- これがきっかけで彼女と会った。— Thanks to this opportunity, I met her.
79 | 0.86

812 授業 jugyou *n.* class, lesson at school
- 授業は九時から始まる。— Classes begin at 9 a.m.
79 | 0.80

813 亡くなる nakunaru *v.* die, pass away
- 昨日、祖父が亡くなりました。— My grandfather passed away yesterday.
79 | 0.85

814 止める tomeru *v.* stop
- あのビルの前で止めてください。— Stop in front of that building, please.
79 | 0.91

815 不思議 fushigi *n.* wonder *na-adj.* wonderful, strange, mysterious
- 不思議な経験をした。— I had a wonderful experience.
79 | 0.92

816 茶 cha *n.* tea; brown
- これは濃い茶だ。— This is strong tea.
79 | 0.90

817 直接 chokusetsu *n., adv.* directly, direct
- 彼女に直接頼むつもりだ。— I will ask her directly.
79 | 0.91

818 バス basu *n.* bus
- バスに乗った。— I got on the bus.
79 | 0.87

819 効果 kouka *n.* effectiveness, effect
- 効果が出るには時間が掛かる。— It needs time to take effect.
79 | 0.98

820 現実 genjitsu *n.* reality, actuality
- 理想は現実とは違う。— There is a gap between ideal and reality.
79 | 0.96

821 触れる fureru *v.* touch; experience
- 展示品に手を触れるな。— Don't touch the exhibits.
78 | 0.96

822 飼う kau *v.* keep, have, breed
- 猫を二匹飼っている。— We have two cats.
78 | 0.68

823 しゃべる shaberu *v.* talk, chat
- 昼ご飯を食べながら友達としゃべるのは楽しい。— It's fun to chat with friends over lunch.
78 | 0.76

824 国民 kokumin *n.* nation, people (of country), public
- 彼女は国民の支持を得ている。— She is supported by the nation.
78 | 0.68

825 さす sasu *v.* shine; pour; put
- 日が差してきた。— The sun began to shine.
78 | 0.97

826 やり方 yari-kata *n.* way of doing, how to, approach
- やり方を変えるべきだ。— You should change your approach.
78 | 0.90

827 ずいぶん zuibun *adv.* very, pretty, quite
- 今日はずいぶん暖かい。— It is quite warm today.
78 | 0.91

828 日本語 nihon go, nippon go *n.* Japanese (language)
- 日本語を勉強したい。— I want to learn Japanese.
78 | 0.91

829 十月 juu gatsu *n.* October
- 十月の第二月曜日は体育の日だ。— The second Monday of October is Sports Day.
77 | 0.72

830 気分 kibun *n.* feeling, mood
- 気分は良くなりましたか。— Are you feeling better now?
77 | 0.89

831 開発(する) kaihatsu(suru) *n.* development *v.* develop
- 新製品を開発しています。— We are developing a new product.
77 | 0.83

832 殺す korosu *v.* kill
- 多くの人々がテロリストによって殺された。— Many people were killed by a terrorist.
77 | 0.83

833 特徴 tokuchou *n.* characteristic, feature
- この大学にはいくつかの特徴がある。— This university has several distinctive features.
77 | 0.96

834 神 kami *n.* God, deity, spirit
- 人々が平和を神に祈る。— Many people pray to God for peace.
77 | 0.77 | BK

835 暮らす kurasu *v.* live
- みんな幸せに暮らしたいと思っている。— Everyone wishes to live a happy life.
77 | 0.91

836 飛ぶ tobu *v.* fly
- 鳥が飛んでいる。— The birds are flying.
77 | 0.93

837 終わり owari *n.* end
- あと三日で今年も終わりになる。— This year will come to an end in three days.
77 | 0.88

838 雑誌 zasshi *n.* magazine
- どんな雑誌を読みますか。— What kind of magazines do you read?
76 | 0.85

839 怒る okoru *v.* get angry
- 彼女は昨夜のことをまだ怒っている。— She is still angry about last night.
76 | 0.83

840 整備(する) seibi(suru) *n.* maintenance, service *v.* prepare
- この道路はかなりの整備が必要だ。— This road requires a good deal of maintenance.
76 | 0.43 | OF

841 んと nto *interj.* well
- 「何をしていたの。」「んと、家でごろごろしてた」— "What did you do?" "Well, I spent my time idly at home."
76 | 0.14 | SP

842 建物 tatemono *n.* building
- この建物は修理が必要だ。— This building needs repair.
76 | 0.97

843 発見（する） hakken(suru) *n.* discovery *v.* discover
- アメリカ大陸はコロンブスによって発見された。— America was discovered by Columbus.
76 | 0.98

844 相談（する） soudan(suru) *n.* consultation *v.* consult
- その件は全員で相談しましょう。— Let's decide the matter in consultation with all members.
76 | 0.86

845 連絡（する） renraku(suru) *n.* connection, contact *v.* contact
- 彼女から連絡がない。— There is no contact from her.
76 | 0.92

846 止まる tomaru *v.* stop
- この電車は次の駅は止まらない。— This train doesn't stop at the next station.
76 | 0.92

847 一生懸命 isshou kenmei *na-adj.* hard, as hard as one can
- 彼は一生懸命働いている。— He works hard.
75 | 0.74

848 用意（する） youi(suru) *n.* preparation *v.* prepare
- 事前に書類を用意した。— I prepared the documentation beforehand.
75 | 0.95

849 変 hen *na-adj.* strange, unusual, funny
- 変な音が聞こえる。— I can hear a strange noise.
75 | 0.80

850 十二月 juu ni gatsu *n.* December
- 十二月はお歳暮の季節です。— December is the season of year-end gifts in Japan.
75 | 0.75

851 学ぶ manabu *v.* learn
- 両親から多くのことを学んだ。— I learned a great deal from my parents.
75 | 0.88

852 突然 totsuzen *adv.* suddenly
- 電車が突然止まった。— The train stopped suddenly.
75 | 0.92

853 首 kubi *n.* neck, head; firing, sacking (of an employee)
- 彼女の首は細い。— She has a slender neck.
75 | 0.81

854 設定（する） settei(suru) *n.* establishment *v.* establish, set
- エアコンを28度に設定する。— I will set the air conditioner to 28 degrees.
75 | 0.95

855 ゆっくり yukkuri *adv.* slowly, leisurely; plenty of time
- もう少しゆっくり話してください。— Would you speak a little more slowly?
75 | 0.91

856 目指す mezasu *v.* aim, go toward
- 彼らは優勝を目指している。— They are aiming for the championship.
75 | 0.87

857 したがって shitagat-te *conj.* accordingly, consequently
- これは労働ビザではありません。したがって、働くことはできません。— This is not a working visa, therefore you can't work.
75 | 0.77

858 一月 ichi gatsu *n.* January
- 一月第二月曜日は成人の日です。— The second Monday in January is Coming-of-Age Day.
75 | 0.73

859 成す nasu *v.* form, constitute
- 彼らは会社の中核を成している。— They constitute the heart of the company.
75 | 0.82

860 集める atsumeru *v.* gather, collect
- 彼は切手を集めている。— He collects stamps.
74 | 0.98

861 失う ushinau *v.* lose
- 妻を事故で失った。— I lost my wife in a traffic accident.
74 | 0.94

862 光 hikari *n.* light
- 光が部屋に差し込んだ。— The light came into the room.
74 | 0.92

863 並ぶ narabu *v.* line, stand in line
- 彼は有名人を見ようと通りに並んだ。— He stood in line on the street to see the celebrities.
74 | 0.97

864 八月 hachi gatsu *n.* August
- お盆は八月十三日から十六日までです。— The Bon festival takes place from August 13 to 16.
74 | 0.72

865 とく toku *aux.* [shortened form of "te oku"]
- それやっとくから。— I'll do that for later.
74 | 0.71

866 七月 shichi gatsu *n.* July
- 七月中旬に梅雨が明けた。— The rainy season ended in mid-July.
74 | 0.73

867 美しい utsukushii *i-adj.* beautiful
- 美しい自然に囲まれている。— It is surrounded by beautiful nature.
74 | 0.90

868 五月 go gatsu *n.* May
- 五月は山が新緑で覆われる。— The mountains are covered with fresh green foliage in May.
74 | 0.76

869 優しい yasashii *i-adj.* gentle, tender, kind, friendly
- 彼女は心が優しい。— She has a tender heart.
74 | 0.91

870 タバコ tabako *n.* cigarette, tobacco
- 煙草に火をつけた。— I lit a cigarette.
74 | 0.86

871 後ろ ushiro *n.* behind, back
- 男の子は母親の後ろに隠れた。— The boy hid behind his mother.
73 | 0.89

872 六月 roku gatsu *n.* June
- 日本では六月上旬から梅雨です。— It is the rainy season from the beginning of June in Japan.
73 | 0.73

873 異なる kotonaru *v.* be different
- 私の意見はあなたの意見と異なります。— My opinion is different from your opinion.
73 | 0.87

874 十一月 juu ichi gatsu *n.* November
- 十一月二十三日は勤労感謝の日です。— November 23 is Labor Thanksgiving Day.
73 | 0.73

875 新た arata *na-adj.* another
- 彼は新たな課題に取り組んでいる。— He is tackling a new challenge.
73 | 0.82

876 飛行機 hikouki *n.* airplane
- 飛行機が離陸した。— The plane took off.
73 | 0.75

877 (お)婆さん (o)-baa-san *n.* old lady; grandmother
- 困っているお婆さんを助けた。— I helped an old lady who was in trouble.
73 | 0.75

878 至る itaru *v.* lead to, get
- この道は日本橋に至る。— This road leads to Nihonbashi.
73 | 0.90

879 午前 gozen *n.* morning, a.m.
- 会議は四月十五日の午前です。— The meeting will be on the morning of April 15.
73 | 0.26 | NM

880 育てる sodateru *v.* bring up, train, develop
- 私は祖母に育てられました。— I was brought up by my grandmother.
73 | 0.95

881 種類 shurui *n.* kind, sort, variety
- 庭には多くの種類の花が植えられている。— In the garden are planted many varieties of flowers.
73 | 0.99

882 商品 shouhin *n.* goods, item of merchandise
- 商品を注文した。— I ordered goods.
73 | 0.95

883 生じる shoujiru, shouzuru *v.* bring about, cause, arise
- これが原因で多くの問題が生じた。— This caused many problems.
73 | 0.69

884 イギリス igirisu *n.* United Kingdom, Britain, England
- イギリスと日本は海に囲まれた島国だ。— Britain and Japan are island nations surrounded by sea.
72 | 0.92

885 大好き daisuki *na-adj.* love
- 大好きです。— I love it!
72 | 0.79

886 語る kataru *v.* talk, tell
- 彼は真実を語った。— He told the truth.
72 | 0.80

887 胸 mune *n.* chest, heart
- 胸がどきどきしています。— My heart is beating so fast.
72 | 0.85

888 頼む tanomu *v.* ask, order
- 教授に講演を頼んだ。— I asked the professor to give a talk.
72 | 0.88

889 体験(する) taiken(suru) *n.* experience *v.* experience, have experience of
- 私にとって貴重な体験でした。— It was a valuable experience for me.
72 | 0.90

890 材料 zairyou *n.* materials, ingredient
- 料理の材料を準備する。— I will prepare the ingredients for cooking.
72 | 0.94

891 広がる hirogaru *v.* spread, stretch
- 田んぼが広がっている。— Rice fields stretch out.
72 | 0.96

892 きちんと kichinto *adv.* precisely, accurately, neatly
- 彼の部屋はきちんと片付けられている。— His room is neatly arranged.
72 | 0.98

893 そちら sochira *pron.* your place; there; you
- そちらの天気はどうですか。— How is the weather up there?
72 | 0.63

894 勝つ katsu *v.* win, defeat
- 私の好きなチームが試合に勝った。— My favorite team won the game.
72 | 0.88

895 運動（する） undou(suru) *n.* exercise *v.* exercise, move
- 運動する必要がある。— I need some exercise.
72 | 0.98

896 捨てる suteru *v.* throw away, abandon
- 彼女は古い雑誌を捨てた。— She threw away old magazines.
72 | 0.92

897 幸せ shiawase *na-adj.* happy *n.* happiness; fortune, luck
- お二人の幸せを祈ります。— I wish you both every happiness.
72 | 0.87

898 通す toosu *v.* pass, show . . . into
- 彼女は友達を部屋に通した。— She showed her friends into the room.
72 | 0.95

899 横 yoko *n.* side, beside
- 彼女は娘の横に寝ている。— She sleeps beside her daughter.
71 | 0.93

900 伴う tomonau *v.* accompany, involve
- 台風には大雨が伴う。— Heavy rain accompanies a typhoon.
71 | 0.71

901 命 inochi *n.* life
- 命を大切にすべきだ。— You should value your life.
71 | 0.95

902 流れ nagare *n.* stream, flow, current
- 時代の流れに乗ったほうがいい。— You should keep up with the current of the times.
71 | 0.99

903 育つ sodatsu *v.* grow up
- 私は京都で育った。— I grew up in Kyoto.
71 | 0.90

904 ちなみに chinami ni *conj.* by the way, incidentally
- ちなみに、彼はまだ独身です。— Incidentally, he is still single.
71 | 0.61 | WB

905 予定（する） yotei(suru) *n.* plan, schedule *v.* plan
- 週末は特に予定はありません。— I have no special plans for the weekend.
71 | 0.89

906 決して kesshite *adv.* never, by no means
- 決してあきらめないでください。— Never give up.
71 | 0.94

907 馬 uma *n.* horse
- 叔父は馬を飼っている。— My uncle keeps horses.
71 | 0.85

908 完全 kanzen *na-adj.* perfect, complete
- 仕事はまだ完全に終わっていない。— My work is not completely finished yet.
71 | 0.97

909 学生 gakusei *n.* student
- 学生たちはよくこのレストランに来る。— Students often come to this restaurant.
70 | 0.93

910 風 kaze *n.* wind
- 風が強い。— The wind is blowing hard.
70 | 0.92

911 性格 seikaku *n.* character, personality
- 彼はよい性格の人だ。— He has a good personality.
70 | 0.97

912 死 shi *n.* death
- 人々は彼女の死を悲しんだ。— People mourned her death.
70 | 0.82

913 位置（する） ichi(suru) *n.* position, location *v.* be located
- GPSで車両の位置を特定する。— GPS identifies the location of vehicles.
70 | 0.98

914 発展（する） hatten(suru) *n.* development *v.* develop, expand
- この国は急速に発展している。— This country is developing rapidly.
70 | 0.87

915 おかしい okashii *i-adj.* funny, amusing
- 何がそんなにおかしいの。— What's so funny?
70 | 0.94

916 近所 kinjo *n.* neighborhood
- 近所に大きなスーパーマーケットがある。— There is a big supermarket in my neighborhood.
70 | 0.77

917 一本 ip-pon *n.* one (long/cylindrical object)
- それ一本ください。— Give me one of those, please.
70 | 0.93

918 張る haru *v.* stretch, put up
- 彼は木の間にロープを張った。— He stretched a rope between the trees.
70 | 0.93

919 ご飯 gohan *n.* rice, meal
- ご飯を炊いた。— I cooked rice.
70 | 0.80

920 危険 kiken *n.* danger, hazard *na-adj.* dangerous
- 一人でそこに行くのは危険です。— It's dangerous to go there alone.
69 | 0.99

921 かしら kashira *p. disc.* I wonder
- その話本当かしら。— I wonder if the story is true.
69 | 0.83

922 すなわち sunawachi *conj.* that is (to say), namely
- その教授は文化の重要な一部、すなわち言語を研究している。— The professor studies one of the most important aspects of human culture, namely, language.
69 | 0.69 | BK

923 海外 kaigai *n.* overseas, abroad, foreign
- 家族で休暇を海外で過ごした。— I took an overseas holiday with my family.
69 | 0.97

924 教育(する) kyouiku(suru) *n.* education *v.* educate
- 良い教育を受けた。— I had a good education.
69 | 0.88

925 想像(する) souzou(suru) *n.* imagination, image *v.* imagine
- 想像以上に難しい仕事だった。— It was a more difficult task than I imagined.
69 | 0.92

926 実は jitsu wa *adv.* actually, in fact
- 実は、お願いがあります。— Actually, I need a favor.
69 | 0.85

927 許す yurusu *v.* allow, permit, forgive
- 父は私が車を運転するのを許してくれない。— My father won't allow me to drive a car.
69 | 0.96

928 表 hyou *n.* table, chart
- 彼はデータを表にまとめた。— He made a table of the data.
68 | 0.67

929 文化 bunka *n.* culture
- それぞれの国には違った文化がある。— Each country has a different culture.
68 | 0.94

930 八 hachi *n.* eight
- 表八を見なさい。— Look at Table 8.
68 | 0.89

931 食べ物 tabemono *n.* food
- 嫌いな食べ物がありますか。— Are there any foods you don't like?
68 | 0.83

932 借りる kariru *v.* borrow, rent
- 友達から本を借りた。— I borrowed a book from my friend.
68 | 0.94

933 だけれど da keredo *conj.* despite, though
- 退屈だけれど読まないといけない。— I have to read it though it's boring.
68 | 0.87

934 準備(する) junbi(suru) *n.* preparation *v.* prepare
- 何も準備をする時間がなかった。— I had no time to make any preparations.
68 | 1.00

935 二月 ni gatsu *n.* February
- 二月が一年も最も寒い月です。— February is the coldest month of the year.
68 | 0.71

936 や ya *aux.* COPULA (dialectal)
- それなんや？ たこ焼きや。— What's that? It's takoyaki.
68 | 0.71

937 月 tsuki *n.* month; moon
- 月が出た。— The moon has risen.
68 | 0.92

938 世の中 yononaka *n.* world, society
- 世の中にはいろいろな人がいる。— It takes all sorts of people to make a world.
68 | 0.86

939 インターネット intaanetto *n.* Internet
- 多くの人はインターネットで情報を探す。— Many people look for information on the Internet.
68 | 0.96

940 春 haru *n.* spring
- 春には桜が咲く。— In spring, the cherry blossoms bloom.
68 | 0.93

941 旅 tabi *n.* trip, journey
- 彼は旅に出た。— He went on a trip.
68 | 0.91

942 二年 ni nen *n.* two years
- コンクールは二年に一度開催される。— The competition is held once every two years.
68 | 0.97

943 寒い samui *i-adj.* cold
- 寒くなってきた。— It is getting cold.
68 | 0.78

944 年 nen *n.* year
- 年何回そこに行きますか？— How many times a year do you go there?
68 | 0.97

945 同様 douyou *na-adj.* similar, same
- 同様の意見です。— I have the same opinion.
67 | 0.87

946 一般 ippan *n.* general
- ここは一般の人は入れません。— The general public is not allowed in here.
67 | 0.95

947 第一 dai-ichi *n.* first
- 健康が第一だ。— Nothing is more important than health.
67 | 0.65

948 三年 san nen *n.* three years
- 石の上にも三年。— Three years on a stone. (Perseverance prevails).
67 | 0.97

949 申す mousu *v.* say, be (humble)
- 山田太郎と申します。— My name is Taro Yamada.
67 | 0.67

950 押す osu *v.* push, press
- 押さないでください。— Don't push, please.
67 | 0.94

951 責任 sekinin *n.* responsibility
- 責任は私にあります。— The responsibility lies with me.
67 | 0.93

952 選択（する）sentaku(suru) *n.* selection, choice *v.* choose
- ビジネスコースを選択するつもりだ。— I will choose the business course.
67 | 0.96

953 負ける makeru *v.* lose, be beaten
- 私たちのチームは試合に負けた。— Our team lost the game.
67 | 0.90

954 技術 gijutsu, gijitsu *n.* technique, skill
- 新しい技術を身につけたい。— I want to acquire new skills.
66 | 0.93

955 一般的 ippan-teki *na-adj.* general, common, ordinary
- 一般的な方法だ。— This is the general method.
66 | 0.99

956 そば soba *n.* side, beside
- 女の子が母親のすぐ側に座っている。— A girl is seated right beside her mother.
66 | 0.86

957 減る heru *v.* decrease, become less
- 人口が減っている。— The population is decreasing.
66 | 0.98

958 記事 kiji *n.* article
- 新聞の記事でそのニュースを知った。— I learned about the news from a newspaper article.
66 | 0.85

959 本人 honnin *n.* person himself/herself, person in question
- 本人次第だね。— It's up to the person himself.
66 | 0.98

960 焼く yaku *v.* roast, bake
- 彼はケーキを焼いた。— He baked a cake.
66 | 0.89

961 たまに tamani *adv.* occasionally, once in a while
- たまに居酒屋でお酒を飲む。— I drink in a pub once in a while.
66 | 0.71

962 慣れる nareru *v.* get used to
- 大阪の生活に慣れてきた。— I am getting used to life in Osaka.
66 | 0.84

963 もしくは moshikuwa *conj.* or, otherwise
- 注文はメール、もしくはファックスで送ってください。— Please send your order by e-mail or fax.
66 | 0.72

964 出会う deau *v.* meet, come across
- その時に彼女はご主人と出会った。— That was when she met her husband.
66 | 0.91

965 推進（する）suishin(suru) *n.* propulsion *v.* promote, drive
- 我が社は省エネを推進している。— Our company is promoting energy saving.
66 | 0.36 | OF

966 自ら mizukara *n.* personally, oneself, own
- 彼女自らが失敗を招いた。— She brought this failure on herself.
66 | 0.88

967 作業（する） sagyou(suru) *n.* operation, work *v.* work
- 彼は作業を終えた。— He got his work finished.
66 | 0.99

968 私自身 watashi jishin *n.* myself, my own
- これは私自身の問題です。— This is my own problem.
66 | 0.77

969 たび tabi *n.* every time
- この写真を見るたびにあなたを思い出す。— Every time I look at this photo, I will think of you.
66 | 0.97

970 付き合う tsukiau *v.* associate with, go out with, go along with
- 私は若い人たちと付き合うのが好きだ。— I like to associate with young people.
65 | 0.76

971 半分 hanbun *n.* half
- 彼女はケーキを半分に切った。— She cut the cake in half.
65 | 0.95

972 条件 jouken *n.* condition
- 良い条件の仕事を見つけた。— I found a job with good conditions.
65 | 0.95

973 医者 isha *n.* doctor
- 父は医者です。— My father is a doctor.
65 | 0.82

974 振る furu *v.* wave, shake, swing
- 彼に手を振った。— I waved at him.
65 | 0.88

975 関心 kanshin *n.* interest
- 温暖化についての関心が高まっている。— People are taking a growing interest in global warming.
65 | 0.94

976 表示（する） hyouji(suru) *n.* indication *v.* display, indicate
- 画面にメッセージが表示されている。— The message is displayed on the screen.
65 | 0.90

977 秋 aki *n.* autumn, fall
- 秋には紅葉する。— In the fall, the leaves turn yellow and red.
65 | 0.93

978 明るい akarui *i-adj.* bright, light; cheerful
- 明るい未来に目を向ける。— I look toward a bright future.
65 | 0.94

979 趣味 shumi *n.* hobby
- 趣味で絵を描いています。— I paint as a hobby.
65 | 0.83

980 生徒 seito *n.* student, pupil
- 生徒は誰もその質問に答えられなかった。— No students were able to answer the question.
65 | 0.96

981 相当（する） soutou(suru) *na-adj.* considerable *n.* equivalence *v.* be equivalent *adv.* considerably, pretty
- 彼は相当英語がうまい。— He speaks English pretty well.
65 | 0.85

982 従う shitagau *v.* obey, follow
- 法律には従わなければならない。— You must obey the law.
65 | 0.71

983 検討（する） kentou(suru) *n.* consideration, discussion examination *v.* consider, discuss
- その問題については今検討しています。— The matter is now under consideration.
65 | 0.61

984 占める shimeru *v.* occupy, account for
- 高齢者が全人口の40パーセントを占める。— Elderly people account for more than 40 percent of the total population.
65 | 0.46 | OF

985 まさに masani *adv.* exactly
- それがまさに聞きたかったことなんです。— That's exactly what I wanted to ask you about.
64 | 0.95

986 選手 senshu *n.* player, athlete
- 大きくなったら、野球選手になる。— I'm going to be a baseball player when I grow up.
64 | 0.84

987 以下 ika *n.* below, the following
- 以下の質問にお答えください。— We would like you to answer the following questions.
64 | 0.61

988 大きさ ooki-sa *n.* size
- それは卵と同じくらいの大きさです。— It is about the size of an egg.
64 | 1.00

989 調査（する）chousa(suru) n. investigation v. investigate, inquire, explore
- 警察は事故の原因を調査している。— The police are investigating the cause of the accident.
64 | 0.63

990 分 bun adv., n. part, share, portion
- 私の分は自分で払います。— I'll pay my share.
64 | 0.97

991 実家 jikka n. one's parents' home
- ずいぶん長い間実家に戻っていない。— I haven't visited my parents in ages.
64 | 0.72

992 発表（する）happyou(suru) n. announcement, publication v. announce, publish
- 先ほど選挙の結果が発表されました。— The result of the election was just announced.
64 | 0.94

993 むしろ mushiro adv. rather, if anything
- 量よりむしろ質のほうが大切だ。— Quality is important rather than quantity.
64 | 0.93

994 作成（する）sakusei(suru) n., v. make, create
- 最近自分のウェブサイトを作成しました。— I created my own website recently.
64 | 0.78

995 名 na n. name
- 父の名は利行、母の名は愛子です。— My father's name is Toshiyuki, and my mother's name is Aiko.
64 | 0.82

996 確保（する）kakuho(suru) n. securement, reservation v. secure, maintain, guarantee
- 政府は国民の安全を確保しなければならない。— The government must secure people's safety.
64 | 0.66

997 まるで marude adv. just like, quite
- まるで映画の話のようですね。— It's just like a movie story.
64 | 0.83

998 運ぶ hakobu v. carry, transport, move
- この荷物を車に運んでください。— Please carry this baggage to the car.
64 | 0.94

999 こともある koto mo aru cp. sometimes, can be
- ここは雪がたくさん降ることもあります。— It sometimes snows a lot here.
64 | 0.85

5 Countries

(frequency per million words)

日本 nihon, nippon 770.457 **Japan**
アメリカ amerika 234.057 **America**
中国 chuugoku 123.164 **China**[1]
イギリス igirisu 72.499 **United Kingdom, Britain, England**
フランス furansu 59.678 **France**
ドイツ doitsu 48.680 **Germany**
韓国 kankoku 45.434 **Korea, South Korea, Republic of Korea**
米国 beikoku 39.373 **United States**
オーストラリア oosutoraria 36.606 **Australia**
イタリア itaria 31.627 **Italy**
インド indo 30.446 **India**
カナダ kanada 24.434 **Canada**
ロシア roshia 22.357 **Russia**
スペイン supein 19.989 **Spain**
ソ連 soren 18.798 **Soviet Union**
タイ tai 18.259 **Thailand**
台湾 taiwan 18.113 **Taiwan**
北朝鮮 kitachousen 16.683 **Democratic People's Republic of Korea, North Korea**
英国 eikoku 15.828 **United Kingdom, Britain**
ベトナム betonamu 15.215 **Vietnam**
アフリカ afurika 15.083 **Africa**
エジプト ejiputo 14.587 **Egypt**
ブラジル burajiru 14.293 **Brazil**
スイス suisu 13.297 **Switzerland**
イラク iraku 12.359 **Iraq**
オランダ oranda 12.293 **Netherlands**
ニュージーランド nyuujiirando 10.795 **New Zealand**
シンガポール shingapooru 10.662 **Singapore**
フィリピン firipin 10.506 **Philippines**
メキシコ mekishiko 10.088 **Mexico**
朝鮮 chousen 9.417 **Korea**
イラン iran 8.342 **Iran**
スウェーデン suweeden 8.327 **Sweden**
インドネシア indoneshia 7.588 **Indonesia**

1 May include instances of *chuugoku* meaning the region in Japan.

1000 てはいけない、ちゃいけない te wa ike nai, cha ike nai *cp.* must not, should not
- 約束を忘れてはいけない。— You must not forget your promise.
64 | 0.91

1001 正しい tadashii *i-adj.* right, accurate, proper
- 三つの中から正しい答えを選びなさい。— Select the right answer from the three options.
64 | 0.97

1002 ほぼ hobo *adv.* about, nearly, almost
- 私は毎日ほぼ同じ時間に起きます。— I wake up at about the same time every morning.
64 | 0.95

1003 表わす arawasu *v.* show, express, symbolize
- この言葉は私の気持ちをよく表している。— These words really express my feelings.
64 | 0.88

1004 毎年 maitoshi *adv., n.* every year, annually
- 私の家族は毎年海外に行きます。— My family goes abroad every year.
63 | 0.97

1005 文字 moji *n.* letter, character, writing
- 世界には文字を持たない言語も多くある。— There are many languages in the world that have no writing.
63 | 0.92

1006 空 sora *n.* sky, air
- 空には雲が一つもない。— There is not a cloud in the sky.
63 | 0.90

1007 に対し ni taishi *cp.* toward; against; in contrast to
- 皆会社に対し多くの不満を持っていた。— Everyone had many complaints against the company.
63 | 0.57

1008 明日 asu *adv., n.* tomorrow
- 明日は晴れるでしょう。— It will be fine tomorrow.
63 | 0.49 | WB

1009 役割 yakuwari *n.* part, role
- 彼はプロジェクトで重要な役割を果たしている。— He plays an important role in this project.
63 | 0.80

1010 地球 chikyuu *n.* earth, globe
- 月は地球の周りを回っている。— The moon orbits the earth.
63 | 0.95

1011 公園 kouen *n.* park
- 公園で散歩するのが好きだ。— I like having a walk in the park.
63 | 0.90

1012 個人 kojin *n.* individual
- 参加するかどうかは個人の自由だ。— It's up to individuals whether to participate or not.
63 | 0.99

1013 やら yara *p.* and, or
- 掃除やら洗濯やらやることが多い。— I have many things to do, such as cleaning the house and doing the washing.
63 | 0.85

1014 消える kieru *v.* go off; disappear
- 急に電気が消えてしまった。— The light suddenly went out.
63 | 0.89

1015 激しい hageshii *i-adj.* fierce, intense, severe
- 背中に激しい痛みを感じた。— I felt an intense pain in my back.
63 | 0.95

1016 短い mijikai *i-adj.* short
- あの髪の短い女の子が私の娘です。— That girl with short hair is my daughter.
63 | 0.99

1017 薬 kusuri *n.* medicine
- この薬は一日三回飲んでください。— Take this medicine three times a day.
63 | 0.88

1018 試合 shiai *n.* match, game, bout
- 試合は六時に始まります。— The game will start at six.
63 | 0.84

1019 成長(する) seichou(suru) *n.* growth *v.* grow
- 子どもは成長が早い。— Children grow quickly.
63 | 1.00

1020 おなか onaka *n.* stomach, belly
- ちょっとおなかが痛いんです。— I have a little pain in my stomach.
62 | 0.79

1021 機能(する) kinou(suru) *n.* function, capability, feature *v.* function, work
- この新しいモデルのほうが機能が多い。— This new model has more features.
62 | 0.92

1022 ボール booru *n.* ball
- ゴールに向けてボールを蹴った。— I kicked the ball toward the goal.
62 | 0.89

1023 少年 shounen *n.* boy, juvenile
- 野球は日本の少年に最も人気のあるスポーツの1つだ。— Baseball is one of the most popular sports among boys in Japan.
62 | 0.93

1024 方向 houkou *n.* direction, course
- 方向が全然わからなくなった。— I have lost all sense of direction.
- 62 | 0.89

1025 遅い osoi *i-adj.* late; slow
- 父はいつも帰りが遅い。— My father always comes home late.
- 62 | 0.91

1026 資料 shiryou *n.* document, material, data
- 論文を書くための資料を集めている。— I'm collecting material for my thesis.
- 62 | 0.50 | OF

1027 タイプ（する） taipu(suru) *n.* type *v.* type
- あの子は僕のタイプじゃないよ。— She is not my type.
- 62 | 0.92

1028 扱う atsukau *v.* deal with, handle, treat
- それは丁寧に扱ってください。— Please treat it carefully.
- 62 | 0.97

1029 指摘（する） shiteki(suru) *n.* designation *v.* point out, indicate
- 何か誤りがあったら指摘してください。— Please point out any errors to me.
- 62 | 0.66

1030 ヨーロッパ yooroppa *n.* Europe
- 友達に会いにヨーロッパへ行った。— I went to Europe to see some friends.
- 62 | 0.93

1031 除く nozoku *v.* remove; except; get rid of
- 彼の作文は多少の間違いを除いてすばらしかった。— His composition was excellent except for a few errors.
- 62 | 0.71

1032 それら sore-ra *pron.* those, these, they
- それらは全てうそだ。— These are all lies.
- 62 | 0.89

1033 ご存じ go-zonji *n.* know, knowing (honorific)
- ご存じのように日本語には文字が三種類あります。— As you may know, there are three different types of Japanese characters.
- 62 | 0.89

1034 意外 igai *na-adj.* unexpected, surprising
- 彼が反対しなかったのは意外だった。— It was surprising that he didn't object.
- 61 | 0.88

1035 一週間 is-shukan *n.* one week
- 来月一週間休みを取るつもりです。— I will take a week off next month.
- 61 | 0.79

1036 何回 nan kai *n.* how many times
- 何回その映画を見たの？— How many times have you seen the movie?
- 61 | 0.83

1037 政府 seifu *n.* government
- 政府は来年消費税を上げるかもしれない。— The government may raise the consumer tax next year.
- 61 | 0.69

1038 分ける wakeru *v.* divide, distribute; classify
- クラスを二つのグループに分けた。— They divided the class into two groups.
- 61 | 0.98

1039 計画（する） keikaku(suru) *n.* project, schedule, plan *v.* plan
- お正月の計画を立てる。— I make plans for the New Year.
- 61 | 0.87

1040 段階 dankai *n.* grade, stage, step
- それはまだ準備の段階にある。— It's now at the preparation stage.
- 61 | 0.88

1041 量 ryou *n.* quantity, volume, amount
- 最近ごみの量が増えた。— The quantity of garbage has increased recently.
- 61 | 1.00

1042 田舎 inaka *n.* countryside; one's hometown
- 私は田舎で育ちました。— I grew up in the coutryside.
- 61 | 0.67

1043 感動（する） kandou(suru) *n.* deep emotion *v.* be impressed, be moved
- 私はその話を聞いて感動した。— I was deeply moved by the story.
- 61 | 0.85

1044 スポーツ supootsu *n.* sports
- どんなスポーツをしますか。— What kind of sports do you do?
- 61 | 0.90

1045 感覚 kankaku *n.* sense; sensation, feeling
- 彼女は色に対する感覚が鋭い。— She has a keen sense of color.
- 61 | 0.94

1046 地元 jimoto *n.* home area, local area
- これは地元で一番にぎやかな通りです。— This is the busiest street in the local area.
- 61 | 0.96

1047 勝手 katte *na-adj.* on one's own, at one's convenience
- 何でも勝手に決めないで。— Don't decide everything on your own.
- 60 | 0.87

1048 さすが sasuga *adv.* as might be expected, as one would expect
- さすが彼は会社のことは何でも知っている。— As might be expected, he knows all about the company.
60 | 0.85

1049 寂しい sabishii *i-adj.* lonely, lonesome
- 一人暮らしをするのは寂しい。— It is lonely to live all by oneself.
60 | 0.78

1050 再び futatabi *adv.* again, once more
- 彼は再び仕事を始めた。— He has started to work again.
60 | 0.90

1051 利く kiku *v.* act, work
- ブレーキが利くかどうか確かめて。— Check to see if the brakes are working.
60 | 0.90

1052 勤める tsutomeru *v.* be employed, work for
- 大企業に勤めたいと思っている。— I want to work for a big company.
60 | 0.91

1053 吸う suu *v.* breathe in, sip, smoke
- 深く息を吸ってください。— Breathe in deeply, please.
60 | 0.81

1054 流す nagasu *v.* flush; pour; drain
- このボタンを押して流してください。— Please push this button to flush.
60 | 0.96

1055 希望(する) kibou(suru) *n.* hope, wish, request *v.* hope, wish, desire
- 留学するという希望を捨ててはいけない。— You should not give up hope of studying abroad.
60 | 0.94

1056 急 kyuu *na-adj.* urgent, sudden; steep; sharp
- 急な仕事が入ってしまった。— Some urgent business has come up.
60 | 0.92

1057 勧める susumeru *v.* encourage, recommend
- 友人にこの本を読むよう勧められた。— I was encouraged to read this book by a friend.
60 | 0.91

1058 年齢 nenrei *n.* age, years
- 彼女は年齢より若く見える。— She looks younger than her age.
60 | 0.96

1059 フランス furansu *n.* France
- それはフランスに行った時に撮った写真です。— That's a picture I took when I went to France.
60 | 0.96

1060 仕方 shikata *n.* way, method
- クレジットカードは人々の買い物の仕方を変えた。— Credit cards have changed the way people shop.
59 | 0.97

1061 なし nashi *n.* without, no
- 彼女はあいさつもなしに部屋に入った。— She entered the room without saying hello.
59 | 0.98

1062 さて sate *conj.* well, now
- さて次は何をしようかな。— Now, what should I do next?
59 | 0.84

1063 疲れる tsukareru *v.* get tired
- 疲れたら寝てもいいですよ。— You can sleep if you get tired.
59 | 0.81

1064 落とす otosu *v.* drop, lose, turn down
- コップを落とさないように気をつけなさい。— Be careful not to drop your cup.
59 | 0.93

1065 人気 ninki *n.* popularity
- その歌手は若い女性の間で人気が高まっている。— That singer has increased in popularity among young women.
59 | 0.85

1066 弱い yowai *i-adj.* weak, faint, light
- うちの息子は意志が弱い。— My son is weak-willed.
59 | 0.97

1067 まとめる matomeru *v.* summarize, settle, gather
- 話す前に自分の意見をまとめてください。— Gather your thoughts before you speak.
59 | 0.97

1068 格好 kakkou *n.* appearance, shape, look
- もっと格好に気をつかったほうがいいよ。— You should pay more attention to your appearance.
59 | 0.88

1069 渡る wataru *v.* cross, go across
- 通りを渡るときは注意しなさい。— You must be careful when you cross the road.
59 | 0.96

1070 患者 kanja *n.* patient, case
- 医者は患者に適切な情報を与えるべきだ。— Doctors should give appropriate information to the patient.
59 | 0.86

1071 壁 kabe *n.* wall, barrier
- その絵を壁に掛けてくれませんか。— Would you hang the painting on the wall for me?
59 | 0.89

1072 道路 douro *n.* road, way, street
- 道路が混んでいるみたいだ。— The road seems to be crowded.

59 | 0.95

1073 参る mairu *v.* go, come, visit (humble); be in trouble, be embarrassed
- 私が駅までお迎えに参ります。— I will come to meet you at the station.

59 | 0.52 | OF

1074 反対(する) hantai(suru) *n.* opposition, contrast, objection *v.* oppose
- 彼らの結婚には多くの反対があった。— There was a lot of opposition to their marriage.

59 | 0.98

1075 他人 tanin *n.* others, unrelated person, stranger
- 他人のことは気にしないで。— Don't worry about others.

59 | 0.94

1076 提供(する) teikyou(suru) *n.* offer *v.* supply, sponsor
- 我が社では新しいお客様に無料サービスを提供しています。— We offer a free service for our new customers.

59 | 0.79

1077 空気 kuuki *n.* air, atmosphere
- 山の中は空気がきれいだ。— The air is clean in the mountains.

59 | 0.97

1078 去年 kyonen *adv., n.* last year
- 私は去年日本に来ました。— I came to Japan last year.

58 | 0.86

1079 肩 kata *n.* shoulder
- 肩が凝ってきた。— My shoulders are getting stiff.

58 | 0.86

1080 知れる shireru *v.* come out, come to light, be discovered
- その事実が知れたら大問題になるだろう。— If that fact comes to light, it will be a big issue.

58 | 0.75

1081 匂い nioi *n.* smell, odor, scent
- 台所からいい匂いがする。— There is a good smell coming from the kitchen.

58 | 0.89

1082 銀行 ginkou *n.* bank
- 銀行にお金を引き出しに行く。— I'll go to the bank to withdraw some money.

58 | 0.99

1083 実現(する) jitsugen(suru) *n.* realization, implementation *v.* realize, put into practice
- 夢の実現のために努力する。— I make every effort for the realization of my dream.

58 | 0.86

1084 ありがとう arigatou *interj.* thank you
- ご親切にありがとうございます。— Thank you for your kindness.

58 | 0.86

1085 購入(する) kounyuu(suru) *n.* buying *v.* purchase, buy
- 去年、自宅を購入しました。— I bought the house last year.

58 | 0.81 | WB

1086 十年 juu nen *n.* ten years, decade
- 私は十年前に母を亡くした。— I lost my mother a decade ago.

58 | 0.96

1087 右 migi *n.* right
- 次の角を右に曲がってください。— Please turn right at the next corner.

58 | 0.92

1088 全体 zentai *n.* total, whole, entire
- 戦争は世界全体に影響を与えた。— The war affected the world as a whole.

58 | 0.81

1089 話題 wadai *n.* topic, subject
- 話題を変えましょう。— Let's change the subject.

58 | 0.93

1090 認識(する) ninshiki(suru) *n.* recognition, awareness *v.* recognize, be aware
- たばこは健康に悪いという認識が広がっている。— There is a growing recognition that smoking damages health.

58 | 0.85

1091 安心(する) anshin(suru) *n.* peace of mind, relief *v.* feel relieved
- その知らせを聞いて安心しました。— I felt relieved to hear the news.

58 | 0.97

1092 雪 yuki *n.* snow
- 今夜は少し雪が降るかもしれない。— We might have some snow tonight.

58 | 0.95

1093 ポイント pointo *n.* point
- 最大のポイントはコストの安さです。— The most important point is the low cost.

58 | 0.89

1094 十 juu *num.* ten
- 彼女には十に一つの可能性しかない。— She has one chance in ten.

58 | 0.94

1095 仲間 nakama *n.* company, fellow, mate, group
- 彼は仕事の仲間に人気がある。— He's popular among his fellow workers.
57 | 0.95

1096 かつ katsu *conj.* besides, also, as well
- 彼は画家でありかつ作家でもある。— He is an illustrator and also a writer.
57 | 0.68

1097 知識 chishiki *n.* knowledge, information
- コンピューターに関する知識が全くない。— I have no knowledge of computers.
57 | 0.99

1098 多少 tashou *adv., n.* more or less; somewhat; a little
- 私はスペイン語を多少知っています。— I know a little Spanish.
57 | 0.93

1099 緑 midori *n.* green; greenery
- 緑の地球を大切にしよう。— We must look after the green earth.
57 | 0.94

1100 解決(する) kaiketsu(suru) *n.* solution, settlement *v.* solve, settle
- その問題を解決するのは難しかった。— It was difficult to solve the problem.
57 | 0.93

1101 狭い semai *i-adj.* narrow, small
- どうやったら狭い部屋を広く見せられるだろう。— How can I make my small room look larger?
57 | 0.96

1102 一時間 ichi jikan *n.* one hour
- 一時間以上も待たされた。— I was made to wait for over an hour.
57 | 0.90

1103 失敗(する) shippai(suru) *n.* failure, mistake *v.* fail
- 失敗から学ぶことができる。— You can learn from your mistakes.
57 | 0.96

1104 いきなり ikinari *adv.* suddenly, without notice
- 彼女はいきなり会社をクビになった。— She was fired without notice.
57 | 0.89

1105 成功(する) seikou(suru) *n.* success, achievement *v.* succeed
- 成功したいならもっと努力しなさい。— If you want to succeed, you must work harder.
57 | 0.95

1106 マンション manshon *n.* apartment, condominium, flat
- 彼は高層マンションに住んでいる。— He lives in a high-rise apartment.
57 | 0.87

1107 協力(する) kyouryoku(suru) *n.* cooperation, collaboration *v.* cooperate, collaborate
- ご協力ありがとうございました。— Thank you for your cooperation.
57 | 0.77

1108 伯父 oji *n.* uncle
- 伯父さんからお小遣いをもらった。— I got some pocket money from my uncle.
57 | 0.83

1109 時々 tokidoki *adv.* sometimes, once in a while, on occasion
- 息子は時々私に会いに来てくれる。— My son comes to see me once in a while.
57 | 0.92

1110 産む, 生む umu *v.* give birth; produce
- 彼女は男の子を産んだ。— She gave birth to a baby boy.
- 彼らは良い結果を生んだ。— They produced good results.
57 | 0.97

1111 卒業(する) sotsugyou(suru) *n.* graduation *v.* graduate
- 昨年大学を卒業しました。— I graduated from university last year.
57 | 0.87

1112 降る furu *v.* fall, come down
- 雪が静かに降り続いている。— The snow keeps falling silently.
57 | 0.91

1113 野菜 yasai *n.* vegetable
- 毎日野菜を食べるようにしています。— I try to eat vegetables every day.
57 | 0.95

1114 自分自身 jibun-jishin *n.* oneself
- 結婚相手は自分自身で決めなさい。— You must choose your marriage parter by yourself.
56 | 0.84

1115 報告(する) houkoku(suru) *n.* report, information, account *v.* inform
- 何かあったらすぐに報告してください。— If anything happens, please report it immediately.
56 | 0.83

1116 落ち着く ochitsuku *v.* settle, calm down
- 地震の時人々は落ち着いていた。— People stayed calm at the time of the earthquake.
56 | 0.95

1117 決定(する) kettei(suru) *n.* decision, determination *v.* decide, determine
- 決定する前によく考えてください。— Think carefully before you make a decision.
56 | 0.81

1118 割合 wariai *adv.* comparatively *n.* ratio, percentage
- 世界の人口は一日に約百人の割合で増加している。 — The world population grows at a rate of around one hundred people a day.
56 | 0.53 | OF

1119 移動(する) idou(suru) *n.* movement *v.* transfer, move, migrate
- その鳥は日本から東南アジアまで移動する。 — The birds migrate from Japan to Southeast Asia.
56 | 0.99

1120 いまだ imada *adv.* still, yet, so far
- 真実はいまだ謎のままだ。 — The truth is still a mystery.
56 | 0.95

1121 血 chi *n.* blood
- 傷から血が出ている。 — The wound is bleeding.
56 | 0.86

1122 応ずる、応じる ouzuru, oujiru *v.* answer, respond, accept
- そんな要求に応ずる必要はない。 — You are not required to respond to such a demand.
56 | 0.73

1123 涙 namida *n.* tear
- 彼女の目から涙が流れた。 — Tears flowed from her eyes.
56 | 0.88

1124 表情 hyjoujou *n.* expression, facial expression, look
- 彼女は悲しそうな表情をしていた。 — She had a sad expression.
56 | 0.79

1125 ああ aa *adv.* like that
- ああいう服が着たいなあ。 — I wish I could wear something like that.
56 | 0.71

1126 逃げる nigeru *v.* run away, escape
- 犯人はお金を持って逃げた。 — The criminals escaped with the money.
56 | 0.90

1127 次第 shidai *adv.* depend on; as soon as *n.* order
- 結論が出次第ご連絡します。 — We will contact you as soon as a conclusion is reached.
56 | 0.87

1128 楽 raku *na-adj.* comfort, ease, comfortable
- 想像していたような楽な仕事ではなかった。 — It wasn't as easy a job as I expected.
56 | 0.88

1129 やがて yagate *adv.* soon, before long, after all
- やがて雨が降り始めました。 — Soon, it began to rain.
56 | 0.78 | BK

1130 ではありません, じゃありません de wa ari mase n, ja ari mase n *cp.* not, no
- 年をとるのは悪いことではありません。 — Getting old is not a bad thing.
55 | 0.97

1131 かつて katsute *adv.* once, before, ever, former
- この町はかつてこの国の首都だった。 — This town was once the capital of the country.
55 | 0.90

1132 ごみ gomi *n.* rubbish, garbage, trash
- ごみはごみ箱に捨ててください。 — Please put the garbage in the trash can.
55 | 0.84

1133 警察 keisatsu *n.* police
- 警察はまだ犯人を見つけられていない。 — The police still can't find the criminal.
55 | 0.96

1134 兄 ani *n.* elder brother
- 私には兄が二人います。 — I have two older brothers.
55 | 0.85

1135 くれる kureru *v.* give
- これは祖父がくれた時計です。 — This is the watch my grandfather gave me.
55 | 0.84

1136 代わり kawari *n.* substitute, replacement, alternative
- 肉の代わりに豆腐を使うこともできます。 — You can use tofu instead of meat.
55 | 0.94

1137 外国 gaikoku *n.* foreign country
- 祖母は外国に行ったことがない。 — My grandmother has never been to a foreign country.
55 | 0.91

1138 細かい komakai *i-adj.* small, fine; trivial; sensitive
- まずは玉ねぎを細かく切ってください。 — First of all, chop an onion finely.
55 | 0.98

1139 静か shizuka *na-adj.* quiet, silent
- もう少し静かにしてくれませんか。 — Would you mind being a little more quiet?
55 | 0.91

1140 腰 koshi *n.* back, lower back, waist, hip
- 腰をひねって左足を上げて。 — Twist your waist and raise your left leg.
55 | 0.85

1141 開催（する）kaisai(suru) *n.* holding, opening *v.* hold, open
- 多くの日本の学校は十月に運動会を開催する。— Many schools in Japan hold athletic meetings in October.
55 | 0.66

1142 瞬間 shunkan *adv., n.* moment, instant, second
- 彼女は私を見た瞬間ほほえんだ。— The moment she saw me, she smiled.
55 | 0.91

1143 近付く chikazuku *v.* approach, get closer to
- 今まさに春が近付いてきている。— Now that spring is approaching.
55 | 0.92

1144 わずか wazuka *na-adj.* a few, a little, a bit *adv.* only
- 試験にわずか33パーセントの学生しか合格しなかった。— Only 33 percent of students passed the exam.
55 | 0.92

1145 暗い kurai *i-adj.* dark; depressed
- 母はまだ暗いうちに起きる。— My mother gets up while it's still dark.
55 | 0.90

1146 届く todoku *v.* reach, arrive
- 荷物は時間通りに届いた。— The package has arrived on time.
55 | 0.83

1147 窓 mado *n.* window
- 泥棒は窓を割って侵入した。— The thief broke in through a window.
55 | 0.88

1148 ストレス sutoresu *n.* stress
- どうやってストレスを解消していますか。— How do you reduce your stress?
55 | 0.87

1149 伸ばす nobasu *v.* extend, lengthen; postpone
- 教師たちは生徒の個性を伸ばそうと努力している。— The teachers are trying to develop more individuality in their pupils.
54 | 0.96

1150 ドア doa *n.* door
- ドアを閉めて鍵をかけた。— I closed the door and locked it.
54 | 0.80

1151 森 mori *n.* forest, woods, grove
- 子どもの頃よく森へ出かけてちょうを捕っていた。— When I was a kid, I used to go into the woods and collect butterflies.
54 | 0.90

1152 目標 mokuhyou *n.* goal, objective, target
- 毎年正月にその年の目標を決める。— I set my goals for the year at New Year every year.
54 | 0.96

1153 本来 honrai *adv., n.* originally, essentially, by nature, proper
- この絵本は本来子供向けに書かれた。— This picture book was originally written for children.
54 | 0.99

1154 重い omoi *i-adj.* heavy, important
- 重いスーツケースを持って空港へ行く。— I went to the airport with a heavy suitcase.
54 | 0.97

1155 変更（する）henkou(suru) *n.* change, modification, revision *v.* change, revise
- もし予定に変更があればできるだけ早く知らせてください。— If your plans change, please notify us as soon as possible.
54 | 0.86

1156 感謝（する）kansha(suru) *n.* gratitude, appreciation *v.* thank, be grateful
- アドバイスをいただき感謝しています。— I really appreciate your advice.
54 | 0.94

1157 腕 ude *n.* arm; skill, ability
- 彼は腕を組んで考えていた。— He was thinking with his arms folded.
54 | 0.84

1158 手術（する）shujutsu(suru) *n.* surgery, operation *v.* operate
- 祖父は手術を受けるために入院した。— My grandfather went to the hospital for an operation.
54 | 0.84

1159 当たり前 atarimae *na-adj.* natural, usual, common, ordinary
- これは日本では当たり前のことだ。— This is something natural in Japan.
54 | 0.93

1160 時点 jiten *n.* point in time, as of
- 今年三月の時点でこれが世界で最も高い建物です。— As of this March, this is the tallest building in the world.
54 | 0.97

1161 一日 tsuitachi *n.* first (date)
- 来月の一日から駅でたばこを吸うことは禁止されます。— From the first of next month, it will be illegal to smoke in stations.
54 | 0.63

1162 馬鹿 baka *na-adj.* foolish *n.* fool
- 彼を信じるなんて、私はなんて馬鹿なんだ。 — How foolish I am to believe him.
54 | 0.84

1163 忙しい isogashii *i-adj.* busy, occupied
- 彼はどんなに忙しくても自分でご飯を作る。 — No matter how busy he is, he always cooks for himself.
54 | 0.87

1164 おく oku *v.* at; in; on
- この会場において国際会議が行われる。 — The international conference will be held in this hall.
54 | 0.44

1165 愛する aisuru *v.* love, care
- 愛する人をなくすのはとてもつらい経験だ。 — Losing loved ones is a very hard experience.
54 | 0.89

1166 それでは、それじゃ sore de wa, sore ja *conj.* then, well, so
- それでは次の質問に移りましょう。 — Well, let's move on to the next question.
54 | 0.92

1167 遠い tooi *i-adj.* far, distant
- 私の職場は駅から遠い。 — My office is a long way from the station.
53 | 0.94

1168 苦労（する）kurou(suru) *n.* hardship, difficulty, trouble *v.* have trouble, have a hard time
- 仕事に復帰するのに苦労した。 — I had trouble getting back to work.
53 | 0.91

1169 押さえる osaeru *v.* press down, hold
- ドアを押さえておいてくれますか。 — Can you hold the door for me?
53 | 0.95

1170 課題 kadai *n.* subject; assignment, task
- 課題を明日までに終えないといけない。 — I need to finish my assignment by tomorrow.
53 | 0.79

1171 とともに to tomo ni *cp.* together with, with
- 年齢とともに視力が落ちた。 — My eyesight deteriorated with age.
53 | 0.33 | OF

1172 見つかる mitsukaru *v.* be found, be discovered
- 新しい星が見つかった。 — A new star was discovered.
53 | 0.92

1173 うそ uso *n.* lie, falsehood
- 彼女は両親にうそをついて出かけた。 — She lied to her parents and went out.
53 | 0.89

1174 仰る ossharu *v.* say, tell, speak (honorific)
- おっしゃっていることがよくわかりません。 — I don't understand what you're saying.
53 | 0.66

1175 主張（する）shuchou(suru) *n.* argument, claim *v.* argue, insist
- 大臣は政治改革が必要だと主張した。 — The minister argued that political reform was necessary.
53 | 0.90

1176 施設 shisetsu *n.* facility, institution, plant
- 会員だけがこの施設を使える。 — Only members can make use of these facilities.
53 | 0.79

1177 チェック（する）chekku(suru) *n., v.* check
- リストの中の自分の名前をチェックしてください。 — Please check your name on the list.
53 | 0.93

1178 一ヶ月 ik-kagetsu *n.* one month
- 一ヶ月で外国語を習得するのは不可能だ。 — It's impossible to master a foreign language in a month.
53 | 0.82

1179 ものの monono *p. conj.* but, although, despite
- 試合には勝ったものの彼は満足していなかった。 — Although he won the game, he was not satisfied.
53 | 0.82

1180 展開（する）tenkai(suru) *n.* development *v.* develop, unfold
- 今後の展開を楽しみにしています。 — We look forward to future developments.
53 | 0.92

1181 事業 jigyou *n.* business, enterprise, project
- 私は友人と事業を始めることにした。 — I decided to start a business with a friend of mine.
53 | 0.61

1182 データ deeta *n.* data
- データを集めるために実験を行った。 — We conducted an experiment to collect the data.
52 | 0.94

1183 役 yaku *n.* part, role, duty
- その芝居では男性が女性の役を演じる。 — Men play women's roles in the play.
52 | 0.94

1184 伸びる nobiru *v.* grow, stretch, extend
- その会社の売り上げは伸びている。 — The sales of the company are growing.
52 | 1.00

1185 通常 tsuujoo *adv., n.* normally, ordinary, regular
- 通常届くのに一週間かかります。— Normally, it takes one week to arrive.
52 | 0.99

1186 ピアノ piano *n.* piano
- 昔ピアノを習っていた。— I used to take piano lessons.
52 | 0.77

1187 行為 koui *n.* action; motion; behavior
- 自分の行為には責任がある。— You are responsible for your own actions.
52 | 0.86

1188 悩む nayamu *v.* be worried, be troubled, suffer
- 一人で悩まないでください。— Please don't suffer alone.
52 | 0.86

1189 第二 dai-ni *n.* second, secondary; another
- ここはこの国第二の都市です。— This is the second biggest city in the country.
52 | 0.47 | OF

1190 議論（する）giron(suru) *n.* argument, discussion, controversy *v.* discuss
- 議論の主な焦点は環境問題だ。— Their discussions mainly focus on environmental matters.
52 | 0.66

1191 記録（する）kiroku(suru) *n.* record, document *v.* record, write down
- 彼は100メートル走で世界記録を出した。— He set a world record in the 100 meter dash.
52 | 0.96

1192 当てる ateru *v.* hit, put, expose, guess
- ボールを友達の頭に当ててしまった。— I hit my friend's head with a ball.
52 | 0.97

1193 出来事 dekigoto *n.* event, affair, happening
- その歴史的出来事についてはほとんど記録がない。— There are very few records of the historic event.
52 | 0.90

1194 温かい atatakai *i-adj.* warm, genial
- 彼の家で温かい歓迎を受けた。— I received a warm welcome at his house.
52 | 0.92

1195 おかげ okage *n.* thanks, virtue
- あなたが手伝ってくれたおかげで商売で成功することができた。— Thanks to your help, I've been able to succeed in business.
52 | 0.90

1196 安全 anzen *na-adj.* safe *n.* safety, security
- この車は安くてとても安全だ。— This car is cheap and very safe.
52 | 0.86

1197 眺める nagameru *v.* see, view, gaze
- 窓から山々を眺めることができる。— You can see mountains from the window.
52 | 0.88

1198 いかに ikani *adv.* how, in what way
- 人間はいかに生きるべきだろうか。— How should human beings live?
52 | 0.95

1199 設置（する）setchi(suru) *n.* installation *v.* set up, place
- この店にはビデオカメラが設置されています。— A video camera is set up in the store.
52 | 0.69

1200 極めて kiwamete *adv.* very, extremely
- この犬はこの物語の中で極めて重要な役割を果たしている。— This dog plays an extremely important role in the story.
52 | 0.71

1201 入院（する）nyuuin(suru) *n.* hospitalization, admission to hospital *v.* hospitalize
- 彼は入院しなければならなかった。— He had to be hospitalized.
52 | 0.88

1202 積極的 sekkyoku-teki *na-adj.* active, positive, aggressive
- このクラスでは積極的な参加が求められます。— Your active participation is required in this class.
52 | 0.71

1203 事故 jiko *n.* accident, incident, trouble
- 事故は真夜中に起きた。— The accident occurred at midnight.
52 | 0.97

1204 たたく tataku *v.* slap, hit, knock, clap
- 音楽に合わせて手をたたこう！— Let's clap hands to the music!
52 | 0.90

1205 としても to shi te mo *cp.* assuming, even if
- それが本当だとしても言い訳にはならない。— Even if it's true, it is no excuse.
52 | 0.94

1206 会話（する）kaiwa(suru) *n.* conversation *v.* talk, chat
- 彼と会話を続けるのは難しい。— It's difficult to carry on a conversation with him.
51 | 0.90

1207 方々 katagata *n.* people
- 多くの方々がこの企画にご参加くださっています。— A lot of people have joined the project.
51 | 0.86

6 Emotions

(frequency per million words)

(心情・気分) (Feelings)

気持ち kimochi 327.991 **feeling**
心 kokoro 311.791 **mind, thought, feeling, heart**
気分 kibun 77.348 **feeling, mood**
性格 seikaku 70.200 **character, personality**
心理 shinri 10.465 **psychology**
心地 kokochi 7.917 **feelings**
機嫌 kigen 7.698 **temper, mood**
情 jou 7.174 **emotion**
心情 shinjou 5.298 **mentality**
情緒 joucho 3.440 **emotion**
気性 kishou 2.241 **temperament**

(心的態度など) (Attitude/mental state)

期待(する) kitai(suru) 93.563 **expectation; expect**
希望(する) kibou(suru) 59.760 **hope, wish, request; hope, wish, desire**
我慢(する) gaman(suru) 43.158 **patience, endurance, tolerance; be patient, endure**
願い negai 26.887 **wish, hope**
勇気 yuuki 25.496 **courage, bravery**
覚悟(する) kakugo(suru) 21.238 **readiness, preparedness; be ready**
確信(する) kakushin(suru) 16.729 **conviction; be convinced**
動機 douki 13.877 **motive**
意欲 iyoku 12.834 **will, motivation**
情熱 jounetsu 10.501 **passion**
緊張感 kinchou-kan 9.635 **tension**
やる気 yaruki 8.307 **motivation, enthusiasm**
望み nozomi 7.084 **hope**
願望(する) ganbou 6.300 **desire**

(ネガティブな気持ち) (Negative feelings)

嫌 iya, ya 141.232 **unpleasant, disagreeable**
辛い tsurai 133.413 **hard, difficult, painful**
心配(する) shinpai(suru) 119.840 **anxious, worried; anxiety, worry, care; worry, be anxious**
怖い kowai 110.664 **frightening, scary, be terrified**
不安 fuan 95.516 **anxiety, concern**
悲しい kanashii 86.265 **sad, unhappy**
寂しい sabishii 60.226 **lonely, lonesome**
嫌い kirai 44.328 **dislike, hate**
苦しい kurushii 41.468 **painful, hard, difficult**
恥ずかしい hazukashii 41.457 **ashamed, embarrassed**

迷惑(する) meiwaku 35.411 **troublesome, annoying; annoyance, nuisance, trouble; be inconvenienced**
不満 fuman 25.587 **dissatisfaction, discontent; discontented**
悔しい kuyashii 22.275 **regrettable, frustrating; feel regret**
やばい yabai 18.359 **risky, chancy**
苦痛 kutsuu 15.479 **pain**
羨ましい urayamashii 14.925 **envious, enviable**
孤独 kodoku 14.837 **lonely**
情けない nasakenai 10.948 **miserable**
面倒くさい mendou-kusai 8.453 **troublesome**
空しい munashii 6.379 **empty**
不快 fukai 6.270 **annoying**
不愉快 fu-yukai 6.003 **irritating**
哀れ aware 5.461 **pitiful**
憂鬱 yuutsu 3.834 **depressing**
腹立たしい haradatashii 3.702 **exasperating**
憎い nikui 2.192 **hateful**
憎たらしい nikutarashii 1.339 **unlovable**
忌々しい imaimashii 1.098 **annoying**
ばからしい bakarashii 1.093 **stupid**
憎らしい nikurashii 0.610 **annoying**

(ネガティブな気持ち・名詞) (Negative feelings: nouns)

ショック shokku 40.389 **shock**
悩み nayami 24.777 **trouble, worry**
恐怖 kyoufu 23.827 **fear, dread, terror**
怒り ikari 23.773 **anger, rage, fury**
悲しみ kanashimi 18.796 **sadness, grief**
苦しみ kurushimi 13.163 **suffering, agony**
寂しさ sabishi-sa 10.964 **loneliness**
辛さ tsura-sa 9.521 **pain**
怖さ kowa-sa 6.681 **fear**
恨み urami 5.417 **grudge**
悲しさ kanashi-sa 3.943 **grief**
焦り aseri 3.187 **irritation**
妬み netami 1.221 **jealousy**

(ネガティブな気持ち・動詞) (Negative feelings: verbs)

心配(する) shinpai(suru) 119.840 **anxious, worried; anxiety, worry, care; worry, be anxious**
困る komaru 116.479 **have difficulty, be in trouble**

泣く naku 80.656 cry
苦労（する）kurou(suru) 53.251 hardship, difficulty, trouble; have trouble, have a hard time
悩む nayamu 52.134 be worried, be troubled, suffer
緊張（する）kinchou(suru) 40.327 tension; get tense
けんか（する）kenka(suru) 34.306 fight, quarrel
苦しむ kurushimu 23.752 feel pain, suffer
恐れる osoreru 22.114 fear, be afraid
飽きる akiru 21.308 tire, weary, be tired of, get bored
落ち込む ochikomu 20.803 sink, go down, be depressed
叱る shikaru 20.381 scold, admonish
嫌う kirau 19.205 hate, detest
後悔（する）koukai(suru) 18.596 repentance, regret; regret
嫌がる iyagaru 16.639 be reluctant, hate
焦る aseru 16.264 be in a hurry; be impatient; be eager
狂う kuruu 13.635 go mad
がっかりする gakkarisuru 13.013 be disappointed
痛む itamu 12.249 ache, hurt, pain
嫉妬（する）shitto(suru) 6.308 envy
恨む uramu 5.671 feel bitter about
絶望（する）zetsubou(suru) 5.528 feel hopeless
いらいら（する）iraira(suru) 4.538 annoy
威張る ibaru 3.266 domineer
妬む netamu 1.252 envy

(中立的な気持ち) (Feelings: neutral)
大丈夫 daijoubu 104.664 safe, all right
驚く odoroku 92.702 be surprised
びっくり（する）bikkuri(suru) 90.027 surprise, amaze
不思議 fushigi 78.685 wonder, wonderful, strange, mysterious
涙 namida 56.089 tear
緊張する kinchou(suru) 40.327 tension; get tense
迷う mayou 33.003 get lost; cannot decide
必死 hisshi 29.360 desperate
平気 heiki 28.188 insensitive, fine; calmness
騒ぐ sawagu 20.968 make noise, fuss
自慢（する）jiman(suru) 19.447 pride, boast; boast, brag
驚き odoroki 18.810 surprise, amazement
本気 honki 18.657 seriousness, earnestness; serious, earnest

慎重 shinchou 17.442 careful, discreet
どきどきする dokidoki-suru 11.311 throb, beat fast
呑気 nonki 3.608 easy-going

(ポジティブな気持ち) (Positive feelings)
好き suki 403.262 favorite, like, love
楽しい tanoshii 279.007 pleasant, happy, enjoyable
面白い omoshiroi 185.642 interesting, fun, funny
嬉しい ureshii 179.753 glad, happy
大好き daisuki 72.435 love
幸せ shiawase 71.615 happy; happiness; fortune, luck
おかしい okashii 69.942 funny, amusing
安心 anshin(suru) 57.707 peace of mind, relief, feel relieved
幸い saiwai 31.549 lucky, fortunate; happiness; fortunately
ありがたい arigatai 25.459 kind, welcome
快適 kaiteki 17.738 comfortable
気軽 kigaru 15.406 light-hearted, feel free
幸福 koufuku 15.068 happiness
望ましい nozomashii 13.762 desirable
おかしな okashina 10.736 funny, ridiculous
好ましい konomashii 6.130 favourable
心地よい kokochiyoi 5.874 comfortable
快い kokoroyoi 5.782 pleasant, agreeable
愉快 yukai 4.377 fun
愛しい itoshii 2.826 dear, beloved

(ポジティブな気持ち・名詞) (Positive feelings: nouns)
感謝 kansha(suru) 53.973 gratitude, appreciation; thank, be grateful
愛 ai 44.480 love, affection
喜び yorokobi 42.029 pleasure, delight
恋 koi 24.645 love (romantic)
憧れ akogare 20.254 admiration
尊敬（する）sonkei(suru) 17.425 respect; respect
面白さ omoshiro-sa 10.915 interest, fun
嬉しさ ureshi-sa 7.917 pleasure
敬意 keii 4.997 respect

(ポジティブな気持ち・動詞) (Positive feelings: verbs)
楽しむ tanoshimu 160.936 enjoy, have a good time
喜ぶ yorokobu 85.561 be glad, rejoice
感動（する）kandou(suru) 60.932 deep emotion; be impressed, be moved

安心(する) anshin(suru) 57.707 peace of mind, relief; feel relieved
落ち着く ochitsuku 56.434 settle, calm down
愛する aisuru 53.613 love, care
満足(する) manzoku(suru) 25.212 satisfaction; be satisfied
ほっとする hottosuru 19.582 be relieved
尊敬(する) sonkei(suru) 17.425 respect; respect
憧れる akogareru 14.879 long for; admire
わくわく(する) wakuwaku suru 11.553 be bubbling; be excited
微笑む hohoemu 11.405 smile

(人の性格) (Personality)
厳しい kibishii 95.794 strict (also hard)
優しい yasashii 73.588 gentle, tender
明るい akarui 64.806 cheerful (also bright, light)
細かい komakai 55.013 sensitive (also small, fine; trivial)
暗い kurai 54.779 depressed (also dark)
温かい atatakai 51.916 warm, genial
積極的 sekkyoku-teki 51.747 active, positive, aggressive
正直 shoujiki 42.378 honesty; honest, truthful; honestly
冷たい tsumetai 38.726 cold
真面目 majime 25.525 serious; steady; honest
素直 sunao 25.412 obedient, tame

親切 shinsetsu 19.764 kind
穏やか odayaka 18.858 calm, peaceful (also mild)
おとなしい otonashii 16.214 gentle, well-behaved, quiet
さっぱり sappari 15.862 frank
わがまま wagamama 14.329 selfish, disobedient; selfishness
しつこい shitsukoi 8.632 persistent (also over-rich (food))
率直 sotchoku 8.262 candid, frank
陽気 youki 7.803 cheerful, lively
大雑把 oozappa 6.147 rough
頑固 ganko 5.203 stubborn
誠実 seijitsu 4.870 honest
消極的 shoukyoku-teki 3.656 passive
狡い zurui 2.845 shrewd
意地悪 ijiwaru 2.693 malicious
だらしない darashinai 2.673 untidy
ずうずうしい zuuzuushii 2.541 shameless
寛大 kandai 2.332 forgiving, generous, tolerant
けち kechi 1.953 mean, stingy
嘘つき usotsuki 1.714 lying; liar
軽率 keisotsu 1.349 careless
短気 tanki 1.338 fiery, short-tempered
厚かましい atsukamashii 1.313 presumptuous
朗らか ooraka 1.056 breezy, cheery
純情 junjou 0.390 pure-hearted
そそっかしい sosokkashii 0.348 ditzy, careless, scatterbrained

1208 要る iru *v.* need, want
- 何か要るものある？ — Do you need anything?
51 | 0.95

1209 鳥 tori *n.* bird; poultry
- ここでは珍しい鳥を見ることができます。 — You can see some rare birds here.
51 | 0.88

1210 何とか nan to ka *adv.* somehow *n.* something
- 何とかして時間までに行きます。 — I'll get there in time somehow.
51 | 0.80

1211 市 shi *n.* city, town
- 市は新しい学校を建設することを決定した。 — The city decided to build a new school.
51 | 0.59 | NM

1212 眠る nemuru *v.* sleep
- 昨日の夜、全然眠れなかった。 — I couldn't sleep at all last night.
51 | 0.87

1213 自信 jishin *n.* confidence
- 彼女は自分に自信がないようだ。 — She seems to lack confidence in herself.
51 | 0.95

1214 固い katai *i-adj.* hard, solid, stiff
- この岩はとても固い。 — This rock is very hard.
51 | 0.94

1215 戦後 sengo *adv., n.* postwar, after the war
- この国は戦後大きく変化した。 — This country has changed greatly since the war.
51 | 0.94

1216 値段 nedan *n.* price, value, cost
- 手ごろな値段でおいしい料理が味わえる。— You can enjoy delicious food at a reasonable price.

51 | 0.87

1217 通じる tsuujiru *v.* lead; communicate, understand
- 駅へ通じる道はいつも混雑している。— The street leading to the station is always crowded.

51 | 0.92

1218 動かす ugokasu *v.* move, shift, operate
- 自動車を動かしてください。— Please move your car.

51 | 0.96

1219 トイレ toire *n.* toilet, restroom, bathroom
- トイレはどちらでしょうか。— Could you tell me where the restroom is?

51 | 0.87

1220 あんな anna *adn.* such, like that
- 私もあんな車がほしいなあ。— I want a car like that.

51 | 0.86

1221 避ける sakeru *v.* avoid, keep away from
- 彼に避けられているような気がする。— I feel like he is avoiding me.

51 | 0.97

1222 お勧め（する） o-susume(suru) *n.* recommendation, advice *v.* recommend, advise
- お勧めのものはありますか。— Do you have any recommendations?

51 | 0.67 | WB

1223 野球 yakyuu *n.* baseball
- 小さいときに野球を始めました。— I started playing baseball when I was a small boy.

51 | 0.77

1224 穴 ana *n.* hole, pit
- ケーブルをつなぐために壁に穴を開けなければならなかった。— I had to make a hole in a wall to connect a cable.

51 | 0.92

1225 クリック（する） kurikku(suru) *n., v.* click
- ここをクリックしてファイルを開いてください。— Click here to open the file.

51 | 0.54 | WB

1226 捕らえる toraeru *v.* catch, grasp, seize, arrest
- 警察は犯人を捕らえるためにわなをしかけた。— The police set a trap to catch the criminal.

51 | 0.90

1227 昨年 sakunen *adv., n.* last year
- 昨年この地域で大地震がありました。— There was a major earthquake in this area last year.

50 | 0.80

1228 減少（する） genshou(suru) *n.* decrease, reduction *v.* decline, decrease
- この町では犯罪が40パーセント減少した。— Crime has decreased by 40 percent in this town.

50 | 0.49 | OF

1229 洗う arau *v.* wash
- 食べる前に必ず手を洗ってね。— Be sure to wash your hands before you eat.

50 | 0.92

1230 左 hidari *n.* left
- その棚を左に動かしてください。— Please move the shelf to the left.

50 | 0.87

1231 珍しい mezurashii *i-adj.* rare, unusual, unique
- あいつがこんなに早く起きるなんて珍しいね。— It's unusual for him to get up so early.

50 | 0.91

1232 尋ねる tazuneru *v.* ask, look for
- 誰かに道を尋ねてきたらどうですか。— Why don't you go and ask someone for directions?

50 | 0.83

1233 一言 hitokoto *n.* one word, single word, brief comment
- 彼はいつも一言多い。— He always says one word too many.

50 | 0.98

1234 男の子 otokonoko *n.* boy, male child
- うちには男の子が二人います。— We have two boys.

50 | 0.88

1235 制度 seido *n.* system, institution
- 今の制度を変えるのは簡単ではない。— It's not easy to change the present system.

50 | 0.76

1236 買い物（する） kaimono(suru) *n.* shopping *v.* go shopping
- 彼女はスーパーへ買い物に行った。— She went shopping at a supermarket.

50 | 0.86

1237 チーム chiimu *n.* team
- 私たちはチームとして仕事をした。— We worked together as a team.

50 | 0.86

1238 登場（する） toujou(suru) *n.* entry, appearance *v.* appear, emerge
- 彼女は美しいドレスを着てパーティーに登場した。— She appeared at the party wearing a beautiful dress.

50 | 0.82

1239 期間 kikan *n.* period, term, interval
- 契約の期間を延長したいです。— I'd like to extend the period of the contract.
50 | 0.89

1240 金額 kingaku *n.* amount of money
- 金額を確認してここにサインしてください。— Please confirm the amount of money and sign here.
50 | 0.85

1241 塩 shio *n.* salt
- 塩取ってくれる？ — Can you pass me the salt?
50 | 0.94

1242 奥 oku *n.* inner part, back; bottom
- 奥に詰めてもらえますか。— Could you please move to the rear?
50 | 0.88

1243 九 kyuu *num.* nine
- 十から一を引くと九になる。— If you subtract one from ten, you get nine.
50 | 0.88

1244 まだまだ madamada *adv.* still, still more
- まだまだやることがたくさんある。— There are still more things to be done.
49 | 0.92

1245 習う narau *v.* take lessons, be taught, learn
- どのくらい日本語を習っていますか。— How long have you been learning Japanese?
49 | 0.69

1246 番組 bangumi *n.* show, program
- いつでも好きな番組を楽しむことができます。— You can enjoy your favorite program at any time.
49 | 0.88

1247 一時 ichiji *adv., n.* at one time, temporary, for a while
- 彼は一時インドに帰国するつもりだ。— He will be going back to India for a while.
49 | 0.54 | NM

1248 ケース keesu *n.* case
- それはかなり珍しいケースだ。— That's a rather unusual case.
49 | 0.97

1249 傾向 keikou *n.* tendency, trend, inclination
- 日本人には他の人と同じことをしていると安心する傾向がある。— Japanese have a tendency to feel comfortable when doing the same thing as everyone else.
49 | 0.86

1250 日々 hibi *adv.* every day, daily *n.* days
- 日々の生活にストレスを感じる人は多い。— Many people feel stressed in their daily lives.
49 | 0.94

1251 拡大（する）kakudai(suru) *n.* enlargement, expansion *v.* enlarge, expand
- 我が社は海外での事業を拡大しています。— Our company is expanding its overseas business.
49 | 0.71

1252 レベル reberu *n.* level
- この教科書は中級のレベルの学習者向けです。— This textbook is for learners at the intermediate level.
49 | 0.98

1253 よろしく yoroshiku *adv.* well, properly, best regards
- 彼によろしくお伝えください。— Please give him my best regards.
49 | 0.56 | WB

1254 疑問 gimon *n.* question, problem, doubt
- いくつかの疑問が解決されないまま残っている。— Some questions remain unanswered.
49 | 0.99

1255 それなり sore-nari *n.* in itself, as it is, in its way
- あの映画はそれなりに楽しかった。— That movie was fun in its own way.
49 | 0.90

1256 現状 genjou *n.* present condition, existing state
- 我々は世界の現状を理解しなければならない。— We must understand the present state of the world.
49 | 0.86

1257 ドイツ doitsu *n.* Germany
- 私はドイツで三年間働いていた。— I was working in Germany for three years.
49 | 0.96

1258 取り上げる toriageru *v.* pick up, adopt; take away
- その番組ではある話題を取り上げて議論する。— They pick up on some topic and discuss it in the program.
48 | 0.95

1259 主に omo ni *adv.* mainly, for the most part, chiefly
- この店は主に輸入品を扱っている。— This shop deals mainly with imported goods.
48 | 0.98

1260 伯母 oba *n.* aunt
- 伯母の家に遊びに行った。— I went to visit my aunt.
48 | 0.84

1261 パン pan *n.* bread
- 私は時々うちでパンを焼く。— I sometimes bake bread at home.
48 | 0.86

1262 クラス kurasu *n.* class
- 調査の結果をクラスで発表する。— I'll present the results of my research to the class.
48 | 0.86

1263 肉 niku *n.* meat, flesh, fat
- お肉は食べられないんです。— I can't eat meat.
48 | 0.91

1264 なるべく narubeku *adv.* as . . . as possible, if possible
- なるべく多くの情報を集めてください。— You should gather as much information as possible.
48 | 0.91

1265 指 yubi *n.* finger
- 紙で指を切ってしまった。— I cut my finger on some paper.
48 | 0.88

1266 態度 taido *n.* attitude, manner, behavior
- あの人態度が悪いと思わない？— Don't you think he has a bad attitude?
48 | 0.95

1267 地 chi *n.* earth, ground, land, place
- 彼らは新しい定住の地を見つけなければならなかった。— They had to find a new place to settle down.
48 | 0.90

1268 全国 zenkoku *n.* nationwide, whole country, national
- インフルエンザが全国に広がった。— The flu has spread nationwide.
48 | 0.82

1269 答え kotae *n.* answer, solution
- 私は答えが分からなかった。— I didn't know the answer.
48 | 0.98

1270 世話（する） sewa(suru) *n.* care *v.* take care of, look after
- 彼女は子供達の世話をしている。— She looks after her children.
48 | 0.93

1271 差 sa *n.* difference, gap, margin
- たくさん練習する人としない人の間には差がつく。— There will be a big gap between people who practice a lot and people who do not.
48 | 0.98

1272 一切 issai *adv., n.* all, entirely, not . . . at all
- いくら掛かるかは一切気にしません。— I don't care at all how much it will cost.
48 | 0.98

1273 食う kuu *v.* eat, consume
- あの車はかなりガソリンを食う。— That car eats up a lot of gas.
48 | 0.88

1274 文章 bunshou *n.* sentence; writing, text
- 彼のレポートは簡潔な文章で書かれていた。— His report was written in concise sentences.
48 | 0.97

1275 背景 haikei *n.* background, context, setting
- 山を背景にして写真を撮った。— We took pictures with mountains in the background.
48 | 0.88

1276 負担（する） futan(suru) *n.* burden, load, charge *v.* bear
- 子どもたちの負担になりたくない。— I don't want to be a burden to my children.
48 | 0.87

1277 事情 jijou *n.* circumstance, situation, reason
- 事情があって仕事をやめなければならなかった。— I had to give up my job because of circumstances.
48 | 0.95

1278 メンバー menbaa *n.* member, participant
- クラブにはメンバーが100人以上います。— There are more than one hundred members in the club.
48 | 0.94

1279 ようやく youyaku *adv.* at last, gradually, barely
- ようやく全て終わった。— It is finally all over.
48 | 0.92

1280 地方 chihou *n.* area, district, countryside
- 多くの労働者が地方から都市へ出てくる。— Many workers come from the rural areas to the cities.
48 | 0.92

1281 豊か yutaka *na-adj.* abundant, plentiful, rich
- 私の故郷は緑の豊かな所です。— My hometown is rich in greenery.
48 | 0.93

1282 助ける tasukeru *v.* help, rescue, save
- 売り上げの一部は難民を助けるために使われます。— A portion of our sales will be used to help refugees.
48 | 0.94

1283 詰まる tsumaru *v.* be blocked, be packed, be clogged
- トイレが詰まったみたいだ。— The toilet seems blocked.
47 | 0.91

1284 一個 ik-ko *n.* one, piece
- 一個いくらですか。— How much for one?
47 | 0.93

1285 大阪 oosaka *n.* Osaka
- 大阪は商業の都市として知られていた。— Osaka was known as a commercial city.
47 | 0.98

1286 果たす hatasu *v.* carry out, achieve, fulfil
- 自分の責任は果たしたと思っている。— I believe I've carried out my responsibilities.
47 | 0.84

1287 支える sasaeru *v.* support, hold, sustain
- 家族を支えるために働き始めました。— I started working to support my family.
47 | 0.94

1288 抱える kakaeru *v.* hold, carry, employ
- 母親は赤ちゃんを両腕に抱えていた。— The mother held her baby in her arms.
47 | 0.97

1289 大分 daibu, daibun *adv.* very, a lot, much
- 大分気分が良くなった。— I feel much better now.
47 | 0.74

1290 追う ou *v.* follow, chase, pursue
- 彼は流行を追うのが好きだ。— He likes to follow fashion.
47 | 0.94

1291 権利 kenri *n.* right, claim, entitlement
- 他人の権利を侵害してはならない。— You must not violate the rights of others.
47 | 0.82

1292 何々 naninani *pron.* such and such, this and that
- 「何々が好きだ」と彼に答えた。— I answered him, "I like such and such".
47 | 0.21 | SP

1293 計算（する）keisan(suru) *n.* calculation *v.* calculate, count, figure
- 彼女は計算がとても得意だ。— She is very good at calculating.
47 | 0.93

1294 痛み ita-mi *n.* pain, ache
- これは痛みを和らげるための薬です。— This is a drug to relieve pain.
47 | 0.90

1295 返す kaesu *v.* return; repay; turn over
- 本は必ず期限までに返すように。— Be sure to return the book by the deadline.
47 | 0.95

1296 庭 niwa *n.* garden, yard
- 庭の手入れをするのが趣味です。— My hobby is looking after my garden.
47 | 0.89

1297 納得（する）nattoku(suru) *n.* agreement *v.* understand, be convinced
- 病院側の説明には納得していない。— I'm not convinced by the hospital's explanation.
47 | 0.98

1298 組織（する）soshiki(suru) *n.* organization, structure *v.* organize
- 彼はとうとう組織のトップに立った。— Finally, he got to the head of the organization.
47 | 0.87

1299 能力 nouryoku *n.* ability, capacity, power; proficiency
- 子どもたちは新しい環境に適応する能力が高い。— Children have a great capacity to adapt to new environments.
47 | 0.93

1300 人口 jinkou *n.* population
- 世界の人口は増加し続けている。— The global population keeps growing.
47 | 0.84

1301 薄い usui *i-adj.* thin, light, weak
- このコンピューターは雑誌のように薄い。— This computer is as slim as a magazine.
47 | 0.94

1302 注 chuu *n.* note, annotation, comment
- 注は文書の最後に付けて下さい。— You should put the notes at the end of the text.
46 | 0.38 | OF

1303 二回 ni kai *n.* twice
- この薬を一日二回飲んでください。— You should take this medicine twice a day.
46 | 0.93

1304 治療（する）chiryou(suru) *n.* cure, treatment, therapy *v.* treat, cure
- 今がんの治療を受けている。— I'm receiving treatment for cancer.
46 | 0.95

1305 昼 hiru *n.* noon; daytime
- 夫は仕事に行っていて昼は家にいません。— My husband is at work in the daytime and isn't at home.
46 | 0.83

1306 を通じて o tsuuji te *cp.* throughout, across, through
- 私たちは共通の友人を通じて知り合いました。— We met each other through mutual friends.
46 | 0.80

1307 せっかく sekkaku *adv.* with effort, take the trouble to
- せっかく外国に来たのだからそこの文化を知る努力をしよう。— As I've made the effort to come all the way to a foreign country, I should try to understand their culture.
46 | 0.95

1308 赤い akai *i-adj.* red
- 彼女は寝不足で赤い目をしていた。— She had red eyes because of lack of sleep.
46 | 0.89

1309 比較的 hikaku-teki *na-adj.* comparative, relative
- 郊外の家賃はほかの地域に比べると比較的高い。— Rents in the suburbs are relatively high compared to other areas.
46 | 0.96

1310 サービス（する）saabisu(suru) *n.* service *v.* attend, serve
- この店はきめ細かいサービスで有名だ。— This restaurant is famous for its fine service.
46 | 0.96

1311 何人 nan-nin *n.* how many people
- ご家族は何人ですか。— How many people are there in your family?
46 | 0.91

1312 荷物 nimotsu *n.* baggage, parcel, burden
- 荷物はホテルに届けてください。— Please deliver the baggage to my hotel.
46 | 0.83

1313 魅力 miryoku *n.* charm, attraction, appeal
- この町の魅力は親切な人々です。— The charm of this town lies in the kind people.
46 | 0.85

1314 現場 genba *n.* field, scene, spot
- 自動車事故の現場を見てしまった。— I happened to see the scene of the car accident.
46 | 0.99

1315 道具 dougu *n.* tool, instrument
- この道具は使い方によって危険なこともあります。— This tool can be dangerous, depending on how it is used.
46 | 0.84

1316 遠く touku *adv.* far, remote *n.* distance
- 老人は遠くを見つめながら座っていた。— The old man was sitting on a bench looking into the distance.
46 | 0.88

1317 中学 chuugaku *n.* junior high school
- 息子は来年から中学に行きます。— My son will enter junior high school next year.
46 | 0.84

1318 村 mura *n.* village
- この村ではまだ外国人は珍しいようだ。— It still seems to be rare to see foreigners in this village.
46 | 0.90

1319 システム shisutemu *n.* system
- 多くの会社がその新しいシステムを導入している。— Many companies have introduced the new system.
46 | 0.97

1320 あそこ asoko *pron.* there, over there
- かつてあそこには大きな家がありました。— There used to be a large house over there.
46 | 0.88

1321 十時 juu ji *n.* ten o'clock
- 十時にお客様と会う約束があります。— I have an appointment with a client at ten o'clock.
45 | 0.28 | NM

1322 息 iki *n.* breath, respiration
- 駅まで走ったら息が切れてしまった。— I was out of breath after running to the station.
45 | 0.82

1323 伝わる tsutawaru *v.* spread, descend, travel
- 彼女の死のニュースはすぐに国中に伝わった。— The news of her death spread across the nation immediately.
45 | 0.96

1324 撮影（する）satsuei(suru) *n.* shooting *v.* shoot, photograph
- 来月から映画の撮影が始まります。— We will start shooting the movie next month.
45 | 0.76

1325 指導（する）shidou(suru) *n.* guidance *v.* guide, coach
- 彼から指導を受けるためにこの学校に入った。— I entered this school to receive guidance from him.
45 | 0.75

1326 生かす ikasu *v.* keep alive; make use of
- この貴重な経験を生かすつもりです。— I intend to make use of this valuable experience.
45 | 0.89

1327 韓国 kankoku *n.* Korea, South Korea, Republic of Korea
- 韓国は日本人に人気のある旅行先だ。— Korea is a popular travel destination for Japanese.
45 | 0.94

1328 字 ji *n.* letter, character; handwriting
- 彼女は字がきれいです。— She has good handwriting.
45 | 0.89

1329 指定（する）shitei(suru) *n.* appointment *v.* specify
- その運送会社は指定された日時に届けてくれる。— That shipping company delivers the goods on a specified date and time.
45 | 0.79

1330 経営（する）keiei(suru) *n.* management *v.* manage, run
- 彼には経営の手腕がある。— He has management skills.
45 | 0.94

1331 あらゆる arayuru *adn.* every, all, any
- 兄と僕はあらゆる点で違う。— My elder brother and I are different in every way.
45 | 0.93

1332 価値 kachi *n.* value, worth
- 円の価値が上昇した。— The value of the yen has risen.
45 | 0.95

1333 南 minami *n.* south
- 私は東京の南にある小さい町に住んでいます。— I live in a small town in the south of Tokyo.
45 | 0.92

1334 成立（する）seiritsu(suru) *n.* completion *v.* establish, conclude, come into existence
- 何年もの交渉の末、二人の離婚は成立した。— Their divorce was concluded after years of negotiation.
45 | 0.79

1335 季節 kisetsu *n.* season
- 秋は食べ物がおいしい季節です。— Autumn is the season for good food.
45 | 0.90

1336 導入（する）dounyuu(suru) *n.* introduction *v.* introduce
- その国は新しい税金を導入した。— The country introduced a new tax.
45 | 0.81

1337 ことにする koto ni suru *aux.* decide to, pretend to
- 家を買うことにした。— I decided to buy a house.
45 | 0.82

1338 一枚 ichi-mai *n.* one (sheet, slice)
- 一枚ずつ紙を取ってください。— Take one sheet of paper each, please.
45 | 0.90

1339 い i *p. disc.* QUESTION
- 本当に大丈夫かい。— Are you really alright?
45 | 0.73

1340 先輩 senpai *n.* senior, elder
- この仕事は先輩から紹介された。— I was introduced to this job by a senior student.
45 | 0.82

1341 全員 zen'in *adv., n.* all members, everyone
- このゲームは家族全員で楽しめる。— All the family can enjoy this game.
45 | 0.94

1342 にしても ni shite mo *cp.* even if, even though
- 冗談にしてもそれはひどすぎる。— Even if it's a joke, it's too much.
45 | 0.84

1343 四人 yo-nin *n.* four people
- 家族は二人の息子と妻と私の四人です。— There are four people in my family, two sons, my wife and myself.
45 | 0.94

1344 人物 jinbutsu *n.* person, character
- 彼女は素晴らしい人物だった。— She was a wonderful person.
45 | 0.83

1345 距離 kyori *n.* distance
- ２つの町の距離はだいたい10キロです。— The distance between the two cities is about 10 kilometers.
45 | 0.99

1346 泊まる tomaru *v.* stay
- 友達の家に泊まる予定です。— I will stay at my friend's house.
45 | 0.76

1347 充実（する）juujitsu(suru) *n.* fullness *v.* enrich, fullfill
- 彼は充実した人生を楽しんでいる。— He enjoys a full life.
45 | 0.74

1348 によると ni yoru to *cp.* according to
- この新聞によると また税金が上がるそうだ。— According to this newspaper, taxes are going to be raised again.
45 | 0.93

1349 コミュニケーション（する）komyunikeeshon(suru) *n.* communication *v.* communicate
- 同僚との間にコミュニケーションの問題を感じている。— I feel I have a communication problem with my colleagues.
45 | 0.82

1350 散歩（する）sanpo(suru) *n., v.* walk, stroll
- 散歩の途中で美しい庭を見つけた。— I found a beautiful garden during my walk.
45 | 0.81

1351 グループ guruupu *n.* group, team
- 私たちは五人のグループで働いている。— We are working in a group of five people.
45 | 0.98

1352 黒い kuroi *i-adj.* black
- 黒いのはありますか。— Do you have a black one?
45 | 0.89

1353 九時 ku ji *n.* nine o'clock
- 九時のバスに乗らなくちゃいけない。— I need to take the bus leaving at nine o'clock.
45 | 0.33 | NM

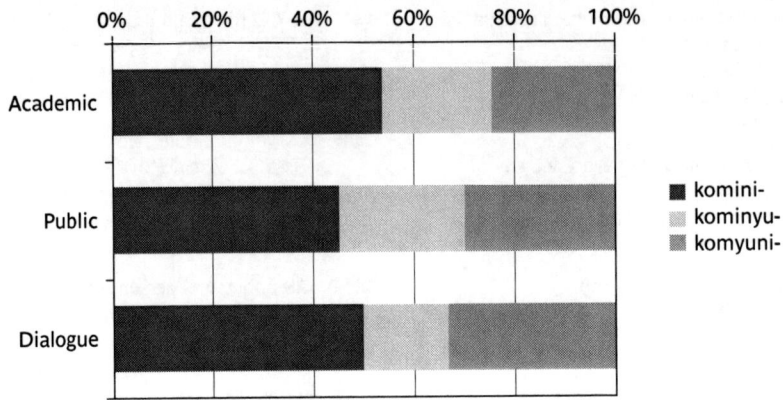

Variants of *komyunikeeshon* (communication): Metathesis between the rhymes of the second and third syllables occur in this loanword.

1354 石 ishi *n.* stone, rock
- この教会は石でできている。— This church is built of stone.
- 45 | 0.89

1355 エネルギー enerugii *n.* energy, power
- エネルギーに関する問題を解決するためには何が必要だろうか。— What needs to be done to solve the energy problems?
- 45 | 0.94

1356 挨拶(する) aisatsu(suru) *n.* greeting *v.* greet
- 私たちは新年の挨拶を交わした。— We exchanged New Year's greetings.
- 45 | 0.93

1357 愛 ai *n.* love, affection
- 子どもたちは親の愛を感じなければならない。— Children need to feel their parents' love.
- 44 | 0.87

1358 比較(する) hikaku(suru) *n.* comparison *v.* compare
- 十年前と比較すると外国人住民の数は非常に増加した。— Compared to ten years ago, the number of foreign residents has increased dramatically.
- 44 | 0.81

1359 結ぶ musubu *v.* tie, connect, unite
- 靴のひもは自分で結べるよね。— You can tie your shoes by yourself, can't you?
- 44 | 0.92

1360 移る utsuru *v.* move, transfer, shift
- あの席に移ってもよろしいですか。— Can I move to that seat?
- 44 | 0.95

1361 従来 juurai *adv., n.* up to now, conventional, traditional
- これは従来の方法よりも効果的だろう。— It will be more efficient than conventional methods.
- 44 | 0.71

1362 嫌い kirai *na-adj.* dislike, hate
- 何か嫌いな食べ物がありますか。— Are there any foods you don't like?
- 44 | 0.77

1363 注目(する) chuumoku(suru) *n.* attention *v.* pay attention, watch
- 政治の問題に注目する人が増えている。— The number of people paying attention to politics is increasing.
- 44 | 0.89

1364 携帯(する) keitai(suru) *n.* portable *v.* carry
- 運転するときはいつも免許証を携帯しなさい。— You should carry your driver's license with you whenever you drive.
- 44 | 0.74 | WB

1365 休む yasumu *v.* take a rest, be absent from
- 少し休みましょう。— Let's take a rest for a while.
- 44 | 0.87

1366 甘い amai *i-adj.* sweet; soft
- 甘い物を控えるように言われた。— I was told to cut out sweets.
- 44 | 0.92

1367 最高 saikou *n., na-adj* best, highest
- 私共は世界で最高の技術を使っています。— We use the best technology in the world.
- 44 | 0.94

1368 弟 otouto *n.* younger brother
- これが私の弟です。— This is my younger brother.
44 | 0.89

1369 卵 tamago *n.* egg, spawn
- 卵を割ってボウルに入れてね。— Break some eggs into the bowl.
44 | 0.92

1370 服 fuku *n.* clothes, dress, outfit
- 服を床に散らかさないで！— Don't throw your clothes on the floor!
44 | 0.90

1371 赤ちゃん akachan *n.* baby, infant
- 彼女には五か月の赤ちゃんがいる。— She has a five-month-old baby.
44 | 0.86

1372 始め hajime *adv., n.* beginning, origin
- 毎回授業の始めに小テストがある。— We have a quiz at the beginning of each lesson.
44 | 0.88

1373 要求（する） youkyuu(suru) *n., v.* demand, request, claim
- そんな要求にはこたえられない。— I cannot meet such a demand.
44 | 0.89

1374 紙 kami *n.* paper
- 答えは全てその紙に書いてください。— Write all the answers on the paper.
44 | 0.96

1375 妹 imouto *n.* younger sister
- 妹は中学生です。— My younger sister is a junior high school student.
44 | 0.86

1376 額 gaku *n.* amount of money; frame
- 詳しい額は請求書にかいてあります。— The exact amount was on the invoice.
- 家族の写真を額に入れた。— We put the family photo in a frame.
44 | 0.73

1377 交ぜる mazeru *v.* mix, shuffle
- 彼女は野菜と果物を交ぜてボウルに入れた。— She mixed some vegetables and fruit in the bowl.
44 | 0.90

1378 抱く idaku *v.* have, hold, embrace
- 若者たちは将来に大きな希望を抱いている。— Young people have big hopes for their future.
44 | 0.85

1379 出来上がる dekiagaru *v.* be completed, be finished, be ready
- 晩ご飯が出来上がりましたよ。— Dinner is ready!
44 | 0.94

1380 小説 shousetsu *n.* novel, fiction, story
- 私は家で一日中小説を読んでいた。— I stayed home all day reading novels.
44 | 0.89

1381 訪れる otozureru *v.* visit, call on, arrive
- この国を訪れるのに一番いい季節は春だと思う。— I think spring is the best season to visit the country.
44 | 0.84

1382 汗 ase *n.* sweat, perspiration
- 彼は顔の汗をぬぐった。— He wiped the sweat off his face.
44 | 0.83

1383 特別 tokubetsu *na-adj.* special, particular
- この仕事に特別な技術は必要ありません。— This job doesn't require any special skills.
44 | 0.96

1384 改善（する） kaizen(suru) *n.* improvement, reform *v.* improve
- 患者の症状に改善が見られない。— The patient's symptoms don't show any improvement.
44 | 0.75

1385 休み yasumi *n.* holiday; rest; be closed
- 銀行は日曜日は休みだ。— Banks are closed on Sundays.
44 | 0.77

1386 咲く saku *v.* bloom
- この公園にはさまざまな花が咲く。— Many different flowers bloom in this park.
43 | 0.86

1387 基本 kihon *n.* foundation, basis, basic
- 料理の基本を学びたい。— I want to learn the basics of cooking.
43 | 0.96

1388 暑い atsui *i-adj.* hot, warm
- 今日は特に暑いですね。— It is especially hot today, isn't it?
43 | 0.77

1389 向く muku *v.* turn, face, look
- 彼女は私のほうを向いて泣き出した。— She turned to me and started crying.
43 | 0.90

1390 ますます masumasu *adv.* more and more, increasingly
- ますます多くの人が室内でペットを飼っている。— More and more people are keeping pets indoors.
43 | 0.97

1391 最終的 saishuu-teki *na-adj.* final, last, ultimate
- 最終的な目標は何ですか。— What is your ultimate goal?
43 | 0.95

1392 感情 kanjou *n.* feeling, emotion
- 彼女の感情を傷つけるつもりはなかった。— I had no intention of hurting her feelings.
43 | 0.89

1393 我慢（する） gaman(suru) *n.* patience, endurance, tolerance *v.* be patient, endure
- 彼の失礼な態度にはもう我慢ができない。— I lost patience with his rude attitude.
43 | 0.86

1394 浮かぶ ukabu *v.* float, rise
- たくさんのボートが湖に浮かんでいる。— Many boats are floating on the lake.
43 | 0.86

1395 利益 rieki *n.* profit, benefit, gain
- 株で利益を上げた。— We made a profit on the stock market.
43 | 0.92

1396 先日 senjitsu *adv., n.* the other day, recently
- 先日はありがとうございました。— Thank you very much for the other day.
43 | 0.69 | WB

1397 裏 ura *n.* reverse, back; rear
- 写真の裏に日付を書いた。— I wrote the date on the back of the photograph.
43 | 0.92

1398 もたらす motarasu *v.* bring, cause,
- 天候の変化が農業に深刻な被害をもたらしている。— Climate change has caused serious damage to the farming industry.
43 | 0.84

1399 姉 ane *n.* elder sister
- 姉はもう結婚しています。— My older sister is already married.
43 | 0.80

1400 問う tou *v.* ask, question; charge
- これは人生の意味を問う映画だ。— It's a movie asking the meaning of life.
43 | 0.96

1401 継ぐ tsugu *v.* succeed, take over
- 彼はお父さんの後を継いで社長になる予定だ。— He will succeed his father as company president.
43 | 0.20 | NM

1402 北海道 hokkaidou *n.* Hokkaido
- 北海道は雪がたくさん降る。— They have a lot of snow in Hokkaido.
43 | 0.98

1403 構成（する） kousei(suru) *n.* constitution, structure *v.* compose
- 委員会は二十人の委員によって構成されている。— The committee is composed of twenty members.
43 | 0.88

1404 反応（する） hannou(suru) *n.* reaction, response *v.* respond
- 観客の反応はいかがでしたか。— What kind of reaction have you got from the audience?
43 | 0.97

1405 ナイフ naifu *n.* knife
- 男性がナイフで刺されました。— A man was stabbed with a knife.
43 | 0.58

1406 （お）じいさん (o)-jii-san *n.* grandfather
- おじいさんは年のわりに元気です。— My grandfather is lively for his age.
43 | 0.86

1407 新宿 shinjuku *n.* Shinjuku (place name)
- 新宿駅で電車を乗り換えてください。— Please change trains at Shinjuku station.
43 | 0.68

1408 活用（する） katsuyou(suru) *n.* application *v.* exploit, take advantage of
- この機会を活用すべきだ。— You should take advantage of this opportunity.
42 | 0.68

1409 正直 shoujiki *n.* honesty *na-adj.* honest, truthful *adv.* honestly
- 正直な気持ちを聞かせてほしい。— Please tell me your true feelings.
42 | 0.89

1410 黒 kuro *n.* black
- あの画家は良く黒を使う。— That painter uses black a lot.
42 | 0.68

1411 スーパー suupaa *n.* supermarket
- 毎日同じスーパーで買い物している。— I shop at the same supermarket every day.
42 | 0.81

1412 プロ puro *n.* professional, pro
- 彼は小さいときにダンスを始めてプロになった。— He started dancing when he was little and became a professional.
42 | 0.83

1413 渡す watasu *v.* carry across, hand, transfer
- 私は姉にタオルを渡した。— I handed the towel to my sister.
42 | 0.92

1414 掲げる kakageru *v.* hang out, hold up
- 我々は高い理想を掲げている。— We hold high ideals.
42 | 0.53

1415 京都 kyouto *n.* Kyoto
- 京都にはたくさんの神社やお寺がある。— In Kyoto, there are many shrines and temples.
42 | 0.98

7 Family

(frequency per million words)

子供 kodomo[1] 696.364 child
子 ko 287.056 child
母 haha 232.266 mother
親 oya 215.826 parent
家族 kazoku 208.854 family
父 chichi 193.972 father, dad
子供達 kodomo-tachi 162.141 children
娘 musume 136.502 daughter
母さん (o)kaa-san 130.059 mother, Mom
母親 hahaoya 122.515 mother
主人 shujin[2] 116.857 husband (also shop owner)
夫 otto 104.761 husband
父親 chichioya 98.212 father
息子 musuko[3] 86.575 son
父さん (o)tou-san 82.835 father, Dad
妻 tsuma 81.319 wife
両親 ryoushin 79.599 (both) parents
家庭 katei 79.208 family (also home, household)
(お)婆さん (o)-baa-san[4] 72.953 grandmother (also old lady)
伯父 oji 56.794 uncle
兄 ani 55.213 elder brother
伯母 oba 48.430 aunt
弟 otouto 44.074 younger brother
赤ちゃん akachan 44.024 baby, infant
妹 imouto 43.882 younger sister
姉 ane 42.920 elder sister
(お)じいさん (o)-jii-san[5] 42.582 grandfather
奥さん oku-san 38.364 wife

旦那 danna[6] 38.002 husband
夫婦 fuufu 36.861 (married) couple
兄弟 kyoudai 33.440 brother, sister, sibling
祖母 sobo 32.501 grandmother
孫 mago 31.512 grandchild
親父 oyaji 31.192 father (also old man, boss)
長男 chounan 31.030 eldest son
主婦 shufu 30.765 housewife
ママ mama 27.314 mom, mummy
ペット petto 27.036 pet
親戚 shinseki 24.592 relative
親子 oyako 23.431 parent and child, parents and their children
祖父 sofu 22.823 grandfather
(お)姉さん (o)-nee-san[7] 22.746 elder sister
兄さん (o)nii-san 19.239 elder brother
嫁 yome 17.367 wife, bride; daughter-in-law
パパ papa 17.094 papa, dad
女房 nyoubou 16.752 wife
家内 kanai 14.505 one's family, my wife
お袋 ofukuro 13.977 mother
次男 jinan 12.812 second son
奥様 oku-sama 12.703 wife
赤ん坊 akanbou 11.912 baby
従兄弟 itoko 11.104 cousin
子孫 shison 10.530 descendant (also posterity)
長女 choujo 10.484 eldest daughter
一家 ikka 10.427 family (also house, household)
専業主婦 sengyoushufu 10.417 housewife
新婦 shinpu 10.158 bride

1 Includes *kodomo-san*.
2 Includes *go-shujin*.
3 Includes *musuko-san*.
4 Includes *baa-chan, o-baa-chan, o-baa-san*.
5 Includes *o-jii-san, o-jii-chan, jii-san*.
6 Includes *danna-san* and *dannna-sama*.
7 Includes *o-nee-san, o-nee-chan, nee-chan*.

1416 就職（する）shuushoku(suru) *n.* job hunting *v.* find employment, get a job
- 就職はさらに困難になってきている。— Getting a job is becoming increasingly difficult.
42 | 0.93

1417 立派 rippa *na-adj.* fine, splendid, great
- その学校には立派なプールがある。— The school has a fine swimming pool.
42 | 0.96

1418 舞台 butai *n.* stage, scene
- 彼女が舞台に現れると観客から拍手が沸き起こった。— When she appeared on the stage, the audience burst into applause.
42 | 0.89

1419 現地 genchi *n.* field, on-site, local
- 現地の言葉を知っていたら旅行はもっと楽しくなる。— Traveling becomes more fun if you know the local language.
42 | 0.94

1420 数字 suuji *n.* number, figure
- 正確な数字は覚えていません。— I do not remember the exact number.
42 | 0.86

1421 提出（する）teishutsu(suru) *n.* submission *v.* submit, hand in
- 至急履歴書を提出してください。— Please submit your resume immediately.
42 | 0.77

1422 コンピューター、コンピュータ konpyuutaa, konpyuuta *n.* computer
- コンピューターの電源を切った。— I turned off the computer.
42 | 0.94

1423 東京都 toukyou to *n.* Tokyo, Tokyo metropolitan government, Tokyo metropolitan area
- 東京都が交通事故に関する調査を行いました。— Tokyo metropolitan government has carried out a survey on traffic accidents.
42 | 0.87

1424 から kara *conj.* because
- 今日は何も食べていないからおなかが空いている。— I am hungry because I did not eat anything today.
42 | 0.61

1425 弾く hiku *v.* play (musical instrument)
- 私はときどきピアノを弾く。— I sometimes play the piano.
42 | 0.75

1426 自宅 jitaku *n.* home, house
- もしよろしければご自宅の電話番号を教えてください。— If you don't mind, please tell me your home phone number.
42 | 0.91

1427 腹 hara *n.* belly, stomach
- 腹にパンチをしてみろ。— Punch me in the stomach.
42 | 0.87

1428 喜び yorokobi *n.* pleasure, delight
- 皆さまをお迎えできるのは何よりの喜びです。— It gives me great pleasure to welcome you all.
42 | 0.90

1429 しようがない、しょうがない shiyou ga nai, shou ga nai *i-adj.* it can't be helped, nothing can be done
- 人がミスをするのはしようがない。— It can't be helped that people make errors.
42 | 0.00 | SP

1430 風呂 furo *n.* bath
- お風呂に入った。— I took a bath.
42 | 0.80

1431 香り kaori *n.* smell, scent
- 彼女の香水の香りが好きだ。— I like the smell of her perfume.
42 | 0.85

1432 スキー sukii *n.* ski; skiing
- 今年の冬はスキーに行くつもりだ。— I'm planning to go skiing this winter.
42 | 0.55

1433 構う kamau *v.* mind, care about
- 少々お待ちいただいても構いませんか。— Would you mind waiting a minute?
42 | 0.91

1434 受け入れる ukeireru *v.* receive, accept, agree
- 新しい生活スタイルが受け入れられつつある。— The new lifestyle is being accepted.
42 | 0.97

1435 お菓子 o-kashi *n.* sweets, snack food
- この店にはいろいろなお菓子がある。— There are various kinds of sweets in this shop.
42 | 0.79

1436 無料 muryou *n.* free, no charge
- 六歳以下の子供は入場料が無料です。— Admission is free for children under six.
42 | 0.44 | NM

1437 付き合い tsukiai *n.* association, acquaintance
- 私は近所の人と付き合いがない。— I have nothing to do with my neighborhood.
42 | 0.84

1438 私共 watakushi-domo *pron.* we
- 私共は世界中にサービスを提供しております。— We provide services worldwide.
42 | 0.26 | OF

1439 被害 higai *n.* damage, harm
- 建物には何も被害がなかった。— No damage was done to any of the buildings.
42 | 0.77

1440 椅子 isu *n.* chair
- 椅子を三列に並べてもらえますか。— Will you arrange the chairs in three rows?
42 | 0.88

1441 直す naosu *v.* fix, repair, mend
- 部屋のシャワーを直していただけませんか。— Could you repair the shower in my room?
42 | 0.94

1442 桜 sakura *n.* cherry tree; cherry blossom
- 桜の花の咲く季節が来ました。— The cherry blossom season has come.
42 | 0.89

1443 回答(する) kaitou(suru) *n.* answer, response, reply *v.* answer, respond, reply
- 回答は100人から集められた。— Responses were collected from one hundred people.
42 | 0.61 | WB

1444 ゲーム geemu *n.* game
- 息子はゲームに夢中になっている。— My son really gets into computer games.
42 | 0.90

1445 ことはない koto wa nai *aux.* not have to, there is no need for
- あなたが心配することはないよ。— You don't have to worry about it.
42 | 0.82

1446 個人的 kojin-teki *na-adj.* private, personal, individual
- 個人的な質問をしてもよろしいですか。— Do you mind if I ask you a personal question?
42 | 0.88

1447 活躍(する) katsuyaku(suru) *n.* activity, action *v.* be active, flourish
- 彼女はジャーナリストとして活躍している。— She has been active as a journalist.
42 | 0.90

1448 試験(する) shiken(suru) *n.* exam, test, trial *v.* examine
- 彼女は試験に受かった。— She passed the exam.
42 | 0.87

1449 身近 mijika *na-adj.* familiar, close
- 日本人にとって米は最も身近な食べ物だ。— Rice is the most familiar food for Japanese.
42 | 0.91

1450 苦しい kurushii *i-adj.* painful, hard, difficult
- 生きるのが苦しい。— Life is hard.
41 | 0.94

1451 恥ずかしい hazukashii *i-adj.* ashamed, embarrassed
- 道で転んだ時、恥ずかしかった。— I was embarrassed when I stumbled on the street.
41 | 0.85

1452 金 kin *n.* gold, money
- この指輪は金でできている。— This ring is made of gold.
41 | 0.26 | NM

1453 ただ tada *n.* just, mere, only
- 私たちはただの友達です。— We are just friends.
41 | 0.88

1454 検査(する) kensa(suru) *n.* inspection *v.* inspect
- その車は詳細な検査に合格した。— The car passed a close inspection.
41 | 0.97

1455 皮、革 kawa *n.* skin, hide, jacket
- 最初に皮をむいて。— First you have to peel the skin.
41 | 0.92

1456 白 shiro *n.* white; innocence
- ワインは赤と白どちらがいいですか。— Which wine would you prefer, red or white?
41 | 0.68

1457 足りる tariru *v.* be sufficient, be enough, be worthy
- 十ドルで足りるはずだ。— Ten dollars should be enough.
41 | 0.98

1458 代表(する) daihyou(suru) *n.* representative *v.* represent, stand for
- 彼は会社を代表して会議に出る。— He will attend the conference representing the company.
41 | 0.93

1459 夕方 yuugata *adv., n.* evening
- 明日の夕方までにこの仕事を終えなければならない。— I have to finish this work by tomorrow evening.
41 | 0.85

1460 下がる sagaru *v.* fall, drop, step back
- 気温が下がっている。— The temperature is falling.
41 | 0.97

1461 実感(する) jikkan(suru) *n.* real feeling *v.* actually feel
- その薬の効果を実感できない。— I can't actually feel the effect of the medicine.
41 | 0.92

1462 有する yuusuru *v.* have
- すべての人は対等の権利を有する。— All people have equal rights.
41 | 0.58

1463 抜く nuku *v.* pull, extract
- 彼はワインの瓶からコルクを抜いた。— He pulled the cork from a wine bottle.
41 | 0.94

1464 回す mawasu *v.* turn, rotate, spin
- 彼女は静かにノブを回してドアを開けた。— She turned the knob quietly and opened the door.
41 | 0.97

1465 敵 teki *n.* enemy, opponent
- 敵をたくさん作ってしまった。— I have made so many enemies.
41 | 0.81

1466 側 gawa *n.* side
- その問題についてはどちらの側にもつかない。— I will not take sides on the matter.
41 | 0.97

1467 分かれる wakareru *v.* divide, split, part
- その問題については意見が分かれると思う。— I think opinions will be divided on the issue.
41 | 0.98

1468 見つめる mitsumeru *v.* stare, gaze
- 男はただ子供たちを見つめていた。— The man was just staring at the children.
41 | 0.70

1469 祭り matsuri *n.* festival
- 娘と近所の祭りに出かけた。— I went to a neighborhood festival with my daughter.
41 | 0.88

1470 抜ける nukeru *v.* fall out; come loose; be omitted; leave
- ストレスのせいで髪が抜けてしまった。— The stress made my hair fall out.
41 | 0.92

1471 仕様 shiyou *n.* style, specification, method
- この車は日本の仕様に合わせて作られた。— This car was made to Japanese specifications.
41 | 0.94

1472 最大 saidai *n.* biggest, largest
- 結婚は人生で最大のイベントと言われている。— Marriage is said to be the biggest event in one's life.
41 | 0.96

1473 スタート（する）sutaato(suru) *n.* start *v.* get off, start
- 走者は良いスタートを切った。— The runner got off to a good start.
41 | 0.91

1474 なり nari *p.* or, whether or not
- 具合が悪い時は誰かに相談するなり病院に行くなりしなさい。— When you feel ill, you should talk to someone or go to hospital.
41 | 0.81

1475 沖縄 okinawa *n.* Okinawa
- 沖縄は一年中暖かい。— Okinawa is warm all year round.
41 | 0.98

1476 設ける moukeru *v.* institute, set up
- 話し合いの場を設ける必要がある。— We need to arrange a meeting.
41 | 0.80

1477 でもって de mot-te *cp.* by, with, in
- 彼らは残り物を新聞紙でもって包んで家に持って帰った。— They wrapped the leftovers in newspaper and took them home.
41 | 0.00 | SP

1478 幼稚園 youchi-en *n.* preschool, kindergarten
- 息子は二年間幼稚園に通っている。— My son has been going to preschool for two years.
41 | 0.90

1479 二度 ni do *n.* twice
- パリへ二度行ったことがある。— I have been to Paris twice.
41 | 0.96

1480 処理（する）shori(suru) *n.* management, processing *v.* manage, process
- このコンピューターはデータの処理が遅い。— This computer processes data very slowly.
41 | 0.81

1481 困難 konnan *n.* difficulty *na-adj.* difficult
- 彼らはこれまで多くの困難を乗り越えてきた。— They have overcome a lot of difficulties.
41 | 0.82

1482 あくまで akumade *adv.* only, to the last
- これはあくまで私個人の意見です。— This is just my personal opinion.
41 | 0.99

1483 分野 bun'ya *n.* field, discipline
- 彼は様々な分野で活躍している。— He is active in various fields.
40 | 0.78

1484 間違う machigau *v.* be wrong, make a mistake
- 彼の意見は間違っている。— His opinion is wrong.
40 | 0.92

1485 姿勢 shisei *n.* posture, attitude
- 彼は姿勢がいい。— He has good posture.
40 | 0.95

1486 ショック shokku *n.* shock
- 彼はそのニュースを聞いてショックを受けた。— He was shocked by the news.
40 | 0.84

1487 暇 hima *na-adj.*, *n.* free, not busy
- 今晩暇ですか。— Are you free tonight?
40 | 0.83

1488 つい tsui *adv.* without thinking, unintentionally
- つい、笑ってしまった。— I laughed in spite of myself.
40 | 0.93

1489 土 tsuchi *n.* soil
- 植木鉢に新しい土を入れた。— I put new soil in the flower pot.
40 | 0.95

1490 隠す kakusu *v.* hide, conceal
- 彼はその本をベッドの下に隠した。— He hid the book under the bed.
40 | 0.90

1491 緊張（する）kinchou(suru) *n.* tension *v.* get tense
- 私は人前で話すとき緊張してしまう。— I become nervous when I speak in front of other people.
40 | 0.93

1492 それとも sore to mo *conj.* or
- 彼の考えに賛成ですか、それとも反対ですか。— Are you for or against his idea?
40 | 0.75

1493 帰り kaeri *n.* return
- 彼女は夫の帰りを待った。— She waited for her husband's return.
40 | 0.77

1494 三日 mik-ka *n.* third (date); three days
- 三日続けて雨が降った。— Rain fell for three days straight.
40 | 0.76

1495 戦う tatakau *v.* fight
- 彼らは自由のために戦った。— They fought for freedom.
40 | 0.91

1496 単に tanni *adv.* just, simply
- この料理は単においしいだけでなく体にもいい。— This dish is not only delicious but healthy too.
40 | 0.96

1497 席 seki *n.* seat
- 自分の席に戻りなさい。— Go back to your seat.
40 | 0.92

1498 つる tsuru *v.* hang; fish
- 彼は首をつって自殺した。— He hanged himself.
- 川でマスを釣る。— Fish for trout in a river.
40 | 0.84

1499 達する tassuru *v.* reach
- 2011年に世界人口は七十億人に達した。— The world population reached seven billion in 2011.
40 | 0.83

1500 小学生 shougaku-sei *n.* elementary school student, primary school pupil
- 私の息子は小学生だ。— My son is in elementary school.
40 | 0.83

1501 ついに tsuini *adv.* at last, finally
- 彼の夢がついに実現した。— His dream has come true at last.
40 | 0.88

1502 具合 guai *n.* condition
- 具合が良くありません。— I don't feel well.
40 | 0.96

1503 歯 ha *n.* tooth
- 私は一日に二回歯を磨く。— I brush my teeth twice a day.
40 | 0.92

1504 ベッド beddo *n.* bed
- 犬が私のベッドで寝ている。— My dog is sleeping in my bed.
40 | 0.79

1505 無事 buji *adv.* safely *n.* safety *na-adj* safe
- 大地震が起きたが、家族は皆無事だった。— A big earthquake happened, but all my family was safe.
40 | 0.83

1506 身体 shintai *n.* body
- 人間の身体の約60パーセントから70パーセントは水分である。— 60 to 70 percent of the human body is water.
40 | 0.82

1507 何年 nan nen *n.* what year, how many years
- 何年ぐらい東京に住んでいますか。— How many years have you been in Tokyo?
40 | 0.88

1508 星 hoshi *n.* star
- 今夜は星が見えない。— I can't see the stars tonight.
40 | 0.94

1509 携帯電話 keitai denwa *n.* cell phone
- あとで私の携帯電話に電話してください。— Call me later on my cell phone.
40 | 0.87

1510 砂糖 satou *n.* sugar
- 彼女はコーヒーに砂糖とミルクを入れる。— She puts milk and sugar in her coffee.
40 | 0.90

1511 切れる kireru *v.* expire, run out
- 運転免許証の期限が来週で切れる。— My driver's license will expire next week.
40 | 0.92

1512 維持（する）iji(suru) *n.* maintenance, preservation *v.* keep, maintain
- 毎朝ジョギングをして健康を維持している。— I keep fit by jogging every morning.
40 | 0.83

1513 高さ taka-sa *n.* height
- このテーブルはちょうどいい高さだ。— This table is the right height for me.
40 | 0.94

1514 太陽 taiyou *n.* sun
- 地球は太陽の周りを回っている。— The earth goes around the sun.
40 | 0.99

1515 会場 kaijou *n.* hall; site
- 会場は人でいっぱいだ。— The hall is full of people.
40 | 0.47 | NM

1516 素敵 suteki *na-adj.* lovely, nice, wonderful
- 素敵な指輪ですね。— That's a lovely ring.
40 | 0.81

1517 湯 yu *n.* hot water
- 鍋で湯を沸かしてください。— Please boil water in a pot.
40 | 0.89

1518 そもそも somosomo *adv., n.* in the first place
- そもそもそんなことをするべきではなかった。— You shouldn't have done that in the first place.
40 | 0.99

1519 約束（する）yakusoku(suru) *n.* promise, appointment *v.* promise, make an appointment
- 約束は守らなければならない。— You have to keep your promise.
40 | 0.96

1520 ワイン wain *n.* wine
- パーティーでワインを飲んだ。— I drank wine at the party.
40 | 0.84

1521 高校生 koukou-sei *n.* high school student
- 彼らはまだ高校生だ。— They are still high school students.
40 | 0.93

1522 イベント ibento *n.* event
- お祭りの期間中、様々なイベントが行われる。— A variety of events are featured during the festival.
40 | 0.82

1523 二日 futsu-ka *n.* second (date); two days
- 私は1972年の一月二日に生まれた。— I was born on January 2 in 1972.
39 | 0.68

1524 売れる ureru *v.* sell
- この本は最近よく売れている。— This book is selling well these days.
39 | 0.92

1525 少なくとも sukunaku tomo *adv.* at least
- 少なくとも毎月一冊は本を読む。— I read at least one book every month.
39 | 0.89

1526 米国 beikoku *n.* United States
- 米国大統領が来日中だ。— The President of the United States is in Japan.
39 | 0.82

1527 周囲 shuui *n.* surroundings
- その家は周囲を森に囲まれていた。— The house was surrounded by the forest.
39 | 0.87

1528 伺う ukagau *v.* ask, inquire (humble)
- 教授の研究について伺う。— I will ask the professor about his research.
39 | 0.60 | OF

1529 引っ越す hikkosu *v.* move (house)
- 来月、東京に引っ越す。— I am moving to Tokyo next month.
39 | 0.62

1530 二十年 nijuu nen *n.* twenty years
- 私たちが結婚して二十年になる。— It's been twenty years since we got married.
39 | 0.70

1531 たまる tamaru *v.* accumulate, build up
- 彼はストレスがたまると怒りっぽくなる。— He tends to get angry quickly when stress builds up.
39 | 0.90

1532 精神的 seishin-teki *na-adj.* spiritual
- 彼は精神的な柱だ。— He is a spiritual leader.
39 | 0.90

1533 中学校 chuugakkou *n.* junior high school
- 妹が中学校に入った。— My sister entered junior high school.
39 | 0.86

1534 仲良く nakayoku *adv.* friendly
- 彼女は誰とでもすぐに仲良くなる。— She makes friends with everyone straight away.
39 | 0.74

1535 言い方 ii-kata *n.* way to say
- もっと自然な言い方がありますか。— Is there a more natural way to say it?
39 | 0.94

1536 バランス baransu *n.* balance
- 栄養のバランスを考えて食べましょう。— Eat taking nutritional balance into account.
39 | 0.96

1537 五年 go nen *n.* five years
- 私はフランス語を五年勉強した。— I studied French for five years.
39 | 0.93

1538 安定(する) antei(suru) *n.* stability *v.* become stable
- 将来は安定した仕事につきたい。— I hope to get a stable job in the future.
39 | 0.88

1539 完成(する) kansei(suru) *n.* completion *v.* complete
- その橋は完成までに約三年かかるだろう。— It will take about three years to complete the bridge.
39 | 0.95

1540 我が家 wagaya *n.* one's house, one's family, one's home
- 私は友人を我が家に招待した。— I invited my friend to my house.
39 | 0.74

1541 見かける mikakeru *v.* see
- この写真の猫を見かけたら、お電話ください。— Please call me if you see the cat in this picture.
39 | 0.83

1542 広げる hirogeru *v.* spread, expand
- 彼女は机に新聞を広げた。— She spread a newspaper on the desk.
39 | 0.95

1543 参考 sankou *n.* reference
- この本は私の研究に参考になる。— This book is a useful reference for my research.
39 | 0.86

1544 たとえ tatoe *adv.* even if
- たとえ両親が反対しても私は行く。— I will go even if my parents are against it.
39 | 0.90

1545 受け取る uketoru *v.* get, accept
- この手紙を受け取ったらすぐに返事をください。— Please write back to me as soon as you get this letter.
39 | 0.96

1546 冷たい tsumetai *i-adj.* cold
- 何か冷たいものが飲みたいなあ。— I want to drink something cold.
39 | 0.90

1547 望む nozomu *v.* hope
- 世界中の人が平和を望んでいる。— People around the world hope for peace.
39 | 0.97

1548 適用(する) tekiyou(suru) *n.* application *v.* apply
- その規則はこの場合には適用されない。— The rule doesn't apply in this case.
39 | 0.66

1549 宗教 shuukyou *n.* religion
- 宗教を信じない人もいる。— Some people don't believe in any religion.
39 | 0.87

1550 一年間 ichi nenkan *n.* one year
- 一年間ありがとうございました。— Thank you for everything you've done for me over the last year.
39 | 0.93

1551 範囲 han'i *n.* extent, range
- 次の試験の範囲はどこですか。— What's going to be in the next exam?
39 | 0.90

1552 接する sessuru *v.* adjoin, come in contact
- 私はあまり外国人と接する機会がない。— I don't have many opportunities to meet foreigners.
39 | 0.95

1553 戻す modosu *v.* put back, restore
- 本は元の場所に戻してください。— Please put the book back where it was.
39 | 0.94

1554 すっかり sukkari *adv.* entirely, completely
- 彼女の誕生日をすっかり忘れていた。— I completely forgot her birthday.
39 | 0.86

1555 低下(する) teika(suru) *n., v.* decline, fall
- 最近、この国では出生率が低下している。— Recently the birth rate has been declining in this country.
39 | 0.69

1556 政治 seiji *n.* politics
- 彼は政治に興味がなかった。— Politics didn't interest him.
39 | 0.97

1557 なんら nanra *adv.* nothing
- この計画はなんら問題はない。— There is nothing wrong with this plan.
39 | 0.92

1558 取り組む torikumu *v.* tackle, deal with
- 彼は十年以上環境問題に取り組んできた。— He has tackled environmental issues for over ten years.
39 | 0.73

1559 余裕 yoyuu *n.* leeway
- 予算に余裕がある。— I have some leeway in my budget.
38 | 0.95

1560 パリ pari *n.* Paris
- 彼は今パリにいる。— He is in Paris now.
38 | 0.87

1561 にて nite *p. case* by; in; at
- メールにて結果をお知らせください。— Please let me know the results by e-mail.
38 | 0.87

1562 奥さん oku-san *n.* wife
- 彼女はよい奥さんになるだろう。— She'll make a good wife.
38 | 0.85

1563 遅れる okureru *v.* be late, be delayed
- 彼はよく学校に遅れる。— He is often late for school.
38 | 0.99

1564 担当（する）tantou(suru) *n.* charge *v.* be in charge of
- 田中先生が私のクラスを担当している。— Miss Tanaka is in charge of my class.
38 | 0.97

1565 向上（する）koujou(suru) *n.* improvement, progress *v.* improve, advance
- 彼の英語力は大きく向上した。— His English improved greatly.
38 | 0.67

1566 機械 kikai *n.* machine
- この機械は大きい木を切るのに使われる。— This machine is used for cutting large trees.
38 | 0.95

1567 ＣＤ shiidii *n.* compact disk
- このＣＤを借りてもいいですか。— May I borrow this CD?
38 | 0.79

1568 寄る yoru *v.* stop by; move to one side
- 家に帰る途中でコンビニに寄った。— I stopped by a convenience store on the way home.
38 | 0.86

1569 都市 toshi *n.* city
- 東京は日本最大の都市である。— Tokyo is the largest city in Japan.
38 | 0.82

1570 費用 hiyou *n.* cost
- このシステムはかなり費用がかかる。— The system costs a lot.
38 | 0.82

1571 運転（する）unten(suru) *n.* driving, operation *v.* drive
- 日本では十八歳になると車を運転できる。— In Japan, you can drive when you turn eighteen.
38 | 0.98

1572 生地 kiji *n.* cloth, material; dough
- この生地でスカートを作るつもりだ。— I'm going to use this material to make a skirt.
38 | 0.77

1573 さあ saa *interj.* come on, now, well
- さあ、もう寝なさい。— Now it's time to go to bed.
38 | 0.87

1574 だけでなく dake de naku *cp.* not only
- 肉だけでなく、野菜も食べなさい。— Eat not only meat, but also vegetables.
38 | 0.79

1575 予想（する）yosou(suru) *n.* expectation *v.* expect
- 結果は予想したとおりだった。— The result was as we expected.
38 | 0.95

1576 一層 issou *adv., n.* more
- 今後、問題は一層深刻化するだろう。— The problems will become more severe in the future.
38 | 0.64

1577 旦那 danna *n.* husband
- 私のだんなは優しい。— My husband is kind.
38 | 0.49 | WB

1578 経る heru *v.* pass through, experience
- 彼女はつらい体験を経て精神的に強くなった。— She became mentally strong after going through hardship.
38 | 0.94

1579 揃う sorou *v.* become complete; be equal
- 必要なものはすべてそろった。— I've got everything in order.
38 | 0.92

1580 下げる sageru *v.* lower; hang
- エアコンの温度を下げてくれる？— Can you lower the temperature of the air conditioner for me?
38 | 0.97

1581 誘う sasou *v.* invite
- 彼女を家に誘った。— I invited her to my house.
38 | 0.90

1582 重ねる kasaneru *v.* stack; repeat
- 彼はテーブルの上の皿を重ねた。— He stacked the dishes on the table.
38 | 0.95

1583 採用（する）saiyou(suru) *n.* adoption, employment *v.* employ
- 彼女は秘書として採用された。— She was employed as a secretary.
38 | 0.92

1584 価格 kakaku *n.* price
- 輸入品の価格が下がっている。— Prices of imported goods have fallen.
38 | 0.90

1585 飾る kazaru *v.* decorate
- 机の上にきれいな花が飾ってあった。— There were beautiful flowers on the desk.
38 | 0.89

1586 がん gan *n.* cancer.
- 彼女はがんで死んだ。— She died of cancer.
38 | 0.91

1587 土 do *n.* Saturday
- この土日は夜勤だ。— I'll be on night duty this coming Saturday and Sunday.
38 | 0.17 | NM

1588 週 shuu *n.* week
- 彼は週に一度手紙をくれる。— He writes me once a week.
38 | 0.92

1589 細い hosoi *i-adj.* thin, narrow, slender
- 彼女は足が細い。— She has slender legs.
38 | 0.94

1590 直る naoru *v.* be repaired; be corrected; get better
- 車がやっと直った。— The car is fixed at last.
38 | 0.78

1591 単純 tanjun *na-adj.* simple
- 彼女は子供のように単純だ。— She is as simple as a child.
38 | 0.96

1592 ファックス(する) fakkusu(suru) *n.* fax *v.* fax
- それをファックスで送ってください。— Please send it to me by fax.
38 | 0.20 | NM

1593 アルバイト arubaito *n.* part-time job
- 彼は車を買うためにアルバイトをしている。— He has a part-time job so that he can buy a car.
38 | 0.75

1594 北 kita *n.* north
- カナダはアメリカの北にある。— Canada is to the north of the United States.
38 | 0.92

1595 一生 isshou *n.* life
- 彼女は一生独身だった。— She remained single all her life.
38 | 0.90

1596 ファン fan *n.* fan
- 昔から彼のファンです。— I have been a fan of him for a long time.
38 | 0.80

1597 及ぶ oyobu *v.* reach
- 台風の被害は関東地方にも及んだ。— The damage from the typhoon reached as far as the Kanto area.
38 | 0.87

1598 後 nochi *n., adv.* after, later
- 明日は晴れのち曇りでしょう。— Tomorrow, it will be fine and later cloudy.
38 | 0.83

1599 調子 choushi *n.* condition, tone
- 最近体の調子があまりよくない。— Recently my physical condition has not been very good.
38 | 0.89

1600 基準 kijun *n.* standard
- この建物は安全基準を満たしている。— This building meets safety standards.
38 | 0.77

1601 植物 shokubutsu *n.* plant
- 植物は水がなければ枯れてしまう。— Plants die without water.
38 | 0.97

1602 契約(する) keiyaku(suru) *n., v.* contract
- わが社はこの会社と契約を結んだ。— We made a contract with this company.
37 | 0.95

1603 組む kumu *v.* pair with; cross
- 彼は腕を組んで座っていた。— He was sitting with his arms folded.
37 | 0.97

1604 叫ぶ sakebu *v.* shout
- 彼は助けを求めて叫んだ。— He shouted for help.
37 | 0.78

1605 若者 wakamono *n.* youth
- 彼は若者に人気がある。— He is popular among young people.
37 | 0.95

1606 手段 shudan *n.* means
- ことばはコミュニケーションの手段だ。— Language is a means of communication.
37 | 0.94

1607 下ろす orosu *v.* take down; unload; withdraw; fillet (fish); grate
- 銀行にお金を下ろしに行った。— I went to the bank to withdraw some money.
37 | 0.89

1608 明治 meiji *n.* Meiji (period)
- この人は明治時代の小説家だ。— This person was a novelist in the Meiji period.
37 | 0.85

8 Food

(frequency per million words)

(主な食材) (Major foods)

魚 sakana 98.845 fish
野菜 yasai 56.585 vegetable
肉 niku 48.365 meat, flesh, fat
卵 tamago 44.064 egg (also spawn)
米 kome 29.271 rice
牛乳 gyuunyuu 28.931 (cow's) milk
果物 kudamono 18.890 fruit
粉 kona 16.999 flour (also powder)
小麦粉 komugiko 16.621 flour
缶詰 kanzume 15.731 canned food
チーズ chiizu 14.283 cheese
蜂蜜 hachimitsu 12.410 honey
納豆 nattou 11.055 fermented soybeans
具 gu 10.981 ingredient
飯 meshi 10.943 rice
生クリーム namakuriimu 10.844 fresh cream
鮎 ayu 10.700 sweet fish, ayu
麺 men 10.604 noodles
パスタ pasuta 10.291 pasta
餅 mochi 9.509 rice cake
豆腐 toufu 9.278 tofu, bean curd
乳製品 nyuusei-hin 2.242 dairy products

(肉・魚) (Meat, fish)

エビ ebi 14.089 shrimp, prawn
豚肉 butaniku 9.192 pork
牛肉 gyuuniku 8.921 beef
烏賊 ika 8.475 cuttlefish
鮪 maguro 6.145 tuna
鶏肉 toriniku 3.806 chicken[1]
鰹 katsuo 3.753 bonito
鮭 sake 3.641 salmon
鯖 saba 2.714 mackerel
鰯 iwashi 2.708 sardine
鯵 aji 2.110 horse mackerel
サンマ sanma 2.106 saury
イクラ ikura 1.882 salted salmon roe
鱈 tara 0.634 cod

(野菜・果物) (Vegetables, fruits)

米 kome 29.271 rice
りんご ringo 26.742 apple
玉ねぎ tamanegi 24.225 onion
にんにく nin'niku 18.755 garlic
人参 ninjin 18.177 carrot
大根 daikon 18.030 Japanese radish, radish
トマト tomato 17.557 tomato
栗 kuri 14.519 chestnut
じゃが芋 jagaimo 12.678 potato
豆 mame 11.462 bean, pea
レモン remon 11.087 lemon
カボチャ kabocha 10.644 pumpkin
バナナ banana 10.386 banana
生姜 shouga 10.208 ginger
キャベツ kyabetsu 9.831 cabbage
サラダ sarada 9.605 salad
葱 negi 9.044 leek
きゅうり kyuuri 8.969 cucumber
柿 kaki 8.588 persimmon
桃 momo 8.492 peach
オレンジ orenji 7.150 orange
ホウレン草 houren-sou 6.835 spinach
トウモロコシ toumorokoshi 5.459 corn
茸 kinoko 4.635 mushroom
苺 ichigo 4.531 strawberry
茄子 nasu 4.513 eggplant
ミカン mikan 4.098 tangerine
西瓜 suika 3.714 watermelon
レタス retasu 3.541 lettuce
葡萄 budou 3.525 grapes
梨 nashi 2.744 pear
サクランボ sakuranbo 1.422 cherry

(食事) (Meals)

夕食 yuushoku 21.036 dinner
朝食 choushoku 15.741 breakfast
昼食 chuushoku 11.871 lunch
おやつ oyatsu 7.920 snack
昼ご飯 hirugohan 6.093 lunch
朝ご飯 asagohan 5.242 breakfast
晩ご飯 bangohan 3.766 dinner
間食 kanshoku 2.119 eating between meals

(調味料) (Spices, sauces)

酒 sake 109.387 alcohol; sake, rice wine
塩 shio 49.640 salt
砂糖 satou 39.891 sugar
油 abura 29.989 oil
バター bataa 21.788 butter
しょう油 shouyu 16.869 soy sauce
ソース soosu 16.860 sauce (also source)

胡椒 koshou 15.730 pepper
酢 su 15.266 vinegar
マヨネーズ mayoneezu 3.858 mayonnaise
ケチャップ kechappu 2.725 ketchup

(料理・調理済みの食品) (Cooked dishes)
パン pan 48.415 bread
弁当[2] bentou[2] 28.633 boxed lunch
カレー karee 22.104 curry
スープ suupu 21.786 soup
ラーメン raamen 15.996 Chinese noodles
餃子 gyouza 11.780 Chinese dumplings
お好み焼き okonomiyaki 10.217 okonomiyaki (Japanese-style savoury pancake with vegetables, meat, seafood etc.)
デザート dezaato 9.830 dessert
スパゲッティー supagettii 9.684 spaghetti
豆腐 toufu 9.278 tofu, bean curd
刺身 sashimi 9.194 sliced raw fish
おかず okazu 9.192 food, side dish
うどん udon 8.685 udon, thick white noodles
サンドイッチ sandoitchi 7.444 sandwich
蕎麦 soba 6.974 buckwheat noodles
焼肉 yakiniku 6.550 grilled meat
味噌汁 miso shiru 6.241 miso soup
煮物 nimono 6.137 stewed food
天ぷら tenpura 6.052 tempura
寿司 sushi 5.093 sushi
ハンバーグ hanbaagu 4.613 hamburger steak
焼きそば yakisoba 4.119 fried soba
ステーキ suteeki 3.396 steak
焼き鳥 yakitori 3.355 chicken pieces grilled on a skewer
炒飯 chaahan 3.348 (Chinese) fried rice
おでん oden 2.582 winter stew of vegetables, hard-boiled eggs, konnyaku etc.
ハンバーガー hanbaagaa 2.412 hamburger
とんかつ tonkatsu 2.273 pork cutlets
すき焼き sukiyaki 1.832 sukiyaki
オムレツ omuretsu 1.386 omelette
牛丼 gyuudon 1.190 bowl of rice topped with beef
カツ丼 katsudon 0.885 bowl of rice topped with pork cutlets
肉じゃが nikujaga 0.628 meat and potato stew
親子丼 oyako-don 0.415 bowl of rice topped with chicken and egg
海老フライ ebi furai 0.390 fried prawns
茶碗蒸し chawan mushi 0.384 savoury egg custard
カキフライ kaki furai 0.195 fried oysters

(菓子類) (Sweets, confectionery)
ケーキ keeki 19.666 cake
チョコレート chokoreeto 9.408 chocolate
クッキー kukkii 6.321 cookie
飴 ame 3.987 candy, sweet
団子 dango 2.882 dumpling
ドーナツ doonatsu 2.647 donut
ビスケット bisuketto 2.241 biscuit
ガム gamu 2.149 gum
饅頭 manjuu 2.138 steamed bun with bean-jam filling
ポテトチップ poteto chippu 1.497 potato chip, crisp
煎餅 senbei 1.374 rice cracker

(食・その他) (Others)
食べ物 tabemono 68.105 food
餌 esa 35.240 feed (also bait)
生 nama 32.938 raw, fresh, live
食料 shokuryou 26.687 food
新鮮 shinsen 24.954 fresh
食品 shokuhin 22.872 food
栄養 eiyou 19.037 nutrition
食材 shokuzai 16.172 ingredient, foodstuff
食 shoku 13.349 meal, diet
食生活 shoku-seikatsu 13.213 eating habits
飲み物 nomimono 12.301 drink
飲み込む nomikomu 11.004 swallow
食欲 shokuyoku 10.434 appetite
腐る kusaru 9.539 rot, decay, go off
食物 shokumotsu 9.099 food, dish

(調理) (Cooking)
切る kiru 166.834 cut
料理(する) ryouri(suru) 103.435 cooking, dish; cook
焼く yaku 66.249 roast, bake
下ろす orosu 37.198 fillet (fish); grate (also take down; unload; withdraw)
鍋 nabe 36.824 pan, pot; hot-pot
炒める itameru 29.537 fry, stir-fry
沸く waku 29.364 boil (also be in uproar)
巻く maku 29.150 roll up, wind up (also wear around)
煮る niru 24.930 boil, cook
潰す tsubusu 22.001 smash; crush, squash (also ruin)

茹でる yuderu 20.445 boil
漬ける tsukeru 18.893 soak; pickle
焼ける yakeru 16.380 be burned; be roasted
    (also be sunburned)
刻む kizamu 16.188 cut into fine pieces
    (also engrave; tick)
レシピ reshipi 9.898 recipe
オーブン oobun 9.771 oven
煮込む nikomu 9.698 stew
こねる koneru 9.316 knead, squeeze, work
蒸す musu 4.979 steam
炙る aburu 2.633 broil

(調理器具) (Kitchen utensils)
ボール booru 62.319 bowl[3]
鍋 nabe 36.824 pan, pot (also hot-pot)
フライパン furaipan 15.873 frying pan
瓶 bin 11.965 bottle
包丁 houchou 11.322 kitchen knife
ざる zaru 5.724 basket
炊飯器 suihan-ki 3.487 rice cooker
おたま o-tama 2.017 ladle
菜箸 saibashi 0.708 large chopsticks for cooking

(食器) (Tableware)
ナイフ naifu 42.637 knife
皿 sara 25.487 plate, dish
器 utsuwa 16.649 container

グラス gurasu 11.259 glass
箸 hashi 10.435 chopsticks
カップ kappu 10.080 cup
スプーン supuun 7.934 spoon
フォーク fooku 6.553 fork
茶碗 chawan 5.421 rice bowl
コップ koppu 5.351 glass
椀 wan 4.049 bowl

(飲み物) (Drinks)
水 mizu 282.138 water
酒 sake 109.387 alcohol, sake, rice wine
茶 cha[4] 78.641 tea (also brown)
ワイン wain 39.622 wine
コーヒー koohii 36.298 coffee
ビール biiru 35.890 beer
牛乳 gyuunyuu 28.931 (cow's) milk
紅茶 koucha 20.633 tea
アルコール arukooru 12.038 alcohol
ジュース juusu 10.589 juice
ミルク miruku 10.530 milk
日本酒 nihonshu 10.377 sake
ウイスキー uisukii 6.610 whiskey
焼酎 shouchuu 4.029 Japanese spirits
コーラ koora 2.802 cola
緑茶 ryokucha 2.504 green tea
ウーロン茶 uuron cha 1.929 Oolong tea
ジンジャーエール jinjaa eeru 0.098 ginger ale

1 toriniku 9169.
2 Includes お o-bentou.
3 May include the meaning of "ball" as in a ball game.
4 Includes お茶 o-cha.

1609 形成（する） keisei(suru) *n.* formation *v.* take form
  • 教育の目的は人格の形成である。— The object of education is to form character.
  37 | 0.73

1610 マンガ manga *n.* comics, cartoon
  • 彼はいつもマンガを読んでいる。— He's always reading comics.
  37 | 0.83

1611 ドラマ dorama *n.* TV drama, drama
  • 日本のドラマを見た。— I watched a Japanese TV drama.
  37 | 0.79

1612 いよいよ iyoiyo *adv.* finally, at last
  • いよいよ私の番が来た。— Finally it was my turn.
  37 | 0.96

1613 高齢者 kourei-sha *n.* senior citizen
  • 高齢者の割合が高くなっている。— The percentage of senior citizens is increasing.
  37 | 0.79

1614 無駄 muda *na-adj* useless, futile *n.* waste
  • 彼に頼んでも無駄だ。— It's useless asking him.
  37 | 0.97

1615 髪 kami *n.* hair
- 彼女は髪が長い。— She has long hair.
37 | 0.81

1616 管理（する）kanri(suru) *n.* control, management *v.* manage, control
- 危機管理が大きな関心事である。— Our major concern is crisis management.
37 | 0.91

1617 サッカー sakkaa *n.* football, soccer
- 私の国ではサッカーはテニスより人気がある。— Soccer is more popular than tennis in my country.
37 | 0.82

1618 工場 koujou *n.* factory
- 彼は工場で働いている。— He works in a factory.
37 | 0.94

1619 正確 seikaku *na-adj.* correct, exact, accurate
- 正確な値段は覚えていない。— I do not remember the exact price.
37 | 0.96

1620 夫婦 fuufu *n.* (married) couple
- その夫婦は仲がいい。— The couple get along well.
37 | 0.99

1621 監督（する）kantoku(suru) *n.* manager, director, proctor, invigilator *v.* supervise, direct
- 彼は有名な映画監督だ。— He is a famous film director.
37 | 0.97

1622 鍋 nabe *n.* pan, pot; hot-pot
- 鍋に水を入れてください。— Put water into the pot.
37 | 0.91

1623 バイト baito *n.* part-time job
- いいバイトを見つけた。— I found a good part-time job.
37 | 0.61

1624 十分 jup-pun, jip-pun *n.* ten minutes
- 学校までバスで十分かかる。— It takes ten minutes to get to school by bus.
37 | 0.88

1625 外す hazusu *v.* undo; take off, remove
- 彼女はジャケットのボタンを外した。— She undid the buttons of her jacket.
37 | 0.93

1626 何でも nan de mo *adv.* anything; nothing; everything
- ここには何でもある。— This place has everything.
37 | 0.77

1627 階段 kaidan *n.* stairs
- 彼は階段を上った。— He went up the steps.
37 | 0.90

1628 オーストラリア oosutoraria *n.* Australia
- 私はオーストラリアから来ました。— I am from Australia.
37 | 0.88

1629 そこで soko de *conj.* so
- テストの点が悪かった。そこで、もっと勉強することにした。— I got a bad grade on my test, so I have decided to study harder.
37 | 0.00 | SP

1630 オーケー ookee *n.* O.K.
- 「五時ごろに来て。」「オーケー。じゃ、五時に。」— "Come around five." "OK. See you then."
37 | 0.78

1631 発達（する）hattatsu(suru) *n.* development *v.* develop
- 技術はどんどん発達している。— Technology is developing quite fast.
37 | 0.92

1632 適当 tekitou *na-adj.* proper, appropriate, suitable; irresponsible, whimsical
- サーモンは適当な大きさに切ってください。— Cut the salmon into pieces of an appropriate size.
37 | 0.94

1633 戦い tatakai *n.* fight, battle
- 彼にとって厳しい戦いになるだろう。— It will be a hard fight for him.
37 | 0.92

1634 はさむ hasamu *v.* put in, sandwich between; catch in
- ドアに指をはさまれてしまった。— I got my fingers caught in the door.
36 | 0.94

1635 鼻 hana *n.* nose
- 鼻がつまっている。— My nose is stuffed up.
36 | 0.89

1636 会 kai *n.* meeting, gathering
- 彼女はその会に出席した。— She attended the meeting.
36 | 0.75

1637 数年 suu nen *n.* several years
- 数年前東京に住んでいた。— I lived in Tokyo a few years ago.
36 | 0.86

1638 現代 gendai *n.* the present age, today
- 現代はコンピューターとインターネットの時代だ。— Today is the age of computers and the Internet.
36 | 0.93

1639 回復（する）kaifuku(suru) *n.* recovery *v.* recover
- 景気はゆっくり回復しているように見える。— The economy appears to be recovering slowly.
36 | 0.91

1640 すみません sumi mase n *interj.* thank you; I am sorry; excuse me
- すみません、トイレはどこですか。— Excuse me, where is the restroom?
36 | 0.68 | WB

1641 コーヒー koohii *n.* coffee
- 私は毎朝コーヒーを飲む。— I drink coffee every morning.
36 | 0.90

1642 塗る nuru *v.* spread; paint
- パンにバターを塗った。— I spread the butter on the bread.
36 | 0.92

1643 老人 roujin *n.* old person, the old
- 老人には運動が必要だ。— Old people need exercise.
36 | 0.89

1644 共通（する）kyoutsuu(suru) *n., v.* common
- これは世界共通の問題である。— This is a common problem all over the world.
36 | 0.96

1645 一瞬 isshun *n., adv.* a moment, an instant
- 君なら一瞬でわかってしまうだろう。— You'd understand in an instant.
36 | 0.86

1646 面倒 mendou *na-adj.* troublesome *n.* bother, care
- この天気では外に出るのが面倒だ。— It's too much trouble to go out in this kind of weather.
36 | 0.88

1647 開始（する）kaishi(suru) *n.* beginning, start *v.* begin, start
- 試合は午後一時に開始される。— The match begins at 1 p.m.
36 | 0.85

1648 翌日 yokujitsu *n.* next day
- カメラを買ったが、その翌日になくしてしまった。— I bought a camera, but I lost it the next day.
36 | 0.95

1649 しまう shimau *v.* put away
- お皿を食器棚にしまった。— I put the dishes away in the cupboard.
36 | 0.80

1650 商店街 shouten-gai *n.* shopping street
- 近くに商店街がある。— There is a shopping street near by.
36 | 0.80

1651 原則 gensoku *n.* principle
- 原則として、短期滞在ビザからほかのビザには変更できない。— In principle, short-term visas cannot be changed to visas with other statuses.
36 | 0.79

1652 販売（する）hanbai(suru) *n.* sale *v.* sell
- チケットは本日九時から販売いたします。— Tickets go on sale at 9 a.m. today.
36 | 0.92

1653 諦める akirameru *v.* give up, quit
- 途中であきらめないで。— Don't give up halfway through.
36 | 0.86

1654 場面 bamen *n.* scene, sight
- 私はこの映画のこの場面が好きだ。— I like this scene in the movie.
36 | 0.98

1655 障害 shougai *n.* obstacle, handicap
- 彼は障害を乗り越えて、夢を実現した。— He got over difficulties, and made his dream come true.
36 | 0.86

1656 やや yaya *adv.* a little, slightly
- 彼は標準よりやや背が高い。— He is a little taller than average.
36 | 0.92

1657 一定（する）ittei(suru) *n., v.* a certain, fixed, constant
- 会社員は、一定の年齢になれば退職しなければならない。— An employee must retire at a certain age.
36 | 0.80

1658 いかが ikaga *na-adj.* how
- コーヒーはいかがですか。— Would you like some coffee?
36 | 0.79

1659 上手 jouzu *na-adj.* good, skillful
- 彼女は絵が上手だ。— She is good at drawing.
36 | 0.93

1660 関連（する）kanren(suru) *n.* relation, connection *v.* be related, be connected
- その二つの事件は関連がある。— The two incidents are connected.
36 | 0.73

1661 笑顔 egao *n.* smile
- 彼女は笑顔で私にあいさつをした。— She greeted me with a smile.
36 | 0.84

1662 真ん中 mannaka *n.* middle
- 彼は部屋の真ん中にテーブルを置いた。— He set up a table in the middle of the room.
36 | 0.86

1663 ビール biiru *n.* beer
- 彼はビールを二本飲んだ。— He drank two bottles of beer.

36 | 0.93

1664 正月 shougatsu *n.* New Year
- 正月は毎年、家族と過ごす。— I spend New Year with my family every year.

36 | 0.82

1665 すら sura *p.* even
- 彼は自分の名前すら書けない。— He cannot even write his own name.

36 | 0.95

1666 デザイン(する) dezain(suru) *n.* design *v.* design
- このデザインは女性によく合う。— This design is suitable for women.

36 | 0.76

1667 わざわざ wazawaza *adv.* take the trouble, especially
- 今日はわざわざ会ってくれてありがとう。— Thank you for taking the trouble to see me today.

36 | 0.91

1668 あふれる afureru *v.* overflow, be filled with
- 公園は花であふれている。— The park is filled with flowers.

36 | 0.87

1669 葉 ha *n.* leaf
- 秋になると木の葉が赤くなる。— The leaves turn red in the fall.

35 | 0.93

1670 種 shu *n.* kind, species
- 私はこの種の仕事に慣れていない。— I am not used to this kind of work.

35 | 0.95

1671 迷惑(する) meiwaku(suru) *na-adj.* troublesome, annoying *n.* annoyance, nuisance, trouble *v.* be inconvenienced
- ご迷惑をおかけして申し訳ありません。— I'm sorry to trouble you.

35 | 0.91

1672 つかむ tsukamu *v.* catch, grasp
- 警官は彼の腕をつかんだ。— The policeman caught him by the arm.

35 | 0.89

1673 締める shimeru *v.* tie; tighten
- 私は毎日ネクタイを締める。— I wear a tie every day.

35 | 0.91

1674 ラジオ rajio *n.* radio
- 毎晩ラジオを聞いている。— I listen to the radio every night.

35 | 0.90

1675 入る iru *v.* come in, enter; join
- 郷に入れば郷に従え。— When in Rome, do as the Romans do.

35 | 0.23 | SP

1676 じっと(する) jitto(suru) *adv., v.* still, fixedly, intently
- ちょっとじっとしていてください。— Keep still for a moment.

35 | 0.78

1677 うなずく unazuku *v.* nod
- 彼は時々うなずきながら私の話を聞いた。— He listened to my story nodding his head occasionally.

35 | 0.50 | BK

1678 餌 esa *n.* feed; bait
- 昨日うさぎの餌を買った。— I bought feed for my rabbit yesterday.

35 | 0.91

1679 背中 senaka *n.* back
- 時々背中が痛い。— I have a pain in my back sometimes.

35 | 0.87

1680 両方 ryouhou *n.* both
- 犬も猫も両方好きだ。— I like both dogs and cats.

35 | 0.99

1681 床 yuka *n.* floor
- コップを床に落としてしまった。— I dropped my glass on the floor.

35 | 0.84

1682 囲む kakomu *v.* surround
- その町は山に囲まれている。— The town is surrounded by mountains.

35 | 0.94

1683 並べる naraberu *v.* arrange; line up; enumerate
- 私は本を色別に並べた。— I arranged my books by color.

35 | 0.95

1684 黙る damaru *v.* hold one's tongue, become silent
- 黙って聞きなさい。— Hold your tongue and listen to me.

35 | 0.82

1685 きり kiri *p.* only
- 私達は二人きりになった。— We were left alone.

35 | 0.97

1686 風景 fuukei *n.* scenery, landscape
- 私は窓から風景を見ていた。— I was looking at the landscape out of the window.

35 | 0.93

1687 ごとし gotoshi *aux.* like, as if (Classical)
- 光陰矢のごとし。— Time flies like an arrow.

35 | 0.75

1688 保存(する) hozon(suru) *n.* preservation, storage *v.* preserve, store
- ワインを暗いところに保存しておきなさい。 — Store wine in a dark place.
35 | 0.96

1689 社長 shachou *n.* company president
- 彼は旅行会社の社長だ。 — He is the president of a travel company.
35 | 0.94

1690 目立つ medatsu *v.* be conspicuous, stand out
- ポスターは目立つ場所に貼らなければならない。 — The poster must be prominently displayed.
35 | 0.97

1691 保護(する) hogo(suru) *n.* protection *v.* protect
- この地域の野生動物は法律で保護されている。 — The wildlife in this area is protected by law.
35 | 0.84

1692 確実 kakujitsu *na-adj.* certain, sure
- 彼が試験に合格するのは確実だ。 — It is certain that he will pass the test.
35 | 0.97

1693 経済 keizai *n.* economy; finance
- 今その国は経済の状態が悪い。 — The country is in a bad economic state now.
35 | 0.78

1694 等 tou *suffix* and so on
- 氏名、所属、住所、等をお知らせください。 — Please let us know your name, affiliation, address, and so on.
35 | 0.77

1695 演奏(する) ensou(suru) *n.* (musical) performance *v.* perform, play
- 素晴らしい演奏だった。 — It was a wonderful performance.
35 | 0.93

1696 増やす fuyasu *v.* increase, add
- 友達をもっと増やしたい。 — I want to have more friends.
35 | 0.99

1697 温泉 onsen *n.* hot spring, spa
- 日本にはたくさん温泉がある。 — There are a lot of hot springs in Japan.
35 | 0.86

1698 工夫(する) kufuu(suru) *n.* device, idea *v.* devise, plan
- 何かうまい工夫はありませんか。 — Have you got any good ideas?
35 | 0.92

1699 触る sawaru *v.* touch
- 絵に触らないでください。 — Please don't touch the paintings.
35 | 0.88

1700 教室 kyoushitsu *n.* classroom, ... school
- この教室はとても小さい。 — This classroom is very small.
35 | 0.89

1701 登録(する) touroku(suru) *n.* registration, entry *v.* register, enroll
- 当サイトのご利用には登録が必要です。 — Registration is required to use this website.
35 | 0.88

1702 長さ naga-sa *n.* length
- その川の長さは367キロメートルだ。 — The river is 367 kilometers in length.
35 | 0.98

1703 資格 shikaku *n.* qualification; capacity
- 彼は1992年に弁護士の資格を取った。 — He qualified as a lawyer in 1992.
35 | 0.98

1704 明確 meikaku *na-adj.* clear, definite
- 明確な答えが見つからない。 — I can't find a definite answer.
35 | 0.83

1705 記載(する) kisai(suru) *n.* registration entry *v.* record, write down
- パスポートの記載どおりにローマ字氏名を入力してください。 — Enter your name as it is printed in your passport.
35 | 0.86

1706 肌 hada *n.* skin
- タバコは肌によくないですよ。 — Smoking isn't good for your skin.
35 | 0.73

1707 倒れる taoreru *v.* fall (down), collapse
- その木は台風で倒れてしまった。 — The tree fell down in a typhoon.
35 | 0.91

1708 症状 shoujou *n.* symptom
- どのような症状がありますか。 — What symptoms do you have?
35 | 0.87

1709 普及(する) fukyuu(suru) *n.* spread, diffusion *v.* spread
- インターネットは急速に普及した。 — The Internet has spread rapidly.
35 | 0.84

1710 すると suru to *conj.* then, if so
- 彼は穴の中を見た。すると、かわいいねずみが出てきた。 — He looked into the hole. Then, a cute mouse came out.
35 | 0.67

1711 優れる sugureru *v.* be superior
- 肉体的強さという点で男性は女性より優れている。 — Men are superior to women in terms of physical strength.
35 | 0.90

1712 返事（する）henji(suru) *n.* answer, reply *v.* answer, reply
- 名前を呼ばれたら返事をしてください。— Answer when your name is called.
34 | 0.87

1713 職場 shokuba *n.* workplace
- 今度の職場は家の近くだ。— My new workplace is near my home.
34 | 0.95

1714 取り出す toridasu *v.* take out, extract
- 彼女はバッグからカメラを取り出した。— She took her camera out of the bag.
34 | 0.91

1715 骨 hone *n.* bone
- 足の骨が折れている。— A bone in my foot is broken.
34 | 0.94

1716 平和 heiwa *n.* peace *na-adj.* peaceful
- 日本は平和な国だ。— Japan is a peaceful country.
34 | 0.98

1717 間違い machigai *n.* mistake, error
- 私の手紙に間違いがあったら直してくれませんか。— Could you correct any mistakes in my letter?
34 | 0.98

1718 まい mai *aux.* INTENTION OF NEGATION
- 彼女には何も言うまいと思った。— I don't think I'll tell her anything.
34 | 0.70

1719 けんか（する）kenka(suru) *n.* fight, quarrel *v.* fight, quarrel
- 子供達はいつもけんかしている。— My children fight all the time.
34 | 0.87

1720 偉い erai *i-adj.* great, big
- いつもお母さんのお手伝いをして偉いね。— It is great that you always help your mother.
34 | 0.89

1721 くださる kudasaru *v.* give (honorific)
- 先生が本をくださいました。— The teacher gave me a book.
34 | 0.67

1722 熱い atsui *i-adj.* hot, heated
- このお茶はとても熱い。— This tea is very hot.
34 | 0.89

1723 当日 toujitsu *n.* that day, current day
- 試験の当日に病気になってしまった。— I got sick on the very day of the exam.
34 | 0.70

1724 残り nokori *n.* rest, remainder
- 宿題の残りをやりなさい。— Do the rest of your homework.
34 | 0.99

1725 支援（する）shien(suru) *n.* support, assistance *v.* support, assist
- 皆様方のご支援に深く感謝いたします。— We really appreciate your support.
34 | 0.73

1726 実行（する）jikkou(suru) *n.* practice *v.* carry out
- 彼らは計画を実行した。— They carried out the plan.
34 | 0.94

1727 握る nigiru *v.* hold, grasp, clasp
- ハンドルを両手でしっかり握ってください。— Please hold the steering wheel firmly with both hands.
34 | 0.90

1728 出会い deai *n.* encounter
- 最近出会いがない。— I have had no opportunities to meet new people recently.
34 | 0.88

1729 体重 taijuu *n.* (body) weight
- 体重が全然減らなかった。— I didn't lose any weight at all.
34 | 0.90

1730 上司 joushi *n.* boss
- その件については上司に相談しなければなりません。— I need to talk to my boss about it.
34 | 0.87

1731 結論 ketsuron *n.* conclusion
- 結論を出すのは難しい。— It is hard to come to any conclusions.
34 | 0.95

1732 け ke *p. disc.* QUESTION ABOUT SOMETHING SPEAKER FORGOT
- 今日は何曜日だったっけ。— What day is it today?
34 | 0.68

1733 テーブル teeburu *n.* table
- テーブルの上にお皿がある。— There is a plate on the table.
34 | 0.83

1734 盛ん sakan *na-adj.* popular; active; prosperous
- この国ではサッカーが大変盛んだ。— Soccer is very popular in this country.
34 | 0.93

1735 急ぐ isogu *v.* hurry
- 電車に乗ろうと急いだ。— I hurried to catch a train.
34 | 0.96

1736 ともかく tomokaku *adv.* in any case, anyway
- できるかどうかわからないけど、ともかくやってみます。— I don't know if I can, but I'll try anyway.
34 | 0.92

1737 犯人 hannin *n.* criminal, culprit
- 犯人がつかまった。— The criminal has been arrested.
34 | 0.91

1738 熱 netsu *n.* fever; heat
- 少し熱があるみたい。— I seem to have a slight fever.
34 | 0.97

1739 犯罪 hanzai *n.* crime, offense
- 最近、少年犯罪が増えている。— Juvenile crime is on the increase these days.
34 | 0.95

1740 批判(する) hihan(suru) *n.* criticism *v.* criticize
- 日本の英語教育は長い間批判されてきた。— English-language education in Japan has been criticized for a long time.
34 | 0.93

1741 出発(する) shuppatsu(suru) *n.* departure *v.* leave
- このバスは何時に出発するんですか。— What time does this bus leave?
34 | 0.97

1742 遊び asobi *n.* play, game
- これは小さな女の子の遊びだ。— This is a game played by little girls.
34 | 0.95

1743 教師 kyoushi *n.* teacher
- 母は小学校の教師です。— My mother is a primary school teacher.
34 | 0.90

1744 横浜 yokohama *n.* Yokohama
- 今日は横浜に買い物に行く。— I will go shopping in Yokohama today.
34 | 0.85

1745 脳 nou *n.* brain
- 彼は脳の機能について研究している。— He studies brain function.
34 | 0.92

1746 レストラン resutoran *n.* restaurant
- そのビルの中にいくつかレストランがある。— There are several restaurants in the building.
34 | 0.87

1747 そろそろ sorosoro *adv.* soon; slowly
- そろそろ行かないと。— I have to go soon.
34 | 0.84

1748 日曜日 nichiyou bi *n.* Sunday
- 銀行は日曜日は休みだ。— Banks are closed on Sundays.
34 | 0.91

1749 けが(する) kega(suru) *n.* injury *v.* hurt, injure
- けがをしないように気をつけてね。— Be careful not to get hurt.
34 | 0.92

1750 兄弟 kyoudai *n.* brother; sister; sibling
- 彼には兄弟がいますか。— Does he have any brothers or sisters?
33 | 0.86

1751 楽器 gakki *n.* musical instrument
- 何か楽器をやってる? — Do you play any instruments?
33 | 0.79

1752 保つ tamotsu *v.* keep, maintain
- 健康を保つために運動する。— I exercise to keep healthy.
33 | 0.96

1753 自動車 jidou-sha *n.* car
- この工場では月に三万台の車を生産している。— This factory produces 30,000 cars per month.
33 | 0.89

1754 ほんの honno *adn.* just, nothing but, only
- 「もっとビールをどうですか。」「じゃ、ほんの少しお願いします。」— "Would you like some more beer?" "Well, just a little, please."
33 | 0.91

1755 カメラ kamera *n.* camera
- 新しいカメラがほしい。— I want a new camera.
33 | 0.89

1756 寺 tera *n.* temple
- 京都の寺はたくさんの観光客でにぎわっています。— The temples in Kyoto are crowded with lots of tourists.
33 | 0.86

1757 ビデオ bideo *n.* video
- その映画は二、三年前にビデオで見た。— I saw the movie on video two or three years ago.
33 | 0.91

1758 適切 tekisetsu *na-adj.* suitable, proper
- 適切な食事と適切な運動が重要だ。— Proper diet and exercise are important.
33 | 0.57

1759 見事 migoto *na-adj.* excellent *adv.* completely
- 彼女のスピーチは見事だった。— Her speech was excellent.
33 | 0.89

1760 底 soko *n.* bottom; sole
- 心の底から彼女を愛している。— I love her from the bottom of my heart.
33 | 0.94

1761 刺激（する）shigeki(suru) *n., v.* stimulate, incite, excite
- 彼女には彼らとの議論がいい刺激になったようだ。— She seems to be stimulated by discussion with them.
33 | 0.95

1762 勢い ikioi *n.* speed; force; vigor
- その会社はすごい勢いで成長している。— The company is growing at great speed.
33 | 0.94

1763 吹く fuku *v.* blow; breathe out; play (musical instrument)
- 強い風が吹いている。— A strong wind is blowing.
33 | 0.94

1764 今日 konnichi *adv.* today, these days
- 今日世界経済はますます悪化している。— The world economy is getting worse these days.
33 | 0.81

1765 迷う mayou *v.* get lost; cannot decide
- それを買うかどうか迷っている。— I cannot decide whether to buy one or not.
33 | 0.84

1766 背 se *n.* stature; back
- 彼女は背が低い。— She is short (in stature).
33 | 0.83

1767 生 nama *n.* raw; fresh; live
- その魚は生で食べられる。— The fish can be eaten raw.
33 | 0.90

1768 訴える uttaeru *v.* sue; complain; appeal
- 彼女は上司をセクハラで訴えた。— She sued her boss for sexual harassment.
33 | 0.97

1769 精神 seishin *n.* mind, spirit
- 助け合いの精神を忘れてはいけない。— Do not forget the spirit of cooperation.
33 | 0.93

1770 把握（する）haaku(suru) *n.* grasp *v.* grasp
- まだ状況が把握できていない。— I have not yet grasped the situation.
33 | 0.76

1771 対する taisuru *v.* toward, against; compare, receive
- 彼女は誰に対しても親切だ。— She is kind to everyone.
33 | 0.78

1772 十二 juu ni *n.* twelve
- 十と十一と十二の合計は三十三だ。— The sum of ten, eleven, and twelve is thirty-three.
33 | 0.89

1773 じゃ ja *aux.* COPULA is, are
- なんじゃ、こりゃ。— What the hell is this?
33 | 0.77

1774 地震 jishin *n.* earthquake
- 昨夜大きな地震があった。— There was a big earthquake last night.
33 | 0.93

1775 応援（する）ouen(suru) *n.* support *v.* cheer, support
- 私たちは大声で自分たちのチームを応援した。— We cheered loudly for our team.
33 | 0.87

1776 人類 jinrui *n.* human race, mankind
- 世界平和は人類の夢だ。— World peace is the dream of mankind.
33 | 0.89

1777 上昇（する）joushou(suru) *n.* rise *v.* rise
- 最近物価が上昇している。— Prices are rising these days.
33 | 0.64

1778 空間 kuukan *n.* space
- ペットのための快適な空間を作りましょう。— Make a nice comfortable space for your pet.
33 | 0.91

1779 複雑 fukuzatsu *na-adj.* complicated, complex
- その二つの国の関係は複雑だ。— The relationship between the two countries is complicated.
33 | 0.97

1780 特定（する）tokutei(suru) *n.* specific *v.* specify
- 多くの日本人は特定の宗教を信じていない。— Many Japanese don't believe in a particular religion.
33 | 0.88

1781 高める takameru *v.* raise
- この国における女性の地位を高める必要がある。— We need to raise the status of women in this country.
33 | 0.86

1782 以外 igai *n.* except
- 土曜と日曜以外は毎朝四時に起きている。— I get up at 4 a.m. every day except for Saturdays and Sundays.
33 | 0.93

1783 観点 kanten *n.* viewpoint, standpoint
- この問題を別の観点から見てみましょう。— Let us look at the issue from another viewpoint.
33 | 0.52

1784 努める tsutomeru *v.* make efforts
- 今後もサービスの向上に努めてまいります。
— We will make every effort to improve our service.
33 | 0.56 | OF

1785 二時間 ni jikan *n.* two hours
- 毎日二時間通勤します。— I commute for two hours every day.
33 | 0.89

1786 きつい kitsui *i-adj.* tight; hard, severe; strong
- このシャツは少しきつい。— This shirt is a little tight.
33 | 0.86

1787 祖母 sobo *n.* grandmother
- 祖母は九十九歳まで生きました。— My grandmother lived to be ninety-nine years old.
33 | 0.73

1788 プラス（する）purasu(suru) *n.* plus, benefit *v.* benefit, add to
- この経験は自分の将来にプラスになるだろう。
— This experience will benefit your future.
32 | 0.93

1789 大抵 taitei *adv.* usually
- 朝ごはんはたいてい七時に食べる。— I usually have breakfast at seven o'clock.
32 | 0.86

1790 狙う nerau *v.* aim at
- 彼は優勝を狙っている。— He is aiming to win the championship.
32 | 0.90

1791 知り合い shiriai *n.* acquaintance
- その花屋は父の知り合いだ。— The florist is my father's acquaintance.
32 | 0.81

1792 迫る semaru *v.* approach, draw near; demand
- 申し込みの締め切り日が迫っている。
— The deadline for applications is drawing near.
32 | 0.94

1793 どうぞ douzo *adv.* please
- どうぞこちらにお掛けください。— Please have a seat here.
32 | 0.86

1794 消す kesu *v.* put out, turn off; erase
- 部屋を出るときは電気を消してください。
— Please turn off the lights when you leave the room.
32 | 0.90

1795 唯一 yuiitsu *n., adv.* only
- 最近は食べることが唯一の楽しみだ。
— Eating is my only pleasure these days.
32 | 0.96

9 Furniture

(frequency per million words)

(家具・家電など) (Furniture, electric appliances)

電話 denwa 224.921 **telephone**
テレビ terebi 173.941 **television, TV**
パソコン pasokon 95.766 **personal computer**
コンピューター konpyuutaa, konpyuuta 42.124 **computer**
椅子 isu 41.671 **chair**
ベッド beddo 40.082 **bed**
テーブル teeburu 33.838 **table**
冷蔵庫 reizou-ko 27.601 **refrigerator**
布団 futon 26.572 **futon, Japanese-style bedding**
机 tsukue 25.556 **desk**
時計 tokei 22.236 **clock (also watch)**
鏡 kagami 21.819 **mirror**
家具 kagu 13.256 **furniture**
DVD diibuidii 13.053 **DVD**
畳 tatami 13.019 **tatami mat**
ソファー sofaa 12.258 **sofa**
棚 tana 11.393 **shelf, shelves**
カーテン kaaten 10.953 **curtain(s)**
壺 tsubo 9.912 **pot, vase**
エアコン eakon 8.880 **air-conditioning, air conditioner**
洗濯機 sentaku ki 7.748 **washing machine**
クーラー kuuraa 6.441 **air conditioner**
箪笥 tansu 5.298 **chest of drawers**
スピーカー supiikaa 5.032 **speaker(s)**
掃除機 souji ki 3.787 **vacuum cleaner**
暖房 danbou 3.688 **heating**
本棚 hondana 3.559 **bookshelf**
冷房 reibou 3.359 **air conditioning**
アイロン airon 3.353 **iron**
プリンター purintaa 2.191 **printer**
扇風機 senpuu ki 2.161 **fan**
ヒーター hiitaa 1.288 **heater**

1796 連中 renchuu *n.* company, crowd; those guys
- 彼は悪い連中と付き合っている。— He is mixed up with bad guys.

32 | 0.75

1797 青い aoi *i-adj.* blue; pale; unripe
- 彼は青いシャツを着ている。— He is wearing a blue shirt.

32 | 0.91

1798 終了(する) shuuryou(suru) *n.* end *v.* end, be over
- 会議はもう終了いたしました。— The meeting is already over.

32 | 0.90

1799 をもって o mot-te *cp.* by; with; as of
- 本日をもって退職いたします。— I will be leaving the company as of today.

32 | 0.80

1800 前提 zentei *n.* assumption, premise
- 全ての講義は予習を前提に進めます。— All lectures proceed on the assumption that you have prepared beforehand.

32 | 0.83

1801 四つ yot-tsu *n.* four
- この町には学校が四つある。— There are four schools in this town.

32 | 0.40

1802 未来 mirai *n.* future
- 君には明るい未来がある。— You have a bright future.

32 | 0.93

1803 僕ら boku-ra *pron.* we
- 僕らはおばあちゃんが大好き。— We love my grandmother.

32 | 0.84

1804 立ち上がる tachiagaru *v.* stand up, rise
- 彼女は突然立ち上がって行ってしまった。— She suddenly stood up and left.

32 | 0.75

1805 同 dou *n.* same
- 私も彼と同意見です。— I have the same opinion as him.

32 | 0.60

1806 推移(する) suii(suru) *n.* transition, change *v.* change, shift
- 図9は人口の推移を表したものである。— Figure 9 shows the changes in population.

32 | 0.24 | OF

1807 なくす nakusu *v.* lose
- 財布をなくしてしまったみたいだ。— I seem to have lost my wallet.

32 | 0.97

1808 有効 yuukou *na-adj.* valid; effective
- そのチケットは四十八時間有効です。— The ticket is valid for forty-eight hours.

32 | 0.91

1809 次々 tsugitsugi *adv.* one after another
- お客さんが次々と入って来た。— Customers came in one after another.

32 | 0.92

1810 上で ue de *cp.* after; in the context of
- 両親と相談した上で決めます。— I will decide after consulting with my parents.

32 | 0.74

1811 国内 kokunai *n.* domestic, home
- 彼の国内政策は批判されている。— His domestic policy has been criticized.

32 | 0.88

1812 が ga *conj.* but
- 旅行に行きたい。が、時間がない。— I want to travel, but I have no time.

32 | 0.75

1813 都合(する) tsugou(suru) *n.* convenience, circumstances *v.* arrange *adv.* altogether
- 都合がいいのはいつですか。— When is it convenient for you?

32 | 0.95

1814 主な omona *adn.* main, chief
- その事故の主な原因はまだわかっていない。— The main cause of the accident is still unknown.

32 | 0.81

1815 ふと futo *adv.* casually; suddenly
- 家に帰る途中でふと約束を思い出した。— I suddenly remembered the appointment on the way home.

32 | 0.85

1816 四年 yo nen *n.* four years
- 私たちが結婚して四年になる。— We have been married for four years.

32 | 0.94

1817 無視(する) mushi(suru) *n., v.* neglect, ignore
- クラスの友達から無視された。— I was ignored by my classmates.

32 | 0.93

1818 一気 ikki *adv., n.* at a stretch, in one gulp
- 彼女は水を一気に飲み干した。— She drank a glass of water in one gulp.

32 | 0.91

1819 手続き tetsuzuki *n.* procedure, formalities
- 次に、婚姻届の手続きについてご説明します。— Next, I will explain the procedures for marriage notification.

32 | 0.88

1820 波 nami *n.* wave
- 今日は波が高い。— The waves are high today.
32 | 0.98

1821 仲 naka *n.* relations, terms
- 彼女はクラスのほとんどの人と仲がいい。— She is on friendly terms with most of her classmates.
32 | 0.86

1822 中学生 chuugaku-sei *n.* junior high school student
- 私はそのころ中学生だった。— I was a junior high school student then.
32 | 0.94

1823 イタリア itaria *n.* Italy
- イタリアの首都はローマだ。— The capital of Italy is Rome.
32 | 0.98

1824 のぞく nozoku *v.* look through, look down; drop in
- 彼女は窓から中をのぞいた。— She looked in through the window.
32 | 0.88

1825 誕生（する）tanjou(suru) *n.* birth *v.* be born, be created
- 地球が誕生したの四十五億年前だ。— The earth was born 4.5 billion years ago.
32 | 0.93

1826 汚い kitanai *i-adj.* dirty; unfair; vulgar
- 汚いから、触ったらいけません。— It's dirty, don't touch it.
32 | 0.75

1827 畑 hatake *n.* field (for fruit, vegetables); garden
- 今年の夏、畑にそばの種をまいた。— I seeded the field with buckwheat this summer.
32 | 0.94

1828 履く haku *v.* put on, wear
- 彼女はいつもジーンズを履いている。— She always wears jeans.
32 | 0.88

1829 膝 hiza *n.* knee, lap
- 転んでひざをけがしてしまった。— I fell and injured my knee.
32 | 0.87

1830 提案（する）teian(suru) *n.* proposal *v.* propose
- 彼の提案には賛成できません。— I cannot agree to his proposal.
32 | 0.89

1831 業務 gyoumu *n.* business, work
- これも私たちにとって重要な業務である。— This is also important business for us.
32 | 0.51 | OF

1832 幸い saiwai *na-adj.* lucky, fortunate *n.* happiness *adv.* fortunately
- 兄は交通事故に遭ったが、幸いなことに、軽いけがで済んだ。— My brother had a car accident but luckily he was only slightly injured.
32 | 0.95

1833 かわいそう kawaisou *na-adj.* pitiful, miserable
- 彼女がかわいそうだ。— I feel sorry for her.
32 | 0.80

1834 画像 gazou *n.* picture, image
- 画像をクリックすると次のページに進みます。— Click any picture to go to the next page.
32 | 0.66 | WB

1835 孫 mago *n.* grandchild
- 彼女は十人の孫がいる。— She has ten grandchildren.
32 | 0.88

1836 つなぐ tsunagu *v.* connect, tie
- 犬を庭の木につないだ。— I tied my dog to the tree in the yard.
32 | 0.94

1837 包む tsutsumu *v.* wrap
- プレゼント用に包んでもらえますか。— Can you wrap them for a gift?
32 | 0.85

1838 思い切る omoikiru *v.* give up; venture
- 思い切って会議で自分の意見を言った。— I ventured to give my opinion at the conference.
31 | 0.96

1839 事態 jitai *n.* situation
- これは深刻な事態だ。— This is a serious situation.
31 | 0.83

1840 夜中 yonaka *n.* middle of the night
- 夜中に目が覚めた。— I woke up in the middle of the night.
31 | 0.78

1841 改める aratameru *v.* change; reform
- 彼は上司に対する態度を改めるべきだ。— He has to change his attitude toward his boss.
31 | 0.86

1842 集中（する）shuuchuu(suru) *n.* concentration *v.* concentrate
- 宿題に集中できない。— I can't concentrate on my homework.
31 | 0.98

1843 両手 ryoute *n.* both hands, both arms
- 両手でしっかり持って。— Hold it firmly with both hands.
31 | 0.78

1844 指示（する） shiji(suru) *n.* instruction, direction *v.* instruct, direct
- 係員の指示に従ってください。— Please follow the attendant's instructions.

31 | 0.93

1845 結婚式 kekkon shiki *n.* wedding ceremony
- 私は先月結婚式を挙げました。— I got married last month.

31 | 0.80

1846 虫 mushi *n.* insect, bug; worm
- 母は本当に虫が嫌いだ。— My mother really doesn't like insects.

31 | 0.88

1847 バイク baiku *n.* motorcycle, motorbike
- 私はバイクに乗れない。— I can't ride a motorcycle.

31 | 0.79

1848 確立（する） kakuritsu(suru) *n.* establishment *v.* establish
- この制度は1990年に確立された。— The system was established in 1990.

31 | 0.78

1849 到着（する） touchaku(suru) *n.* arrival *v.* arrive
- 飛行機は時間通りに到着した。— The plane arrived on time.

31 | 0.88

1850 かく kaku *v.* scratch; paddle; shovel
- かゆくてもかいてはいけない。— You mustn't scratch, even if it's itchy.

31 | 0.89

1851 痩せる yaseru *v.* become thin, lose weight
- 一週間で五キロ痩せた。— I lost five kilos in a week.

31 | 0.84

1852 親父 oyaji *n.* father; old man; boss
- 彼は彼の親父さんにそっくりだ。— He resembles his father.

31 | 0.84

1853 なくてはいけない naku te wa ike nai *cp.* have to, must
- 毎日学校に行かなくてはいけない。— I have to go to school every day.

31 | 0.00 | SP

1854 試す tamesu *v.* try, attempt
- いろいろな方法を試してみたが、全部だめだった。— I tried lots of methods but nothing worked.

31 | 0.86

1855 終える oeru *v.* finish, end
- 彼は高校を終えて大学に進んだ。— He finished high school and went to university.

31 | 0.95

1856 遥か haruka *na-adj.* faraway, far
- 遥か昔のことのようだ。— It seems like ages ago.

31 | 0.89

1857 受験（する） juken(suru) *n.* examination *v.* take an examination
- 彼女は二月に高校を受験する。— She will take the high school entrance exam in February.

31 | 0.74

1858 医師 ishi *n.* doctor
- その場合は直ちに医師の診断を受けてください。— In such cases, consult a physician immediately.

31 | 0.89

1859 バンド bando *n.* band; belt
- このバンドは日本でとても人気がある。— This band is very popular in Japan.

31 | 0.72

1860 体力 tairyoku *n.* physical strength
- 彼女は体力がない。— She lacks physical strength.

31 | 0.96

1861 国家 kokka *n.* state, country, nation
- 彼らは国家のために戦い、死んでいった。— They fought and died for their nation.

31 | 0.86

1862 ソフト sofuto *n.* software *na-adj.* soft
- 新しいソフトを買った。— I bought some new software.
- ソフトな肌触り。— The touch is soft.

31 | 0.84

1863 長男 chounan *n.* eldest son
- 長男はフランスで芸術を学んでいる。— The eldest son is studying art in France.

31 | 0.86

1864 0 rei *n.* zero
- テストで0点をとった。— I got zero in that test.

31 | 0.81

1865 さっき sakki *adv., n.* a little while ago
- さっき、君のお母さんに会ったよ。— I saw your mother just now.

31 | 0.79

1866 ごく goku *adv.* very
- 私はごく普通の家庭で育った。— I grew up in a very average household.

31 | 0.93

1867 入力（する） nyuuryoku(suru) *n.* input *v.* type
- 彼はコンピューターにデータを入力した。— He input the data on the computer.

31 | 0.95

1868 CM shiiemu *n.* commercial
- このCM面白いと思わない？ — Don't you think this commercial is funny?
31 | 0.68

1869 十一 juu ichi *n.* eleven
- その町まで十一キロある。 — It's eleven kilometers to the town.
31 | 0.87

1870 チャンス chansu *n.* chance
- もう一度チャンスをください。 — Please give me another chance.
31 | 0.93

1871 別れる wakareru *v.* part; divorce, break up
- 彼らは先月別れてしまった。 — They broke up last month.
31 | 0.79

1872 昼間 hiruma *n.* daytime
- そのバーは昼間は閉まっている。 — The bar is closed in the daytime.
31 | 0.93

1873 生産（する） seisan(suru) *n.* production *v.* produce
- その車の生産は2000年に始まった。 — The production of the automobile started in 2000.
31 | 0.77

1874 要 you *n.* in short
- 行きたくないわけではない。要はお金の問題だ。 — That's not to say that I don't want to go to. In short, it's an issue of money.
31 | 0.83

1875 収める osameru *v.* obtain, gain; put; keep
- その映画は大成功を収めた。 — The movie was a great success.
31 | 0.86

1876 掃除（する） souji(suru) *n.* cleaning *v.* clean
- 部屋を掃除しなさい。 — Clean your room.
31 | 0.85

1877 強化（する） kyouka(suru) *n., v.* tighten, strengthen
- 空港の警備が強化された。 — The security at the airport has been tightened.
31 | 0.59

1878 主婦 shufu *n.* housewife
- 母は主婦です。 — My mother is a housewife.
31 | 0.92

1879 徐々 jojo *n.* gradually
- 景気は徐々に回復してきている。 — The economy is gradually recovering.
31 | 1.00

1880 メーカー meekaa *n.* maker, manufacturer
- この会社は日本のカメラのメーカーだ。 — This company is a Japanese camera manufacturer.
31 | 0.90

1881 あり得る ari eru *v.* be possible, be likely, be probable
- 何だってあり得るよ。 — Anything is possible.
31 | 0.85

1882 記す shirusu *v.* write down; mark
- この資料にはジョンは1800年ごろ生まれたと記されている。 — In this document, it is written that John was born around 1800.
31 | 0.74

1883 うわさ（する） uwasa(suru) *n.* gossip, rumor *v.* talk about
- 彼についていろいろうわさが流れている。 — Various rumors about him are going around.
31 | 0.90

1884 保険 hoken *n.* insurance
- レンタカーを借りる時はいつも保険に入る。 — I always buy insurance when I rent a car.
31 | 0.92

1885 規制（する） kisei(suru) *n.* regulation *v.* regulate
- マラソン大会のため、交通が規制される。 — Traffic will be restricted because of the marathon.
31 | 0.72

1886 もの mono *p.* because
- 「どうしてパーティーに行かないの。」「だって、忙しいもの。」 — "Why don't you come to the party?" "Because I'm busy."
31 | 0.71

1887 感想 kansou *n.* feeling, impression
- この本の感想はどうですか？ — What is your impression of this book?
31 | 0.94

1888 左右（する） sayuu(suru) *n.* right and left *v.* determine, influence
- この試験の結果が私の将来を左右する。 — This exam result will determine my future.
31 | 0.93

1889 促進（する） sokushin(suru) *n.* promotion *v.* promote
- 政府は自然エネルギーの利用を促進するべきだ。 — The government should promote the use of natural energy.
31 | 0.41 | OF

1890 景色 keshiki *n.* scenery, view, scene
- 景色のいい部屋がいいなあ。 — I'd like a room with a good view.
31 | 0.84

1891 味わう ajiwau *v.* taste, savor
- ゆっくり食べて、よく味わってね。— Eat slowly and savor the taste.
30 | 0.94

1892 アジア ajia *n.* Asia
- 中国はアジアで一番広い国だ。— China is the largest country in Asia.
30 | 0.95

1893 交流(する) kouryuu(suru) *n.* interchange, exchange *v.* interact
- 両国は交流が盛んだ。— There is an active exchange between the two countries.
30 | 0.87

1894 報道(する) houdou(suru) *n.* report *v.* report
- 彼の死は新聞でも報道された。— His death was reported in the newspapers.
30 | 0.96

1895 当初 tousho *n.* beginning, original *adv.* at first
- 留学の当初の目的は法律を勉強することだった。— My original aim in studying abroad was to study law.
30 | 0.96

1896 インド indo *n.* India
- 日本はインドから紅茶を輸入している。— Japan imports tea from India.
30 | 0.95

1897 観察(する) kansatsu(suru) *n.* observation *v.* observe
- 私はその植物の成長を7週間観察した。— I observed the growth of the plants for seven weeks.
30 | 0.93

1898 電気 denki *n.* electricity; electric light
- 電気を消すのを忘れないでね。— Don't forget to turn the light off.
30 | 0.97

1899 癖 kuse *n.* habit, peculiarity
- 彼女は爪をかむくせがある。— She has a habit of biting her nails.
30 | 0.84

1900 たいした taishita *adn.* not big, not much; great, quite
- たいしたことじゃないよ。— It's not such a big deal.
30 | 0.87

1901 あり方 ari-kata *n.* way something ought to be, state of things
- 彼は教育のあり方についての意見を述べた。— He expressed his view about how education ought to be.
30 | 0.70

1902 どころ dokoro *p.* far from, on the contrary, can't even
- 彼はワインどころかビールも飲まない。— He doesn't even drink beer, let alone wine.
30 | 0.91

1903 好み konomi *n.* liking, taste
- 彼の好みに合ったワインを買う。— I bought a bottle of wine that suits his taste.
30 | 0.87

1904 はまる hamaru *v.* fit; fall; be addicted to
- 鍵がはまらない。— The key won't fit.
30 | 0.78

1905 早速 sassoku *adv.* at once, lose no time in doing
- 彼は職場に来ると早速仕事を始めた。— He began to work right away as soon as he arrived at the office.
30 | 0.90

1906 支払う shiharau *v.* pay
- 料金は日曜日までにお支払いください。— Please pay the bills by Sunday.
30 | 0.94

1907 市民 shimin *n.* resident (of a city), citizen
- 市民は図書館の資料が無料で借りられる。— Residents of this city can borrow books from the library for free.
30 | 0.52

1908 メリット meritto *n.* merit, advantage
- パッケージツアーのメリットは安全なことだ。— The advantage of a package tour is safety.
30 | 0.97

1909 近年 kinnen *adv.* in recent years
- 近年旅行者の数が大きく増加した。— The number of tourists has increased greatly in recent years.
30 | 0.62

1910 分かりやすい wakari-yasui *i-adj.* easy to understand.
- この辞書の例はわかりやすい。— The examples in this dictionary are easy to understand.
30 | 0.97

1911 製品 seihin *n.* product
- 日本には外国の製品がたくさんある。— There are plenty of foreign products in Japan.
30 | 0.94

1912 果たして hatashite *adv.* really; just as one thought
- 彼らが言うことが果たして本当なのかわからない。— I don't know if what they are saying is really true.
30 | 0.99

1913 得意 tokui *na-adj.* be good at, be proud *n.* customer
- 私、料理は得意なんです。— I am good at cooking.
30 | 0.84

1914 二週間 ni shuukan *n.* two weeks
- 車を二週間借りた。— I rented a car for two weeks.
30 | 0.83

1915 問い合わせ toiawase *n.* inquiry
- お問い合わせ、ありがとうございます。— Thank you for your inquiry.
30 | 0.16 | NM

1916 あっ a *interj.* Ah!, Oh!, Hey!
- あっ、電話だ。— Oh, the phone's ringing.
30 | 0.77

1917 何だか nan da ka *adv.* somewhat; somehow
- なんだか今日は気分が悪い。— For some reason, I feel sick today.
30 | 0.60

1918 過程 katei *n.* process
- 彼はチョコレートを作る過程を説明した。— He explained the process of making chocolate.
30 | 0.88

1919 仕組み shikumi *n.* structure, mechanism
- その国の政治の仕組みを理解するのは難しい。— It's difficult to understand the political structure of the country.
30 | 0.88

1920 慌てる awateru *v.* be flustered, be in a hurry
- 慌ててやると間違えてしまいますよ。— You make mistakes if you do things in a hurry.
30 | 0.84

1921 ざるを得ない zaru o e nai *cp.* have to, cannot help doing
- その会社は生産を縮小せざるをえないだろう。— The company would have to cut back its production.
30 | 0.88

1922 措置（する） sochi(suru) *n.* measure *v.* take measures
- 政府は適切な措置を取らなかった。— The government didn't take proper measures.
30 | 0.32 | OF

1923 油 abura *n.* oil
- フライパンに油をひいてください。— Put oil in a frying pan.
30 | 0.98

1924 半年 hantoshi *n.* half a year
- 妹はイギリスに半年住んでいた。— My younger sister lived in England for six months.
30 | 0.87

1925 視線 shisen *n.* eyes, gaze, look
- 全員の視線が彼に向けられた。— Everyone's eyes turned to him.
30 | 0.69

1926 構造 kouzou *n.* structure
- この建物は構造が複雑だ。— The structure of this building is complex.
30 | 0.91

1927 筋肉 kinniku *n.* muscle
- 筋肉をつけるためにトレーニングをしている。— I have been working out to develop my muscles.
30 | 0.93

1928 少々 shoushou *adv.* a little, a minute
- 少々お待ちいただけますか。— Would you please wait a minute?
30 | 0.90

1929 対策 taisaku *n.* measure
- 何か対策を考えなければならない。— We must consider some measures.
30 | 0.69

1930 濃い koi *i-adj.* thick; strong; heavy; deep
- コーヒーは濃いのが好きだ。— I like strong coffee.
30 | 0.93

1931 異常 ijou *na-adj.* abnormal *n.* disorder
- 機械に異常が見つかった。— There is something wrong with the machine.
30 | 0.95

1932 図書館 tosho-kan *n.* library
- 彼女は今図書館で勉強している。— She is studying in the library now.
30 | 0.89

1933 靴 kutsu *n.* shoe
- 新しい靴をはいてみました。— I tried putting on the new shoes.
30 | 0.89

1934 おそれ osore *n.* fear, danger
- 今晩は激しい雨が降るおそれがあります。— There is a risk of heavy rain tonight.
30 | 0.81

1935 二階 ni kai *n.* second floor
- 私の部屋は二階です。— My room is on the second floor.
30 | 0.73

1936 あえて aete *adv.* dare
- 私はその時あえて何も言わなかった。— I didn't dare say anything at that time.
30 | 0.99

1937 三回 san kai *n.* three times
- 私は富士山に三回登りました。— I climbed Mt. Fuji three times.
30 | 0.96

1938 引っ越し（する）hikkoshi(suru) *n.* moving, removal *v.* move house
- 春に引っ越しをする。— We're going to move out in spring.
30 | 0.71

1939 失礼（する）shitsurei(suru) *n.* rudeness, impoliteness *v.* be rude, be impolite *na-adj.* rude, impolite *interj.* Excuse me
- 失礼ですが、お名前は。— Excuse me, may I have your name, please?
30 | 0.91

1940 太る futoru *v.* get fat, gain weight
- 一年で十キロも太ってしまった。— I have gained ten kilos in one year.
30 | 0.82

1941 街, 町 machi *n.* town, city
- 東京はとても大きい街だ。— Tokyo is a very big city.
30 | 0.76

1942 いったん ittan *adv.* once; for a moment
- 彼女はいったん話し始めると止まらない。— Once she starts talking, she doesn't stop.
30 | 0.96

1943 取り入れる toriireru *v.* take in; adopt; harvest
- 日本は西洋の習慣や文化を取り入れた。— Japan adopted Western customs and culture.
30 | 0.93

1944 モテる moteru *v.* be popular
- モテて、モテて、困ってしまう。— I'm so popular among girls, it's a bit embarrassing.
30 | 0.97

1945 都会 tokai *n.* city
- 都会より田舎のほうが好きだ。— I like the countryside better than cities.
30 | 0.79

1946 大量 tairyou *n., na-adj.* large quantity, a lot
- 日本は大量の魚を消費する。— Japan consumes a lot of fish.
30 | 0.98

1947 発言（する）hatsugen(suru) *n.* remark *v.* speak
- 彼は会議中全く発言しなかった。— He did not speak at all during the meeting.
30 | 0.95

1948 炒める itameru *v.* fry, stir-fry
- 鶏肉を色が変わるまで炒めてください。— Stir-fry the chicken until it turns brown.
30 | 0.91

1949 投げる nageru *v.* throw; give up
- 彼はボールを投げて窓を割った。— He broke the window by throwing a ball.
30 | 0.93

1950 玄関 genkan *n.* entrance, front door
- 玄関の鍵がかかっている。— The entrance was locked.
30 | 0.89

1951 一種 isshu *n.* kind, sort, species
- それは一種の差別だ。— That's a kind of discrimination.
29 | 0.94

1952 世代 sedai *n.* generation
- 彼は若い世代に人気がある。— He is popular with the younger generation.
29 | 0.96

1953 にあたって ni atat-te *cp.* at the time of
- 登録にあたって料金のお支払方法をお選びいただきます。— At the time of registration, you must select a payment method.
29 | 0.66

1954 申し込み moushikomi *n.* application
- ツアーのお申し込みは明日までです。— Applications for the tour are accepted until tomorrow.
29 | 0.21 | NM

1955 高まる takamaru *v.* rise, heighten, grow
- 近年、ゴルフの人気が高まっている。— In recent years golf has grown in popularity.
29 | 0.79

1956 証明（する）shoumei(suru) *n.* proof *v.* prove
- あなたの収入を証明する書類が必要です。— You will need documents that prove your income.
29 | 0.98

1957 沸く waku *v.* boil; be in uproar
- お湯が沸いた。— The water is boiling.
29 | 0.90

1958 必死 hisshi *na-adj.* desperate
- 彼は岸まで必死で泳いだ。— He swam desperately to shore.
29 | 0.91

1959 真剣 shinken *na-adj.* serious
- 自分の人生について真剣に考えなさい。— Think seriously about your life.
29 | 1.00

1960 まさか masaka *adv.* surely not, cannot possibly *n.* the worst
- まさか彼がやったんじゃないよね？ — No way. He didn't do that, did he?
29 | 0.88

1961 ごめんなさい gomen nasai *interj.* I'm sorry, Excuse me
- 遅くなってごめんなさい。— I'm sorry I'm late.
29 | 0.72

1962 画面 gamen *n.* screen
- この携帯電話は画面が広くて使いやすい。— This cell phone has a large screen and is easy to use.
29 | 0.89

1963 米 kome *n.* rice
- この地方のお米はおいしい。— Rice from this region tastes great.
29 | 0.96

1964 成果 seika *n.* result, product
- 努力したけど何の成果もなかった。— My efforts yielded no results.
29 | 0.85

1965 物語 monogatari *n.* tale, story
- 寝る前に子供に物語を読んでやる。— I read a story to my child at bedtime.
29 | 0.92

1966 日時 nichiji *n.* date and time
- 次の会議の日時は郵便でお知らせします。— You will be notified of the date and time of the next meeting by mail.
29 | 0.10 | NM

1967 来年 rainen *n.* next year
- 私は来年大学を卒業する。— I will graduate from university next year.
29 | 0.82

1968 巻く maku *v.* roll up, wind up; wear around
- 彼は首に白いタオルを巻いている。— He wore a white towel around his neck.
29 | 0.93

1969 こっち kotchi *pron.* here; this; I; we
- こっちに来て手伝って。— Come on over and give me a hand.
29 | 0.73

1970 必ずしも kanarazu shimo *adv.* not necessarily, not always
- 英語のスペルと発音は必ずしも同じではない。— English spelling and pronunciation are not always the same.
29 | 0.79

1971 たっぷり tappuri *adv.* full, plenty *n.* fullness
- このスープは野菜がたっぷり入っている。— This soup is full of vegetables.
29 | 0.81

1972 はやる hayaru *v.* be fashionable, be popular, go around
- 短いスカートが今はやっている。— Short skirts are in fashion now.
29 | 0.77

1973 恐ろしい osoroshii *i-adj.* terrible, frightful, amazing, awful
- がんは恐ろしい病気だ。— Cancer is a terrible disease.
29 | 0.82

1974 中身 nakami *n.* contents; substance
- この箱の中身は何だろう。— What's in this box?
29 | 0.97

1975 スピード supiido *n.* speed
- この車、どのくらいスピードが出るの。— How fast is this car?
29 | 0.95

1976 一歩 ip-po *n.* step
- もう一歩も歩けない。— I can't walk another step.
29 | 0.97

1977 牛乳 gyuunyuu *n.* (cow's) milk
- 私は朝食に牛乳を飲む。— I have milk for breakfast.
29 | 0.92

1978 否定(する) hitei(suru) *n.* denial, negative *v.* deny
- その男は車を盗んだことを否定した。— The man has denied that he stole the car.
29 | 0.92

1979 踏まえる fumaeru *v.* be based on
- この分析結果を踏まえて結論を出します。— I conclude that based on the results of the analysis.
29 | 0.51 | OF

1980 若干 jakkan *adv.* slightly *n.* a little, few, some
- 人口が若干増加した。— The city's population had increased slightly.
29 | 0.86

1981 箱 hako *n.* box, case
- 私はその箱を開けた。— I opened the box.
29 | 0.93

1982 テニス tenisu *n.* tennis
- 明日一緒にテニスをしませんか。— Do you want to play tennis together tomorrow?
29 | 0.69

1983 アパート apaato *n.* apartment
- 私はアパートに一人で住んでいる。— I live on my own in an apartment.
29 | 0.87

1984 面接(する) mensetsu(suru) *n.* interview *v.* interview
- 今日アルバイトの面接を受けた。— I was interviewed for a part-time job today.
29 | 0.86

1985 住民 juumin *n.* inhabitant, resident
- 地元の住民はその計画に反対している。— The local residents are opposed to the plan.
29 | 0.77

1986 て参る te mairu *cp.* begin to, come to; have been; go and come (humble)
- 店長を呼んでまいりますので少々お待ちください。— Just a moment, I'll go and bring our manager.
29 | 0.00 | SP

1987 ギター gitaa *n.* guitar
- 私の趣味はギターを弾くことです。— My hobby is playing the guitar.
29 | 0.74

1988 要素 youso *n.* element, factor
- 睡眠は健康のための重要な要素である。— Sleeping is an important factor for health.
29 | 0.93

1989 泳ぐ oyogu *v.* swim
- 海で泳ぎたいなあ。— I want to swim in the sea.
29 | 0.87

1990 大勢 oozei *n.* a large number of, many
- 大勢の人にこの歌を聞いてもらいたい。— I hope that many people will hear this song.
29 | 0.94

1991 習慣 shuukan *n.* custom, habit
- 日本にはチップを渡す習慣がない。— Japanese do not have a custom of tipping.
29 | 0.92

1992 込める komeru *v.* put into, pour into
- 彼は感情を込めて歌を歌った。— He put emotion into his singing.
29 | 0.91

1993 風邪 kaze *n.* cold
- 風邪を引かないように気をつけてね。— Be careful not to catch a cold.
29 | 0.81

1994 調整（する） chousei(suru) *n.* adjustment *v.* adjust
- あなたと会えるようにスケジュールを調整します。— I will adjust my schedule to meet you.
29 | 0.88

1995 踊る odoru *v.* dance
- 一晩中カラオケを歌ったり踊ったりした。— I danced and sang karaoke all night.
29 | 0.91

1996 とも tomo *p.* all, both
- 遅くとも10時までには帰りなさい。— Come home by ten o'clock at the latest.
29 | 0.89

1997 タクシー takushii *n.* taxi
- タクシーで病院に行った。— I took a taxi to the hospital.
29 | 0.88

1998 教会 kyoukai *n.* church
- 毎週日曜に教会に行く。— I go to church every Sunday.
29 | 0.84

1999 攻撃（する） kougeki(suru) *n.* attack *v.* attack
- 彼らは敵を攻撃した。— They attacked the enemy.
29 | 0.92

10 Greetings

(frequency per million words)

（挨拶言葉・応答詞）
えー, ええ **ee** 8635.612 **er?, what?; well, yes**
うん **un** 291.385 **yes, yeah**
いや **iya** 138.900 **no**
ありがとう **arigatou** 58.125 **thank you**
それでは, それじゃ **sore de wa, sore ja** 53.578 **then, well, so**
やすみ **yasumi**[1] 43.540 **holiday (also rest; be closed)**
すみません **sumimasen** 36.308 **thank you; I am sorry; excuse me**
どうぞ **douzo** 32.431 **please**
失礼（する） **shitsurei(suru)** 29.672 **excuse me (also rude, impolite)**
願い（する） **negai**[2] 26.887 **wish, hope**
おい **oi** 20.862 **hey**

ただいま **tadaima** 17.147 **I'm back! (also now, just now, at once)**
ごめん **gomen** 15.735 **pardon, sorry [to decline]**
ううん **uun** 14.576 **no; well**
いえ **ie** 13.929 **no**
いいえ **iie** 12.298 **no**
おはよう **ohayou** 10.148 **good morning**
こんにちは **konnichiwa** 10.010 **hello, good afternoon**
いやあ **iyaa** 9.453 **well, sorry**
おめでとう **omedetou** 9.423 **congratulations**
こんばんは **konbanwa** 5.746 **good evening**
お疲れ様 **o-tsukare-sama** 4.405 **thank you (for your hard work)**
どうも **doumo** N/A **thank you**

1 Includes おやすみ *o-yasumi*.
2 Includes お願い *o-negai*.

2000 五時 go ji *n.* five o'clock
- 彼は五時ごろ戻ります。— He'll be back around five o'clock.
29 | 0.49 | NM

2001 （お）弁当 (o)-bentou *n.* boxed lunch
- お弁当を買いに行く。— I'm going to get a lunch box.
29 | 0.83

2002 方達 kata-tachi *n.* people (honorific)
- 私はその方達に大変感謝しています。— I am very grateful to those people.
29 | 0.18 | SP

2003 久しぶり hisashiburi *n.* after a long time
- 彼女から久しぶりに電話が来た。— I had a call from her for the first time in a long time.
29 | 0.68

2004 とたん totan *n.* as soon as
- 警察官を見たとたん、彼は逃げ出した。— As soon as he saw the policeman he ran away.
29 | 0.85

2005 要する yousuru *v.* need, take
- 世界経済は回復するのに数年を要します。— The global economy will need several years to recover.
29 | 0.66

2006 幅 haba *n.* width, breadth; difference; latitude
- その橋は幅が二十メートルある。— The bridge is twenty meters in width.
29 | 0.97

2007 周辺 shuuhen *n.* outskirts, around
- そのホテルの周辺にはたくさんの店やレストランがある。— The area around the hotel has many shops and restaurants.
29 | 0.96

2008 十日 too-ka *n.* tenth (date); ten days
- 十一月十日までにお返事をください。— Please respond by November 10.
29 | 0.63

2009 取得（する） shutoku(suru) *n.* acquisition *v.* acquire
- その国への入国はビザの取得が必要です。— You need to acquire a visa to enter the country.
29 | 0.86

2010 挑戦（する） chousen(suru) *n.* challenge *v.* challenge, try
- 若い人には新しいことに挑戦してほしい。— I want young people to try new things.
29 | 0.88

2011 独立（する） dokuritsu(suru) *n.* independence *v.* be independent
- 子供達はもう独立していて、主人と二人で暮らしている。— My children are already independent and I live with my husband, just the two of us.
28 | 0.94

2012 収入 shuunyuu *n.* income
- 私より妻のほうが収入が多い。— My wife's income is more than mine.
28 | 0.96

2013 ぜ ze *p.* EMPHASIS
- やったぜ！— I made it!
28 | 0.68

2014 市場 shijou *n.* market
- この製品はまだ市場には出ていない。— This product is not on the market yet.
28 | 0.90

2015 着物 kimono *n.* kimono
- 母はいつも家で着物を着ている。— My mother always wears a kimono at home.
28 | 0.87

2016 メニュー menyuu *n.* menu
- メニューを見せてください。— Can I see the menu?
28 | 0.89

2017 夏休み natsuyasumi *n.* summer holiday
- 息子は夏休みを楽しみにしている。— My son is looking forward to the summer holidays.
28 | 0.86

2018 壊す kowasu *v.* break; impair; upset
- 友達の時計を壊してしまった。— I broke my friend's watch.
28 | 0.87

2019 なさる nasaru *v.* do (honorific)
- デザートは何になさいますか。— What would you like for dessert?
28 | 0.94

2020 仮 kari *n.* temporary, provisional; assumed
- これは仮のタイトルです。— This is a provisional title.
28 | 0.94

2021 かえって kaette *adv.* on the contrary, rather
- タクシーで行ったらかえって時間がかかってしまった。— I went by taxi but on the contrary it took longer.
28 | 0.95

2022 関する kansuru *v.* be related to, be concerned with
- 当社の製品に関するお問い合わせはメールにて受け付けております。— For all questions related to our products, feel free to email us.
28 | 0.61

2023 輸入（する）yu'nyuu(suru) *n., v.* import
- 日本はブラジルからコーヒーを輸入している。— Japan imports coffee from Brazil.
28 | 0.55

2024 満たす mitasu *v.* fill, satisfy, meet
- 応募者は次の条件を満たしていることが必要です。— The applicant must satisfy the following requirements.
28 | 0.94

2025 いわば iwaba *adv.* so to speak, as it were
- 彼はいわば日本のエジソンだ。— He is a Japanese Edison, as it were.
28 | 0.74

2026 スタッフ sutaffu *n.* staff
- スタッフをもっと募集しなければならない。— We need to recruit more staff.
28 | 0.89

2027 住所 juusho *n.* address
- 住所をいただけますか？ — Could you give us your address?
28 | 0.75

2028 平気 heiki *na-adj.* insensitive, fine *n.* calmness
- 平気なふりをした。— I pretended to be fine.
28 | 0.85

2029 コース koosu *n.* course, route, lane
- この音楽学校には子供のためのコースもある。— This music school has a course for kids too.
28 | 0.83

2030 訪ねる tazuneru *v.* visit, go to see
- このツアーでは、京都のお寺や神社を訪ねます。— On this tour, you visit temples and shrines in Kyoto.
28 | 0.85

2031 鍵 kagi *n.* key
- 部屋に鍵を忘れてしまった。— I left my key in my room.
28 | 0.91

2032 世界中 sekai-juu *n.* around the world, throughout the world
- 彼女は飛行機で世界中を旅行した。— She traveled all over the world by air.
28 | 0.96

2033 下手 heta *na-adj.* not good at, poor, bad, unskilled
- 彼は野球が下手だ。— He is not good at baseball.
28 | 0.85

2034 詩 shi *n.* poem, poetry
- 彼は多くの詩を書いた。— He wrote a lot of poems.
28 | 0.90

2035 経過（する）keika(suru) *n.* progress, development *v.* pass
- 試合開始から十分が経過しました。— Ten minutes have passed since the game started.
28 | 0.81

2036 整える totonoeru *v.* arrange, prepare
- 次の試合に向けてコンディションを整えておかなければ。— I have to prepare my physical condition for the next match.
28 | 0.95

2037 ツアー tsuaa *n.* tour
- スキーツアーに参加したいんですが。— I'd like to join the ski tour.
28 | 0.78

2038 西 nishi *n.* west
- その町は東京の西にある。— The town is located in west Tokyo.
28 | 0.94

2039 事項 jikou *n.* matter, fact, item
- 審議事項は以上です。— That's all the items we have to discuss.
28 | 0.29 | OF

2040 塾 juku *n.* cram school
- 彼は一週間に四日塾に通っている。— He goes to a cram school four days a week.
28 | 0.71

2041 去る saru *v., adn.* leave, pass, be gone
- 彼は六十歳でこの世を去った。— He passed away at the age of sixty.
28 | 0.92

2042 五人 go-nin *n.* five people
- 私の学校には外国人の先生が五人いる。— There are five foreign teachers at my school.
28 | 0.94

2043 入り口 iriguchi *n.* entrance
- ビルの入り口の前で待っていてください。— Please wait for me at the entrance of the building.
28 | 0.93

2044 改めて aratamete *adv.* over again; some other time
- 後ほど改めてお電話いたします。— I will call you back later.
28 | 0.86

2045 県 ken *n.* prefecture
- 日本には四十三の県がある。— There are forty-three prefectures in Japan.
28 | 0.87

2046 断る kotowaru *v.* decline, refuse, reject, turn down; ask permission; give notice
- デートを断られてしまった。— I got turned down for a date.
28 | 0.90

2047 事務所 jimu-sho *n.* office
- 彼は昨年東京に事務所を開いた。 — He opened an office in Tokyo last year.

28 | 0.98

2048 大さじ oosaji *n.* tablespoon
- カップ一杯の牛乳に大さじ一杯の酢を加えてください。 — Add one tablespoon vinegar to one cup of milk.

28 | 0.77

2049 整理（する）seiri(suru) *n.* arrangement *v.* arrange, put in order, dispose of
- 今日自分の本棚を整理した。 — I arranged my bookshelf today.

28 | 0.92

2050 耐える taeru *v.* stand, endure, bear
- 彼女と別れるなんて耐えられない。 — I can't stand losing her.

28 | 0.93

2051 職員 shokuin *n.* staff member
- この市役所には英語が話せる職員が二名おります。 — There are two members of staff at this city hall who speak English.

28 | 0.70

2052 コメント（する）komento *n.* comment *v.* comment
- その件については今はコメントできません。 — I can't comment on that right now.

28 | 0.78

2053 五分 go fun *n.* five minutes
- 電車が五分遅れている。 — The train is five minutes late.

28 | 0.89

2054 発揮（する）hakki(suru) *n.* exhibition, show *v.* display, exhibit
- 彼が実力を発揮できるといいんですが。 — I hope he can show his true ability.

28 | 0.90

2055 閉じる tojiru *v.* close, shut
- 教科書を閉じてください。 — Close your textbooks.

28 | 0.85

2056 芝居 shibai *n.* play, drama
- 友達と芝居を見に行った。 — I went to see a play with my friend.

28 | 0.66

2057 分析（する）bunseki(suru) *n.* analysis *v.* analyze
- この機械は食品の味や成分を分析することができる。 — The machine can analyze the ingredients and taste of foods.

28 | 0.85

2058 解釈（する）kaishaku(suru) *n.* interpretation *v.* interpret
- この文章はいくつかの解釈が可能だ。 — Several different interpretations are possible for this sentence.

28 | 0.87

2059 奪う ubau *v.* rob, take by force; fascinate
- 彼らは自由と権利をうばわれた。 — They were deprived of their rights and freedom.

28 | 0.93

2060 三ヶ月 san kagetsu *n.* three months
- 日本に来てから三ヶ月が過ぎた。 — Three months have passed since I came to Japan.

28 | 0.93

2061 注文（する）chuumon(suru) *n.* order *v.* order
- 私はコーヒーを三つ注文した。 — I ordered three coffees.

28 | 0.91

2062 傷 kizu *n.* injury; scratch; bruise; flaw; stain
- この車は傷がある。 — This car has a scratch.

28 | 0.91

2063 外国人 gaikoku-jin *n.* foreigner
- 最近外国人のお客さんの数が多くなっている。 — Recently the number of foreign customers has been increasing.

28 | 0.92

2064 八時 hachi ji *n.* eight o'clock
- 授業は八時に始まる。 — The class starts at eight.

28 | 0.51 | NM

2065 冷蔵庫 reizou-ko *n.* refrigerator
- 冷蔵庫からビールを出して。 — Get a beer out of the refrigerator.

28 | 0.89

2066 任せる makaseru *v.* entrust, leave
- それは私に任せて。 — Leave it to me.

28 | 0.96

2067 配慮（する）hairyo(suru) *n.* consideration *v.* consider
- 我が社は環境に十分配慮しております。 — My company is greatly concerned about the environment.

28 | 0.67

2068 赤 aka *n.* red
- 好きな色は赤です。 — My favorite color is red.

28 | 0.94

2069 かぶる kaburu *v.* put on, cover
- 外に出るなら帽子をかぶりなさい。 — Put your hat on if you go outside.

28 | 0.94

2070 海外旅行 kaigai ryokou *n.* travel abroad, foreign trip
- 今年の夏海外旅行に行くつもりだ。— I am going to travel abroad this summer.

28 | 0.67

2071 営業（する） eigyou(suru) *n.* business, sales *v.* do business
- 私は営業を担当しています。— I am in charge of sales.

28 | 0.97

2072 水 sui *n.* Wed(nesday)
- 授業は水曜にあります。— The class will be held on Wednesday.

28 | 0.15 | NM

2073 なるほど naruhodo *adv.* I see, indeed, to be sure, of course
- なるほど。それで彼のことが嫌いなんだ。— I see. That's why you hate him.

27 | 0.92

2074 空港 kuukou *n.* airport
- 空港に友達を見送りに行った。— I went to the airport to see my friend off.

27 | 0.91

2075 交換（する） koukan(suru) *n.* exchange *v.* exchange
- クリスマスにはパーティーをしてプレゼントを交換する。— We have a party and exchange gifts at Christmas.

27 | 0.92

2076 生える haeru *v.* grow, sprout, cut (teeth),
- 息子はまだ歯が生えていない。— My son hasn't cut his first tooth yet.

27 | 0.89

2077 防ぐ fusegu *v.* defend, protect; prevent, keep away
- 彼らは交通事故を防ぐためのキャンペーンを始めた。— They began a campaign to prevent traffic accidents.

27 | 0.91

2078 ホームページ hoomupeeji *n.* home page
- 詳しくは弊社のホームページをご覧ください。— For more details, visit our website.

27 | 0.77

2079 妊娠（する） ninshin(suru) *n.* pregnancy *v.* get pregnant
- 彼女は妊娠している。— She is pregnant.

27 | 0.80

2080 貸す kasu *v.* lend, rent
- ペンを貸していただけますか。— Would you lend me your pen?

27 | 0.95

2081 ママ mama *n.* mom, mummy
- おやすみなさい、ママ。— Good night, mom.

27 | 0.82

2082 空く aku *v.* become vacant, be free
- この後空いてる？— Are you free after this?

27 | 0.88

2083 危ない abunai *i-adj.* dangerous, risky; questionable
- そこに一人で行くのは危ないよ。— It's dangerous to go there alone.

27 | 0.89

2084 まっすぐ massugu *n.* straight, direct *adv.* honest
- まっすぐ歩けないほど彼は酔っ払った。— He got so drunk that he was unable to walk straight.

27 | 0.91

2085 映像 eizou *n.* picture, image, video
- 防犯カメラの映像が証拠として使われた。— Video from a security camera was used as evidence.

27 | 0.93

2086 壊れる kowareru *v.* be broken, be damaged; be destroyed
- コンピュータが壊れている。— My computer is broken.

27 | 0.85

2087 破壊（する） hakai(suru) *n.* destruction, demolition *v.* destroy, demolish
- 私たちは自然環境を破壊している。— We are destroying the natural environment.

27 | 0.95

2088 削除（する） sakujo(suru) *n.* deletion *v.* delete
- このファイルは削除してください。— Please delete this file.

27 | 0.50 | WB

2089 派遣（する） haken(suru) *n., v.* dispatch, send
- 多くの国が日本に救助隊を派遣した。— Many countries sent rescue teams to Japan.

27 | 0.87

2090 カード kaado *n.* card
- カードで払ってもいいですか。— Can I pay by credit card?

27 | 0.92

2091 改正（する） kaisei(suru) *n.* amendment *v.* amend
- その法律は1999年に改正された。— The law was amended in 1999.

27 | 0.54 | OF

2092 世間 seken *n.* world, public, society
- 世間の目なんて気にしない。— I don't care how society sees us.

27 | 0.91

2093 手伝う tetsudau *v.* help
- 宿題を手伝ってくれませんか。— Can you help with my homework?

27 | 0.89

2094 社員 shain *n.* employee, member of staff
- 彼はうちの社員です。— He is an employee of our company.
27 | 0.99

2095 月 getsu *n.* Monday, Mon.
- ごみの日は月・木です。— The garbage collection days are Monday and Thursday.
27 | 0.15 | NM

2096 信頼(する) shinrai(suru) *n., v.* trust, rely on
- 彼は上司から信頼されている。— He is trusted by his boss.
27 | 0.96

2097 沿う sou *v.* go along; in line with, according to, meet
- 私達は川に沿って歩いた。— We walked along the river.
27 | 0.89

2098 輝く kagayaku *v.* shine, glitter, twinkle, glow
- たくさんの星が空に輝いている。— Many stars are shining in the sky.
27 | 0.82

2099 三時 san ji *n.* three o'clock
- 三時までに必ず来てください。— Be sure to come here by three o'clock.
27 | 0.35 | NM

2100 ペット petto *n.* pet
- ペットを飼おうと思っている。— I think I'll get a pet.
27 | 0.75

2101 世 yo *n.* world, public; age, reign
- その大学は十一万人以上の卒業生を世に送り出した。— The university has turned out over 110,000 graduates.
27 | 0.86

2102 不可能 fu-kanou *na-adj.* impossible *n.* impossibility
- アイディアはすばらしいが、不可能だ。— The idea is wonderful, but it's impossible.
27 | 0.94

2103 襲う osou *v.* attack, hit; seize
- 昨夜女性が三人の男に襲われた。— A woman was attacked by three men last night.
27 | 0.90

2104 問 mon *n.* question number; counter for questions
- テストで一問だけ間違えてしまった。— I got only one answer incorrect in the test.
27 | 0.27 | NM

2105 サイト saito *n.* website
- 面白いサイトを見つけた。— I found an interesting site on the web.
27 | 0.40 | WB

2106 ボランティア borantia *n.* volunteer
- ボランティアの人たちが公園の掃除を手伝っている。— Volunteers are helping to clean up the park.
27 | 0.89

2107 問題点 mondai ten *n.* problem, point at issue
- この計画の問題点は費用だ。— The problem of this plan is the cost.
27 | 0.82

2108 一人一人 hitorihitori *n.* one by one, each (people)
- 私は子供達一人一人に手紙を書いた。— I wrote a letter to each of my children.
27 | 0.91

2109 サイズ saizu *n.* size
- もっと大きいサイズがありますか。— Do you have a larger size?
27 | 0.80

2110 建設(する) kensetsu(suru) *n.* construction *v.* build, construct
- 新しい空港の建設は1999年に始まった。— The construction of the new airport started in 1999.
27 | 0.78

2111 線 sen *n.* line
- 紙に鉛筆で一本線を引いてください。— Draw a line on the paper with a pencil.
27 | 0.96

2112 子育て kosodate *n.* child rearing, bringing up one's child
- 子育ては長くて大変な仕事だ。— Child rearing is a long, hard job.
27 | 0.88

2113 (お)願い(する) (o)negai(suru) *n., v.* wish, hope
- ついに私の願いがかなった。— At last my wish came true.
27 | 0.95

2114 よろしい yoroshii *i-adj.* all right, good, may (I) (formal)
- ひとつお願いしてもよろしいですか。— May I ask you a favor?
27 | 0.84

2115 二十分 nijup-pun, nijip-pun, *n.* twenty minutes
- 彼は二十分遅れて着いた。— He arrived twenty minutes late.
27 | 0.84

2116 モデル moderu *n.* model
- この携帯電話は最新モデルです。— This phone is the latest model.
27 | 0.90

2117 余計 yokei *na-adj.* additional, extra
- その本に余計にお金を払ってしまった。— I paid more than enough for the book.
27 | 0.92

2118 引き続く hikitsuzuku *v.* continue; follow
- 今年も引き続きご支援をお願いいたします。— We would appreciate your continued support this year.
27 | 0.50 | OF

2119 移す utsusu *v.* move, transfer, shift
- 彼は事務所をパリからベルリンに移した。— He transferred his office from Paris to Berlin.
27 | 0.97

2120 募集(する) boshuu(suru) *n.* recruitment *v.* recruit
- ちょうど今、その会社が社員を募集している。— Right now, the company is recruiting new staff.
27 | 0.52 | NM

2121 りんご ringo *n.* apple
- 果物でりんごが一番好き。— I like apples best of all the fruits.
27 | 0.91

2122 まずい mazui *i-adj.* not taste good; awkward
- まずい!また遅刻だ。— Oh no! I'm late again.
27 | 0.89

2123 食料 shokuryou *n.* food, provisions
- 私はキャンプのとき、たくさん食料を持って行く。— I take a lot of food when I go camping.
27 | 0.80

2124 優勝(する) yuushou(suru) *n.* championship, victory *v.* win
- 彼女はスピーチコンテストで優勝した。— She won the speech contest.
27 | 0.75

2125 間 kan *n.* during; between
- このバスは東京、大阪間を走っている。— This bus runs between Tokyo and Osaka.
27 | 0.89

2126 属する zokusuru *v.* belong to, be a member of
- 彼はサッカーチームに属している。— He plays in a soccer team.
27 | 0.82

2127 豊富 houfu *na-adj.* rich, abundant
- 彼は経験が豊富だ。— He has a lot of experience.
27 | 0.92

2128 消費者 shouhi-sha *n.* consumer
- 我々は消費者のニーズに対応しなければならない。— We must meet the needs of consumers.
27 | 0.77

2129 喉 nodo *n.* throat; voice
- 喉が痛い。— I have a sore throat.
27 | 0.86

2130 布団 futon *n.* futon, Japanese-style bedding
- 布団に寝るのは心地好い。— It is comfortable to sleep on a futon.
27 | 0.84

2131 十五分 juu go fun *n.* fifteen minutes
- 15分電車が遅れた。— The train was fifteen minutes late.
27 | 0.85

2132 宇宙 uchuu *n.* universe, space
- 宇宙には何百万もの星がある。— There are millions of stars in the universe.
27 | 0.95

2133 同じく onajiku *adv.* likewise, like, as
- 彼も私と同じく疲れているはずだ。— I'm sure he is as tired as I am.
27 | 0.98

2134 資金 shikin *n.* funds
- 資金が足りなかったため、計画は失敗してしまった。— Owing to a shortage of funds our project failed.
27 | 0.84

2135 しかたない shikatanai *i-adj.* It can't be helped, be beyond any help, I can't help …
- この問題についてこれ以上考えてもしかたない。— There is no point in dwelling on this matter any more.
27 | 0.75

2136 料金 ryoukin *n.* charge, fee, fare
- 料金は着いてから払ってください。— Pay your fee when you get there.
27 | 0.87

2137 デパート depaato *n.* department store
- デパートに買い物に行った。— I went shopping at a department store.
26 | 0.78

2138 地図 chizu *n.* map
- 迷わないように地図を持って行って。— Take a map with you so that you don't get lost.
26 | 0.99

2139 唇 kuchibiru *n.* lip
- 寒くて唇が青くなった。— It was so cold that my lips were turning blue.
26 | 0.68

2140 釣り tsuri *n.* fishing
- 先週近くの川に釣りに行った。— I went fishing in a nearby river last week.
26 | 0.76

2141 十五日 juu go nichi *n.* fifteenth (date); fifteen days
- 両親は三月十五日まで日本にいた。— My parents stayed in Japan until March 15.
26 | 0.54

2142 駅前 ekimae *n.* in front of the station
- 昨日の晩は駅前のホテルに泊まった。— I stayed at a hotel in front of the station last night.
26 | 0.66

2143 つつある tsutsu aru *cp.* be in the process of doing, be doing
- 日本では子供の数が減りつつある。— In Japan, the number of children is decreasing.
26 | 0.75

2144 ご覧 goran *n.* looking, seeing (honorific)
- 結果はご覧の通りです。— The results are like this, as you can see.
26 | 0.78

2145 大会 taikai *n.* convention, mass meeting, tournament
- 彼女は昨年五つの大会で優勝した。— She won five tournaments last year.
26 | 0.79

2146 拾う hirou *v.* pick up, gather, pick out
- 駐車場で誰かの財布を拾った。— I found someone's wallet in the car park.
26 | 0.89

2147 いざ iza *adv.* when one comes to, if compelled
- いざというときのためにお金を貯めている。— I set aside some money just in case of an emergency.
26 | 0.93

2148 二番目 ni ban-me *n.* second
- 大阪は日本で二番目に大きい都市です。— Osaka is the second largest city in Japan.
26 | 0.85

2149 良さ yo-sa *n.* good point, good
- このワインは味の良さで知られている。— This wine is known for its good taste.
26 | 0.90

2150 たって tat-te *p.* even if
- 走ったって間に合わない。— Even if you ran, you couldn't make it.
26 | 0.92

2151 素材 sozai *n.* material
- あなたの洋服の素材は何ですか。— What material are your clothes made of?
26 | 0.84

2152 設立(する) setsuritsu(suru) *n.* establishment *v.* establish, set up
- 彼は新しい会社を設立した。— He set up a new company.
26 | 0.79

2153 なので na no de *conj.* because, as
- 彼はまだ高校生なので、お酒を飲ませてはいけない。— We should not let him drink alcohol, because he is still a high school student.
26 | 0.49 | WB

2154 絞る shiboru *v.* squeeze
- このレモンを絞ってください。— Please squeeze the juice from this lemon.
26 | 0.99

2155 ところで tokoro de *conj.* by the way, well
- ところで、明日は何か予定がありますか。— By the way, do you have any plans for tomorrow?
26 | 0.84

2156 江戸 edo *n.* Edo
- 東京は昔、江戸と呼ばれていた。— Tokyo was called Edo in the past.
26 | 0.86

2157 下る kudaru *v.* go down
- 彼は自転車で坂を下っていた。— He went down the hill on a bicycle.
26 | 0.90

2158 二十 nijuu *num.* twenty
- この容器は20リットル入る。— This container can hold twenty liters.
26 | 0.87

2159 反映(する) han'ei(suru) *n.* reflection *v.* reflect
- 世論はなかなか政治には反映されない。— It takes time for public opinions to be reflected in politics.
26 | 0.77

2160 天気 tenki *n.* weather
- 天気がよければ富士山が見える。— If the weather is good, you can see Mt. Fuji.
26 | 0.72

2161 作家 sakka *n.* writer
- 彼女は有名な作家です。— She is a famous writer.
26 | 0.86

2162 減らす herasu *v.* reduce, cut down
- 予算が減らされた。— The budget has been cut.
26 | 0.97

2163 十五 juu go *n.* fifteen
- この土地は15ヘクタールある。— This land is fifteen hectares.
26 | 0.90

2164 ゴルフ gorufu *n.* golf
- 父の趣味はゴルフです。— My father's hobby is playing golf.
26 | 0.84

2165 敷く shiku *v.* spread, lay
- 床にカーペットを敷いた。— I spread a carpet on the floor.
26 | 0.94

2166 合格（する）goukaku(suru) *n.* passing an exam *v.* pass an exam
- 弟はその試験に合格した。— My brother passed the exam.
26 | 0.93

2167 日常 nichijou *n., adv.* everyday, daily, usually
- それが彼の日常の仕事だ。— That's his daily work.
26 | 0.97

2168 毎回 maikai *n.* every time
- 雨が降ると毎回屋根が漏る。— The roof leaks every time it rains.
26 | 0.80

2169 影 kage *n.* shadow
- 木の影が地面に映っている。— The shadow of a tree falls on the ground.
26 | 0.86

2170 うるさい urusai *i-adj.* noisy; annoying
- うるさいな、ほっといてよ。— Don't bother me. Just leave me alone.
26 | 0.85

2171 法 hou *n.* law
- 法の下に人は平等だ。— All men are equal under the law.
26 | 0.82

2172 罪 tsumi *n.* crime; guilt
- 彼は罪を認めた。— He pleaded guilty.
26 | 0.90

2173 まるい marui *i-adj.* round, circular
- 子供達はまるくなって座った。— The children sat in a circle.
26 | 0.92

2174 団体 dantai *n.* party, group, organization
- 彼らは団体で京都観光に行った。— They went on a group tour to Kyoto.
26 | 0.85

2175 詳細 shousai *n.* details *na-adj.* detailed
- 彼はその出来事について詳細に説明した。— He explained in detail what was going on.
26 | 0.80

2176 洋服 youfuku *n.* clothes, suit, dress
- その洋服を着ると素敵に見えますよ。— You look great in the dress.
26 | 0.87

2177 承知（する）shouchi(suru) *n.* agreement *v.* agree, understand
- 承知しました。— I understand.
26 | 0.58

2178 多数 tasuu *n.* many, a number of
- その事故で多数の死者が出た。— Many people died in the accident.
26 | 0.89

2179 運営（する）un'ei(suru) *n.* management *v.* manage, run
- そのイベントはうまく運営されている。— The event is well managed.
26 | 0.82

2180 生き方 iki-kata *n.* way of life
- いろいろな生き方がある。— There are many ways of life.
26 | 0.95

2181 備える sonaeru *v.* get something ready, prepare
- 災害に備えて水や食料を買っておく。— I store water and food ready for a disaster.
26 | 0.87

2182 おしゃれ oshare *na-adj.* fashionable, smart
- おしゃれなレストランで夕食を食べる。— We have dinner at a fashionable restaurant.
26 | 0.79

2183 住宅 juutaku *n.* house, residence
- 住宅を購入するお金がない。— I don't have enough money to buy a house.
26 | 0.83

2184 考慮（する）kouryo(suru) *n.* thought *v.* think over, consider
- その点については十分考慮するつもりです。— I will give careful consideration to that point.
26 | 0.81

2185 働き hataraki *n.* work
- 朝は頭の働きが良い。— My brain works well in the morning.
26 | 0.93

2186 踏む fumu *v.* step on, tread on
- 誰かに足を踏まれた。— Somebody stepped on my foot.
26 | 0.96

2187 ファイル fairu *n.* file
- そのファイルを取ってください。— Please pass me that file.
26 | 0.84

2188 有り ari *v., n.* exist; live
- 異議あり！— Objection!
26 | 0.89

2189 要因 youin *n.* factor, main cause
- その問題には複雑な要因がからんでいる。— There are some complicated factors involved in the problem.
26 | 0.79

2190 わし washi *n.* I (used by old men)
- わしは若い頃漁師じゃった。— I was a fisherman when I was young.
26 | 0.63

2191 火 ka *n.* fire; Tuesday, Tue.
- 毎週火、水、木は大学へ行く。— I go to the university on Tuesday, Wednesday, and Thursday every week.
26 | 0.15 | NM

2192 偶然 guuzen *adv.* by chance *n.* chance, accident
- 偶然、駅で彼女と会った。— I met her by chance at the station.
26 | 0.89

2193 だって dat-te *conj.* because, but
- 「どうして食べないの」「だって、ダイエット中なんだもん」 — "Why don't you eat it?" "Because I'm on a diet."
26 | 0.75

2194 不満 fuman *n.* dissatisfaction, discontent *na-adj.* discontented
- 彼女は不満ばかり言う。— She always complains.
26 | 0.99

2195 クラブ kurabu *n.* club
- 学校で何のクラブに入ろうか考えている。— I'm thinking about which club I should join at school.
26 | 0.85

2196 懐かしい natsukashii *i-adj.* nostalgic
- 故郷が懐かしい。— I feel nostalgic about my home town.
26 | 0.86

2197 ページ peeji *n.* page
- 教科書の五ページを開けてください。— Open your textbook at page five.
26 | 0.86

11 House

(frequency per million words)

(住居) (Housing)
家 ie 443.741 **house, home**
部屋 heya 190.494 **room**
マンション manshon 56.961 **apartment, condominium, flat**
窓 mado 54.582 **window**
ドア doa 54.383 **door**
トイレ toire 50.843 **toilet, restroom, bathroom**
庭 niwa 46.799 **garden, yard**
風呂 furo 41.992 **bath**
我が家 wagaya 38.965 **one's house, one's family, one's home**
階段 kaidan 36.668 **stairs**
床 yuka 35.172 **floor**
玄関 genkan 29.521 **entrance, front door**
アパート apaato 28.864 **apartment**
住宅 juutaku 25.745 **house, residence**
扉 tobira 22.815 **door**
廊下 rouka 22.782 **corridor**
屋根 yane 20.859 **roof top**
柱 hashira 20.110 **pillar, post**
門 mon 18.381 **gate**
お宅 otaku 17.893 **your house**

台所 daidokoro 17.509 **kitchen**
天井 tenjou 17.383 **ceiling**
地下 chika 16.304 **basement (also underground)**
ガラス garasu 15.612 **glass**
団地 danchi 14.957 **housing development**
シャワー shawaa 14.522 **shower**
室内 shitsunai 12.384 **indoor**
ベランダ beranda 12.006 **porch, balcony**
屋敷 yashiki 11.255 **mansion, residence, estate**
社宅 shataku 9.222 **company house**
居間 ima 8.674 **living room**
寝室 shinshitsu 8.182 **bedroom**
風呂場 furoba 3.005 **bathroom**
洗面所 senmen-jo 2.000 **lavatory**

(暮らし・その他) (Living, etc.)
住む sumu 362.306 **live**
暮らす kurasu 76.712 **live**
引っ越し(する) hikkoshi(suru) 29.672 **moving, removal; move house**
住所 juusho 28.208 **address**
暮らし kurashi 20.363 **life, livelihood**
家賃 yachin 13.963 **rent**
大家 ooya[1] 11.607 **landlord, owner**

[1] Includes 大家さん *ooya-san*.

2198 止む yamu *v.* stop
- 雨が止んだ。— It has stopped raining.
26 | 0.94

2199 外れる hazureru *v.* be off, get out of place, be dislocated
- 笑いすぎてあごが外れた。— I laughed too much and dislocated my jaw.
26 | 0.96

2200 経済的 keizai-teki *na-adj.* economical; economic; financial
- 日本はその国に経済的な援助を行っている。— Japan gives the country financial support.
26 | 0.95

2201 机 tsukue *n.* desk
- 机に向かって仕事をしなければならない。— I have to sit at the desk and work.
26 | 0.90

2202 使い方 tsukai-kata *n.* how to use
- 新しい携帯電話の使い方がわからない。— I don't know how to use my new cell phone.
26 | 0.98

2203 ハワイ hawai *n.* Hawaii
- 休みはハワイに行く。— I will go to Hawaii for the holiday.
26 | 0.86

2204 予算 yosan *n.* estimate, budget
- 予算の規模を縮小しなければならない。— We have to squeeze the budget.
26 | 0.83

2205 真面目 majime *na-adj.* serious; steady; honest
- 彼は真面目な人だ。— He is a serious person.
26 | 0.88

2206 勇気 yuuki *n.* courage, bravery
- 彼女は勇気がある。— She is brave.
25 | 0.94

2207 皿 sara *n.* plate, dish
- この料理を皿に盛りつけてください。— Please put this food on the plate.
25 | 0.93

2208 ありがたい arigatai *i-adj.* kind, welcome
- ありがたいことに雨が止んだ。— Luckily the rain has stopped.
25 | 0.95

2209 視点 shiten *n.* viewpoint
- 別の視点から考えてみましょう。— Let's think about it from another point of view.
25 | 0.89

2210 素直 sunao *na-adj.* obedient, tame
- 彼女はとても素直です。— She is very obedient.
25 | 0.91

2211 表面 hyoumen *n.* surface, outside, appearance
- この紙の表面はざらざらしている。— The surface of this paper is rough.
25 | 0.98

2212 コピー（する） kopii(suru) *n., v.* copy
- この書類をコピーしてください。— Please copy this document.
25 | 0.90

2213 削る kezuru *v.* save; sharpen, plane
- 鉛筆を削ってください。— Please sharpen a pencil for me.
25 | 0.95

2214 部活 bukatsu *n.* club
- 放課後は部活があるので、息子はいつも五時ごろ帰ってきます。— My son usually comes home around 5 p.m., because he participates in club activities after school.
25 | 0.52

2215 サラリーマン sarariiman *n.* salaried worker, office worker
- 父はサラリーマンです。— My father is an office worker.
25 | 0.89

2216 制限（する） seigen(suru) *n.* restriction *v.* limit, restrict
- その国との貿易は制限されている。— Trade with the country is restricted.
25 | 0.89

2217 実験（する） jikken(suru) *n.* experimentation *v.* experiment
- 彼らは実験室で実験している。— They are doing an experiment in the lab.
25 | 0.89

2218 ニューヨーク nyuuyooku *n.* New York
- 田中さんはニューヨークへ出張しています。— Mr. Tanaka is in New York on business.
25 | 0.92

2219 確かめる tashikameru *v.* confirm, make sure
- ドアに鍵をかけたか確かめましたか。— Did you make sure you locked the door?
25 | 0.93

2220 東 higashi *n.* east
- 太陽は東から昇る。— The sun rises in the east.
25 | 0.90

2221 主人公 shujin-kou *n.* hero, heroine
- この映画の主人公は誰ですか。— Who is the heroine of this film?
25 | 0.90

2222 もっとも mottomo *conj.* though, although
- もっとも彼の言うことは正しいが、私は賛成できない。— Though what he said is right, I can't agree.
25 | 0.78

2223 アメリカ人 amerika-jin *n.* American (person)
- 彼はアメリカ人です。— He is an American.
25 | 0.82

2224 テスト(する) tesuto(suru) *n.* test *v.* test
- 数学のテストを受けた。— I took a math test.
25 | 0.93

2225 高校時代 koukou jidai *n.* high school days
- 高校時代はとても楽しかった。— My high school days were very happy.
25 | 0.59

2226 満足(する) manzoku(suru) *n.* satisfaction *v.* be satisfied
- 私は今の生活に満足している。— I'm satisfied with my life now.
25 | 0.93

2227 愛情 aijou *n.* love, affection
- 愛情をこめて料理を作る。— I cook with love.
25 | 0.92

2228 微妙 bimyou *na-adj.* delicate, subtle
- それは微妙な問題だ。— That is a delicate issue.
25 | 0.89

2229 生み出す umidasu *v.* create, invent
- そのアーティストはここで多くの作品を生みだした。— The artist created a lot of works here.
25 | 0.90

2230 ビル biru *n.* building
- ここに新しいビルが建設される。— A new building will be built here.
25 | 0.94

2231 あらかじめ arakajime *adv.* beforehand, in advance
- そのイベントに参加する場合は、あらかじめ私に知らせてください。— Please let me know in advance if you participate in the event.
25 | 0.94

2232 財産 zaisan *n.* property; fortune
- 彼女の財産はどのくらいあるんだろう。— What is the value of her fortune?
25 | 0.88

2233 証拠 shouko *n.* evidence
- 証拠が明らかなので、彼は有罪になるだろう。— The evidence is clear, so he will be found guilty.
25 | 0.91

2234 我 ware *pron.* I; oneself
- 金もうけに我を忘れてしまった。— I got carried away with making money.
25 | 0.77

2235 訓練(する) kunren(suru) *n.* training *v.* train
- その犬はよく訓練されている。— The dog is well trained.
25 | 0.95

2236 区別(する) kubetsu(suru) *n.* distinction *v.* distinguish
- この偽物は本物と区別がつかない。— I can't distinguish this fake from the real thing.
25 | 0.90

2237 四日 yok-ka *n.* fourth (date); four days
- あと四日しかない。— We have only four days left.
25 | 0.64

2238 サークル saakuru *n.* circle, club
- 私はテニスのサークルに入りたい。— I want to join a tennis club.
25 | 0.66

2239 皆様 mina-sama *n.* everybody
- 皆様、お早うございます。— Good morning, everybody.
25 | 0.78

2240 光景 koukei *n.* sight, spectacle
- それは不思議な光景だった。— It was a strange sight.
25 | 0.88

2241 パターン pataan *n.* pattern
- 彼の小説のストーリーはいつも同じパターンの繰り返しだ。— The stories of his novels all follow the same pattern.
25 | 0.97

2242 シーン shiin *n.* scene
- 映画のこのシーンが好きです。— I like this scene in the film.
25 | 0.86

2243 新鮮 shinsen *na-adj.* fresh
- この魚は新鮮ですか。— Is this fish fresh?
25 | 0.87

2244 恵まれる megumareru *v.* be blessed
- 恵まれない子供達のために寄付した。— I made a donation for unfortunate children.
25 | 0.98

2245 煮る niru *v.* boil, cook
- 水を加えて十分ぐらい煮てください。— Add some water, and cook for ten minutes.
25 | 0.92

2246 旨 mune *n.* effect; principle
- 学校はその生徒に退学になる旨を警告した。— The school warned the student that he would be expelled.
25 | 0.55

2247 反省（する）hansei(suru) *n.* soul-searching, reflection *v.* reflect on
- 前回の反省を生かして作業する。— He works making the best use of reflections on previous issues.
25 | 0.99

2248 放送（する）housou(suru) *n.* broadcasting, telecasting *v.* broadcast
- ドラマの再放送を見る。— I watch a repeat broadcast of the TV drama.
25 | 0.93

2249 人間関係 ningen kankei *n.* interpersonal relationship
- いい人間関係を作るには信頼が大切だ。— Trust is vital in order to establish a good relationship.
25 | 0.94

2250 ボタン botan *n.* button
- シャツからボタンがとれた。— A button came off the shirt.
25 | 0.86

2251 少女 shoujo *n.* girl
- あのピアノを弾いている少女はまだ八歳だ。— The girl who's playing the piano is only eight.
25 | 0.82

2252 命ずる meizuru *v.* order
- 自衛隊の出動を命じた。— He ordered the dispatch of the Self-Defense Force.
25 | 0.72

2253 自己 jiko *n.* oneself, self
- 自己を肯定することは大切だ。— It's important to hold a positive view of yourself.
25 | 0.80

2254 ロンドン rondon *n.* London
- 来月、ロンドンに留学する。— From next month, I'll be studying in London.
25 | 0.87

2255 端 hashi *n.* end, tip, edge
- きれの両端を持って伸ばす。— I stretch the cloth, holding the ends.
25 | 0.91

2256 加わる kuwawaru *v.* increase, add; join
- クラスに新しい生徒が加わる。— A new member is joining our class.
25 | 0.92

2257 規模 kibo *n.* scale
- 会社の規模を拡大する。— He expanded the scale of the company.
25 | 0.82

2258 悩み nayami *n.* trouble, worry
- 悩みを友人に相談する。— I'll speak to my friend about my worries.
25 | 0.94

2259 鳴る naru *v.* sound; ring
- 誰かの携帯電話が鳴っている。— Someone's cell phone is ringing.
25 | 0.87

2260 運 un *n.* luck, fortune
- 彼女は運がいい。— She is lucky.
25 | 0.84

2261 ルール ruuru *n.* rule
- クラブのルールをみんなで決める。— The rules of the club are made by all the members.
25 | 0.98

2262 妙 myou *na-adj.* strange, curious
- 妙なうわさを耳にした。— I heard a strange rumor.
25 | 0.85

2263 告げる tsugeru *v.* tell, announce
- 医者は彼女の病気について家族に告げた。— The doctor told her family about her illness.
25 | 0.83

2264 恋 koi *n.* love (romantic)
- 彼女は今恋をしている。— She's in love with someone now.
25 | 0.82

2265 現象 genshou *n.* phenomenon, happening; phase
- 小さな現象だが、丁寧に観察することが大事だ。— Although this is a minor phenomenon, it requires careful observation.
25 | 0.91

2266 ベース beesu *n.* base, basis
- このスープのベースとなるのは、しょうゆだ。— Soy sauce forms the base for this soup.
25 | 0.94

2267 ネット netto *n.* net
- ネットで友達とチャットする。— My friend and I chat online.
25 | 0.63 | WB

2268 許可（する）kyoka(suru) *n.* permission, leave *v.* permit, authorize
- 車を止めるには、許可が必要だ。— You need permission to park your car there.
25 | 0.68

2269 商売 shoubai *n.* business
- 新しい商売を始める準備をする。— We've been preparing for a new business.
25 | 0.91

2270 積む tsumu *v.* pile up, heap up; acquire, accumulate
- 失敗しても経験を積むことは大切だ。— It is important to gain some experience even if you fail.
25 | 0.97

2271 文句 monku *n.* words; complaint
- 彼は一言も文句を言わない。— He never makes any complaints.
25 | 0.88

2272 発想 hassou *n.* idea, conception
- 柔軟な発想が求められる。— Flexible ideas are needed.
25 | 0.97

2273 見なす minasu *v.* be considered, look upon
- 入金した日を契約初日とみなします。— The day on which the payment is made is considered to be the first day of the contract.
25 | 0.69

2274 親戚 shinseki *n.* relative
- お正月に親戚が集まる。— Our relatives will gather together for New Year.
25 | 0.84

2275 大幅 oohaba *na-adj.* steep, big, sharp
- 経営について大幅な見直しをする。— They will carry out a major review of management.
25 | 0.63

2276 アドバイス adobaisu *n.* advice
- 周りからのアドバイスを参考にする。— I take everyone's advice into account.
25 | 0.78

2277 ダイエット(する) daietto(suru) *n.* diet *v.* go on a diet
- 今年こそダイエットをする。— I'll go on a diet this year.
25 | 0.75

2278 生命 seimei *n.* life
- 彼女は今、生命の危機にさらされている。— Her life is in danger now.
25 | 0.88

2279 中央 chuuou *n.* center *adj.* central
- あの公園の中央に像がある。— There is a statue in the center of that park.
24 | 0.90

2280 発行(する) hakkou(suru) *n.* publication, issue *v.* publish, issue
- 新しい問題集が出版社から発行される。— A new issue of the exam practice book will come out.
24 | 0.87

2281 ほめる homeru *v.* praise, speak well, commend
- あの人はいつも周りの人をほめる。— She always speaks well of others.
24 | 0.90

2282 カナダ kanada *n.* Canada
- カナダへ語学留学へ行く。— I'll be travelling to Canada to study English.
24 | 0.91

2283 請求(する) seikyuu(suru) *n.* demand, request, charge *v.* demand, claim
- 代金を請求する。— A request for payment has been made.
24 | 0.86

2284 企画(する) kikaku(suru) *n.* planning *v.* plan
- 彼らは、新入社員を歓迎する企画を準備している。— They are planning a welcome event for new recruits.
24 | 0.91

2285 話し合う hanashiau *v.* talk, discuss
- 大切なことはみんなで話し合おう。— Let's discuss important issues with everyone.
24 | 0.97

2286 注ぐ sosogu *v.* flow into; water; pour
- ビールをコップに注ぐ。— He's pouring beer into a glass.
24 | 0.92

2287 増す masu *v.* increase
- 緊張が増していく。— Tension has been increasing.
24 | 0.95

2288 浴びる abiru *v.* bathe; pour
- シャワーを浴びるね。— I'll take a shower.
24 | 0.94

2289 縁 en *n.* chance, fate, destiny
- 私はお金に縁がない。— I am hopeless when it comes to making money.
24 | 0.89

2290 吐く haku *v.* exhale, breathe out; vomit; spit
- 気持ち悪くて、トイレで吐いた。— I was sick and threw up in the toilet.
24 | 0.91

2291 渋谷 shibuya *n.* Shibuya (place name)
- 渋谷で友達とよく買い物をする。— I often go shopping with friends in Shibuya.
24 | 0.74

2292 間違える machigaeru *v.* make a mistake
- いつも同じ漢字を間違える。— I always make the same kanji mistakes.
24 | 0.84

2293 セット setto *n.* set
- ハンバーガーセットを注文する。— We ordered a hamburger set meal.
24 | 0.88

2294 てはならない te wa nara nai *cp.* must not, should not
- お酒を飲んだら、車を運転してはならない。— You should not drive when you drink.
24 | 0.76

2295 明かり akari *n.* light
- 明かりをつける。— I turn the light on.
24 | 0.86

2296 玉ねぎ tamanegi *n.* onion
- 玉ねぎを切ってフライパンで炒めてください。— Chop an onion and fry it in a frying pan.
24 | 0.94

2297 しかない shika nai *cp.* can't but, can only, have no choice
- 今やるしかない。— We must do it now.
24 | 0.82

2298 合計(する) goukei(suru) *n.* sum total *v.* total
- 彼の部屋には合計百冊以上の本がある。— He has a total of over a hundred books in his room.
24 | 0.82

2299 良し yoshi *i-adj.* good, OK
- よし、これでおしまい。— OK, that's it.
24 | 0.94

2300 二本 ni hon *n.* two (long/cylindrical objects)
- ビールを二本飲む。— I drink two bottles of beer.
24 | 0.94

2301 御 o *prefix* POLITENESS
- お食事はいかがですか。— Would you like something to eat?
24 | 0.51

2302 貴重 kichou *na-adj.* precious, valuable
- 貴重な経験を積む。— I will gain valuable experience.
24 | 0.97

2303 引っ張る hipparu *v.* pull
- このチームを引っ張るためには強いリーダーシップが必要だ。— He needs a strong character to lead the team.
24 | 0.96

2304 城 shiro *n.* castle
- この城は江戸時代に築かれた。— This castle was built in the Edo period.
24 | 0.87

2305 対処(する) taisho(suru) *n.* handling, coping *v.* deal with
- 緊急時の対処法について学ぶ。— We learn how to deal with emergencies.
24 | 0.74

2306 覆う oou *v.* cover
- 仮面で顔を覆って変装する。— I cover my face with a mask to disguise myself.
24 | 0.90

2307 教授 kyouju *n.* professor
- 教授の書いた論文を読んでいる。— I'm reading the article written by the professor.
24 | 0.85

2308 橋 hashi *n.* bridge
- 橋の上で花火を見た。— We watched the fireworks from the bridge.
24 | 0.95

2309 巨大 kyodai *na-adj.* huge, enormous, gigantic
- 巨大なプロジェクトを任される。— He is assigned a huge project.
24 | 0.88

2310 あちらこちら achirakochira *pron.* here and there
- いなくなった愛犬を、あちらこちら探し回った。— I searched everywhere for my missing dog.
24 | 0.47

2311 苦手 nigate *na-adj.* not good at, weak point
- 私は英語が苦手です。— I'm not good at English.
24 | 0.82

2312 スタイル sutairu *n.* style, body, figure
- 彼女はスタイルがいい。— She has a great body.
24 | 0.80

2313 テント tento *n.* tent
- テントを川のそばに張った。— We put up a tent near the river.
24 | 0.69

2314 ユダヤ人 yudaya-jin *n.* Jew
- ユダヤ人の友達を訪ねる。— I visit my Jewish friend.
24 | 0.61

2315 主 nushi *n.* head, master
- この家の主は今出かけています。— The owner of the house has been away.
24 | 0.75

2316 意志 ishi *n.* will, willpower
- 彼は強い意志を持っている。— He has a strong will.
24 | 0.88

2317 容易 youi *na-adj.* easy
- あの人を説得するのは容易ではない。— It's not easy to persuade him.
24 | 0.83

2318 しばしば shibashiba *adv.* always, often
- 祖母は記憶をなくすことがしばしばある。— My grandmother very often loses her memory.
24 | 0.82

2319 のんびり nonbiri *adv.* tranquil, leisurely, easygoing
- のんびり休日を過ごした。— I spent my holiday in a leisurely way.
24 | 0.84

2320 話しかける hanashikakeru *v.* speak to
- 迷子になっている子に、店員がやさしく話しかけた。— A shop assistant spoke gently to the child who was lost.
24 | 0.87

2321 揃える soroeru *v.* arrange, prepare
- 生活必需品をそろえる。— We provide daily necessities.
24 | 0.94

2322 毎月 maitsuki *n.* every month
- 毎月家賃を支払う。— I pay the rent every month.
24 | 0.77

2323 礼 rei *n.* bow; courtesy
- 学生たちは先生に礼をした。— Students bowed to their teacher.
24 | 0.90

2324 つぶやく tsubuyaku *v.* mutter, murmur
- 彼は小さな声でつぶやいた。— He muttered in a low voice.
24 | 0.56

2325 抵抗（する）teikou(suru) *n.* resistance *v.* resist, offer opposition
- 彼らは政府の弾圧に抵抗した。— They resisted the government's oppression.
24 | 0.94

2326 十一時 juu ichi ji *n.* eleven o'clock
- 十一時までに家に帰る必要がある。— I need to go home by eleven o'clock.
24 | 0.37 | NM

2327 恐怖 kyoufu *n.* fear, dread, terror
- 恐怖でからだが震えた。— My body shivered with fear.
24 | 0.85

2328 支配（する）shihai(suru) *n.* rule, control *v.* rule, control, govern
- 植民地支配についての本を読む。— I'm reading a book about colonial rules.
24 | 0.81

2329 右手 migite *n.* right hand
- 右手で鞄を持つ。— I hold my bag with my right hand.
24 | 0.82

2330 親しい shitashii *i-adj.* close, friendly
- 親しい友人と一緒に食事をした。— I had dinner with close friends.
24 | 0.88

2331 間違い無い machigai nai *i-adj.* must be
- 彼女が彼の娘であることは間違いない。— Without doubt she's his daughter.
24 | 0.83

2332 禁止（する）kinshi(suru) *n.* prohibition, ban *v.* prohibit, ban
- これらのことは禁止されています。— These things are prohibited.
24 | 0.92

2333 怒り ikari *n.* anger, rage, fury
- 怒りの手紙を送った。— I sent her an angry letter.
24 | 0.82

2334 本格的 honkaku-teki *na-adj.* genuine, real; full-scale
- やっと本格的に動き始めた。— They finally started to move in earnest.
24 | 0.98

2335 命令（する）meirei(suru) *n.* order, command, direction *v.* order, command
- 上司からの命令に従って仕事する。— I work following my boss's orders.
24 | 0.78

2336 四時 yo ji *n.* four o'clock
- 四時に仕事が終わる。— Work finishes at four o'clock.
24 | 0.33 | NM

2337 援助（する）enjo(suru) *n.* assistance, aid, support *v.* help, support, assist
- さまざまな国から援助を受ける。— They receive aid from different countries.
24 | 0.84

2338 二人共 futari-tomo *adv.* both of them, two people
- 二人とも高校の時の同級生だ。— They were both my high school classmates.
24 | 0.84

2339 好む konomu *v.* like, be fond of, love, care
- 辛い料理を好んでいる。— He is fond of spicy foods.
24 | 0.92

2340 苦しむ kurushimu *v.* feel pain, suffer
- 食糧不足に苦しんでいる人を助けたい。— I want to help people suffering from food shortages.
24 | 0.98

2341 見方 mi-kata *n.* point of view, way of looking
- 人によって、ものの見方は違う。— Each person has a different point of view.
24 | 0.97

2342 介護（する）kaigo(suru) *n.* nursing, care *v.* nurse, look after
- 母の介護に必要なお金を計算する。— I calculate how much money I will need for my mother's care.
24 | 0.93

2343 成績 seiseki *n.* record, result, grade, mark
- 彼女は成績優秀で表彰される。— She is commended for high grades.
24 | 0.96

2344 広告（する）koukoku(suru) *n.* advertisement, flyer *v.* advertise
- 広告を見て、買い物に行く。— I always check flyers when I go shopping.
24 | 0.99

2345 本日 honjitsu *n.* today
- 本日は晴天です。— It's sunny today.
24 | 0.64 | WB

2346 強調（する）kyouchou(suru) *n.* emphasis, stress *v.* emphasize, stress
- 講師は大事なポイントを強調する。— The lecturer emphasizes crucial points.
24 | 0.87

2347 大いに ooini *adv.* very, greatly
- この勉強法は大いに役に立つだろう。— This study skill will be very helpful for you.
24 | 0.93

2348 たまる tamaru *v.* bear, endure
- 負けてたまるか。— There's absolutely no way I'm losing the competition
24 | 0.87

2349 お子さん o-ko-san *n.* (someone else's) child
- お子さんは今、いくつですか。— How old are your children?
24 | 0.76

2350 実態 jittai *n.* actual situation
- その機関の実態を知ったら、驚くだろう。— You'd be surprised if you knew the organization's real situation.
24 | 0.61

2351 によれば ni yore ba *cp.* according to, ...say
- 天気予報によれば、明日は晴れるだろう。— According to the forecast, it will be sunny tomorrow.
24 | 0.72

2352 隠れる kakureru *v.* be hidden, hide
- 彼は茂みの陰に隠れた。— He hid himself behind the shrubs.
24 | 0.92

2353 埋める umeru *v.* cover, bury
- 車は雪に埋まってしまった。— Cars were buried in the snow.
24 | 0.96

2354 トップ toppu *n.* top
- その会社のトップがまた変わった。— The head of the company has changed again.
24 | 0.87

2355 依頼（する）irai(suru) *n.* request *v.* request, ask
- 出版者は新しい本の出版を彼女に依頼した。— A publisher asked her for a new book.
24 | 0.97

2356 もはや mohaya *adv.* now, already; not ... any longer
- もはや増税は避けられないだろう。— A tax increase will no longer be avoidable.
24 | 0.80

2357 真 shin *n.* truth; reality
- 真の自由を手に入れるために、努力を続ける。— They continue to strive to obtain true freedom.
24 | 0.88

2358 出産（する）shussan(suru) *n.* birth *v.* give birth
- 旦那さんが出産に立ち会う。— Her husband will attend the baby's birth.
23 | 0.93

2359 達成（する）tassei(suru) *n.* achievement, attainment *v.* achieve, attain
- 目標を達成するために一生懸命働く。— I work very hard to achieve my goals.
23 | 0.82

2360 申請（する）shinsei(suru) *n.* application, petition *v.* apply
- 奨学金を申請したが、却下された。— I applied for a scholarship but I was rejected.
23 | 0.74

2361 知り合う shiriau *v.* get to know
- 新しい友達と知り合う。— I got to know some new friends.
23 | 0.84

2362 親子 oyako *n.* parent and child, parents and children
- 親子で公園に出かける。— The parents and children will go out to the park.
23 | 0.74

2363 取り組み torikumi *n.* match; approach
- 仕事への取り組み方が評価された。— They evaluated my approach towards work highly.
23 | 0.63

2364 招く maneku *v.* invite
- このままでは最悪の事態を招くだろう。— This will cause the worst situation if nothing is done.
23 | 0.92

2365 二十日 hatsu-ka *n.* twentieth (date); twenty days
- 毎月二十日に給料が振り込まれる。— My salary is paid on the twentieth of each month.
23 | 0.52

2366 政治家 seiji-ka *n.* politician
- 彼の夢は政治家になることだ。— His dream is to become a politician.
23 | 0.99

2367 飛び出す tobidasu *v.* spring out; come rushing out
- 目の前に急に子供が飛び出してきた。— A child rushed out suddenly right in front of me.
23 | 0.93

2368 陥る ochiiru *v.* fall into
- あの会社は経営危機に陥っている。— That company has been in bad shape.
23 | 0.96

2369 寄せる yoseru *v.* let come near, bring near; put; be dependent on
- 彼女はあの人に大きな信頼を寄せている。— She puts a great deal of trust in him.
23 | 0.88

2370 定員 teiin *n.* capacity (people)
- この企画はすでに定員オーバーです。— This event is already overbooked.
23 | 0.16 | NM

2371 駐車場 chuusha-jou *n.* parking space, parking lot, car park
- 駅前の駐車場を探している。— I'm looking for a parking lot around the station.
23 | 0.92

2372 彼氏 kareshi *n.* boyfriend
- 彼氏を親に紹介する。— I will introduce my boyfriend to my parents.
23 | 0.42 | WB

2373 式 shiki *n.* ceremony
- 正式な式に着ていく服を探している。— I'm looking for some clothes for formal occasions.
23 | 0.92

2374 によっては ni yotte wa *cp.* depending on
- 人によっては、これをおいしいという。— It varies from person to person, but some people find this tasty.
23 | 0.00 | SP

2375 蓋 futa *n.* lid
- 鍋に蓋をしなさい。— Cover the pan with a lid.
23 | 0.95

2376 実 mi *n.* seed; berry; fruit; nut; pulp
- この木は実がたくさんなる。— This tree bears a lot of fruit.
23 | 0.44 | SP

2377 社会人 shakai-jin *n.* adult; full member of society
- 弟はこの四月に社会人になる。— My brother will start working this April.
23 | 0.80

2378 墓 haka *n.* grave
- 墓参りに行った。— I visited the grave.
23 | 0.88

2379 十三 juu san *num.* thirteen
- 十三は不吉な数字だと思う人もいる。— There are some people who believe that thirteen is an unlucky number.
23 | 0.86

2380 宿 yado *n.* inn, hotel
- 静かな宿に泊まった。— I stayed in a quiet hotel.
23 | 0.88

2381 都心 toshin *n.* city center, downtown area
- 都心は家賃が高い。— Rents are expensive in the city center.
23 | 0.72

2382 二ヶ月 ni kagetsu *n.* two months
- 二ヶ月間出張に出かける。— I'll go on a business trip for two months.
23 | 0.88

2383 役立つ yakudatsu *v.* useful
- このサイトには役立つ情報がたくさん出ている。— This website has plenty of useful information.
23 | 0.94

2384 土曜日 doyou bi *n.* Saturday
- 土曜日に美容室に行く。— I'll go to a hair salon on Saturday.
23 | 0.88

2385 労働者 roudou-sha *n.* laborer, working man
- その会社は海外からの労働者を受け入れる。— The company accepts laborers from overseas.
23 | 0.75

2386 五日 itsu-ka *n.* fifth (date); five days
- 五月五日はこどもの日だ。— May 5 is Children's Day.
23 | 0.58

2387 発売（する）hatsubai(suru) *n.* sale *v.* sell, put on sale
- 新しい本が販売される。— A new book will be on sale.
23 | 0.73

2388 成り立つ naritatsu *v.* be concluded; consist of
- この企画は、たくさんの人の努力で成り立っています。— This event is built on the efforts of many people.
23 | 0.95

2389 人数 ninzuu *n.* number of people
- 彼はグループの人数を数える。— He counts the number of people in the group.
23 | 0.98

2390 物質 busshitsu *n.* matter, material
- 彼は物質の変化について実験する。— He carries out experiments on changes in matter.
23 | 0.90

2391 温度 ondo *n.* temperature; heat
- 外の温度を測ろう。— Let's check the temperature outside.
23 | 0.99

2392 性質 seishitsu *n.* nature, disposition
- その二つの問題は性質が違う。— The two problems are different in nature.
23 | 0.83

2393 方針 houshin *n.* course, line; policy, plan; principle
- 会社は方針を発表した。— The company announced their plan.
23 | 0.84

2394 ひたすら hitasura *adv.* determinedly, earnestly
- ひたすら前だけを見て頑張った。— I looked ahead determinedly and persevered.
23 | 0.90

2395 秘密 himitsu *n.* secret, confidence
- 秘密は守ります。— I'll keep your secret.
23 | 0.91

2396 該当(する) gaitou(suru) *n.* fall under, be applicable, correspond
- その条件に該当する人は少なかった。— There were only a few people who were eligible.
23 | 0.67

2397 案内 annai *n.* guidance; guide, sign
- 案内がわかりにくい。— The guide is not clear.
23 | 0.91

2398 基礎 kiso *n.* basis, basics, foundation
- 中学校で英語の基礎を学ぶ。— We learn the basics of English in junior high school.
23 | 0.87

2399 単なる tannaru *adn.* mere, simple
- 単なる勘違いでは済まない。— You cannot leave it as simply a mistake.
23 | 0.91

12 Leisure

(frequency per million words)

映画 eiga 138.825 movie
歌 uta 100.936 song
雑誌 zasshi 76.477 magazine
趣味 shumi 64.787 hobby
ピアノ piano 52.202 piano
買い物(する) kaimono(suru) 49.847 shopping; go shopping
ゲーム geemu 41.637 game
マンガ manga 37.071 comics, cartoon
ドラマ dorama 37.050 TV drama, drama
ラジオ rajio 35.379 radio
温泉 onsen 34.820 hot spring, spa
楽器 gakki 33.416 musical instrument
ビデオ bideo 33.248 video
ギター gitaa 28.790 guitar
踊る odoru 28.694 dance
海外旅行 kaigairyokou 27.545 travel abroad, foreign trip
釣り tsuri 26.484 fishing
クラブ kurabu 25.580 club
キャンプ kyanpu 22.494 camp
チケット chiketto 19.381 ticket
観光(する) kankou(suru) 18.728 sightseeing; go sightseeing
レース reesu 18.073 race[1]
花火 hanabi 18.057 fireworks
コンサート konsaato 17.004 concert
カラオケ karaoke 16.224 karaoke
演劇 engeki 15.855 drama, play
パチンコ pachinko 15.122 pachinko, Japanese pinball
競馬 keiba 14.832 horse racing
将棋 shougi 14.492 shogi, Japanese chess
DVD diibuidii 13.053 DVD
ミュージカル myuujikaru 12.653 musical
読書 dokusho 11.646 reading
ジャズ jazu 11.349 jazz
ダンス dansu 11.124 dancing
ドライブ doraibu 10.447 drive
絵画 kaiga 10.284 painting, picture
ショー shoo 10.210 show
アニメ anime 9.953 animation
三味線 shamisen 9.411 shamisen
ボーリング booringu 8.759 bowling
ショッピング shoppingu 7.329 shopping
手芸 shugei 1.369 handicrafts

1 This count may include レース as "lace".

2400 草 kusa n. grass, weed
- 彼は庭の草むしりをしている。— He is weeding the garden.
23 | 0.90

2401 食品 shokuhin n. food
- バランスよく食品を選ぶ。— I select food for a well-balanced diet.
23 | 0.97

2402 トラブル toraburu n. trouble
- その生徒はよくトラブルを起こす。— The student often causes trouble.
23 | 0.95

2403 植える ueru v. plant
- 庭に桜を植える。— I will plant a cherry tree in the garden.
23 | 0.94

2404 定義 teigi n. definition
- 用語の定義を正確にしなさい。— You should define the terms more precisely.
23 | 0.85

2405 盛り上がる moriagaru v. swell, rise; liven up
- 今年の同窓会は、盛り上がった。— This year's reunion was successful.
23 | 0.90

2406 祖父 sofu n. grandfather
- 祖父は八十歳だ。— My grandfather is eighty years old.
23 | 0.80

2407 扉 tobira n. door
- 扉を開けると、冷たい風が入ってきた。— The cold wind blew in when I opened the door.
23 | 0.86

2408 僕達 boku-tachi pron. we (used by male speakers)
- 僕達はみんな野球をやっている。— We all play baseball.
23 | 0.85

2409 にわたって ni watat-te cp. throughout, over a period of
- 将来にわたって安定を保障する会社は、どこにもない。— There is no company that assures employees' benefits in the long term.
23 | 0.85

2410 廊下 rouka n. corridor
- 廊下を走ると危ないです。— It is dangerous to run down the corridor.
23 | 0.81

2411 要請 yousei n. request
- お客からの要請にはできるだけ早く対応する。— We respond to our customers' requests as quickly as possible.
23 | 0.56

2412 (お)姉さん (o)-nee-san n. elder sister
- あなたのお姉さんと友達になりたい。— I want to make friends with your sister.
23 | 0.59

2413 プログラム puroguramu n. program
- 新しいプログラムをダウンロードした。— I downloaded a new program.
23 | 0.96

2414 職業 shokugyou n. occupation, trade, profession
- 将来どんな職業に就きたいですか。— What kind of job do you want to have in the future?
23 | 0.99

2415 限界 genkai n. limit, boundary
- 自分の限界に挑戦したい。— I want to challenge the limits of my abilities.
23 | 0.98

2416 地位 chii n. rank, position
- 地位と名誉があっても、幸せとは限らない。— People with status and prestige are not necessarily happy.
23 | 0.84

2417 負う ou v. take, assume
- 彼は大きな責任を負っている。— He has a great responsibility.
23 | 0.91

2418 何しろ nanishiro adv. anyhow, anyway
- 何しろ、この仕事は今日中に終わらせなければならない。— I need to finish this up today anyway.
23 | 0.85

2419 何と nan to adv. how, what
- なんと素晴らしい歌だろう。— What a beautiful song!
23 | 0.74

2420 エンジン enjin n. engine
- エンジンのトラブルで車が動かない。— The car won't move because of a problem with the engine.
23 | 0.86

2421 コンビニ konbini n. convenience store
- コンビニで夕食を買う。— I buy some food for supper in a convenience store.
23 | 0.74

2422 質 shitsu n. nature, quality
- 商品の質の向上を目指す。— They aim to improve the quality of their products.
23 | 0.96

2423 漢字 kanji n. kanji, Chinese character
- 私は漢字が苦手です。— I'm not good at Chinese characters.
23 | 0.95

2424 政策 seisaku *n.* policy
- 日本の教育政策についての記事を読む。— I read an article about Japanese education policies.
23 | 0.84

2425 本物 honmono *n.* real (thing), genuine
- 彼女に本物のダイヤをプレゼントした。— I gave her a real diamond ring.
23 | 0.88

2426 作り出す tsukuridasu *v.* make, create
- 彼はこの工房で毎日新しい作品を作り出す。— He creates new pieces every day in this studio.
23 | 0.91

2427 解消(する) kaishou(suru) *n.* cancellation, annulment; cancel, dissolve
- ストレスを解消するには、スポーツするのが効果的だ。— Exercising is an effective way to get rid of stress.
23 | 0.91

2428 キャンプ kyanpu *n.* camp
- キャンプ場でバーベキューをする。— We will have a barbecue at a camping site.
22 | 0.79

2429 アルバム arubamu *n.* album
- 私は彼氏に子供のころのアルバムを見せた。— I showed my boyfriend albums of my childhood photos.
22 | 0.78

2430 運命 unmei *n.* destiny, fate
- 私たちは二度と会えない運命かもしれない。— We may not be destined to see each other again.
22 | 0.85

2431 に違いない ni chigai nai *aux.* must be, no doubt that
- 彼女は日本人にちがいない。— She must be Japanese.
22 | 0.56

2432 発する hassuru *v.* emit, release
- 地震速報が発せられた。— An earthquake alert was issued.
22 | 0.87

2433 ロボット robotto *n.* robot
- 彼はロボットの開発をしている。— He is working on developing robots.
22 | 0.70

2434 水分 suibun *n.* water, moisture
- 暑い日はこまめに水を飲んで、水分を補給してください。— On hot days, please drink plenty of water and stay hydrated.
22 | 0.90

2435 天皇 tennou *n.* Emperor
- 彼女は天皇の即位式を見に行った。— She went to see the enthronement ceremony of the emperor.
22 | 0.76

2436 布 nuno *n.* cloth
- 市場で布を買う。— I buy cloth at the market.
22 | 0.98

2437 生物 seibutsu *n.* living thing; biology
- 生物に関する本を読む。— I read a book about living things.
22 | 0.86

2438 根 ne *n.* root
- 木を根から掘り起こす。— I dig up a tree by the roots.
22 | 0.95

2439 信用(する) shinyou suru *n.* trust, rely on
- 先生はいつも彼を信用する。— The teacher always trusts him.
22 | 0.96

2440 ロシア roshia *n.* Russia
- ロシア文学を読む。— I read Russian literature.
22 | 0.97

2441 農業 nougyou *n.* agriculture
- 両親は農業を営んでいる。— My parents are engaged in agriculture.
22 | 0.73

2442 思想 shisou *n.* thought, idea
- 政治思想について話し合う。— We are discussing political ideas.
22 | 0.80

2443 丁寧 teinei *na-adj.* careful, polite
- 彼は丁寧な口調で話す。— He speaks in a polite tone.
22 | 0.94

2444 種 tane *n.* seed
- 母は庭に野菜の種をまく。— My mother sows vegetable seeds in the garden.
22 | 0.91

2445 書類 shorui *n.* document
- 必要書類を用意しなさい。— Prepare the required documents.
22 | 0.96

2446 疑う utagau *v.* suspect, doubt
- 私たちは彼の発言を疑う。— We doubt his words.
22 | 0.91

2447 神様 kami-sama *n.* god, God
- 彼は神様を信じている。— He believes in God.
22 | 0.89

2448 悔しい kuyashii *i-adj.* regrettable, frustrating; feel regret
- なんて悔しいんだろう！ — How frustrating!

22 | 0.83

2449 農家 nouka *n.* farmer
- この町は農家が多い。 — There are many farmers in this town.

22 | 0.87

2450 市町村 shi chou son *n.* municipality
- 市町村合併について会議を開く。 — We are having a meeting about merging municipalities.

22 | 0.47 | OF

2451 被害者 higai-sha *n.* victim
- あの事件の被害者は、六十歳の女性だった。 — The victim of that incident was a sixty year-old woman.

22 | 0.90

2452 時計 tokei *n.* watch; clock
- 時計を見る。 — I look at my watch.

22 | 0.94

2453 雲 kumo *n.* cloud
- 今日は雲がひとつもない。 — There are no clouds today.

22 | 0.88

2454 ぱっと patto *adv.* suddenly
- 面白いアイディアがぱっと思いついた。 — I suddenly got an interesting idea.

22 | 0.67

2455 メッセージ messeeji *n.* message
- 彼の携帯にメッセージをおくった。 — I sent a message to his cell phone.

22 | 0.92

2456 いじめ ijime *n.* bullying
- いじめは最悪な行為だ。 — Bullying is the worst act.

22 | 0.92

2457 離婚(する) rikon(suru) *n.* divorce *v.* divorce, get divorced
- あの夫婦は去年離婚した。 — That couple divorced last year.

22 | 0.90

2458 効果的 kouka-teki *na-adj.* effective
- 効果的な方法を見つけた。 — I found an effective method.

22 | 0.88

2459 掲載(する) keisai(suru) *n.* publication *v.* publish, print
- 彼の書いた記事が新聞に掲載された。 — The article that he wrote was published in the newspaper.

22 | 0.75

2460 しょっちゅう shotchuu *adv.* often, always
- 彼はしょっちゅう遅刻する。 — He is always late.

22 | 0.76

2461 オリンピック orinpikku *n.* Olympics
- 東京は次のオリンピックの開催地に立候補する。 — Tokyo is running to be the venue for the next Olympics.

22 | 0.72

2462 操作(する) sousa(suru) *n.* operation *v.* operate
- 彼はあのロボットの操作方法についてたずねる。 — He asks about the operation of that robot.

22 | 0.96

2463 知恵 chie *n.* wisdom
- お年寄りの知恵は尊重すべきだ。 — The wisdom of elderly people should be respected.

22 | 0.98

2464 伝統 dentou *n.* tradition
- 伝統を守るのは大切だ。 — It is important to keep traditions.

22 | 0.89

2465 留まる todomaru *v.* stay
- その場所に一週間とどまった。 — I stayed at that place for a week.

22 | 0.81

2466 受かる ukaru *v.* pass
- 彼は大学の試験に受かった。 — He passed the university examination.

22 | 0.47

2467 恐れる osoreru *v.* fear, be afraid
- 彼は奥さんを恐れている。 — He is afraid of his wife.

22 | 0.86

2468 著しい ichijirushii *i-adj.* significant
- あの会社の成長は著しい。 — The improvement of that company is tremendous.

22 | 0.52

2469 カレー karee *n.* curry
- カレーは私の好物だ。 — Curry is my favorite food.

22 | 0.80

2470 ウインドウズ uindouzu *n.* Windows
- ウインドウズをパソコンにインストールした。 — I installed Windows on my PC.

22 | 0.81

2471 救う sukuu *v.* save, rescue
- 彼は私を救った。 — He saved me.

22 | 0.93

2472 助かる tasukaru *v.* survive, be saved; be helpful
- 彼のおかげで助かった。— I survived thanks to him.
22 | 0.88

2473 巡る meguru *v.* go around
- 世界遺産をめぐるのが好きだ。— I like visiting world heritage sites.
22 | 0.89

2474 予約(する) yoyaku(suru) *n.* reservation *v.* reserve, book
- コンサートの予約をした。— I made a reservation for the concert.
22 | 0.79

2475 響く hibiku *v.* affect
- その言葉が心に響いていた。— The words got to my heart.
22 | 0.88

2476 事前 jizen *n.* prior
- 事前に準備することがとても大切だ。— Preparation in advance is very important.
22 | 0.84

2477 進行(する) shinkou(suru) *n.* progression *v.* progress
- 結婚式の進行について確認する。— They check on the progress of the wedding.
22 | 0.93

2478 解説(する) kaisetsu(suru) *n.* explanation, comment, description *v.* explain
- 名画の解説書を読んだ。— I read an explanatory leaflet about the famous pictures.
22 | 0.85

2479 潰す tsubusu *v.* smash; crush, squash; ruin
- 空き缶を足でつぶす。— I squashed an empty can with my foot.
22 | 0.92

2480 二時 ni ji *n.* two o'clock
- 二時にうちに帰る。— I go back home at two o'clock.
22 | 0.42 | NM

2481 行事 gyouji *n.* event
- お正月は日本で一番大きな行事だ。— New Year holidays are the biggest event in Japan.
22 | 0.94

2482 男女 danjo *n.* men and women
- この学校は男女共学だ。— This school is open to men and women.
22 | 0.97

2483 メイン mein *n.* main
- メイン料理はこれからだ。— The main dish is coming soon.
22 | 0.82

2484 かむ kamu *v.* bite; chew
- 猫が急に噛み付いた。— The cat bit me suddenly.
22 | 0.92

2485 温める atatameru *v.* warm, heat
- 彼の夕食をレンジであたためた。— I heated his dinner in the microwave.
22 | 0.95

2486 概念 gainen *n.* notion, idea, concept
- 彼らはこの事業の中心概念を理解する。— They understand the main concept of this event.
22 | 0.81

2487 重視(する) juushi(suru) *n.* respect *v.* make a point of, consider important
- 仕事を選ぶ時、彼はいつも給料を重視する。— When he chooses a job, he considers salary important.
22 | 0.87

2488 複数 fukusuu *n.* plural
- この単語の複数形を知っていますか。— Do you know the plural form of this word?
22 | 0.94

2489 三十 sanjuu *num.* thirty
- もうすぐ三十になる。— I will be thirty soon.
22 | 0.94

2490 興奮(する) koufun(suru) *n.* excitement *v.* be excited
- 彼はそれを聞いて非常に興奮した。— He was so excited to hear that.
22 | 0.86

2491 突っ込む tsukkomu *v.* thrust, stick; dip; shove
- 彼はポケットに手を突っ込んだ。— He shoved his hands in his pockets.
22 | 0.94

2492 牛 ushi *n.* cattle, cow, ox
- 彼らは牧場で牛を見る。— They see cattle at the stock farm.
22 | 0.96

2493 鏡 kagami *n.* mirror
- 彼女は毎日鏡を見る。— She looks in the mirror every day.
22 | 0.93

2494 ないし naishi *conj.* or, otherwise
- 砂糖の代わりに蜂蜜、ないし果物を入れてください。— Please add honey or fruit instead of sugar.
22 | 0.75

2495 二千年 nisen nen *n.* two thousand years
- 二千年前の本を見つける。— I found a book from two thousand years ago.
22 | 0.92

2496 煙 kemuri *n.* smoke, fumes; fog
- 彼らは台所から煙が出ているのを見つけた。— He found the smoke was coming from the kitchen.
22 | 0.92

2497 参照(する) sanshou(suru) *n.* reference *v.* consult, refer
- 辞書を参照しなさい。— Consult a dictionary.
22 | 0.84

2498 価値観 kachi-kan *n.* sense of values
- 価値観は人によって違う。— Values vary from person to person.
22 | 0.95

2499 バター bataa *n.* butter
- パンにバターをつけて食べる。— I eat bread with butter.
22 | 0.92

2500 スープ suupu *n.* soup
- 母がスープを作っている。— My mother is making soup.
22 | 0.86

2501 自殺(する) jisatsu(suru) *n.* suicide *v.* commit suicide
- 彼は自殺した。— He committed suicide.
22 | 0.97

2502 トラック torakku *n.* truck
- あのトラックは私の父のだ。— That truck is my father's.
22 | 0.96

2503 委員 iin *n.* committee member; councillor
- みんな彼を委員に選んだ。— Everyone selected him as a committee member.
22 | 0.28 | OF

2504 行政 gyousei *n.* administration, government
- 地方行政のための選挙が行われる。— The election for a local government will be held.
22 | 0.80

2505 一年生 ichi nen-sei *n.* first grade, first year
- 彼の子供は小学一年生だ。— His child is in the first grade of elementary school.
22 | 0.89

2506 犯す okasu *v.* commit, offend; break
- あの人は十年前に罪を犯した。— That person committed a crime ten years ago.
22 | 0.90

2507 膨らむ fukuramu *v.* swell, expand
- 春になるとつぼみが膨らみ始める。— In spring, buds start swelling.
22 | 0.95

2508 とうとう toutou *adv.* finally
- とうとう彼は医者になった。— Finally, he became a doctor.
22 | 0.87

2509 このごろ konogoro *n.* these days
- このごろ彼の様子がおかしい。— He acts funny these days.
22 | 0.88

2510 女子 joshi *n.* woman, girl
- 女子サッカーで日本が優勝した。— The Japanese team won the women's football tournament.
22 | 0.80

2511 ＪＲ jeiaaru *n.* Japan Railways (JR)
- いつもＪＲを使って会社へ行く。— I always use JR to go to the office.
22 | 0.77

2512 言語 gengo *n.* language, tongue, speech
- 日本語は彼の第二言語だ。— Japanese is his second language.
22 | 0.84

2513 とる toru *aux.* [shortened form of "teoru"]
- わしは何も悪いことはしとらん。— I'm not doing anything wrong.
22 | 0.88

2514 以来 irai *n.* since
- あの地震以来、一人で寝るのが怖い。— Since that earthquake, I'm afraid of sleeping alone.
22 | 0.95

2515 市内 shinai *n.* within the city
- 友達に市内を案内する。— I will guide my friend around the city.
22 | 0.39 | NM

2516 しかしながら shikashi nagara *aux.* however, but
- 彼の能力はまだまだだ。しかしながら, 可能性は感じられる。— He is not competent enough yet. However, he has potential.
22 | 0.55

2517 針 hari *n.* needle; stitch
- 針で指を刺した。— I pricked my finger with a needle.
21 | 0.91

2518 集団 shuudan *n.* group, mass
- 集団旅行に参加した。— I joined the group tour.
21 | 0.93

2519 体調 taichou *n.* physical condition
- 最高の体調でゲームに参加する。— I will participate in the game in top physical condition.
21 | 0.85

2520 三年間 san nenkan *n.* three years
- 三年間海外で生活した。— I lived abroad for three years.
21 | 0.93

2521 手前 temae *n.* this side
- 手前の机にあります。— It is on the desk in the foreground.
21 | 0.91

2522 幼い osanai *i-adj.* young, immature, childish
- 幼いとき、よく姉と一緒にこの公園で遊んだ。— When I was young, I often played in this park with my older sister.
21 | 0.90

2523 説 setsu *n.* theory; explanation
- 人々はそれについて異なる説を唱えている。— People give different explanations about it.
21 | 0.90

2524 神社 jinja *n.* shrine
- お正月に神社へ行く。— We go to shrines at New Year.
21 | 0.89

2525 列車 ressha *n.* train
- 駅に列車が入ってきた。— There is a train coming into the station.
21 | 0.95

2526 夢中 muchuu *n., na-adj.* crazy about, obsessed with
- 彼は今日本のアニメに夢中だ。— Now he is crazy about Japanese animation.
21 | 0.89

2527 トレーニング toreeningu *n.* training
- 彼は毎日のトレーニングを欠かさない。— He never misses training every day.
21 | 0.83

2528 よほど、よっぽど yohodo, yoppodo *adv.* very, greatly
- 彼はよほど怒っているらしい。— He seems very angry.
21 | 0.90

2529 どうせ douse *adv.* anyway
- どうせだめだ。— It's impossible, anyway.
21 | 0.89

2530 坂 saka *n.* slope, hill
- 坂をあがると私の家があります。— When you go up the hill, you'll find my house.
21 | 0.82

2531 検索（する） kensaku(suru) *n.* search *v.* search, look up
- インターネット検索で、レストランを見つける。— I found a restaurant by an Internet search.
21 | 0.69

2532 アップ（する） appu(suru) *n.* raise *v.* go up
- 今月から給料がアップした。— Salaries went up from this month.
21 | 0.72

2533 絶える taeru *v.* cease, fail
- 昨日、祖父が病院で息絶えた。— My grandfather took his last breath in hospital yesterday.
21 | 0.90

2534 三十一日 sanjuu ichi nichi *n.* thirty-first (date); thirty one days
- 十二月三十一日は、大晦日だ。— December 31 is New Year's Eve.
21 | 0.51 | NM

2535 取材（する） shuzai(suru) *n.* interview, report *v.* gather information
- 新しいプロジェクトについて、取材を受けた。— I was interviewed about a new project.
21 | 0.80

2536 ぶつかる butsukaru *v.* strike, bump, collide
- 壁にぶつかった。— I bumped into the wall.
21 | 0.91

2537 曲がる magaru *v.* bend, wind; turn
- 角を曲がると、郵便局がある。— When you turn the corner, you'll find the post office.
21 | 0.93

2538 ては te wa *p., conj.* alternately do . . . and . . .
- 彼女は彼の写真を見ては溜息をついた。— She sighed whenever she saw his photo.
21 | 0.01 | SP

2539 前年 zennen *n.* previous year, year before
- 今年の売り上げは前年を上回った。— This year's sales have exceeded the previous year's.
21 | 0.35 | OF

2540 飽きる akiru *v.* tire, weary, be tired of, get bored
- そのゲームにも飽きてきた。— I get bored with that game.
21 | 0.79

2541 三十日 sanjuu nichi *n.* thirtieth (date); thirty days
- 三十日に家へ帰る。— I go back to my hometown on the 30th.
21 | 0.56 | NM

2542 分類（する） bunrui(suru) *n.* classification *v.* classify
- 本の細かい分類については、司書に聞いてください。— Please ask a librarian about detailed book classification.
21 | 0.87

2543 どっち dotchi *pron.* which
- どっちの航空券が安いですか？— Which airplane ticket is cheaper?
21 | 0.62

2544 自分なり jibun-nari *n.* in one's own way
- 自分なりにやってみます。— I'll do it in my own way.
21 | 0.78

2545 覚悟（する）kakugo(suru) *n.* readiness, preparedness *v.* be ready
- 病気について聞いた時、彼は死を覚悟した。— When he heard he was ill, he prepared himself to die.
21 | 0.91

2546 糸 ito *n.* thread, string
- 太い糸で洋服を縫っている。— I am sewing clothes with thick thread.
21 | 0.96

2547 逮捕（する）taiho(suru) *n.* arrest *v.* arrest
- 彼はとうとう逮捕された。— He was finally arrested.
21 | 0.95

2548 収まる osamaru *v.* hold, pack
- 本は全部この箱に収まるだろう。— This box will hold all the books.
21 | 0.93

2549 交渉（する）koushou(suru) *n.* negotiation, treaty *v.* negotiate
- この会議では交渉がとても重要だ。— Negotiation is so important in this meeting.
21 | 0.89

2550 枝 eda *n.* branch, twig, bough
- 木の枝に鳥が止まっている。— The bird is on the tree branch.
21 | 0.90

2551 なにより nani yori *adv.* above all, chiefly, more than anything
- 彼は何よりもビールが好きだ。— He loves beer more than anything.
21 | 0.81

2552 教科書 kyouka-sho *n.* textbook
- 教科書を机の上に出してください。— Please have your textbook ready on the desk.
21 | 0.96

2553 六時 roku ji *n.* six o'clock
- 毎朝六時に起きる。— I wake up at six o'clock every morning.
21 | 0.64

2554 取り引き torihiki *n.* business, dealing, trade
- 彼は公正な取引が行われているか調査する。— He investigates whether they have fair trade or not.
21 | 0.84

2555 免許 menkyo *n.* license, permit
- 運転免許を取りに行く。— I'll go and get a driver's license.
21 | 0.90

2556 講ずる kouzuru *v.* take
- 早急に措置を講ずる必要がある。— It is necessary to take measures immediately.
21 | 0.26 | OF

2557 太い futoi *i-adj.* thick; heavy; bold
- ボードに太い線を書いてください。— Draw a thick line on the board.
21 | 0.94

2558 開く aku *v.* open
- 突然、ドアが開いた。— Suddenly the door opened.
21 | 0.18 | SP

2559 及ぼす oyobosu *v.* influence, affect
- 二酸化炭素ガスは地球温暖化に重大な影響を及ぼす。— CO2 gas has a significant effect on global warming.
21 | 0.76

2560 千円 sen en *n.* one thousand yen
- お父さんは子供に千円あげた。— The father gave the children one thousand yen.
21 | 0.63

2561 独自 dokuji *na-adj.* original, own
- 独自の方法で英語を勉強する。— I study English in my own way.
21 | 0.92

2562 夕食 yuushoku *n.* dinner
- 夕食の用意をしなさい。— Get ready for dinner.
21 | 0.88

2563 震える furueru *v.* shake, tremble
- 手が震えた。— My hands were trembling.
21 | 0.79

2564 心臓 shinzou *n.* heart
- 彼は心臓麻痺で死んだ。— He died of a heart attack.
21 | 0.88

2565 世界的 sekai-teki *na-adj.* world, global
- 世界的に有名なピアニストのコンサートへ行く。— I will go to a concert by a world-famous pianist.
21 | 0.92

2566 所属（する）shozoku(suru) *n.* affiliation *v.* attach, be attached, belong
- 広報課の所属になった。— I have been assigned to the Public Relations section.
21 | 0.98

2567 騒ぐ sawagu *v.* make a noise, make a fuss
- 隣の人が大声で騒いでいる。— The neighbors are making a loud noise.
21 | 0.89

2568 そっと sotto *adv.* softly, lightly
- 彼は病人を起こさないようにそっと歩いた。— He walked softly so as not to awaken the sick man.
21 | 0.84

2569 溜める tameru *v.* save, store, accumulate
- 若いうちに知識をためておきなさい。— Accumulate knowledge while you are young.
21 | 0.89

2570 晩 ban *n.* night, evening
- 昨日の晩、彼女が家に来た。— She came to my house last night.
21 | 0.86

2571 小屋 koya *n.* hut, cabin, barn, shed
- 彼は小屋で暮らしている。— He lives in a hut.
21 | 0.74

2572 会議 kaigi *n.* meeting
- 私たちは会議に出席している。— We are attending the meeting.
21 | 0.93

2573 個性 kosei *n.* personality, character
- 個性を伸ばすことは大切だ。— It is important to develop our personalities.
21 | 0.96

2574 たがる tagaru *aux.* want to
- 妹は一緒に行きたがった。— My younger sister wanted to go with me.
21 | 0.89

2575 理想 risou *n.* ideal, dream
- 彼らはみんなから理想の夫婦と呼ばれている。— Everyone calls them an ideal couple.
21 | 0.94

2576 給料 kyuuryou *n.* salary
- 今日給料をもらう。— I will get my salary today.
21 | 0.93

2577 マスコミ masukomi *n.* mass media, mass communication
- 将来マスコミの仕事をしたい。— I would like to work in the field of mass communication in the future.
21 | 0.99

2578 おい oi *interj.* hey
- おい、そこに入ってはいけないよ！— Hey, don't go in there!
21 | 0.81

2579 屋根 yane *n.* roof
- 屋根の上に猫がいる。— There is a cat on the roof.
21 | 0.91

2580 クリスマス kurisumasu *n.* Christmas
- 私たちはクリスマスの歌を歌う。— We will sing a Christmas song.
21 | 0.84

2581 重なる kasanaru *v.* pile up; conspire
- たくさん箱が重なっている。— There is a big pile of boxes.
21 | 0.98

2582 各地 kakuchi *n.* each place
- 各地で名産を食べる。— In each place, I eat the food that is famous there.
21 | 0.93

2583 落ち込む ochikomu *v.* sink, go down; be depressed
- テストのことで、彼はとても落ち込んでいる。— He's very depressed about the exam.
21 | 0.99

2584 進化(する) shinka(suru) *n.* evolution *v.* evolve, develop
- 人間の進化について学ぶ。— I study human evolution.
21 | 0.94

2585 とんでも tondemo *adv.* unexpected; outrageous, very offensive
- そのかばんはとんでもない値段だ。— The bag is an outrageous price.
21 | 0.94

2586 思い付く omoitsuku *v.* think of, guess, conceive
- 名案を思いついた。— I thought of a good idea.
21 | 0.90

2587 新幹線 shin-kansen *n.* bullet train
- 私たちは新幹線で旅行します。— We will travel by bullet train.
21 | 0.90

2588 第三 dai-san *n.* third
- 第三者からの意見は貴重だ。— Comments from third parties are important.
21 | 0.52

2589 数える kazoeru *v.* count, number
- 小銭の数を数えなさい。— Count the number of coins.
21 | 0.97

2590 公開(する) koukai(suru) *n.* exhibition, presentation *v.* release
- その映画は日本で初めて公開された。— The film was first released in Japan.
21 | 0.92

2591 地面 jimen *n.* ground, land
- 地面はまだ濡れている。— The ground is still wet.
21 | 0.89

2592 貢献(する) kouken(suru) *n.* contribution, service *v.* contribute
- 彼はこのプロジェクトに大きく貢献した。— He contributed greatly to this project.
21 | 0.87

2593 台風 taifuu *n.* typhoon
- 島は台風に襲われた。— The island was hit by a typhoon.
21 | 0.94

2594 映る utsuru *v.* reflect
- ひまわりが水に映っている。— The sunflowers are reflected in the water.
21 | 0.93

2595 大臣 daijin *n.* Cabinet minister, minister of state
- 彼は大臣になった。— He was appointed a Cabinet minister.
21 | 0.22 | OF

2596 十四 juu shi *num.* fourteen
- 十四歳までアメリカで暮らした。— I lived in the United States until I was fourteen years old.
21 | 0.86

2597 入学(する) nyuugaku(suru) *n.* (school etc.) entrance, admission *v.* enter (school etc.)
- おいが小学校へ入学する。— My nephew will enter elementary school.
21 | 0.91

13 Occupations

(frequency per million words)

先生 sensei 315.291 teacher
医者 isha[1] 65.367 doctor
アルバイト arubaito 37.664 part-time job
社長 shachou 35.023 company president
教師 kyoushi 33.621 teacher
医師 ishi 31.117 doctor
職員 shokuin 27.797 staff member
モデル moderu 26.831 model
作家 sakka 26.147 writer
サラリーマン sarariiman 25.365 salaried worker, office worker
政治家 seiji-ka 23.356 politician
労働者 roudou-sha 23.070 laborer, working man
農家 nouka 22.270 farmer
大臣 daijin 20.672 Cabinet minister, a minister of state
弁護士 bengo-shi 20.387 lawyer, counsellor
王 ou 20.358 king, monarch
講師 koushi 20.239 speaker, lecturer
役者 yakusha 20.218 actor, actress
専門家 senmon-ka 19.904 expert, specialist
看護婦 kango-fu[2] 18.178 nurse (female)
従業員 juugyou-in 17.370 employee, worker
経営者 keiei-sha 16.273 manager, proprietor
アーティスト aatisuto 15.056 artist
首相 shushou 14.629 prime minister
王様 ousama 14.100 king
大統領 daitouryou 13.792 President
軍隊 guntai 13.294 army, troops
研究者 kenkyuu-sha 12.761 researcher
運転手 unten-shu 12.514 driver
公務員 koumu-in 12.261 civil servant, government employee

自衛隊 jieitai 12.248 Self-Defense Forces
記者 kisha 11.734 journalist, reporter
担当者 tantou-sha 11.472 person in charge
歌手 kashu 11.120 singer
職人 shokunin 10.994 craftsman, workman
俳優 haiyuu 10.511 actor
裁判官 saiban-kan 10.275 judge
農民 noumin 10.269 farmer
兵士 heishi 10.020 soldier
芸能人 geinou-jin 10.019 entertainer
ドライバー doraibaa 9.967 driver
学者 gakusha 9.934 scholar
議員 giin 9.826 member of Diet/Congress/Parliament
武士 bushi 9.558 warrior, samurai
警察官 keisatsu-kan 9.547 policeman
将軍 shougun 9.360 general
店員 ten'in 9.202 clerk, sales assistant
画家 gaka 8.852 artist, painter
デザイナー dezainaa 5.901 designer
建築家 kenchiku-ka 5.847 architect
音楽家 ongaku-ka 4.876 musician
会社員 kaisha-in 4.580 office worker
ジャーナリスト jaanarisuto 3.960 journalist
美容師 biyou-shi 3.912 hairdresser
駅員 eki-in 2.340 station staff
外交官 gaikou-kan 2.308 diplomat
スポーツ選手 supootsu senshu 2.193 athlete
銀行員 ginkou-in 1.979 bank clerk
エンジニア enjinia 1.838 engineer
調理師 chouri-shi 1.204 cook

1 Includes お医者さん *o-isha-san*.
2 Includes 看護婦さん *kango-fu-san*.

2598 紅茶 koucha *n.* tea (black)
- 紅茶とケーキを注文した。— I ordered tea and a piece of cake.
21 | 0.74

2599 控える hikaeru *v.* abstain, hold back, refrain
- タバコは控えてください。— Please refrain from smoking.
21 | 0.94

2600 促す unagasu *v.* urge
- 政府は次の地震について人々に注意を促した。— The government drew people's attention to the next earthquake.
21 | 0.90

2601 何事 nanigoto *n.* what
- 何事ですか? — What's the matter?
21 | 0.90

2602 プレゼント purezento *n.* present
- 私は彼に誕生日プレゼントを渡す。— I'll give him a birthday present.
21 | 0.75

2603 配る kubaru *v.* deal, distribute, deliver
- 彼は駅前でチラシを配った。— He distributed flyers in front of the station.
21 | 0.96

2604 改革(する) kaikaku(suru) *n.* reform *v.* make reforms
- 国民は行政改革を願っている。— People in our country wish for administrative reforms.
21 | 0.76

2605 一致(する) itchi(suru) *n.* agreement, accord *v.* consent, agree
- あなたのやっていること言っていることは一致していない。— What you do is not consistent with what you say.
21 | 0.88

2606 ゼロ zero *n.* zero
- ゼロカロリーの食べ物を食べている。— I'm eating foods with zero calories.
21 | 1.00

2607 義務 gimu *n.* duty, obligation
- 親には子供を育てる義務がある。— Parents have an obligation to bring up their children.
21 | 0.84

2608 出席(する) shusseki(suru) *n.* attendance *v.* attend
- 先生は授業の最初に出席をとる。— The teacher checks the attendance at the beginning of the class.
21 | 0.97

2609 十人 juu-nin *n.* ten people
- クラスには生徒が10人いる。— There are ten students in the class.
21 | 0.83

2610 処分(する) shobun(suru) *n.* disposal, disposition *v.* dispose of
- その家族は財産処分について話し合った。— The family discussed how to dispose of their property.
21 | 0.78

2611 年間 nenkan *n.* year; annual
- これが年間計画です。— This is the annual plan.
21 | 0.88

2612 広島 hiroshima *n.* Hiroshima
- 広島に原爆ドームを見に行く。— I will go to Hiroshima to see the Atomic Bomb Dome.
20 | 0.94

2613 NHK enueichikei, enuechikei *n.* Nihon Hoso Kyokai (Japan Broadcasting Corporation)
- 七時のＮＨＫのニュースをいつも見てます。— I always watch NHK news at seven o'clock.
20 | 0.95

2614 設計(する) sekkei(suru) *n.* plan, design *v.* plan, design
- 庭を設計するのが彼の仕事です。— His job is to design gardens.
20 | 0.94

2615 飛び込む tobikomu *v.* dive, plunge
- プールに飛び込むのは危険です。— It is dangerous to dive into the pool.
20 | 0.87

2616 邪魔(する) jama(suru) *n.* obstacle, disturbance, interruption *v.* disturb, interrupt
- 邪魔しないで。— Do not disturb.
20 | 0.88

2617 ゆでる yuderu *v.* boil
- ジャガイモを三十分ゆでなさい。— Boil the potatoes for thirty minutes.
20 | 0.91

2618 プール puuru *n.* pool
- プールで泳ぐのが好きだ。— I like swimming in the pool.
20 | 0.91

2619 弁護士 bengo-shi *n.* lawyer, counsellor
- 彼は弁護士になるために勉強している。— He is studying to become a lawyer.
20 | 0.95

2620 叱る shikaru *v.* scold, admonish
- 遅刻してしかられた。— I was scolded for being late.
20 | 0.92

2621 恋人 koibito *n.* lover, boyfriend, girlfriend
- 私の恋人はとても親切だ。— My boyfriend is really kind.
20 | 0.86

2622 暮らし kurashi *n.* life, livelihood
- いい暮らしをするために、がんばる。 — We work hard to have a good life.
20 | 0.80

2623 王 ou *n.* king, monarch
- あの国の王様に会う。 — We will meet the king of that country.
20 | 0.79

2624 真似(する) mane(suru) *n.* imitation, mimicry, impersonation *v.* imitate, copy
- 妹が芸能人の真似をする。 — My sister mimics entertainers.
20 | 0.90

2625 税金 zeikin *n.* tax
- 毎年税金を払わなければならない。 — Every year we have to pay tax.
20 | 0.95

2626 預ける azukeru *v.* leave, check, deposit
- ホテルのクロークに所持品を預けた。 — I left my things in the cloakroom at the hotel.
20 | 0.95

2627 柔らかい yawarakai *i-adj.* soft, tender
- やわらかいクッションを買った。 — I bought a soft cushion.
20 | 0.93

2628 物事 monogoto *n.* thing
- 彼は物事を苦にしない。 — He does not take things too seriously.
20 | 0.96

2629 相変わらず ai-kawara zu *adv* as ever, as usual, the same, as before [always]
- 相変わらず彼は元気だ。 — He is fine, as always.
20 | 0.84

2630 年金 nenkin *n.* pension, annuity
- 彼は年金で暮らしている。 — He lives on a pension.
20 | 0.81

2631 やりとり yaritori *n.* exchange, interchange
- メールでやり取りをする。 — We exchange emails.
20 | 0.99

2632 ホーム hoomu *n.* platform
- 駅のホームで人を待っている。 — I am waiting for someone on the station platform.
20 | 0.91

2633 頼る tayoru *v.* depend, turn to, trust
- 彼以外に頼れる友人は一人もいない。 — I have no friends to turn to, except for him.
20 | 0.98

2634 学生時代 gakusei jidai *n.* student days, university days
- 彼は学生時代はサッカー部に入っていた。 — He was on a soccer team in his school days.
20 | 0.73

2635 憧れ akogare *n.* admiration
- 木田先生は私たちの憧れのまとでした。 — Mrs. Kida was the object of admiration among all of us.
20 | 0.84

2636 内側 uchigawa *n.* inside, interior, inner
- 内側を見せてください。 — Let me see the inside.
20 | 0.91

2637 講師 koushi *n.* speaker, lecturer
- 彼は大学の講師です。 — He is a lecturer at university.
20 | 0.43 | NM

2638 池 ike *n.* pond
- 庭園の真ん中に大きな池がある。 — There is a big pond in the middle of the garden.
20 | 0.91

2639 接続(する) setsuzoku(suru) *n.* connection *v.* connect
- 部屋からインターネットに接続できます。 — You can connect to the Internet from your room.
20 | 0.95

2640 役者 yakusha *n.* actor, actress
- 私の兄は役者になった。 — My brother became an actor.
20 | 0.71

2641 光る hikaru *v.* shine, glitter, twinkle
- 星が光っている。 — The stars are shining.
20 | 0.85

2642 富士山 fuji-san *n.* Mt. Fuji
- 私たちは昨年夏に富士山に登った。 — We climbed Mt. Fuji last summer.
20 | 0.86

2643 必要性 hitsuyou-sei *n.* necessity
- 私たちはテレビの必要性について議論する。 — We discuss the necessity of television.
20 | 0.80

2644 七時 shichi ji *n.* seven o'clock
- 七時に起きる。 — I wake up at seven o'clock.
20 | 0.61

2645 としたら to shi tara *p. conj.* if so
- 明日死ぬとしたら、何がしたいですか。 — If you were going to die tomorrow, what would you want to do?
20 | 0.71

2646 出演(する) shutsuen(suru) *n.* appearance, broadcast *v.* appear (on stage, TV)
- 彼はよくテレビに出演する。— He often appears on television.
20 | 0.67

2647 柱 hashira *n.* pillar, post
- あの神社の中心に大きな柱がある。— There is a big pillar in the center of the shrine.
20 | 0.93

2648 間に合う maniau *v.* catch, get, make it
- 電車に間に合った。— I caught the train OK.
20 | 0.96

2649 年代 nendai *n.* era; generation; date
- 彼の年代ではこのことは理解できない。— Men of his generation would never understand this.
20 | 0.85

2650 鉄 tetsu *n.* iron, steel
- 鉄は熱いうちに打て。— Strike while the iron is hot.
20 | 0.96

2651 継続(する) keizoku(suru) *n.* continuation *v.* continue
- 継続することが大切である。— It's important to keep it going.
20 | 0.85

2652 特殊 tokushu *na-adj.* special
- この部屋は特殊な目的のために作られた。— This room was designed for a special purpose.
20 | 0.98

2653 引き上げる hikiageru *v.* pull up; increase, raise
- 政府は消費税を5パーセント引き上げる。— The government will increase the consumption tax by 5 percent.
20 | 0.90

2654 スペイン supein *n.* Spain
- スペイン料理が好きです。— I like Spanish food.
20 | 0.95

2655 裁判 saiban *n.* trial; judgment; justice
- 裁判が開かれる。— The court is in session.
20 | 0.92

2656 はあ haa *interj.* oh, Oh boy, Oh dear
- はー、今日も疲れた。— Oh dear, I'm so tired today.
20 | 0.75

2657 上回る uwamawaru *v.* exceed, surpass
- 去年は、出生率が死亡率を上回った。— Last year, the birth rate exceeded the death rate.
20 | 0.68

2658 地下鉄 chika-tetsu *n.* subway, underground
- 地下鉄の駅を探した。— I looked for the subway station.
20 | 0.88

2659 専門家 senmon-ka *n.* expert, specialist
- 専門家に意見を聞いた。— I asked the specialist for advice.
20 | 0.88

2660 内部 naibu *n.* inside, interior
- 内部のものの仕業に違いない。— This must have been done by an insider.
20 | 0.91

2661 割る waru *v.* break; crack
- 窓ガラスをうっかり割ってしまった。— I broke the window by mistake.
20 | 0.99

2662 スペース supeesu *n.* space, room
- もう一人乗れるだけのスペースがありますか？ — Is there enough space for one more person?
20 | 0.92

2663 結果的 kekka-teki *na-adj.* result
- 結果的に、みんなその案に賛成した。— As a result, everyone agreed to the proposal.
20 | 0.97

2664 飲める nomeru *v.* be able to drink
- あのバーでは、珍しいビールが飲める。— We can drink special beer in that bar.
20 | 0.80

2665 割 wari *n.* cost, rate
- あのレストランは、高い割にはおいしくない。— The restaurant is expensive and the food is not worth it.
20 | 0.86

2666 日記 nikki *n.* diary
- 毎日日記を書く。— I keep a diary every day.
20 | 0.88

2667 担う ninau *v.* cover, carry, take
- 彼女は学校で重要な役割を担っている。— She plays a prominent role in our school.
20 | 0.84

2668 揺れる yureru *v.* shake, wave, swing
- 子供が枝にぶらさがって揺れている。— The child was swinging on a branch.
20 | 0.90

2669 彼 kare *pron.* he; boyfriend
- 彼は三十歳だ。— He is thirty years old.
20 | 0.81

2670 一匹 ip-piki *n.* one (animal)
- 犬を一匹飼っている。— I have a dog as a pet.
20 | 0.84

2671 憲法 kenpou *n.* constitution
- この権利は憲法の下に保障されている。— This is guaranteed under the Constitution.
20 | 0.80

2672 件 ken *n.* affair, matter, issue
- あの件について、家族で話し合った。— We had a discussion about that issue in our family.
20 | 0.81

2673 江戸時代 edo jidai *n.* Edo era
- 江戸時代の書物を探す。— I'm looking for a book about the Edo era.
20 | 0.96

2674 むく muku *v.* peel, pare
- リンゴの皮をむく。— I peel apples.
20 | 0.91

2675 親切 shinsetsu *na-adj.* kind
- 彼女は親切で頭がいい。— She is kind and smart.
20 | 0.85

2676 埼玉県 saitama ken *n.* Saitama prefecture
- 埼玉県は東京都の隣だ。— Saitama prefecture is located next to Tokyo.
20 | 0.91

2677 急速 kyuusoku *na-adj.* rapid, speedy
- あの国は急速な発展を遂げた。— The country underwent rapid industrialization.
20 | 0.72

2678 燃える moeru *v.* burn, flame, glow, be on fire
- 家が燃えている。— The house is burning.
20 | 0.94

2679 末 sue *n.* end, last
- 先月の末からずっと寒さが続いている。— It's been very cold since the end of last month.
20 | 0.97

2680 胃 i *n.* stomach, belly
- 胃が痛い。— I have a stomachache.
20 | 0.92

2681 九州 kyuushuu *n.* Kyushu
- 彼は飛行機で九州まで行く。— He goes to Kyushu by plane.
20 | 1.00

2682 ブログ burogu *n.* blog
- ブログに写真を投稿する。— I posted photos to a blog.
20 | 0.11 | WB

2683 にすぎない ni sugi nai *aux.* just, mere
- ほんの憶測にすぎない。— It's a mere guess.
20 | 0.71

2684 想定(する) soutei(suru) *n.* assumption, supposition *v.* assume, suppose
- 私たちは成功するという想定でことをすすめます。— I will proceed on the assumption that we will succeed.
20 | 0.89

2685 学習(する) gakushuu(suru) *n.* learning, study *v.* learn, study
- 毎日新しいことを学習する。— We learn new things every day.
20 | 0.84

2686 ケーキ keeki *n.* cake
- 彼の誕生日にケーキを作る。— I will make a cake for his birthday.
20 | 0.83

2687 六年 roku nen *n.* six years
- 六年間、小学校に通う。— We go to elementary school for six years.
20 | 0.93

2688 袋 fukuro *n.* bag, sack, pouch
- 袋いっぱいのジャガイモを使った。— I used a sack of potatoes.
20 | 0.93

2689 医療 iryou *n.* medical care, medical treatment
- 医療費はとても高い。— Medical fees are really high.
20 | 0.88

2690 増大(する) zoudai(suru) *n.* increase, growth; increase, grow
- 凶悪犯罪が増大している。— Brutal crimes are increasing.
20 | 0.46

2691 競争(する) kyousou(suru) *n.* competition, contest *v.* compete
- その産業での競争は激しい。— The competition in that industry is fierce.
20 | 0.91

2692 投資(する) toushi(suru) *n.* investment *v.* invest
- 新しいプロジェクトに投資する。— I invested in the new project.
20 | 0.87

2693 ほっとする hottosuru *v.* be relieved
- 彼の姿を見てほっとした。— I was relieved when I saw him.
20 | 0.88

2694 お土産 o-miyage *n.* present, souvenir
- 旅行先で家族へのお土産を買った。— I bought some souvenirs for my family while traveling.
20 | 0.80

2695 記述（する） kijutsu(suru) *n.* description, account *v.* describe
- 自分の生い立ちについて詳細を記述する。— I will describe my background.
20 | 0.83

2696 謝る ayamaru *v.* apologize
- 彼は自分の失敗について謝った。— He apologized for his mistakes.
20 | 0.85

2697 にもかかわらず ni mo kakawara zu *p. conj.* in spite of, though, despite
- 病気にもかかわらず、会議に出席した。— He attended the meeting in spite of his illness.
20 | 0.79

2698 獲得（する） kakutoku(suru) *n.* acquisition *v.* get, gain
- 彼のゴールは富を獲得することだ。— His goal is to acquire wealth.
20 | 0.89

2699 見直す minaosu *v.* review, look over
- もう一度丁寧に見直してください。— Please look it over again carefully.
20 | 0.91

2700 無人 mujin *n.* uninhabited, empty
- その駅は、無人だった。— The station was deserted.
20 | 0.37

2701 心がける kokorogakeru *v.* be careful, be prudent
- 安全運転を心がける。— I am always careful to drive safely.
20 | 0.91

2702 テープ teepu *n.* tape
- テープを再生してください。— Please play the tape back.
19 | 0.93

2703 七日 nanoka *n.* seventh (date); seven days
- 一週間は七日間だ。— One week has seven days.
19 | 0.53

2704 二つ目 futa-tsu-me *n.* second
- 二つ目の角を曲がって。— Turn at the second corner.
19 | 0.73

2705 板 ita *n.* board, plate
- その家の屋根は、薄い板で作られている。— The roof of this house is made of thin board.
19 | 0.94

2706 自慢（する） jiman(suru) *n.* pride, boast *v.* boast, brag
- これは彼の自慢の車です。— This is a car he is proud of.
19 | 0.87

2707 前項 zenkou *n.* previous page
- 条件については前項で述べている。— The conditions are described on the previous page.
19 | 0.13 | OF

2708 選挙 senkyo *n.* election
- 次の選挙は来年行われる。— The next election will be held next year.
19 | 0.97

2709 更新（する） koushin(suru) *n.* renewal *v.* renew, update
- 契約の更新を行ってください。— Please renew your contract.
19 | 0.79

2710 IT aitii *n.* IT
- 彼はIT関連企業に就職する。— He will be employed at an IT company.
19 | 0.84

2711 あちら achira *pron.* that way; that place, there; that
- あちらの門へ行って下さい。— Please go to that gate.
19 | 0.63

2712 受け止める uketomeru *v.* take, catch
- 彼はボールを片手で受け止めた。— He caught the ball with one hand.
19 | 0.94

2713 景気 keiki *n.* business conditions, economy
- 来年は景気がよくなることを祈っている。— We hope that business will pick up next year.
19 | 0.82

2714 二十五日 nijuu go nichi *n.* twenty-fifth (date); twenty-five days
- 今月の二十五日に子供が生まれた。— This child was born on the twenty-fifth of this month.
19 | 0.48 | NM

2715 根拠 konkyo *n.* ground, evidence
- その話は何の根拠もない。— The story has no basis.
19 | 0.89

2716 チケット chiketto *n.* ticket
- コンサートのチケットを買う。— I'm going to buy a ticket for the concert.
19 | 0.77

2717 民間 minkan *n.* private, non government
- 政府はそのプロジェクトに民間の投資を望んでいる。— The government hopes that the private sector will invest in the project.
19 | 0.66

2718 口調 kuchou *n.* tone, voice
- 彼女は丁寧な口調で話す。— She speaks in a polite tone.
19 | 0.56

2719 ふさわしい fusawashii *i-adj.* suitable, appropriate
- 彼はこのプロジェクトにもっともふさわしい人物だ。— He is the most suitable person for this project.
19 | 0.90

2720 といっても to it-te mo *p.* even though
- 祝日といっても、特に特別なことはない。— There is nothing special going on in particular, even though it's a national holiday.
19 | 0.89

2721 眼鏡 megane *n.* glasses, spectacles
- 新しい眼鏡が必要だ。— I need a new pair of glasses.
19 | 0.87

2722 脇 waki *n.* side
- 車を脇に寄せた。— I pulled over to the side.
19 | 0.90

2723 持ち込む mochikomu *v.* bring, import
- このレストランには、自分でワインを持ち込むことができる。— We can bring our own wine to this restaurant.
19 | 0.98

2724 全身 zenshin *n.* all over, whole body
- 雨で全身が濡れてしまった。— I got wet with rain from top to toe.
19 | 0.83

2725 兄さん nii-san *n.* elder brother
- 兄さんは頼りがいがある。— My elder brother is a man you can count on.
19 | 0.57

2726 予測（する）yosoku(suru) *n.* prospect *v.* predict, estimate
- 予測を誤ってしまった。— We were mistaken in our estimate.
19 | 0.92

2727 あれ are *interj.* Oh
- あれ？髪の毛切った？— Oh? Did you have your hair cut?
19 | 0.79

2728 つながり tsunagari *n.* connection, relation
- 彼とは血のつながりがある。— I am related to him by blood.
19 | 0.96

2729 欠ける kakeru *v.* lack; chip
- グラスの端が欠けた。— The edge of the glass got chipped.
19 | 0.98

2730 嫌う kirau *v.* hate, detest
- 彼は変化を嫌う。— He hates changes.
19 | 0.85

2731 保険料 hoken-ryou *n.* insurance premium
- 保険料を支払わないといけない。— I have to pay insurance fees.
19 | 0.71

2732 飛ばす tobasu *v.* let fly, fly
- その子は紙飛行機を飛ばした。— The child flew a paper airplane through the air.
19 | 0.94

2733 教わる osowaru *v.* learn
- 友達に日本語を教わる。— I learn Japanese from my friend.
19 | 0.81

2734 三十年 sanjuu nen *n.* thirty years
- 私達は三十年間お互いのことを知っている。— We have known each other for thirty years.
19 | 0.95

2735 後半 kouhan *n.* latter half, second half
- ゲームの後半戦が始まった。— The second half of the game began.
19 | 0.97

2736 たく taku *v.* burn
- 母は毎日線香をたく。— My mother burns incense every day.
19 | 0.89

2737 何日 nan nichi *n.* many days; how many days
- 彼は何日も待っていた。— He had been waiting for many days.
19 | 0.84

2738 防止（する）boushi(suru) *n.* prevention *v.* prevent
- 交通事故の防止について努力しなければならない。— We should make efforts to prevent traffic accidents.
19 | 0.56

2739 遺伝子 iden-shi *n.* gene
- 彼は遺伝子交換について調べている。— He investigates gene exchange.
19 | 0.91

2740 本屋 hon-ya *n.* bookshop
- 時間があったので本屋に立ち寄った。— I still had time, so I called in at a bookshop.
19 | 0.72

2741 明日 asu *n.* tomorrow
- 明日から学校が始まる。— School starts tomorrow.
19 | 0.69

2742 早め hayame *n.* early
- 少し早めに夕食の準備をした。— I prepared supper a little earlier than usual.
19 | 0.85

2743 独特 dokuji *na-adj.* peculiar, unique; personal
- それは私の独自の意見です。— This is my personal opinion.
19 | 0.93

2744 今夜 kon'ya *n.* tonight
- 今夜はすき焼きを食べる。— I'm going to eat sukiyaki tonight.
19 | 0.65

2745 ゆえ yue *n.* reason; therefore
- 彼の作品はその斬新さゆえに批判されることもあった。— His works of art were sometimes criticized because of their novelty.
19 | 0.79

2746 リズム rizumu *n.* rhythm
- リズムに乗ってダンスした。— We danced to the rhythm.
19 | 0.97

2747 突く tsuku *v.* push; prick
- 後ろから突かれて、私は倒れた。— Pushed hard from behind, I fell forward.
19 | 0.84

2748 魂 tamashii *n.* soul, spirit
- もっと魂を入れて仕事をしなさい。— Work with all your heart and soul.
19 | 0.78

2749 滞在(する) taizai(suru) *n.* stay, visit *v.* stay, visit, stop
- イギリス滞在中に彼に会った。— I met him during my stay in England.
19 | 0.89

2750 連携(する) renkei(suru) *n.* cooperation *v.* work together with
- 周囲との連携が不可欠だ。— It is important to cooperate with people around you.
19 | 0.62

2751 ライブ raibu *n.* live (music)
- たまにライブを聴きに行く。— I sometimes go and listen to live music.
19 | 0.69

2752 演ずる enzuru *v.* play, perform
- 彼女がヒロインを演ずる。— She will play the heroine.
19 | 0.85

2753 廃止(する) haishi(suru) *n.* abolition *v.* repeal
- そのシステムはずいぶん前に廃止された。— That system was abolished a long time ago.
19 | 0.81

2754 復活(する) fukkatsu(suru) *n.* revival, restoration *v.* revive, restore
- その町の復活を願う。— We hope for the town's recovery.
19 | 0.95

2755 借金(する) shakkin(suru) *n.* debt, loan *v.* borrow (money)
- 全ての借金を返し終わった。— He finished paying back all his debts.
19 | 0.97

2756 常識 joushiki *n.* common sense, general knowledge
- 彼は常識が全くない。— He has no common sense at all.
19 | 0.96

2757 闇 yami *n.* darkness, dark
- 闇の中を車で走った。— We drove through the darkness.
19 | 0.71

2758 見守る mimamoru *v.* watch, observe
- 母は子供を絶えず見守る。— Mother always watches over her children.
19 | 0.96

2759 不便 fuben *n.* inconvenience *na-adj.* inconvenient
- 家が不便なところにある。— The house is inconveniently situated.
19 | 0.73

2760 栄養 eiyou *n.* nutrition
- こんな食事では栄養が足りない。— You cannot get enough nutrition from a meal like this.
19 | 0.96

2761 フランス語 huransu go *n.* French language
- 大学でフランス語を勉強する。— I study French at university.
19 | 0.76

2762 アクセス akusesu *n.* access
- カフェでアクセスポイントを探した。— I looked for an access point in the café.
19 | 0.95

2763 PC piishii *n.* personal computer
- 自分のPCで仕事をする。— I work with my own PC.
19 | 0.35 | WB

2764 不幸 fukou *na-adj.* unhappiness, misfortune
- 彼は自分の不幸を嘆いた。— He regretted his misfortune.
19 | 0.94

2765 こだわる kodawaru *v.* stick to; be particular about
- 彼は細部にこだわる。— He is meticulous about it.
19 | 0.89

2766 カット katto *n.* cut
- 私は髪の毛をカットしてもらった。— I had my hair cut.
19 | 0.91

2767 乾く kawaku v. dry
- この生地は乾くのが早い。— This cloth dries quickly.
19 | 0.90

2768 おまけ omake n. addition, free gift
- お菓子のおまけを集める。— I collect free gifts that come inside boxes of sweets.
19 | 0.83

2769 をはじめ o hajime p. starting with . . . , including
- 校長をはじめとして、学校全体がその案に賛成した。— The entire school, including the principal, agreed with that idea.
19 | 0.74

2770 ついで tsuide n. on one's way, along the way
- ついでに、友達のうちへ寄った。— I stopped at a friend's house along the way.
19 | 0.87

2771 名称 meishou n. name
- 台湾の正式名称は何ですか。— What is the official name of Taiwan?
19 | 0.89

2772 鍛える kitaeru v. train, discipline
- 体を鍛えないといけない。— I must get in shape.
19 | 0.87

2773 大学生 daigaku-sei n. college student, university student
- 彼は来年大学生になる。— He will be a college student next year.
19 | 0.91

2774 左手 hidarite n. left hand; on one's left
- 新幹線から富士山が左手に見える。— We can see Mt. Fuji on our left from the bullet train.
19 | 0.86

2775 乾燥(する) kansou(suru) n. dryness v. dry
- 肌が乾燥して困る。— I have a problem with my dry skin.
19 | 0.94

2776 たった tatta adv. just, only
- たった今彼は帰りました。— He went home just now.
19 | 0.76

2777 およそ oyoso adv. around, about
- 彼はおよそ五年間海外で生活した。— He spent about five years abroad.
19 | 0.93

2778 八日 you-ka n. eighth (date); eight days
- 今月の八日が締め切りだ。— The deadline is the eighth of this month.
19 | 0.49 | NM

2779 ぴったり pittari adv. tight; exactly
- この靴は私にぴったりだ。— These shoes are perfect for me.
19 | 0.85

2780 添える soeru v. attach, add
- 申込書には写真を添えて下さい。— Attach the photograph to your application form.
19 | 0.76

2781 ノート nooto n. notebook
- ノートを持ってくるように。— Be sure to bring a notebook.
19 | 0.95

2782 配置(する) haichi(suru) n. arrangement, layout v. arrange
- 家具の配置を考えるのが好きです。— I like to think about the furniture layout.
19 | 0.89

2783 輸出(する) yushutsu(suru) n. exportation v. export
- その会社は自動車を海外に輸出している。— The company exports cars to foreign countries.
19 | 0.58

2784 陰 kage n. shade, shadow; behind someone's back
- 陰で悪口を言うな。— Don't speak ill of others behind their backs.
19 | 0.85

2785 漬ける tsukeru v. soak; pickle
- 一晩水に漬けておいた豆を使って調理した。— I cooked beans soaked in water overnight.
19 | 0.86

2786 果物 kudamono n. fruit
- スーパーで果物を買ってきて。— Go and get some fruit at the supermarket.
19 | 0.90

2787 個々 koko n. individual, each
- 個々の事例について調べる必要がある。— We must examine individual cases.
19 | 0.83

2788 十六日 juu roku nichi n. sixteenth (date); sixteen days
- 今月の十六日は彼の誕生日だ。— The 16th of this month is his birthday.
19 | 0.45 | NM

2789 電話番号 denwa bangou n. telephone number
- 電話番号を教えてくれませんか。— Could you tell me your telephone number?
19 | 0.63

2790 混む komu *v.* be crowded
- 電車が大変混んでいる。— The train is very crowded.
19 | 0.76

2791 築く kizuku *v.* build, have
- 彼らは新しい家庭を築き始めた。— They started to build a new family.
19 | 0.94

2792 穏やか odayaka *na-adj.* mild; calm, peaceful
- 彼は穏やかな口調で話をする。— He speaks in a calm tone of voice.
19 | 0.92

2793 結び付く musubitsuku *v.* join, be connected with
- 逮捕に結びつく重要な情報だ。— That is very important imformation that is connected to the person's arrest.
19 | 0.90

2794 崩れる kuzureru *v.* crumble, collapse
- 需要と供給のバランスが崩れることになる。— That will lead to an imbalance of demand and supply.
19 | 0.99

14 Plants

(frequency per million words)

(植物) (Plants)

桜 sakura 41.650 **cherry tree, cherry blossom**
紅葉 kouyou(suru)¹ 15.310 **autumn leaves; put on fall colors**
竹 take 14.096 **bamboo**
バラ bara 13.691 **rose**
梅 ume 9.941 **plum, Japanese apricot**
杉 sugi 9.391 **Japanese cedar**
桃 momo 8.492 **peach**
菊 kiku 8.187 **chrysanthemum**
稲 ine 6.485 **rice plant**
芝 shiba 6.133 **turf, lawn**
蓮 hasu 5.298 **lotus**
チューリップ chuurippu 3.115 **tulip**
ユリ yuri 2.903 **lily**
苔 koke 2.822 **moss**
アジサイ ajisai 2.799 **hydrangea**
イチョウ ichou 2.701 **ginkgo**
ツバキ tsubaki 2.372 **camellia**
ヒマワリ himawari 2.244 **sunflower**
コスモス kosumosu 2.155 **cosmos**
レンゲ renge 1.494 **Chinese milk vetch**
ケヤキ keyaki 1.476 **Japanese zelcova**
スミレ sumire 1.330 **violet**
白樺 shirakaba 1.289 **white birch**
アサガオ asagao 1.262 **morning glory**
つつじ tsutsuji 1.232 **azalea**
タンポポ tanpopo 1.208 **dandelion**
スイセン suisen 0.897 **narcissus**
シクラメン shikuramen 0.482 **cyclamen**
クスノキ kusunoki 0.360 **camphor tree**
キンモクセイ kin mokusei 0.305 **fragrant olive**

(植物に関わる動詞) (Verbs related to plants)

伸びる nobiru 52.364 **grow (also stretch, extend)**
咲く saku 43.480 **bloom**
植える ueru 22.840 **plant**
栽培(する) saibai(suru) 12.969 **cultivation; cultivate**
枯れる kareru 9.251 **wither, die**
蒔く maku 4.794 **sow**
茂る shigeru 4.786 **grow thick**
発芽(する) hatsuga(suru) 2.641 **sprout**
萎れる shioreru 1.043 **wilt**

(植物・部分) (Plants: parts)

実 mi 187.389 **seed; berry; fruit; nut (also pulp)**
花 hana 148.735 **flower**
葉 ha 35.460 **leaf**
種 tane² 35.411 **seed**
根 ne 22.397 **root**
枝 eda 21.183 **branch, twig, bough**
芽 me 11.472 **bud, shoot**
花粉 kafun 8.649 **pollen**
茎 kuki 7.775 **stem**
苗 nae 6.521 **young plant**
つぼみ tsubomi 6.301 **bud, shoot**
幹 miki 6.099 **trunk**
花弁 kaben 6.012 **petal**
梢 kozue 1.519 **treetop**

1 Reading: *kouyou*; if read as *momiji*, the ranking is 22873.
2 Reading changed from *shu* to *tane*.

2795 届ける todokeru v. deliver; send; report
- 落し物を交番に届けた。— I reported some lost property to the police box.
19 | 0.93

2796 プレー puree n. play
- 彼の素晴らしいプレーで、チームは優勝した。— Thanks to his great play, his team won the championship.
19 | 0.84

2797 進歩(する) shinpo(suru) n. progress, advance v. progress, advance
- 医学の進歩は著しい。— Medical advances are just amazing.
19 | 0.95

2798 百 hyaku num. hundred
- 百歳まで生きる。— I will live to be a hundred years old.
19 | 0.87

2799 (お)尻 (o)-shiri n. hips
- 彼女はお尻の形がきれいに見えるズボンを履いている。— She's wearing trousers that make her hips look good.
19 | 0.86

2800 汚れる yogoreru v. dirty, soil
- 彼はいつも穴の空いた汚れたジーンズをはいている。— He always wears torn, dirty jeans.
19 | 0.93

2801 産業 sangyou n. industry
- 多くのアフリカの国では産業が発達していない。— In many African countries industry is underdeveloped.
19 | 0.72

2802 前日 zenjitsu n. eve, previous day
- 前日に発表の練習をする。— They practiced their presentations the previous day.
19 | 0.94

2803 吸収(する) kyuushuu(suru) n. absorption, assimilation v. absorb, assimilate
- この布は汗をよく吸収する。— This material absorbs perspiration well.
19 | 0.98

2804 驚き odoroki n. surprise, amazement
- 彼が独身だったなんて驚きだ。— It was a surprise to learn that he was still single.
19 | 0.89

2805 ソ連 soren n. Soviet Union
- ソ連の崩壊に皆驚いた。— Everyone was surprised at the collapse of the Soviet Union.
19 | 0.64

2806 悲しみ kanashimi n. sadness, grief
- 彼女は毎日悲しみにくれていた。— She passed every day lost in her grief.
19 | 0.90

2807 十一日 juu ichi nichi n. eleventh (date); eleven days
- 十一日から学校が始まる。— School starts on the eleventh.
19 | 0.47 | NM

2808 最低 saitei n. minimum, lowest
- 最低五万円は必要だ。— It will cost a minimum of fifty thousand yen.
19 | 0.96

2809 十六 juu roku num. sixteen
- 彼女の十六歳の誕生日を祝う。— We will celebrate her sixteenth birthday.
19 | 0.88

2810 にんにく nin'niku n. garlic
- 料理ににんにくを使う。— We use garlic in cooking.
19 | 0.85

2811 順番 junban n. turn, order
- ようやく彼女の順番になった。— At last her turn came.
19 | 0.94

2812 裁判所 saiban-sho n. court, courthouse
- これは裁判所が課した罰金です。— This is the fine imposed by the court.
19 | 0.74

2813 観光(する) kankou(suru) n. sightseeing v. go sightseeing
- 北海道へ観光に行く。— We will go to Hokkaido to go sightseeing.
19 | 0.94

2814 申し訳 moushiwake n. excuse, apology
- まことに申し訳ありません。— I do apologize.
19 | 0.88

2815 葉っぱ happa n. leaf
- 葉っぱが全て落ちてしまった。— The leaves have all fallen.
19 | 0.79

2816 生き物 ikimono n. creature, life
- あらゆる生き物を大切にしなさい。— Care about all living things.
19 | 0.95

2817 演出(する) enshutsu(suru) n., v. direction, direct
- 彼が演出を担当します。— He is in charge of stage direction.
19 | 0.80

2818 ですが desu ga conj. but, however
- まだ冬ですが、春のように暖かい。— It is still winter, but the weather is warm like spring.
19 | 0.71

2819 本気 honki *n.* seriousness, earnestness *na-adj.* serious, earnest
- 私は本気です。— I am serious.
19 | 0.84

2820 三年生 san nen-sei *n.* third grade, third year
- 三年生から英語を勉強する。— They start studying English from third grade.
19 | 0.85

2821 記入(する) kinyuu(suru) *n.* entry *v.* fill in
- 書類に名前を記入しなさい。— Fill in your name on the form.
19 | 0.50

2822 見上げる miageru *v.* look up; respect
- 空を見上げてごらん。— Look up at the sky.
19 | 0.79

2823 話し合い hanashiai *n.* discussion, meeting
- 話し合いを2時間した。— We had a meeting for two hours.
19 | 0.90

2824 値 atai *n.* price
- 野菜の値段が上がっている。— Vegetable prices are increasing.
19 | 0.79

2825 一人暮らし hitorigurashi *n.* living alone, single life
- その老婦人は一人暮らしだ。— The old lady lives alone.
19 | 0.88

2826 趣旨 shushi *n.* purpose, intention, point
- 趣旨がよくわからなかった。— I couldn't get the point.
19 | 0.55

2827 柔らかい yawarakai *i-adj.* soft
- このパンはとてもやわらかい。— This bread is very soft.
19 | 0.89

2828 舌 shita *n.* tongue
- 舌を出してください。— Stick out your tongue.
19 | 0.84

2829 三時間 san jikan *n.* three hours
- 三時間仕事をする。— I work for three hours.
19 | 0.83

2830 後悔(する) koukai(suru) *n.* repentance, regret *v.* regret
- くだらない間違いをしたことを後悔する。— I regret making such a silly mistake.
19 | 0.82

2831 詰める tsumeru *v.* plug, pack, stuff
- お菓子を袋に詰める。— We pack sweets into a bag.
19 | 0.99

2832 勝利 shouri *n.* victory, triumph, winning
- そのチームは勝利を収めた。— The team won a victory.
19 | 0.88

2833 自覚(する) jikaku(suru) *n.* consciousness, awareness *v.* realize
- 自分の限界を自覚しなさい。— You should realize your own limits.
19 | 0.98

2834 今朝 kesa *n.* this morning
- 今朝から雨が降っている。— It has been raining since this morning.
19 | 0.54

2835 総合的 sougou-teki *na-adj.* synthetic, integrated, comprehensive
- 統合的なスキルを身につけるべきだ。— You should acquire integrated skills.
19 | 0.44 | OF

2836 美しさ utsukushi-sa *n.* beauty
- 彼女の美しさは比類がない。— Her beauty is beyond compare.
19 | 0.89

2837 法人 houjin *n.* corporation
- 法人の設立を申請する。— I apply for the establishment of a corporation.
19 | 0.40

2838 滑る suberu *v.* slide, slip; be slippery
- 雨の後は道路が滑る。— The road is slippery after the rain.
19 | 0.94

2839 極端 kyokutan *na-adj.* extreme
- それは極端すぎる。— That's going too far.
19 | 0.98

2840 留学(する) ryuugaku(suru) *n., v.* study abroad
- 留学を決めた。— I decided to study abroad.
19 | 0.85

2841 念 nen *n.* sense, feeling
- 私は彼女に尊敬の念を抱いている。— I have a sense of respect for her.
18 | 0.94

2842 銀座 ginza *n.* Ginza (place name)
- 銀座へ出かける。— We are going out to Ginza.
18 | 0.81

2843 十五年 juu go nen *n.* fifteen years
- 十五年後の日本について予想する。— They imagine what Japan will be like after fifteen years.
18 | 0.92

2844 漂う tadayou *v.* drift, float
- おいしいカレーのにおいが漂ってくる。— The scent of delicious curry is in the air.
18 | 0.81

2845 測る hakaru *v.* measure; weigh
- その人は家の高さを測っている。— The person is measuring the height of a house.
18 | 0.95

2846 永遠 eien *n.* eternity, permanence
- 芸術は永遠だ。— Art is eternal.
18 | 0.90

2847 十四日 juu yok-ka *n.* fourteenth (date); fourteen days
- 十四日に友達と会う。— I will meet my friend on the fourteenth.
18 | 0.51

2848 取り戻す torimodosu *v.* take back, repossess
- 彼はやっと自信を取り戻した。— He got back his confidence.
18 | 0.95

2849 いっぺん ip-pen *n.* at the same time; altogether
- ネットで別々に注文した品物がいっぺんに届いた。— The items I ordered separately on the internet arrived all at the same time.
18 | 0.81

2850 門 mon *n.* gate
- 彼は私を門の前で待ってる。— He is waiting for me in front of the gate.
18 | 0.85

2851 伸び nobi *n.* growth
- この木は驚くほど伸びが速い。— This tree grows surprisingly fast.
18 | 0.35 | OF

2852 たどる tadoru *v.* follow, trace, search
- 彼らは足跡をたどって、犯罪者を見つけた。— They found the criminal by following his footprints.
18 | 0.92

2853 事例 jirei *n.* case
- 過去の事例を調べる。— I will investigate past cases.
18 | 0.74

2854 どなた donata *pron.* who
- どなたですか。— Who is this?
18 | 0.72

2855 やばい yabai *i-adj.* risky, chancy
- やばい仕事に手を出す。— He is involved in risky business.
18 | 0.68

2856 冗談 joudan *n.* joke
- 彼は冗談ばかり言っている。— He is always making jokes.
18 | 0.85

2857 巣 su *n.* nest
- 鳥が巣を作っている。— A bird is making a nest.
18 | 0.87

2858 進展（する） shinten(suru) *n.* progress, development, evolution *v.* develop, progress, advance
- 私たちは自分たちのビジネスを進展させる必要がある。— We need to develop our business.
18 | 0.49

2859 手伝い tetsudai *n.* help
- 母の料理の手伝いをした。— I helped my mother with the cooking.
18 | 0.93

2860 死亡（する） shibou(suru) *n.* death, decease *v.* die
- 彼はバスの事故で死亡した。— He died in a bus accident.
18 | 0.88

2861 細胞 saibou *n.* cell
- 人間の体はたくさんの細胞でできている。— The human body is made up of many cells.
18 | 0.90

2862 犠牲 gisei *n.* sacrifice, expense
- 戦争で多くの人が犠牲になった。— A great many lives were sacrificed during the war.
18 | 0.93

2863 殴る naguru *v.* hit, strike
- 彼は友達の顔を殴った。— He hit his friend's face.
18 | 0.90

2864 前後 zengo *n.* back and forth
- 腕を前後に動かす。— We are moving our arms back and forth.
18 | 0.98

2865 対立（する） tairitsu(suru) *n.* opposition, conflict *v.* be opposed to
- その二人の意見は対立していた。— The two people's opinions stood in opposition.
18 | 0.89

2866 六日 mui-ka *n.* sixth (date); six days
- 六日まで学校で勉強する。— I study at school until the sixth.
18 | 0.52

2867 比率 hiritsu *n.* ratio, proportion
- この事務所の男女の比率が逆転した。— The male-female ratio in this office has reversed itself.
18 | 0.49

2868 タイ tai *n.* Thailand
- タイへ旅行に行く。— I'm going on a trip to Thailand.
18 | 0.97

2869 放つ hanatsu *v.* fly, loose
- その蛍は美しい光を放っている。— The firefly is giving off a beautiful light.
18 | 0.81

2870 香港 honkon *n.* Hong Kong
- 香港へ観光に行く。— I will go to Hong Kong to go sightseeing.
18 | 0.98

2871 湖 mizuumi *n.* lake
- 私たちは湖で釣りをしている。— We are fishing on the lake.
18 | 0.88

2872 稼ぐ kasegu *v.* earn
- お金を稼ぐために働く。— I work to earn money.
18 | 0.91

2873 出現(する) shutsugen(suru) *n.* appearance, dawn, birth, advent *v.* appear
- インターネットの出現によって、社会は変わった。— With the advent of the Internet, our society has changed.
18 | 0.86

2874 真実 shinjitsu *n.* truth, reality
- 真実を話します。— I'll tell you the truth.
18 | 0.82

2875 前回 zenkai *n.* last time, previous time
- 前回は会議は9時から始まった。— The meeting started at nine o'clock last time.
18 | 0.85

2876 工事(する) kouji(suru) *n.* construction, work *v.* construct
- あのビルは、まだ工事中だ。— The building is still under construction.
18 | 0.90

2877 科学 kagaku *n.* science
- この問題は現代科学では解明されていない。— This problem is not solved by modern science.
18 | 0.93

2878 順 jun *n.* order
- 先着順にプレゼントがもらえる。— These presents are given on a first-come-first-served basis.
18 | 0.81

2879 読者 dokusha *n.* reader
- この雑誌の読者はほとんどが十代だ。— The readers of this magazine are mostly teenagers.
18 | 0.71

2880 不足(する) fusoku(suru) *n.* lack, shortage *v.* be insufficient
- 住宅の不足が深刻だ。— The housing shortage is serious.
18 | 0.94

2881 社会的 shakai-teki *na-adj.* social
- 社会的な責任を負う。— We all have social responsibility.
18 | 0.87

2882 限定(する) gentei(suru) *n.* restriction, limitation *v.* restrict, limit
- 訪問時間は三十分に限定されている。— Visiting time is limited to thirty minutes.
18 | 0.94

2883 劇団 gekidan *n.* theater company
- 私は劇団に所属している。— I am a member of the theater company.
18 | 0.59

2884 看護婦 kango-fu *n.* nurse (female)
- 彼女はベテランの看護婦だ。— She is a veteran nurse.
18 | 0.89

2885 人参 ninjin *n.* carrot
- にんじんが好きだ。— I like carrots.
18 | 0.93

2886 一面 ichimen *n.* side, facet
- 物事の一面だけをみて、判断してはいけない。— Don't make a decision based on only one side of things.
18 | 0.97

2887 生涯 shougai *n.* life, lifetime; career
- 彼は幸せな生涯を送った。— He lived a happy life.
18 | 0.89

2888 意思 ishi *n.* will, intention
- 彼らは意思の疎通がうまくいっていない。— They do not understand each other.
18 | 0.92

2889 追加(する) tsuika(suru) *n.* addition, supplement *v.* add, supplement
- 追加の注文はできるだけ早くお願いします。— Please place additional orders as soon as possible.
18 | 0.91

2890 台湾 taiwan *n.* Taiwan
- 私は今週台湾へ行く。— I will go to Taiwan this week.
18 | 0.99

2891 日常生活 nichijou seikatsu *n.* daily life
- 日常生活を楽しんでいる。— She is really enjoying her daily life.
18 | 0.93

2892 拭く fuku *v.* wipe, dry
- 母が布巾でお皿を拭いている。— My mother is drying dishes with a cloth.
18 | 0.89

2893 レース reesu *n.* race
- マラソンレースに参加する。— I will participate in a marathon race.
18 | 0.79

2894 民族 minzoku *n.* people, race, nation
- その地域の民族は、違う言葉を話す。— The peoples in that area speak different languages.
18 | 0.90

2895 天 ten *n.* sky, heaven
- 天の星を見る。— I look at the stars in the sky.
18 | 0.77

2896 花火 hanabi *n.* firework
- 花火を見に行く。— I will go to watch the fireworks.
18 | 0.82

2897 項目 koumoku *n.* item, heading
- 必要な項目を考える。— I think about the items that we need.
18 | 0.94

2898 動向 doukou *n.* trend, movement
- 彼らは今後の動向を知らせる。— They advise on future trends.
18 | 0.42

2899 にしろ ni shiro *p. conj.* even if
- 故意じゃないにしろ、罪は罪だ。— A crime is a crime even if you did it unintentionally.
18 | 0.78

2900 日頃 higoro *n.* every day
- 彼は日頃から走っている。— He runs every day.
18 | 0.86

2901 砂 suna *n.* sand
- 砂が目に入った。— The sand got into my eyes.
18 | 0.95

2902 大根 daikon *n.* Japanese radish, radish
- 大根を使って料理をする。— I cook using Japanese radishes.
18 | 0.90

2903 感激(する) kangeki(suru) *n.* deep emotion *v.* be impressed
- その日感激したことについて日記を書いた。— I wrote in my diary about things that impressed me that day.
18 | 0.81

2904 浮く uku *v.* float, suspend
- 海にたくさんごみが浮いている。— Lots of garbage is floating on the sea.
18 | 0.93

2905 まして mashite *adv.* much less, much more
- 彼女は丁寧な言葉も知らないし、まして礼儀は知るはずもない。— She doesn't even know polite language, much less good manners.
18 | 0.93

2906 リスク risuku *n.* risk
- リスクを最小限に抑える。— I will minimize the risk.
18 | 0.93

2907 引っ掛かる hikkakaru *v.* catch; be caught
- 彼はよく詐欺にひっかかる。— He is often caught committing fraud.
18 | 0.92

2908 オークション ookushon *n.* auction
- オークションで一億円で落札された。— It was knocked down for 100 million yen at auction.
18 | 0.34 | WB

2909 二十一日 nijuu ichi nichi *n.* twenty-first (date); twenty-one days
- 二十一日にもう一度来てください。— Come again on the twenty-first.
18 | 0.52

2910 ほら hora *interj.* Look!
- ほら、あそこにあるよ。— Look! It is over there.
18 | 0.83

2911 を通して o tooshi te *cp.* according to; through
- 人を通して聞いたところ、彼は元気そうだ。— According to what I have heard from others, he is well.
18 | 0.00 | SP

2912 武器 buki *n.* weapon
- 兵士は武器を構えた。— The soldiers held the weapons.
18 | 0.97

2913 都内 tonai *n.* in the city
- 都内を散策する。— We are walking around the city.
18 | 0.83

2914 違反(する) ihan(suru) *n.* violation *v.* violate
- 重大な違反があった。— There was a serious violation.
18 | 0.58

2915 すっきり(する) sukkiri(suru) *adv., v.* feel refreshed
- 新鮮な空気を吸うとすっきりする。— A breath of fresh air makes me feel refreshed.
18 | 0.83

2916 十二日 juu ni nichi *n.* twelfth (date), twelve days
- 十二日の便で国に帰ります。— I will go back to my country on the flight on the twelfth.
18 | 0.50 | NM

2917 別に betsu ni *adv.* (not) particularly
- 別に構いません。— I don't mind particularly.
18 | 0.76

2918 十八日 juu hachi nichi *n.* eighteenth (date); eighteen days
- 次の会議は十八日です。— We'll have the next meeting on the eighteenth.
18 | 0.49 | NM

2919 お宅 o-taku *n.* your house
- 明日、お宅へ伺います。— I'll visit your house tomorrow.
18 | 0.91

2920 交通 koutsuu *n.* traffic; transportation
- ここは交通の便が悪い。— Public transportation is very poor in this area.
18 | 0.93

2921 業界 gyoukai *n.* business world
- 姉は映画業界で働いている。— My older sister works in the movie world.
18 | 0.98

2922 解放(する) kaihou(suru) *n.* liberation *v.* liberate
- 人質の解放をめざす。— We work for the liberation of the hostage.
18 | 0.89

2923 需要 juyou *n.* demand
- エネルギーの需要が急速に伸びている。— Demand for energy is rapidly growing.
18 | 0.65

2924 高度 koudo *n.* altitude *na-adj.* high, advanced
- 製造には高度な技術が必要だ。— A high level of skill is required to produce it.
18 | 0.81

2925 帰国(する) kikoku(suru) *n., v.* going/coming back to one's own country
- 留学していた弟が先週帰国した。— My younger brother who was studying abroad came back home last week.
18 | 0.95

2926 午前中 gozen-chuu *n.* in the morning, throughout the morning
- 午前中に病院へ行った。— I went to the hospital in the morning.
18 | 0.92

2927 実践(する) jissen(suru) *n., v.* practice
- 実践を通して技術を学んだ。— I learned the technique through practice.
18 | 0.88

2928 深刻 shinkoku *na-adj.* serious
- 事態は深刻だ。— The situation is serious.
18 | 0.90

2929 十八 juu hachi *num.* eighteen
- 十八の国から参加者が集まった。— The participants gathered from eighteen countries.
18 | 0.89

2930 関係者 kankei-sha *n.* person concerned
- 関係者以外は立入禁止である。— No unauthorized entry.
18 | 0.87

2931 追いかける oikakeru *v.* run after, chase
- パトカーが信号無視をした車を追いかけた。— A police car chased after the car which ignored the traffic lights.
18 | 0.90

2932 作用(する) sayou(suru) *n.* action *v.* act
- この物質は人体に有害な作用を及ぼす。— This material has harmful effects on the human body.
18 | 0.89

2933 毎週 maishuu *adv.* every week
- 毎週月曜日にミーティングがある。— We have a meeting every Monday.
18 | 0.80

2934 五つ itsu-tsu *n.* five
- リンゴを五つ買った。— I bought five apples.
18 | 0.97

2935 頻繁 hinpan *na-adj.* frequent
- この交差点では事故が頻繁に起こる。— Traffic accidents occur frequently at this crossing.
18 | 0.96

2936 差別(する) sabetsu(suru) *n.* discrimination *v.* discriminate
- 不当な差別を受けた。— I was discriminated against unjustly.
18 | 0.98

2937 大声 oogoe *n.* loud voice
- 誰かが大声で叫んだ。— Someone cried out.
18 | 0.81

2938 長年 naganen *adv.* long time; many years
- A国とB国は長年にわたり対立している。— Country A and Country B have been at odds for many years.
18 | 0.96

2939 固まり katamari *n.* mass, lump
- 屋根から大きな雪の固まりが落ちてきた。— A large mass of snow fell from the roof.
18 | 0.90

2940 快適 kaiteki *na-adj.* comfortable
- そのホテルは清潔で快適だった。— The hotel was clean and comfortable.
18 | 0.92

2941 あいつ aitsu *pron.* that fellow; that thing
- あいつには負けたくない。— I don't want to be beaten by that fellow.
18 | 0.74

2942 研修(する) kenshuu(suru) *n.* training *v.* study
- 三日間の研修を受けた。— I joined in the three-day training.
18 | 0.89

2943 沈む shizumu *v.* sink, go down
- その船は海の底に沈んだ。— The ship sank to the bottom of the sea.
18 | 0.95

2944 男子 danshi *n.* boy, man
- このクラスは女子より男子のほうが多い。— There are more boys than girls in this class.
18 | 0.80

2945 爪 tsume *n.* nail; claw
- 伸びた爪を切った。— I cut my long nails.
18 | 0.85

2946 青年 seinen *n.* young man
- 彼は真面目な青年だ。— He is an honest young man.
18 | 0.90

2947 捕まえる tsukamaeru *v.* catch, arrest
- 警察が犯人を捕まえた。— The police arrested a criminal.
18 | 0.93

2948 こいつ koitsu *pron.* this fellow; this thing
- こいつは駄目だ。— This fellow is no good.
18 | 0.83

2949 氷 koori *n.* ice
- ジュースに氷を入れますか。— Do you put ice in the juice?
18 | 0.95

2950 十七日 juu shichi nichi *n.* seventeenth (date); seventeen days
- 十七日に予約した。— I made a reservation for the seventeenth.
18 | 0.46 | NM

2951 鋭い surudoi *i-adj.* sharp, pointed
- このナイフは刃が鋭い。— This knife has a sharp blade.
18 | 0.77

2952 いじめる ijimeru *v.* torment, bully, tease
- 動物をいじめてはいけない。— You must not torment animals.
18 | 0.88

2953 業者 gyousha *n.* dealer, agent, operator
- この部屋の掃除は業者に頼んである。— I asked the cleaning company to clean this room.
18 | 0.96

2954 大半 taihan *n.* better part, most part
- 猫は一日の大半を寝て過ごす。— The cat spends most of the day sleeping.
18 | 0.96

2955 作り上げる tsukuri-ageru *v.* make up, build up
- 一年かけてこのシステムを作り上げた。— We spent one year building up this system.
18 | 0.94

2956 三つ目 mit-tsu-me *n.* third
- 三つ目の交差点を左に曲がってください。— Turn left at the third crossing.
18 | 0.74

2957 称する shou suru *v.* call; pretend
- 彼は関係者と称して、立入禁止区域に入っていった。— He pretended to be a member of staff and got into the restricted area.
18 | 0.88

2958 とすれば to sure ba *p. conj.* if that is the case
- 一つだけ選ぶとすれば、これだ。— If I choose only one, I choose this.
18 | 0.76

2959 支持(する) shiji(suru) *n.* support *v.* support
- この大統領は絶大な支持を受けている。— This President receives great support.
18 | 0.90

2960 九日 kokono-ka *n.* ninth (date); nine days
- 九日は私の誕生日だった。— The ninth was my birthday.
18 | 0.46 | NM

2961 雌 mesu *n.* female animal
- この猫は雄ですか、雌ですか。— Is this cat male or female?
18 | 0.96

2962 跡 ato *n.* track, trail; mark, sign
- タイヤの跡が残っている。— There are tire tracks left behind.
18 | 0.92

2963 トマト tomato *n.* tomato
- トマトのサラダを食べた。— I ate a tomato salad.
18 | 0.92

2964 エピソード episoodo *n.* episode, anecdote
- 彼には面白いエピソードがたくさんある。— He has a lot of interesting anecdotes.
18 | 0.89

2965 真 makoto *n.* truth, fact
- それは真か。— Is it the truth?
18 | 0.85

2966 訪問(する) houmon(suru) *n.* visit, call *v.* visit, call (on)
- 首相がA国を訪問した。— The prime minister visited Country A.
18 | 0.94

2967 スピーチ supiichi *n.* speech
- 友人に結婚式のスピーチを頼んだ。— I asked my friend to make a speech at the wedding ceremony.
18 | 0.54

2968 一見 ikken *adv.* at a glance
- 一見同じようだが、実は違う。— They look the same at first glance, but in fact they are different.
18 | 0.91

2969 足元 ashimoto *n.* at one's feet; step
- 足元に転がってきたボールを拾った。— I picked up the ball which rolled to my feet.
18 | 0.87

2970 台所 daidokoro *n.* kitchen
- 母は台所にいます。— My mother is in the kitchen.
18 | 0.91

2971 ねばならない ne ba nara nai *cp.* must, have to
- これだけは言わねばならない。— I must say only this.
18 | 0.67

2972 毛 ke *n.* hair; fur; wool
- この犬は毛がやわらかい。— This dog has soft fur.
18 | 0.92

2973 一点 it-ten *n.* point, single point
- 皆の関心は、その一点に集中した。— Everybody's interest was concentrated on that point.
18 | 0.96

2974 二十三日 nijuu san nichi *n.* twenty-third (date); twenty-three days
- 二十三日は空いていますか。— Are you free on the twenty-third?
17 | 0.51 | NM

2975 支給（する）shikyuu(suru) *n.* provision, payment *v.* provide, pay
- 通勤手当が支給される。— A commutation allowance is paid.
17 | 0.77

2976 経費 keihi *n.* expense, cost
- この計画には莫大な経費がかかる。— This plan requires huge expense.
17 | 0.69

2977 晴れる hareru *v.* clear up, be dispelled; be refreshed
- 天気予報によると、今日は晴れるそうです。— According to the weather forecast, it will be fine today.
17 | 0.84

2978 感心（する）kanshin(suru) *n.* admiration *v.* admire
- 彼の努力に感心した。— I admired his effort.
17 | 0.88

2979 ポケット poketto *n.* pocket
- 彼はポケットから何か取り出した。— He took something out from his pocket.
17 | 0.86

2980 決意（する）ketsui(suru) *n.* determination *v.* resolve
- 彼の決意は固いようだ。— His determination seems to be firm.
17 | 0.94

2981 法則 housoku *n.* law
- ニュートンは万有引力の法則を発見した。— Newton discovered the law of universal gravitation.
17 | 0.94

2982 とはいえ to wa ie *p. conj.* though, however
- 失敗したとはいえ、よく頑張った。— Though you failed, you did your best.
17 | 0.79

2983 資産 shisan *n.* assets, property
- 彼は十分な資産がある。— He has enough assets.
17 | 0.85

2984 慎重 shinchou *na-adj.* careful, discreet
- 慎重に検討するべきだ。— You should examine it carefully.
17 | 0.89

2985 二十四日 nijuu yok-ka *n.* twenty-fourth (date); twenty-four days
- 二十四日は忙しい。— I will be busy on the twenty-fourth.
17 | 0.50

2986 尊敬（する）sonkei(suru) *n.* respect *v.* respect
- 私は彼を尊敬している。— I respect him.
17 | 0.93

2987 尽くす tsukusu *v.* do one's best, devote; exhaust
- 勝つために全力を尽くすつもりだ。— I will do my best to win.
17 | 0.96

2988 謎 nazo *n.* mystery, riddle
- ついに事件の謎が解けた。— The mystery of the murder was finally solved.
17 | 0.85

2989 田んぼ tanbo *n.* rice field
- うちは田んぼに囲まれている。— My house is surrounded by rice fields.
17 | 0.89

2990 評判 hyouban *n.* reputation; popularity
- 評判どおりあの店の料理はおいしかった。— The food at that restaurant was as delicious as reputed.

17 | 0.89

2991 寒さ samu-sa *n.* cold
- 今年の冬は寒さが厳しい。— It is bitterly cold this winter.

17 | 0.93

2992 天井 tenjou *n.* ceiling
- この家は天井が高い。— This house has high ceilings.

17 | 0.88

2993 池袋 ikebukuro *n.* Ikebukuro (place name)
- 池袋のデパートで買い物をした。— I did my shopping at a department store in Ikebukuro.

17 | 0.55

2994 せめて semete *adv.* at least, at most
- 次のテストではせめて七十点は取りたい。— I want to get 70 marks at least in the next test.

17 | 0.93

2995 喫茶店 kissa-ten *n.* tearoom, coffee shop, café
- 喫茶店でコーヒーを飲んだ。— I had some coffee in a cafe.

17 | 0.78

2996 従業員 juugyou-in *n.* employee, worker
- このホテルの従業員はみんな若い。— All the employees in this hotel are young.

17 | 0.95

2997 嫁 yome *n.* wife; bride; daughter-in-law
- 嫁と姑はいい関係だ。— My wife and my mother have a good relationship.

17 | 0.82

2998 浮かべる ukaberu *v.* float; show; imagine
- 子供達が池に船を浮かべて遊んでいる。— Children are playing, floating a boat on the pond.

17 | 0.67

2999 災害 saigai *n.* disaster, calamity
- いつ大きな災害が起きるかわからない。— Nobody knows when a great disaster will happen.

17 | 0.55

3000 国際的 kokusai-teki *na-adj.* international
- 解決には国際的な協力が必要だ。— International cooperation is necessary for the solution.

17 | 0.63

3001 髪の毛 kaminoke *n.* hair
- 床に髪の毛が落ちている。— Hair has fallen on the floor.

17 | 0.84

3002 ないといけない nai to ike nai *cp.* must, have to
- 仕事に行かないといけない。— I have to go to work.

17 | 0.00 | SP

3003 加入（する）kanyuu(suru) *n.* admission, joining *v.* join
- 健康保険に加入する。— I will join the health insurance scheme.

17 | 0.80

3004 受け付け uketsuke *n.* acceptance, information desk, reception (desk)
- 受け付けは昨日締め切られました。— The deadline for accepting applications was yesterday.

17 | 0.47

3005 玉 tama *n.* ball; coin
- 子供達が小さい玉を転がして遊んでいる。— Children are playing, rolling small balls.

17 | 0.91

3006 型 kata *n.* model, pattern, type
- 古い型のパソコンを安く買った。— I bought an old model of PC cheaply.

17 | 0.94

3007 順調 junchou *na-adj.* satisfactory, favorable, smooth
- 新事業は順調なスタートを切った。— The new business made a favorable start.

17 | 0.97

3008 専門 senmon *n.* specialty, speciality
- 彼女の専門は法律だ。— Her specialty is law.

17 | 0.96

3009 供給（する）kyoukyuu(suru) *n., v.* supply
- 需要が急増して、供給が追いつかない。— Demand has increased rapidly and supply cannot keep up.

17 | 0.70

3010 振り furi *n.* pretence
- 私は知らない振りをした。— I pretended not to know.

17 | 0.87

3011 売り上げ uriage *n.* sales
- 売り上げが20パーセント伸びた。— Sales were up 20 percent.

17 | 0.97

3012 建築（する）kenchiku(suru) *n.* architecture, construction *v.* build
- ここにマンションが建築される予定だ。— An apartment building will be built here.

17 | 0.95

3013 利用者 riyou-sha *n.* user
- このサービスの利用者は毎年増えている。— The number of users of this service increases every year.

17 | 0.85

15 School

(frequency per million words)

(学校) (Educational institution)
学校 gakkou 253.320 school
大学 daigaku 189.107 university, college
高校 koukou 113.696 high school
小学校 shou-gakkou 108.930 elementary school, primary school
中学 chuugaku 45.672 junior high school
幼稚園 youchi-en 40.674 preschool, kindergarten
中学校 chuu-gakkou 39.208 junior high school
塾 juku 27.985 cram school
予備校 yobi-kou 13.192 cram school preparing for university entrance examinations
保育園 hoiku-en 11.445 nursery school, day care
専門学校 senmon gakkou 10.359 technical school, college, vocational school
短大(短期大学) tandai 6.537 junior college
女子大 joshi-dai 3.113 women's college
男子校 danshi-kou 1.400 boys' school
女子校 joshi-kou 1.186 girls' school

(活動・行事) (Activity, event)
試験 shiken 41.520 exam
夏休み natsuyasumi 28.409 summer holiday
クラブ kurabu 25.580 club
部活 bukatsu 25.367 club
サークル saakuru 25.032 club (also circle)
合宿(する) gasshuku(suru) 14.060 training camp; stay together in a camp
運動会 undou kai 9.504 sports meeting
修学旅行 shuugaku ryokou 6.590 school trip
卒業式 sotsugyou shiki 5.847 graduation ceremony
春休み haruyasumi 5.515 spring vacation
入学式 nyuugaku shiki 4.724 entrance ceremony
学園祭 gakuen-sai 3.890 school festival
遠足 ensoku 3.722 excursion
冬休み fuyuyasumi 3.092 winter vacation
入学試験(入試) nyuugaku shiken[1] 1.093 entrance examination
課外活動 kagai katsudou 0.831 after-school activities

(学生・教師) (Student, teacher)
学生 gakusei 70.489 student
生徒 seito 64.735 student, pupil
先輩 senpai 44.955 senior, elder
小学生 shougaku-sei 40.165 elementary school student
高校生 koukou-sei 39.618 high school student
教師 kyoushi 33.621 teacher
中学生 chuugaku-sei 31.659 junior high school student
教授 kyouju 24.094 professor
講師 koushi 20.239 lecturer (also speaker)
大学生 daigaku-sei 18.951 college student, university student
後輩 kouhai 14.052 junior
同級生 doukyuu-sei 13.340 classmate
児童 jidou 12.446 school child
同期 douki 11.922 same period, same class
園児 enji 1.655 kindergarten child

(授業・クラス・学年など) (Course, class, grade)
授業 jugyou 78.805 class, lesson at school
クラス kurasu 48.384 class
登録(する) touroku(suru) 34.738 registration, entry; register, enroll
出席(する) shusseki(suru) 20.523 attendance; attend
単位 tan'i 16.581 unit, credit
講義 kougi 11.230 lecture
学部 gakubu 9.367 faculty, department
学年 gakunen 9.039 grade, year
専攻(する) senkou(suru) 6.174 major
欠席(する) kesseki(suru) 3.280 absence; be absent

---

[1] nyuushi is ranked 6376.

3014 多様 tayou *na-adj.* various
- 多様なニーズに応える努力をする。— I make efforts to meet various needs.
17 | 0.64

3015 地方公共団体 chihou koukyou dantai *n.* local public body
- 国から地方公共団体へ補助金が交付される。— A subsidy is issued from the state to the local public body.
17 | 0.31 | OF

3016 じゃん jan *p. disc.* isn't it
- いいじゃん。— It's good, isn't it?
17 | 0.65

3017 鉄道 tetsudou *n.* railroad, railway
- 開通したばかりの鉄道を利用した。— I used the railroad which had just been opened.
17 | 0.90

3018 誕生日 tanjou bi *n.* birthday
- 今日は弟の誕生日だ。— It is my younger brother's birthday today.
17 | 0.83

3019 五十年 gojuu nen *n.* fifty years
- この問題の解決までに五十年かかった。— It took fifty years to solve this problem.
17 | 0.60

3020 役員 yakuin *n.* official, director
- 会社の役員が集まった。— The directors of the company gathered.
17 | 0.79

3021 設備 setsubi *n.* equipment, facilities
- あの病院は設備が整っている。— That hospital is well-equipped.
17 | 0.87

3022 悪化（する）akka(suru) *n.* change for the worse *v.* worsen
- 治安が悪化している。— Public safety is deteriorating.
17 | 0.89

3023 用 you *n.* something to do; use
- 用があって、行けないんです。— I can't go because I have something to do.
17 | 0.89

3024 ただいま tadaima *adv.* now, just now, at once; I'm back!
- ただいま参ります。— I'm coming just now.
17 | 0.46

3025 十三日 juu san nichi *n.* thirteenth (date); thirteen days
- 十三日の金曜日は不吉だ。— Friday the thirteenth is an unlucky date.
17 | 0.46 | NM

3026 遺跡 iseki *n.* ruins, remains
- 父は古代の遺跡を訪ねるのが好きだ。— My father likes visiting ancient ruins.
17 | 0.85

3027 消費（する）shouhi(suru) *n.* consumption *v.* consume
- この村の人々は魚を多く消費する。— The people of this village consume a lot of fish.
17 | 0.78

3028 模様 moyou *n.* pattern, design, look
- 彼は不思議な模様の服を着ていた。— He wore clothes of a strange design.
17 | 0.94

3029 深める fukameru *v.* deepen
- 環境問題への理解を深めたい。— I want to deepen my understanding of environmental problems.
17 | 0.80

3030 パパ papa *n.* papa, dad
- うちのパパは優しい。— My dad is kind.
17 | 0.80

3031 文 bun *n.* sentence
- わかりにくいので、この文を直してください。— Please correct this sentence because it is difficult to understand.
17 | 0.88

3032 中国人 chuugoku-jin *n.* Chinese (person)
- 彼は中国人だ。— He is Chinese.
17 | 0.89

3033 活性化（する）kassei-ka(suru) *n.* revitalization *v.* revitalize
- 経済を活性化する政策が必要だ。— Policies to revitalize the economy are required.
17 | 0.82

3034 聖書 seisho *n.* Bible
- 毎日聖書を読む。— I read the Bible every day.
17 | 0.71

3035 神経 shinkei *n.* nerve
- 歯医者で歯の神経を抜いた。— I had root canal treatment at the dentist.
17 | 0.90

3036 混乱（する）konran(suru) *n.* confusion *v.* get confused
- 混乱して、何も考えられない。— I'm confused, so I can't think about anything.
17 | 0.89

3037 ど do *p.* but (Classical)
- 声は聞こえど姿は見えない。— I can hear a voice, but I can't see anyone.
17 | 0.91

3038 癒す iyasu *v.* heal, cure, recover from
- ゆっくり休んで、仕事のストレスを癒した。— I took a good rest and recovered from work-related stress.

17 | 0.87

3039 磨く migaku *v.* polish, brush; improve
- 寝る前に歯を磨く。— I brush my teeth before going to bed.

17 | 0.92

3040 動作(する) dousa(suru) *n.* movement, operation *v.* operate
- パソコンの動作が遅くなった。— The PC was running slowly.

17 | 0.93

3041 コンサート konsaato *n.* concert
- 一緒にクラシックのコンサートに行かない？ — Would you like to come to a classical music concert with me?

17 | 0.84

3042 粉 kona *n.* flour, powder
- 食後にこの粉の薬を飲んでください。— Take this powdered medicine after meals.

17 | 0.92

3043 身長 shinchou *n.* height
- 彼は身長が180センチ以上ある。— He is over 180 centimeters tall.

17 | 0.93

3044 賛成(する) sansei(suru) *n.* agreement *v.* agree
- この意見に賛成の人は手を挙げてください。— Please raise your hand if you agree with this opinion.

17 | 0.90

3045 形態 keitai *n.* form
- 現代はさまざまな雇用形態がある。— There are various forms of employment in the present day.

17 | 0.78

3046 につれて ni tsure te *cp.* as
- 人口の増加につれて、様々な問題が出てきた。— As the population increased, various problems emerged.

17 | 0.91

3047 部下 buka *n.* subordinate
- この仕事は部下に任せよう。— I will entrust this job to my subordinate.

17 | 0.83

3048 二十世紀 nijis-seiki *n.* twentieth century
- この戦争は二十世紀の初めに起きた。— This war happened at the beginning of the twentieth century.

17 | 0.83

3049 ひょっとする hyotto suru *v.* perhaps
- ひょっとしたらこれは偽物かもしれない。— This may possibly be an imitation.

17 | 0.86

3050 勤務(する) kinmu(suru) *n.* service, duty, work *v.* work, serve
- 父は勤務中に倒れた。— My father fell while on duty.

17 | 0.96

3051 恋愛(する) ren'ai(suru) *n.* love (romantic) *v.* love
- 彼女からよく恋愛について相談された。— I was often consulted by her about love.

17 | 0.81

3052 都道府県 to dou fu ken *n.* prefectures
- 日本には都道府県が四十七ある。— There are forty-seven prefectures in Japan.

17 | 0.35 | OF

3053 誤解(する) gokai(suru) *n.* misunderstanding *v.* misunderstand
- あいまいな言い方は誤解を招く。— Vague expressions cause misunderstanding.

17 | 0.97

3054 直前 chokuzen *n.* just before
- 出発の直前まで、行くかどうか悩んだ。— I worried about whether or not to go until just before departure.

17 | 0.97

3055 平均(する) heikin(suru) *n.* average *v.* average
- 睡眠時間は平均すると一日六時間ぐらいだ。— I sleep six hours a night on average.

17 | 0.87

3056 出身 shusshin *n.* hometown; alma mater
- ご出身はどちらですか。— Where are you from?

17 | 0.83

3057 区 ku *n.* ward, district
- この区には外国人が多く住んでいる。— Many foreigners live in this ward.

17 | 0.70

3058 しょう油 shouyu *n.* soy sauce
- さしみにしょう油をつけて食べる。— I eat sashimi with soy sauce.

17 | 0.92

3059 こつ kotsu *n.* knack
- この料理を上手に作るこつを教えてください。— Teach me the knack of making this dish well.

17 | 0.82

3060 翻訳(する) hon'yaku(suru) *n.* translation *v.* translate
- ロシア文学の翻訳をやっています。— I do translation of Russian literature.

17 | 0.88

3061 ぼおっと bootto *adv.* vacantly; dimly
- 彼女は窓の外をぼおっと見ていた。— She looked vacantly out of the window.
17 | 0.00 | SP

3062 ソース soosu *n.* sauce; source
- このステーキのソースがおいしい。— The sauce on this steak is delicious.
17 | 0.85

3063 二十二日 nijuu ni nichi *n.* twenty-second (date); twenty-two days
- 彼の帰国日は22日です。— He will return on the twenty-second.
17 | 0.50

3064 固まる katamaru *v.* harden; become certain
- 卵が固まったら、火を止めてください。— When the egg hardens, turn off the heat.
17 | 0.97

3065 ステージ steeji *n.* stage
- ステージに上がってください。— Please come up onto the stage.
17 | 0.87

3066 ストーリー sutoorii *n.* story
- この映画のストーリーを簡単に教えてください。— Tell me the story of this film briefly.
17 | 0.86

3067 越す kosu *v.* cross, pass
- この鳥は毎年この地方で冬を越す。— These birds pass the winter in this district every year.
17 | 0.98

3068 まとまる matomaru *v.* be well arranged; be united; be settled
- みんなの意見がなかなかまとまらない。— Everyone's opinions are not readily united.
17 | 0.99

3069 始まり hajimari *n.* beginning, origin
- 新しい一日の始まりだ。— It's the beginning of a new day.
17 | 0.95

3070 解く toku *v.* untie; solve; remove
- 彼はすらすらとその問題を解いた。— He solved the question easily.
17 | 0.94

3071 別れ wakare *n.* parting, farewell
- 彼女に別れを告げた。— I said good-bye to my girlfriend.
17 | 0.86

3072 女房 nyoubou *n.* wife
- うちの女房は倹約家だ。— My wife is thrifty.
17 | 0.79

3073 才能 sainou *n.* talent, ability
- このピアニストは素晴らしい才能を持っている。— This pianist has a splendid talent.
17 | 0.89

3074 背後 haigo *n.* back; background
- この事件の背後に潜む問題を明らかにしよう。— Let's clarify the problem underlying this case.
17 | 0.66

3075 通過（する）tsuuka(suru) *n.* passage *v.* pass
- この電車は今、A駅を通過しています。— This train is passing station A now.
17 | 0.99

3076 確信（する）kakushin(suru) *n.* conviction *v.* be convinced
- 確信を持って「そうだ」と言える。— I can say "Yes, it is." with conviction.
17 | 0.91

3077 株 kabu *n.* stump; stock, share
- A社の株を買った。— I bought stocks in Company A.
17 | 0.91

3078 いまさら imasara *adv.* now (after such a long time)
- そんなこと、いまさら彼女に聞けないよ。— I can't ask her such a thing now.
17 | 0.88

3079 強力 kyouryoku *na-adj.* strong, powerful
- 彼は強力なリーダーシップを持っている。— He has a strong leadership.
17 | 0.89

3080 神戸 koube *n.* Kobe
- 小さい頃、神戸に住んでいた。— When I was a child, I lived in Kobe.
17 | 0.97

3081 見出だす miidasu *v.* find, discover
- 多くの人々がそこに価値を見出した。— Many people found the value in it.
17 | 0.88

3082 北朝鮮 kitachousen *n.* Democratic People's Republic of Korea, North Korea
- A氏は北朝鮮で生まれた。— Mr. A was born in North Korea.
17 | 0.77

3083 側面 sokumen *n.* side; flank
- さまざまな側面から考える必要がある。— It is necessary to think about it from various sides.
17 | 0.87

3084 誇り hokori *n.* pride, honor
- 息子を誇りに思う。— I'm proud of my son.
17 | 0.93

3085 作り tsukuri *n.* make, construction
- このスーツの作りはいかがですか。— Do you like the make of this suit?
17 | 0.93

3086 米 bei *n.* meter
- この土地の広さは二十平米だ。— The area of this land is twenty square meters.
17 | 0.85

3087 崩壊（する）houkai(suru) *n., v.* collapse
- そのビルは地震で崩壊した。— The building collapsed in the earthquake.
17 | 0.96

3088 二十一 nijuuichi *num.* twenty-one
- このお祭りは21回目です。— This festival has been held twenty-one times.
17 | 0.75

3089 直ちに tadachini *adv.* immediately, directly
- このような行為は直ちにやめるべきだ。— You must stop doing this immediately.
17 | 0.65

3090 バッグ baggu, bakku *n.* bag
- 有名ブランドのバッグがほしい。— I want a name-brand bag.
17 | 0.59

3091 本書 honsho *n.* this book
- その答えは本書を読めばわかる。— You will understand the answer if you read this book.
17 | 0.45

3092 器 utsuwa *n.* container
- 余った料理を器に入れて持って帰った。— I put the leftovers into a container and took it home.
17 | 0.81

3093 血液 ketsueki *n.* blood
- 大量の血液が必要だ。— A large quantity of blood is needed.
17 | 0.95

3094 衝撃 shougeki *n.* shock, impact
- その事件に強い衝撃を受けた。— I was greatly shocked by the affair.
17 | 0.92

3095 嫌がる iyagaru *v.* be reluctant; hate
- 息子が幼稚園へ行くのを嫌がる。— My son is reluctant to go to nursery school.
17 | 0.84

3096 製造（する）seizou(suru) *n.* production *v.* produce
- 医薬品の製造に携わっている。— I am engaged in the production of pharmaceutical products.
17 | 0.90

3097 とりわけ toriwake *adv.* especially
- この地域の夏はとりわけ暑い。— It is especially hot in this area in summer.
17 | 0.78

3098 小麦粉 komugi ko *n.* (wheat) flour
- 鶏肉に小麦粉をまぶして、油で揚げた。— I coated the chicken in flour, then fried it.
17 | 0.86

3099 気配 kehai *n.* indication, sign
- 人の気配を感じて、振り返った。— Feeling there was someone behind me, I looked back.
17 | 0.79

3100 理論 riron *n.* theory
- 彼は独自の理論を打ち立てた。— He established an original theory.
17 | 0.82

3101 流行（する）ryuukou(suru) *n.* fashion, epidemic *v.* come into fashion, be rife
- 最新の流行を取り入れた商品です。— This is a product which incorporates the latest fashion.
17 | 0.93

3102 見解 kenkai *n.* opinion, view
- 両者の間には見解の相違があるようだ。— There seems to be a difference of opinion between the two.
17 | 0.77

3103 承認（する）shounin(suru) *n.* approval *v.* approve
- 議会の承認を得なければならない。— The approval of the assembly is required.
17 | 0.62

3104 いかにも ikani mo *adv.* indeed, really, just
- 彼はいかにも高そうなスーツを着ていた。— He wore a suit which looked really expensive.
17 | 0.69

3105 単位 tan'i *n.* unit, credit
- 長さの単位は国によって違う。— The unit of length differs from country to country.
17 | 0.91

3106 掘る horu *v.* dig
- 庭に穴を掘って、生ごみを埋めた。— I dug a hole in the garden and buried the kitchen garbage in it.
17 | 0.95

3107 歌詞 kashi *n.* song lyrics
- 間違えないように、歌詞を見ながら歌った。— In order not to make a mistake, I looked at the lyrics while singing.
17 | 0.79

3108 絡む karamu *v.* get entangled, involve; pick a quarrel
- さまざまな問題が複雑に絡んでいる。— It is complicated by various problems.
17 | 0.99

3109 文明 bunmei *n.* civilization
- ここに高度な文明を持つ国が存在した。— A country with an advanced civilization existed here.
17 | 0.84

3110 長崎 nagasaki *n.* Nagasaki
- 長崎は坂が多い町だ。— Nagasaki is a town of many hills.
17 | 0.95

3111 構える kamaeru *v.* get set, get ready; set up
- 記者たちは一斉にカメラを構えた。— Reporters held up cameras all at once.
17 | 0.91

3112 わー waa *interj.* wow!
- わー、きれい! — Wow! How beautiful!
17 | 0.85

3113 発音(する) hatsuon(suru) *n.* pronunciation *v.* pronounce
- 正しく発音できません。— I can't pronounce it correctly.
17 | 0.90

3114 共有(する) kyouyuu(suru) *n., v.* share
- みんなで情報を共有する。— We share the information with each other.
17 | 0.97

3115 勝負(する) shoubu(suru) *n.* victory or defeat, match *v.* play
- チャンピオンに勝負を挑んだ。— He challenged the champion to a match.
17 | 0.83

3116 住まい sumai *n.* house, residence
- 郊外に住まいを構えた。— I set up home in the suburbs.
17 | 0.95

3117 二十八日 nijuu hachi nichi *n.* twenty-eighth (date); twenty-eight days
- 母の誕生日は4月28日です。— My mother's birthday is April 28.
17 | 0.53

3118 重大 juudai *na-adj.* serious, important
- この事件は国際関係に重大な影響を及ぼす。— This case has a serious effect on international relations.
17 | 0.75

3119 各国 kak-koku *n.* each country, various countries
- 会議のために各国の代表が集まる。— The representatives from each country gather to hold a meeting.
17 | 0.70

3120 無理矢理 muriyari *adv.* forcibly, against one's will
- 欲しくもないものを無理矢理買わされた。— I was made to buy something that I didn't want against my will.
17 | 0.86

3121 五百円 gohyaku en *n.* five hundred yen
- 今日は五百円の弁当を買って食べた。— Today I bought and ate a five-hundred-yen box lunch.
17 | 0.52

3122 出品(する) shuppin(suru) *n.* exhibit *v.* submit
- 私の絵がコンテストに出品されることになった。— My painting will be submitted to the contest.
16 | 0.28 | WB

3123 祈る inoru *v.* pray, wish
- 世界の平和を祈る。— I pray for world peace.
16 | 0.87

3124 三番目 san ban-me *n.* third
- 三番目の兄は両親と一緒に住んでいる。— My third older brother lives with my parents.
16 | 0.84

3125 メモ(する) memo(suru) *n.* memo *v.* take notes
- メモをとりながら、講演を聞いた。— I took notes while listening to the lecture.
16 | 0.97

3126 平日 heijitsu *n.* weekday
- 平日の昼間はうちにいないことが多い。— I'm often away from home in the daytime on weekdays.
16 | 0.82

3127 支払い shiharai *n.* payment
- 家賃の支払いが遅れた。— Payment of the rent was late.
16 | 0.91

3128 皮膚 hifu *n.* skin
- 目の周りは皮膚が薄い。— The skin around the eyes is thin.
16 | 0.90

3129 反面 hanmen *n.* other side
- 嬉しい反面、少し悲しい。— I'm glad, but on the other hand slightly sad.
16 | 0.91

3130 代表的 daihyou-teki *na-adj.* representative, typical
- トマトは代表的な夏野菜だ。— Tomatoes are typical summer vegetables.
16 | 0.96

3131 整う totonou *v.* be ready; be well-regulated
- 準備が整うまで少々お待ちください。— Please wait a moment until the preparations are complete.
16 | 0.97

3132 初心者 shoshin-sha *n.* beginner
- これは初心者向けのクラスです。— This is a class for beginners.
16 | 0.75

3133 たどり着く tadoritsuku *v.* finally arrive at, struggle along to
- ようやく頂上にたどり着いた。— I finally arrived at the top.
16 | 0.88

3134 焼ける yakeru *v.* be burned; be roasted; be sunburned
- 火事で家が焼けた。— My house was burnt by the fire.
16 | 0.88

3135 合併(する) gappei(suru) *n.* combination, merger *v.* combine, merge
- 合併により、A市はB市になった。— City A became City B in the merger.
16 | 0.88

3136 ウサギ usagi *n.* rabbit
- 彼女はウサギを飼っている。— She keeps a rabbit.
16 | 0.92

3137 徹底(する) tettei(suru) *n.* thoroughgoing, out-and-out *v.* be thorough
- 情報管理の徹底に努めています。— We strive for in-depth information management.
16 | 0.78

3138 脱ぐ nugu *v.* take off
- ここで靴を脱いでください。— Please take off your shoes here.
16 | 0.85

3139 八年 hachi nen *n.* eight years
- その本を書くのに八年かかった。— It took me eight years to write the book.
16 | 0.80

3140 ですけれど desu keredo *conj.* but
- 一時間お待ちしました。ですけれど、いらっしゃいませんでした。— I waited for him for an hour, but he didn't come.
16 | 0.06 | SP

3141 意 i *n.* mind; will; sense
- 感謝の意を込めて、先生に花を贈った。— With a sense of gratitude, we gave our teacher flowers.
16 | 0.86

3142 自民党 jimin-tou *n.* Liberal Democratic Party
- 当時は自民党の天下だった。— The Liberal Democratic Party was in charge then.
16 | 0.92

3143 地下 chika *n.* basement; underground
- このビルの地下に駐車場があります。— There is parking in the basement of this building.
16 | 0.99

3144 構築(する) kouchiku(suru) *n.* construction *v.* construct
- 完全なシステムの構築を目指します。— I aim at the construction of a complete system.
16 | 0.74

3145 両者 ryousha *n.* both, the two
- 両者の違いははっきりしている。— The difference between the two is clear.
16 | 0.81

3146 適する tekisuru *v.* suit, fit
- この仕事は私に適した仕事ではないと思う。— I think this job does not suit me.
16 | 0.96

3147 引き受ける hikiukeru *v.* undertake
- この仕事は彼が引き受けてくれた。— He undertook this work.
16 | 0.95

3148 番号 bangou *n.* number
- 彼に教えてもらった番号は間違っていた。— The number that he had told me was wrong.
16 | 0.95

3149 経営者 keiei-sha *n.* manager, proprietor
- 経営者の責任を追及するつもりだ。— I'm going to pursue the question of the responsibility of the manager.
16 | 0.95

3150 焦る aseru *v.* be in a hurry; be impatient; be eager
- そんなに焦らなくてもいいだろう。— You do not need to get impatient like that.
16 | 0.82

3151 論文 ronbun *n.* essay, thesis, paper, dissertation
- 年内にこの論文を書き上げたい。— I want to finish writing this paper by the end of the year.
16 | 0.90

3152 タイミング taimingu *n.* timing
- 帰るタイミングを逃してしまった。— My timing was bad and I missed my chance to leave.
16 | 0.89

3153 百パーセント hyaku paasento *n.* one hundred percent
- 果汁100パーセントのジュースを飲む。— I drink 100 percent fruit juice.

16 | 0.98

3154 週末 shuumatsu *n.* weekend
- 充実した週末を過ごした。— I spent a full weekend.

16 | 0.81

3155 出品者 shuppin-sha *n.* exhibitor
- この展覧会は出品者が多い。— There are many exhibitors at this exhibition.

16 | 0.11 | WB

3156 二十六日 nijuuroku nichi *n.* twenty-sixth (date); twenty-six days
- ミーティングは26日でいいですか？— Can we have a meeting on the twenty-sixth?

16 | 0.47 | NM

3157 正式 seishiki *na-adj.* formal, official
- 政府から正式な発表があった。— The government gave us the official announcement.

16 | 0.99

3158 カラオケ karaoke *n.* karaoke
- ゆうべカラオケに行った。— I went to karaoke last night.

16 | 0.77

3159 退職（する）taishoku(suru) *n.* retirement, resignation *v.* retire, resign
- 今月末で退職することにした。— I decided to resign from the job at the end of this month.

16 | 0.98

3160 満ちる michiru *v.* be full; rise
- この町は活気に満ちている。— This town is full of energy.

16 | 0.79

3161 おとなしい otonashii *i-adj.* gentle, well behaved, quiet
- この子はおとなしい性格だ。— This boy has a quiet character.

16 | 0.85

3162 知人 chijin *n.* acquaintance
- 知人の紹介で彼と知り合った。— I got to know him though an introduction from an acquaintance.

16 | 0.91

3163 刻む kizamu *v.* cut into fine pieces; engrave; tick
- 私は野菜を刻んで炒めた。— I cut vegetables into fine pieces and fried them.

16 | 0.90

3164 十九日 juuku nichi *n.* nineteenth (date); nineteen days
- 出産予定は今月の19日です。— The baby's due date is the nineteenth of this month.

16 | 0.44 | NM

3165 千葉県 chiba ken *n.* Chiba prefecture
- 千葉県の出身です。— I'm from Chiba prefecture.

16 | 0.95

3166 食材 shokuzai *n.* ingredient, foodstuff
- この料理は新鮮な食材を使っている。— This dish was cooked with fresh ingredients.

16 | 0.86

3167 携わる tazusawaru *v.* participate, be engaged
- 彼は新しいシステムの開発に携わっている。— He is engaged in the development of the new system.

16 | 0.93

3168 組み合わせ kumiawase *n.* combination, matching
- この色の組み合わせが気に入っている。— I like this combination of colors.

16 | 0.93

3169 冷静 reisei *na-adj.* calm
- 焦ると冷静な判断ができなくなる。— A calm judgment isn't possible when I'm in a hurry.

16 | 0.94

3170 台詞 serifu *n.* lines, speech, words
- 主人公の最後の台詞が印象的だった。— The hero's last lines were impressive.

16 | 0.86

3171 コート kooto *n.* coat; court
- 毛皮のコートを着た女性が見えますか。— Can you see a woman in a fur coat?

16 | 0.86

3172 二年生 ni nen-sei *n.* second grade, second year
- 小学二年生のときから、ピアノを習っている。— Since I was in the second grade of elementary school, I have been learning to play the piano.

16 | 0.91

3173 ロック rokku *n.* rock; lock
- これはロックの名曲だ。— This is one of the masterpieces of rock music.

16 | 0.88

3174 国会 kokkai *n.* national assembly, Diet
- この問題は国会でたびたび取り上げられている。— This issue is often taken up in the Diet.

16 | 0.57

3175 編む amu *v.* knit, braid
- 母がセーターを編んでくれた。— My mother knit a sweater for me.

16 | 0.79

3176 破る yaburu *v.* tear; break; beat
- 不要な書類を破って捨てた。— I tore up and threw away the unnecessary documents.
16 | 0.94

3177 真っ赤 makka *na-adj.* bright red; downright
- 彼の顔が真っ赤になった。— His face turned bright red.
16 | 0.89

3178 意図 ito *n.* intention
- 作者の意図が不明だ。— The intention of the author is not clear.
16 | 0.89

3179 さらす sarasu *v.* expose
- 風雨にさらされて、自転車がさびてしまった。— My bicycle got rusty because it had been exposed to wind and rain.
16 | 0.89

3180 手間 tema *n.* labour; time
- 手間がかかる仕事だった。— It was a time-consuming job.
16 | 0.93

3181 可愛がる kawaigaru *v.* love, treat with affection
- 祖母は私たちを可愛がってくれた。— My grandmother loved us.
16 | 0.81

3182 森林 shinrin *n.* forest, woods
- そこには広大な森林が広がっていた。— A vast forest lay there.
16 | 0.58

3183 マイナス mainasu *n.* minus
- 今日の気温はマイナスになる予想だ。— Today's temperature is expected to be below zero.
16 | 0.95

3184 ラーメン raamen *n.* Chinese noodles
- おいしいラーメンを食べました。— I ate delicious Chinese noodles.
16 | 0.69

3185 帽子 boushi *n.* hat, cap
- 彼はいつも帽子をかぶっている。— He always wears a hat.
16 | 0.90

3186 オープン（する）oopun(suru) *n., v.* open
- 駅前に新しくオープンしたお店に行った。— I went to the newly opened shop in the station square.
16 | 0.77

3187 名古屋 nagoya *n.* Nagoya
- 名古屋まで新幹線で行った。— I went to Nagoya by bullet train.
16 | 0.93

3188 離す hanasu *v.* separate, divide; keep apart
- 貴重品は体から離さないでください。— Please do not leave your valuables unattended.
16 | 0.92

3189 数値 suuchi *n.* numerical value; score, count
- 白血球が高い数値を示している。— The white blood cell count is high.
16 | 0.82

3190 熱心 nesshin *na-adj.* eager, enthusiastic
- 彼はガイドの説明を熱心に聞いている。— He listens eagerly to the guide's explanation.
16 | 0.94

3191 見直し minaoshi *n.* review, reconsideration
- 現行の制度の大幅な見直しが行われた。— The major review of the current system was carried out.
16 | 0.65

3192 盗む nusumu *v.* steal
- 自転車を盗まれた。— I had my bicycle stolen.
16 | 0.90

3193 一冊 is-satsu *n.* one (book)
- 週に一冊本を読む。— I read one book a week.
16 | 0.90

3194 強さ tsuyo-sa *n.* strength, power
- あのチームは圧倒的な強さで優勝した。— That team won the championship with overwhelming strength.
16 | 0.96

3195 紐 himo *n.* string; lace
- 靴の紐を結びなおした。— I retied my shoes.
16 | 0.94

3196 岩 iwa *n.* rock
- 崖から巨大な岩が転がり落ちた。— A huge rock hurtled down the cliff.
16 | 0.87

3197 ミス（する）misu(suru) *n.* mistake *v.* make a mistake
- 敗因はミスが多かったことだ。— The cause of our defeat is that there were many mistakes.
16 | 0.90

3198 移行（する）ikou(suru) *n., v.* shift
- 新システムへの移行はうまく進んでいる。— The shift to the new system is being carried out smoothly.
16 | 0.88

3199 味方（する）mikata(suru) *n.* supporter *v.* support
- 母だけが味方になってくれた。— Only my mother supported me.
16 | 0.87

16 Shops

(frequency per million words)

スーパー suupaa 42.355 **supermarket**[1]
商店街 shouten-gai 36.035 **shopping street**
レストラン resutoran 33.579 **restaurant**
デパート depaato 26.498 **department store**
コンビニ konbini 22.588 **convenience store**
本屋 hon'ya 19.148 **bookshop**
喫茶店 kissa-ten 17.371 **tearoom, coffee shop, café**
オープン(する) oopun(suru) 15.976 **open**
カフェ kafe 14.252 **café**
食堂 shokudou 11.776 **cafeteria**
バー baa 10.085 **bar**
居酒屋 izakaya 9.307 **(Japanese style) bar, tavern**
美容院 biyou-in 6.110 **beauty salon**
百貨店 hyakka-ten 5.352 **department store**
薬局 yakkyoku 4.806 **pharmacy**
寿司屋 sushi-ya 4.083 **sushi restaurant**
魚屋 sakana-ya 3.613 **fish store, fishmonger**
蕎麦屋 soba-ya 3.452 **soba restaurant**
ラーメン屋 raamen-ya 2.915 **ramen restaurant**
百円ショップ hyaku en shoppu 2.326 **hundred-yen store**
ファミレス famiresu 2.303 **casual dining restaurant**
八百屋 yaoya 2.004 **vegetable store, greengrocer**
肉屋 niku-ya 1.699 **meat shop, butcher**
和菓子屋 wa gashi-ya 1.608 **Japanese-style confectionery store**
花屋 hana-ya 1.519 **florist**
中華料理店 chuuka ryouri-ten 1.112 **Chinese restaurant**
電気屋 denki-ya 0.806 **electrical store**
クリーニング屋 kuriiningu-ya 0.685 **laundry**
パチンコ店 pachinko-ten[2] 0.647 **pachinko (Japanese pinball) parlor**
ケーキ屋 keeki-ya 0.630 **cake shop**
ファーストフード店 faasuto fuudo-ten 0.550 **fast-food restaurant**
キオスク kiosuku 0.434 **kiosk**
ディスカウントストア deisukaunto sutoa 0.159 **discount store**
カラオケ店 karaoke-ten 0.067 **karaoke bar**

1 スーパー may include meanings other than "supermarket".
2 pachinko-ya is ranked 5855.

3200 純粋 junsui *na-adj.* pure; genuine
- 彼は素朴で純粋な人だ。— He is a person who is unsophisticated and pure.
16 | 0.96

3201 転勤(する) tenkin(suru) *n.* transfer (job) *v.* be transferred
- 夫が大阪に転勤になった。— My husband was transferred to Osaka.
16 | 0.73

3202 ビートルズ biitoruzu *n.* Beatles
- ビートルズは最も偉大な音楽家の一つだ。— The Beatles are one of the greatest musicians.
16 | 0.53

3203 フライパン furaipan *n.* frying pan
- フライパンで焼いてください。— Roast it in a frying pan.
16 | 0.89

3204 一階 ik-kai *n.* first floor (US), ground floor (UK)
- 山田さんはこのアパートの一階に住んでいる。— Mr. Yamada lives on the first floor of this apartment block.
16 | 0.85

3205 さっぱり sappari *adv.* not at all
- さっぱり理解できない。— I can't understand it at all.
16 | 0.91

3206 正面 shoumen *n.* front
- 今、ホテルの正面にいます。— I'm at the front of the hotel now.
16 | 0.88

3207 演劇 engeki *n.* drama, play
- 今週末、演劇を見に行く。— I will go to see a play this weekend.
16 | 0.74

3208 疲れ tsukare *n.* fatigue, exhaustion, tiredness
- 最近疲れがたまっている。— I've been very tired lately.
16 | 0.87

3209 経緯 keii *n.* details, process
- どんな経緯があったかは知らない。— I don't know what kind of process there was.
16 | 0.90

3210 探る saguru *v.* fumble; probe
- 彼はポケットを探って、鍵を取り出した。— He fumbled in his pocket, and took out the key.

16 | 0.87

3211 数学 suugaku *n.* mathematics
- 私は数学が苦手です。— I'm very bad at mathematics.

16 | 0.92

3212 関わり kakawari *n.* relation, connection
- この問題は家庭環境と密接な関わりがある。— This problem is closely related to one's home environment.

16 | 0.90

3213 英国 eikoku *n.* United Kingdom, Britain
- 英国式の庭園を散策した。— I took a walk in a British-style garden.

16 | 0.95

3214 巻き込む makikomu *v.* involve
- 旅先でトラブルに巻き込まれてしまった。— I got caught up in some trouble while traveling.

16 | 0.95

3215 退院(する) taiin(suru) *n.* leaving hospital *v.* be discharged from hospital
- 彼はもうすぐ退院できるだろう。— He will be able to leave hospital soon.

16 | 0.83

3216 覚え oboe *n.* memory
- そんなことを言った覚えはない。— I don't have any memory that I said such a thing.

16 | 0.85

3217 優秀 yuushuu *na-adj.* excellent
- 彼は優秀な人物だ。— He is an excellent person.

16 | 0.98

3218 リラックス(する) rirakkusu(suru) *n., v.* relax
- お茶を飲んで、リラックスする。— I relax drinking tea.

16 | 0.81

3219 施策 shisaku, sesaku *n.* policy, measure
- 新たな施策を講じる必要がある。— It is necessary to take new measures.

16 | 0.38 | OF

3220 瞳 hitomi *n.* pupil; eye
- 少女はつぶらな瞳で私を見つめた。— The girl stared at me with cute round eyes.

16 | 0.70

3221 二十七日 nijuushichi nichi *n.* twenty-seventh (date); twenty-seven days
- 今月27日までにお支払いください。— Please pay by the twenty-seventh of this month.

16 | 0.50

3222 権限 kengen *n.* authority, power
- この国では大統領が強大な権限を持つ。— The President has great power in this country.

16 | 0.68

3223 十七 juu nana *num.* seventeen
- 十七は恋多き年だ。— Seventeen is an age full of romance.

16 | 0.84

3224 展示(する) tenji(suru) *n.* display, exhibition *v.* display, exhibit
- 博物館で興味深い展示を見た。— I saw an interesting exhibition at the museum.

16 | 0.58

3225 三歳 san-sai *n.* three years old
- 彼女には三歳の娘がいる。— She has a three-year-old daughter.

16 | 0.85

3226 朝食 choushoku *n.* breakfast
- 近くの喫茶店で遅い朝食をとった。— I had a late breakfast at a coffee shop nearby.

16 | 0.88

3227 診断(する) shindan(suru) *n.* diagnosis *v.* diagnose
- ただの風邪だと診断された。— My illness was diagnosed as just a cold.

16 | 0.93

3228 ご免 gomen *n.* pardon, sorry, [to decline]
- 人前で歌うなんてご免だ。— I'm definitely not going to sing in public.

16 | 0.76

3229 缶詰 kanzume *n.* canned food
- 缶詰のフルーツを食べた。— I ate canned fruit.

16 | 0.81

3230 こしょう koshou *n.* pepper
- 塩とこしょうを振ってから焼いてください。— Grill after sprinkling with salt and pepper.

16 | 0.91

3231 潰れる tsubureru *v.* be crushed; go bankrupt; become useless
- 不景気で多くの店や会社が潰れた。— Many shops and companies went bankrupt because of the depression.

16 | 0.94

3232 海岸 kaigan *n.* seashore, seaside
- 海岸沿いにおしゃれなレストランが並んでいる。— There are stylish restaurants along the shore.

16 | 0.96

3233 領域 ryouiki *n.* territory, field
- この研究結果は様々な領域に影響を及ぼすだろう。— These research results will influence various fields.

16 | 0.82

3234 出版（する）shuppan(suru) *n.* publication *v.* publish
- 彼女の自伝が出版された。— Her autobiography was published.
16 | 0.90

3235 映画館 eiga-kan *n.* movie theater, cinema
- 映画館で新作映画を見た。— I watched a new film at the movie theater.
16 | 0.80

3236 気温 kion *n.* temperature
- 明日は気温が下がるそうだ。— I heard that the temperature will go down tomorrow.
16 | 0.90

3237 由来（する）yurai(suru) *n.* origin, history *v.* originate
- 私の名前の由来を聞かれた。— I was asked about the origin of my name.
16 | 0.95

3238 引き起こす hikiokosu *v.* raise, cause
- 政府の発表が混乱を引き起こした。— The government's announcement caused confusion.
16 | 0.88

3239 筋 suji *n.* tendon; line; reason
- 彼の話は筋が通っていない。— What he says is illogical.
16 | 0.97

3240 ガラス garasu *n.* glass
- ボールで窓ガラスを割ってしまった。— I broke a pane of glass with a ball.
16 | 0.95

3241 同意（する）doui(suru) *n.* agreement, consent *v.* agree
- 本人の同意を得なければできない。— You can't do it without his consent.
16 | 0.80

3242 土日 donichi *n.* Saturday and Sunday
- 今度の土日はどちらも空いている。— I am free on both this Saturday and Sunday.
16 | 0.69

3243 認定（する）nintei(suru) *n.* authorization *v.* authorize
- この機関は国の認定を受けている。— This organization received the authorization from the state.
16 | 0.67

3244 おもちゃ omocha *n.* toy
- 息子は一人でおもちゃで遊んでいる。— My son is playing alone with toys.
16 | 0.88

3245 島 tou *n.* island
- ハワイ島のホテルに一週間滞在した。— I stayed at a hotel on Hawaii Island for a week.
16 | 0.00 | SP

3246 丘 oka *n.* hill
- 彼の家は小高い丘の上にある。— His house is on a small hill.
16 | 0.88

3247 二年間 ni nenkan *n.* two years
- 2005年から2007年までの二年間、カナダに住んでいた。— I lived in Canada for two years from 2005 to 2007.
16 | 0.95

3248 メディア media *n.* media
- メディアを通して、世界中の出来事を知ることができる。— Through the media, we can learn of events that have happened all over the world.
16 | 0.94

3249 一台 ichi dai *n.* one (machine/vehicle)
- 田舎では一人一台車を持っていることも珍しくない。— It is not unusual to have one car each in the countryside.
16 | 0.93

3250 翌年 yokunen *n.* the next year, the following year
- 知り合った翌年に二人は結婚した。— They married the year after they had got to know each other.
16 | 0.90

3251 酸素 sanso *n.* oxygen
- 有酸素運動は体にいい。— Aerobic exercise is good for one's health.
16 | 0.91

3252 よし yoshi *interj.* All right!, Good!
- よし、行くぞ。— All right. Let's go!
16 | 0.83

3253 いまや ima ya *adv.* now
- 先生に怒られてばかりいた彼が、いまや大企業の社長だ。— The one who often made teachers angry is now the president of a big company.
16 | 0.76

3254 贅沢 zeitaku *n.* luxury *na-adj.* luxurious
- 贅沢な暮らしがしたい。— I would like to live in luxury.
16 | 0.89

3255 金融機関 kin'yuu kikan *n.* financial institution
- 彼女は金融機関への就職を希望している。— She hopes to find a job with a financial institution.
16 | 0.84

3256 百円 hyaku en *n.* one hundred yen
- 百円足りないので、貸してくれませんか。— I'm a hundred yen short, so will you lend me it?

16 | 0.78

3257 黄色 kiiro *n.* yellow
- 好きな色は黄色です。— My favorite color is yellow.

16 | 0.95

3258 制定（する） seitei(suru) *n.* enactment *v.* enact
- この法律は1964年に制定された。— This law was enacted in 1964.

16 | 0.79

3259 文書 bunsho *n.* document; writing
- 結果は文書でお知らせします。— We will inform you of the result in writing.

15 | 0.81

3260 初期 shoki *n.* early days, initial stage
- この家は昭和の初期に建てられた。— This house was built in the early Showa period.

15 | 0.95

3261 ぬれる nureru *v.* get wet
- 雨で靴がぬれた。— The shoes had gotten wet in the rain.

15 | 0.84

3262 はがき hagaki *n.* postcard
- 旅先の友人からはがきが届いた。— I received a postcard from a friend who is traveling.

15 | 0.63

3263 巨人 kyojin *n.* giant
- 大昔、この地方には巨人が住んでいたという言い伝えがある。— There is a legend that a giant lived in this district a long long time ago.

15 | 0.81

3264 俺達 ore-tachi *n.* we (used by male speakers)
- 俺達も知らない。— We don't know, either.

15 | 0.75

3265 苦痛 kutsuu *n.* pain
- この治療法は激しい苦痛を伴う。— This cure is accompanied by intense pain.

15 | 0.89

3266 パワー pawaa *n.* power
- あの歌手の歌にはパワーを感じる。— I feel the power in that singer's singing.

15 | 0.85

3267 いかなる ikanaru *adn.* what kind of, any
- いかなる理由があろうと、許されない。— It is not allowed, for any reason whatsoever.

15 | 0.77

3268 あちこち achikochi *pron.* here and there, everywhere
- 最近、あちこちでこの店を見かける。— Recently I see this shop here and there.

15 | 0.76

3269 実力 jitsuryoku *n.* real ability
- 本番では実力が出し切れなかった。— I couldn't show my real ability during the performance.

15 | 0.91

3270 面する men-suru *v.* face
- この町は海に面している。— This town faces the sea.

15 | 0.90

3271 もったいない mottai nai *i-adj.* wasteful; too good
- 週末を寝て過ごすのはもったいない。— It is wasteful to spend the weekend sleeping.

15 | 0.84

3272 港 minato *n.* harbour, port
- 船が港に着いた。— The ship arrived at the port.

15 | 0.95

3273 片方 katahou *n.* one side; the other one
- 靴下が片方なくなった。— I lost one of the socks.

15 | 0.95

3274 最悪 saiaku *na-adj.* worst
- 最悪の事態は免れた。— We avoided the worst situation.

15 | 0.90

3275 ぎりぎり girigiri *adv.* barely
- 終電にぎりぎり間に合った。— I was barely in time for the last train.

15 | 0.95

3276 二十九日 nijuu ku nichi *n.* twenty-ninth (date); twenty-nine days
- 今月29日は祝日だ。— We have a national holiday on the 29th this month.

15 | 0.49

3277 市販（する） shihan(suru) *n.* on the market *v.* market
- この薬は市販されている。— This medicine is on the market.

15 | 0.87

3278 この世 konoyo *n.* this world
- 彼は昨日この世を去った。— He departed this world yesterday.

15 | 0.62

3279 片手 katate *n.* one hand
- 彼女は片手で卵が割れる。— She is able to break an egg with one hand.

15 | 0.83

3280 サイン（する）sain(suru) n. signature, autograph v. sign
- 手紙の最後にサインを書いた。— I wrote my signature at the end of the letter.
15 | 0.91

3281 キリスト教 kirisuto-kyou n. Christianity
- 彼はキリスト教の教えを忠実に守っている。— He faithfully follows the teachings of Christianity.
15 | 0.89

3282 年寄り toshiyori n. old people, the elderly
- お年寄りに席を譲りましょう。— Please give up these seats to elderly people.
15 | 0.95

3283 気軽 kigaru na-adj. light-hearted, feel free
- 困った時は、気軽に連絡してください。— If you have a problem, feel free to contact me.
15 | 0.75

3284 鳴く naku v. cry, sing
- 遠くで鳥が鳴いている。— Birds are singing in the distance.
15 | 0.87

3285 呼吸（する）kokyuu(suru) n. breath v. breathe
- うまく呼吸ができなくて、苦しい。— I can't breathe well, and it's painful.
15 | 0.95

3286 コーナー koonaa n. corner
- 本屋の雑誌コーナーで立ち読みをする。— I stand reading at the magazine section of the bookstore.
15 | 0.80

3287 徒歩 toho n. on foot, walk
- 駅からレストランまでは徒歩五分です。— It is five minutes' walk from the station to the restaurant.
15 | 0.80

3288 延長（する）enchou(suru) n. extension v. extend
- 申し込み期間が一週間延長した。— The application period has been extended one more week.
15 | 0.88

3289 眠い nemui i-adj. sleepy
- 徹夜明けなので、とても眠い。— I've stayed awake all night, so I'm very sleepy.
15 | 0.40 | WB

3290 厚い atsui i-adj. thick; kind; abundant
- 冬になると、この湖には厚い氷が張る。— When winter comes, thick ice stretches across this lake.
15 | 0.92

3291 二千二年 nisen ni nen n. 2002 (year)
- 2002年に通貨ユーロが欧州12ヶ国で流通し始めた。— In 2002, the euro entered circulation in twelve European countries.
15 | 0.91

3292 中小企業 chuushou kigyou n. small and medium-sized enterprises
- 中小企業の倒産が相次いだ。— Small and medium-sized enterprises went bankrupt one after another.
15 | 0.45

3293 浅草 asakusa n. Asakusa (place name)
- 浅草は観光客が多い。— There are many tourists in Asakusa.
15 | 0.65

3294 完璧 kanpeki na-adj. perfect
- 彼女の演奏は完璧だった。— Her performance was perfect.
15 | 0.90

3295 傷付ける kizutsukeru v. hurt; damage
- 車を傷付けられた。— My car was damaged.
15 | 0.93

3296 とく toku n., adj. [shortened form of "teoku"]
- ご飯炊けたら先食べといて。— When the rice is ready, go ahead and eat.
15 | 0.89

3297 あご ago n. jaw, chin
- あの人はあごに小さな傷がある。— That person has a small injury on the chin.
15 | 0.85

3298 紅葉（する）kouyou(suru) n. autumn leaves v. put on fall colors
- 山に紅葉を見に行った。— I went to the mountains to see the fall colors.
15 | 0.85

3299 では de wa p. in; on; as for
- デザインではこの車が一番いい。— As for the design, this car is the best.
15 | 0.01 | SP

3300 信仰（する）shinkou(suru) n. religious faith v. believe
- 私たちは信仰の自由が認められている。— We have freedom of religious belief granted as a right.
15 | 0.87

3301 ねた neta n. material; ingredient
- このすし屋は新鮮なねたを使っている。— This sushi restaurant uses fresh ingredients.
15 | 0.76

3302 雇う yatou v. employ, hire
- 新しいアルバイトを雇うことにした。— I decided to employ a new part-time worker.
15 | 0.92

3303 雄 osu *n.* male animal
- この犬は雄です。 — This dog is male.

15 | 0.91

3304 欧米 oubei *n.* Europe and America
- この会には欧米の研究者が多く集まった。 — Many European and American researchers gathered at this meeting.

15 | 0.96

3305 運用（する）un'you(suru) *n.* making use of *v.* manage
- 資金を賢く運用しましょう。 — Let's manage your funds judiciously.

15 | 0.51

3306 酢 su *n.* vinegar
- この料理には酢が少し入っている。 — There is a little vinegar in this dish.

15 | 0.58

3307 半ば nakaba *n.* half, middle *adv.* partly
- 彼は1980年代半ばに日本に来た。 — He came to Japan in the mid-1980s.

15 | 0.88

3308 印象的 inshou-teki *na-adj.* impressive
- それは印象的な光景だった。 — It was an impressive view.

15 | 0.82

3309 権力 kenryoku *n.* power, authority
- 当時、皇帝が強大な権力を握っていた。 — In those days, the emperor had great power.

15 | 0.82

3310 拒否（する）kyohi(suru) *n.* refusal *v.* refuse, reject
- 彼はその申し出を強く拒否した。 — He strongly rejected the proposal.

15 | 0.94

3311 空く suku *v.* become empty, be free; get hungry
- お腹が空いた。 — I got hungry.

15 | 0.80

3312 ビジネス bijinesu *n.* business
- 何かビジネスを始めようと思っています。 — I'm thinking of setting up some kind of business.

15 | 0.96

3313 幅広い habahiroi *i-adj.* wide, broad
- この商品は幅広い年齢層で人気がある。 — This product is popular among a wide age range.

15 | 0.82

3314 アイデア aidea *n.* idea
- いいアイデアがなかなか浮かばない。 — A good idea doesn't readily occur to me.

15 | 0.94

3315 十二時 juu ni ji *n.* twelve o'clock
- 昼休みは十二時から一時までです。 — The lunch break is from 12:00 to 1:00.

15 | 0.68

3316 ベトナム betonamu *n.* Vietnam
- おいしいベトナム料理を食べました。 — I ate delicious Vietnamese food.

15 | 0.93

3317 落札（する）rakusatsu(suru) *n.* successful bid *v.* make a successful bid
- その絵は彼が落札した。 — He made a successful bid for that picture.

15 | 0.22 | WB

3318 出場（する）shutsujou(suru) *n.* participation *v.* participate
- このチームが世界大会に出場する。 — This team will participate in the world tournament.

15 | 0.67

3319 だます damasu *v.* cheat, trick, deceive
- 彼女の嘘にまんまと騙されてしまった。 — I was thoroughly deceived by her lie.

15 | 0.91

3320 片付ける katazukeru *v.* put in order, tidy; clear away; finish
- 部屋を片付けなさい。 — Tidy up your room.

15 | 0.89

3321 組み合わせる kumiawaseru *v.* combine, put together, match
- 木とガラスを組み合わせて、テーブルを作った。 — I combined wood and glass to make a table.

15 | 0.91

3322 むろん muron *adv.* of course
- そんなことはむろん分かっている。 — Of course, I understand such a thing.

15 | 0.70

3323 雇用（する）koyou(suru) *n.* employment *v.* employ
- 雇用を創出するための対策が必要だ。 — Measures to create employment are needed.

15 | 0.68

3324 乗り越える norikoeru *v.* climb over; overcome
- 塀を乗り越えて、彼はその家に侵入した。 — Climbing over the wall, he broke into the house.

15 | 0.97

3325 休日 kyuujitsu *n.* holiday, day off
- 忙しいときは、休日にも出勤する。 — When I am busy with work, I go to work even on days off.

15 | 0.92

3326 寝袋 nebukuro *n.* sleeping bag
- キャンプでは、テントを張って、寝袋で寝た。 — At the camp, we pitched a tent and slept in sleeping bags.
15 | 0.30

3327 疑い utagai *n.* doubt, suspicion
- 彼の行為は法律違反の疑いがある。 — His conduct is suspected of being a violation of the law.
15 | 0.92

3328 引き出す hikidasu *v.* pull out, bring out; withdraw
- どうしたら能力を最大限に引き出せるか。 — How can we draw out the full potential?
15 | 0.92

3329 折 ori *n.* occasion, opportunity
- 彼には折を見て連絡しよう。 — I will call him at a suitable opportunity.
15 | 0.86

3330 印刷(する) insatsu(suru) *n.* printing *v.* print
- 招待状の印刷はもう済んでいる。 — The printing of the letter of invitation has already been finished.
15 | 0.93

3331 こなす konasu *v.* cope with; finish
- 与えられた仕事をこなすので精一杯だ。 — It is all I can do to finish the work I have been given.
15 | 0.88

3332 パチンコ pachinko *n.* pachinko, Japanese pinball
- 暇なときにパチンコをやる。 — I play pachinko when I have time.
15 | 0.59

3333 導く michibiku *v.* guide, lead
- 何が彼を成功に導いたのだろうか。 — What is it that led him to success?
15 | 0.86

3334 中止(する) chuushi(suru) *n.* cancellation *v.* cancel, call off
- 旅行は中止になった。 — The trip has been called off.
15 | 0.94

3335 連続(する) renzoku(suru) *n.* continuation, succession *v.* continue
- 山田さんは三日連続で会社を休んでいる。 — Mr. Yamada has been absent from work for three successive days.
15 | 0.99

3336 折る oru *v.* break; fold; bend
- 足の骨を折った。 — I broke my leg.
15 | 0.94

3337 関西 kansai *n.* Kansai region
- 彼は関西の生まれだ。 — He was born in the Kansai region.
15 | 0.88

3338 単語 tango *n.* word
- 毎日十個ずつ単語を覚える。 — I learn ten words a day.
15 | 0.92

3339 曖昧 aimai *na-adj.* vague, ambiguous
- 彼の返事は曖昧だった。 — His answer was vague.
15 | 0.97

3340 死体 shitai *n.* dead body
- 山で死体が見つかった。 — A dead body was found on the mountain.
15 | 0.65

3341 アフリカ afurika *n.* Africa
- 先月、初めてアフリカを訪れた。 — I visited Africa for the first time last month.
15 | 0.95

3342 なくてはならない naku te wa nara nai *cp.* must
- もう行かなくてはならない。 — I must go now.
15 | 0.93

3343 幸福 koufuku *n.* happiness
- 科学は人類に幸福をもたらすと考えられている。 — It is thought that science brings happiness to the human race.
15 | 0.85

3344 説得(する) settoku(suru) *n.* persuasion *v.* persuade
- こんな説明では彼を説得できないだろう。 — We can't persuade him with such an explanation.
15 | 0.97

3345 籠もる komoru *v.* shut oneself up; be full of
- 弟は部屋に籠ったまま出てこない。 — My younger brother shut himself up in his room and doesn't come out.
15 | 0.88

3346 レッスン ressun *n.* lesson
- 毎週一回ピアノのレッスンを受けている。 — I take a piano lesson once a week.
15 | 0.84

3347 放置(する) houchi(suru) *n.* leaving something as it is *v.* neglect
- 治療しないでそのまま放置した。 — I didn't take any medical treatment and left things to take their course.
15 | 0.96

3348 危機 kiki *n.* crisis, critical moment
- その動物は絶滅の危機にひんしている。 — The animal is on the brink of extinction.
15 | 0.93

3349 アーティスト aatisuto *n.* artist
- これは著名なアーティストの作品だ。— This is a work by a well-known artist.
15 | 0.80

3350 子達 ko-tachi *n.* children
- この子達は誰ですか。— Who are these children?
15 | 0.75

3351 編集（する） henshuu(suru) *n.* editing *v.* edit
- 雑誌の編集に携わったことがある。— I have been involved in the editing of a magazine.
15 | 0.94

3352 くっ付く kuttsuku *v.* stick, keep close; go out
- 靴にガムがべったりくっ付いている。— Some chewing gum is stuck tight to my shoe.
15 | 0.86

3353 取り付ける toritsukeru *v.* install, arrange
- 部屋にエアコンを取り付けてもらった。— I had an air-conditioner installed in the room.
15 | 0.95

3354 原稿 genkou *n.* manuscript, draft
- 昨日スピーチの原稿を書いた。— I wrote the draft of the speech yesterday.
15 | 0.86

3355 象徴（する） shouchou(suru) *n.* symbol *v.* symbolize
- 鳩は平和の象徴だ。— The dove is a symbol of peace.
15 | 0.88

3356 説く toku *v.* explain; preach; persuade
- 彼は教会で聖書の教えを説いている。— He preaches the teachings of the Bible at church.
15 | 0.77

3357 服装 fukusou *n.* clothes, dress
- カジュアルな服装で構いません。— You can dress casually.
15 | 0.87

3358 見学（する） kengaku(suru) *n.* studying by observation, field trip *v.* visit for study, go on a field trip
- 来週自動車工場の見学に行く。— We have a field trip to the car factory next week.
15 | 0.91

3359 六人 roku-nin *n.* six (people)
- 六人のグループを作ってください。— Please form groups of six.
15 | 0.92

3360 中野 nakano *n.* Nakano (place name)
- 以前、中野区に住んでいた。— I lived in Nakano Ward before.
15 | 0.61

3361 応募（する） oubo(suru) *n.* application *v.* apply for
- 応募の締め切りは今週の金曜日です。— The deadline for applications is this Friday.
15 | 0.74

3362 ラッキー rakkii *na-adj.* lucky
- 雨が降らなかったのはラッキーだった。— It was lucky that it didn't rain.
15 | 0.75

3363 二回目 ni kai-me *n.* second time
- このレストランに来るのは二回目だ。— It is the second time I have been to this restaurant.
15 | 0.87

3364 棒 bou *n.* stick, pole, bar
- 子どもが棒で犬を叩いている。— A child is beating a dog with a stick.
15 | 0.94

3365 こととなる koto to naru *aux.* it has been decided that
- 来週出張に行くこととなった。— It has been decided that I will go on a business trip next week.
15 | 0.48

3366 固定（する） kotei(suru) *n.* fixing *v.* fix
- 地震に備えて、家具を固定しておく。— I will secure the furniture in case of an earthquake.
15 | 0.96

3367 告白（する） kokuhaku(suru) *n.* confession *v.* confess
- ずっと好きだった人に告白した。— I confessed my love to the person whom I had liked for a long time.
15 | 0.75

3368 圧倒的 attou-teki *na-adj.* overwhelming
- 反対する人のほうが圧倒的に多かった。— There was an overwhelmingly large number of people who objected to it.
15 | 0.97

3369 策定（する） sakutei(suru) *n.* settling on *v.* settle on
- 現在、基本計画の策定を進めている。— We are settling on the basic plan now.
15 | 0.50

3370 矛盾（する） mujun(suru) *n.* contradiction, conflict *v.* contradict
- 彼の話は矛盾だらけだ。— What he says is full of contradictions.
15 | 0.92

3371 引き取る hikitoru *v.* take back, collect; leave
- フロントへ預けた荷物を引き取りに行く。— I will go to the front desk to collect the baggage which I left there.
15 | 0.98

3372 保証(する) hoshou(suru) n. guarantee v. guarantee
- 必ず成功するという保証はない。— There is no guarantee that you will definitely succeed.
15 | 0.94

3373 団地 danchi n. housing development
- この団地は1980年代につくられた。— This housing development was built in the 1980s.
15 | 0.71

3374 会長 kaichou n. president, chairperson
- A氏が会長に就任した。— Mr. A was installed as president.
15 | 0.91

3375 利点 riten n. advantage
- この方法には利点がいくつかある。— There are several advantages to this method.
15 | 0.96

3376 ジャンル janru n. genre, category
- いろいろなジャンルの音楽を聞く。— I listen to various genres of music.
15 | 0.84

3377 縦 tate n. length; height; vertical
- 日本の新聞はふつう縦に書いてある。— Japanese newspapers are usually written vertically.
15 | 0.86

3378 隙間 sukima n. crevice, opening, gap
- カーテンの隙間から外が見える。— I can see the outside through a gap in the curtains.
15 | 0.96

3379 歴史的 rekishi-teki na-adj. historical, historic
- 彼は歴史的偉業を成し遂げた。— He accomplished a historic achievement.
15 | 0.92

3380 羨ましい urayamashii i-adj. envious; enviable
- 毎年海外旅行ができる友人が羨ましい。— I'm envious of the friend who can travel abroad every year.
15 | 0.83

3381 ガス gasu n. gas
- この部屋はガスくさい。— This room smells of gas.
15 | 0.99

3382 ウイルス uirusu n. virus
- この病気はウイルスの感染によって起こる。— This disease is caused by a viral infection.
15 | 0.93

3383 公表(する) kouhyou(suru) n. publication v. make public
- 容疑者の名前は公表されていない。— The name of the suspect wasn't made public.
15 | 0.79

3384 二千一年 nisen ichi nen n. 2001 (year)
- 2001年から二十一世紀が始まる。— The twenty-first century begins in 2001.
15 | 0.88

3385 古く furuku n. ancient times adv. anciently
- この寺は古くからここにある。— This temple has been here since ancient times.
15 | 0.95

3386 潜る moguru v. dive; go underground
- 海に潜って、きれいな魚を見た。— I dived in the sea and saw beautiful fishes.
15 | 0.82

3387 一万円 ichi man en n. ten thousand yen
- 今では一万円でデジタルカメラが買える。— You can buy a digital camera for 10,000 yen now.
15 | 0.89

3388 意義 igi n. meaning, significance
- この国で国際会議が開かれる意義は大きい。— Holding the international conference in this country has great significance.
15 | 0.85

3389 憧れる akogareru v. long for; admire
- こんな生活に憧れる。— I long for such a life.
15 | 0.88

3390 前向き maemuki na-adj. facing forward; positive
- 彼女は明るく前向きな性格だ。— Her character is cheerful and positive.
15 | 0.98

3391 ゆったり yuttari adv. comfortably; calm; loose
- 祖父はソファーにゆったりと座っていた。— My grandfather was sitting comfortably on a sofa.
15 | 0.89

3392 漏れる moreru v. leak, escape; be omitted
- おわんの底から水が漏れている。— Water is leaking from the bottom of the soup bowl.
15 | 0.94

3393 品物 shinamono n. goods, article
- 頼んでいた品物が今日届いた。— The article which I have ordered arrived today.
15 | 0.96

3394 前述(する) zenjutsu(suru) n., v. above-mentioned, mentioned above
- その原因は前述の通りだ。— The cause is as mentioned above.
15 | 0.80

3395 あら ara interj. Oh! (used by female speakers)
- あら、ここにいたの。— Oh, you are here.
15 | 0.82

3396 OS ooesu *n.* operating system
- OSは何をお使いですか？ — Which OS do you use?

15 | 0.76

3397 まとも matomo *na-adj.* direct; honest; proper
- 彼女の顔がまともに見られなかった。 — I couldn't see her face directly.

15 | 0.88

3398 入手（する） nyuushu(suru) *n.* acquisition *v.* get, obtain
- 原料の入手が困難になった。 — It became difficult to get the ingredients.

15 | 0.98

3399 二十代 nijuu dai *n.* twenties
- 二十代は経験が少なかった。 — I was inexperienced when I was in my twenties.

15 | 0.92

3400 孤独 kodoku *na-adj.* lonely
- 彼女は見知らぬ土地で孤独だった。 — She was lonely in a strange city.

15 | 0.87

3401 平等 byoudou *n.* equality *na-adj.* equal
- この会社は男女平等を推進している。 — This company promotes gender equality.

15 | 0.94

17 Sports

(frequency per million words)

(スポーツ) (Sports)

野球 yakyuu 50.721 **baseball**
スキー sukii 41.962 **ski, skiing**
サッカー sakkaa 36.918 **football, soccer**
テニス tenisu 28.871 **tennis**
ゴルフ gorufu 26.100 **golf**
マラソン marason 12.635 **marathon**
プロ野球 puroyakyuu 12.173 **professional baseball**
体育 taiiku, taiku 11.652 **physical education, gymnastics**
剣道 kendou 10.199 **kendo**
水泳 suiei 9.365 **swimming**
バレーボール bareebooru 8.409 **volleyball**
ボート booto 8.216 **boat**
体操 taisou(suru) 8.169 **gymnastics, calisthenics**
ボクシング bokushingu 7.802 **boxing**
柔道 juudou 6.869 **judo**
相撲 sumou 5.233 **sumo**
ラグビー ragubii 4.683 **rugby**
バドミントン badominton 4.672 **badminton**
卓球 takkyuu 3.839 **table tennis**
バスケットボール basukettobooru 2.793 **basketball**
F1 efuwan 2.111 **Formula 1**
スケート sukeeto 1.925 **skating**
プロレス puroresu 1.824 **pro wrestling**
フットボール futtobooru 1.141 **football**
ホッケー hokkee 0.752 **hockey**
レスリング resuringu 0.555 **wrestling**

(スポーツ・施設) (Sports facilities)

プール puuru 20.431 **pool**
コート kooto 16.109 **court (also coat)**
スキー場 sukii-jou 11.240 **ski area, ski resort**
グラウンド guraundo 10.098 **ground, playground, sports field**
体育館 taiiku-kan, taik-kan 9.468 **gym**
スタジアム sutajiamu 2.400 **stadium**
競技場 kyougi-jou 1.013 **sports field**

(スポーツ・イベント) (Sports events)

試合 shiai 62.626 **match, game, bout**
大会 taikai 26.430 **tournament (also convention, mass meeting)**
オリンピック orinpikku 22.153 **Olympics**
ワールドカップ waarudo-kappu 11.196 **World Cup**

(スポーツ・動詞) (Sports: verbs)

練習（する） renshuu(suru) 111.668 **practice, training; practice, train**
勝つ katsu 71.815 **win, defeat**
運動（する） undou(suru) 71.739 **exercise, move**
負ける makeru 66.824 **lose, be beaten**
泳ぐ oyogu 28.766 **swim**
優勝（する） yuushou(suru) 26.684 **championship, victory; win**
トレーニング（する） toreeningu 21.436 **training**
プレー（する） puree 18.844 **play**
出場（する） shutsujou(suru) 15.201 **participation; participate**
競う kisou 7.475 **compete**
引き分け hikiwake 1.728 **draw**

3402 崩す kuzusu *v.* destroy; put into disorder; change
- 山を崩して、道路を作った。— They cut a road through the mountain.
15 | 0.94

3403 競馬 keiba *n.* horse racing
- 兄は時々競馬に行く。— My older brother sometimes goes to the races.
15 | 0.71

3404 格好良い kakkou yoi, kakkoii *i-adj.* cool, good-looking
- 友達のお兄さんは格好良い。— My friend's older brother is good-looking.
15 | 0.55

3405 交わす kawasu *v.* exchange
- 彼とは挨拶を交わす程度の関係だ。— I only know him well enough to exchange greetings.
15 | 0.85

3406 伝統的 dentou-teki *na-adj.* traditional
- これは日本の伝統的な遊びです。— This is a traditional game in Japan.
15 | 0.92

3407 パーティー paatii *n.* party
- 昨日のパーティーは楽しかった。— I enjoyed yesterday's party.
15 | 0.88

3408 役目 yakume *n.* duty, role
- しつけは親の役目だ。— Disciplining their children is a duty of the parents.
15 | 0.93

3409 通知（する）tsuuchi(suru) *n.* notice, notification *v.* notify
- 大学から合格の通知が届いた。— Notification that I had passed the exam reached me from the university.
15 | 0.74

3410 要望（する）youbou(suru) *n.* demand *v.* make demands
- 客からの要望に応えた。— We met the customers' demand.
15 | 0.67

3411 をめぐる o meguru *cp.* over, concerning
- 新しい制度をめぐる議論が活発だ。— There is a lively debate over a new system.
15 | 0.75

3412 営む itonamu *v.* run a business; engage in; hold a ceremony
- この村は農業を営んでいる人が多い。— There are many people engaged in agriculture in this village.
15 | 0.77

3413 パート paato *n.* part; part-time
- 私は一番高いパートを歌う。— I sing the highest part.
15 | 0.92

3414 手のひら tenohira *n.* palm of the hand
- 掌に載るくらい小さい子犬をもらった。— I got a puppy which is so small that it fits on the palm of my hand.
15 | 0.84

3415 地上 chijou *n.* ground
- 鳥が地上に降りてきた。— The birds came down onto the ground.
15 | 0.91

3416 踊り odori *n.* dance
- 最後にみんなで踊りを踊った。— Everyone did a dance at the end.
15 | 0.87

3417 押し付ける oshitsukeru *v.* press against, force
- 彼はたばこを灰皿に押し付けた。— He stubbed out the cigarette in the ashtray.
15 | 0.94

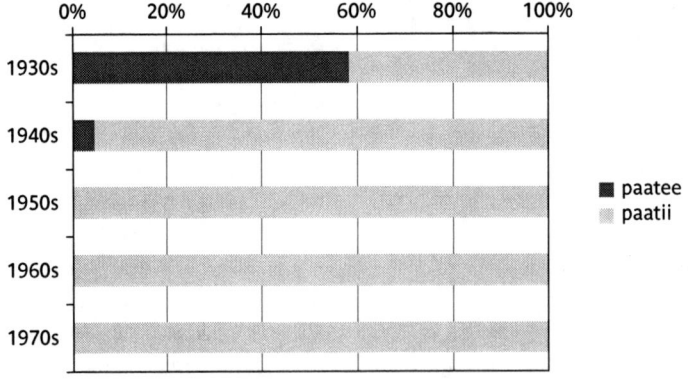

Variation of *paatii* (party): Elderly speakers born in the 1940s or earlier often pronounce the English loan word *party* as *paatee*, because traditional Japanese does not have the syllable /ti/. Younger speakers use the new variant of *paatii* which is closer to the English pronunciation.

3418 溶ける tokeru *v.* melt, thaw; dissolve
- 暖かくなって、湖の氷が溶け始めた。— It became warm, so the ice on the lake has begun to melt.

15 | 0.99

3419 奇妙 kimyou *na-adj.* strange, odd
- この村では時々奇妙な現象が起こる。— A strange phenomenon sometimes happens in this village.

15 | 0.71

3420 最中 saichuu *n.* in the middle of
- 式の最中に花嫁が倒れてしまった。— The bride fell down in the middle of the ceremony.

15 | 0.96

3421 定着（する）teichaku(suru) *n.* fixing *v.* fix; become established
- この制度はまだ十分に定着していない。— This system isn't yet sufficiently established.

15 | 0.88

3422 依然 izen *adv.* still, as before
- 依然として赤字が続いている。— The deficit still continues.

15 | 0.63

3423 素早い subayai *i-adj.* quick
- 政府の対応は素早かった。— The government dealt with it quickly.

15 | 0.83

3424 そこらへん sokora hen *n.* around there; such a matter
- 「ハサミ、どこ？」「そこらへんにない？」— "Where are the scissors?" "I think they are around there."

15 | 0.59

3425 有利 yuuri *na-adj.* profitable, advantageous
- これはこちらにとって有利な条件である。— These are favorable conditions for us.

15 | 0.95

3426 水準 suijun *n.* standard, level
- この地域はまだ生活水準が低い。— The standard of living is still low in this area.

15 | 0.48

3427 じっくり jikkuri *adv.* without haste, deliberately
- じっくり絵を見ることができなかった。— I wasn't able to have a good look at the paintings.

15 | 0.92

3428 首相 shushou *n.* prime minister
- 首相が会見を行った。— The prime minister held a press conference.

15 | 0.85

3429 レコード rekoodo *n.* record
- 私の趣味は古いレコードを集めることだ。— My hobby is collecting old records.

15 | 0.88

3430 際に sai ni *p.* when
- 今度会った際に、お渡しします。— I will hand it to you when I see you next.

15 | 0.84

3431 滅多 metta *na-adj.* rash, thoughtless; seldom
- こんなチャンスは滅多にない。— Such a chance seldom comes.

15 | 0.87

3432 機関 kikan *n.* engine; organization; facilities
- 将来は国際的な機関で働きたい。— I want to work in an international organization in the future.

15 | 0.69

3433 手作り tezukuri *n.* handmade, homemade
- 母が手作りのケーキを送ってくれた。— My mother sent me her homemade cake.

15 | 0.84

3434 提示（する）teiji(suru) *n.* presentation *v.* present
- 身分証の提示を求められた。— I was asked to present my ID.

15 | 0.87

3435 エジプト ejiputo *n.* Egypt
- エジプトへピラミッドを見に行きたい。— I want to go to Egypt to see the pyramids.

15 | 0.88

3436 下町 shitamachi *n.* Shitamachi (place name); traditional working-class neighborhood
- A氏は東京の下町で生まれ育った。— Mr. A was born and raised in Shitamachi in Tokyo.

15 | 0.58

3437 ううん uun *interj.* no; well
- 「食べる？」「ううん、食べない。」— "You want to try a taste?" "No, thanks."

15 | 0.58

3438 優先（する）yuusen(suru) *n.* priority *v.* have priority
- 人命を何よりも優先する。— Human life has priority over all other things.

15 | 0.98

3439 大部分 dai-bubun *n.* majority *adv.* mostly
- 日本の国土の大部分を山が占めている。— Mountains occupy the greater part of the Japanese landmass.

15 | 0.75

3440 戦前 senzen *n.* pre-war
- この店は戦前から続く名店だ。— This is a well-known restaurant which has been in business since before the war.

15 | 0.93

3441 制作（する）seisaku(suru) *n.* production *v.* produce
- この作品は十年前に制作された。— This work of art was produced ten years ago.
15 | 0.91

3442 いい加減 ii kagen *na-adj.* irresponsible, groundless
- いい加減なことを言わないでください。— Don't talk irresponsibly.
15 | 0.95

3443 後者 kousha *n.* the latter
- 私なら後者を選ぶ。— I would choose the latter.
15 | 0.86

3444 五十 gojuu *num.* fifty
- 今年、五十になった。— I turned fifty this year.
15 | 0.96

3445 入り込む hairikomu *v.* go into; come into
- 冷たい空気が部屋に入り込んでくる。— Cold air comes into the room.
15 | 0.91

3446 シャワー shawaa *n.* shower
- 出かける前にシャワーを浴びる。— I take a shower before going out.
15 | 0.87

3447 栗 kuri *n.* chestnut
- この栗はおいしい。— These chestnuts are delicious.
15 | 0.79

3448 札幌 sapporo *n.* Sapporo (place name)
- 来月、札幌へ雪まつりを見に行くつもりだ。— I'm going to go to Sapporo to see the snow festival next month.
15 | 0.93

3449 主体 shutai *n.* main constituent; subject
- この活動の主体は学生だ。— The subjects of this activity are students.
15 | 0.85

3450 家内 kanai *n.* one's family; my wife
- 来週、家内の実家に行くことになっている。— I am scheduled to visit my wife's parents' house next week.
15 | 0.77

3451 看板 kanban *n.* signboard, billboard; attraction
- あそこにその店の看板が見える。— You can see the signboard of the shop over there.
14 | 0.93

3452 将棋 shougi *n.* shogi, Japanese chess
- 祖父と父はよく一緒に将棋をさしている。— My grandfather and my father often play shogi together.
14 | 0.66

3453 家事 kaji *n.* housework
- 家事は分担してやるべきだ。— We should share the housework.
14 | 0.98

3454 捕まる tsukamaru *v.* be caught, be arrested; hold
- 犯人がついに捕まった。— The criminal was arrested at last.
14 | 0.90

3455 他方 tahou *n.* the other side
- 一方は成功し、他方は失敗した。— One side succeeded, the other side failed.
14 | 0.54

3456 交通事故 koutsuu jiko *n.* traffic accident
- 今朝、交通事故に遭った。— I had a traffic accident this morning.
14 | 0.83

3457 手順 tejun *n.* order, process, plan
- 手順に従って、組み立ててください。— Please assemble according to the instructions.
14 | 0.96

3458 コスト kosuto *n.* cost
- この計画はコストがかかりすぎる。— This plan costs too much.
14 | 0.94

3459 余る amaru *v.* be left over; be too many
- パーティーで余った料理をもらって帰った。— I took home the food left over at the party.
14 | 0.97

3460 輪 wa *n.* circle, ring; loop
- 輪になって座りましょう。— Let's sit down in a circle.
14 | 0.91

3461 ならびに narabi ni *conj.* and, both . . . and
- これは第四条ならびに第五条に規定されている。— This is prescribed in Articles 4 and 5.
14 | 0.31

3462 男達 otoko-tachi *n.* men
- 男達は楽しそうに酒を飲んでいた。— The men were drinking liquor happily.
14 | 0.55

3463 地名 chimei *n.* place name
- この地名の由来を知っていますか。— Do you know the origin of this place name?
14 | 0.91

3464 合意（する）goui(suru) *n.* mutual agreement *v.* agree
- 交渉は合意に至らなかった。— The negotiations didn't reach a mutual agreement.
14 | 0.63

3465 大手 oote *n.* major companies
- 彼は大手の出版社に勤めている。— He works for a major publishing company.
14 | 0.88

3466 本番 honban *n.* performance
- リハーサルなしで本番に臨んだ。— I did the performance without rehearsal.
14 | 0.81

3467 同僚 douryou *n.* colleague
- 職場の同僚と食事に行った。— I went to eat with a work colleague.
14 | 0.92

3468 楽しさ tanoshi-sa *n.* pleasure, charm
- これも旅の楽しさだ。— This is also the pleasure of travelling.
14 | 0.86

3469 丈夫 joubu *na-adj.* strong; healthy
- この素材は丈夫で長持ちだ。— This material is strong and durable.
14 | 0.90

3470 技 waza *n.* skill, technique, trick
- これは職人の巧みな技によって作り出された。— This was created by the wonderful skill of the craftsman.
14 | 0.86

3471 たちまち tachimachi *adv.* in a moment, at once; suddenly
- 彼女の顔はたちまち赤くなった。— Her face suddenly turned red.
14 | 0.64

3472 仕上げる shiageru *v.* finish, complete
- 今日中にこのレポートを仕上げてしまおう。— I will finish this report today!
14 | 0.83

3473 回収（する）kaishuu(suru) *n.* collection *v.* collect
- 今日はごみの回収はない。— The garbage won't be collected today.
14 | 0.98

3474 再生（する）saisei(suru) *n.* rebirth *v.* regenerate
- わが国の経済の再生には何が必要か。— What is necessary for the rebirth of our country's economy?
14 | 0.90

3475 わがまま wagamama *na-adj.* selfish, disobedient *n.* selfishness
- あの人はわがままだ。— That person is selfish.
14 | 0.81

3476 小さじ kosaji *n.* teaspoon
- 肉に小さじ一の塩を振ってください。— Sprinkle one teaspoon of salt on the meat.
14 | 0.83

3477 コントロール（する）kontorooru(suru) *n.* control *v.* control
- 車がコントロールを失った。— The car had lost control.
14 | 0.92

3478 深夜 shin'ya *n.* middle of the night
- パーティーは深夜まで続いた。— The party continued until very late at night.
14 | 0.92

3479 なおかつ naokatsu *adv.* besides, and yet
- この店の料理はおいしくて、なおかつ安い。— The food at this restaurant is delicious, yet cheap.
14 | 0.86

3480 活発 kappatsu *na-adj.* lively, active; brisk
- 活発にボランティア活動を行う。— We are active in volunteer work.
14 | 0.88

3481 芸術 geijutsu *n.* art
- 彼は芸術に造詣が深い。— He has a deep knowledge of art.
14 | 0.92

3482 ブラジル burajiru *n.* Brazil
- ワールドカップでブラジルが優勝した。— Brazil won the championship at the World Cup.
14 | 0.96

3483 施行（する）shikou(suru) *n.* enforcement *v.* enforce
- この法律は去年施行された。— This law was enforced last year.
14 | 0.51

3484 チーズ chiizu *n.* cheese
- ハムとチーズのサンドイッチを作った。— I made a sandwich with ham and cheese.
14 | 0.89

3485 教え oshie *n.* teaching, lesson, doctrine
- 先人の教えには従うものだ。— We should follow our predecessors' teaching.
14 | 0.87

3486 追及（する）tsuikyuu(suru) *n.* pursuit *v.* pursue the question
- メディアは首相の責任を厳しく追及した。— The media pursued the question of the prime minister's responsibility.
14 | 0.95

3487 今月 kongetsu *n.* this month
- 今月、新しい家に引っ越す。— I move into a new house this month.
14 | 0.67

3488 仙台 sendai *n.* Sendai (place name)
- 仙台の七夕祭りは有名だ。— The Star Festival in Sendai is famous.
14 | 0.88

3489 特許 tokkyo *n.* patent
- 新技術の特許を取った。— We obtained a patent on our new technology.

14 | 0.86

3490 株式 kabushiki *n.* stock, shares
- その会社は株式を公開した。— The company floated its shares on the stock market.

14 | 0.72

3491 労働（する） roudou(suru) *n., v.* work, labor
- 工場で労働する。— I work in a factory.

14 | 0.87

3492 カフェ kafe *n.* café
- 友達とカフェでコーヒーを飲んだ。— I drank coffee in a café with a friend.

14 | 0.81

3493 シンプル shinpuru *na-adj.* simple
- シンプルなデザインの家具を買った。— I bought furniture of a simple design.

14 | 0.63

3494 規則 kisoku *n.* rule, regulation
- 規則を守ってください。— Please follow the regulations.

14 | 0.93

3495 客観的 kyakkan-teki *na-adj.* objective
- 客観的に見たら、私は間違っているのかもしれない。— If I look at it objectively, I might be wrong.

14 | 0.96

3496 帰宅（する） kitaku(suru) *n.* coming home *v.* come home
- 仕事で帰宅が遅くなってしまった。— I ended up coming home late because of the work.

14 | 0.71

3497 つくづく tsukuzuku *adv.* thoroughly, deeply, carefully
- 家族のありがたみをつくづく感じる。— I feel deeply the importance of the family.

14 | 0.79

3498 一つ目 hito-tsu-me *n.* first
- 一つ目の角を右に曲がると、ありますよ。— You will find it when you turn right at the first corner.

14 | 0.68

3499 汚染（する） osen(suru) *n.* pollution *v.* pollute
- この川の水は汚染されている。— This river is polluted.

14 | 0.73

3500 転換（する） tenkan(suru) *n.* conversion *v.* convert, change
- その車は方向を転換した。— The car changed direction.

14 | 0.76

3501 たんぱく質 tanpaku-shitsu *n.* protein
- 良質なたんぱく質を摂りましょう。— Take high quality protein.

14 | 0.96

3502 Eメール ii meeru *n.* e-mail
- 友達にEメールを送った。— I sent an e-mail to my friend.

14 | 0.57

3503 予防（する） yobou(suru) *n.* prevention *v.* prevent
- 風邪の予防のために、手洗いとうがいをしている。— To prevent colds, I wash my hands and gargle.

14 | 0.87

3504 頬 hoo *n.* cheek
- 涙が彼女の頬を伝った。— Tears streamed down her cheeks.

14 | 0.56

3505 面積 menseki *n.* area, size
- 世界で一番面積が広い国はロシアだ。— The country with the largest area in the world is Russia.

14 | 0.81

3506 大正 taishou *n.* Taisho era
- 祖父は大正生まれだ。— My grandfather was born in the Taisho era.

14 | 0.83

3507 固める katameru *v.* make something hard, strengthen
- 彼は恋人に真実を告げる決意を固めた。— He determined to tell his girlfriend the truth.

14 | 0.94

3508 反する han-suru *v.* go against, be contrary
- この報道には事実に反する部分がある。— There are parts of this news report that contradict the facts.

14 | 0.89

3509 振るう furuu *v.* flourish, prosper
- インフルエンザが猛威を振るっている。— Influenza is spreading like wildfire.

14 | 0.92

3510 宣言（する） sengen(suru) *n.* declaration *v.* declare
- A国はB国からの独立を宣言した。— Country A declared independence from country B.

14 | 0.94

3511 直後 chokugo *n.* immediately after, just after
- 彼は病院に運ばれた直後に亡くなったそうだ。— He died soon after he was taken to hospital.

14 | 0.94

3512 ねえ nee *interj.* hey
- ねえ、聞いてよ。— Hey, listen!

14 | 0.57

3513 せいぜい seizei *adv.* at most
- その子はせいぜい十歳ぐらいにしか見えない。— She only looks around ten years old at most.
14 | 0.88

3514 特性 tokusei *n.* character, property
- この薬品には油を溶かす特性がある。— This chemical has the property of dissolving oil.
14 | 0.79

3515 解散（する）kaisan(suru) *n.* dissolution *v.* dissolve, break up
- 議会が解散し、選挙が行われることになった。— They decided to dissolve the parliament, and another election will take place.
14 | 0.94

3516 貧しい mazushii *i-adj.* poor
- 彼は貧しい人々を救済する活動をしている。— He is active in helping people in poverty.
14 | 0.88

3517 回転（する）kaiten(suru) *n.* revolution *v.* revolve, turn round, spin
- ヘリコプターのプロペラが回転し始めた。— The rotor blades of the helicopters started spinning.
14 | 0.93

3518 マナー manaa *n.* manners
- 最近、マナーが悪い乗客が増えた。— There is an increasing number of bad-mannered passengers these days.
14 | 0.90

3519 いちいち ichiichi *adv.* one by one; everything
- 英語の発音をいちいち直されて、嫌な気分になった。— I was upset because he corrected everything about my English pronunciation.
14 | 0.92

3520 政令 seirei *n.* government ordinance
- このことは政令で定められている。— This is regulated by a government ordinance.
14 | 0.14 | OF

3521 王様 ousama *n.* king
- 彼は王様のように振る舞う。— He acts like a king.
14 | 0.81

3522 折れる oreru *v.* break
- 転んで足の骨が折れた。— I fell over and broke my leg.
14 | 0.91

3523 竹 take *n.* bamboo
- 竹でおもちゃを作った。— We made a toy out of bamboo.
14 | 0.90

3524 暴力 bouryoku *n.* violence
- 彼は酒に酔って暴力を振るい、警察に捕まった。— He got drunk, and was arrested for being violent.
14 | 0.91

3525 えび ebi *n.* prawn, shrimp
- 昼ご飯はえびフライを食べた。— I had some fried prawns for lunch.
14 | 0.93

3526 担任 tannin *n.* class teacher
- 昨日、小学校のときの担任の先生に偶然会った。— I bumped into my elementary school teacher yesterday.
14 | 0.86

3527 角度 kakudo *n.* angle
- この角度からは見えづらい。— It's hard to see it from this angle.
14 | 0.98

3528 革命 kakumei *n.* revolution
- その国では去年革命が起こった。— There was a revolution in the country last year.
14 | 0.77

3529 合宿（する）gasshuku(suru) *n.* training camp *v.* stay together in a camp
- この夏はクラブの合宿に参加する予定だ。— I'm planning to attend the club's training camp this summer.
14 | 0.61

3530 後輩 kouhai *n.* one's junior
- 仕事の帰りに、会社の後輩と飲みに行った。— I went for a drink with my junior colleague after work.
14 | 0.82

3531 一連 ichiren *n.* course of, series of
- 一連の事件の経緯を簡単に説明します。— I'll briefly explain the course of the series of events.
14 | 0.89

3532 自動的 jidou-teki *na-adj.* automatic
- 自動的に電気がついた。— The light turned on automatically.
14 | 0.97

3533 郵便局 yuubin kyoku *n.* post office
- 郵便局から荷物を送った。— I sent a parcel from the post office.
14 | 0.85

3534 概要 gaiyou *n.* outline, summary
- 新制度の概要をご説明します。— I will provide an overview of the new program.
14 | 0.66

3535 ローマ rooma *n.* Rome
- ローマはイタリアの首都だ。— Rome is the capital of Italy.
14 | 0.94

3536 にわたる ni wataru *cp.* ranging, covering
- あの会社は多岐にわたる事業を展開している。— That company owns a wide range of businesses.
14 | 0.68

3537 体制 taisei *n.* system, structure
- その会社は経営の体制を立て直した。— The company reorganized their management structure.
14 | 0.71

3538 セックス（する）sekkusu(suru) *n.* sex *v.* have sex
- お互い合意の上でないセックスは犯罪だ。— Sex without mutual consent is a criminal offence.
14 | 0.72

3539 上記 jouki *n.* the above, above-mentioned
- ご質問は上記メールアドレスまでお問い合わせください。— If you have any queries, please contact us at the above e-mail address.
14 | 0.88

3540 何時 nan ji *n.* what time
- この店は何時に閉店しますか。— What time does the store close?
14 | 0.74

3541 親友 shin'yuu *n.* best friend, close friend
- 二十年来の親友の結婚式に出席した。— I attended the wedding of my best friend of twenty years.
14 | 0.88

3542 お袋 ofukuro *n.* mother
- 夕べお袋から電話があった。— Last night, there was a phone call from Mom.
14 | 0.61

3543 所有（する）shoyuu(suru) *n.* ownership *v.* own
- 祖父はこの近くに土地を所有している。— My grandfather owns land near here.
14 | 0.94

3544 進出（する）shinshutsu(suru) *n.* advance *v.* launch into
- A社は世界二十か国に進出している。— Company A has launched its business in twenty countries.
14 | 0.91

3545 大げさ oogesa *na-adj.* exaggerated
- 彼は小さな傷に大げさに騒いでいる。— He's making too much fuss about a small scar.
14 | 0.88

3546 測定（する）sokutei(suru) *n.* measurement *v.* measure
- その研究者は二酸化炭素の濃度を測定した。— The researcher measured the density of carbon dioxide.
14 | 0.84

3547 そこそこ sokosoko *adv.* about; in a hurry; all right
- 多くはないが、そこそこの収入がある。— It's not a lot but I have a reasonable income.
14 | 0.77

3548 論ずる ronzuru *v.* argue, discuss
- 国の習慣について論ずるのは難しい。— It's difficult to discuss the customs of the country.
14 | 0.72

3549 家賃 yachin *n.* rent
- この部屋は家賃が高い。— The rent for this room is expensive.
14 | 0.97

3550 蛇 hebi *n.* snake
- 蛇にかまれた。— I was bitten by a snake.
14 | 0.89

3551 自身 jishin *n.* oneself
- 自分自身を客観的に見ることは難しい。— It is hard to see ourselves objectively.
14 | 0.93

3552 譲る yuzuru *v.* give; sell; offer
- 電車でお年寄りに席を譲った。— I offered my seat to an elderly person on the train.
14 | 0.97

3553 修理（する）shuuri(suru) *n.* repair *v.* repair
- そのパソコンは修理が必要だ。— The PC needs a repair.
14 | 0.90

3554 遡る sakanoboru *v.* go back; be retroactive
- この祭りの起源は江戸時代まで遡る。— This festival can be traced back to the Edo period.
14 | 0.96

3555 加工（する）kakou(suru) *n.* processing *v.* process
- この製品は特殊な加工が施されている。— This product is made by a unique process.
14 | 0.98

3556 鶏 niwatori *n.* chicken; baby bird
- 隣のうちは鶏を飼っている。— My neighbor keeps chickens.
14 | 0.94

3557 保護者 hogo-sha *n.* protector
- 未成年者の参加には、保護者の同意が必要である。— Parental consent is required for the attendance of minors.
14 | 0.45

3558 いえ ie *interj.* no
- 「取引先からの書類、もう届いた？」「いえ、まだ届いていません。」— "Have we received the documents from the customer?" "No, we haven't yet."
14 | 0.76

3559 施す hodokosu *v.* give, do, apply, add
- 城の室内は豪華な装飾が施されていた。— The inside of the castle was lavishly decorated.
14 | 0.76

3560 人材 jinzai *n.* talented people
- わが社には優秀な人材が必要だ。— Our company needs talented people.
14 | 0.85

3561 かすか kasuka *na-adj.* a few, a little
- そのことはかすかに覚えている。— I vaguely remember that.
14 | 0.61

3562 取り込む torikomu *v.* take in
- 洗濯物を取り込んだ。— I took the washing in.
14 | 0.98

3563 排除(する) haijo(suru) *n.* removal *v.* remove
- その可能性を完全に排除することはできない。— We cannot completely eliminate the possibility.
14 | 0.88

3564 育成(する) ikusei(suru) *n.* cultivation *v.* bring up, cultivate, mold
- この会社は若手社員の育成に力を入れている。— This company makes great efforts to cultivate young talents.
14 | 0.69

3565 移転(する) iten(suru) *n., v.* move
- 事務所が隣のビルに移転することになった。— They decided to move the office to the building next door.
14 | 0.76

3566 動機 douki *n.* motive
- 警察は犯行の動機を調べている。— The police are investigating the motive for the offence.
14 | 0.94

3567 兼ねる kaneru *v.* combine; serve both
- 趣味と実益を兼ねて、中国語を習っている。— For enjoyment combined with usefulness, I am learning Chinese.
14 | 0.97

3568 ネットワーク nettowaaku *n.* network
- 子育て支援のためのネットワークの構築を目指す。— They aim to build a network for parenting support.
14 | 0.86

3569 自立(する) jiritsu(suru) *n.* independence *v.* be independent
- 早く自立したいと思っている。— I want to be independent as soon as I can.
14 | 0.92

3570 ハムスター hamusutaa *n.* hamster
- 妹はハムスターを飼っている。— My sister has a hamster.
14 | 0.42

3571 でかい dekai *i-adj.* big, huge
- あいつは体がでかい。— He is huge.
14 | 0.82

3572 下す kudasu *v.* give, issue; make a decision
- 裁判所は全員無罪という判決を下した。— The court delivered a verdict of not guilty for all of them.
14 | 0.90

3573 やたら yatara *adv.* freely, thoughtlessly
- 彼は一人暮らしなのに、やたら大きいテレビを持っている。— He has an excessively huge TV though he lives on his own.
14 | 0.85

3574 二十五 nijuu go *num.* twenty-five
- この教室には机といすが二十五ずつある。— There are twenty-five sets of desks and chairs in this classroom.
14 | 0.82

3575 黄色い kiiroi *i-adj.* yellow
- 一面に黄色い花が咲いていた。— Yellow flowers bloomed all over.
14 | 0.91

3576 確率 kakuritsu *n.* probability
- たんに確率の問題だ。— It's simply a matter of probability.
14 | 0.95

3577 ペース peesu *n.* pace
- 自分のペースで無理なく走りましょう。— Run at your own pace without straining.
14 | 0.91

3578 大統領 daitouryou *n.* President
- この公園に大統領が訪れた。— The President visited this park.
14 | 0.96

3579 スムーズ sumuuzu *na-adj.* smooth
- 新システムへの移行はスムーズに進んだ。— The transition to the new system went smoothly.
14 | 0.96

3580 欠点 ketten *n.* fault, defect; drawback, weak point
- この装置の欠点は大きすぎることだ。— The weak point of the machine is being too big.
14 | 0.94

3581 適正 tekisei *na-adj.* appropriate, proper, reasonable
- この評価は適正だと思う。— The evaluation is reasonable.
14 | 0.47

3582 千葉 chiba *n.* Chiba
- 東京ディズニーランドは千葉にある。— Tokyo Disneyland is located in Chiba.
14 | 0.92

3583 望ましい nozomashii *i-adj.* desirable
- 実務経験があることが望ましい。— Work experience is desirable.
14 | 0.73

3584 鳴らす narasu *v.* ring
- チャイムを鳴らしたが、誰も出てこなかった。— I rang the doorbell but nobody answered.
14 | 0.90

3585 ブランド burando *n.* brand
- あれは有名なブランドのバッグらしい。— That looks like a famous brand bag.
14 | 0.81

3586 学問 gakumon *n.* study, learning
- 大学に入った彼は、学問に励んだ。— He pursued academic work at the university.
14 | 0.87

3587 共同 kyoudou *n.* cooperation; common
- 共同トイレが嫌で寮を出た。— I hated the shared toilets and moved out of the dorm.
14 | 0.81

3588 取り除く torinozoku *v.* remove
- 私は魚の骨を取り除くのが苦手だ。— I'm not good at removing fish bones.
14 | 0.96

3589 不可欠 fukaketsu *na-adj.* indispensable
- この活動の成功には、地域住民の協力が不可欠だ。— In order to make the activity successful, support from local residents is indispensable.
14 | 0.78

3590 十九 juu kyuu *num.* nineteen
- 彼女は十九で結婚した。— She got married when she was nineteen.
14 | 0.88

3591 神奈川県 kanagawa ken *n.* Kanagawa Prefecture
- 伯母は神奈川県に住んでいる。— My aunt lives in Kanagawa.
14 | 0.94

3592 二十二 nijuu ni *num.* twenty-two
- 普通二十二で大学を卒業する。— They usually graduate from college when they are twenty-two.
14 | 0.72

3593 ばれる bareru *v.* come out, be discovered
- 浮気はすぐにばれる。— Your affair will come out soon.
14 | 0.73

3594 乗り込む norikomu *v.* board, get into
- 突然乗り込んできた男が、バスをハイジャックした。— The man who had suddenly broken in hijacked the bus.
14 | 0.85

3595 欠かせる kakaseru *v.* cause to lack
- これは日本料理には欠かせない食材です。— This ingredient is indispensable for Japanese cuisine.
14 | 0.89

3596 窓口 madoguchi *n.* window, counter
- お支払いはあちらの窓口でお願いいたします。— Please proceed to the counter over there for payment.
14 | 0.65

3597 収穫（する）shuukaku(suru) *n., v.* harvest
- 秋は米の収穫の季節だ。— Fall is the season of the rice harvest.
14 | 0.89

18 Taste

(frequency per million words)

おいしい oishii 209.947 **delicious, tasty**
薄い usui 133.412 **weak (also thin, light)**
甘い amai 46.509 **sweet (also soft)**
濃い koi 44.152 **strong (also thick, heavy, deep)**
まずい mazui 29.815 **not taste good (also awkward)**
すっきり（する）sukkiri(suru) 26.700 **feel refreshed**
さっぱり（する）sappari(suru) 17.958 **not at all**
爽やか sawayaka 15.862 **fresh**
しつこい shitsukoi 9.387 **over-rich (food) (also persistent)**
苦い nigai 8.632 **bitter**

渋い shibui 6.760 **astringent**
辛い karai 5.376 **spicy, hot**
濃厚 noukou 4.173 **strong (also thick, heavy, deep)**
酸っぱい suppai 3.047 **sour**
まろやか maroyaka 2.106 **mild**
しょっぱい shoppai 1.864 **salty**
淡泊 tanpaku 1.410 **light**
甘酸っぱい amazuppai 1.148 **sour-sweet**
あぶらっこい aburakkoi 1.081 **oily**
えぐい egui 0.642 **harsh**
塩からい shiokarai 0.494 **salty**

3598 バラ bara *n.* rose
- バラの花束をもらった。— I got a bunch of roses.
14 | 0.74

3599 血管 kekkan *n.* blood vessel
- 彼女の腕は細く、血管が透けて見える。— Her arm is so thin that blood vessels can be seen.
14 | 0.87

3600 方言 hougen *n.* dialect
- 家族と話すときは方言を使う。— I speak in local dialect when talking to my family members.
14 | 0.77

3601 時間帯 jikan-tai *n.* time (period), time zone
- 今は電車が一番混む時間帯だ。— Trains get most crowded at this time of day.
14 | 0.91

3602 全体的 zentai-teki *na-adj.* whole, overall
- まず、全体的な作業手順を説明します。— I'll explain the whole procedure first of all.
14 | 0.98

3603 割れる wareru *v.* split; break
- 強風で窓ガラスが割れた。— The window was shattered by a strong wind.
14 | 0.92

3604 抽選(する) chuusen(suru) *n.* lottery *v.* draw lots
- 抽選でダイヤモンドが当たった。— I won a diamond ring in a draw.
14 | 0.27 | NM

3605 手法 shuhou *n.* technique, method
- この布は伝統的な手法で染められている。— This cloth is dyed using a traditional method.
14 | 0.90

3606 肉体 nikutai *n.* body
- 彼は強じんな肉体の持ち主だ。— He has a strong body.
14 | 0.70

3607 生き生き ikiiki *adv.* lively, fresh
- 学生達は休み時間の間は生き生きしています。— The students are lively during the break.
14 | 0.71

3608 狂う kuruu *v.* go mad
- 毎日忙しすぎて、気が狂いそうだ。— It's been so hectic every day and it's driving me mad.
14 | 0.88

3609 一口 hitokuchi *n.* bite, sip, mouthful
- 彼はそのケーキを一口で食べた。— He ate the cake in one bite.
14 | 0.94

3610 協議(する) kyougi(suru) *n.* consultation, discussion *v.* consult, discuss
- この点については、関係機関と協議の上、決定したいと思います。— As for this issue, we'll make a decision after consultation with the relevant institutions.
14 | 0.54

3611 重要性 juuyou-sei *n.* importance
- 彼はチャレンジすることの重要性を説いた。— He argued the importance of giving things a try.
14 | 0.72

3612 発酵(する) hakkou(suru) *n.* fermentation *v.* ferment
- 納豆は大豆を発酵させた食品だ。— Natto is made from fermented soy beans.
14 | 0.74

3613 繰り返し kurikaeshi *n.* repetition
- 同じ毎日の繰り返しに飽きた。— I'm fed up with the same routine every day.
14 | 0.98

3614 入札(する) nyuusatsu(suru) *n.* bid, tender *v.* bid, tender
- 入札の結果、A社が工事を請け負うことになった。— Company A was assigned the construction by bid.
14 | 0.48 | WB

3615 覚める sameru *v.* wake up
- 夕べは夜中に何度も目が覚めてしまった。— I woke up several times last night.
14 | 0.85

3616 ベスト besuto *n.* best; vest
- 選手たちは皆ベストを尽くして戦った。— All the athletes competed giving their best.
14 | 0.78

3617 羽根 hane *n.* wing; feather
- 鳥が羽根を広げて飛び立とうとしている。— A bird is about to spread its wings and fly.
14 | 0.93

3618 背負う seou *v.* carry something on one's back
- あのリュックを背負っている人が山田さんです。— The man with a backpack is Mr. Yamada.
14 | 0.93

3619 いつか istu ka *adv.* someday
- いつか真実が分かるだろう。— You will know the truth someday.
14 | 0.75

3620 次回 jikai *n.* next time
- 次回のミーティングは来週の木曜日です。— Our next meeting will be held next Thursday.
13 | 0.82

3621 基盤 kiban *n.* base, basis
- 地震によって多くの人々が生活の基盤を失った。— Many people lost the foundations of their lives due to the earthquake.

13 | 0.82

3622 丸 maru *n.* circle, ring
- 当てはまる項目をすべて丸で囲んでください。— Circle all the items that are applicable.

13 | 0.95

3623 感染(する) kansen(suru) *n.* infection *v.* contract, catch, be infected
- インフルエンザに感染した。— I got infected with flu.

13 | 0.91

3624 尊重(する) sonchou(suru) *n.* respect *v.* give something serious consideration
- 第三者の意見も尊重されるべきだ。— The opinions of third parties should also be given serious consideration.

13 | 0.79

3625 オフィス ofisu *n.* office
- オフィスの中は禁煙です。— No smoking in the office.

13 | 0.96

3626 否 ina *n.* no
- 実現が可能か否かを検討する。— We will discuss whether or not it's feasible.

13 | 0.78

3627 素人 shirouto *n.* amateur, beginner
- 僕はゴルフに関しては素人だ。— I am an amateur at golf.

13 | 0.91

3628 十七歳 juu nana-sai *n.* seventeen years old
- 十七歳のとき、初めて海外旅行をした。— I traveled abroad for the first time when I was seventeen.

13 | 0.89

3629 一環 ikkan *n.* part of
- このプロジェクトは政策の一環として行われる。— This project will be carried out as a part of the policy.

13 | 0.75

3630 洗濯(する) sentaku(suru) *n.* washing *v.* wash
- 今日は天気がいいから洗濯しよう。— I should do the laundry as the weather is fine today.

13 | 0.90

3631 争う arasou *v.* compete
- 去年もこの二チームが優勝を争った。— These two teams competed for the championship last year as well.

13 | 0.98

3632 一時的 ichiji-teki *na-adj.* temporary
- この薬を飲めば一時的に症状は緩和する。— The symptoms will be temporarily alleviated if you take this medication.

13 | 0.98

3633 観光客 kankou kyaku *n.* tourist
- 観光客が一番多い季節は春だ。— Spring is the season which has the largest number of visitors.

13 | 0.97

3634 主要 shuyou *na-adj.* major, main
- 川崎市は日本の主要な工業都市である。— Kawasaki is a major industrial city in Japan.

13 | 0.68

3635 魅力的 miryoku-teki *na-adj.* charming, attractive
- 彼女は魅力的だ。— She is charming.

13 | 0.88

3636 外側 sotogawa *n.* outside
- 窓の外側が汚れている。— The outside of the window is dirty.

13 | 0.95

3637 勘違い(する) kanchigai(suru) *v.* misunderstand, mistake
- 約束の時間を勘違いして、遅刻してしまった。— I had mistaken the time of the appointment, so I came late.

13 | 0.81

3638 この間 kono aida *n.* a few days ago *adv.* recently, lately
- この間までは寒かったが、今は暖かい。— It was cold until recently, but it's warm now.

13 | 0.00 | SP

3639 臭い kusai *i-adj.* smelly
- 靴を脱いだら、足が臭かった。— My feet were smelly when I took my shoes off.

13 | 0.76

3640 手元 temoto *n.* at hand, with one
- お手元の資料をご覧ください。— Please take a look at your handout.

13 | 0.98

3641 食 shoku *n.* meal, diet
- 彼女は食が細い。— She eats very little.

13 | 0.84

3642 ため息 tameiki *n.* sigh
- 彼は通帳の残高を見て、ため息をついた。— Looking at the balance on the bank statement, he sighed.

13 | 0.64

3643 急激 kyuugeki *na-adj.* sudden; drastic
- 環境の急激な変化でストレスを感じる。— I feel under stress because of the sudden change of environment.

13 | 0.87

3644 お仕舞い o-shimai *n.* end, conclusion
- 彼はもうお仕舞いだ。— It's all over with him now.
13 | 0.89

3645 修正（する）shuusei(suru) *n.* revision *v.* revise
- スピーチの原稿に修正を加えた。— I revised the draft speech.
13 | 0.93

3646 たいして taishite *adv.* (not) very much
- あのレストランは有名だが、料理はたいしておいしくない。— That restaurant is famous but their food is not that great.
13 | 0.82

3647 インタビュー（する）intabyuu(suru) *n., v.* interview
- 大統領が記者のインタビューに答えた。— The president answered questions in a press interview.
13 | 0.92

3648 同級生 doukyuu-sei *n.* classmate
- 久しぶりに高校時代の同級生が集まった。— There was a reunion of my high school classmates for the first time in ages.
13 | 0.87

3649 受け継ぐ uketsugu *v.* inherit
- この伝統は脈々と受け継がれてきた。— The tradition has been handed down from generation to generation.
13 | 0.93

3650 重さ omo-sa *n.* weight
- この鞄の重さは20キロ以上ある。— The weight of the bag is over twenty kilos.
13 | 0.99

3651 町作り machizukuri *n.* town development
- 市長は町作りに熱心だ。— The mayor devotes himself to the development of the town.
13 | 0.52

3652 削減（する）sakugen(suru) *n.* cut, reduction *v.* cut, slash
- 機械化により、生産コストの削減を目指す。— They aim to slash the production costs through mechanization.
13 | 0.78

3653 顧客 kokyaku *n.* customer
- 顧客を獲得するため、キャンペーンを行う。— We'll launch a campaign to gain new customers.
13 | 0.87

3654 爆発（する）bakuhatsu(suru) *n.* explosion *v.* explode
- 近くの工場で爆発が起こった。— There was an explosion in a nearby factory.
13 | 0.97

3655 スイス suisu *n.* Switzerland
- この時計はスイス製だ。— This watch is made in Switzerland.
13 | 0.94

3656 うかがう ukagau *v.* peep, peer; watch for (a chance)
- ドアの隙間から中の様子をうかがった。— I peered inside through the door.
13 | 0.85

3657 軍隊 guntai *n.* army, troops
- テロ活動を阻止するため軍隊が送られた。— Troops were sent in order to deter the terrorist activities.
13 | 0.88

3658 そいつ soitsu *n.* that guy
- そいつ、誰だ？— Who is that guy?
13 | 0.77

3659 試みる kokoromiru *v.* try
- 別の視点から分析を試みた。— I tried to make an analysis from a different view point.
13 | 0.84

3660 決心（する）kesshin(suru) *n.* resolution *v.* decide
- 十年付き合った後結婚する決心を固めた。— We decided to get married after being together for ten years.
13 | 0.82

3661 所得 shotoku *n.* income
- その国は国民一人当たりの所得が低い。— The average annual income of that country is low.
13 | 0.71

3662 難い gatai *suffix* hard to ...
- それはにわかには信じ難い出来事だ。— It's an incident which is hard to believe.
13 | 0.32

3663 リーダー riidaa *n.* leader
- 彼は営業チームのリーダーとして活躍している。— He works as the leader of the sales team.
13 | 0.93

3664 調理（する）chouri(suru) *n.* cooking *v.* cook
- 魚を買って、家で調理した。— I bought a fish and cooked it at home.
13 | 0.95

3665 地区 chiku *n.* area
- 市のスポーツ大会に、この地区の代表として出場する。— I'm taking part in the city's sports competition as a local representative.
13 | 0.90

3666 家具 kagu *n.* furniture
- 新居の家具を買いそろえた。— We bought furniture for our new place.
13 | 0.91

3667 自治体 jichi tai *n.* municipality
- 国や自治体が環境問題に取り組む。— The government and municipalities tackle environmental problems.

13 | 0.89

3668 剣 ken *n.* sword
- ペンは剣よりも強し。— The pen is mightier than the sword.

13 | 0.65

3669 介護保険 kaigo hoken *n.* nursing care insurance
- 四十歳以上は介護保険料を払う義務がある。— People over forty are obliged to pay for nursing care insurance.

13 | 0.85

3670 キス（する）kisu(suru) *n., v.* kiss
- 彼は彼女の頬にキスをした。— He kissed her on the cheek.

13 | 0.67

3671 不況 fukyou *n.* recession
- この不況を乗り切るために、わが社は何をするべきだろうか。— What does our company need to do in order to survive the current recession?

13 | 0.94

3672 松 matsu *n.* pine
- 海岸に沿って、松の林が続いている。— Pine forest extends along the coast.

13 | 0.94

3673 停止（する）teishi(suru) *n.* stop, suspension *v.* stop, suspend
- そのレストランは営業の停止を命じられた。— The restaurant was ordered to suspend business.

13 | 0.83

3674 古代 kodai *n.* ancient times
- 古代、日本には文字がなかった。— Japanese had no characters in ancient times.

13 | 0.88

3675 四十 shijuu *num.* forty
- 四十を越えると肉体的に弱さを覚える。— When you are over forty, you start to feel physically weak.

13 | 0.94

3676 シリーズ shiriizu *n.* series
- このドラマシリーズは十年以上続いている。— This drama series has been broadcast for over ten years.

13 | 0.79

3677 食生活 shoku seikatsu *n.* eating habits
- 日本人の食生活は戦後大きく変化した。— Since WWII, Japanese eating habits have changed dramatically.

13 | 0.94

3678 申し込む moushikomu *v.* apply
- 近所のジムに入会を申し込んだ。— I applied for membership of a local gym.

13 | 0.77

3679 デビュー（する）debyuu(suru) *n.* debut *v.* make one's debut
- その歌手は昨年デビューしたばかりだ。— The singer just made her debut last year.

13 | 0.82

3680 足る taru *v.* be enough; deserve
- 彼は信頼に足る人物だ。— He deserves your trust.

13 | 0.96

3681 四十年 yonjuu nen *n.* forty years
- この家は築四十年だ。— This house is forty years old.

13 | 0.87

3682 思い込む omoikomu *v.* be obsessed with the idea
- 彼は勝手にそう思い込んでいる。— He is so obsessed with the idea.

13 | 0.85

3683 予備校 yobi-kou *n.* cram school preparing for university entrance examinations
- 高校卒業後、一年間予備校に通った。— After I graduated from high school, I went to a university entrance private preparatory school for a year.

13 | 0.54

3684 膨大 boudai *na-adj.* enormous
- この病気の治療には膨大な費用がかかる。— It costs an enormous amount to cure this disease.

13 | 0.93

3685 統一（する）touitsu(suru) *n., v.* unity
- 分裂していた国家が統一した。— Two divided states have reunited.

13 | 0.92

3686 寿命 jumyou *n.* life expectancy
- 男性より女性のほうが寿命が長い。— Life expectancy for women is longer than it is for men.

13 | 0.92

3687 根本的 konpon-teki *na-adj.* fundamental, basic
- 彼の言っていることは根本的に間違っている。— What he is saying is basically wrong.

13 | 0.97

3688 幕府 bakufu *n.* shogunate
- 徳川幕府は本拠地を江戸（東京）に置いた。— The Tokugawa shogunate located their headquarters in Edo (Tokyo).

13 | 0.73

3689 苦しみ kurushimi *n.* suffering, agony
- 彼は家族を失う苦しみを味わった。— He went through the agony of losing his family.
13 | 0.93

3690 要件 youken *n.* important matter; requirement
- 次の要件を満たした方のみ、応募できます。— Only those who meet the following requirements are eligible to apply.
13 | 0.74

3691 図表 zuhyou *n.* chart
- 調査の結果を図表で示した。— The research results are shown in charts.
13 | 0.41

3692 逃れる nogareru *v.* escape
- 彼は迫害を逃れるため、他国へ亡命した。— He sought refuge in another country to avoid persecution.
13 | 0.87

3693 反対側 hantai gawa *n.* opposite side
- そのホテルは道を挟んで反対側にある。— The hotel is located across the street.
13 | 0.89

3694 プロジェクト purojekuto *n.* project
- 新しいプロジェクトが開始した。— A new project has been launched.
13 | 0.92

3695 励ます hagemasu *v.* cheer up, encourage
- お互いに励まし合いながら、私たちは救助を待った。— We encouraged each other while we waited for rescue.
13 | 0.91

3696 存ずる zonzuru *v.* know
- 詳しいことは存じておりません。— I am not certain about the details.
13 | 0.40

3697 辞書 jisho *n.* dictionary
- 言葉の意味を辞書で引いた。— I looked up the meaning of the word in a dictionary.
13 | 0.83

3698 中国語 chuugoku go *n.* Chinese language
- 中国語を習っている。— I'm learning Chinese.
13 | 0.88

3699 までもない made mo nai *cp.* needless
- その重要性をいまさら語るまでもないだろう。— It's needless at this stage to mention its significance.
13 | 0.74

3700 カラス karasu *n.* crow
- カラスがごみをあさっている。— Crows are pecking through the garbage.
13 | 0.91

3701 問い toi *n.* question
- この問いに答えられる者はいなかった。— There was no one who could answer this question.
13 | 0.84

3702 派手 hade *na-adj.* flamboyant, flashy
- 彼女の服装はいつも派手だ。— Her outfits are always flashy.
13 | 0.88

3703 DVD diibuidii *n.* DVD
- DVDで映画を見た。— I watched a film on DVD.
13 | 0.50 | WB

3704 発明(する) hatsumei(suru) *n.* invention *v.* invent
- これは画期的な発明だ。— This is an epoch-making invention.
13 | 0.88

3705 大学時代 daigaku jidai *n.* college days, university days
- 大学時代にラグビーをやっていました。— I played rugby in college.
13 | 0.62

3706 干す hosu *v.* dry
- 今から洗濯物を干します。— I'll hang up the washing to dry.
13 | 0.84

3707 披露宴 hirou en *n.* wedding reception
- 教会での結婚式の後、ホテルで披露宴を行った。— After the ceremony in church, we held the wedding reception in a hotel.
13 | 0.66

3708 気候 kikou *n.* climate
- この地方の気候は温暖で過ごしやすい。— The climate in this region is warm and comfortable.
13 | 0.96

3709 非難(する) hinan(suru) *n.* criticism *v.* criticize
- 彼の発言は激しい非難を浴びた。— His account was bitterly criticized.
13 | 0.88

3710 唱える tonaeru *v.* recite; advocate
- 異議を唱える者はいなかった。— No one raised an objection.
13 | 0.86

3711 作者 sakusha *n.* author
- この俳句の作者は不明だ。— The author of this haiku is unknown.
13 | 0.95

3712 助け tasuke *n.* help, assistance
- 近くにいた人に助けを求めた。— I sought assistance from a passer-by.
13 | 0.88

3713 に比べて ni kurabe te *cp.* compared to
- 五十年前に比べて、人々の生活は豊かになった。— Compared to fifty years ago, people have affluent lives.

13 | 0.00 | SP

3714 関東 kantou *n.* Kanto region
- この味付けは関東風だ。— This flavoring is Kanto-style.

13 | 0.95

3715 なめる nameru *v.* lick; suck
- 喉の調子が悪いので、あめをなめている。— I'm sucking a candy as I have a sore throat.

13 | 0.84

3716 不明 fumei *na-adj., n.* unknown, unidentified
- 昨夜の列車事故の原因は不明だった。— The cause of the train accident last night was unknown.

13 | 0.92

3717 スケジュール sukejuuru *n.* schedule
- 来週のスケジュールを立てた。— I drew up next week's schedule.

13 | 0.96

3718 差し出す sashidasu *v.* hold out
- 彼は右手を差し出し、握手を求めた。— He held out his right hand and offered a handshake.

13 | 0.72

3719 外部 gaibu *n.* outside
- このことを外部に漏らしてはいけない。— You must not leak this to outsiders.

13 | 0.92

3720 ネズミ nezumi *n.* rat; mouse
- 部屋にネズミが出た。— A rat appeared in my room.

13 | 0.92

3721 ニーズ niizu *n.* needs
- 顧客のニーズを満たす製品の開発が必要だ。— It is necessary to develop a product that meets our customers' needs.

13 | 0.67

3722 現金 genkin *n.* cash
- 多額の現金を持ち歩くのは危ない。— It is not safe to carry a large amount of cash.

13 | 0.97

3723 彼女達 kanojo-tachi *n.* they (female)
- 彼女達は自分たちの可能性を知らない。— Those girls do not know their potential.

13 | 0.83

3724 故郷 kokyou *n.* home town
- 故郷を離れて十年になる。— It's been ten years since I left home.

13 | 0.84

3725 畳 tatami *n.* tatami mat
- 畳の上に布団を敷いて寝る。— I spread my bedding on the tatami and sleep in it.

13 | 0.90

3726 がっかり(する) gakkari(suru) *v.* be disappointed
- サッカーの試合に負けてがっかりした。— I was disappointed to lose the soccer game.

13 | 0.84

3727 しも shimo *p.* EMPHASIS (Classical)
- 誰しも一つや二つは秘密がある。— Anyone has a secret or two.

13 | 0.96

3728 福祉 fukushi *n.* welfare
- 長引く不況のため福祉の予算が削減された。— The budget for welfare was slashed because of the prolonged recession.

13 | 0.76

3729 上下 jouge *n.* up and down
- 船が激しく上下に揺れている。— The ship is being tossed about violently.

13 | 0.94

3730 汚れ yogore *n.* dirt
- 何度洗っても汚れが取れない。— I can't get rid of the dirt no matter how many times I wash it.

13 | 0.93

3731 書き込む kakikomu *v.* write in, jot down
- カレンダーに予定を書き込んでおく。— I'll jot down the schedule on the calendar.

13 | 0.93

3732 栽培(する) saibai(suru) *n.* cultivation *v.* cultivate
- この地方ではぶどうや桃などの果物の栽培が盛んだ。— Cultivation of fruits such as grapes and peaches is thriving in this region.

13 | 0.88

3733 視野 shiya *n.* perspective, view
- 留学の経験が彼の視野を広げた。— Experience of studying abroad broadened his perspective.

13 | 0.97

3734 隅 sumi *n.* corner
- 観葉植物を部屋の隅に置いた。— I placed a potted plant in the corner of the room.

13 | 0.84

3735 保障(する) hoshou(suru) *n., v.* guarantee
- 憲法で基本的人権が保障されている。— Fundamental human rights are guaranteed by the consititution.

13 | 0.85

3736 三十代 sanjuu dai *n.* thirties
- 彼は三十代半ばだろう。— He is probably in his mid-thirties.
13 | 0.92

3737 バック(する) bakku(suru) *n.* back, background *v.* reverse, back
- 富士山をバックに母の写真を撮った。— I took a picture of my mother with Mt. Fuji in the background.
13 | 0.85

3738 一斉 issei *n.* all at once
- 観客は一斉に拍手した。— The audience applauded all at once.
13 | 0.94

3739 お盆 (o)-bon *n.* Bon Festival, Obon
- 毎年八月のお盆の期間中は駅がたくさんの人で混雑する。— During Obon in August every year the train stations are always crowded with many people.
13 | 0.91

3740 審査(する) shinsa(suru) *n.* examination *v.* examine
- 空港で入国審査を受ける。— People go through a visa inspection at the airport.
13 | 0.85

3741 ゆとり yutori *n.* have something to spare
- 今は旅行に行くだけの経済的ゆとりがない。— I have no spare money to travel at the moment.
13 | 0.94

3742 打ち込む uchikomu *v.* devote oneself
- ずっと仕事に打ち込んできた。— I've always devoted myself to work.
13 | 0.93

3743 福岡 fukuoka *n.* Fukuoka (place name)
- 来週出張で福岡に行く。— I'm going on a business trip to Fukuoka next week.
13 | 0.95

3744 通勤(する) tsuukin(suru) *n., v.* commute
- 片道一時間以上かけて通勤している。— I spend over one hour commuting each way.
13 | 0.90

3745 準用(する) jun'you(suru) *n., v.* apply mutatis mutandis, with necessary modification
- 規則を準用してよろしい。— You can apply the rule with modifications.
13 | 0.11 | OF

3746 右側 migigawa *n.* right side
- この国では、車は右側を走る。— Vehicles keep to the right in this country.
13 | 0.96

3747 推測(する) suisoku(suru) *n.* assumption, guess *v.* guess, presume
- 勝手な推測でものを言ってはいけない。— You shouldn't say things based on unwarranted assumptions.
13 | 0.93

3748 ライン rain *n.* line
- ラインの後ろでお待ちください。— Please wait behind the line.
13 | 0.79

3749 預かる azukaru *v.* keep, look after
- ホテルに荷物を預かってもらった。— We asked the hotel to look after our luggage.
13 | 0.99

3750 美術館 bijutsu-kan *n.* art gallery, museum of art
- 先週末、上野の美術館に行った。— I went to an art gallery in Ueno last weekend.
13 | 0.87

3751 二個 ni-ko *n.* two (pieces, things)
- ケーキを二個食べた。— I had two pieces of cake.
13 | 0.97

3752 冷やす hiyasu *v.* keep cool, cool
- 冷蔵庫でジュースを冷やしておく。— I keep juice cool in the fridge.
13 | 0.92

3753 仏教 bukkyou *n.* Buddhism
- 日本に仏教が伝来したのは六世紀のことだ。— It was in the sixth century that Buddhism was introduced into Japan.
13 | 0.83

3754 接触(する) sesshoku(suru) *n.* touch, contact *v.* touch
- 電源が入らないのは接触が悪いせいかもしれない。— Maybe the power's not getting through because of a bad contact.
13 | 0.94

3755 意欲 iyoku *n.* will, motivation
- この生徒は学ぶ意欲がないようだ。— This pupil seems to lack motivation to study.
13 | 0.92

3756 本音 honne *n.* true feeling; truth
- 彼女は本音で語り合える友人だ。— She is the kind of friend with whom I can talk about my true feelings.
13 | 0.93

3757 二種類 ni shurui *n.* two kinds
- 大きく二種類に分類した。— We divided them roughly into two groups.
13 | 0.97

3758 主役 shuyaku *n.* main character
- その映画で主役を演じた俳優の名前が思い出せない。— I cannot remember the name of the actor who played the main character in the movie.
13 | 0.89

3759 次男 jinan *n.* second son
- 彼は次男だ。— He is the second son of the family.
13 | 0.87

3760 多々 tata *adv.* many
- 反省すべき点が多々ある。— There are many points to reconsider.
13 | 0.86

3761 定期的 teiki-teki *na-adj.* regular
- 定期的に健康診断を受けている。— I regularly have medical examinations
13 | 0.98

3762 しめる shimeru *aux.* (Classical)
- その失敗が彼を死に至らしめた。— The failure led him to his death.
13 | 0.73

3763 通り過ぎる toorisugiru *v.* pass, go past
- 目の前をものすごいスピードで自転車が通り過ぎていった。— A bicycle went past right in front of me at a terrific speed.
13 | 0.84

3764 スーツ suutsu *n.* suit
- あの黒いスーツを着ている人が山田さんです。— The man in a black suit is Mr. Yamada.
13 | 0.85

3765 形式 keishiki *n.* form
- 形式にとらわれすぎないほうがいい。— Excessive adherence to form is not good.
13 | 0.89

3766 ピンク pinku *n.* pink
- 桜が咲いて、河川敷が一面ピンクに染まった。— As the cherry trees were in full bloom, the whole river bank was coloured pink.
13 | 0.70

3767 七年 shichi nen *n.* seven years
- 七年働いた会社を辞めた。— I left the company where I worked for seven years.
13 | 0.73

3768 生きがい ikigai *n.* pupose in life, something to live for
- 何か生きがいを見つけたい。— I want to find a purpose in life.
13 | 0.91

3769 にぎやか nigiyaka *na-adj.* busy, bustling
- ここは町で一番にぎやかな通りだ。— This is the busiest street in the town.
13 | 0.91

3770 結成（する）kessei(suru) *n.* formation *v.* form, organize
- 去年、この会社に労働組合が結成された。— Last year, a trade union was formed in this company.
13 | 0.93

3771 研究者 kenkyuu-sha *n.* researcher
- A大学の研究者らが最新の研究成果を発表した。— Researchers from University A published their latest findings.
13 | 0.71

3772 名付ける nazukeru *v.* name
- 息子は犬を「ハチ」と名付けて、かわいがっている。— My son named the dog Hachi and takes good care of him.
13 | 0.88

3773 信号 shingou *n.* traffic light, signal
- こちらの人々は車が来なければ信号を無視して道路を渡る。— People here cross the street ignoring the traffic lights if there are no cars coming.
13 | 0.95

3774 就職活動（する）shuushoku katsudou(suru) *n.* job-hunting *v.* look for a job
- 彼は就職活動中だ。— He's been job-hunting.
13 | 0.65

3775 捜査（する）sousa(suru) *n.* criminal investigation *v.* investigate
- 警察は慎重に捜査を進めている。— The police are carrying out a careful investigation.
13 | 0.80

3776 現に genni *adv.* as a matter of fact, actually
- 現に汚染は隣接県まで拡大している。— As a matter of fact, the pollution has spread to neighboring prefectures.
13 | 0.69

3777 黒人 koku-jin *n.* black person
- この黒人女性歌手の名前を知っていますか。— Do you know the name of this black female singer?
13 | 0.85

3778 事柄 kotogara *n.* matter, issue
- このページには、特に重要な事柄についてまとめてあります。— This page outlines particularly important issues.
13 | 0.84

3779 早く hayaku *n.* early, soon
- 父は毎日朝早くから夜遅くまで働いている。— My father works from early in the morning to late at night every day.
13 | 0.96

3780 速度 sokudo *n.* speed
- その車はカーブの手前で速度を落とした。 — The car reduced its speed before the bend.

13 | 0.94

3781 奥様 oku-sama *n.* wife (honorific)
- 奥様はお元気でいらっしゃいますか。 — How is your wife?

13 | 0.87

3782 まれ mare *na-adj.* rare
- これは極めてまれなケースだ。 — This is a very rare case.

13 | 0.91

3783 じゃが芋 jagaimo *n.* potato
- じゃが芋の皮をむいてください。 — Please peel the potatoes.

13 | 0.92

3784 数多く kazuooku *adv.* many, a number of
- この町には歴史的な建造物が数多く残っている。 — There are many historical buildings left in this town.

13 | 0.80

3785 ひそか hisoka *na-adj.* secret, confidential *adv.* secretly
- そうなることをひそかに期待している。 — I'm secretly looking forward to it.

13 | 0.82

3786 照らす terasu *v.* light
- 海が太陽の光に照らされて輝いている。 — The sea glitters, lit up by the sun.

13 | 0.85

3787 ミュージカル myuujikaru *n.* musical
- ニューヨークでミュージカルを見た。 — I saw a musical in New York.

13 | 0.64

3788 怪しい ayashii *i-adj.* eerie; doubtful
- 店内は怪しい雰囲気があった。 — Inside the store there was an eerie atmosphere.

13 | 0.80

3789 友 tomo *n.* friend
- 私は良き友を得たと思う。 — I believe that I've made a good friend.

13 | 0.94

3790 傾ける katamukeru *v.* tilt, incline
- 傘を前に傾けて歩いた。 — I walked with my umbrella tilted forward.

13 | 0.89

3791 鉛筆 enpitsu *n.* pencil
- 鉛筆で書いてください。 — Please write in pencil.

13 | 0.88

3792 判決（する）hanketsu(suru) *n.* decision *v.* decide
- 最高裁は無罪判決を言い渡した。 — The supreme court announced a decision of "not guilty".

13 | 0.88

3793 マラソン marason *n.* marathon
- 今度マラソンに挑戦する。 — I'll compete in a marathon soon.

13 | 0.60

3794 広さ hiro-sa *n.* area; width; extent
- 家族五人が住むだけの広さが必要だ。 — We need enough room for a family of five to live in.

13 | 0.96

3795 リスト risuto *n.* list
- 必要な材料のリストを作った。 — I made a list of the necessary ingredients.

13 | 0.94

3796 振り向く furimuku *v.* look around, turn around
- 名前を呼ばれて、後ろを振り向いた。 — I looked round as someone was calling my name.

13 | 0.73

3797 二歳 ni-sai *n.* two years old
- この子は二歳になったばかりだ。 — She has just turned two.

13 | 0.80

3798 関与（する）kan'yo(suru) *n.* participation *v.* participate
- A氏がこの事件に関与している疑いが強まった。 — Suspicion about Mr A's involvement in this case increased.

13 | 0.84

3799 遂げる togeru *v.* achieve
- この会社は数年で急速な成長を遂げた。 — The company has achieved rapid growth in the past few years.

13 | 0.92

3800 二十人 nijuu-nin *n.* twenty people
- 夕べの飲み会には二十人ぐらい集まった。 — We had about twenty people at the party last night.

13 | 0.43

3801 タオル taoru *n.* towel
- 手を洗ってタオルで拭いた。 — I washed my hands and dried them with a towel.

13 | 0.80

3802 一泊 ip-paku *n.* one night stay
- 週末を利用して、一泊旅行に出かける。 — We'll make an overnight trip over the weekend.

13 | 0.83

19 Time

(frequency per million words)

(時間) (Time)
時 toki 2513.857 time
日 hi 435.812 day, sun
時間 jikan 423.024 time
年 toshi 148.875 year (also age)
午後 gogo 118.217 afternoon
午前 gozen 72.809 morning
年間 nenkan 20.515 year, annual
世紀 seiki 5.590 century
秒 byou 1.074 second
週間 shuukan 0.403 week

(時間帯) (Period of time)
夜 yoru 220.255 night, evening
朝 asa 187.099 morning
昼 hiru 46.287 noon; daytime
夕方 yuugata 41.221 evening
夜中 yonaka 31.427 middle of the night
深夜 shin'ya 14.318 middle of the night
早朝 souchou 10.333 early morning
明け方 akegata 3.432 dawn
真昼 mahiru 0.823 midday

(今週・先週・来週) (Week)
先週 senshuu 10.029 last week
今週 konshuu 9.963 this week
来週 raishuu 8.573 next week

(今月・先月・来月) (Month)
今月 kongetsu 14.267 this month
来月 raigetsu 6.136 next month
先月 sengetsu 5.769 last month

(今年・去年・来年) (Year)
今年 kotoshi 135.708 this year
去年 kyonen 58.482 last year
来年 rainen 29.188 next year
一昨年 issaku nen 4.557 year before last
再来年 sarai-nen 0.795 year after next

(毎〜) (Every . . .)
毎日 mainichi 211.838 every day
毎年 maitoshi 63.465 every year, annually
毎週 maishuu 17.765 every week
毎朝 maiasa 12.069 every morning
毎晩 maiban 3.983 every night

(月) (Months)
四月 shi-gatsu 99.944 April
三月 san-gatsu 91.185 March
九月 ku-gatsu 78.931 September
十月 juu-gatsu 77.383 October
十二月 juuni-gatsu 75.337 December
一月 ichi-gatsu 74.787 January
八月 hachi-gatsu 74.100 August
七月 shichi-gatsu 73.955 July
五月 go-gatsu 73.788 May
六月 roku-gatsu 73.301 June
十一月 juuichi-gatsu 73.110 November
二月 ni-gatsu 68.017 February

(今朝・今晩) (Tonight, etc.)
今夜 kon'ya 19.129 tonight
今朝 kesa 18.571 this morning
今晩 konban 3.796 this evening, tonight

(曜日) (Days of the week)
日曜日 nichiyou bi 33.511 Sunday
土曜日 doyou bi 23.085 Saturday
金曜日 kinyou bi 10.836 Friday
月曜日 getsuyou bi 9.933 Monday
火曜日 kayou bi 4.496 Tuesday
水曜日 suiyou bi 2.685 Wednesday
木曜日 mokuyou bi 2.600 Thursday
曜日 you bi 2.210 day

(季節) (Seasons)
夏 natsu 124.770 summer
冬 fuyu 81.166 winter
春 haru 67.796 spring
秋 aki 64.919 autumn, fall

3803 ごちそう(する) gochisou(suru) n. feast
v. give a dinner, treat
- ゆうべは友達の家で晩ご飯をごちそうになった。— I was invited to dinner at my friend's place.
13 | 0.86

3804 的確 tekikaku, tekkaku na-adj. precise, exact
- 彼女のアドバイスは的確だった。— Her advice was right.
13 | 0.62

3805 運転手 unten-shu n. driver
- タクシーの運転手においしいお店を教えてもらった。— We asked the taxi driver to give us the name of a good restaurant.
13 | 0.82

3806 各種 kakushu n. various, all sorts of
- この施設は必要な各種設備が整っている。— This facility has all sorts of equipment.
13 | 0.59

3807 録音(する) rokuon(suru) n., v. record
- 会議を録音しておいた。— We have the meeting tape recorded
13 | 0.93

3808 沈黙(する) chinmoku(suru) n. silence
v. be silent
- しばらく沈黙が続いた。— The silence continued for a while.
13 | 0.68

3809 再度 saido adv. twice, again
- 再度見直すと、また間違いが見つかった。— As we read it for the second time, some other mistakes were found.
12 | 0.92

3810 以後 igo adv. after this, since then
- それ以後彼は姿を見せていない。— Since then, he hasn't turned up.
12 | 0.90

3811 熊 kuma n. bear
- 村に熊が出て、人を襲った。— A bear appeared in a village and attacked someone.
12 | 0.99

3812 八王子 hachiouji n. Hachioji (place name)
- 八王子市は東京の南西部にある。— Hachioji is located in south-west Tokyo.
12 | 0.50

3813 贈る okuru v. give (as a present), send
- 定年退職した母にプレゼントを贈った。— I sent a gift to my mother who retired.
12 | 0.79

3814 林 hayashi n. grove, forest, wood
- この山には杉の林が広がっている。— A cedar forest covers this mountain.
12 | 0.87

3815 懸念(する) kenen(suru) n. fear v. fear
- 円高の輸出産業に与える影響が懸念されている。— The impact of the strong yen on the export market is a matter of concern.
12 | 0.81

3816 燃やす moyasu v. burn
- 薪を燃やして暖をとった。— We burned firewood and kept ourselves warm.
12 | 0.95

3817 枠 waku n. frame
- この家の窓枠は白く塗ってある。— The window frames of this house are painted white.
12 | 0.97

3818 児童 jidou n. pupil
- この小学校の児童は全部で三十人だ。— There are a total of thirty pupils in this elementary school.
12 | 0.69

3819 真っ白 masshiro na-adj. pure white
- 窓の外は一面真っ白な雪景色だった。— Outside the window everything was completely covered in pure white snow.
12 | 0.88

3820 さっと satto adv. quickly
- さっとシャワーを浴びて、家を出た。— I had a quick shower and went out.
12 | 0.88

3821 定年(する) teinen(suru) n. retirement v. retire
- 今月父は定年を迎えた。— My father reached retirement age this month.
12 | 0.93

3822 育児(する) ikuji(suru) n. childcare v. take care of a child
- 育児休暇を一年取った。— I took one year childcare leave.
12 | 0.96

3823 蹴る keru v. kick
- 思い切りボールを蹴った。— He kicked the ball hard.
12 | 0.92

3824 蜂蜜 hachimitsu n. honey
- パンに蜂蜜を塗った。— I spread honey on bread.
12 | 0.80

3825 度々 tabitabi adv. often
- 度々お電話してすみません。— I am sorry to call you so often.
12 | 0.99

3826 完了(する) kanryou(suru) n. complete
v. complete
- 手続きの完了までもう少しかかりそうだ。— It looks like it will take a little while until the process is completed.
12 | 0.92

3827 二十三 nijuu san *num.* twenty-three
- 東京には二十三の区がある。— There are twenty-three wards in Tokyo.
12 | 0.75

3828 通訳 tsuuyaku *n.* interpreter
- 通訳なしでは会議が行えない。— We cannot have meetings without an interpreter.
12 | 0.89

3829 飼い主 kainushi *n.* pet owner
- ペットの面倒を見ることは、飼い主の義務だ。— It is the owners' duty to take care of their pets.
12 | 0.83

3830 傍ら katawara *n.* side, besides
- 道の傍らにうずくまっている子どもがいた。— There was a child crouching by the roadside.
12 | 0.75

3831 宣伝(する) senden(suru) *n.* advertisement *v.* advertise
- 最近この製品が派手に宣伝されている。— This product has been advertised heavily recently.
12 | 0.96

3832 室内 shitsunai *n.* indoor
- 隣の家では、室内で犬を飼っている。— Our neighbor keeps a dog indoors.
12 | 0.89

3833 会員 kaiin *n.* member
- 会員になると、割引などのサービスが受けられる。— You are privileged to receive offers including discounts when you become a member.
12 | 0.89

3834 思考(する) shikou(suru) *n.* thought *v.* think
- 彼は柔軟な思考の持ち主だ。— He has flexible ideas.
12 | 0.82

3835 衣装 ishou *n.* costume
- パレードの参加者は色とりどりの衣装を身にまとっていた。— Participants in the parade dressed in colorful costumes.
12 | 0.89

3836 足す tasu *v.* add
- 味が薄いから、もう少ししょう油を足したほうがいい。— It's a bit tasteless, so you should add a little more soy sauce.
12 | 0.96

3837 シャツ shatsu *n.* shirt
- みんな白い長袖のシャツを着ている。— Everybody is wearing white long-sleeved shirts.
12 | 0.71

3838 イラク iraku *n.* Iraq
- イラクは石油産出国だ。— Iraq is an oil producer.
12 | 0.90

3839 取り扱う toriatsukau *v.* handle, treat
- 顧客の個人情報は適切に取り扱わなければならない。— Customers' personal information must be handled with care.
12 | 0.86

3840 わざと wazato *adv.* intentionally
- 彼女はわざとジュースをこぼした。— She spilled the juice on purpose.
12 | 0.86

3841 前年度 zen nendo *n.* preceding year
- 前年度に比べて、売り上げが倍増した。— The sales have doubled since the preceding year.
12 | 0.26 | OF

3842 新郎 shinrou *n.* groom, bridegroom
- 結婚式は新郎の挨拶から始まった。— The wedding reception started with the groom's speech.
12 | 0.46

3843 幹部 kanbu *n.* executive
- このことは幹部社員しか知らなかった。— Only the executive staff knew this.
12 | 0.95

3844 シェア(する) shea(suru) *n., v.* share
- わが社の製品は市場の80%のシェアを占めている。— Our product accounts for a 80 percent share of the market.
12 | 0.58

3845 ガソリン gasorin *n.* gasoline, petrol
- ガソリンを入れてから、ドライブに出発しよう。— Let's fill up with gasoline and then go for a drive.
12 | 0.92

3846 記念(する) kinen(suru) *n.* commemoration *v.* commemorate
- 今日の記念に集合写真を撮った。— We took a group photograph to commemorate today.
12 | 0.84

3847 強烈 kyouretsu *na-adj.* strong, intense
- その言葉は私に強烈な印象を残した。— The words left me with a strong impression.
12 | 0.88

3848 俳句 haiku *n.* haiku (Japanese poem of seventeen syllables)
- 祖父の趣味は俳句を詠むことだ。— My grandfather's hobby is composing haiku.
12 | 0.84

3849 特色 tokushoku *n.* characteristic, feature
- この点がこの大学の最大の特色である。 — This is the chief characteristic of the university.
12 | 0.83

3850 引退（する） intai(suru) *n.* retirement *v.* retire
- 彼のような人気も実力もあった選手が引退して、少し寂しい。 — It's a shame that an athlete as popular and talented as him is retiring.
12 | 0.92

3851 飲み物 nomimono *n.* drink
- 何か冷たい飲み物を買ってきて。 — Go and buy me a cold drink.
12 | 0.85

3852 いいえ iie *interj.* no
- 「コーヒーはいかがですか」「いいえ、けっこうです」 — "Would you like some coffee?" "No, thank you."
12 | 0.68

3853 部 bu *n.* division, department, section; club
- 午後の部は1時から始まります。 — The afternoon session will begin at 1pm.
12 | 0.59

3854 オランダ oranda *n.* the Netherlands, Holland
- 江戸時代に日本はオランダと交易を行っていた。 — Japan carried on trade with the Netherlands in the Edo period.
12 | 0.98

3855 華やか hanayaka *na-adj.* gorgeous
- 華やかな衣装を着た歌手がステージに登場した。 — A singer in a gorgeous costume appeared on the stage.
12 | 0.84

3856 高価 kouka *na-adj.* expensive
- こんな高価なものをいただくわけにはいきません。 — I cannot accept such an expensive gift.
12 | 0.95

3857 なじむ najimu *v.* become accustomed
- 新しい職場に早くなじむよう、努力する。 — I will try my best to adapt to the new workplace as soon as possible.
12 | 0.95

3858 誇る hokoru *v.* be proud, boast
- 日本車は世界に誇る製品の一つだ。 — Japanese automobiles are one of our world-class products.
12 | 0.82

3859 左側 hidarigawa *n.* left, left side
- 二分ほど歩くと、左側に郵便局がある。 — If you walk about two minutes, you will see the post office on your left.
12 | 0.96

3860 浮気 uwaki *n.* affair
- 夫の浮気に気づいた。 — I realized that my husband is having an affair.
12 | 0.68

3861 デート（する） deeto(suru) *n., v.* date
- 彼らは初めてデートした。 — They went on a first date.
12 | 0.81

3862 抑制（する） yokusei(suru) *n.* control, restraint *v.* control, restrain
- 彼は怒りを抑制した。 — He controlled his anger.
12 | 0.77

3863 好奇心 kouki-shin *n.* curiosity
- この子は好奇心が旺盛だ。 — She is full of curiosity.
12 | 0.91

3864 公務員 koumu-in *n.* civil servant, government employee
- 公務員は安定した仕事だ。 — Being a civil servant is a steady job.
12 | 0.85

3865 列 retsu *n.* line
- 列に並んでください。 — Please stand in line.
12 | 0.95

3866 ソファー sofaa *n.* sofa
- 私はソファーに座った。 — I sat on a sofa.
12 | 0.84

3867 初日 shonichi *n.* first day
- 連休の初日はどこも道が込んでいる。 — Traffic is busy everywhere on the first day of a long holiday.
12 | 0.88

3868 プロセス purosesu *n.* process
- 基本的なプロセスは次の通りだ。 — The basic process is as follows.
12 | 0.86

3869 郊外 kougai *n.* suburb
- 私は東京の郊外に住んでいる。 — I live in a suburb of Tokyo.
12 | 0.89

3870 六十 rokujuu *num.* sixty
- 節分に豆を六十食べた。 — I ate sixty beans at Setsubun (festival marking end of winter and coming of spring).
12 | 0.98

3871 痛む itamu *v.* ache, hurt, pain
- 歯が痛む。 — My tooth aches.
12 | 0.86

3872 自衛隊 jiei-tai *n.* Self-Defense Forces
- 政府は自衛隊を送り込んだ。 — The government sent the Self-Defense Forces.
12 | 0.73

3873 尽きる tsukiru *v.* run out
- 食料が尽きかけている。— We are running out of food.

12 | 0.97

3874 国連 kokuren *n.* United Nations
- その提案は国連に提出された。— The proposal was submitted to the United Nations.

12 | 0.70

3875 手軽 tegaru *na-adj.* light; simple; reasonable
- このコンピューターは手軽な値段で気に入った。— This computer appealed to me because of its reasonable price.

12 | 0.86

3876 町並み machinami *n.* street, row of town houses
- 町並みが美しい。— The streets are lined with neat rows of stores and houses.

12 | 0.91

3877 推定（する）suitei(suru) *n.* presumption, estimation *v.* presume, estimate
- この村の人口はおよそ五万人と推定されている。— The population of this village is estimated to be approximately 50,000.

12 | 0.82

3878 ちまう chimau *aux.* do something completely
- やる気がないなら、やめちまえ！— If you don't want to do it, just quit!

12 | 0.72

3879 文部省 monbu-shou *n.* Ministry of Education, Culture, Sports
- 文部省は日本の大学のレベルをもっと宣伝するべきだ。— The Ministry of Education needs to promote the standards of Japanese universities more.

12 | 0.31

3880 結びつける musubitsukeru *v.* connect, tie, bind
- 二つの証拠を結び付けて考えることができない。— I cannot connect these two pieces of evidence.

12 | 0.90

3881 例外 reigai *n.* exception
- 例外は認められない。— No exception should be made.

12 | 0.90

3882 プロ野球 puro yakyuu *n.* professional baseball
- 最近のプロ野球はおもしろい。— Professional baseball has been interesting recently.

12 | 0.78

3883 二枚 ni-mai *n.* two (sheets)
- 映画のチケットが二枚ある。— There are two movie tickets.

12 | 0.89

3884 まさしく masashiku *adv.* surely, exactly
- それはまさしく私が言おうとしていたことです。— That's exactly what I've been trying to say.

12 | 0.93

3885 変わり kawari *n.* change
- 「お変わりありませんね」— "You haven't changed much."

12 | 0.95

3886 用事 youji *n.* business
- 彼は用事で呼び出された。— He was called away on business.

12 | 0.85

3887 効率 kouritsu *n.* efficiency
- 仕事の効率を上げる必要がある。— We need to increase work efficiency.

12 | 0.99

3888 クリア（する）kuria(suru) *n.* clearing, clearance *na-adj., v.* clear
- 難しい問題をクリアした。— I solved a difficult problem.

12 | 0.89

3889 だけど da kedo *conj.* but, however
- 行きたくなかった。だけど行ってよかった。— I didn't want to go. However, I'm glad I did.

12 | 0.48

3890 財布 saifu *n.* wallet
- 財布を家に忘れた。— I left my wallet at home.

12 | 0.88

3891 徹底的 tettei-teki *na-adj.* thorough, complete
- 部屋を徹底的に掃除した。— I gave a room a thorough cleaning.

12 | 0.95

3892 直面（する）chokumen(suru) *n.* confrontation *v.* confront, face
- 彼は危険に直面している。— He is facing danger.

12 | 0.88

3893 己 onore *n.* oneself (first person pronoun)
- 己に負けるな。— Don't give in to your weakness.

12 | 0.70

3894 目安 meyasu *n.* standard, criterion
- 何を目安に大学を選びますか。— By what criteria will you choose the university?

12 | 0.95

3895 目覚める mezameru *v.* wake up
- 真夜中に目が覚めた。— I woke up in the middle of the night.

12 | 0.90

3896 等しい hitoshii *i-adj.* equal
- この二本の線は長さが等しい。— These two lines are equal in length.
12 | 0.80

3897 休憩（する） kyuukei(suru) *n.* rest, break *v.* take a rest
- ちょっと休憩しましょう。— Let's take a rest.
12 | 0.91

3898 一日中 ichinichi-juu *n.* all day
- 一日中雨が降り続いた。— It was raining all day.
12 | 0.02 | SP

3899 有無 umu *n.* existence, presence
- 欠席の有無を確かめた。— I checked whether everyone was there or not.
12 | 0.83

3900 HP hoomupeeji *n.* home page
- 毎日ホームページを更新している。— I'm updating my home page every day.
12 | 0.43 | WB

3901 不要 fuyou *na-adj.* unnecessary
- 予約は不要だ。— Reservations are not required.
12 | 0.72

3902 猿 saru *n.* monkey
- 猿も木から落ちる。— Even monkeys fall from trees.
12 | 0.95

3903 従事（する） juuji(suru) *n.* engagement in *v.* be engaged in
- 医療に従事している。— I'm engaged in medical services.
12 | 0.68

3904 蓄積（する） chikuseki(suru) *n.* storage, accumulation *v.* store, accumulate
- 知識の蓄積は大切だ。— Accumulation of knowledge is important.
12 | 0.89

3905 よみがえる yomigaeru *v.* revive, come back
- この写真で記憶がよみがえってきた。— The memories came back to me as I looked at this photo.
12 | 0.84

3906 年賀状 nenga-jou *n.* New Year's card
- 忙しくて、まだ年賀状を書いていない。— I've been busy, so I haven't written New Year's cards yet.
12 | 0.76

3907 バブル baburu *n.* bubble
- バブルの崩壊が起こった。— The collapse of the bubble economy occurred.
12 | 0.89

3908 毎朝 maiasa *adv., n.* every morning
- 毎朝、ジョギングをしている。— I go jogging every morning.
12 | 0.87

3909 地味 jimi *na-adj.* simple
- 彼は地味な暮らしをしていた。— He lived a very simple life.
12 | 0.91

3910 文学 bungaku *n.* literature
- 私は英文学について研究している。— I study English literature.
12 | 0.83

3911 Tシャツ tii shatsu *n.* T-shirt
- 私はいつもTシャツで寝ている。— I always sleep in a T-shirt.
12 | 0.78

3912 放る houru *v.* throw; leave something undone
- ボールを壁に放り投げた。— I threw a ball against the wall.
12 | 0.93

3913 攻める semeru *v.* attack
- 私達は相手チームを攻めた。— We attacked the opposing team.
12 | 0.91

3914 位置付ける ichi zukeru *v.* rank; evaluate
- この研究をどう位置付けますか。— How would you evaluate this research?
12 | 0.79

3915 四回 yon kai *n.* four times
- 私は富士山に四回登った。— I climbed Mt. Fuji four times.
12 | 0.94

3916 マーク maaku *n.* mark
- 会社のマークを箱に印刷した。— The company's trademark is printed on the box.
12 | 0.83

3917 アルコール arukooru *n.* alcohol
- 彼女はアルコールが全然飲めない。— She can't drink alcohol at all.
12 | 0.96

3918 優しさ yasashi-sa *n.* kindness
- 彼の優しさを忘れないだろう。— I won't forget his kindness.
12 | 0.95

3919 漠然 bakuzen *adv.* vague, obscure
- 漠然とした答えしかわからない。— I can only give a vague answer.
12 | 0.88

3920 偉大 idai *na-adj.* great, grand
- 彼は偉大な音楽家だ。— He is a great musician.
12 | 0.84

3921 脂肪 shibou *n.* fat
- 脂肪の取りすぎに注意しなさい。— Be careful not to take too much fat.
12 | 0.94

3922 言い出す ii dasu *v.* propose, suggest
- 彼女はゲームをしようと言い出した。— She proposed playing a game.
12 | 0.81

3923 青 ao *n.* blue
- 今日私は青の服を着ています。— I'm wearing blue today.
12 | 0.91

3924 キーワード kii waado *n.* keyword
- キーワードを使って質問に答えなさい。— Answer the questions using the keywords.
12 | 0.92

3925 ベランダ beranda *n.* porch, balcony, veranda
- ベランダのいすに座って、本を読んだ。— I sat on a chair on the balcony and read a book.
12 | 0.83

3926 炎 honoo *n.* flame
- ろうそくの炎が消えた。— The candle flame went out.
12 | 0.78

3927 交付(する) koufu(suru) *n.* issue *v.* issue, grant
- パスポートが交付された。— My passport has been issued.
12 | 0.59

3928 証言(する) shougen(suru) *n.* evidence *v.* give testimony
- 私はその事故について証言した。— I gave testimony about the accident.
12 | 0.89

3929 敏感 binkan *na-adj.* sensitive
- 私は暑さ寒さに敏感だ。— I'm sensitive to heat and cold.
12 | 0.96

3930 鮮やか azayaka *na-adj.* vivid, lively; skillful
- 今日は鮮やかな赤い服を着ていた。— She was wearing bright red clothes today.
12 | 0.86

3931 解明(する) kaimei(suru) *n.* clarification *v.* solve
- 私達は謎を解明しなければならない。— We must solve a mystery.
12 | 0.86

3932 方式 houshiki *n.* method
- 新しい方式が病院に導入された。— New methods were introduced into the hospital.
12 | 0.86

3933 瓶 bin *n.* bottle
- 彼はビールの瓶の栓を抜いた。— He opened the cap of the beer bottle.
12 | 0.93

3934 そっくり sokkuri *na-adj.* resembling, just like *adv.* altogether
- 彼女は母親にそっくりだ。— She looks just like her mother.
12 | 0.86

3935 縛る shibaru *v.* bind, tie
- 古新聞を縛った。— I tied up the old newspapers.
12 | 0.93

3936 実情 jitsujou *n.* case, actual situation
- 実情はそうではない。— That is not the case.
12 | 0.64

3937 円 en *n.* yen; circle
- 空港で円をドルに替えた。— I converted yen into dollars at the airport.
12 | 0.96

3938 化粧(する) keshou(suru) *n.* makeup *v.* put on makeup
- 寝る前に化粧を落としなさい。— Take off your makeup before going to bed.
12 | 0.86

3939 二十四 nijuu shi *num.* twenty-four
- 彼は二十四で大学院修士課程を修了した。— He finished his master's course when he was twenty-four.
12 | 0.80

3940 数々 kazukazu *n.* many, numerous
- 不平不満は数々ある。— There are many complaints.
12 | 0.88

3941 持参(する) jisan(suru) *n.* bringing, taking *v.* bring, take
- 筆記用具を持参してください。— Please bring your writing materials.
12 | 0.48

3942 引用(する) in'you(suru) *n.* quotation *v.* quote
- そのエッセイは引用文で始まっている。— The essay starts with a quotation.
12 | 0.80

3943 同期 douki *n.* same period, same class
- 私達は同期の出身です。— We are in the same class at school.
12 | 0.83

3944 健全 kenzen *na-adj.* healthy
- 彼は健全な生活を送っている。— He is leading a healthy life.
12 | 0.66

3945 西洋 seiyou *n.* the West
- 日本は西洋の多大な影響を受けた。— Japan was greatly influenced by the West.
12 | 0.89

3946 プレッシャー puresshaa *n.* pressure
- 正直に話すようにプレッシャーをかけた。— I put a lot of pressure on him to tell the truth.
12 | 0.84

3947 赤ん坊 akanbou *n.* baby
- 赤ん坊が生まれた。— A baby was born.
12 | 0.75

3948 打ち合わせ uchiawase *n.* meeting
- 十時から打ち合わせが入っています。— I have a meeting from ten o'clock.
12 | 0.95

3949 欲望 yokubou *n.* desire, passion
- 彼は欲望をコントロールすることができなかった。— His couldn't control his desire.
12 | 0.72

3950 軍 gun *n.* army
- 彼は軍に入隊した。— He joined the army.
12 | 0.85

3951 パス（する）pasu(suru) *n., v.* pass
- 彼にボールをパスした。— I passed the ball to him.
12 | 0.89

3952 頼り tayori *n.* support, dependence
- 彼は私の頼りだった。— I counted on him.
12 | 0.92

3953 扱い atsukai *n.* treatment
- 日本で親切な扱いを受けた。— I was treated kindly when I was in Japan.
12 | 0.97

3954 本質 honshitsu *n.* nature, essence
- 本質をついた質問だ。— That's an essential question.
12 | 0.85

3955 市役所 shi yakuhso *n.* city hall
- 今日市役所に行かなければならない。— I must go to city hall today.
12 | 0.42

3956 車両 sharyou *n.* car, carriage
- この新幹線は十六車両ある。— This bullet train is a sixteen-car train.
12 | 0.92

3957 株価 kabuka *n.* stock prices
- 株価が下がった。— The stock prices declined.
12 | 0.90

3958 昼食 chuushoku *n.* lunch
- もう昼食は食べましたか。— Have you already had lunch?
12 | 0.85

3959 注射 chuusha *n.* injection
- この注射はあまり痛くない。— This injection won't hurt much.
12 | 0.87

3960 臨む nozomu *v.* face
- そのホテルは海を臨んでいる。— The hotel faces the sea.
12 | 0.96

3961 職 shoku *n.* job, work
- 去年から新しい職に就いている。— I have had a new job since last year.
12 | 0.97

3962 見た目 mi ta me *n.* appearance, looks
- 人を見た目で判断するな。— Don't judge a person by how they look.
12 | 0.79

3963 アピール（する）apiiru(suru) *n.* appeal *v.* appeal
- もっと自分をアピールした方がいい。— You should make yourself more appealing.
12 | 0.87

3964 三分の一 san-bun no ichi *n., num.* one-third
- 国土の三分の一は海に囲まれている。— About one-third of the country is surrounded by sea.
12 | 0.93

3965 全国的 zenkoku-teki *na-adj.* nationwide
- そのニュースは全国的に放送された。— The news was broadcast nationwide.
12 | 0.78

3966 豚 buta *n.* pig
- 彼は豚を飼っている。— He breeds pigs.
12 | 0.92

3967 資本 shihon *n.* capital
- このプロジェクトはさらなる資本を産み出す。— This project will create more capital.
12 | 0.77

3968 思いやり omoiyari *n.* consideration
- みんなにもっと思いやりの気持ちを持ちなさい。— Have more consideration for everyone.
12 | 0.94

3969 見通し mitooshi *n.* prospect, outlook
- 将来の国の見通しは明るい。— The outlook for the country's future is bright.
12 | 0.76

3970 十二年 juu ni nen *n.* twelve years
- 日本の義務教育は十二年だ。— Compulsory education in Japan lasts for twelve years.
12 | 0.77

3971 きっちり kitchiri *adv.* tightly
- 彼女はドアをきっちり閉めた。— She closed the door tightly.
12 | 0.96

3972 砂漠 sabaku *n.* desert
- 見渡す限り砂漠が広がっている。— The desert stretches as far as we can see.
12 | 0.91

3973 エレベーター erebeetaa *n.* elevator
- 三階までエレベーターに乗った。— I took the elevator to the third floor.
12 | 0.92

3974 浅い asai *i-adj.* shallow
- プールの浅いところへ行った。— I went to the shallow end of the pool.
12 | 0.97

3975 カバー kabaa *n.* cover
- 車にカバーをかぶせた。— I put a cover over my car.
12 | 0.96

3976 交代(する) koutai(suru) *n.* change, shift *v.* take turns
- 私達は交代で運転した。— We took turns at driving.
12 | 0.97

3977 資源 shigen *n.* resource
- オーストラリアは天然資源に恵まれている。— Australia is rich in natural resources.
12 | 0.79

3978 現実的 genjitsu-teki *na-adj.* realistic
- 彼の夢がより現実的になった。— His dream became more realistic.
12 | 0.97

3979 苦笑 kushou *v.* wry smile
- 彼はそれを聞いて苦笑した。— When he heard that he gave a wry smile.
12 | 0.54

3980 餃子 gyouza *n.* Chinese dumpling
- 家で餃子を作った。— I made some Chinese dumplings at home.
12 | 0.74

3981 食堂 shokudou *n.* cafeteria, dining room
- 食堂はどこですか。— Where is the cafeteria?
12 | 0.89

3982 もっぱら moppara *adv.* entirely
- 彼らは結婚するというもっぱらのうわさだ。— Everyone is saying that they are going to get married.
12 | 0.92

3983 締結(する) teiketsu(suru) *n.* conclusion *v.* conclude
- 政府は友好条約を締結した。— The government concluded a treaty of friendship.
12 | 0.48

3984 裸 hadaka *n.* naked, nude
- 温泉は裸で入浴してください。— Please bathe naked in the hot spring.
12 | 0.86

3985 そうこう soukou *adv.* in the meantime
- そうこうするうちに、日が暮れてしまった。— In the meantime it became dark.
12 | 0.56

3986 イライラ(する) iraira(suru) *v.* be annoyed, be irritated, be impatient
- 隣の部屋の騒音はイライラする。— My next-door neighbor's noise is annoying.
12 | 0.83

3987 収集(する) shuushuu(suru) *n.* collection *v.* collect
- ゴミの収集は毎週火曜日です。— Garbage collection is every Tuesday.
12 | 0.79

3988 記者 kisha *n.* journalist, reporter
- 私は政治記者になりたい。— I want to be a political journalist.
12 | 0.88

3989 脱出(する) dasshutsu(suru) *n.* escape *v.* escape, break out
- 彼は刑務所から脱出した。— He broke out of prison.
12 | 0.90

3990 呼び出す yobidasu *v.* call, summon
- 友達を呼び出しカラオケへ行った。— I called my friend and we went to karaoke.
12 | 0.93

3991 主流 shuryuu *n.* mainstream
- 高校では制服が主流だ。— In high schools, school uniform is mainstream.
12 | 0.97

3992 さほど sahodo *adv.* (not) particularly
- お酒がさほど好きじゃありません。— I am not particularly fond of sake.
12 | 0.93

3993 事務 jimu *n.* office work
- 事務は機械化されつつある。— Office work is becoming mechanized.
12 | 0.68

3994 付け加える tsukekuwaeru *v.* add
- 何か付け加えることはありませんか。— Would you like to add anything?
12 | 0.88

3995 国々 kuniguni *n.* countries
- 私は様々な国々を旅行した。— I've traveled in various countries.
12 | 0.83

3996 地球上 chikyuu-jou *n.* on the earth
- 地球上には七つの大陸がある。— There are seven continents on the earth.
12 | 0.91

20 Transportation

(frequency per million words)

(交通手段) (Means of transportation)

車 kuruma 271.365 car (also wheel)
電車 densha 96.469 train
自転車 jitensha 82.341 bicycle
船 fune 78.934 ship, boat
バス basu 78.568 bus
飛行機 hikouki 72.986 airplane
自動車 jidousha 33.399 car
バイク baiku 31.302 motorcycle, motorbike
タクシー takushii 28.660 taxi
トラック torakku 21.776 truck
列車 ressha 21.445 train
新幹線 shin-kansen 20.774 bullet train
地下鉄 chika-tetsu 19.942 subway, underground
鉄道 tetsudou 17.210 railroad, railway
車両 sharyou 11.876 car
救急車 kyuukyuu-sha 11.281 ambulance
乗り物 norimono 9.688 vehicle (also (amusement park) ride)
フェリー ferii 9.574 ferry
国鉄 kokutetsu 8.704 national railway
汽車 kisha 8.686 train
急行 kyuukou 7.641 express train
ヘリコプター herikoputaa 6.705 helicopter
特急 tokkyuu 3.653 limited express
ロケット roketto 3.377 rocket
オートバイ ootobai 3.051 motorcycle
私鉄 shitetsu 2.077 private railway
モノレール monoreeru 1.950 monorail

(交通・駅、道路など) (Station, road, etc.)

駅 eki 139.266 station
空港 kuukou 27.467 airport
駅前 ekimae 26.478 in front of the station
交通 koutsuu 17.879 traffic; transportation
交通事故 koutsuu jiko 14.462 traffic accident
切符 kippu 10.927 ticket
高速道路 kousoku douro 10.719 freeway
歩道 hodou 9.921 sidewalk, pavement
線路 senro 9.166 track, railroad
飛行場 hikou-jou 6.956 airport
改札 kaisatsu 3.043 ticket gate
プラットホーム purattohoomu 1.405 platform
踏切 fumikiri 0.951 (railroad) crossing
停留所 teiryuu-jo 0.543 bus stop

(交通・動詞) (Traffic, transportation: verbs)

乗る noru 326.215 ride, get on, take
降りる oriru 85.817 go/come down, get off
乗せる noseru 82.381 take on, put on, pick up
運転(する) unten(suru) 38.154 driving, operation; drive
降ろす orosu 37.198 take down, unload (also withdraw)
乗り込む norikomu 13.698 board, get into
往復(する) oufuku(suru) 11.094 round trip
乗り換える norikaeru 10.762 change, transfer
渋滞(する) juutai(suru) 9.967 traffic jam, delay; be delayed
着陸(する) chakuriku(suru) 4.307 land
乗車(する) jousha(suru) 3.320 get on a train/bus
下車(する) gesha(suru) 2.901 get off
停車(する) teisha(suru) 2.342 stop
離陸(する) ririku(suru) 2.039 take off
渡航(する) tokou(suru) 1.649 make a voyage
搭乗(する) toujou(suru) 1.343 board, get into
降車(する) kousha(suru) 0.159 get off a train/bus

3997 大企業 dai-kigyou *n.* big business
• 兄は大企業に就職した。— My elder brother got a position in a big company.
12 | 0.74

3998 倒す taosu *v.* knock down
• 彼はボクシングでチャンピオンを倒した。— He knocked down the champion in a boxing match.
12 | 0.90

3999 写る utsuru *v.* photograph
• 彼女はきれいに写っていた。— She photographed very well.
12 | 0.86

4000 漏らす morasu *v.* betray
• 彼女は彼の秘密を漏らした。— She betrayed his secret.
12 | 0.84

4001 上達(する) joutatsu(suru) *n.* improvement *v.* improve, progress
• 彼女は中国語が上達している。— She is improving in her Chinese.
12 | 0.80

4002 故郷 furusato *n.* hometown
• 故郷を離れるのは寂しい。— I feel sad that I left my hometown.
12 | 0.88

4003 行使 koushi(suru) *n.* exercise
- 投票権を行使した。— They exercised the right to vote.

12 | 0.75

4004 表明（する）hyoumei(suru) *n.* expression, manifestation *v.* express, manifest
- 大統領は遺憾の意を表明した。— The President expressed his regret.

12 | 0.83

4005 体育 taiiku, taiku *n.* physical education, gymnastics
- 体育の授業は必修です。— The physical education lesson is a compulsory subject.

12 | 0.87

4006 読書 dokusho *n.* reading
- 読書の秋です。— Fall is the best season for reading.

12 | 0.92

4007 都 miyako *n.* capital
- パリはファッションの都だ。— Paris is the fashion capital.

12 | 0.74

4008 ずれる zureru *v.* be out of step, slip
- あなたの考えは今の時代からずれている。— Your ideas are out of step with the times.

12 | 0.95

4009 通用（する）tsuuyou(suru) *n.* currency *v.* accept, obtain
- この店ではクレジットカードしか通用しない。— This shop accepts only credit cards.

12 | 0.97

4010 支障 shishou *n.* obstacle
- 校長の考えはよい教育の支障となっている。— The principal's ideas are an obstacle to good education.

12 | 0.83

4011 カウンター kauntaa *n.* counter
- カウンターで支払ってください。— Please pay at the counter.

12 | 0.84

4012 大規模 dai-kibo *na-adj.* large-scale
- 大規模に店を経営している。— He is doing business on a large scale.

12 | 0.78

4013 大家さん ooya-san *n.* landlord, owner
- 大家さんは家賃を上げたいそうだ。— The landlord says he wants to raise the rent.

12 | 0.72

4014 昨夜 sakuya *n.* last night
- 昨夜はほとんど眠れなかった。— I slept very little last night.

12 | 0.57

4015 角 kado *n.* corner
- あの角を右に曲がってください。— Please turn right at the corner.

12 | 0.89

4016 ニコニコ（する）nikoniko(suru) *v.* smile *adv.* smiling
- その赤ちゃんはいつもニコニコしている。— The baby is always smiling.

12 | 0.88

4017 三日間 mik-kakan *n.* three days
- 三日間晴れが続いた。— The weather stayed fine for three days.

12 | 0.83

4018 撫でる naderu *v.* stroke
- 子猫は撫でられるのが好きだ。— The kitten loves being stroked.

12 | 0.82

4019 金利 kinri *n.* interest
- 銀行は金利を上げた。— The bank raised the rate of interest.

12 | 0.86

4020 わくわく（する）wakuwaku(suru) *v.* be bubbling; be excited
- 明日は遠足なのでわくわくする。— I am excited about tomorrow's day trip.

12 | 0.82

4021 仮定（する）katei(suru) *n.* assumption, supposition *v.* assume, suppose
- その話が本当だと仮定しよう。— Let's suppose the story is true.

12 | 0.85

4022 引きずる hikizuru *v.* drag, trail
- 彼女の長いドレスは床を引きずっていた。— Her long dress trailed on the floor.

12 | 0.91

4023 バラバラ barabara *na-adj.* separate
- 私は家族とバラバラに住んでいる。— I live separate from my family.

12 | 0.99

4024 依存（する）izon(suru) *n.* dependence, reliance *v.* depend, rely
- 彼女の助けに依存できない。— You can't rely on her help.

12 | 0.78

4025 様 sama *n.* Mr., Mrs., Miss., Ms.
- スミス様、フロントまでお越し下さい。— Mr. Smith, please come to the front desk.

12 | 0.86

4026 同居（する）doukyo(suru) *n.* coexistence, living together *v.* live together, live with
- 兄は両親と同居している。— My elder brother lives with our parents.

12 | 0.98

4027 スカート sukaato *n.* skirt
- 彼女は今日ロングスカートをはいている。— She is wearing a long skirt today.

12 | 0.64

4028 柄 gara *n.* pattern, character
- 彼女は花柄のドレスを着ている。— She is wearing a floral-patterned dress.

12 | 0.86

4029 回数 kaisuu *n.* frequency
- 今年は日本は地震の回数が多い。— The frequency of earthquakes in Japan is higher this year.

12 | 0.99

4030 ユーザー yuuzaa *n.* user
- ここにユーザーのフルネームを入れてください。— Please type the user's full name here.

12 | 0.88

4031 筆者 hissha *n.* writer, author
- 筆者が言おうとしていることがわからない。— I don't understand what the writer is trying to say.

12 | 0.67

4032 筆 fude *n.* brush
- カンバスに筆を走らせた。— I swept a brush across the canvas.

11 | 0.95

4033 制約(する) seiyaku(suru) *n.* restriction, constraint *v.* restrict, constrain
- ここでの生活は時間的な制約がない。— Life here has no time constraints.

11 | 0.82

4034 絵本 ehon *n.* picture book
- 子供に絵本を読んであげた。— I read my child a picture book.

11 | 0.61

4035 町中 machinaka *n.* downtown
- 町中に住んでいます。— I'm living downtown.

11 | 0.88

4036 著者 chosha *n.* author, writer
- この本の著者は誰ですか。— Who is the author of this book?

11 | 0.78

4037 芽 me *n.* bud, shoot
- 芽が出て花が咲いた。— Buds appeared and blossomed.

11 | 0.96

4038 担当者 tantou-sha *n.* person in charge
- 担当者が説明するでしょう。— The man in charge will explain.

11 | 1.00

4039 嵐 arashi *n.* storm
- 嵐の前の静けさだった。— It was the calm before the storm.

11 | 0.82

4040 厚生省 kousei-shou *n.* Ministry of Welfare
- 厚生省は在宅ケアを推進した。— The Ministry of Welfare promoted home care.

11 | 0.42

4041 豆 mame *n.* bean, pea
- 豆から豆腐を作った。— I made bean curd from soy beans.

11 | 0.87

4042 損 son *n.* loss, damage
- もし今買わなかったら大変な損になるでしょう。— If you don't buy it now, it will be a great loss.

11 | 0.94

4043 肝心 kanjin *na-adj.* main, essential, important
- 肝心なことはすぐにそれを実行することだ。— What is the most important thing is that you do it at once.

11 | 0.97

4044 保育園 hoiku-en *n.* nursery school, day care
- 子供を保育園に迎えに行った。— I picked up my child from day care.

11 | 0.78

4045 ポスト posuto *n.* post, postbox, mailbox
- 今日手紙をポストに投函した。— I took a letter to the post today.

11 | 0.94

4046 呼びかける yobikakeru *v.* call out, appeal
- 道路の向こう側から呼びかけた。— I called a man from across the street.

11 | 0.87

4047 余談 yodan *n.* digression
- 余談だが、彼の名前は長い。— By the way, he has a long name.

11 | 0.68

4048 凝る koru *v.* be absorbed, be devoted; become stiff
- 彼が何か始めると凝る性質だ。— When he begins to do anything, he devotes himself to it.

11 | 0.89

4049 水道 suidou *n.* water supply
- 水道が止まった。— Our water supply was cut off.

11 | 0.93

4050 人形 ningyou *n.* doll
- 彼女は色々な人形を持っている。— She has a variety of dolls.

11 | 0.90

4051 狙い nerai *n.* aim, target
- この論文の狙いはいい。— The aim of this essay is good.
11 | 0.85

4052 決断(する) ketsudan(suru) *n.* decision *v.* decide
- それはいい決断だ。— You made a good decision.
11 | 0.96

4053 大切さ taisetsu-sa *n.* importance
- 先生は日々の練習の大切さを強調した。— The teacher stressed the importance of daily practice.
11 | 0.80

4054 よそ yoso *n.* other, elsewhere
- この商品はよそでは買えません。— You can't buy this item at other shops.
11 | 0.95

4055 蚊 ka *n.* mosquito
- 昨日の夜はたくさん蚊に刺された。— I was bitten by mosquitoes a lot last night.
11 | 0.84

4056 監視(する) kanshi(suru) *n.* observation *v.* watch
- 彼を厳しく監視しなければならない。— We have to keep him under observation.
11 | 0.86

4057 同年 dounen *n.* same year
- 私達は同年に会社に入った。— We were employed in the same year.
11 | 0.64

4058 あっさり assari *adv.* easily, flatly, simple, plain
- 私はあっさりした料理が好きだ。— I prefer plain food.
11 | 0.84

4059 微笑む hohoemu *v.* smile
- 母は優しく微笑んだ。— Mother smiled kindly.
11 | 0.59

4060 駆け付ける kaketsukeru *v.* run, rush
- 警察は現場に駆け付けた。— The police rushed to the scene.
11 | 0.89

4061 ゴール gooru *n.* goal
- 選手はゴールを決めた。— The player scored a goal.
11 | 0.84

4062 三本 san-bon *n.* three (long/cylindrical objects)
- 鉛筆を三本ください。— Please give me three pencils.
11 | 0.96

4063 棚 tana *n.* shelf
- 棚の上に本がある。— The books are on the shelf.
11 | 0.92

4064 しっぽ shippo *n.* tail
- 犬がしっぽを振った。— The dog wagged its tail.
11 | 0.85

4065 虐待(する) gyakutai(suru) *n.* abuse *v.* abuse
- 子供の虐待は深刻な問題だ。— Child abuse is a serious problem.
11 | 0.91

4066 然り shikari *v. (Classical)* to be so
- 親が親なら子供も然りだ。— If the parents do not behave well, the children will be like them.
11 | 0.87

4067 正常 seijou *na-adj.* normal
- 体温は正常です。— Body temperature is normal.
11 | 0.96

4068 配布(する) haifu(suru) *n.* distribution *v.* distribute
- 先生は遠足のチラシを配布した。— The teacher distributed handouts about the excursion.
11 | 0.57

4069 持ち上げる mochiageru *v.* lift, raise
- この重い荷物を持ち上げてください。— Please lift this heavy baggage.
11 | 0.91

4070 見送る miokuru *v.* see off
- 友達を空港まで見送りに行った。— I went to see my friend off at the airport.
11 | 0.92

4071 引き継ぐ hikitsugu *v.* take over
- 息子が会社を引き継いだ。— His son took over the company.
11 | 0.94

4072 違和感 iwa kan *n.* uncomfortable feeling
- 右腕に違和感を感じた。— I felt discomfort in my right arm.
11 | 0.90

4073 ジャズ jazu *n.* jazz
- 彼はジャズに夢中だ。— He is keen on jazz.
11 | 0.85

4074 次いで tsuide *adv.* next, after that
- アマゾン川はナイル川に次いで長い川だ。— The Amazon is the longest river in the world after the Nile.
11 | 0.49

4075 向き muki *n.* direction, aspect; suitable
- この家は南向きだ。 — This house has a southern aspect.

11 | 0.87

4076 五年間 go nenkan *n.* five years
- 私は五年間日本語を勉強している。 — I have been studying Japanese for five years.

11 | 0.75

4077 安全性 anzen-sei *n.* safety, security
- コンピューターの安全性を高めなければならない。 — I must improve my computer security.

11 | 0.62

4078 国境 kokkyou *n.* border
- 国境を越えた。 — I crossed the border.

11 | 0.92

4079 包丁 houchou *n.* kitchen knife
- この包丁はよく切れる。 — This kitchen knife can cut very well.

11 | 0.89

4080 キー kii *n.* key
- 彼は車のキーを回した。 — He turned the key.

11 | 0.85

4081 どきどき(する) dokidoki(suru) *v.* throb, beat fast
- 階段を上っただけで、心臓がどきどきした。 — My heart pounded simply because I went up the stairs.

11 | 0.86

4082 賑わう nigiwau *v.* be crowded with
- ビーチはたくさんの人で賑わっていた。 — The beach was crowded with many people.

11 | 0.81

4083 地獄 jigoku *n.* hell
- 彼女にとって学校は地獄だ。 — The school is hell for her.

11 | 0.84

4084 豪華 gouka *na-adj.* luxurious, gorgeous
- ハワイで豪華なホテルに泊まった。 — I stayed in a luxury hotel in Hawaii.

11 | 0.92

4085 救急車 kyuukyuu-sha *n.* ambulance
- 救急車を呼んでください。 — Please call an ambulance.

11 | 0.88

4086 十年間 juu nenkan *n.* ten years
- 彼は十年間先生をしている。 — He has been teaching for ten years.

11 | 0.83

4087 不動産 fu-dousan *n.* real estate, property
- 最近不動産の価値が高くなった。 — The value of real estate has increased recently.

11 | 0.99

4088 広まる hiromaru *v.* spread, get around
- そのうわさはすぐ広まった。 — The rumor got around quickly.

11 | 0.97

4089 外出(する) gaishutsu(suru) *n.* going out, outing *v.* go out
- 彼女はめったに外出しない。 — She seldom goes out.

11 | 0.93

4090 グラス gurasu *n.* glass
- グラスにワインを注いだ。 — I poured wine into a glass.

11 | 0.63

4091 曲げる mageru *v.* bend, twist
- 体を曲げて伸ばしましょう。 — Bend your body and stretch.

11 | 0.91

4092 屋敷 yashiki *n.* mansion, residence, estate
- なんて素敵なお屋敷なんでしょう！ — What a wonderful residence you have!

11 | 0.66

4093 専門的 senmon-teki *na-adj.* technical, academic
- 専門的な経験がない人は雇えません。 — We can't employ anyone who lacks technical experience.

11 | 0.88

4094 切り替える kirikaeru *v.* switch, change
- 明かりを赤から緑に切り替えた。 — The lights switched from red to green.

11 | 0.93

4095 染める someru *v.* dye, color
- 私の母は白髪を黒く染めた。 — My mum dyed her white hair black.

11 | 0.89

4096 スキー場 sukii-jou *n.* ski ground, ski resort
- 私達はスキー場で偶然会いました。 — We happened to meet at a ski resort.

11 | 0.72

4097 ヒント hinto *n.* hint, clue
- 彼にヒントを与えた。 — I gave him a hint.

11 | 0.90

4098 講義 kougi *n.* lecture
- 有名な教授の講義を書き留めた。 — I took notes of the famous professor's lecture.

11 | 0.92

4099 裏切る uragiru *v.* betray
- 友達の信頼を裏切らないようにしなさい。 — Never betray the trust of your friends.

11 | 0.90

4100 余地 yochi *n.* room, space
- 疑う余地はない。— There is no room for doubt.
11 | 0.90

4101 富む tomu *v.* be rich (in); grow
- この野菜はビタミンCに富んでいる。— This vegetable is rich in vitamin C.
11 | 0.94

4102 手書き tegaki *n.* handwriting
- 彼女はいつもきれいな手書きの文字を書きます。— She always writes in neat handwriting.
11 | 0.67

4103 ブーム buumu *n.* boom
- 今は世界的な健康ブームだ。— Nowadays, there is a worldwide health boom.
11 | 0.84

4104 ワールドカップ waarudo kappu *n.* World Cup
- このチームはワールドカップで優勝した。— This team won the championship in the World Cup.
11 | 0.72

4105 鬼 oni *n.* ogre, devil, demon
- 野球のコーチは鬼の形相で叫んだ。— My baseball coach shouted with a face like thunder.
11 | 0.86

4106 ホール hooru *n.* hall
- このホールは500人収容できる。— This hall can hold 500 people.
11 | 0.93

4107 似合う niau *v.* suit
- その帽子はよくお似合いです。— That hat suits you well.
11 | 0.76

4108 節約(する) setsuyaku(suru) *n.* saving, economy *v.* save, economize on
- 水を節約して使ってください。— Please use the water sparingly.
11 | 0.99

4109 実績 jisseki *n.* achievement
- 今年彼は素晴らしい実績をあげている。— He has an impressive record of achievement this year.
11 | 0.82

4110 訳す yakusu *v.* translate
- 英語を日本語に訳した。— I translated English into Japanese.
11 | 0.87

4111 奴ら yatsu-ra *n.* guys, fellows
- 悪い奴らと遊ぶな。— Don't mess around with bad guys.
11 | 0.79

4112 キッチン kitchin *n.* kitchen
- キッチンからいいにおいがした。— A good smell came from the kitchen.
11 | 0.82

4113 課する kasuru *v.* assign, charge, impose
- あの会社は社員にとても厳しいノルマを課しているそうだ。— The company has imposed a very strict quota on the workers.
11 | 0.80

4114 養う yashinau *v.* bring up, keep, support
- 彼は大家族を養っている。— He has a large family to support.
11 | 0.98

4115 別々 betsubetsu *na-adj.* separate, individual
- 別々に払います。— We will pay separately.
11 | 0.97

4116 手足 teashi *n.* limb
- 彼は手足が大きい。— He has large limbs.
11 | 0.90

4117 物価 bukka *n.* prices
- 今月は物価が上がった。— This month prices have gone up.
11 | 0.75

4118 部品 buhin *n.* parts, components
- この会社は自動車の部品を作っている。— This company makes components for automobiles.
11 | 0.99

4119 最適 saiteki *na-adj.* best, optimum
- 彼女はこの会社に最適な人だ。— She is the best person for this company.
11 | 0.91

4120 宿題 shukudai *n.* homework
- 宿題がたくさんある。— We have a lot of homework.
11 | 0.87

4121 氏名 shimei *n.* name
- ここに住所・氏名を書きなさい。— Write your name and address here.
11 | 0.54

4122 ダンス dansu *n.* dancing
- 彼はダンスに夢中だ。— He is crazy about dancing.
11 | 0.88

4123 溶かす tokasu *v.* dissolve; melt
- フライパンにバターを溶かした。— I melted butter in a frying pan.
11 | 0.99

4124 人種 jinshu *n.* race
- アメリカには様々な人種がいます。— There are various races in the United States of America.
11 | 0.82

4125 歌手 kashu *n.* singer
- 彼は美しい声の歌手だ。— He is a singer with a beautiful voice.
11 | 0.86

4126 銀 gin *n.* silver
- 私はオリンピックで銀メダルを取った。— I won a silver medal in the Olympics.
11 | 0.96

4127 ルート ruuto *n.* route
- 山頂に登る新しいルートを登った。— I climbed a new route to the top of the mountain.
11 | 0.99

4128 第一号 dai-ichi gou *n.* first
- 第一号の受賞者だ。— You are the first recipient of the prize.
11 | 0.45

4129 従兄弟 itoko *n.* cousin
- 彼らは私の従兄弟です。— They are my cousins.
11 | 0.80

4130 概ね oomune *adv.* mostly, mainly, generally
- 私の勘は概ね当たっている。— My hunch proved mainly right.
11 | 0.69

4131 往復 oufuku *n.* round trip
- 往復切符をください。— A return ticket, please.
11 | 0.94

4132 起源 kigen *n.* origin
- この言葉の起源はドイツ語だ。— This word is German in origin.
11 | 0.92

4133 広場 hiroba *n.* square, plaza
- その広場に鳩がたくさんいる。— There are many pigeons in the square.
11 | 0.80

4134 レモン remon *n.* lemon
- 彼女は紅茶にレモンをしぼった。— She squeezed a lemon for tea.
11 | 0.88

4135 円滑 enkatsu *na-adj.* smooth
- 料理の手順が円滑に進んだ。— The cooking process went smoothly.
11 | 0.37

4136 広大 koudai *na-adj.* vast, huge, extensive
- サハラは広大な砂漠だ。— The Sahara is a vast desert.
11 | 0.95

4137 TV terebi *n.* television
- テレビで野球の試合を見た。— I watched a baseball game on TV.
11 | 0.39 | WB

4138 カップル kappuru *n.* couple
- 彼らはお似合いのカップルだ。— They make a good couple.
11 | 0.89

4139 納豆 nattou *n.* fermented soybeans
- 納豆はねばねばしている。— Fermented soybeans are sticky.
11 | 0.82

4140 堂々 doudou *adv.* nobly, openly
- 彼は堂々と振る舞っていた。— He was acting nobly.
11 | 0.95

4141 肝臓 kanzou *n.* liver
- この薬は肝臓に効きます。— These pills act on the liver.
11 | 0.90

4142 味わえる ajiwaeru *v.* can taste, can enjoy
- このレストランは南国の雰囲気が味わえます。— You can enjoy a tropical atmosphere at this restaurant.
11 | 0.85

4143 電源 dengen *n.* power supply
- コンピューターの電源を入れた。— I turned on the power to the computer.
11 | 0.84

4144 分割（する） bunkatsu(suru) *n.* division *v.* divide
- 分割払いでお願いします。— I will pay by installments, please.
11 | 0.93

4145 縮小（する） shukushou(suru) *n.* reduction *v.* reduce
- 画像を縮小して送ってください。— Please reduce image size before sending.
11 | 0.72

4146 練る neru *v.* knead; polish; elaborate
- 私達は計画を細かく練る必要があります。— We need to refine the plan in detail.
11 | 0.93

4147 飲み込む nomikomu *v.* swallow
- 私は急いで飴を飲み込んだ。— I swallowed a candy hastily.
11 | 0.83

4148 職人 shokunin *n.* craftsman, workman
- 彼は立派な職人だ。— He is a fine craftsman.
11 | 0.86

4149 十三年 juu san nen *n.* thirteen years
- 日本へ来て十三年経ちます。— It is thirteen years since I came to Japan.
11 | 0.73

4150 キャラクター kyarakutaa *n.* character
- この漫画のキャラクターは子供たちに人気があります。— This cartoon character is popular among children.
11 | 0.87

4151 大地 daichi *n.* earth, ground
- 雪が大地を覆った。— Snow covered the ground.
11 | 0.86

4152 具 gu *n.* ingredient
- すべての具を混ぜて煮てください。— Please combine all the ingredients and simmer.
11 | 0.81

4153 戸惑う tomadou *v.* confuse, puzzle
- 彼女はその状況に戸惑った。— She was confused by the situation.
11 | 0.90

4154 寂しさ sabishi-sa *n.* loneliness
- お酒で寂しさを紛らわした。— I drank my loneliness away.
11 | 0.81

4155 吐く tsuku *v.* tell (a lie); sigh
- 彼女は深いため息を吐いた。— She gave a deep sigh.
11 | 0.95

4156 カーテン kaaten *n.* curtain
- カーテンを開けましょうか。— Shall I open the curtains?
11 | 0.88

4157 情けない nasakenai *i-adj.* miserable
- 情けない姿をしているね。— You look so miserable.
11 | 0.89

4158 飯 meshi *n.* rice
- 同じ釜の飯を食べた仲間だ。— We eat at the same table.
11 | 0.92

4159 幼児 youji *n.* infant
- 毎日幼児のための食事を作っています。— I make food for infants every day.
11 | 0.78

4160 法案 houan *n.* bill
- 法案は国会を通過した。— The bill cleared the Diet.
11 | 0.37

4161 病 yamai *n.* illness, disease
- その病の原因は何ですか。— What is the cause of that disease?
11 | 0.90

4162 切符 kippu *n.* ticket
- 飛行機の切符を予約した。— I booked an airline ticket.
11 | 0.87

4163 消滅（する） shoumetsu(suru) *n.* disappearance *v.* disappear
- 酸素がなかったら生き物は消滅していただろう。— Without oxygen, living things would have disappeared.
11 | 0.84

4164 障害者 shougai-sha *n.* disabled person, handicapped person
- 障害者のための学校を始めた。— I started a school for handicapped people.
11 | 0.80

4165 台 dai *n.* stand, rack
- 台に楽譜を載せた。— I put the music on a music stand.
11 | 0.90

4166 面白さ omoshiro-sa *n.* interest, fun
- あの小説の面白さがわからない。— I don't understand what's interesting about that novel.
11 | 0.92

4167 生まれ umare *n.* birth; birthplace
- 彼は東京生まれだ。— He was born in Tokyo.
11 | 0.88

4168 保有（する） hoyuu(suru) *n.* possession *v.* hold, possess
- 自分の会社の株を保有しています。— I hold shares in my own company.
11 | 0.71

4169 反発（する） hanpatsu(suru) *n.* repulsion, resistance *v.* react, resist, rebel, repel
- 私は親の考えに反発した。— I rebelled against my parents' way of thinking.
11 | 0.94

4170 アレンジ（する） arenji(suru) *n.* arrangement *v.* arrange
- プレゼントでアレンジされた花をもらった。— I got an arrangement of flowers as a present.
11 | 0.74

4171 しつけ shitsuke *n.* tacking (sewing); discipline
- 彼は家でのしつけの良さがわかります。— You can see that he's had good discipline at home.
11 | 0.97

4172 指導者 shidou-sha *n.* leader, coach
- 彼は有名な指導者だ。— He is a famous leader.
11 | 0.92

4173 原理 genri *n.* principle
- 彼はてこの原理を使って石を動かした。— He moved the stone using the principle of the lever.
11 | 0.86

4174 東南アジア tounan ajia *n.* Southeast Asia
- 東南アジアへ旅行に行きます。— I will travel to Southeast Asia.
- 11 | 0.89

4175 ID aidii *n.* identification, ID
- IDカードを見せてください。— Please show me your ID card.
- 11 | 0.27 | WB

4176 金属 kinzoku *n.* metal
- 金属バットは重いです。— A metal baseball bat is heavy.
- 11 | 0.95

4177 しわ shiwa *n.* wrinkle, line
- 祖母の顔はしわだらけだ。— My grandmother has lots of lines on her face.
- 11 | 0.93

4178 思い浮かべる omoiukaberu *v.* recall, remember
- 私は家族の顔を思い浮かべた。— I remembered the faces of my family.
- 11 | 0.88

4179 一分 ip-pun *n.* one minute
- 私の家は駅から徒歩一分です。— My house is about one minute's walk from the station.
- 11 | 0.89

4180 当面 toumen *n.* present, current; for the time being
- 当面の問題は失業についてです。— The current problem concerns unemployment.
- 11 | 0.70

4181 貯金 chokin *n.* savings, deposit
- 彼女の貯金は少ない。— She has few savings.
- 11 | 0.86

4182 技術的 gijutsu-teki *na-adj.* technical, practical
- この作業は技術的に不可能だ。— This operation is technically impossible.
- 11 | 0.81

4183 四歳 yon-sai *n.* four years old
- 私のペットは四歳になりました。— My pet has turned four years old.
- 11 | 0.84

4184 ダンボール danbooru *n.* cardboard
- この部屋に積み上げられたダンボールの山がある。— There are piles of cardboard boxes in this room.
- 11 | 0.83

4185 生クリーム nama kuriimu *n.* fresh cream
- ケーキに苺と生クリームをのせた。— I put strawberries and fresh cream on the cake.
- 11 | 0.79

4186 名乗る nanoru *v.* give one's name
- 彼はどうして偽名を名乗ったのだろうか。— I wonder why he gave a false name.
- 11 | 0.86

4187 金曜日 kin'you bi *n.* Friday
- 彼女は毎週金曜日に買い物へ行きます。— She goes shopping every Friday.
- 11 | 0.80

4188 生き残る ikinokoru *v.* survive
- 私はその事故で生き残った。— I survived the accident.
- 11 | 0.94

4189 演技 engi *n.* performance
- 彼女のスケートの演技はすばらしかった。— Her skating performance was brilliant.
- 11 | 0.83

4190 取り巻く torimaku *v.* surround, enclose
- 大学に入ると、彼を取り巻く環境が変化した。— When he entered university, the environment surrounding him changed.
- 11 | 0.80

4191 体質 taishitsu *n.* constitution (physical)
- 湿気の多い気候は彼の体質に合わなかった。— The humid climate did not agree with his constitution.
- 11 | 0.99

4192 ドイツ語 doitsu go *n.* German (language)
- ドイツ語を話すのは苦手だ。— I'm poor at speaking German.
- 11 | 0.80

4193 仕方が無い shikata ga nai *cp.* cannot be helped, no use
- そこへ行っても仕方がない。— It's no use going there.
- 11 | 0.00 | SP

4194 参加者 sanka-sha *n.* participant
- その講演会の参加者の大部分は女性だった。— The majority of the participants at the lecture meeting were women.
- 11 | 0.69

4195 第三者 dai-san-sha *n.* outsider, third party
- 第三者として意見を聞かせてください。— Please give us your opinion as a third party.
- 11 | 0.90

4196 感性 kansei *n.* sensitivity, sensibility
- 彼は音楽に対する鋭い感性を持っている。— He has an acute sensitivity for music.
- 11 | 0.90

4197 谷 tani *n.* valley; ravine, gorge
- 川は谷の中を曲がりくねっている。— The river winds through the valley.
- 11 | 0.94

21 Weather

(frequency per million words)

(天気) (Weather)
雨 ame 86.231 rain
雪 yuki 57.578 snow
雲 kumo 22.224 cloud
台風 taifuu 20.680 typhoon
嵐 arashi 11.467 storm
霧 kiri 9.710 fog
暑さ atsu-sa 9.434 heat
日差し hizashi 9.128 sunshine
雷 kaminari 7.774 thunder
晴れ hare 5.766 clear weather
大雨 ooame 5.276 heavy rain
梅雨 tsuyu 4.553 rainy season
曇り kumori 2.720 cloudy weather
大雪 ooyuki 2.541 heavy snow
快晴 kaisei 2.404 fine weather
小雨 kosame 2.020 light rain
霜 shimo 1.787 frost

(寒暖) (Temperature/Light)
寒い samui 67.689 cold
明るい akarui 64.806 bright, light (also cheerful)
暗い kurai 54.779 dark (also depressed)
温かい atatakai 51.916 warm (also genial)
暑い atsui 43.369 hot, warm
冷たい tsumetai 38.726 cold
寒さ samu-sa 17.384 cold
冷える hieru 10.468 chill, become cold, feel cold
涼しい suzushii 9.822 cool
蒸し暑い mushiatsui 1.917 hot and stuffy

(天気・気候・気温) (Climate)
天気 tenki 26.179 weather
気温 kion 15.657 temperature
気候 kikou 13.047 climate
天候 tenkou 10.141 weather

4198 本社 honsha *n.* head office
• 彼は本社から九州支社に転勤になった。— He was transferred from the head office to a branch in Kyushu.
11 | 0.98

4199 都度 tsudo *n.* every time
• 彼は上京の都度お土産を持って来てくれる。— Every time he comes up to Tokyo, he brings us a souvenir.
11 | 1.00

4200 ぼんやり(する) bon'yari(suru) *adv.* vacantly, vaguely, dimly *v.* be vague, be blurred
• 彼女は授業中ぼんやり窓の外を見ていた。— She was idly looking out of the window in class.
11 | 0.71

4201 死者 shisha *n.* dead
• この事故で死者と行方不明者が多数出た。— There were many dead and missing people as a result of the accident.
11 | 0.79

4202 四季 shiki *n.* four seasons
• 日本は四季がはっきりしています。— The four seasons are clearly defined in Japan.
11 | 0.86

4203 倒産(する) tousan(suru) *n.* bankruptcy *v.* go bankrupt
• その会社は倒産した。— The company went bankrupt.
11 | 0.99

4204 ニュージーランド nyuujiirando *n.* New Zealand
• ニュージーランドの首都はウェリントンです。— The capital of New Zealand is Wellington.
11 | 0.87

4205 センター sentaa *n.* center
• 私は今、国際交流のセンターで働いています。— I'm working at the Center for International Exchange now.
11 | 0.92

4206 保全(する) hozen(suru) *n.* preservation, maintenance *v.* preserve, maintain
• 彼はこの島で環境の保全のために働いている。— He is working to preserve the environment on this island.
11 | 0.48

4207 結合(する) ketsugou(suru) *n.* combination *v.* combine, join
• ロープウェイで二つの島を結合させた。— The two islands were linked with a ropeway.
11 | 0.73

4208 発送(する) hassou(suru) *n., v.* send, ship, dispatch
• 結婚式の招待状を昨日発送しました。— I sent out the wedding invitations yesterday.
11 | 0.51

4209 パンツ pantsu *n.* pants, trousers; shorts, underpants
- 今日の彼女はパンツとジャケットで出社した。— She came to the office wearing pants and a jacket today.
11 | 0.63

4210 ぐるぐる guruguru *adv.* round and round
- 犬は庭をぐるぐる駆け回った。— The dog ran round and round the garden.
11 | 0.86

4211 ナンバー nanbaa *n.* number
- ひき逃げの車のナンバーを書き留めた。— I wrote down the number of the hit-and-run driver's car.
11 | 0.76

4212 持ち主 mochinushi *n.* owner
- この別荘の持ち主は誰ですか。— Who owns this cottage?
11 | 0.86

4213 到底 toutei *adv.* (cannot) possibly, no matter how
- 彼の行動は到底理解できない。— I can't possibly understand his behavior.
11 | 0.90

4214 夕日 yuuhi *n.* evening sun, sunset
- 私は今までこんなきれいな夕日を見たことがない。— I have never seen such a beautiful sunset.
11 | 0.89

4215 乗り換える norikaeru *v.* change, transfer
- 次の駅で電車からバスに乗り換えなければならない。— We have to change from the train to a bus at the next station.
11 | 0.87

4216 リストラ risutora *n.* restructuring, downsizing
- 我が社は不況のためリストラしなければならない。— Our company has to downsize because of the recession.
11 | 0.96

4217 答弁 touben *n.* answer, defense
- 首相に替わって大臣が答弁に立った。— The Minister stood up to answer for the Prime Minister.
11 | 0.18 | OF

4218 哲学 tetsugaku *n.* philosophy
- 私の兄は哲学を専攻しています。— My brother is majoring in philosophy.
11 | 0.84

4219 おかしな okashina *adn.* funny, ridiculous
- 彼はおかしな格好をしていたのでからかった。— I teased him because he was wearing funny clothes.
11 | 0.93

4220 当事者 touji-sha *n.* parties concerned
- 彼はその事件の当事者として法廷に立った。— He stood up in court as a party directly concerned with the affair.
11 | 0.75

4221 シーズン shiizun *n.* season
- 桜のシーズンはたくさんの人で賑わいます。— The cherry blossom season is busy with lots of people.
11 | 0.76

4222 品 shina *n.* goods, article
- この店では色々な品を売っています。— They sell articles of all kinds at this shop.
11 | 0.84

4223 高速道路 kousoku douro *n.* freeway
- 高速道路は帰省の車で渋滞した。— The freeway was congested with cars returning home.
11 | 0.89

4224 一員 ichiin *n.* member
- 彼は野球部の一員だ。— He is a member of the baseball club.
11 | 0.96

4225 確定(する) kakutei(suru) *n.* determination, decision *v.* determine, decide
- 彼の落選が確定した。— It was determined that he had lost the election.
11 | 0.84

4226 委員会 iin kai *n.* committee
- 委員会で今年の予算は承認された。— The budget for this year was approved by the committee.
11 | 0.56

4227 混ぜ合わせる mazeawaseru *v.* mix
- 二つのものを混ぜ合わせると危険です。— It's dangerous to mix the two.
11 | 0.87

4228 興味深い kyoumi bukai *i-adj.* interesting
- 美術館に興味深い絵画が展示されています。— There are some interesting exhibits in the art museum.
11 | 0.81

4229 あれこれ arekore *adv.* this and that
- 休み時間に学生たちはあれこれと話しています。— Students are talking about this and that during recess.
11 | 0.91

4230 分布(する) bunpu(suru) *n.* distribution *v.* distribute
- その植物は世界中に広く分布しています。— The plant is distributed widely throughout the world.
11 | 0.74

4231 観客 kankyaku *n.* audience
- 演奏者の登場で観客は静まり返った。— The audience fell silent when the player entered.
11 | 0.82

4232 鮎 ayu *n.* sweetfish, ayu
- 夏休みに川で鮎を釣った。— I fished for ayu in the river during the summer holidays.
11 | 0.79

4233 正午 shougo *n.* noon, midday
- 会議は正午まで続いた。— The meeting ran on until midday.
11 | 0.14 | NM

4234 首都 shuto *n.* capital city
- 東京は日本の首都だ。— Tokyo is the capital of Japan.
11 | 0.91

4235 体内 tainai *n.* inside the body
- マラソン選手は体内にエネルギーを蓄えている。— The marathon runners are storing energy in the body.
11 | 0.94

4236 調和(する) chouwa(suru) *n.* harmony, balance *v.* harmonize, match
- あの旅館は景色と調和していた。— That inn was in harmony with the scenery.
11 | 0.80

4237 権威 ken'i *n.* authority
- 私の兄は科学の権威です。— My brother is an authority on science.
11 | 0.85

4238 シンガポール shingapooru *n.* Singapore
- シンガポールはマーライオンが有名です。— Singapore is famous for the Merlion.
11 | 0.93

4239 酔う you *v.* get drunk, feel sick
- 彼は酔っても態度が変わらない。— His behavior doesn't change even when he has been drinking.
11 | 0.87

4240 最低限 saitei-gen *n.* minimum
- 来月の出費は最低限に抑えなければならない。— You must keep your expenditure next month to a minimum.
11 | 0.95

4241 傷つく kizutsuku *v.* be injured, be hurt
- 彼女は彼の乱暴な言葉で傷ついた。— She was hurt by his rude words.
11 | 0.87

4242 カボチャ kabocha *n.* pumpkin
- ハロウィーンでカボチャのスープを作った。— I made pumpkin soup for Halloween.
11 | 0.88

4243 老後 rougo *n.* old age
- 老後は気楽に過ごしたいです。— I want to live comfortably in my old age.
11 | 0.98

4244 当てはまる atehamaru *v.* apply
- 彼が言ったことは学生にも当てはまる。— What he has said applies to the student too.
11 | 0.98

4245 害 gai *n.* harm, damage
- たばこは健康に害があるので気をつけましょう。— Please be careful because smoking is harmful to your health.
11 | 0.91

4246 稽古(する) keiko(suru) *n.* practice, exercise *v.* practice
- 娘は五歳からピアノの稽古をしている。— My daughter has been practicing on the piano since she was five years old.
11 | 0.87

4247 一位 ichi-i *n.* first prize
- 彼女はヴァイオリンコンテストで一位になった。— She won first prize in a violin contest.
11 | 0.79

4248 率いる hikiiru *v.* head, lead, command
- 私は学生を率いて博物館へ行った。— I led my students to the museum.
11 | 0.80

4249 前者 zensha *n.* former
- この二つの案のうち、私は前者より後者の方がいい。— Of these two plans, I prefer the latter to the former.
11 | 0.82

4250 数人 suu-nin *n.* several people
- 今日は数人の学生が欠席した。— Several students were absent today.
11 | 0.94

4251 創造(する) souzou(suru) *n.* creation *v.* create
- 神は天と地を創造した。— God created heaven and earth.
11 | 0.87

4252 届け出 todokede *n.* report, notification
- 今日結婚の届け出を出した。— I submitted a marriage notification today.
11 | 0.60

4253 荻窪 ogikubo *n.* Ogikubo (place name)
- 荻窪で有名なラーメン店に行って食べた。— We went to eat at a famous noodle shop in Ogikubo.
11 | 0.29

4254 スイッチ suitchi *n.* switch
- このスイッチを押せばカーテンが開きます。— If you press this switch the curtains will open.
11 | 0.92

4255 試み kokoromi *n.* attempt, try
- 彼は三度目の試みで試験に合格した。— He passed the exam on his third attempt.
11 | 0.88

4256 歩む ayumu *v.* walk, go through
- 離婚してお互いに新しい人生を歩んだ。— We divorced and each went on to lead a new life.
11 | 0.93

4257 立ち止まる tachidomaru *v.* stop, pause
- 彼はたばこを吸うために立ち止まった。— He stopped to smoke.
11 | 0.76

4258 いまいち imaichi *adv.* not quite, not really
- 彼の指導はいまいち理解できない。— I don't really understand his teaching.
11 | 0.45

4259 麺 men *n.* noodles
- 麺は一分だけゆでてください。— Please boil the noodles for one minute only.
11 | 0.72

4260 不安定 fu-antei *na-adj.* unstable, uneasy
- 日本の経済は不安定な状態になった。— The Japanese economy became unstable.
11 | 0.97

4261 原点 genten *n.* starting point, origin
- 迷った時は原点に立ち返らなければならない。— You must go back to the starting point when you can't make up your mind.
11 | 0.95

4262 一向 ikkou *adv.* (not) at all; completely
- この薬を飲んだが一向に効かなかった。— I took the medicine but it did not work at all.
11 | 0.91

4263 それゆえ sore yue *adv.* therefore, thus
- 地震が起こった。それゆえに多くの人が帰宅できなかった。— There was an earthquake. Therefore, many people were unable to return home.
11 | 0.58

4264 ジュース juusu *n.* juice
- そのジュースは少し酸っぱいです。— This juice tastes a little sour.
11 | 0.84

4265 軽減(する) keigen(suru) *n.* reduction *v.* reduce
- 国民は税の軽減を希望しています。— The public are hoping for a tax reduction.
11 | 0.77

4266 不自由 fu-jiyuu *n.* inconvenience; disability
- 水が不足すると不自由します。— A water shortage causes inconvenience.
11 | 0.94

4267 悲鳴 himei *n.* scream
- 深夜悲鳴を聞いて駆け付けた。— I heard a scream late at night and ran to help.
11 | 0.72

4268 落札者 rakusatsu-sha *n.* successful bidder
- アメリカの落札者がその絵を買った。— The successful American bidder bought the picture.
11 | 0.03 | WB

4269 融資(する) yuushi(suru) *n.* loan *v.* loan, lend
- 銀行から融資を受けた。— I got a loan from the bank.
11 | 0.78

4270 破綻(する) hatan(suru) *n.* bankruptcy, collapse *v.* fail, go bankrupt
- 国の財政は破綻寸前である。— The nation's finances are on the verge of collapse.
11 | 1.00

4271 二千八年 nisen hachi nen *n.* 2008 (year)
- 二千八年に世界金融危機に直面した。— We faced a global financial crisis in 2008.
11 | 0.29 | WB

4272 アドレス adoresu *n.* address
- メールのアドレスを教えてください。— Please tell me your email address.
11 | 0.58

4273 励む hagemu *v.* work hard, make efforts
- 息子は日々学業に励んでいる。— My son is studying hard every day.
11 | 0.90

4274 双方 souhou *n.* both sides, both parties
- この問題は双方との話し合いによって解決しなければならない。— This problem needs to be solved by discussion with both sides.
11 | 0.89

4275 原爆 genbaku *n.* atomic bomb
- 原爆が広島に落とされた。— The atomic bomb was dropped on Hiroshima.
11 | 0.82

4276 傘 kasa *n.* umbrella
- 電車に傘を忘れた。— I left my umbrella on the train.
11 | 0.90

4277 チャレンジ charenji *n.* challenge
- オリンピック選手は世界記録にチャレンジした。— The Olympic athlete challenged the world record.
11 | 0.90

4278 炭 sumi *n.* charcoal
- 彼は山で竹を焼いて炭を作った。— He burned bamboo to make charcoal in the mountain.
11 | 0.74

4279 不意 fui *na-adj.* sudden, unexpected *n.* suddenness
- 昨日家に不意の来客が来た。— An unexpected visitor came to my house yesterday.
11 | 0.49

4280 リサイクル（する） risaikuru(suru) *n.* recycling *v.* recycle
- 空き缶をリサイクルします。— We recycle waste cans.
11 | 0.90

4281 ミルク miruku *n.* milk
- 床にミルクをこぼした。— I spilled milk on the floor.
11 | 0.87

4282 子孫 shison *n.* descendant; posterity
- 彼は有名な政治家の子孫です。— He is a descendant of a famous politician.
11 | 0.95

4283 近頃 chikagoro *n.* recently, lately
- 彼女は近頃太ってきた。— She has put on weight recently.
11 | 0.90

4284 鞄 kaban *n.* bag
- 教科書は鞄の中です。— The textbook is in the bag.
11 | 0.89

4285 五千円 gosen en *n.* five thousand yen
- 友達の誕生日に五千円のプレゼントを買った。— I bought a present for five thousand yen for my friend's birthday.
11 | 0.76

4286 圧力 atsuryoku *n.* pressure, stress
- 本当の事を話すように彼に圧力をかけた。— I put pressure on him to tell the truth.
11 | 0.95

4287 斜め naname *n.* diagonal
- 斜めに線をひいた。— I drew a diagonal line.
11 | 0.95

4288 補助（する） hojo(suru) *n.* help, aid, assistance *v.* help, aid, assist
- 父は国から補助を受けている。— My father is receiving financial assistance from the state.
11 | 0.63

4289 改良 kairyou *n.* improvement
- この機械は日々いろいろと改良されている。— These machines are being improved in various ways from day to day.
11 | 0.91

4290 俳優 haiyuu *n.* actor
- 彼は俳優の卵だ。— He is a budding actor.
11 | 0.86

4291 フィリピン firipin *n.* Philippines
- 私達はフィリピンのセブ島で挙式した。— We had a wedding ceremony on the island of Cebu in the Philippines.
11 | 0.93

4292 効率的 kouritsu-teki *na-adj.* efficient
- 勉強は効率的にしなければならない。— You should study in an efficient manner.
11 | 0.59

4293 情熱 jounetsu *n.* passion
- 彼の仕事への情熱は貪欲だ。— His passion for work is insatiable.
11 | 0.92

4294 七人 shichi-nin *n.* seven people
- 『七人の侍』は有名な映画だ。— "Seven Samurai" is a famous movie.
11 | 0.97

4295 焦点 shouten *n.* focus
- カメラの焦点を合わせた。— I brought the camera into focus.
10 | 0.92

4296 旅館 ryokan *n.* inn, Japanese-style hotel
- ここは伝統的な日本の旅館です。— This is a traditional Japanese inn.
10 | 0.99

4297 食卓 shokutaku *n.* dining table
- 食卓にごちそうが並べてあった。— The dining table was spread with a feast.
10 | 0.89

4298 歩き回る arukimawaru *v.* walk about
- ペットが部屋の中を自由に歩き回っている。— My pet walks around the room freely
10 | 0.82

4299 悲劇 higeki *n.* tragedy
- シェイクスピアのマクベスは悲劇です。— Shakespeare's Macbeth is a tragedy.
10 | 0.91

4300 長女 choujo *n.* eldest daughter
- 去年、長女が誕生した。— The eldest daughter was born last year.
10 | 0.87

4301 議会 gikai *n.* Diet, Parliament, Congress
- 今議会は開会中です。— The Diet is now in session.
10 | 0.84

4302 侵入（する） shinnyuu(suru) *n.* invasion *v.* break into, invade
- 泥棒が裏口から侵入した。— The thief broke in the back door.
10 | 0.88

4303 盛る moru *v.* serve, heap
- 茶碗にご飯を盛ってください。— Please serve rice in a bowl.

10 | 0.82

4304 転ずる tenzuru *v.* switch, shift
- 責任を私に転ずるのはやめてください。— Stop shifting the responsibility onto me.

10 | 0.65

4305 祭る matsuru *v.* enshrine; worship; deify
- この神社に誰が祭られていますか。— What deity is worshipped at this shrine?

10 | 0.86

4306 笑み emi *n.* smile
- 彼女はいつも顔に笑みをたたえていた。— She always wears a smile on her face.

10 | 0.53

4307 三度 san do *n.* three times
- 一日に三度の食事は大切だ。— It is important to have three meals a day.

10 | 0.93

4308 冷える hieru *v.* chill, become cold, feel cold
- 今朝はだいぶ冷えますね。— It's quite chilly this morning, isn't it?

10 | 0.93

4309 案 an *n.* plan, proposal, idea
- 彼の案は会議で採決された。— His proposal was adopted at the meeting.

10 | 0.87

4310 心理 shinri *n.* psychology
- 私は彼の心理がわからない。— I cannot understand his psychology.

10 | 0.92

4311 縫う nuu *v.* sew
- 母は私にドレスを縫ってくれた。— My mother sewed me a dress.

10 | 0.99

4312 おしゃべり(する) o-shaberi(suru) *n.* chat, talk *v.* chat, talk
- 彼女は授業中おしゃべりをしていた。— She was talking in class.

10 | 0.89

4313 次ぐ tsugu *v.* next to, after
- インドは中国に次ぐ人口の多い国だ。— India is the second most populated country, after China.

10 | 0.73

4314 復帰(する) fukki(suru) *n.* return, comeback *v.* return, come back, make a comeback
- 彼女は今年から舞台に復帰した。— She made a comeback on the stage this year.

10 | 0.96

4315 衝突(する) shoutotsu(suru) *n.* collision *v.* collide, clash
- 店から出てきた男と衝突した。— I collided with a man who came out of a shop.

10 | 0.93

4316 持ち出す mochidasu *v.* carry out, take out
- こっそりお金を持ち出すところを見られた。— I was seen taking out the money secretly.

10 | 0.89

4317 浸かる tsukaru *v.* be flooded; soak
- 私は肩までお湯に浸かった。— I soaked in the bath up to my shoulders.

10 | 0.90

4318 ドライブ(する) doraibu *n., v.* drive
- 新しい車でドライブに出かけませんか。— Would you like to go for a drive in my new car?

10 | 0.85

4319 テキスト tekisuto *n.* textbook
- 授業が始まる前にテキストを買ってください。— Please buy the textbook before the class starts.

10 | 0.88

4320 変動(する) hendou(suru) *n.* change, fluctuation, movement *v.* change, fluctuate
- 金の価格は日々変動している。— The price of gold is fluctuating daily.

10 | 0.71

4321 吸い込む suikomu *v.* breathe in; suck up
- 私達は新鮮な山の空気を吸い込んだ。— We breathed in fresh mountain air.

10 | 0.86

4322 木々 kigi *n.* trees
- 公園には木々が生い茂っている。— Trees grow luxuriantly in the park.

10 | 0.86

4323 ヒット hitto *n.* hit
- 彼はヒットを放った。— He got a hit.

10 | 0.82

4324 箸 hashi *n.* chopsticks
- 彼は箸が上手に使えない。— He can't use chopsticks well.

10 | 0.91

4325 食欲 shokuyoku *n.* appetite
- 今日は食欲がない。— I have no appetite today.

10 | 0.85

4326 語 go *n.* word; language
- この語はどういう意味ですか。— What does this word mean?

10 | 0.74

4327 通信 tsuushin *n.* correspondence, communication
- 弟は通信で勉強しています。 — My younger brother is taking a correspondence course.
10 | 0.76

4328 一家 ikka *n.* family, house, household
- 母は一家を切り盛りしている。 — My mother manages the household.
10 | 0.89

4329 怒鳴る donaru *v.* shout
- 私に怒鳴らないでください。 — Please don't shout at me.
10 | 0.74

4330 二十一年 nijuu ichi nen *n.* twenty-one years
- この家は築二十一年です。 — This house is twenty-one years old.
10 | 0.23 | NM

4331 専業主婦 sengyou shufu *n.* housewife, homemaker
- 母は専業主婦です。 — My mother is a housewife.
10 | 0.83

4332 滝 taki *n.* waterfall
- 橋の上の方に滝があります。 — There's a waterfall above the bridge.
10 | 0.92

4333 ひねる hineru *v.* twist
- ランニングで足首を捻った。 — I twisted my ankle while running.
10 | 0.86

4334 身分 mibun *n.* position, status
- 身分が違うので彼女と結婚できない。 — I can't marry her because of the difference in social status.
10 | 0.89

4335 敷地 shikichi *n.* site, ground
- ここは大学の敷地だ。 — Here are the school grounds.
10 | 0.97

4336 冷める sameru *v.* cool, get cold
- 冷めないうちにどうぞ召し上がってください。 — Please eat before it gets cold.
10 | 0.89

4337 ブルー buruu *n.* blue
- この赤ちゃんの目はブルーだ。 — This baby has blue eyes.
10 | 0.78

4338 先進国 senshin-koku *n.* developed country
- 先進国は発展途上国を援助しなければならない。 — The developed countries must aid the developing countries.
10 | 0.78

4339 バナナ banana *n.* banana
- 私はリンゴよりバナナが好きです。 — I like bananas better than apples.
10 | 0.85

4340 取り扱い toriatsukai *n.* treatment, handling
- その花瓶の取り扱いに注意してください。 — Please take care handling that vase.
10 | 0.67

4341 フィルム firumu *n.* film
- フィルムを現像しに行きます。 — I will go to get the film developed.
10 | 0.87

4342 日本酒 nihon-shu *n.* sake, Japanese rice wine
- 父は毎晩日本酒を飲んでいます。 — My father drinks sake every night.
10 | 0.88

4343 WWW daburyuudaburyuudaburyuu *n.* World Wide Web
- WWWサーバーにアクセスする。 — We will access the WWW server.
10 | 0.38 | WB

4344 透明 toumei *na-adj.* transparent, clear
- この湖はとても透明だ。 — This lake is very clear.
10 | 0.99

4345 即 soku *adv.* at once, immediately
- そのサッカー選手はレッドカードで即退場させられた。 — The soccer player was sent off the pitch immediately with a red card.
10 | 0.88

4346 克服(する) kokufuku(suru) *n.* conquest *v.* conquer, overcome
- 彼女は食べ物の好き嫌いを克服した。 — She has overcome food likes and dislikes.
10 | 0.97

4347 専門学校 senmon gakkou *n.* technical school, college, vocational school
- 弟は専門学校で美術を専攻している。 — My younger brother is majoring in art at college.
10 | 0.69

4348 六十歳 rokujus-sai *n.* sixty years old
- 彼は六十歳で定年を迎えた。 — He retired at sixty.
10 | 0.95

4349 朝日 asahi *n.* rising sun, morning sun
- 窓から朝日が差し込んだ。 — The morning sun came in the window.
10 | 0.87

4350 スタジオ sutajio *n.* studio
- 今日私達はスタジオで雑誌の撮影だ。 — We will take magazine photographs in a studio today.
10 | 0.84

4351 長期 chouki *n.* long term
- 私は長期の休暇を取った。— I took a long holiday.
10 | 0.88

4352 美人 bijin *n.* beautiful woman, beauty
- 彼女は本当に美人だ。— She is a real beauty.
10 | 0.79

4353 筆記用具 hikki yougu *n.* stationery, writing materials
- 就職試験に筆記用具を持ってきてください。— Please bring writing materials to the employment exam.
10 | 0.49

4354 石油 sekiyu *n.* oil
- 石油の値段が値上がりした。— The price of oil has gone up.
10 | 0.84

4355 早朝 souchou *n.* early morning
- 彼は早朝の始発の電車に乗った。— He took the first train in the early morning.
10 | 0.92

4356 店内 tennai *n.* inside a shop
- 店内には二人客がいた。— There were two customers in the store.
10 | 0.80

4357 賃金 chingin *n.* salary, wage
- 低い賃金で働きたくない。— I don't want to work for a low wage.
10 | 0.71

4358 見回す mimawasu *v.* look around, look about
- 彼は忘れ物がないかあたりを見回した。— He looked around to see whether he had left anything behind.
10 | 0.61

4359 日程 nittei *n.* schedule, itinerary
- 旅行の日程を来週に変更した。— I changed the schedule of my trip to next week.
10 | 0.63

4360 応用(する) ouyou(suru) *n.* application *v.* apply
- 科学は日常生活に応用できる。— Science can be applied to daily life.
10 | 0.93

4361 真っ暗 makkura *na-adj.* black *n.* pitch-dark
- 帰ってきたとき部屋は真っ暗だった。— The room was in darkness when I came home.
10 | 0.86

4362 眉 mayu *n.* eyebrow
- 彼は眉をしかめて考えた。— He knitted his brows in thought.
10 | 0.62

4363 レンズ renzu *n.* lens
- カメラのレンズを磨いた。— I polished the camera lens.
10 | 0.84

4364 五回 go kai *n.* five times
- 私達は週に五回英語の授業があります。— We have five English lessons a week.
10 | 0.88

4365 俗 zoku *n.*, *na-adj.* common, popular
- 俗にお金持ちと呼ばれる人はお金に細かい。— People who are commonly called the rich are tight with their money.
10 | 0.91

4366 パスタ pasuta *n.* pasta
- この店のパスタとピザはおいしい。— The pasta and pizza at this shop are tasty.
10 | 0.80

4367 差し込む sashikomu *v.* insert, plug in; come in, shine in
- 電話のプラグをコンセントに差し込んだ。— I put the telephone plug into the outlet.
10 | 0.91

4368 性能 seinou *n.* performance, capability
- 電気自動車の性能がよくなってきています。— The performance of electric cars has improved.
10 | 0.94

4369 絵画 kaiga *n.* painting, picture
- オークションでその絵画を手に入れた。— I obtained the painting at an auction.
10 | 0.87

4370 刀 katana *n.* sword
- 侍は刀をさやに納めた。— The samurai sheathed his sword.
10 | 0.69

4371 理念 rinen *n.* philosophy
- 彼女の教育理念は私と違う。— Her eductional philosophy is different from mine.
10 | 0.84

4372 裁判官 saiban-kan *n.* judge
- 裁判官はすべての人に公平であるべきだ。— A judge should be fair to all people.
10 | 0.79

4373 戦略 senryaku *n.* strategy
- 私達は会社経営の戦略を立てた。— We worked out a company management strategy.
10 | 0.90

4374 核 kaku *n.* nucleus, core
- 我が国は核の持ち込みを禁止しています。— Bringing nuclear weapons into our country is prohibited.
10 | 0.94

4375 農民 noumin *n.* farmer
- 農民は自給自足している。— The farmer is self-sufficient.
- 10 | 0.75

4376 コンクリート konkuriito *n.* concrete
- 土台はコンクリートで固められています。— The foundation is bedded in concrete.
- 10 | 0.94

4377 環境問題 kankyou mondai *n.* environmental problem
- 私達は環境問題にもっと関心を持つべきです。— We should be more interested in environmental problems.
- 10 | 0.82

4378 ライター raitaa *n.* lighter
- ライターを持っていますか。— Do you have a lighter?
- 10 | 0.81

4379 手入れ teire *n.* repair, maintenance
- 友人の家には手入れの行き届いた庭がある。— There is a well-kept garden at my friend's house.
- 10 | 0.98

4380 判定(する) hantei(suru) *n.* decision, judgment *v.* decide, judge
- 相撲の勝敗はビデオの判定となった。— The sumo match result was a video decision.
- 10 | 0.91

4381 帯びる obiru *v.* have a trace of, be tinged with
- トマトは赤みを帯びてきた。— The tomatoes were tinged with red.
- 10 | 0.83

4382 日曜 nichiyou *n.* Sunday
- 毎週日曜だけ料理をする。— I cook only every Sunday.
- 10 | 0.87

4383 昨今 sakkon *n.* nowadays
- 昨今物価が非常に高い。— Nowadays, the prices are very expensive.
- 10 | 0.98

4384 対話(する) taiwa(suru) *n.* dialogue, conversation *v.* converse, discuss
- 親は子供ときちんと対話する事が大切だ。— It is important for parents to interact properly with their children.
- 10 | 0.90

4385 帯 obi *n.* kimono sash, belt
- 着物の帯を固く締めた。— I tied the kimono sash tight.
- 10 | 0.89

4386 お好み焼き okonomiyaki *n.* okonomiyaki (Japanese-style savoury pancake with vegetables, meat, seafood etc.)
- お好み焼きは広島と大阪が有名だ。— Okonomiyaki is famous in Hiroshima and Osaka.
- 10 | 0.66

4387 羊 hitsuji *n.* sheep
- オーストラリアで羊の毛を刈った。— I sheared sheep in Australia.
- 10 | 0.90

4388 前半 zenhan *n.* first half
- サッカーの前半は勝っていた。— We were winning in the first half of the soccer game.
- 10 | 0.95

4389 ショー shoo *n.* show
- 私はそのテレビのショーに興奮した。— I was excited by the TV show.
- 10 | 0.84

4390 研究所 kenkyuu-jo, kenkyuu-sho *n.* research institute, laboratory
- 研究所は家の隣にある。— The laboratory is next to my house.
- 10 | 0.72

4391 生姜 shouga *n.* ginger
- 紅茶に生姜を入れて飲んだ。— I drank tea with ginger in.
- 10 | 0.89

4392 冒頭 boutou *n.* beginning
- 彼は会見の冒頭で謝罪した。— He apologized at the beginning of the interview.
- 10 | 0.93

4393 メジャー mejaa *n.* major; measure
- あの歌手はメジャーになった。— That singer became a major figure.
- 10 | 0.93

4394 公演 kouen *n.* performance
- 来週その演劇は大阪で公演します。— The theater is playing in Osaka next week.
- 10 | 0.83

4395 剣道 kendou *n.* kendo
- 彼女は剣道を習っている。— She is learning kendo.
- 10 | 0.77

4396 倉庫 souko *n.* warehouse, storehouse
- 米は倉庫に貯蔵してある。— The rice is stored in warehouses.
- 10 | 0.94

4397 浴衣 yukata *n.* yukata, cotton kimono
- 私は浴衣で花火を見に行った。— I went to see the fireworks in my yukata.
- 10 | 0.82

22 Words including letters of the alphabet (frequency per million words)

CD **shiidii** 38.257 **CD, compact disk**
CM **shiiemu** 30.977 **commercial**
JR **jeiaaru** 21.628 **Japan Railways, JR**
NHK **enueichikei, enuechikei** 20.461 **Nihon Housou Kyoukai (Japan Broadcasting Corporation)**
IT **aitii** 19.424 **IT**
PC **piishii** 19.003 **PC, personal computer**
OS **ooesu** 14.864 **OS, operating system**
Eメール **iimeeru** 14.225 **e-mail**
DVD **diibuidii** 13.053 **DVD**
HP **hoomupeeji** 12.100 **home page**
Tシャツ **tii shatsu** 12.061 **T-shirt**
TV **terebi** 11.076 **TV, television**
ID **aidii** 10.876 **ID, identification**
DNA **dii-enu-ee** 9.602 **DNA, deoxyribonucleic acid**
OB **oobii** 9.068 **OB (old boy), alumnus**
URL **yuuaarueru** 8.746 **URL, Uniform Resource Locator**
PHS **piieichiesu** 5.149 **Personal Handy phone System**
PTA **piitiiee** 4.272 **Parent-Teacher Association**
MD **emudii** 3.598 **minidisc**
MC **emushii** 2.473 **Master of Ceremonies**
F1 **efuwan** 2.111 **Formula 1**
CA **shiiei** 1.726 **cabin attendant**
SOS **esuooesu** 1.638 **SOS (emergency call)**
DS **diiesu** 1.622 **Nintendo DS (game machine)**
X線 **ekkususen** 1.605 **x-ray**
SE **esuii** 1.421 **systems engineer**
JA **jeiee** 1.311 **Japan Agricultural Cooperatives**
AI **eiai** 1.285 **artificial intelligence**
FIFA **fifa** 1.180 **FIFA (International Federation of Association Football)**
Yシャツ **waishatsu** 1.112 **dress shirt**
PV **piibui** 1.055 **promotional video**
DV **diibui** 0.872 **domestic violence**
PDF **piidiiefu** 0.799 **PDF**
OG **oogii** 0.703 **old girl, former female student**
SNS **esuenuesu** 0.226 **Social Networking Service**
WC **daburyuushii** 0.098 **WC**

4398 直径 chokkei *n.* diameter
- 直径5センチの円を描きなさい。— Please draw a circle five centimeters in diameter.
10 | 0.96

4399 残業 zangyou *n.* overtime work
- 私は残業で疲れていた。— I was tired from working overtime.
10 | 0.81

4400 殺人 satsujin *n.* murder
- 彼は殺人の罪で起訴された。— He was indicted for murder.
10 | 0.93

4401 判明（する）hanmei(suru) *n.* proving *v.* turn out, identify
- その噂は嘘であると判明した。— The rumor turned out to be false.
10 | 0.94

4402 統合（する）tougou(suru) *n.* integration *v.* integrate, combine
- 二つの会社を一つに統合した。— The two companies were integrated into one.
10 | 0.82

4403 水気 mizuke *n.* moisture
- 豆腐の水気を切った。— I drained the tofu.
10 | 0.83

4404 我ら ware-ra *pron.* we
- 我らの罪を許したまえ。— Forgive us our trespasses.
10 | 0.58

4405 原料 genryou *n.* raw material, ingredient
- チョコレートの原料はカカオです。— The raw material for chocolate is cocoa.
10 | 0.92

4406 群れ mure *n.* group; herd
- 牛の群れが牧場で草を食べていた。— A herd of cows was grazing in the meadow.
10 | 0.93

4407 新婦 shinpu *n.* bride
- 新婦が着たドレスはとても美しかった。— The dress that the bride wore was very beautiful.
10 | 0.56

4408 持ち物 mochimono *n.* personal belongings
- 自分の持ち物を忘れないでください。— Please don't leave any personal belongings behind.
10 | 0.31

4409 転がる korogaru *v.* roll
- ボールが道路の向こう側に転がっていった。— The ball rolled across the road.
10 | 0.83

4410 おはよう ohayou *interj.* good morning
- 「皆さん、おはよう」と先生が言った。— The teacher said, "Good morning, everyone".
10 | 0.65

4411 二匹 ni-hiki *n.* two (animals)
- 彼は犬を二匹飼っている。— He has two dogs.
10 | 0.80

4412 天候 tenkou *n.* weather
- 五月は天候の変化が激しい。— There is a big change in the weather in May.
10 | 0.97

4413 危険性 kiken-sei *n.* danger
- 医者は喫煙の危険性について警告した。— The doctor warned me about the dangers of smoking.
10 | 0.91

4414 創設（する）sousetsu(suru) *n.* foundation, creation *v.* found, create
- 彼がこの学校を創設した人です。— He is the one who founded this school.
10 | 0.66

4415 年末 nenmatsu *n.* end of the year
- 年末はやらなければならないことがたくさんある。— I have a lot of things to do at the end of the year.
10 | 0.90

4416 感 kan *n.* feeling, emotion
- 彼は幸せ感でいっぱいになった。— He was filled with a feeling of happiness.
10 | 0.90

4417 イコール ikooru *n.* equal
- 実力ナンバーワンとチャンピオンはイコールではない。— Being the No.1 player does not always mean being a champion.
10 | 0.46

4418 実質的 jisshitsu-teki *na-adj.* substantial; essential
- 税金は実質的に値上がりするでしょう。— The tax will be raised substantially.
10 | 0.80

4419 響き hibiki *n.* sound; echo
- そのホールはピアノの響きがすばらしかった。— The sound of the piano in the hall was fantastic.
10 | 0.96

4420 六ヶ月 rok-kagetsu *n.* six months
- 彼女は妊娠六ヶ月だ。— She is six months pregnant.
10 | 0.93

4421 プラン puran *n.* plan
- 旅行のプランはもう立てましたか。— Have you made any plans for your trip yet?
10 | 0.94

4422 グラウンド guraundo *n.* ground, playground, sports field
- 放課後はたいていグラウンドで野球をします。— I usually play baseball on the sports field after school.
10 | 0.82

4423 メキシコ mekishiko *n.* Mexico
- メキシコではスペイン語を話します。— People in Mexico speak Spanish.
10 | 0.91

4424 バー baa *n.* bar
- よくバーへワインを飲みに行きます。— I often go to a bar to drink wine.
10 | 0.87

4425 カップ kappu *n.* cup
- 朝食用のカップを二つ買った。— I bought two breakfast cups.
10 | 0.89

4426 訴訟 soshou *n.* suit, action
- 訴訟の弁護を友人の弁護士に頼んだ。— I asked a lawyer friend to defend me in the suit.
10 | 0.88

4427 流通（する）ryuutsuu(suru) *n.* circulation, distribution *v.* circulate, distribute
- このお酒は一般に流通していない。— This alcohol isn't widely distributed.
10 | 0.80

4428 郵送 yuusou *n.* mail, post
- 履歴書を月末までに郵送してください。— Please send your resume by mail by the end of the month.
10 | 0.30 | NM

4429 平ら taira *na-adj.* flat
- 平らな道を自転車で走った。— I went for a bicycle ride on a flat road.
10 | 0.94

4430 赤字 akaji *n.* deficit, loss, (in) the red
- 今月の家計は赤字なので節約しなければならない。— We must make economies because the household budget is in the red this month.
10 | 0.82

4431 二位 ni-i *n.* second place
- 彼はマラソンで二位だった。— He came in second in the marathon.
10 | 0.83

4432 刃物 hamono *n.* cutlery, edged tool, knife
- 刃物を振り回すのは危ない。— Waving a knife around is dangerous.
10 | 0.78

4433 苦情 kujou *n.* complaint
- 店員の対応の悪さについて苦情を言った。— He made a complaint about a clerk's bad attitude.
10 | 0.84

4434 入社(する) nyuusha(suru) *n.* entry to a company *v.* enter a company, get a job
- 彼は大学を卒業した後新聞社に入社した。— He got a job in a newspaper company after graduating from university.
10 | 0.89

4435 役所 yakusho *n.* government office
- 父は役所に勤めています。— My father works for a government office.
10 | 0.95

4436 三百円 sanbyaku en *n.* three hundred yen
- 入館料は一人三百円です。— The entrance fee is three hundred yen per person.
10 | 0.56

4437 チラシ chirashi *n.* flyer, leaflet, handout
- 先生は学園祭のチラシを配った。— The teacher handed out the school festival leaflets.
10 | 0.93

4438 成人(する) seijin(suru) *n.* adult *v.* come of age
- 日本では二十歳で成人となります。— People come of age when they are twenty years old in Japan.
10 | 0.95

4439 工具 kougu *n.* tool
- 工具は安全なところに保管してください。— Please keep tools in a safe place.
10 | 0.62

4440 先週 senshuu *n.* last week
- 先週から風邪でずっと寝込んでいます。— I caught a cold last week and have been in bed ever since.
10 | 0.57

4441 境 sakai *n.* boundary, border
- この道路が両国の境になっています。— This road forms the border between the two countries.
10 | 0.96

4442 国語 kokugo *n.* Japanese language
- 彼女は国語の先生です。— She is a teacher of Japanese.
10 | 0.95

4443 三十人 sanjuu-nin *n.* thirty people
- 私のクラスに三十人の学生が登録した。— There are thirty students registered in my class.
10 | 0.47

4444 兵士 heishi *n.* soldier
- 兵士は敵に銃を向けた。— The soldier aimed his gun at the enemy.
10 | 0.80

4445 芸能人 geinou-jin *n.* entertainer
- 街で芸能人にあったことがありますか。— Have you ever met an entertainer in the streets?
10 | 0.72

4446 こんにちは konnichiwa *interj.* Hello, Good afternoon
- 小さい子が私に「こんにちは」と言った。— The little child said hello to me.
10 | 0.73

4447 ふっと futto *adv.* suddenly
- 彼がふっと現れたのでびっくりした。— I was surprised that he suddenly appeared.
10 | 0.76

4448 日付 hizuke *n.* date, day
- 彼の出国の時間と日付けを教えてください。— Please tell me the time and date of his departure from the country.
10 | 0.92

4449 相違 soui *n.* difference, disagreement
- 私達の間に意見の相違があるようだ。— There seems to be some disagreement between us.
10 | 0.75

4450 決定的 kettei-teki *na-adj.* definitive, absolute
- 被告に有利な決定的証拠がない。— There is no conclusive evidence in favor of the defendant.
10 | 0.88

4451 無意識 mu-ishiki *n.* unconsciousness *na-adj.* unconscious
- 私達は無意識に人を傷つけることがある。— We sometimes hurt other people's feelings unconsciously.
10 | 0.84

4452 友人達 yuujin-tachi *n.* friends
- 友人達とおしゃべりを楽しんだ。— I enjoyed chatting with my friends.
10 | 0.85

4453 債務者 saimu-sha *n.* debtor
- 支払い能力のない債務者にはお金を貸さない。— We won't lend money to an insolvent debtor.
10 | 0.74

4454 四ヶ月 yon kagetsu *n.* four months
- 日本へ来て四ヶ月が経った。— It is four months since I came to Japan.
10 | 0.85

4455 始末(する) shimatsu(suru) *n.* disposal, circumstances *v.* manage, deal with, dispose of
- ゴミの始末をお願いします。— Please dispose of rubbish.
10 | 0.90

4456 合間 aima *n.* interval, pause, spare moment
- 合間にこの仕事をやっておいてください。— Please get this work done when you have some spare time.
10 | 0.87

4457 副作用 fuku-sayou *n.* side effect
- この薬に副作用はありません。— This medicine has no side effects.
10 | 0.93

4458 成分 seibun *n.* ingredient, constituent, component
- 血液の成分は何ですか。— What are the constituents of blood?
10 | 0.97

4459 初 hatsu *n.* first
- 彼女はパイロットになった初の女性です。— She was the first woman to become a pilot.
10 | 0.83

4460 ドライバー doraibaa *n.* driver
- ドライバーは交通規則を守らなければならない。— Every driver must keep to the traffic rules.
10 | 0.82

4461 渋滞(する) juutai(suru) *n.* traffic jam, delay *v.* be delayed
- 私は渋滞に巻き込まれてイベントに遅れた。— I was late for the event because I got caught up in a traffic jam.
10 | 0.89

4462 遠慮(する) enryo(suru) *n.* reserve *v.* hesitate
- 何かあったら遠慮せずに電話してください。— Don't hesitate to call me if you have any problems.
10 | 0.90

4463 印 shirushi *n.* mark, tick, check
- 次の質問を読んで正しいものに印をつけなさい。— Read the following questions and mark the correct answers.
10 | 0.90

4464 今週 konshuu *n.* this week
- 今週はずっと雨が降るでしょう。— It will be raining all this week.
10 | 0.51

4465 慰める nagusameru *v.* console, comfort
- 試験に落ちたことに対して彼を慰めた。— I consoled him about failing the exam.
10 | 0.81

4466 一方的 ippou-teki *na-adj.* unilateral, one-sided
- 彼とけんかして一方的に電話を切られた。— I had a quarrel with him and he hung up on me.
10 | 0.96

4467 開設(する) kaisetsu(suru) *n.* establishment *v.* establish, set up
- この研究所は去年開設された。— This research institute was established last year.
10 | 0.76

4468 アニメ anime *n.* animation
- あのアニメが映画化されると聞いた。— I heard that animation will be made into a movie.
10 | 0.65

4469 さっさと sassato *adv.* quickly
- 母が私に「さっさと宿題をしなさい」と言った。— My mother said to me, "Do your homework quickly".
10 | 0.85

4470 勢力 seiryoku *n.* power, influence, strength
- 彼はテレビ業界での勢力が大きい。— He has great influence in the TV industry.
10 | 0.88

4471 梅 ume *n.* plum, Japanese apricot
- 梅の花が咲く季節がやってきます。— Plum blossom season is coming.
10 | 0.88

4472 霊 rei *n.* spirit, soul
- 死者の霊を慰めるために手を合わせた。— I put my hands together to appease the souls of the dead.
10 | 0.82

4473 予感(する) yokan(suru) *n.* presentiment, foreboding, hunch *v.* have a presentiment/foreboding/hunch
- 私は何か悪いことが起こる予感がした。— I had a presentiment that something bad would happen.
10 | 0.84

4474 学者 gakusha *n.* scholar
- 彼は偉大な学者だ。— He is a great scholar.
10 | 0.83

4475 車椅子 kuruma isu *n.* wheelchair
- おじいさんを車いすに乗せて押した。— I pushed my grandfather in a wheelchair.
10 | 0.96

4476 月曜日 getsuyou bi *n.* Monday
- 月曜日はいつも憂鬱です。— I always feel blue on Mondays.
10 | 0.84

4477 北京 pekin *n.* Beijing
- 2008年に北京でオリンピックが開催された。— The Olympic Games took place in Beijing in 2008.
10 | 0.90

4478 論理 ronri *n.* logic
- ディベートで彼は論理で攻めてきた。— He used logic to pursue his argument in the debate.
10 | 0.77

4479 見込む mikomu *v.* expect, trust
- この天候で電車が遅れるだろうと見込んでいる。— I expect the train will be late because of this weather.
10 | 0.74

4480 四十分 yonjup-pun, yonjip-pun *n.* forty minutes
- 家から大学まで電車で四十分かかる。— It takes forty minutes by train from my home to the university.
10 | 0.90

4481 歩道 hodou *n.* sidewalk, pavement
- 歩道にお金が落ちていた。— I found a coin on the sidewalk.
10 | 0.98

4482 二千 nisen *num.* two thousand
- 二千を超えるファンが空港に集まった。— More than two thousand fans gathered at the airport.
10 | 0.89

4483 政治的 seiji-teki *na-adj.* political
- 彼はテレビでその議論の政治的な解決を説明した。— He explained the political resolution of the dispute on TV.
10 | 0.86

4484 九年 kyuu nen *n.* nine years
- 日本の義務教育は九年だ。— Compulsory education in Japan lasts for nine years.
10 | 0.72

4485 欠く kaku *v.* lack; chip
- 彼の態度は礼儀を欠く行為だ。— His behavior is an act devoid of courtesy.
10 | 0.87

4486 報告書 houkoku-sho *n.* report
- 彼は報告書のデータを集めるのに忙しかった。— He was busy collecting data for his report.
10 | 0.65

4487 近づける chikazukeru *v.* bring close
- 本を目に近づけて読まない方がいい。— You should not hold the book close to your eyes when reading.
10 | 0.96

4488 壺 tsubo *n.* pot, vase
- 彼はとても値打ちのある壺を飾っていた。— He had on display a very valuable vase.
10 | 0.85

4489 講座 kouza *n.* course, lecture
- 私は書道の講座を取っています。— I'm taking the calligraphy course.
10 | 0.54

4490 レシピ reshipi *n.* recipe
- 母から祖母秘伝のレシピを教えてもらった。— I was taught my grandmother's special recipes by my mum.
10 | 0.71

4491 行列（する） gyouretsu(suru) *n.* procession, line, parade *v.* line up, queue
- 駅に切符を買う長い行列ができていた。— A long line of people buying tickets had formed at the station.
10 | 0.89

4492 計上（する） keijou(suru) *n.* appropriation *v.* appropriate
- 震災のための予算が計上された。— The budget was appropriated for the earthquake disaster.
10 | 0.59

4493 受診（する） jushin(suru) *n.* (medical) consultation *v.* consult, have a medical examination
- 午前中に健康診断を受診するつもりだ。— I'm going to have a medical examination in the morning.
10 | 0.51

4494 指揮（する） shiki(suru) *n.* direction, command *v.* conduct, direct
- 彼は巨大プロジェクトを指揮した。— He directed a huge project.
10 | 0.95

4495 保管（する） hokan(suru) *n.* keeping, storage *v.* keep
- パスポートは安全なところに保管しています。— I keep my passport in a safe place.
10 | 0.92

4496 パートナー paatonaa *n.* partner
- 私はテニスで彼女とパートナーを組んだ。— I had her as my partner in a tennis match.
10 | 0.96

4497 発足（する） hossoku(suru) *n.* start *v.* start
- 新しい言語学会が十月から発足する。— The new Linguistic Society will be launched in October.
10 | 0.78

4498 火事 kaji *n.* fire
- 町は火事で全焼した。— The whole town was destroyed by a fire.
10 | 0.91

4499 中世 chuusei *n.* Middle Ages, medieval
- 教会には中世のヨーロッパの生活を描いた絵が掛けられている。— A picture depicting life in medieval Europe hangs in the church.
10 | 0.81

4500 考察(する) kousatsu(suru) n. consideration, examination v. consider, examine
- この論文は研究の動機について考察されていない。— The research motives are not examined in this paper.
10 | 0.73

4501 祝い iwai n. celebration
- 母の八十歳のお祝いをした。— We had a celebration for our mother's eightieth birthday.
10 | 0.83

4502 儲ける moukeru v. profit, earn, gain
- 彼女は株で百万円儲けた。— She made one million yen on the stock market.
10 | 0.96

4503 指差す yubisasu v. point
- 彼は自分の家を指差した。— He pointed at his own house.
10 | 0.59

4504 認可(する) kyoka(suru) n. permission, approval v. permit, approve
- 許可なしでこの教室は使用できない。— No one is to use this classroom without permission.
10 | 0.32

4505 劣る otoru v. be inferior
- 彼の演技は姉のよりも劣っていた。— His performance was inferior to that of his sister.
10 | 0.94

4506 ぶつける butsukeru v. hit; throw
- 彼は車を塀にぶつけてしまった。— He hit his car on the fence.
10 | 0.90

4507 条約 jouyaku n. treaty, agreement
- 我が国は隣国と条約を結んだ。— Our country concluded a treaty with the neighboring country.
10 | 0.54

4508 像 zou n. figure, statue
- 自由の女神の像までフェリーで行った。— I went to the Statue of Liberty by ferry.
10 | 0.89

4509 マッチ(する) matchi(suru) n., v. match
- 客の条件にマッチしたアパートを見つけた。— I found an apartment that matched the client's requirements.
10 | 0.92

4510 二千円 nisen en n. two thousand yen
- 私は友人に二千円貸した。— I lent my friend two thousand yen.
10 | 0.54

4511 キャベツ kyabetsu n. cabbage
- サラダを作るためにキャベツを千切りにした。— I shredded cabbage to make salad.
10 | 0.92

4512 デザート dezaato n. dessert
- 食事の最後に素晴らしいデザートが出た。— A fine dessert was served after the meal.
10 | 0.81

4513 議員 giin n. member of Diet/Congress/Parliament
- 彼は大阪から議員に立候補した。— He stood for the Diet from Osaka.
10 | 0.88

4514 審議(する) shingi(suru) n. discussion, deliberation v. discuss, deliberate
- その事件は来週裁判で審議される。— The case will come up for discussion at the trial next week.
10 | 0.45

4515 涼しい suzushii i-adj. cool
- だんだん涼しくなってきた。— It's gradually getting cooler.
10 | 0.83

4516 性 sei n. sex, gender
- この会社では性による差異がある。— There is gender differentiation in this company.
10 | 0.83

4517 仕草 shigusa n. behavior, gesture
- 私は彼の落ち着かない仕草が好きじゃない。— I don't like his impatient gestures.
10 | 0.85

4518 マスター(する) masutaa(suru) n., v. master
- 中国語の発音をマスターするのは難しい。— Chinese pronunciation is difficult to master.
10 | 0.88

4519 泡 awa n. bubble, foam
- ビールの泡がグラスから溢れた。— The foam on the beer overflowed from the glass.
10 | 0.91

4520 年配 nenpai n. elderly person
- 年配の男性がオフィスにやってきた。— An elderly man turned up at the office.
10 | 0.80

4521 万が一 mangaichi adv. just in case
- 万が一の場合は電話ください。— In case of an emergency, please call me.
10 | 0.96

4522 挙げ句 ageku n. in the end, finally
- 彼は刑務所から逃亡した挙げ句捕まった。— In the end he was arrested after escaping from jail.
10 | 0.89

4523 つなげる tsunageru *v.* connect, tie
- あのアパートはインターネットにつなげるか確かめた。— I checked whether it is possible to connect to the Internet from that apartment.
10 | 0.90

4524 弟子 deshi *n.* pupil, disciple
- 踊りの先生は去年弟子を取った。— The dance teacher took pupils last year.
10 | 0.80

4525 分解(する) bunkai(suru) *n.* analysis *v.* resolve, dismantle, take apart, analyze
- 彼は時計を分解した。— He took the watch apart.
10 | 0.96

4526 一発 ip-patsu *n.* shot, punch
- 右頬に一発パンチをくらった。— I got a punch on the right cheek.
10 | 0.87

4527 ささやく sasayaku *v.* whisper
- 彼女は彼の耳元でささやいた。— She whispered in her boyfriend's ear.
10 | 0.70

4528 調達(する) choutatsu(suru) *n.* supply, procurement *v.* supply, procure
- 当時は食料の調達が難しかった。— It was hard to procure food in those days.
10 | 0.90

4529 二十六 nijuu roku *num.* twenty-six
- アルファベットは二十六文字ある。— There are twenty-six letters in the alphabet.
10 | 0.78

4530 制服 seifuku *n.* uniform
- 私達の学校では制服を着ます。— We wear uniforms at our school.
10 | 0.98

4531 オーブン oobun *n.* oven
- オーブンでケーキを焼いた。— I baked a cake in the oven.
10 | 0.85

4532 パンフレット panfuretto *n.* brochure
- 旅行のパンフレットに目を通した。— I looked through the travel brochures.
10 | 0.97

4533 賞 shou *n.* prize, award
- 彼女はこの小説で賞をもらった。— She received the prize for this novel.
10 | 0.80

4534 白人 hakujin *n.* Caucasian, 'white person'
- 彼は白人の男性と結婚した。— She married a white man.
10 | 0.86

4535 いささか isasaka *adv.* a little, slightly, rather
- 祖父はいささか気難しい。— My grandfather is rather hard to please.
10 | 0.75

4536 先頭 sentou *n.* head, lead
- 私は列の先頭に立った。— I was in the lead.
10 | 0.93

4537 真っ黒 makkuro *na-adj.* black
- トーストを真っ黒に焦がした。— I burned the toast black.
10 | 0.87

4538 すっと sutto *adv.* quickly; quietly; straight
- 彼女はすっと立ち教室から出て行った。— She stood straight up and went out of the classroom.
10 | 0.71

4539 公共 koukyou *n.* public, common
- 公共の場はきれいにしておきましょう。— Let's keep public places clean.
10 | 0.94

4540 貴族 kizoku *n.* noble, nobility, aristocracy
- 彼は貴族として生まれた。— He was nobly born.
10 | 0.88

4541 散る chiru *v.* fall, drop
- 秋が終わり木の葉が散ってしまった。— Autumn ended and the leaves fell from the trees.
10 | 0.90

4542 路地 roji *n.* alley, lane
- 野良猫が路地をうろついている。— Feral cats prowl around the alleys.
10 | 0.79

4543 緑色 midoriiro *n.* green
- 父は塀を緑色に塗った。— My father painted the fence green.
10 | 0.95

4544 逃げ出す nigedasu *v.* run away
- もし英語で話しかけられたら逃げ出すかもしれない。— If someone suddenly spoke to me in English, I might run away.
10 | 0.78

4545 繁栄(する) han'ei(suru) *n.* prosperity *v.* prosper, flourish
- 町は貿易の中心として繁栄した。— The town flourished as a trading center.
10 | 0.90

4546 銃 juu *n.* gun
- 彼は強盗犯に銃を向けた。— He pointed his gun at the robber.
10 | 0.79

4547 今後とも kongo-tomo *adv.* from now on, in the future
- 今後ともよろしくお願いします。— We look forward to working with you in the future.
10 | 0.42

4548 担ぐ katsugu *v.* carry, shoulder
- リュックサックを担いで山に登った。— I shouldered a rucksack and climbed the mountain.
10 | 0.85

4549 撒く maku *v.* scatter, water
- 花壇に水を撒いた。— I watered the flowerbed.
10 | 0.95

4550 合理的 gouri-teki *na-adj.* reasonable, rational
- 合理的に説明をしないとわかりません。— I don't understand if you don't explain rationally.
10 | 0.69

4551 果て hate *n.* the end
- 世界の果てまで彼について行くと決めた。— I resolved to follow him to the ends of the earth.
10 | 0.87

4552 霧 kiri *n.* fog
- ロンドンは濃い霧が一面に立ちこめていた。— London was completely shrouded in thick fog.
10 | 0.87

4553 主催（する）shusai(suru) *n.* promotion, organizing *v.* host, promote, organize
- このパーティーは学生が主催した。— This party was organized by the students.
10 | 0.71

4554 選択肢 sentaku-shi *n.* choices, alternatives
- 学生はいくつかの選択肢の中から授業が選べます。— The student can choose the lessons from several alternatives.
10 | 0.98

4555 密接 missetsu *na-adj.* close
- 両国の関係はますます密接になった。— The two countries have grown increasingly close.
10 | 0.73

4556 煮込む nikomu *v.* stew
- 肉と野菜を煮込んでスープを作った。— I made a soup by stewing the meat and vegetables.
10 | 0.88

4557 表 omote *n.* front; outside, surface
- 表で遊ぶときは注意しなさい。— Be careful when you play outside.
10 | 0.66

4558 錯覚（する）sakkaku(suru) *n.* illusion, delusion, trick *v.* have the illusion/impression
- 目の錯覚で丸く見えた。— It looked round because of an optical illusion.
10 | 0.89

4559 乗り物 norimono *n.* vehicle; (amusement park) ride
- 目的地まで飛行機ではなく他の乗り物で行くことができますか。— Is it possible to get to the destination by some other means of transportation, rather than by airplane?
10 | 0.89

4560 スパゲッティー supagettii *n.* spaghetti
- ミートソースのスパゲッティーを作った。— I cooked spaghetti in a meat sauce.
10 | 0.12 | SP

4561 隣接（する）rinsetsu(suru) *n.* adjacent, adjoin, next to *v.* be adjacent, adjoin, be next to
- フランスはスペインに隣接している。— France is adjacent to Spain.
10 | 0.96

4562 二千三年 nisen san nen *n.* 2003 (year)
- 二千三年に大学を卒業した。— I graduated from university in 2003.
10 | 0.87

4563 ごまかす gomakasu *v.* cheat, deceive
- あの会社は税金をごまかした。— That company cheated on their taxes.
10 | 0.92

4564 テクニック tekunikku *n.* technique
- 彼女のピアノのテクニックは素晴らしい。— Her piano-playing technique is superb.
10 | 0.89

4565 ステップ suteppu *n.* step
- バスのステップを踏み外して恥ずかしかった。— I was embarrassed that I missed the step of the bus.
10 | 0.86

4566 任務 ninmu *n.* duty, task, mission, role
- 作業員は困難な任務を遂行しています。— The workers are carrying out a difficult task.
10 | 0.74

4567 小川 ogawa *n.* stream
- その小川はとても澄んでいる。— The stream is very clear.
10 | 0.95

4568 ロープ roopu *n.* rope
- 洗濯物をロープにかけて干した。— I hung out the washing on the line to dry.
10 | 0.87

4569 到達（する）toutatsu(suru) *n.* arrival *v.* reach
- 彼は去年エベレスト山頂に到達した。— He reached the top of Mt. Everest last year.
10 | 0.91

4570 イエス *iesu n.* yes; Jesus (Christ)
- 私はイエスと答えた。— I said yes.
10 | 0.81

4571 上海 *shanhai n.* Shanghai
- 上海は世界の大都市の一つです。— Shanghai is one of the largest cities in the world.
10 | 0.92

4572 顕著 *kencho na-adj.* conspicuous, remarkable
- 医学は顕著な進歩を遂げた。— Medical science made remarkable progress.
10 | 0.76

4573 生まれ育つ *umaresodatsu v.* be born and raised
- 彼の両親は日本人だがアメリカで生まれ育った。— His parents are Japanese, but he was born and raised in America.
10 | 0.79

4574 ファッション *fasshon n.* fashion
- これが今年の春の流行のファッションです。— This is the latest fashion this spring.
10 | 0.88

4575 緊張感 *kinchou kan n.* tension
- 試合前の緊張感がテレビから伝わった。— I felt the tension before the game from the TV.
10 | 0.92

4576 容器 *youki n.* container, vessel
- お昼の残り物は容器に入れましょう。— I'll put the leftovers from lunch in a container.
10 | 0.98

4577 サポート（する）*sapooto(suru) n.* support *v.* support
- 奥さんは旦那さんをいつもサポートしています。— The wife always supports her husband.
10 | 0.81

4578 転ぶ *korobu v.* fall, slip
- 雪が降っているので転ばないように気をつけてください。— It's snowing, so please watch out that you don't fall.
10 | 0.97

4579 まし *mashi na-adj.* better *n.* increase
- 貯金は少ないが、ないよりはましだ。— My savings are small, but it's better than nothing.
10 | 0.76

4580 東北 *touhoku n.* Northeast, Tohoku region
- 東北の沿岸に津波警報が出た。— A tsunami warning was issued for the Tohoku coast.
10 | 0.97

4581 亡くす *nakusu v.* lose
- 彼は十歳の時、父親を亡くした。— He lost his father when he was ten.
10 | 0.88

4582 サラダ *sarada n.* salad
- もう少しサラダはいかがですか。— Would you like some more salad?
10 | 0.81

4583 注意点 *chuui ten n.* important point
- 明日の試合の注意点を練習した。— I practiced the important points for tomorrow's game.
10 | 0.78

4584 DNA *diienuee n.* DNA, deoxyribonucleic acid
- 警察はDNAの検査の結果を待ちました。— The police were waiting for the results of the DNA tests.
10 | 0.90

4585 米軍 *beigun n.* US armed forces
- 彼は米軍から除隊した。— He was discharged from the US forces.
10 | 0.86

4586 デメリット *demeritto n.* disadvantage
- 田舎での生活はデメリットが多いと思う。— I think living in the countryside has many disadvantages.
10 | 0.89

4587 国道 *kokudou n.* national highway
- 国道沿いに大型スーパーが出店した。— Large supermarkets have opened along the national highways.
10 | 0.95

4588 浸透（する）*shintou(suru) n.* soaking, penetration *v.* soak, penetrate
- この服は水の浸透を妨げます。— These clothes prevent water penetration.
10 | 0.95

4589 合図（する）*aizu(suru) n.* signal, sign *v.* signal, sign
- 彼女は学生に手を上げろと合図した。— She signaled to the students to raise their hands.
10 | 0.85

4590 フェリー *ferii n.* ferry
- 毎朝フェリーで川を渡ります。— I cross the river by ferry every morning.
10 | 0.84

4591 貿易 *boueki n.* trade, commerce
- 日本は外国貿易に頼っている。— Japan depends on foreign trade.
10 | 0.52

4592 照明 *shoumei n.* lighting
- 暗い照明の中本を読まないでください。— Please don't read books in poor light.
10 | 0.91

23 o-/go- (Honorifics)

The items after "お好み焼き" have been re-classified into the headwords without "o-/go-", thus no frequency information is available.

(お〜)
お前 **omae** 109.138 you (colloquial)
おなか **onaka** 62.420 stomach, belly
おしゃれ **oshare** 25.795 fashionable, smart
お子さん **o-ko-san** 23.624 (someone else's) child
お宅 **otaku** 17.893 your house
お袋 **ofukuro** 13.977 mother
お好み焼き **okonomiyaki** 10.217 okonomiyaki (Japanese-style savoury pancake with vegetables, meat, seafood etc.)
お世話 **o-sewa** care, help
お米 **o-kome** rice
お寺 **o-tera** temple
お金 **o-kane** money
お店 **o-mise** store, shop
お母さん **o-kaa-san** mother, Mom
お話 **o-hanashi** talking, talk, story
お互い **o-tagai** each other
お父さん **o-tou-san** father, Dad
お友達 **o-tomodachi** friend
お客さん **o-kyaku-san** guest, customer, visitor
お酒 **o-sake** alcohol, sake; rice wine
お茶 **o-cha** tea
お婆ちゃん **o-baachan** grandma
お客様 **o-kyaku-sama** customer, client, guest
お菓子 **o-kashi** sweets, snack food
お風呂 **o-furo** bath
おうち **o-uchi** house
お祭り **o-matsuri** festival
お湯 **o-yu** hot water
お正月 **o-shougatsu** New Year
お爺ちゃん **o-jii-chan** grandfather
お年寄り **o-toshiyori** old people, senior citizen
お弁当 **o-bentou** boxed lunch
お昼 **o-hiru** noon, daytime
お医者さん **o-isha-san** doctor
お土産 **o-miyage** present, souvenir
お花 **o-hana** flower
お水 **o-mizu** water
お婆さん **o-baa-san** old lady, grandmother
お願い **o-negai** desire, please
お礼 **o-rei** thanks, reward
お部屋 **o-heya** room
お肉 **o-niku** meat
お尻 **o-shiri** hips
お墓 **o-haka** grave
おじいさん **o-jii-san** grandfather
お皿 **o-sara** dish, plate
お客 **o-kyaku** guest, visitor
お仕舞い **o-shimai** end, conclusion
お考え **o-kangae** opinion, thought, idea
お盆 **o-bon** Bon Festival, Obon
お姉ちゃん **o-nee-chan** elder sister
お城 **o-shiro** castle
お砂糖 **o-satou** sugar
お姉さん **o-nee-san** elder sister

(ご〜)
ご意見 **go-iken** opinion, view, idea
ご主人 **go-shujin** landlord, husband
ご飯 **gohan** rice, meal
ご指摘 **go-shiteki** indication
ご家族 **go-kazoku** family
ご両親 **go-ryoushin** parents
ご親戚 **go-shinseki** relatives
ご兄弟 **go-kyoudai** brothers
ご住所 **go-juusho** address
ご結婚 **go-kekkon** marriage
ご無理 **go-muri** force
ご心配 **go-shinpai** anxiety
ご苦労 **go-kurou** labour
ご紹介 **go-shoukai** introduction
ご案内 **go-annai** guidance
ご相談 **go-soudan** consultation
ご予算 **go-yosan** budget
ご職業 **go-shokugyou** occupation
ご質問 **go-shitsumon** question
ご利用 **go-riyou** usage
ご病気 **go-byouki** sickness, illness
ご報告 **go-houkoku** report

4593 招待（する）shoutai(suru) *n.* invitation *v.* invite
- 彼女の結婚式に招待された。— I was invited to her wedding ceremony.
10 | 0.93

4594 年々 nennen *adv.* year after year
- 年々仕事がきつくなる。— My work gets harder year after year.
10 | 0.79

4595 十一年 juu ichi nen *n.* eleven years
- 彼の逃亡生活は十一年に及んだ。— His life as a fugitive lasted eleven years.
10 | 0.69

4596 武士 bushi *n.* warrior, samurai
- 彼は武士のような魂の持ち主だ。— He has a spirit like a samurai warrior.
10 | 0.81

4597 そりゃ sorya *pron.* that is
- そりゃいい考えだね。— That's a good idea.
10 | 0.62

4598 対抗（する）taikou(suru) *n.* competition, rivalry *v.* oppose, rival
- 腕相撲で彼に対抗できる者はいない。— He has no rival in arm wrestling.
10 | 0.93

4599 者達 monotachi *n.* people
- そこに住んでいる者達は工事に反対した。— Those who live there were against the construction work.
10 | 0.56

4600 警察官 keisatsu-kan *n.* police officer
- 警察官は泥棒を逮捕した。— The policeman arrested the thief.
10 | 0.88

4601 丸める marumeru *v.* curl up, wad up
- 猫が体を丸めて眠っている。— A cat is sleeping curled into a ball.
10 | 0.89

4602 最新 saishin *n.* newest, latest
- これが最新の髪型です。— This is the latest hairstyle.
10 | 0.97

4603 他者 tasha *n.* another person, others
- 彼はいつも他者への心遣いを見せる。— He always shows consideration for others.
10 | 0.66

4604 挿入（する）sounyuu(suru) *n.* insertion *v.* insert
- ここにカードを挿入してください。— Please insert the card here.
10 | 0.76

4605 賢い kashikoi *i-adj.* wise, clever
- 彼女はとても美しくて賢い。— She is very beautiful and wise.
10 | 0.92

4606 腐る kusaru *v.* rot, decay, go off
- 果物は日に当たると腐りやすい。— Fruit rots easily in the sun.
10 | 0.89

4607 こだわり kodawari *n.* concern, obsession
- そんな重要じゃない細かいことにこだわりがありません。— I'm not concerned with such unimportant details.
10 | 0.78

4608 悲惨 hisan *na-adj.* miserable
- 彼は晩年悲惨な生活を送った。— He lived his life in misery in his later years.
10 | 0.96

4609 キリスト kirisuto *n.* Christ
- 彼女はキリストの精神を信じている。— She believes in the Christian spirit.
10 | 0.81

4610 辛さ tsura-sa *n.* pain
- 生きることの辛さをまだ知らないでしょう。— You don't know the pain of living yet.
10 | 0.84

4611 二三日 nisan nichi *n.* two or three days
- この論文を2,3日貸していただけますか。— May I borrow this essay for two or three days?
10 | 0.46

4612 講演 kouen *n.* lecture, talk
- 彼らは講演をじっくり聞いていた。— They were listening to the lecture attentively.
10 | 0.63

4613 誤る ayamaru *v.* make a mistake, be wrong
- 彼は仕事の選択を誤った。— He chose the wrong job.
10 | 0.92

4614 人権 jinken *n.* human rights
- 私は人権の侵害に反対だ。— I am against the violation of human rights.
10 | 0.84

4615 両側 ryougawa *n.* both sides
- 通りの両側にホテルがあります。— There are hotels on both sides of the street.
10 | 0.84

4616 餅 mochi *n.* rice cake
- お正月にお餅をついた。— I pounded steamed rice into cakes for New Year.
10 | 0.95

4617 鎌倉 kamakura *n.* Kamakura (place name)
- 鎌倉の有名な神社を観光した。— I went sightseeing at the famous shrine in Kamakura.
10 | 0.91

4618 運動会 undou kai *n.* sports meeting
- 私達は運動会のリレーで優勝した。— We won the relay at the sports meeting.
10 | 0.87

4619 州 shuu *n.* state
- ハワイは最後に合衆国の州となった。— Hawaii was the last state to join the Union.
10 | 0.93

4620 分離(する) bunri(suru) *n.* separation, detachment *v.* separate, detach
- ドレッシングの油は分離します。— The oil in dressing separates from the other ingredients.
10 | 0.87

4621 日常的 nichijou-teki *na-adj.* routine
- これは日常的に飲まれるお茶です。— This is a tea that is drunk routinely.
10 | 0.95

4622 掲示板 keiji-ban *n.* bulletin board, noticeboard
- 掲示板にアルバイトの募集を出した。— I put up a recruitment notice for a part time job on the bulletin board.
9 | 0.76

4623 住宅地 juutaku chi *n.* residential area
- 都会から離れた住宅地に住んでいる。— I live in a residential area outside of the city.
9 | 0.87

4624 亀 kame *n.* turtle, tortoise
- 亀が卵を産み、海に帰って行った。— The turtle laid her eggs and returned to the sea.
9 | 0.86

4625 四十代 yonjuu dai *n.* forties
- 夫は四十代半ばです。— My husband is in his mid-forties.
9 | 0.93

4626 メロディー merodii *n.* melody
- このメロディーは多くの日本人に親しまれている。— This melody is familiar to many Japanese.
9 | 0.77

4627 民衆 minshuu *n.* people, public
- 彼は通りの民衆に向かってスピーチをした。— He gave a speech to the people on the street.
9 | 0.79

4628 吉祥寺 kichijouji *n.* Kichijoji (place name)
- 吉祥寺には大きな池がある公園がある。— There is a park with a big pond in Kichijoji.
9 | 0.52

4629 貫く tsuranuku *v.* persist, stick to; pierce
- 息子は自分の考えを貫いた。— My son stuck to his opinion.
9 | 0.88

4630 新潟 niigata *n.* Niigata (place name)
- 新潟は豪雪地帯の一つです。— Niigata is the one of the areas with heavy snowfall.
9 | 0.94

4631 箇所 kasho *n.* place, point, part
- 間違った箇所を直さなければいけません。— I have to correct the parts that have mistakes.
9 | 0.90

4632 正解(する) seikai(suru) *n.* correct answer *v.* answer correctly
- この問題はほとんどの人が正解だった。— Most people got the correct answer for this question.
9 | 0.83

4633 悟る satoru *v.* realize
- 彼は自分が間違っていることを悟るでしょう。— He will realize that he is wrong.
9 | 0.78

4634 擦る suru *v.* rub, strike; lose
- 彼はマッチを擦った。— He struck a match.
9 | 0.90

4635 体育館 taiiku-kan, taik-kan *n.* gym
- 放課後体育館に集合してください。— Please assemble in the gym after school.
9 | 0.89

4636 再会(する) saikai(suru) *n.* reunion *v.* meet again
- 昔の先生と再会することを楽しみにしています。— I'm looking forward to seeing my old teacher again.
9 | 0.87

4637 儀式 gishiki *n.* ceremony, ritual
- 息子は生まれてすぐ洗礼の儀式をした。— My son was baptized as soon as he was born.
9 | 0.89

4638 いやあ iyaa *interj.* Well, sorry
- 「いやあ遅れてごめん」と彼は言った。— He said, "Oh, I'm sorry to be late."
9 | 0.48

4639 店舗 tenpo *n.* store, shop
- そのすし店は全国に店舗がある。— That sushi restaurant has outlets all over the country.
9 | 0.92

4640 捕われる torawareru *v.* be arrested, be captured, stick to
- 彼は詐欺をして捕われた。— He was arrested for fraud.
9 | 0.92

4641 日本一 nihon ichi *n.* most ... in Japan
- 富士山は日本一高い山です。— Mt. Fuji is the highest mountain in Japan.
9 | 0.88

4642 トンネル tonneru *n.* tunnel
- トンネルを通過すると海が見えてきます。— When you get through the tunnel, you can see the sea.
9 | 0.99

4643 一歳 is-sai *n.* one year old
- 娘の一歳の誕生日を盛大にお祝いした。— We celebrated our daughter's first birthday in grand style.
9 | 0.77

4644 暑さ atsu-sa *n.* heat
- 夏の暑さは嫌いだ。— I hate the heat of summer.
9 | 0.89

4645 ビタミン bitamin *n.* vitamin
- ビタミンの豊富な野菜を食べてください。— Please eat vegetables rich in vitamins.
9 | 0.82

4646 おめでとう o medetou *interj.* congratulations
- 「卒業おめでとう!」「ありがとう。」— "Congratulations on your graduation!" "Thank you."
9 | 0.70

4647 用途 youto *n.* use
- この道具は色々な用途がある。— This tool has many uses.
9 | 0.96

4648 進学(する) shingaku(suru) *n.* going on to the next level of education *v.* go on to the next level of education
- 大学に進学しないのですか。— Won't you go on to university?
9 | 0.98

4649 タイヤ taiya *n.* tire
- 自転車のタイヤに空気を入れた。— I pumped air into the bicycle tire.
9 | 0.78

4650 朝鮮 chousen *n.* Korea
- 朝鮮は南北に分かれている。— Korea is separated into North and South.
9 | 0.89

4651 三味線 shami-sen *n.* shamisen
- 私の弟は三味線を習っています。— My younger brother is learning the shamisen.
9 | 0.62

4652 保険会社 hoken gaisha *n.* insurance company
- 彼は保険会社にその事故を報告した。— He reported the accident to his insurance company.
9 | 0.90

4653 写す utsusu *v.* copy, trace
- 彼はいつも彼女の宿題を写します。— He always copies from her homework.
9 | 0.93

4654 チョコレート chokoreeto *n.* chocolate
- バレンタインに彼にチョコレートを渡した。— I gave him chocolates on Valentine's Day.
9 | 0.89

4655 走り回る hashirimawaru *v.* run around
- 子犬は毎日庭を走り回ります。— The puppy runs around in the garden every day.
9 | 0.89

4656 有力 yuuryoku *na-adj.* powerful, strong, important
- 犯人の有力な手がかりを見つけた。— I found an important clue to the criminal's identity.
9 | 0.94

4657 仕掛け shikake *n.* device, system
- このドアは自動で閉まる仕掛けになっている。— This door has a device so that it shuts automatically.
9 | 0.94

4658 ポスター posutaa *n.* poster
- 映画のポスターを壁に貼った。— I put the movie poster on the wall.
9 | 0.97

4659 杉 sugi *n.* Japanese cedar
- 日本では春に杉の花粉が飛びます。— Japanese cedar pollen is dispersed during spring in Japan.
9 | 0.96

4660 可愛らしい kawairashii *i-adj.* lovely
- 可愛らしい子がテレビでダンスを踊っている。— A lovely girl is dancing on TV.
9 | 0.87

4661 彫刻 choukoku *n.* sculpture, carving
- その美術館にはブロンズの彫刻がある。— There is a bronze sculpture in the museum.
9 | 0.92

4662 眠り nemuri *n.* sleep
- 昨夜は眠りが足りなかった。— I didn't get enough sleep last night.
9 | 0.83

4663 見込み mikomi *n.* hope, chance, expectation
- 彼はその試合に勝てる見込みがない。— He has no chance of winning the match.
9 | 0.87

4664 爽やか sawayaka *na-adj.* fresh, refreshing
- 早朝の爽やかな時にジョギングをしています。— I go jogging in the early morning when it's fresh.
9 | 0.77

4665 就任(する) shuunin(suru) *n.* assumption *v.* assume
- 彼はこの国の首相に就任した。— He assumed the premiership of this country.
9 | 0.85

4666 先端 sentan *n.* tip, point, forefront
- 彼女のファッションは時代の先端をいく。— Her fashions are at the cutting edge.
9 | 0.88

4667 装置（する）souchi(suru) *n.* device, equipment *v.* be equipped with
- 実験室には最新式のシステムが装置してある。— The laboratory is equipped with the latest system.
9 | 0.93

4668 伝説 densetsu *n.* legend, tradition
- 地方には古い伝説がたくさんある。— There are lots of old legends in the region.
9 | 0.83

4669 今頃 imagoro *n.* this time
- 桜は毎年今頃咲く。— The cherry trees bloom around this time of year.
9 | 0.85

4670 学部 gakubu *n.* faculty, department
- 私は学部の二年生です。— I'm a second year undergraduate student.
9 | 0.78

4671 水泳 suiei *n.* swimming
- 彼女は水泳が上手だ。— She is good at swimming.
9 | 0.89

4672 羽目 hame *n.* plight, predicament
- 彼は入院する羽目になった。— He ended up in the hospital.
9 | 0.89

4673 上京（する）joukyou(suru) *n.* coming/going to Tokyo *v.* come/go to Tokyo
- 弟は上京して大学で勉強しています。— My younger brother has come up to Tokyo and is studying at university.
9 | 0.87

4674 ビザ biza *n.* visa
- 今日ビザの申請をするつもりです。— I am going to apply for a visa today.
9 | 0.69

4675 将軍 shougun *n.* general, shogun
- 将軍は敵を攻撃するように命じた。— The general commanded them to attack the enemy.
9 | 0.78

4676 青少年 seishounen *n.* young people, juvenile
- 青少年の犯罪が急速に増加している。— Juvenile delinquency is increasing rapidly.
9 | 0.56

4677 肘 hiji *n.* elbow
- テーブルに肘をついて食べないでください。— Please don't eat with your elbows on the table.
9 | 0.90

4678 延々 en'en *adv.* on and on, dragging on
- その会議は延々五時間続いた。— The meeting went on and on for five hours.
9 | 0.85

4679 食器 shokki *n.* dish
- 食べた後食器を洗ってください。— Please wash the dishes after eating.
9 | 0.91

4680 引き付ける hikitsukeru *v.* attract
- そのお寺は世界中から観光客を引き付けています。— The temple attracts visitors from all over the world.
9 | 0.93

4681 深さ fuka-sa *n.* depth
- その湖の深さは5メートルです。— The lake is five meters deep.
9 | 0.95

4682 ～さん . . . san *suffix* Mr., Mrs., Miss., Ms.
- 田中さんをご紹介します。— May I introduce Mr. Tanaka?
9 | 0.65

4683 パスポート pasupooto *n.* passport
- パスポートを拝見いたします。— Could I please see your passport?
9 | 0.91

4684 ぼろぼろ boroboro *na-adj.* ragged, worn out *adv.* in drops
- 彼はぼろぼろのかばんを使っている。— He's using a worn-out bag.
9 | 0.85

4685 いつ頃 itsu goro *n.* around what time
- いつ頃お伺いすればよろしいですか。— Around what time should I come to your place?
9 | 0.91

4686 二重 ni juu *n.* double
- その箱は二重に包んであった。— The box was wrapped in a double layer of paper.
9 | 0.97

4687 埼玉 saitama *n.* Saitama
- 父は東京から埼玉まで通勤している。— My father commutes from Tokyo to Saitama.
9 | 0.89

4688 いたずら（する）itazura(suru) *n.* mischief, trick, joke *v.* be mischievous, play a trick
- 父は弟のいたずらを怒った。— My father got angry about my younger brother's mischief.
9 | 0.87

4689 受け付ける uketsukeru *v.* accept
- 願書は十一月から受け付けます。— Applications will be accepted from November.
9 | 0.59

4690 こねる koneru *v.* knead, squeeze, work
- 子供が粘土をこねて遊んでいた。— A child was enjoying kneading the clay.
9 | 0.81

4691 這う hau *v.* creep, crawl
- 毛虫が壁を這っています。— A caterpillar is crawling along the wall.
9 | 0.82

4692 ふらふら（する）furafura(suru) *adv.* aimlessly, unsteadily *na-adj.* unsteady on one's feet *v.* stagger, be dizzy
- ふらふら散歩しているうちに道に迷ってしまった。— I got lost as I walked aimlessly.
9 | 0.80

4693 捧げる sasageru *v.* offer, dedicate, sacrifice
- 彼は国のために命を捧げた。— He sacrificed his life for his country.
9 | 0.82

4694 居酒屋 izakaya *n.* (Japanese style) bar, tavern
- 私達は居酒屋で彼の送別会をした。— We had a farewell party for him at a bar.
9 | 0.85

4695 見下ろす miorosu *v.* look down, overlook
- ホテルから町を見下ろすことができます。— The hotel overlooks the town.
9 | 0.74

4696 一貫 ikkan *n.* consistency
- 彼女の考えは一貫している。— She is consistent in her opinions.
9 | 0.74

4697 文献 bunken *n.* literature
- 日本語に関する文献を調べた。— I referred to the literature on Japanese language.
9 | 0.80

4698 やがる yagaru *aux.* VERB SUFFIX (vulgarism)
- 彼は馬鹿なことを言いやがる。— He says stupid things.
9 | 0.60

4699 ワープロ waapuro *n.* word processor
- ワープロで原稿を書いています。— I'm typing a manuscript on a word processor.
9 | 0.83

4700 象 zou *n.* elephant
- 象は鼻が長い。— An elephant has a long trunk.
9 | 0.90

4701 共感（する）kyoukan(suru) *n.* sympathy *v.* sympathize
- 彼のスピーチは聴衆の共感を得た。— His speech got the audience's sympathy.
9 | 0.96

4702 ズボン zubon *n.* pants, trousers
- 今日は寒いのでズボンを履いた。— It's cold today, so I put trousers on.
9 | 0.84

4703 迅速 jinsoku *na-adj.* quick, swift
- 彼はお客様のクレームに対して迅速に対応した。— He dealt promptly with the customer's complaint.
9 | 0.60

4704 豆腐 toufu *n.* tofu, bean curd
- 豆腐は体にいいので毎日食べています。— Tofu is good for your health, so I'm eating it every day.
9 | 0.80

4705 司会（する）shikai(suru) *n.* host, emcee *v.* host, emcee, take the chair
- 彼はそのテレビのショーの司会を何年もした。— He emceed that TV show for years.
9 | 0.84

4706 幸運 kouun *n.* (good) luck, fortune *na-adj.* lucky, fortunate
- 彼女の幸運を祈っています。— I wish her good luck.
9 | 0.83

4707 緩和（する）kanwa(suru) *n.* relaxation, relief *v.* relieve
- その薬を飲めば痛みが緩和します。— If you take the medicine, you will get relief from the pain.
9 | 0.73

4708 鉄板 teppan *n.* hot plate, iron plate
- 鉄板でステーキや野菜を焼いた。— I cooked steak and vegetables on a hot plate.
9 | 0.76

4709 明ける akeru *v.* begin, dawn, break
- もうすぐ夜が明けます。— Day will break soon.
9 | 0.89

4710 反論（する）hanron(suru) *n.* argument, objection *v.* argue, object
- 彼の意見に反論する人はいなかった。— Nobody objected to his opinion.
9 | 0.94

4711 引っ繰り返す hikkurikaesu *v.* overturn, upset, turn over
- 私は茶碗を引っ繰り返してしまった。— I upset the rice bowl.
9 | 0.86

4712 儲かる moukaru *v.* profit, gain
- この商売は儲からない。— This business isn't profitable.
9 | 0.94

4713 久々 hisabisa *n., adv.* for the first time in a long time
- 久々に家でゆっくり過ごした。— I had a relaxed day at home for the first time in ages.

9 | 0.43

4714 効力 kouryoku *n.* effect
- その薬はすぐ効力があった。— The medicine had an immediate effect.

9 | 0.49

4715 枯れる kareru *v.* wither, die
- 雨不足で植物が枯れた。— The plants died for lack of rain.

9 | 0.96

4716 絆 kizuna *n.* tie, bond
- 彼らには友情の絆があった。— There was a bond of friendship between them.

9 | 0.91

4717 相性 aishou *n.* compatibility
- あの夫婦の性格はお互い相性がいい。— That couple's characters are compatible.

9 | 0.78

4718 三分 san pun *n.* three minutes
- カップにお湯を注いだ後、食べるまで三分待ってください。— After pouring the boiling water into the cup, please wait three minutes before eating.

9 | 0.92

4719 砂浜 sunahama *n.* beach, sand
- 子供達が砂浜で遊んでいます。— Children are playing in the sand.

9 | 0.86

4720 責める semeru *v.* accuse, blame
- 彼は彼女の不注意を責めた。— He blamed her carelessness.

9 | 0.88

4721 参加費 sanka-hi *n.* participation fee
- 遠足の参加費はいくらですか。— How much is the participation fee for the excursion?

9 | 0.04 | NM

4722 井戸 ido *n.* well
- 井戸の水を汲んできてください。— Please come to draw water from the well.

9 | 0.89

4723 五十代 gojuu dai *n.* fifties
- 彼女は五十代に見える。— She looks to be in her fifties.

9 | 0.86

4724 債務 saimu *n.* debt, obligation
- 彼は債務を返済する義務があります。— He has an obligation to pay back his debts.

9 | 0.70

4725 寄与（する）kiyo(suru) *n.* contribution *v.* contribute
- 彼は文化の発展に大いに寄与した。— He made a large contribution to cultural development.

9 | 0.49

4726 社宅 shataku *n.* company housing
- 私達家族は社宅に住んでいます。— Our family is living in a company house.

9 | 0.67

4727 下記 kaki *n.* the following, mentioned below
- 下記の質問に答えなさい。— Answer the following questions.

9 | 0.68

4728 委員長 iin-chou *n.* chairperson
- 彼女は委員会の委員長に任命された。— She was named chairperson of the committee.

9 | 0.30

4729 槍 yari *n.* spear
- 槍を使ってイノシシを狩った。— I hunted wild boar with spears.

9 | 0.80

4730 くわえる kuwaeru *v.* take, hold
- 彼はタバコをくわえながら新聞を読んでいた。— He was holding a cigarette and reading a newspaper.

9 | 0.80

4731 店員 ten'in *n.* clerk, sales assistant
- その店員が贈物を包んでくれた。— The salesman wrapped the gift for me.

9 | 0.84

4732 秩序 chitsujo *n.* order, system
- クラスの秩序を乱さないでください。— Please don't disrupt the class.

9 | 0.74

4733 散々 sanzan *adv.* severely, repeatedly
- 私は遅く帰ってきて親に散々叱られた。— I came home late and was scolded severely by my parents.

9 | 0.90

4734 刺し身 sashimi *n.* sashimi
- 私の好きな日本食は刺し身です。— My favorite Japanese food is sashimi.

9 | 0.87

4735 おかず okazu *n.* food, side dish
- おかずばかりでなくご飯も食べなさい。— Eat the rice, not just the side dishes.

9 | 0.87

4736 豚肉 butaniku *n.* pork
- 豚肉より鶏肉が好きです。— I like chicken better than pork.

9 | 0.93

4737 兵 hei *n.* soldier, troops
- アメリカは海外へ兵を送った。— America sent troops overseas.
9 | 0.61

4738 部長 buchou *n.* head of department, manager
- 部長は今席を外しております。— The manager has stepped out for a moment.
9 | 0.98

4739 サミット samitto *n.* summit
- 世界中がサミットに注目しています。— The whole world is focusing its attention on the summit conference.
9 | 0.77

4740 三十歳 sanjus-sai *n.* thirty years old
- 彼女は三十歳になって初めて絵を描き始めた。— Not until she was thirty did she start to paint.
9 | 0.90

4741 二倍 ni bai *n.* twice, double
- 私の収入は去年の二倍です。— My income is double what it was last year.
9 | 0.98

4742 ベンチ benchi *n.* bench
- 彼は酔って公園のベンチで寝てしまった。— He got drunk and slept on a bench in the park.
9 | 0.87

4743 補う oginau *v.* supplement, compensate
- ダイエットにはビタミンを補うほうがいい。— You should supplement your diet with vitamins.
9 | 0.95

4744 投入（する）tounyuu(suru) *n.* investment *v.* throw, invest
- 失点のために新しい投手が投入された。— A new pitcher was brought in because the previous one gave away points to the opposing team.
9 | 0.92

4745 争い arasoi *n.* fight, struggle, competition
- 二国間は経済問題で争いがあった。— The two nations fought over economic issues.
9 | 0.94

4746 センス sensu *n.* sense
- 彼は笑いのセンスがある。— He has a sense of humor.
9 | 0.85

4747 ハード haado *na-adj.* hard, tight
- 明日からの出張はハードな日程だ。— The business trip from tomorrow will be a tight schedule.
9 | 0.83

4748 見逃す minogasu *v.* miss, overlook
- 今回の失敗は見逃してください。— Please overlook my mistake this time.
9 | 0.94

4749 線路 senro *n.* track, railroad
- 線路に入るな。— Keep off the tracks.
9 | 0.94

4750 四年間 yo nenkan *n.* four years
- 大学で四年間医学の勉強をした。— I studied medicine for four years at university.
9 | 0.19 | SP

4751 リンク（する）rinku(suru) *n., v.* link
- このウェブページは自由にリンクしていいですよ。— You may link to this webpage freely.
9 | 0.81

4752 大蔵省 ookura-shou *n.* Ministry of Finance
- 大蔵省がこの国の財産を管理している。— The Ministry of Finance manages national assets.
9 | 0.26

4753 製作（する）seisaku(suru) *n.* production *v.* manufacture
- この工場では自動車の部品を製作しています。— This factory manufactures automobile parts.
9 | 0.85

4754 世帯 setai *n.* household, family
- このマンションには二十世帯が住んでいる。— There are twenty families living in this apartment building.
9 | 0.57

4755 覗き込む nozokikomu *v.* look into
- 歯医者は患者の口の中を覗き込んだ。— The dentist looked into the patient's mouth.
9 | 0.66

4756 区分（する）kubun(suru) *n.* division, classification *v.* separate
- 郵便物を地域別に区分しなければならない。— I must separate the mail according to region.
9 | 0.62

4757 放棄（する）houki(suru) *n.* abandonment, renunciation *v.* abandon, renounce
- 彼は相続財産を放棄することに同意した。— He agreed to renounce his inheritance.
9 | 0.91

4758 転職（する）tenshoku(suru) *n.* change of job *v.* change job
- 彼は転職後、収入が増えた。— His income increased after he changed his job.
9 | 0.89

4759 類い tagui *n.* kind, sort, type
- その生き物は魚の類いだと思われている。— The creature seems to be a kind of fish.
9 | 0.91

4760 活気 kakki *n.* vigor, energy, liveliness
- この町はとても活気がある。— This town is very lively.
9 | 0.88

4761 日差し hizashi *n.* sunshine
- 強い日差しのためサングラスをかけなければならない。— You must wear sunglasses because of the strong sunlight.
9 | 0.90

4762 人格 jinkaku *n.* character, personality
- 彼女は彼の温和な人格に惹かれた。— She was attracted to his gentle character.
9 | 0.90

4763 避難(する) hinan(suru) *n.* evacuation *v.* evacuate
- 地震の後、安全な場所に避難してください。— After an earthquake, please evacuate to a place of safety.
9 | 0.92

4764 ラスベガス rasubegasu *n.* Las Vegas
- 彼はラスベガスで終日カジノを楽しんだ。— He enjoyed the casinos in Las Vegas all day long.
9 | 0.45

4765 鐘 kane *n.* bell, chime
- 教会で結婚式の鐘が鳴っています。— Wedding bells are ringing at the church.
9 | 0.85

4766 若者達 wakamono-tachi *n.* young people
- 多くの若者達がボランティア活動に参加しています。— Many young people are involved in volunteer work.
9 | 0.84

4767 集まり atsumari *n.* meeting, gathering, group
- 趣味の集まりに参加した。— I joined a hobby group.
9 | 0.97

4768 変換(する) henkan(suru) *n.* change, conversion *v.* convert
- 仮名を漢字に変換した。— I converted kana characters into kanji characters.
9 | 0.85

4769 歓迎(する) kangei(suru) *n.* reception, welcome *v.* welcome
- 私達は彼の家族から暖かい歓迎を受けた。— We received a warm welcome from his family.
9 | 0.95

4770 川崎 kawasaki *n.* Kawasaki
- 川崎には工場が多い。— There are a lot of factories in Kawasaki.
9 | 0.92

4771 支出 shishutsu *n.* expenses, payment, expenditure, spending
- 彼は年末の支出を計算した。— He calculated the expenses at the end of the year.
9 | 0.71

4772 軸 jiku *n.* axis; shaft; stem
- 地球は軸を中心に回転します。— The earth rotates on its axis.
9 | 0.95

4773 食物 shokumotsu *n.* food, dish
- 塩分の多い食物は避けましょう。— Try to avoid eating salty food!
9 | 0.84

4774 損害 songai *n.* damage, loss
- 火事で我が家は大きな損害を受けた。— The fire caused great damage to our house.
9 | 0.76

4775 のみならず nomi nara zu *p.* not only ... but, as well as
- 彼は日本のみならず、海外でも有名な学者だ。— He is a famous scholar not only in Japan, but also abroad.
9 | 0.70

4776 正義 seigi *n.* justice, right
- 裁判で正義のために戦う。— I fight for justice in court.
9 | 0.88

4777 一目 hitome *n.* glance
- 私は一目で彼女だとわかった。— I recognized her at first glance.
9 | 0.93

4778 百年 hyaku nen *n.* hundred years, century
- この建物は百年前に建てられた。— This building was built a hundred years ago.
9 | 0.98

4779 ガイド(する) gaido(suru) *n.* guide, conductor *v.* guide
- ガイドが私達を博物館へ案内してくれた。— The guide led us to the museum.
9 | 0.82

4780 大型 oogata *n.* big, large
- 大型の台風が日本に接近しています。— A large-scale typhoon is approaching Japan.
9 | 0.91

4781 頂上 choujou *n.* top, summit
- 山の頂上まで登った。— I climbed to the top of the mountain.
9 | 0.84

4782 睡眠 suimin *n.* sleep
- 疲れているなら睡眠を十分取りなさい。— Please get plenty of sleep if you are tired.

9 | 0.92

4783 緩やか yuruyaka *na-adj.* gentle, soft, mild
- 私の家の前は緩やかな上り坂になっている。— There is a gentle uphill slope in front of my house.

9 | 0.77

4784 相互 sougo *n.* mutual, each other
- 私達は相互の理解を深めるためにもっと話し合うべきだ。— We should discuss more to deepen our mutual understanding.

9 | 0.63

4785 二十七 nijuu nana *num.* twenty-seven
- ここに二十七の国の留学生が在籍しています。— International students from twenty-seven countries are enrolled here.

9 | 0.79

4786 披露（する）hirou(suru) *n.* announcement, introduction *v.* announce, introduce
- 社長は娘の婚約を披露した。— The boss announced the engagement of his daughter.

9 | 0.60

4787 OB oobii *n.* OB (old boy), alumnus
- 就職活動のためOBを訪問した。— I visited an old boy in connection with job hunting.

9 | 0.79

24 Honorific expressions (frequency per million words)

(尊敬語・動詞) (Honorific: verbs)
いらっしゃる irassharu 95.080 **come, go; be**
仰る ossharu 53.051 **say, tell, speak**
くださる kudasaru 34.282 **give**
なさる nasaru 28.392 **do**
召し上がる meshiagaru 3.628 **eat**

(謙譲語・動詞) (Humble: verbs)
おる oru 1498.811 **be, exist**
いただく itadaku 126.270 **get, receive**
あがる agaru 121.202 **take**
申し上げる moushiageru 104.406 **tell, say**
いたす itasu 96.161 **do**
申す mousu 67.133 **say, be**
参る mairu 58.707 **go, come, visit**
伺う ukagau 39.298 **ask, inquire**
承知(する) shouchi(suru) 25.950 **agree, understand**
存ずる zonzuru 13.080 **know**
頂戴（する）choudai(suru) 8.359 **be given, give, have**
差し上げる sashiageru 7.154 **give**
拝見する haikensuru 5.690 **take a look, see, look**
賜る tamawaru 4.044 **to be given**
授かる sazukaru 3.364 **to be blessed with**
かしこまる kashikomaru 2.160 **humble oneself**
参上する sanjousuru 1.160 **come**
拝借する haishakusuru 0.854 **borrow**
拝受する haijusuru 0.116 **receive**
御目にかかる[1] omenikakaru N/A **see**

(丁寧語) (Polite)
ございます gozai masu 427.951 **honorific ending**

(お/ご～)
Most of these items were merged into the forms without "*o-/go-*", thus no frequency information is available.

ご存じ go-zonji 61.585 **know, knowing (honorific)**
ご覧 goran 26.450 **looking, seeing (honorific)**
お話しする o-hanashi suru N/A **talk (humble)**
お願いする o-negai suru N/A **ask, request, pray (humble)**
お勧め（する）o-susume(suru) N/A **recommendation, advice; recommend, advise (humble)**
ご紹介（する）go-shoukai(suru) N/A **introduction; introduce (humble)**
お願い（致す）o-negai-itasu N/A **beg, request (humble)**
お付き合い（する）o-tsukiai(suru) N/A **associate with (humble)**
ご説明（する）go-setsumei N/A **explanation; explain (humble)**
お伺いする o-ukagai suru N/A **visit, come and see; ask (humble)**
お聞きする o-kiki suru N/A **ask (humble)**
ご覧下さる goran kudasaru N/A **please see, please watch (honorific)**

(て～) (te- form)
てくださる te kudasaru 458.279 **honorific ending**
ていただく te itadaku 306.947 **[humble way to say "receive, get"]**
でございます de gozai masu 125.026 **be (formal)**

---

[1] This word is not included in the lemma list of LUWs.

4788 この方 kono kata *pron.* this person
- この方を知りませんでした。— I didn't know this person.
9 | 0.00 | SP

4789 上位 joui *n.* high rank
- 彼女は上位のテニスプレーヤーです。— She is a high-ranking tennis player.
9 | 0.95

4790 リード（する）riido(suru) *n.* lead *v.* take a lead
- 我がサッカーチームが一点リードしていた。— Our soccer team has a one-point lead.
9 | 0.90

4791 心身 shinshin *n.* mind and body
- 徹夜で心身ともに疲れていた。— After staying up all night, he was both mentally and physically exhausted.
9 | 0.88

4792 債権者 saiken-sha *n.* creditor
- 彼は債権者に会社の負債について報告しなければならない。— He must report to the creditors on the company's debt.
9 | 0.71

4793 燃料 nenryou *n.* fuel
- 飛行機に燃料を補給した。— They refueled the airplane.
9 | 0.98

4794 ショップ shoppu *n.* shop
- 最近、新しいコーヒーショップがオープンした。— A new coffee shop opened recently.
9 | 0.59

4795 長官 choukan *n.* director general
- 彼が防衛庁の長官だ。— He is the director general of the Defense Agency.
9 | 0.33

4796 強いる shiiru *v.* force
- 彼は自分の考えを息子に強いた。— He imposed his opinions on his son.
9 | 0.94

4797 シート shiito *n.* seat; sheet
- 子供達は車の後ろのシートに座った。— The children sat on the back seat of the car.
9 | 0.91

4798 追い込む oikomu *v.* drive into
- 不正が明らかになり、社長は辞職に追い込まれた。— Revelations of wrongdoings drove the president of the company to resign.
9 | 0.93

4799 プライド puraido *n.* pride
- 私は彼のプライドを傷つけてしまった。— I hurt his pride.
9 | 0.87

4800 題名 daimei *n.* title
- それは何という題名の本ですか。— What is the title of the book?
9 | 0.90

4801 問い合わせ toiawase *n.* inquiry
- 問い合わせは以下のアドレスにお願いします。— For inquiries, please contact the following address.
9 | 0.09 | NM

4802 葱 negi *n.* leek
- 私は葱が苦手だ。— I don't like leeks.
9 | 0.91

4803 据える sueru *v.* set, place
- この件については腰を据えて議論するべきだ。— We should take time to deliberate this issue.
9 | 0.88

4804 業績 gyouseki *n.* achievements
- 彼は仕事で立派な業績をあげた。— He produced great results at work.
9 | 0.88

4805 起動（する）kidou(suru) *n.* starting *v.* start
- コンピューターを起動させてください。— Start your computers.
9 | 0.72

4806 学年 gakunen *n.* grade, year
- 私達は大学で同じ学年でした。— We were in the same year at university.
9 | 0.86

4807 助成（する）josei(suru) *n.* subsidy *v.* subsidize
- この職業訓練プログラムは政府によって助成されている。— This vocational program is subsidized by the government.
9 | 0.47

4808 天下 tenka *n.* the whole world
- その短距離選手は100メートル走の世界記録を破り、天下に名をとどろかせた。— The sprinter became world-famous by breaking the world record in the 100 meter dash.
9 | 0.73

4809 打ち出す uchidasu *v.* work out, come up with; announce
- 政府は年金制度の新しい政策を打ち出した。— The government came up with a new policy for the pension scheme.
9 | 0.89

4810 栄える sakaeru *v.* prosper, flourish
- ギリシャでは古代文明が栄えた。— Ancient civilization flourished in Greece.
9 | 0.95

4811 科学的 kagaku-teki *na-adj.* scientific
- その理論は科学的に証明されている。— That theory has been scientifically proved.
9 | 0.93

4812 千九百九十九年 sen kyuuhayku kyuujuu kyuu nen *n.* 1999 (year)
- 1999年はいろいろなことがあった。— So many things happened in 1999.

9 | 0.88

4813 庶民 shomin *n.* common people, ordinary people, masses
- バスのような公共交通機関は庶民が利用する。— Ordinary people use public transportation such as buses.

9 | 0.97

4814 千九百九十年 sen kyuuhyaku kyuujuu nen *n.* 1990 (year)
- それは1990年に始まりました。— It began in 1990.

9 | 0.89

4815 乗り出す noridasu *v.* venture out; embark on
- 彼の会社は海外進出に乗り出した。— His company has embarked on overseas expansion.

9 | 0.78

4816 そんなこんな sonnakonna *adv.* what with one thing and another; after many twists and turns
- そんなこんなで旅行は中止になった。— What with one thing and another, the trip was cancelled.

9 | 0.51

4817 覚ます samasu *v.* wake up
- 地震によって目を覚ました。— The earthquake woke me up.

9 | 0.85

4818 住居 jukyo *n.* house
- 被災地では住居が不足している。— The housing supply in the disaster area is insufficient.

9 | 0.92

4819 沸騰(する) futtou(suru) *n.* boiling *v.* boil
- 水は100度で沸騰する。— Water boils at 100 degrees celsius.

9 | 0.96

4820 仕掛ける shikakeru *v.* begin, start; set
- 私はここに罠を仕掛けた。— I set the trap here.

9 | 0.85

4821 一年半 ichi nen han *n.* one year and a half
- そこに1年半滞在しました。— I stayed there for a year and a half.

9 | 0.87

4822 こっそり kossori *adv.* secretly, on the sly
- 恋人の携帯電話をこっそりみたことがある。— I have secretly checked my partner's cell phone.

9 | 0.86

4823 へん hen *aux.* NEGATION (dialectal)
- お好み焼き食べへん。— I won't eat okonomiyaki.

9 | 0.80

4824 組み立てる kumitateru *v.* assemble
- 彼はその複雑な機械を三分間で組み立てることができる。— He can assemble this complicated machine in three minutes.

9 | 0.97

4825 案外 angai *adv.* unexpectedly
- テストは案外難しかった。— The examination was more difficult than I expected.

9 | 0.91

4826 譲渡(する) jouto(suru) *n.* transfer *v.* transfer, hand over
- 彼は娘に全ての株式を譲渡した。— He handed all of his shares over to his daughter.

9 | 0.65

4827 でもある de mo aru *aux.* be ..., too
- 彼女は二児の母親でもある。— She is also a mother of two children.

9 | 0.79

4828 挫折(する) zasetsu(suru) *n.* setback *v.* fail
- 彼は何度も挫折したが諦めなかった。— He faced many setbacks, but never gave up.

9 | 0.90

4829 きゅうり kyuuri *n.* cucumber
- サラダにきゅうりが入っている。— The salad has cucumber in it.

9 | 0.89

4830 検証(する) kenshou(suru) *n.* verification *v.* verify
- 仮説の検証を試みた。— I tried to verify the hypothesis.

9 | 0.89

4831 株主 kabunushi *n.* stockholder, shareholder
- 私はこの会社の株主だ。— I am a stockholder in this company.

9 | 0.79

4832 見渡す miwatasu *v.* look around
- 彼は隠れるところを探して、辺りを見渡した。— He looked around for a place to hide.

9 | 0.90

4833 誓う chikau *v.* vow, swear
- 彼は彼女に永遠の愛を誓った。— He vowed to love her forever.

9 | 0.89

4834 マッサージ(する) massaaji(suru) *n.* massage *v.* massage
- マッサージをしてもらった。— I got a massage.

9 | 0.81

4835 二度目 ni do-me *n.* second time
- 我々の訪英は二度目であった。— That was the second time we visited the U.K.
9 | 0.89

4836 年上 toshiue *n.* older, senior
- 彼の奥さんは彼より年上だ。— His wife is older than him.
9 | 0.82

4837 力強い chikarazuyoi *i-adj.* strong, powerful
- 両親から力強いメッセージを受け取った。— I picked up on the strong message from my parents.
9 | 0.93

4838 ピーク piiku *n.* peak
- 電力の需要はピークに達した。— Demand for electricity reached its peak.
9 | 0.80

4839 みじん切り mijingiri *n.* minced, cut into fine pieces, chopped
- たまねぎをみじん切りにする。— Chop the onions into fine pieces.
9 | 0.89

4840 強める tsuyomeru *v.* strengthen, increase
- 決意を強めた。— I increased my determination.
9 | 0.81

4841 禁煙(する) kin'en(suru) *n.* no-smoking *v.* stop smoking
- 飛行機の中は禁煙です。— Airplanes are non-smoking.
9 | 0.83

4842 厚さ atsu-sa *n.* thickness
- 厚さはどれくらいですか。— How thick is it?
9 | 0.95

4843 十代 juu dai *n.* teen years, teens
- 彼女は十代で家を出た。— She left home when she was in her teens.
9 | 0.91

4844 タレント tarento *n.* celebrity, entertainer
- 彼女はタレントとして活躍している。— She is very busy as a celebrity.
9 | 0.90

4845 ふさぐ fusagu *v.* cover; stop; block
- 彼は両手で耳をふさいだ。— He covered his ears with both hands.
9 | 0.93

4846 ごと -goto *suffix* every
- オリンピックは四年ごとに開催される。— The Olympic Games take place every four years.
9 | 0.97

4847 牛肉 gyuuniku *n.* beef
- 鶏肉と牛肉とどちらになさいますか。— Would you like the chicken or the beef?
9 | 0.97

4848 枠組み wakugumi *n.* frame, framework
- 新たな法的枠組みを作るつもりだ。— We will create a new legal framework.
9 | 0.72

4849 かゆい kayui *i-adj.* itchy
- 蚊に刺されて、かゆい。— I got bitten by a mosquito and it's itchy.
9 | 0.70

4850 七十 nanajuu *num.* seventy
- 私の父は七十で免許をとった。— My father got a driver's license when he was seventy.
9 | 0.97

4851 多様化(する) tayou-ka(suru) *n.* diversification *v.* diversify
- 人々の生活様式が多様化している。— People's lifestyles have diversified.
9 | 0.55

4852 着せる kiseru *v.* put on, dress
- 彼女は娘にコートを着せた。— She dressed her daughter in her coat.
9 | 0.89

4853 インストール(する) insutooru(suru) *n.* installation *v.* install
- 新しいソフトをインストールした。— I installed new software.
9 | 0.69

4854 二年目 ni nen-me *n.* second year
- 私は入社して二年目です。— This is my second year since I joined the company.
9 | 0.88

4855 機構 kikou *n.* mechanism, structure, system
- 彼らは新しい機構を創設した。— They established a new mechanism.
9 | 0.46

4856 着実 chakujitsu *na-adj.* steady
- その国は着実な発展をしている。— The country is achieving steady development
9 | 0.57

4857 世田谷 setagaya *n.* Setagaya (place name)
- 彼女は世田谷に住んでいます。— She lives in Setagaya.
9 | 0.79

4858 里 sato *n.* village, countryside, one's parents' home
- 妻は里に帰っている。— My wife is staying at her parents' home.
9 | 0.72

4859 決まり kimari *n.* regulation; arrangement, settlement
- 市の決まりを守るべきだ。— You should observe city regulations.

9 | 0.97

4860 独身 dokushin *n.* single, unmarried
- しばらくは独身でいたい。— I want to stay single for a while.

9 | 0.86

4861 十八歳 juu has-sai *n.* eighteen years old
- 十八歳未満は入れません。— You cannot enter if you are under eighteen.

9 | 0.97

4862 高齢化(する) kourei-ka(suru) *n.* aging; increase in age
- 高齢化社会に対応しなければならない。— We must prepare for the aging of society.

9 | 0.70

4863 鮮明 senmei *na-adj.* clear, vivid
- テレビの映像は以前より鮮明だ。— Television pictures are much clearer than before.

9 | 0.95

4864 エアコン eakon *n.* air-conditioning, air conditioner
- 彼はエアコンをつけた。— He turned on the air conditioner.

9 | 0.88

4865 期限 kigen *n.* period; deadline; term
- 期限までに課題を仕上げなければならない。— I have to finish my assignment by the deadline.

9 | 0.92

4866 物件 bukken *n.* article, object; property
- 彼は手頃な物件を探している。— He is looking for an affordable property.

9 | 0.93

4867 前条 zenjou *n.* preceding article
- 手数料は前条に規定される通りである。— Our commission fee is as mentioned in the preceding article.

9 | 0.07 | OF

4868 中間 chuukan *n.* middle, halfway
- 名古屋は東京と大阪の中間にある。— Nagoya lies halfway between Tokyo and Kyoto.

9 | 0.99

4869 カラー karaa *n.* color
- 私が小さい頃はカラーの写真はなかった。— We didn't have color photos when I was small.

9 | 0.66

4870 スポーツクラブ supootsu kurabu *n.* sports club, gym
- スポーツクラブに通っている。— I go to a sports club.

9 | 0.61

4871 群馬県 gunma ken *n.* Gunma Prefecture
- 私の母は群馬県出身です。— My mother is from Gunma Prefecture.

9 | 0.94

4872 フルーツ furuutsu *n.* fruit
- フルーツケーキを食べた。— I ate some fruit cake.

9 | 0.83

4873 グラフ gurafu *n.* graph
- グラフを使って気温の変化を説明した。— I explained changes in temperature with a graph.

9 | 0.79

4874 画家 gaka *n.* artist, painter
- この絵を描いた画家を知っていますか。— Do you know the artist who painted this picture?

9 | 0.82

4875 組み込む kumikomu *v.* build in; insert; integrate
- その機能はコンピューターに組み込まれている。— That feature is built into the computer.

9 | 0.92

4876 マイク maiku *n.* microphone
- アナウンサーはマイクに向かって話し続けた。— The announcer kept talking into the microphone.

9 | 0.89

4877 着替える kigaeru *v.* change clothes; get dressed
- 出かける前に服を着替えなくちゃ。— I have to change clothes before going out.

9 | 0.85

4878 計画的 keikaku-teki *na-adj.* planned, deliberate, premeditated
- それは計画的な犯行だったことがわかった。— It was revealed to be a premeditated crime.

9 | 0.52

4879 典型的 tenkei-teki *na-adj.* typical
- これが典型的な日本の住宅です。— This is a typical Japanese-style house.

9 | 0.90

4880 調節(する) chousetsu(suru) *n.* adjustment *v.* adjust
- つまみを回して温度を調節してください。— Turn the knob to adjust the temperature.

9 | 0.95

4881 回避（する）kaihi(suru) *n.* avoidance *v.* avoid
- パイロットたちは事故を回避するためにあらゆる手段をとった。— The pilots used every means to avoid an accident.
9 | 0.95

4882 打ち明ける uchiakeru *v.* speak one's mind; confess
- 彼は私に秘密を打ち明けてくれた。— He confessed his secret to me.
9 | 0.85

4883 書物 shomotsu *n.* book
- これは古代の書物にある物語だ。— This is a story in an ancient book.
9 | 0.74

4884 隙 suki *n.* space, room, gap
- 二人の間に他人が入り込む隙はない。— There is no room for anyone else to step in between the two.
9 | 0.84

4885 範囲内 han'i-nai *n.* in range, within the limits
- 費用は予算の範囲内に収めなければならない。— We should keep the expense within the limits of the budget.
9 | 0.67

4886 遊園地 yuuen chi *n.* amusement park,
- 家族と一緒に遊園地に行った。— I went to an amusement park with my family.
9 | 0.81

4887 六つ mut-tsu *n.* six
- 父は私が六つの時渡米した。— My father went to the States when I was six.
9 | 0.96

4888 二十歳 nijus-sai *n.* twenty years old
- この8月で二十歳になる。— I will be twenty this August.
9 | 0.90

4889 偏見 henken *n.* prejudice, bias
- 彼は若者に偏見を持っているようだ。— He seems to have a prejudice against young people.
9 | 0.97

4890 理屈 rikutsu *n.* reason, logic, theory
- 理屈は正しいが全く現実的ではない。— It's correct in theory, but it's totally impractical.
9 | 0.92

4891 契機 keiki *n.* momentum; opportunity, chance
- 父は退職を契機に料理を始めた。— My father took the opportunity of retirement to begin cooking.
9 | 0.69

4892 一軒 ik-ken *n.* one building
- もう一軒回らないといけない。— I have another house to call at.
9 | 0.46

4893 紛争 funsou *n.* dispute, trouble, strife
- そのNPOは紛争を解決する努力を続けている。— The NPO keeps working to settle the dispute.
9 | 0.70

4894 魔法 mahou *n.* magic
- この化粧品を使うと、魔法のようにきれいになれます。— If you use these cosmetics, you can become beautiful, as if by magic.
9 | 0.80

4895 影響力 eikyou-ryoku *n.* influence, impact
- 彼は国の政治に大きな影響力を持っている。— He has a lot of influence over national politics.
9 | 0.94

4896 触れ合い fureai *n.* touching, contact
- この動物園では動物との触れ合いを楽しむことができる。— People can enjoy contact with animals in this zoo.
9 | 0.78

4897 極力 kyokuryoku *adv.* as much as possible
- そのレストランでは極力地元の食材を使用している。— The restaurant uses local products as much as possible.
9 | 0.96

4898 私立 shiritsu *n.* private
- 私は子どもを私立の学校に入れたい。— I want to send my child to a private school.
9 | 0.89

4899 明記（する）meiki(suru) *n.* writing clearly *v.* write clearly
- 名前と住所を明記してください。— Please write clearly your name and address.
9 | 0.65

4900 塩分 enbun *n.* salt
- 塩分をとりすぎると体に悪い。— Eating food that contains a lot of salt is bad for one's health.
9 | 0.80

4901 同一 douitsu *na-adj.* same, identical
- それは私が失くした時計と同一の物だ。— That is the same watch as the one I lost.
9 | 0.69

4902 顔色 kaoiro *n.* complexion
- 彼は顔色が悪い。— He has a sickly complexion.
9 | 0.77

4903 何せ nanise *adv.* anyhow, after all, in any case
- 何せ朝から晩まで働いて疲れきっているんだ。— Anyhow, I'm tired out from working from morning till night.
9 | 0.84

4904 資する shisuru *v.* contribute
- その発明はあのビジネスに大きく資することになるだろう。— The invention will contribute greatly to the development of that business.
9 | 0.14 | OF

4905 埃 hokori *n.* dust
- 埃だらけになった。— I was covered with dust from head to toe.
9 | 0.90

4906 既存 kizon *n.* existing
- 既存の枠組みを見直すべきだ。— The existing framework should be reexamined.
9 | 0.83

4907 網 ami *n.* net
- たくさんの魚が網にかかった。— A lot of fish were caught in the net.
9 | 0.96

4908 つ tsu *p.* [indicating contrasts or coordinations]
- 走者達は抜きつ抜かれつ先頭を争っている。— The runners are taking the lead and being overtaken alternately.
9 | 0.78

4909 刑事 keiji *n.* police detective
- 刑事が事件について聞き込みをする。— A police detective is carrying out interviews about the incident.
9 | 0.75

4910 ボーリング booringu *n.* bowling
- 日曜日にボーリングに行こう。— Let's go bowling on Sunday.
9 | 0.50

4911 感触 kanshoku *n.* feel, touch
- このかばんは感触がやわらかい。— This bag is soft to the touch.
9 | 0.86

4912 明く aku *v.* open
- 眠くてなかなか目が明かない。— I'm so sleepy that I can't keep my eyes open.
9 | 0.93

4913 人柄 hitogara *n.* personality
- 彼は人柄がいい。— He has a nice personality.
9 | 0.92

4914 各々 onoono *n.* each
- 各々でお昼ご飯は持ってきてください。— Please each bring lunch.
9 | 0.84

4915 職務 shokumu *n.* duty
- 職務について質問する。— He asks about the person's duties.
9 | 0.51

4916 URL yuuaarueru *n.* URL, Uniform Resource Locator
- そのサイトのURLを教えてください。— Please tell me the URL of that site.
9 | 0.55

4917 だし dashi *n.* soup stock
- このカニの出しはおいしい。— The crab soup stock is delicious.
9 | 0.85

4918 六十年 rokujuu nen *n.* sixty years
- この町に住んで六十年だ。— I have lived in this town for sixty years.
9 | 0.52

4919 薄れる usureru *v.* become dim
- あのころの記憶は薄れてしまった。— I have only faded memories of those days.
9 | 0.96

4920 執行(する) shikkou(suru) *n.* execution, enforcement *v.* carry out, enforce
- 政府は刑の執行を延期した。— The government postponed enforcing the sentence.
9 | 0.51

4921 分量 bunryou *n.* quantity, amount
- 材料の分量を量る。— I measure the quantity of materials.
9 | 0.95

4922 大概 taigai *n.* generally
- 大概郵便は十時頃くる。— Generally the mail is delivered about ten o' clock.
9 | 0.73

4923 熱する nessuru *v.* heat
- フライパンを十分熱してから肉を焼いてください。— Please fry the meat after heating the frying pan well.
9 | 0.91

4924 味わい ajiwai *n.* profound, thought-provoking
- 味わい深い言葉だ。— The remark is very profound.
9 | 0.82

4925 中途半端 chuuto hanpa *na-adj.* unfinished, half-done
- 中途半端にするな。— Don't leave things unfinished.
9 | 0.91

4926 はたち hatachi *n.* twenty years old
- 私の娘は今年はたちになった。— My daughter turned twenty this year.
9 | 0.39

4927 一周 is-shuu *n.* one round
- このコースは一周5キロです。— This course is five kilometers from start to finish.
9 | 0.88

4928 異様 iyou *na-adj.* strange
- 異様な光景だった。— It was a strange sight.
9 | 0.86

4929 髭 hige *n.* mustache; beard
- 髭を伸ばす。— He is growing a beard/mustache.
9 | 0.84

4930 支度（する）shitaku(suru) *n.* preparations *v.* prepare
- 支度は終わりましたか。— Did you finish the preparations?
9 | 0.87

4931 留める todomeru *v.* hold, keep
- 被害を最小限に留めることが大切だ。— It is important to keep the damage to a minimum.
9 | 0.88

4932 立ち上げる tachiageru *v.* boot up, start
- 新しい事業を立ち上げる。— We will start up a new business.
9 | 0.90

4933 受賞（する）jushou(suru) *n.* winning a prize *v.* win (receive) a prize, be awarded a prize
- 受賞者がスピーチをした。— A prize winner made a speech.
9 | 0.67

4934 国鉄 kokutetsu *n.* national railway
- あれは国鉄の駅です。— That is a national railway station.
9 | 0.33

4935 乏しい toboshii *i-adj.* few, little
- この国は資源が乏しい。— This country has few natural resources.
9 | 0.92

4936 祝う iwau *v.* celebrate
- 私たちは先日銀婚式を祝った。— We celebrated our silver wedding the other day.
9 | 0.87

4937 倍 bai *n.* times
- 二の二倍は四だ。— Two times two is four.
9 | 0.97

4938 ただただ tadatada *adv.* all (one) can do is, simply, nothing but
- ただただ泣いてばかりいた。— All she could do was cry.
9 | 0.77

4939 業種 gyoushu *n.* category of business, type of industry
- 業種ごとに名刺を並べる。— Arrange the business cards according to the type of business.
9 | 0.70

4940 汽車 kisha *n.* train
- 汽車で旅行に行く。— We will go on a trip by train.
9 | 0.75

4941 うどん udon *n.* udon, thick white noodles
- うどんが好きだ。— I love udon.
9 | 0.77

4942 五歳 go-sai *n.* five years old
- うちの孫は五歳です。— My grandson is five years old.
9 | 0.89

4943 適度 tekido *na-adj.* moderate
- あの食べ物は適度な温度で保つことが大切だ。— It's important to keep that food at a moderate temperature.
9 | 0.92

4944 日中 nitchuu *n.* during the day
- 日中は外に出ない。— I won't go out during the day.
9 | 0.91

4945 作曲（する）sakkyoku(suru) *n.* musical composition *v.* compose
- この曲はモーツァルトが作曲した。— This song was composed by Mozart.
9 | 0.94

4946 大嫌い daikirai *na-adj.* hate
- 私はゴキブリが大嫌いだ。— I hate cockroaches.
9 | 0.81

4947 居間 ima *n.* living room
- 居間で家族と食事をする。— We have dinner in the living room.
9 | 0.83

4948 心境 shinkyou *n.* state of mind
- 彼の心境は変化した。— His mental state has changed.
9 | 0.93

4949 住宅街 juutaku-gai *n.* housing; residential area
- 住宅街にすむ。— He lives in a residential area.
9 | 0.77

4950 無言 mugon *n.* silence, in silence, without speaking
- 彼女は無言のままうなずいた。— She nodded in silence.
9 | 0.77

4951 調味料 choumi-ryou *n.* seasoning, spice
- 足りない調味料を買ってくる。— I will go to buy the seasonings we lack.
9 | 0.93

4952 一回目 ik-kai-me *n.* first time
- 一回目は失敗した。— The first time was a failure.
9 | 0.83

4953 何時間 nanjikan *n.* how many hours
- 何時間待てばいいのだろうか。— I wonder how many hours I will have to wait.
9 | 0.85

4954 みそ miso *n.* miso; key point
- 野菜にみそをつけて食べた。— I ate the vegetables with miso.
9 | 0.91

4955 花粉 kafun *n.* pollen
- 今年は花粉の量が多い。— The pollen count is high this year.
9 | 0.88

4956 抗議（する）kougi(suru) *n.* protest, objection *v.* object
- 彼は強く抗議した。— He protested strongly.
9 | 0.96

4957 あきれる akireru *v.* be amazed, be disgusted
- 彼の非常識な行為にあきれてしまった。— I was disgusted with his senseless behavior.
9 | 0.81

4958 数日 suu-jitsu *n.* few days
- 完成まで数日かかるだろう。— It will take a few days to complete.
9 | 0.84

4959 信念 shinnen *n.* belief, faith
- あの人は強い信念を持っている。— That person has strong faith.
9 | 0.91

4960 イスラエル isuraeru *n.* Israel
- 初めてイスラエルを訪問した。— I visited Israel for the first time.
9 | 0.97

4961 遅く osoku *n.* late
- 夫は遅く帰ってくる。— My husband comes home late.
9 | 0.75

4962 追い詰める oitsumeru *v.* run down, corner
- 犯人はついに追い詰められた。— The criminal was cornered at last.
9 | 0.93

4963 プラスチック purasuchikku *n.* plastic
- プラスチックの玩具は簡単に壊れない。— Plastic toys do not not break easily.
9 | 0.98

4964 しつこい shitsukoi *i-adj.* persistent; over-rich (food)
- セールスマンにしつこく勧誘された。— The salesman persuaded me persistently.
9 | 0.84

4965 塔 tou *n.* tower
- 向こうに塔が二つ建っている。— Two towers stand over there.
9 | 0.87

4966 家 uchi *n.* house, home
- 家においでよ。— Come to my house.
9 | 0.48

4967 六年生 roku nen-sei *n.* sixth grade, sixth year
- 娘は六年生です。— My daughter is in Year Six.
9 | 0.80

4968 手話 shuwa *n.* sign language
- 手話を習いたい。— I want to learn sign language.
9 | 0.76

4969 痛める itameru *v.* hurt
- 腰を痛めてしまった。— I hurt my back.
9 | 0.92

4970 研究開発 kenkyuu kaihatsu *n.* research and development
- ここで新技術の研究開発が行われている。— The research and development of new technology are carried out here.
9 | 0.28

4971 切り取る kiritoru *v.* cut off, tear off
- 新聞記事をはさみで切り取った。— I cut out the newspaper article with scissors.
9 | 0.94

4972 民法 minpou *n.* civil law
- 民法を学ぶ。— I study civil law.
9 | 0.78

4973 返済（する）hensai(suru) *n.* repayment *v.* repay
- 借金を返済した。— I repaid my debts.
9 | 0.93

4974 例える tatoeru *v.* compare
- 人生はよく旅に例えられる。— Our life is often compared to a journey.
9 | 0.97

4975 なじみ najimi *n.* familiarity
- なじみの店で買い物をする。— I shop at familiar shops.
9 | 0.90

4976 二十九 nijuu kyuu *num.* twenty-nine
- 息子は二十九でまだ無職だ。— My son is twenty-nine, but still has no job.
9 | 0.85

4977 地形 chikei *n.* topography, landform
- この辺りの地形は複雑だ。— The topography of this area is complicated.
9 | 0.90

4978 本能 honnou *n.* instinct
- 彼は本能のままに生きている。— He lives by instinct.
9 | 0.81

4979 解除(する) kaijo(suru) *n.* cancellation *v.* cancel, lift
- 規制が解除された。— The regulation was lifted.
9 | 0.87

4980 放出(する) houshutsu(suru) *n.* emission *v.* emit
- 大気中に二酸化炭素を放出する。— It emits carbon dioxide into the atmosphere.
9 | 0.93

4981 にらむ niramu *v.* stare
- 知らない人がこちらをにらんでいる。— A stranger is staring at me.
9 | 0.81

4982 悪魔 akuma *n.* devil, demon
- 彼は悪魔のような人だ。— He is a fiendish person.
9 | 0.66

4983 ハム hamu *n.* ham
- ハムのサラダを作った。— I made a ham salad.
9 | 0.97

4984 診察(する) shinsatsu(suru) *n.* medical examination, consultation *v.* examine
- 専門医の診察を受けたほうがいいだろう。— You'd better consult the specialist.
9 | 0.88

4985 二日目 futsu-ka-me *n.* second day
- プログラムの二日目は大変よかった。— The second day of the program was very good.
9 | 0.76

4986 柿 kaki *n.* persimmon
- 柿を食べた。— I ate persimmons.
9 | 0.84

4987 給付(する) kyuufu(suru) *n.* provision *v.* provide
- 失業保険の給付を受けた。— I was provided with unemployment insurance.
9 | 0.68

4988 署名(する) shomei(suru) *n.* signature *v.* sign
- 千人の署名を集めた。— We collected the signatures of 1,000 people.
9 | 0.87

4989 詩人 shijin *n.* poet
- 彼は有名な詩人だ。— He is a famous poet.
9 | 0.82

4990 しみじみ shimijimi *adv.* keenly, heartily, from one's heart
- 彼女の親切さをしみじみと感じた。— I felt deeply how kind she was.
9 | 0.89

4991 示唆(する) shisa(suru) *n.* suggestion *v.* suggest
- 彼の発言は示唆に富んでいた。— His remarks were full of suggestions.
9 | 0.84

4992 三千円 sanzen en *n.* three thousand yen
- このシャツは三千円です。— This shirt costs three thousand yen.
9 | 0.59

4993 来週 raishuu *n.* next week
- 来週から学校が始まる。— School starts next week.
9 | 0.45

4994 気楽 kiraku *na-adj.* comfortable, easy, easygoing
- 彼女は気楽に話ができる友達だ。— She is a friend that I can talk with comfortably.
9 | 0.89

4995 略 ryaku *n.* omission, abbreviation
- CDは「コンパクトディスク(Compact Disc)」の略だ。— "CD" is an abbreviation for "compact disc."
9 | 0.90

4996 免れる manugareru *v.* escape, avoid
- 最悪の事態は免れた。— We avoided the worst situation.
9 | 0.90

4997 相次ぐ aitsugu *v.* happen one after another
- 不可解な事件が相次いでいる。— Mysterious incidents are happening one after another.
9 | 0.86

4998 一段 ichidan *n.* one step
- 本堂は一段高い場所にある。— The main building is located one level higher.
9 | 0.89

4999 動揺(する) douyou(suru) *n.* unrest *v.* be agitated
- 彼女は激しく動揺した。— She was violently agitated.
9 | 0.89

5000 まあまあ maamaa *na-adj.* so-so, not bad *adv.* fairly, moderately
- レポートの出来はまあまあだった。— The result of the report was not bad.
9 | 0.84

25 Numbers/numerals

(frequency per million words)

(数) (Numbers)

- 一 ichi 583.437 **one**
- 二 ni 573.950 **two**
- 三 san 374.610 **three**
- 四 yon, shi 231.011 **four**
- 五 go 160.153 **five**
- 六 roku 107.727 **six**
- 七 nana 80.622 **seven**
- 八 hachi 68.308 **eight**
- 十 juu 57.551 **ten**
- 九 kyuu 49.528 **nine**
- 十二 juu ni 32.868 **twelve**
- 十一 juu ichi 30.961 **eleven**
- 二十 nijuu 26.221 **twenty**
- 十五 juu go 26.101 **fifteen**
- 十三 juu san 23.159 **thirteen**
- 三十 sanjuu 21.880 **thirty**
- 十四 juu shi 20.664 **fourteen**
- ゼロ zero 20.540 **zero**
- 百 hyaku 18.837 **hundred**
- 十六 juu roku 18.771 **sixteen**
- 十八 juu hachi 17.811 **eighteen**
- 二十一 nijuu ichi 16.672 **twenty-one**
- 十七 juu nana 15.748 **seventeen**
- 五十 gojuu 14.544 **fifty**
- 二十五 nijuu go 13.832 **twenty-five**
- 十九 juu kyuu 13.744 **nineteen**
- 二十二 nijuu ni 13.739 **twenty-two**
- 四十 yonjuu[1] 13.218 **forty**
- 二十三 nijuu san 12.395 **twenty-three**
- 六十 rokujuu 12.253 **sixty**
- 二十四 nijuu shi 11.943 **twenty-four**
- 二千 nisen 9.921 **two thousand**
- 二十六 nijuu roku 9.779 **twenty-six**
- 二十七 nijuu nana 9.071 **twenty-seven**
- 七十 nanajuu 8.913 **seventy**
- 千 sen 8.411 **one thousand**
- 八十 hachijuu 6.736 **eighty**
- 九十 kyuujuu 4.645 **ninety**
- 五百 gohyaku 3.941 **five hundred**
- 五万 goman 3.501 **fifty thousand**
- 万 man 2.016 **ten thousand**
- 五千 gosen 1.813 **five thousand**
- 億 oku 0.672 **one hundred million**

(日) (Days and dates)

- 一日 ichi nichi 135.856 **a day, the day, one day**
- 一日 tsuitachi 53.828 **first (date)**
- 三日 mik-ka 40.309 **third (date), three days**
- 二日 futsu-ka 39.452 **second (date), two days**
- 十日 too-ka 28.551 **tenth (date), ten days**
- 十五日 juu go nichi 26.483 **fifteenth (date), fifteen days**
- 四日 yok-ka 25.041 **fourth (date), four days**
- 二十日 hatsu-ka 23.363 **twentieth (date), twenty days**
- 五日 itsu-ka 23.042 **fifth (date), five days**
- 三十一日 sanjuu ichi nichi 21.388 **thirty-first (date), thirty-one days**
- 三十日 sanjuu nichi 21.298 **thirtieth (date), thirty days**
- 七日 nano-ka 19.465 **seventh (date), seven days**
- 二十五日 nijuu go nichi 19.385 **twenty-fifth (date), twenty-five days**
- 八日 you-ka 18.914 **eighth (date), eight days**
- 十六日 juu roku nichi 18.887 **sixteenth (date), sixteen days**
- 十一日 juu ichi nichi 18.794 **eleventh (date), eleven days**
- 十四日 juu yok-ka 18.398 **fourteenth (date), fourteen days**
- 六日 mui-ka 18.288 **sixth (date), six days**
- 二十一日 nijuu ichi nichi 17.984 **twenty-first (date), twenty-one days**
- 十二日 juu ni nichi 17.940 **twelfth (date), twelve days**
- 十八日 juu hachi nichi 17.898 **eighteenth (date), eighteen days**
- 十七日 juu shichi nichi 17.659 **seventeenth (date), seventeen days**
- 九日 kokono-ka 17.566 **ninth (date), nine days**
- 二十三日 nijuu san nichi 17.496 **twenty-third (date), twenty-three days**
- 二十四日 nijuu yok-ka 17.440 **twenty-fourth (date), twenty-four days**
- 十三日 juu san nichi 17.145 **thirteenth (date), thirteen days**
- 二十二日 nijuu ni nichi 16.853 **twenty-second (date), twenty-two days**

二十八日 nijuu hachi nichi 16.511 twenty-eighth (date), twenty-eight days
二十六日 nijuu roku nichi 16.231 twenty-sixth (date), twenty-six days
十九日 juu ku nichi 16.187 nineteenth (date), nineteen days
二十七日 nijuu shichi nichi 15.780 twenty-seventh (date), twenty-seven days
二十九日 nijuu ku nichi 15.443 twenty-ninth (date), twenty-nine days

(時刻:時) (Time)

一時 ichi ji 49.308 at one time, temporary, for a while
十時 juu ji 45.486 ten o'clock
九時 ku ji 44.725 nine o'clock
五時 go ji 28.644 five o'clock
八時 hachi ji 27.635 eight o'clock
三時 san ji 27.047 three o'clock
十一時 juu ichi ji 23.840 eleven o'clock
四時 yo ji 23.768 four o'clock
二時 ni ji 21.989 two o'clock
六時 roku ji 21.176 six o'clock
七時 shichi ji 20.160 seven o'clock
十二時 juu ni ji 15.223 twelve o'clock
十三時 juu san ji 5.458 1300
十五時 juu go ji 5.027 1500
十六時 juu roku ji 4.495 1600
零時 rei ji 4.464 twelve o'clock, midnight
十四時 juu yo ji 4.269 1400
十八時 juu hachi ji 3.049 1800
二十時 nijuu ji 2.861 2000
十九時 juu ku ji 2.624 1900
二十一時 nijuu ichi ji 2.422 2100
二十二時 nijuu ni ji 1.598 2200
二十三時 nijuu san ji 1.226 2300
二十四時 nijuu yo ji 0.848 2400

(時刻:分) (Time: minutes)

三十分 sanjup-pun, sanjip-pun 95.488 thirty minutes
十分 jup-pun, jip-pun 36.717 ten minutes
五分 go fun 27.764 five minutes
二十分 nijup-pun, nijip-pun 26.833 twenty minutes
十五分 juu go fun 26.569 fifteen minutes
一分 ip-pun 10.863 one minute
四十分 yonjup-pun, yonjip-pun 9.923 forty minutes
三分 san pun 9.245 three minutes
四十五分 yonjuu go fun 4.977 forty-five minutes
五十分 gojup-pun, gojip-pun 4.166 fifty minutes
二十五分 nijuu go fun 3.735 twenty-five minutes
七分 nana fun 3.624 seven minutes
八分 hachi fun, hap-pun 3.294 eight minutes
四分 yon pun 1.759 four minutes
六分 rop-pun 1.668 six minutes
五十五分 gojuu go fun 1.490 fifty-five minutes
三十五分 sanjuu go fun 1.344 thirty-five minutes
九分 kyuu fun 1.130 nine minutes
六十分 rokujup-pun, rokujip-pun 0.714 sixty minutes

(年) (Years)

一年 ichi nen 92.923 one year
二年 ni nen 67.738 two years
三年 san nen 67.168 three years
十年 juu nen 57.931 ten years, a decade
二十年 nijuu nen 39.219 twenty years
五年 go nen 39.090 five years
四年 yo nen 31.857 four years
二千年 nisen nen 21.813 2000 (year); two thousand years
六年 roku nen 19.661 six years
三十年 sanjuu nen 19.168 thirty years
十五年 juu go nen 18.432 fifteen years
五十年 gojuu nen 17.194 fifty years
八年 hachi nen 16.338 eight years
二千二年 nisen ni nen 15.339 2002 (year)
二千一年 nisen ichi nen 14.908 2001 (year)
四十年 yonjuu nen 13.202 forty years
七年 shichi nen 12.782 seven years
十二年 juu ni nen 11.837 twelve years
十三年 juu san nen 10.991 thirteen years
二千八年 nisen hachi nen 10.558 2008 (year)
二十一年 nijuu ichi nen 10.425 twenty-one years
九年 kyuu nen 9.916 nine years
二千三年 nisen san nen 9.676 2003 (year)
十一年 juu ichi nen 9.561 eleven years
百年 hyaku nen 9.090 hundred years, century
千九百九十九年 sen kyuuhyaku kyuujuu kyuu nen 9.023 1999 (year)
千九百九十年 sen kyuuhyaku kyuujuu nen 9.017 1990 (year)

一年半 ichi nen han 8.993 one year and a half
六十年 rokujuu nen 8.743 sixty years
十四年 juu yo nen 7.655 fourteen years
十九年 juu kyuu nen 7.267 nineteen years
十八年 juu hachi nen 6.047 eighteen years
十六年 juu roku nen 6.021 sixteen years
十七年 juu shichi nen 5.540 seventeen years
九十年 kyujuu nen 4.808 ninety years
八十年 hachijuu nen 4.509 eighty years
七十年 nanajuu nen 2.160 seventy years

(期間:月) (Period: months)
一ヶ月 ik-kagetsu 52.896 one month
三ヶ月 san kagetsu 27.664 three months
二ヶ月 ni kagetsu 23.113 two month
六ヶ月 rok-kagetsu 10.099 six months
四ヶ月 yon kagetsu 9.986 four months
十ヶ月 juk-kagetsu 4.699 ten months
八ヶ月 hachi kagetsu 4.148 eight months
五ヶ月 go kagetsu 3.706 five months
七ヶ月 nana kagetsu 3.353 seven months
九ヶ月 kyuu kagetsu 2.534 nine months
十一ヶ月 juu ichi kagetsu 1.014 eleven months
十二ヶ月 juu ni kagetsu 1.001 twelve months

(期間:年) (Period: years)
一年間 ichi nenkan 38.645 one year
三年間 san nenkan 21.469 three years
二年間 ni nenkan 15.569 two years
五年間 go nenkan 11.326 five years
十年間 juu nenkan 11.272 ten years
四年間 yo nenkan 9.152 four years
六年間 roku nenkan 6.284 six years
二十年間 nijuu nenkan 4.526 twenty years
八年間 hachi nenkan 2.756 eight years
七年間 nana nenkan 2.578 seven years
九年間 kyuu nenkan 2.427 nine years
三十年間 sanjuu nenkan 2.419 thirty years
五十年間 gojuu nenkan 1.283 fifty years
百年間 hyaku nenkan 1.259 one hundred years
四十年間 yonjuu nenkan 1.111 forty years
六十年間 rokujuu nenkan 0.685 sixty years
七十年間 nanajuu nenkan 0.098 seventy years
千年間 sen nenkan 0.079 one thousand years
八十年間 hachijuu nenkan N/A eighty years
九十年間 kyuujuu nenkan N/A ninety years

(年齢) (Age)
三歳 san-sai 15.743 three years old
十七歳 juu nana-sai 13.436 seventeen years old
二歳 ni-sai 12.603 two years old
四歳 yon-sai 10.846 four years old
六十歳 rokujus-sai 10.357 sixty years old
一歳 is-sai 9.441 one year old
三十歳 sanjus-sai 9.185 thirty years old
十八歳 juu has-sai 8.893 eighteen years old
二十歳 nijus-sai 8.817 twenty years old
二十歳 hatachi 8.729 twenty years old
五歳 go-sai 8.685 five years old
十五歳 juu go-sai 7.934 fifteen years old
十歳 jus-sai 7.381 ten years old
十九歳 juu kyuu-sai 7.261 nineteen years old
六歳 roku-sai 6.749 six years old
七歳 nana-sai 5.866 seven years old
十六歳 juu roku-sai 5.531 sixteen years old
十四歳 juu yon-sai 5.137 fourteen years old
四十歳 yonjus-sai 4.931 forty years old
十三歳 juu san-sai 4.850 thirteen years old
七十歳 nanajus-sai 4.704 seventy years old
十二歳 juu ni-sai 3.663 twelve years old
九歳 kyuu-sai 3.250 nine years old
五十歳 gojus-sai 3.166 fifty years old
八歳 has-sai 2.541 eight years old
百歳 hyaku-sai 2.536 one hundred years old
八十歳 hachijus-sai 2.459 eighty years old
十一歳 juu is-sai 2.186 eleven years old
九十歳 kyuujus-sai 1.404 ninety years old

(年代) (Generation)
二十代 nijuu dai 14.838 twenties
三十代 sanjuu dai 12.947 thirties
四十代 yonjuu dai 9.496 forties
五十代 gojuu dai 9.225 fifties
十代 juu dai 8.927 teen years, teens
六十代 rokujuu dai 5.215 sixties
七十代 nanajuu dai 1.937 seventies
八十代 hachijuu dai 1.088 eighties
九十代 kyuujuu dai 0.067 nineties

(物を数える) (Counting things)
一つ hito-tsu 714.990 one
二つ futa-tsu 160.938 two
三つ mit-tsu 126.354 three

四つ yot-tsu 32.290 four
五つ itsu-tsu 17.755 five
六つ mut-tsu 8.820 six
七つ nana-tsu 7.156 seven
八つ yat-tsu 4.899 eight
九つ kokono-tsu 2.001 nine
十 too 0.514 ten

(人を数える) (Counting people)
一人 hito-ri 433.912 one person, alone
二人 futa-ri 314.718 two people
三人 san-nin 103.652 three person
四人 yo-nin 44.938 four people
五人 go-nin 27.966 five people
十人 juu-nin 20.522 ten people
六人 roku-nin 15.010 six people
二十人 nijuu-nin 12.580 twenty people
七人 nana-nin 10.501 seven people
三十人 sanjuu-nin 10.021 thirty people
百人 hyaku-nin 8.517 one hundred people
五十人 gojuu-nin 7.012 fifty people
八人 hachi-nin 6.601 eight people
四十人 yonjuu-nin 5.712 forty people
九人 kyuu-nin 3.902 nine people
千人 sen-nin 3.640 one thousand people
六十人 rokujuu-nin 1.832 sixty people
八十人 hachijuu-nin 1.428 eighty people
七十人 nanajuu-nin 0.799 seventy people
九十人 kyuujuu-nin 0.482 ninety people

(回数) (Counting times)
一回 ik-kai 147.084 once
二回 ni kai 46.411 twice
三回 san kai 29.718 three times
四回 yon kai 12.048 four times
五回 go kai 10.293 five times
十回 juk-kai 4.867 ten times
六回 roko-kai 4.557 six times
八回 hachi kai, hak-kai 2.984 eight times
七回 nana kai 2.642 seven times
九回 kyuu kai 2.197 nine times
二十回 nijuk-kai 2.145 twenty times
百回 hyak-kai 1.630 one hundred times
千回 sen kai 1.326 one thousand times
三十回 sanjuk-kai 0.636 thirty times
五十回 gojuk-kai 0.360 fifty times
四十回 yonjuk-kai 0.195 forty times
六十回 rokujuk-kai 0.134 sixty times
七十回 nanajuk-kai 0.073 seventy times

(金額) (Amount of money)
千円 sen en 21.074 one thousand yen
三百円 sanbyaku en 10.038 three hundred yen
五百円 gohyaku en 16.502 five hundred yen
百円 hyaku en 15.513 one hundred yen
一万円 ichiman en 14.888 ten thousand yen
五千円 gosen en 10.527 five thousand yen
二千円 nisen en 9.836 two thousand yen
一円 ichi en 4.253 one yen
五十円 gojuu en 3.548 fifty yen
五円 go en 1.502 five yen
二円 ni en 0.849 two yen

1 Merged into *shijuu*.

Alphabetical index

Lemma, *part of speech*, English gloss, rank

あ

ああ *adv.* like that 1125
あー *interj.* er, uh, um, hmm, ah, oh 74
アーティスト *n.* artist 3349
愛 *n.* love, affection 1357
相変わらず *adv* as ever, as usual, the same, as before [always] 2629
挨拶(する) *n.* greeting *v.* greet 1356
相性 *n.* compatibility 4717
愛情 *n.* love, affection 2227
合図(する) *n.* signal, sign *v.* signal, sign 4589
愛する *v.* love, care 1165
間 *n.* distance; period 209
あいつ *pron.* that fellow; that thing 2941
相次ぐ *v.* happen one after another 4997
相手 *n.* companion; partner 315
アイデア *n.* idea 3314
IT *n.* IT 2710
ID *n.* identification, ID 4175
合間 *n.* interval, pause, spare moment 4456
曖昧 *na-adj.* vague, ambiguous 3339
会う *v.* meet, see 311
合う *v.* fit, suit, agree 697
あえて *adv.* dare 1936
青 *n.* blue 3923
青い *i-adj.* blue; pale; unripe 1797
赤 *n.* red 2068
赤い *i-adj.* red 1308
赤字 *n.* deficit, loss, the red 4430
赤ちゃん *n.* baby, infant 1371
明かり *n.* light 2295
上がる *v.* go up, rise; end; get nervous 557
明るい *i-adj.* bright, light; cheerful 978
赤ん坊 *n.* baby 3947
秋 *n.* autumn, fall 977
明らか *na-adj.* clear, obvious 743
諦める *v.* give up, quit 1653
飽きる *v.* tire, weary, be tired of, get bored 2540
あきれる *v.* be amazed, be disgusted 4957
空く *v.* become vacant, be free 2082

開く *v.* open 2558
明く *v.* open 4912
アクセス *n.* access 2762
悪魔 *n.* devil, demon 4982
あくまで *adv.* only, to the last 1482
挙げ句 *n.* in the end, finally 4522
開ける *v.* open 646
明ける *v.* begin, dawn, break 4709
あげる *v.* raise, lift 225
あご *n.* jaw, chin 3297
憧れ *n.* admiration 2635
憧れる *v.* long for; admire 3389
朝 *n.* morning 378
浅い *i-adj.* shallow 3974
浅草 *n.* Asakusa (place name) 3293
朝日 *n.* rising sun, morning sun 4349
鮮やか *na-adj.* vivid, lively; skillful 3930
足 *n.* foot; leg 427
味 *n.* flavor, taste 668
アジア *n.* Asia 1892
明日 *n.* tomorrow 2741
足元 *n.* at one's feet; step 2969
味わい *n.* profound, thought-provoking 4924
味わう *v.* taste, savor 1891
味わえる *v.* can taste, can enjoy 4142
明日 *adv., n.* tomorrow 1008
預かる *v.* keep, look after 3749
預ける *v.* leave, check, deposit 2626
汗 *n.* sweat, perspiration 1382
焦る *v.* be in a hurry; be impatient; be eager 3150
あそこ *pron.* there, over there 1320
遊び *n.* play, game 1742
遊ぶ *v.* play 396
値 *n.* price 2824
与える *v.* give, present 416
温かい *i-adj.* warm, genial 1194
温める *v.* warm, heat 2485
頭 *n.* head 323
新しい *i-adj.* new, fresh 308
辺り *n.* area around 778
当たり前 *na-adj.* natural, usual, common, ordinary 1159

当たる *v.* hit, bump, touch; guess right, win 487
あちこち *pron.* here and there, everywhere 3268
あちら *pron.* that way; that place, there; that 2711
あちらこちら *pron.* here and there 2310
あっ *interj.* Ah!, Oh!, Hey! 1916
暑い *i-adj.* hot, warm 1388
熱い *i-adj.* hot, heated 1722
厚い *i-adj.* thick; kind; abundant 3290
悪化(する) *n.* change for the worse *v.* worsen 3022
扱い *n.* treatment 3953
扱う *v.* deal with, handle, treat 1028
暑さ *n.* heat 4644
厚さ *n.* thickness 4842
あっさり *adv.* easily, flatly, simple, plain 4058
圧倒的 *na-adj.* overwhelming 3368
アップ(する) *n.* raise *v.* go up 2532
集まり *n.* meeting, gathering, group 4767
集まる *v.* gather, crowd 672
集める *v.* gather, collect 860
圧力 *n.* pressure, stress 4286
当てはまる *v.* apply 4244
当てる *v.* hit, put, expose, guess 1192
後 *n.* after, later 83
跡 *n.* track, trail; mark, sign 2962
アドバイス *n.* advice 2276
アドレス *n.* address 4272
穴 *n.* hole, pit 1224
あなた, あんた *pron.* you 226
兄 *n.* elder brother 1134
アニメ *n.* animation 4468
姉 *n.* elder sister 1399
あの, あのう, あのー *interj.* Excuse me; uh, eh, um, ah, er 21
あの *adn.* that, those 247
アパート *n.* apartment 1983
アピール(する) *n.* appeal *v.* appeal 3963
浴びる *v.* bathe; pour 2288
危ない *i-adj.* dangerous, risky; questionable 2083
油 *n.* oil 1923
アフリカ *n.* Africa 3341
あふれる *v.* overflow, be filled with 1668
甘い *i-adj.* sweet; soft 1366
余り *adv.* the rest *n.* (not) much 153
余る *v.* be left over; be too many 3459
網 *n.* net 4907
編む *v.* knit, braid 3175
雨 *n.* rain 753
アメリカ *n.* America 312
アメリカ人 *n.* American (person) 2223

怪しい *i-adj.* eerie; doubtful 3788
謝る *v.* apologize 2696
誤る *v.* make a mistake, be wrong 4613
鮎 *n.* sweetfish, ayu 4232
歩む *v.* walk, go through 4256
あら *interj.* Oh! (used by female speakers) 3395
洗う *v.* wash 1229
あらかじめ *adv.* beforehand, in advance 2231
嵐 *n.* storm 4039
争い *n.* fight, struggle, competition 4745
争う *v.* compete 3631
新た *na-adj.* another 875
改めて *adv.* over again; some other time 2044
改める *v.* change; reform 1841
あらゆる *adn.* every, all, any 1331
表わす *v.* show, express, symbolize 1003
現われる *v.* appear, come into sight 737
有り *v. n.* exist; live 2188
あり得る *v.* be possible, be likely, be probable 1881
あり方 *n.* way something ought to be, state of things 1901
ありがたい *i-adj.* kind, welcome 2208
ありがとう *interj.* thank you 1084
ある *v.* be (existence), have (possession), happen, occur 25
ある *adn.* one, a, some, a certain 249
あるいは *conj.* or; perhaps, probably, maybe 237
歩き回る *v.* walk about 4298
歩く *v.* walk 292
アルコール *n.* alcohol 3917
アルバイト *n.* part-time job 1593
アルバム *n.* album 2429
あれ *pron.* that 313
あれ *interj.* Oh 2727
あれこれ *adv.* this and that 4229
アレンジ(する) *n.* arrangement *v.* arrange 4170
泡 *n.* bubble, foam 4519
合わせる *v.* join, add up; adjust 519
慌てる *v.* be flustered, be in a hurry 1920
案 *n.* plan, proposal, idea 4309
案外 *adv.* unexpectedly 4825
安心(する) *n.* peace of mind, relief *v.* feel relieved 1091
安全 *na-adj.* safe *n.* safety, security 1196
安全性 *n.* safety, security 4077
安定(する) *n.* stability *v.* become stable 1538
あんな *adn.* such, like that 1220
案内 *n.* guidance; guide, sign 2397

い

い *p. disc.* QUESTION 1339
胃 *n.* stomach, belly 2680
意 *n.* mind; will; sense 3141
いー *interj.* good, great 258
いいえ *interj.* no 3852
いい加減 *na-adj.* irresponsible, groundless 3442
言い方 *n.* way to say 1535
言い出す *v.* propose, suggest 3922
Eメール *n.* e-mail 3502
委員 *n.* committee member; councillor 2503
委員会 *n.* committee 4226
委員長 *n.* chairperson 4728
言う *v.* say, speak, talk 19
家 *n.* house, home 175
いえ *interj.* no 3558
イエス *n.* yes; Jesus (Christ) 4570
以下 *n.* below, the following 987
意外 *na-adj.* unexpected, surprising 1034
以外 *n.* except 1782
いかが *na-adj.* how 1658
生かす *v.* keep alive; make use of 1326
いかなる *adn.* what kind of, any 3267
いかに *adv.* how, in what way 1198
いかにも *adv.* indeed, really, just 3104
怒り *n.* anger, rage, fury 2333
息 *n.* breath, respiration 1322
意義 *n.* meaning, significance 3388
生き生き *adv.* lively, fresh 3607
勢い *n.* speed; force; vigor 1762
生きがい *n.* pupose in life, something to live for 3768
生き方 *n.* way of life 2180
いきなり *adv.* suddenly, without notice 1104
生き残る *v.* survive 4188
生き物 *n.* creature, life 2816
イギリス *n.* United Kingdom, Britain, England 884
生きる *v.* live 296
行く *v.* go; come 48
育児(する) *n.* childcare *v.* take care of a child 3822
育成(する) *n.* cultivation *v.* bring up, cultivate, mold 3564
幾つ *n.* how many, how old 640
いくら *adv.* how much, however 659
池 *n.* pond 2638
池袋 *n.* Ikebukuro (place name) 2993
意見 *n.* opinion, idea 624
以後 *adv.* after this, since then 3810
移行(する) *n.* shift *v.* shift 3198

イコール *n.* equal 4417
いざ *adv.* when one comes to, if compelled 2147
居酒屋 *n.* (Japanese style) bar, tavern 4694
いささか *adv.* a little, slightly, rather 4535
石 *n.* stone, rock 1354
医師 *n.* doctor 1858
意志 *n.* will, willpower 2316
意思 *n.* will, intention 2888
維持(する) *n.* maintenance, preservation *v.* keep, maintain 1512
意識(する) *n.* consciousness, awareness *v.* be conscious 730
いじめ *n.* bullying 2456
いじめる *v.* torment, bully, tease 2952
医者 *n.* doctor 973
衣装 *n.* costume 3835
以上 *n.* more than; mentioned above; since 317
異常 *na-adj.* abnormal *n.* disorder 1931
椅子 *n.* chair 1440
イスラエル *n.* Israel 4960
いずれ *adv.* anyway, sooner or later *pron.* either 616
遺跡 *n.* ruins, remains 3026
以前 *n.* before, formerly 620
依然 *adv.* still, as before 3422
忙しい *i-adj.* busy, occupied 1163
急ぐ *v.* hurry 1735
依存(する) *n.* dependence, reliance *v.* depend, rely, 4024
板 *n.* board, plate 2705
痛い *i-adj.* painful, hurt 776
偉大 *na-adj.* great, grand 3920
抱く *v.* have, hold, embrace 1378
致す *v.* do (humble) 679
いたずら(する) *n.* mischief, trick, joke *v.* be mischievous, play a trick 4688
いただく *v.* get, receive (humble) 537
痛み *n.* pain, ache 1294
痛む *v.* ache, hurt, pain 3871
炒める *v.* fry, stir-fry 1948
痛める *v.* hurt 4969
イタリア *n.* Italy 1823
至る *v.* lead to, get 878
一 *n.* one 144
位置(する) *n.* position, location *v.* be located 913
一位 *n.* first prize 4247
いちいち *adv.* one by one; everything 3519
一員 *n.* member 4224
一応 *adv.* at first glance; at least, just 415
一月 *n.* January 858

一時 *adv., n.* at one time, temporary, for a while 1247
一時間 *n.* one hour 1102
一時的 *na-adj.* temporary 3632
著しい *i-adj.* significant 2468
一台 *n.* one (machine/vehicle) 3249
一段 *n.* one step 4998
位置付ける *v.* rank; evaluate 3914
一度 *n.* once 350
一日 *n.* a day, the day, one day 514
一日中 *n.* all day 3898
一年 *n.* one year 704
一年間 *n.* one year 1550
一年生 *n.* first grade, first year 2505
一年半 *n.* one year and a half 4821
一番 *adv.* number one, first, most 147
一部 *n.* part 635
一枚 *n.* one (sheet, slice) 1338
一万円 *n.* ten thousand yen 3387
一面 *n.* side, facet 2886
一連 *n.* course of, series of 3531
いつ *pron.* when 174
一家 *n.* family, house, household 4328
五日 *n.* fifth (date); five days 2386
いつか *adv.* someday 3619
一回 *n.* once 479
一階 *n.* first floor, ground floor 3204
一回目 *n.* first time 4952
一ケ月 *n.* one month 1178
一環 *n.* part of 3629
一貫 *n.* consistent 4696
一気 *adv., n.* at a stretch, in one gulp 1818
一見 *adv.* at a glance 2968
一軒 *n.* one building 4892
一個 *n.* one, piece 1284
一向 *adv.* (not) at all; completely 4262
いつ頃 *n.* around what time 4685
一切 *adv., n.* all, entirely, not ... at all 1272
一歳 *n.* one year old 4643
一冊 *n.* one (book) 3193
一種 *n.* kind, sort, species 1951
一周 *n.* one round 4927
一週間 *n.* one week 1035
一瞬 *n., adv.* a moment, an instant 1645
一緒 *n.* together, with 222
一生 *n.* life 1595
一生懸命 *na-adj.* hard, as hard as one can 847
一斉 *n.* all at once 3738
一層 *adv., n.* more 1576
一体 *n., adv.* how, what, why, who 705

いったん *adv.* once; for a moment 1942
一致(する) *n.* agreement, accord *v.* consent, agree 2605
五つ *num.* five 2934
一定(する) *n., v.* a certain, fixed, constant 1657
一点 *n.* point, single point 2973
一杯 *n., adv.* cup(ful), glass(ful), be full of, a lot of 419
一泊 *n.* one night stay 3802
一発 *n.* shot, punch 4526
一般 *n.* general 946
一般的 *na-adj.* general, common, ordinary 955
一匹 *n.* one (animal) 2670
一分 *n.* one minute 4179
いっぺん *n.* at the same time; altogether 2849
一歩 *n.* step 1976
一方 *n.* one side *conj.* on the other hand 558
一方的 *na-adj.* unilateral, one-sided 4466
一本 *n.* one (long/cylindrical object) 917
移転(する) *n.* move *v.* move 3565
遺伝子 *n.* gene 2739
糸 *n.* thread, string 2546
意図 *n.* intention 3178
井戸 *n.* well 4722
移動(する) *n.* movement *v.* transfer, move, migrate 1119
従兄弟 *n.* cousin 4129
営む *v.* run a business; engage in; hold a ceremony 3412
否 *n.* no 3626
田舎 *n.* countryside; one's hometown 1042
犬 *n.* dog 390
命 *n.* life 901
祈る *v.* pray, wish 3123
違反(する) *n.* violation *v.* violate 2914
イベント *n.* event 1522
今 *n.* now 69
居間 *n.* living room 4947
いまいち *adv.* not quite, not really 4258
今頃 *n.* this time 4669
いまさら *adv.* now (after such a long time) 3078
いまだ *adv.* still, yet, so far 1120
いまや *adv.* now 3253
意味(する) *n.* meaning, sense *v.* mean 201
イメージ(する) *n.* image *v.* imagine, have an impression 562
妹 *n.* younger sister 1375
嫌 *n., na-adj.* unpleasant, disagreeable 499
いや *interj.* No 501
いやあ *interj.* Well, sorry 4638

嫌がる *v.* be reluctant; hate 3095
癒す *v.* heal, cure, recover from 3038
いよいよ *adv.* finally, at last 1612
異様 *na-adj.* strange 4928
意欲 *n.* will, motivation 3755
依頼（する） *n.* request *v.* request, ask 2355
以来 *n.* since 2514
いらいら（する） *v.* be annoyed, be irritated, be impatient 3986
イラク *n.* Iraq 3838
いらっしゃる *v.* come, go (honorific); be (honorific) 689
入り口 *n.* entrance 2043
医療 *n.* medical care, medical treatment 2689
いる *v.* be, exist; stay 79
要る *v.* need, want 1208
入る *v.* come in, enter; join 1675
入れる *v.* put in; include 164
色 *n.* color 531
いろいろ *adv., na-adj.* various 143
いろんな *adn.* various 203
岩 *n.* rock 3196
祝い *n.* celebration 4501
祝う *v* celebrate 4936
違和感 *n.* uncomfortable feeling 4072
いわば *adv.* so to speak, as it were 2025
いわゆる *adn.* what is called, what you call, so-called 330
印刷（する） *n.* printing *v.* print 3330
印象 *n.* impression 540
印象的 *na-adj.* impressive 3308
インストール（する） *n.* installation *v.* install 4853
インターネット *n.* Internet 939
引退（する） *n.* retirement *v.* retire 3850
インタビュー（する） *n.* interview *v.* interview 3647
インド *n.* India 1896
引用（する） *n.* quotation *v.* quote 3942

う

う *aux.* SOLICITATION 104
ウイルス *n.* virus 3382
ウインドウズ *n.* Windows 2470
うー *interj.* Woo, Oooh 137
ううん *interj.* no; well 3437
上 *n.* top; above; up; on 171
上で *cp.* after; in the context of 1810
植える *v.* plant 2403
伺う *v.* ask, inquire 1528
うかがう *v.* peep, peer; watch for (the chance) 3656
浮かぶ *v.* float, rise 1394
浮かべる *v.* float; show; imagine 2998
受かる *v.* pass 2466
浮く *v.* float, suspend 2904
受け入れる *v.* receive, accept, agree 1434
受け継ぐ *v.* inherit 3649
受け付け *n.* acceptance, information desk, reception (desk) 3004
受け付ける *v.* accept 4689
受け止める *v.* take, catch 2712
受け取る *v.* get, accept 1545
受ける *v.* get, receive, take 187
動かす *v.* move, shift, operate 1218
動き *n.* movement, action, motion 767
動く *v.* move; work (machine) 566
ウサギ *n.* rabbit 3136
牛 *n.* cattle, cow, ox 2492
失う *v.* lose 861
後ろ *n.* behind, back 871
薄い *i-adj.* thin, light, weak 1301
薄れる *v.* become dim 4919
うそ *n.* lie, falsehood 1173
歌 *n.* song 645
歌う *v.* sing 638
疑い *n.* doubt, suspicion 3327
疑う *v.* suspect, doubt 2446
うち *n.* inside; of; before 133
家 *n* house, home 4966
打ち明ける *v.* speak one's mind; confess 4882
打ち合わせ *n.* meeting 3948
内側 *n.* inside, interior, inner 2636
打ち込む *v.* devote oneself 3742
打ち出す *v.* work out, come up with; announce 4809
宇宙 *n.* universe, space 2132
打つ *v.* hit, strike, beat 619
美しい *i-adj.* beautiful 867
美しさ *n.* beauty 2836
移す *v.* move, transfer, shift 2119
写す *v.* copy, trace 4653
訴える *v.* sue; complain; appeal 1768
移る *v.* move, transfer, shift 1360
映る *v.* reflect 2594
写る *v.* photograph 3999
器 *n.* container 3092
腕 *n.* arm; skill, ability 1157
うどん *n.* udon, thick white noodles 4941
促す *v.* urge 2600
うなずく *v.* nod 1677
奪う *v.* rob, take by force; fascinate 2059
馬 *n.* horse 907

うまい *i-adj.* delicious, tasty; good at 357
生まれ *n.* birth; birthplace 4167
生まれ育つ *v.* be born and raised 4573
生まれる *v.* be born 364
海 *n.* sea, ocean 414
生み出す *v.* create, invent 2229
産む、生む *v.* give birth; produce 1110
有無 *n.* existence, presence 3899
梅 *n.* plum, Japanese apricot 4471
埋める *v.* cover, bury 2353
裏 *n.* reverse, back; rear 1397
裏切る *v.* betray 4099
羨ましい *i-adj.* envious; enviable 3380
売り上げ *n.* sales 3011
売る *v.* sell 538
うるさい *i-adj.* noisy; annoying 2170
嬉しい *i-adj.* glad, happy 394
売れる *v.* sell 1524
浮気 *n.* affair 3860
うわさ(する) *n.* gossip, rumor *v.* talk about 1883
上回る *v.* exceed, surpass 2657
うん *interj.* yes, yeah 265
運 *n.* luck, fortune 2260
運営(する) *n.* management *v.* manage, run 2179
運転(する) *n.* driving, operation *v.* drive 1571
運転手 *n.* driver 3805
運動(する) *n.* exercise *v.* exercise, move 895
運動会 *n.* sports meeting 4618
運命 *n.* destiny, fate 2430
運用(する) *n.* making use of *v.* manage 3305

え

絵 *n.* picture, painting 593
エアコン *n.* air-conditioning, air conditioner 4864
永遠 *n.* eternity, permanence 2846
映画 *n.* movie 503
映画館 *n.* movie theater, cinema 3235
影響(する) *n.* influence *v.* affect, influence 468
営業(する) *n.* business, sales *v.* do business 2071
影響力 *n.* influence, impact 4895
英語 *n.* English language 439
英国 *n.* United Kingdom, Britain 3213
映像 *n.* picture, image, video 2085
HP *n.* home page 3900
栄養 *n.* nutrition 2760
えー、ええ *interj.* eh?, what?; well, yes 18
えーと *interj.* well, let me see 90
笑顔 *n.* smile 1661
描く *v.* draw; describe 707

駅 *n.* station 500
駅前 *n.* in front of the station 2142
餌 *n.* feed; bait 1678
エジプト *n.* Egypt 3435
枝 *n.* branch, twig, bough 2550
江戸 *n.* Edo 2156
江戸時代 *n.* Edo era 2673
NHK *n.* Nihon Hoso Kyokai (Japan Broadcasting Corporation) 2613
エネルギー *n.* energy, power 1355
えび *n.* prawn, shrimp 3525
エピソード *n.* episode, anecdote 2964
絵本 *n.* picture book 4034
笑み *n.* smile 4306
偉い *i-adj.* great, big 1720
選ぶ *v.* choose, select 382
得る *v.* get, obtain 380
エレベーター *n.* elevator 3973
縁 *n.* chance, fate, destiny 2289
円 *n.* yen; circle 3937
延々 *adv.* on and on, dragging on 4678
円滑 *na-adj.* smooth 4135
演技 *n.* performance 4189
演劇 *n.* drama, play 3207
演出(する) *n., v.* direction, direct 2817
援助(する) *n.* assistance, aid, support *v.* help, support, assist 2337
エンジン *n.* engine 2420
演ずる *v.* play, perform 2752
演奏(する) *n.* (musical) performance *v.* perform, play 1695
延長(する) *n.* extension *v.* extend 3288
鉛筆 *n.* pencil 3791
塩 *n.* salt 4900
遠慮(する) *n.* reserve *v.* hesitate 4462

お

御 *prefix* POLITENESS PREFIX 2301
おい *interj.* hey 2578
追いかける *v.* run after, chase 2931
追い込む *v.* drive into 4798
おいしい *i-adj.* delicious, tasty 345
追い詰める *v.* run down, corner 4962
追う *v.* follow, chase, pursue 1290
負う *v.* take, assume 2417
王 *n.* king, monarch 2623
応援(する) *n.* support *v.* cheer, support 1775
王様 *n.* king 3521
応ずる、応じる *v.* answer, respond, accept 1122

往復 *n.* round trip 4131
欧米 *n.* Europe and America 3304
応募(する) *n.* application *v.* apply for 3361
応用(する) *n.* application *v.* apply 4360
終える *v.* finish, end 1855
おー *interj.* Oh, Wow! 122
多い *i-adj.* many, much, a lot of 124
大いに *adv.* very, greatly 2347
覆う *v.* cover 2306
OS *n.* operating system 3396
大型 *n.* big, large 4780
大きい *i-adj.* big, large, great 220
大きさ *n.* size 988
大きな *adn.* big, large, great 213
多く *n.* many, most 437
オークション *n.* auction 2908
大蔵省 *n.* Ministry of Finance 4752
オーケー *n.* O.K. 1630
大げさ *na-adj.* exaggerated 3545
大声 *n.* loud voice 2937
大阪 *n.* Osaka 1285
大さじ *n.* tablespoon 2048
オーストラリア *n.* Australia 1628
大勢 *n.* a large number of, many 1990
大手 *n.* major companies 3465
大幅 *na-adj.* steep, big, sharp 2275
OB *n.* OB (old boy), alumnus 4787
オーブン *n.* oven 4531
オープン(する) *n., v.* open 3186
概ね *adv.* mostly, mainly, generally 4130
大家さん *n.* landlord, owner 4013
丘 *n.* hill 3246
おかげ *n.* thanks, virtue 1195
おかしい *i-adj.* funny, amusing 915
おかしな *adn.* funny, ridiculous 4219
犯す *v.* commit, offend; break 2506
おかず *n.* food, side dish 4735
小川 *n.* stream 4567
荻窪 *n.* Ogikubo (place name) 4253
補う *v.* supplement, compensate 4743
沖縄 *n.* Okinawa 1475
起きる *v.* get up; wake; happen 498
置く *v.* put, place; leave 276
おく *v.* at; in; on 1164
奥 *n.* inner part, back; bottom 1242
奥様 *n.* wife (honorific) 3781
奥さん *n.* wife 1562
送る *v.* send; spend (time) 443
贈る *v.* give (as a present), send 3813

遅れる *v.* be late, be delayed 1563
お子さん *n.* (someone else's) child 2349
起こす *v.* wake; raise; cause 614
行なう *v.* do, carry out, hold 146
お好み焼き *n.* okonomiyaki (Japanese-style savoury pancake with vegetables, meat, seafood etc.) 4386
起こる *v.* happen, occur, take place 526
怒る *v.* get angry 839
押さえる *v.* press down, hold 1169
幼い *i-adj.* young, immature, childish 2522
収まる *v.* hold, pack 2548
収める *v.* obtain, gain; put; keep 1875
伯父 *n.* uncle 1108
教え *n.* teaching, lesson, doctrine 3485
教える *v.* teach, tell 267
押し付ける *v.* press against, force 3417
おしゃべり(する) *n.* chat, talk *v.* chat, talk 4312
おしゃれ *na-adj.* fashionable, smart 2182
押す *v.* push, press 950
雄 *n.* male animal 3303
汚染(する) *n.* pollution *v.* pollute 3499
遅い *i-adj.* late; slow 1025
襲う *v.* attack, hit; seize 2103
遅く *n.* late 4961
おそらく *adv.* probably, likely 804
おそれ *n.* fear, danger 1934
恐れる *v.* fear, be afraid 2467
恐ろしい *i-adj.* terrible, frightful, amazing, awful 1973
教わる *v.* learn 2733
お宅 *n.* your house 2919
穏やか *na-adj.* mild; calm, peaceful 2792
陥る *v.* fall into 2368
落ち込む *v.* sink, go down; be depressed 2583
落ち着く *v.* settle, calm down 1116
落ちる *v.* fall, drop 611
仰る *v.* say, tell, speak (honorific) 1174
夫 *n.* husband 621
音 *n.* sound, noise 413
弟 *n.* younger brother 1368
男 *n.* man, male 293
男達 *n.* men 3462
男の子 *n.* boy, male child 1234
落とす *v.* drop, lose, turn down 1064
訪れる *v.* visit, call on, arrive 1381
大人 *n.* adult 700
おとなしい *i-adj.* gentle, well behaved, quiet 3161
踊り *n.* dance 3416
劣る *v.* be inferior 4505
踊る *v.* dance 1995

驚き *n.* surprise, amazement 2804
驚く *v.* be surprised 708
おなか *n.* stomach, belly 1020
同じ *adn.* same 149
同じく *adv.* likewise, like, as 2133
鬼 *n.* ogre, devil, demon 4105
各々 *n.* each 4914
己 *n.* oneself (first person pronoun) 3893
伯母 *n.* aunt 1260
おはよう *interj.* good morning 4410
帯 *n.* kimono sash, belt 4385
帯びる *v.* have a trace of, be tinged with 4381
オフィス *n.* office 3625
お袋 *n.* mother 3542
覚え *n.* memory 3216
覚える *v.* learn, remember, memorize 358
お前 *n.* you (colloquial) 598
おまけ *n.* addition, free gift 2768
おめでとう *interj.* congratulations 4646
思い *n.* thought, mind, heart 455
重い *i-adj.* heavy, important 1154
思い浮かべる *v.* recall, remember 4178
思い切る *v.* give up; venture 1838
思い込む *v.* be obsessed with the idea 3682
思い出す *v.* remember 594
思い付く *v.* think of, guess, conceive 2586
思い出 *n.* memory, reminiscence 653
思いやり *n.* consideration 3968
思う *v.* think, believe; feel; expect 34
思える *v.* it seems that 742
重さ *n.* weight 3650
面白い *i-adj.* interesting; fun; funny 383
面白さ *n.* interest, fun 4166
おもちゃ *n.* toy 3244
表 *n.* front; outside, surface 4557
主な *adn.* main, chief 1814
主に *adv.* mainly, for the most part, chiefly 1259
親 *n.* parent 336
親子 *n.* parent and child, parents and children 2362
親父 *n.* father; old man; boss 1852
泳ぐ *v.* swim 1989
およそ *adv.* around, about 2777
及び *conj.* and, as well as 256
及ぶ *v.* reach 1597
及ぼす *v.* influence, affect 2559
オランダ *n.* Netherlands 3854
折 *n.* occasion, opportunity 3329
下りる *v.* go down; come down 759
オリンピック *n.* Olympics 2461

おる *v.* be, exist (humble) 684
折る *v.* break; fold; bend 3336
俺 *pron.* I (used by male speakers) 363
俺達 *n.* we (used by male speakers) 3264
折れる *v.* break 3522
下ろす *v.* take down; unload; withdraw; fillet (fish); grate 1607
終わり *n.* end 837
終わる *v.* end, finish 200
音楽 *n.* music 494
温泉 *n.* hot spring, spa 1697
温度 *n.* temperature; heat 2391
女 *n.* woman, female 399
女の子 *n.* girl 682

か

か *p. disc.* QUESTION 29
か *p.* if; or 36
火 *n.* fire; Tuesday, Tue. 2191
彼 *pron.* he 2669
蚊 *n.* mosquito 4055
が *p. case* NOMINATIVE 7
が *p. conj.* ADVERSATIVE 37
が *conj.* but 1812
（お）母さん *n.* mother, Mom 528
カーテン *n.* curtain 4156
カード *n.* card 2090
会 *n.* meeting, gathering 1636
害 *n.* harm, damage 4245
会員 *n.* member 3833
絵画 *n.* painting, picture 4369
海外 *n.* overseas, abroad, foreign 923
海外旅行 *n.* travel abroad, foreign trip 2070
改革（する） *n.* reform *v.* make reforms 2604
海岸 *n.* seashore, seaside 3232
会議 *n.* meeting 2572
解決（する） *n.* solution, settlement *v.* solve, settle 1100
介護（する） *n.* nursing, care *v.* nurse, look after 2342
外国 *n.* foreign country 1137
外国人 *n.* foreigner 2063
介護保険 *n.* nursing care insurance 3669
開催（する） *n.* holding, opening *v.* hold, open 1141
解散（する） *n.* dissolution *v.* dissolve, break up 3515
開始（する） *n.* beginning, start *v.* begin, start 1647
会社 *n.* company, firm 240
解釈（する） *n.* interpretation *v.* interpret 2058
回収（する） *n.* collection *v.* collect 3473
外出（する） *n.* going out, outing *v.* go out 4089
解除（する） *n.* cancellation *v.* cancel, lift 4979

解消（する） *n.* cancellation, annulment; cancel, dissolve 2427
会場 *n.* hall; site 1515
回数 *n.* frequency 4029
改正（する） *n.* amendment *v.* amend 2091
解説（する） *n.* explanation, comment, description *v.* explain 2478
開設（する） *n.* establishment *v.* establish, set up 4467
改善（する） *n.* improvement, reform *v.* improve 1384
階段 *n.* stairs 1627
会長 *n.* president, chairperson 3374
快適 *na-adj.* comfortable 2940
回転（する） *n.* revolution *v.* revolve, turn round, spin 3517
ガイド（する） *n.* guide, conductor *v.* guide 4779
回答（する） *n.* answer, response, reply *v.* answer, respond, reply 1443
該当（する） *n.* fall under, be applicable, correspond 2396
飼い主 *n.* pet owner 3829
概念 *n.* notion, idea, concept 2486
開発（する） *n.* development *v.* develop 831
回避（する） *n.* avoidance *v.* avoid 4881
外部 *n.* outside 3719
回復（する） *n.* recovery *v.* recover 1639
解放（する） *n.* liberation *v.* liberate 2922
解明（する） *n.* clarification *v.* solve 3931
買い物（する） *n.* shopping *v.* go shopping 1236
概要 *n.* outline, summary 3534
改良 *n.* improvement 4289
会話（する） *n.* conversation *v.* talk, chat 1206
買う *adv.* buy 192
飼う *v.* keep, have, breed 822
カウンター *n.* counter 4011
返す *v.* return; repay; turn over 1295
かえって *adv.* on the contrary, rather 2021
帰り *n.* return 1493
返る *v.* return 197
変える *v.* change 467
顔 *n.* face 251
顔色 *n.* complexion 4902
香り *n.* smell, scent 1431
画家 *n.* artist, painter 4874
抱える *v.* hold, carry, employ 1288
価格 *n.* price 1584
科学 *n.* science 2877
科学的 *na-adj.* scientific 4811
掲げる *v.* hang out, hold up 1414
欠かせる *v.* cause to lack 3595

鏡 *n.* mirror 2493
輝く *v.* shine, glitter, twinkle, glow 2098
かかる *v.* hang; take; cost 212
関わり *n.* relation, connection 3212
関わる *v.* concern, affect, be involved 665
下記 *n.* the following, mentioned below 4727
柿 *n.* persimmon 4986
鍵 *n.* key 2031
書き込む *v.* write in, jot down 3731
限り *n.* limit 688
限る *v.* limit, restrict 750
書く *v.* write 163
かく *v.* scratch; paddle; shovel 1850
核 *n.* nucleus, core 4374
欠く *v.* lack; chip 4485
家具 *n.* furniture 3666
額 *n.* amount of money; frame 1376
覚悟（する） *n.* readiness, preparedness *v.* be ready 2545
確実 *na-adj.* certain, sure 1692
学者 *n.* scholar 4474
各種 *n.* various, all sorts of 3806
学習（する） *n.* learning, study *v.* learn, study 2685
確信（する） *n.* conviction *v.* be convinced 3076
隠す *v.* hide, conceal 1490
学生 *n.* student 909
学生時代 *n.* student days, university days 2634
拡大（する） *n.* enlargement, expansion *v.* enlarge, expand 1251
各地 *n.* each place 2582
確定（する） *n.* determination, decision *v.* determine, decide 4225
角度 *n.* angle 3527
獲得（する） *n.* acquisition *v.* get, gain 2698
確認（する） *n.* confirmation *v.* confirm 622
学年 *n.* grade, year 4806
学部 *n.* faculty, department 4670
確保（する） *n.* securement, reservation *v.* secure, maintain, guarantee 996
革命 *n.* revolution 3528
学問 *n.* study, learning 3586
確立（する） *n.* establishment *v.* establish 1848
確率 *n.* probability 3576
隠れる *v.* be hidden, hide 2352
影 *n.* shadow 2169
陰 *n.* shade, shadow; behind someone's back 2784
駆け付ける *v.* run, rush 4060
掛ける *v.* hang; take; cost 199
欠ける *v.* lack; chip 2729
過去 *n.* past 740

加工(する) *n.* processing *v.* process 3555
囲む *v.* surround 1682
傘 *n.* umbrella 4276
重なる *v.* pile up; conspire 2581
重ねる *v.* stack; repeat 1582
飾る *v.* decorate 1585
お菓子 *n.* sweets, snack food 1435
歌詞 *n.* song lyrics 3107
家事 *n.* housework 3453
火事 *n.* fire 4498
賢い *i-adj.* wise, clever 4605
歌手 *n.* singer 4125
箇所 *n.* place, point, part 4631
かしら *p. disc.* I wonder 921
貸す *v.* lend, rent 2080
数 *n.* number 623
ガス *n.* gas 3381
数多く *adv.* many, a number of 3784
かすか *na-adj.* a few, a little 3561
数々 *n.* many, numerous 3940
課する *v.* assign, charge, impose 4113
風 *n.* wind 910
風邪 *n.* cold 1993
稼ぐ *v.* earn 2872
画像 *n.* picture, image 1834
数える *v.* count, number 2589
家族 *n.* family 347
ガソリン *n.* gasoline, petrol 3845
方 *n.* person, man 159
肩 *n.* shoulder 1079
型 *n.* model, pattern, type 3006
固い *i-adj.* hard, solid, stiff 1214
課題 *n.* subject; assignment, task 1170
難い *suffix* hard to ... 3662
方々 *n.* people 1207
方達 *n.* people (honorific) 2002
形 *n.* form, shape, figure 205
片付ける *v.* put in order, tidy; clear away; finish 3320
片手 *n.* one hand 3279
刀 *n.* sword 4370
片方 *n.* one side; the other one 3273
固まり *n.* mass, lump 2939
固まる *v.* harden; become certain 3064
傾ける *v.* tilt, incline 3790
固める *v.* make something hard, strengthen 3507
語る *v.* talk, tell 886
傍ら *n.* side, besides 3830
価値 *n.* value, worth 1332
価値観 *n.* sense of values 2498

勝つ *v.* win, defeat 894
かつ *conj.* besides, also, as well 1096
がっかり(する) *v.* be disappointed 3726
活気 *n.* vigor, energy, liveliness 4760
楽器 *n.* musical instrument 1751
担ぐ *v.* carry, shoulder 4548
格好 *n.* appearance, shape, look 1068
学校 *n.* school 295
格好良い *i-adj.* cool, good-looking 3404
各国 *n.* each country, various countries 3119
合宿(する) *n.* training camp *v.* stay together in a camp 3529
活性化(する) *n.* revitalization *v.* revitalize 3033
勝手 *na-adj.* on one's own, at one's convenience 1047
かつて *adv.* once, before, ever, former 1131
カット *n.* cut 2766
活動(する) *n.* activity *v.* be active 685
活発 *na-adj.* lively, active; brisk 3480
カップ *n.* cup 4425
カップル *n.* couple 4138
合併(する) *n.* combination, merger *v.* combine, merge 3135
活躍(する) *n.* activity, action *v.* be active, flourish 1447
活用(する) *n.* application *v.* exploit, take advantage of 1408
家庭 *n.* home, household, family 805
過程 *n.* process 1918
仮定(する) *n.* assumption, supposition *v.* assume, suppose 4021
角 *n.* corner 4015
家内 *n.* one's family; my wife 3450
神奈川県 *n.* Kanagawa Prefecture 3591
悲しい *i-adj.* sad, unhappy 752
悲しみ *n.* sadness, grief 2806
カナダ *n.* Canada 2282
必ず *adv.* always, certainly, surely 391
必ずしも *adv.* not necessarily, not always 1970
かなり *adv.* considerably, rather 206
加入(する) *n.* admission, joining *v.* join 3003
金 *n.* money 250
鐘 *n.* bell, chime 4765
兼ねる *v.* combine; serve both 3567
可能 *na-adj.* possible 690
可能性 *n.* possibility 629
彼女 *pron.* she; girlfriend 244
彼女達 *n.* they (female) 3723
カバー *n.* cover 3975
鞄 *n.* bag 4284
株 *n.* stump; stock, share 3077

カフェ *n.* café 3492
株価 *n.* stock prices 3957
株式 *n.* stock, shares 3490
株主 *n.* stockholder, shareholder 4831
かぶる *v.* put on, cover 2069
花粉 *n.* pollen 4955
壁 *n.* wall, barrier 1071
カボチャ *n.* pumpkin 4242
構う *v.* mind, care about 1433
構える *v.* get set, get ready; set up 3111
鎌倉 *n.* Kamakura 4617
我慢(する) *n.* patience, endurance, tolerance
    v. be patient, endure 1393
神 *n.* God, deity, spirit 834
紙 *n.* paper 1374
髪 *n.* hair 1615
神様 *n.* god, God 2447
髪の毛 *n.* hair 3001
かむ *v.* bite; chew 2484
亀 *n.* turtle, tortoise 4624
カメラ *n.* camera 1755
画面 *n.* screen 1962
かもしれない *cp.* perhaps, maybe 155
かゆい *i-adj.* itchy 4849
通う *v.* attend, go to, commute 627
から *p. case* from 32
から *p. conj.* because, since 61
から *conj.* because 1424
柄 *n.* pattern, character 4028
カラー *n.* color 4869
カラオケ *n.* karaoke 3158
カラス *n.* crow 3700
ガラス *n.* glass 3240
体 *n.* body 286
絡む *v.* get entangled, involve; pick a quarrel 3108
仮 *n.* temporary, provisional; assumed 2020
借りる *v.* borrow, rent 932
軽い *i-adj.* light, slight 806
彼 *pron.* he 158
カレー *n.* curry 2469
彼氏 *n.* boyfriend 2372
彼ら *pron.* they 458
枯れる *v.* wither, die 4715
川 *n.* river, stream 784
皮、革 *n.* skin, hide, jacket 1455
側 *n.* side 1466
可愛い *i-adj.* cute, nice, lovely 691
可愛がる *v.* love, treat with affection 3181
かわいそう *na-adj.* pitiful, miserable 1833

可愛らしい *i-adj.* lovely 4660
乾く *v.* dry 2767
川崎 *n.* Kawasaki 4770
交わす *v.* exchange 3405
代わり *n.* substitute, replacement, alternative 1136
変わり *n.* change 3885
変わる *v.* change 235
間 *n.* during; between 2125
感 *n.* feeling, emotion 4416
がん *n.* cancer. 1586
考え *n.* idea, thought 717
考え方 *n.* way of thinking, attitude 728
考える *v.* think 102
感覚 *n.* sense; sensation, feeling 1045
観客 *n.* audience 4231
環境 *n.* environment 571
環境問題 *n.* environmental problem 4377
関係 *n.* relationship, connection 318
歓迎(する) *n.* reception, welcome *v.* welcome 4769
関係者 *n.* person concerned 2930
感激(する) *n.* deep emotion *v.* be impressed 2903
観光(する) *n.* sightseeing *v.* go sightseeing 2813
観光客 *n.* tourist 3633
韓国 *n.* Korea, South Korea, Republic of Korea 1327
看護婦 *n.* nurse (female) 2884
関西 *n.* Kansai region 3337
観察(する) *n.* observation *v.* observe 1897
監視(する) *n.* observation *v.* watch 4056
感じ *n.* feeling, impression; atmosphere 138
漢字 *n.* kanji, Chinese character 2423
感謝(する) *n.* gratitude, appreciation *v.* thank,
    be grateful 1156
患者 *n.* patient, case 1070
感情 *n.* feeling, emotion 1392
感触 *n.* feel, touch 4911
感じる *v.* feel 210
関心 *n.* interest 975
感心(する) *n.* admiration *v.* admire 2978
肝心 *na-adj.* main, essential, important 4043
関する *v.* be related to, be concerned with 2022
完成(する) *n.* completion *v.* complete 1539
感性 *n.* sensitivity, sensibility 4196
感染(する) *n.* infection *v.* contract, catch,
    be infected 3623
完全 *na-adj.* perfect, complete 908
感想 *n.* feeling, impression 1887
乾燥(する) *n.* dryness *v.* dry 2775
肝臓 *n.* liver 4141
簡単 *na-adj.* easy 400

勘違い(する) v. misunderstand, mistake 3637
缶詰 n. canned food 3229
観点 n. viewpoint, standpoint 1783
関東 n. Kanto region 3714
感動(する) n. deep emotion v. be impressed, be moved 1043
監督(する) n. manager, director, proctor, invigilator v. supervise, direct 1621
頑張る v. do one's best 448
看板 n. signboard, billboard; attraction 3451
幹部 n. executive 3843
完璧 na-adj. perfect 3294
関与(する) n. participation v. participate 3798
管理(する) n. control, management v. manage, control 1616
完了(する) n. complete v. complete 3826
関連(する) n. relation, connection v. be related, be connected 1660
緩和(する) n. relaxation, relief v. relieve 4707

き

気 n. mind, heart 130
木 n. wood; tree 410
キー n. key 4080
黄色 n. yellow 3257
黄色い i-adj. yellow 3575
キーワード n. keyword 3924
議員 n. member of Diet/Congress/Parliament 4513
消える v. go off; disappear 1014
記憶(する) n. memory v. memorize 652
気温 n. temperature 3236
機会 n. opportunity 715
機械 n. machine 1566
議会 n. Diet, Parliament, Congress 4301
着替える v. change clothes; get dressed 4877
企画(する) n. planning v. plan 2284
気軽 na-adj. light-hearted, feel free 3283
期間 n. period, term, interval 1239
機関 n. engine; organization; facilities 3432
危機 n. crisis, critical moment 3348
木々 n. trees 4322
企業 n. company, business 588
聞く, 聴く v. hear; listen; listen to, obey 112
利く v. act, work 1051
危険 n. danger, hazard na-adj. dangerous 920
起源 n. origin 4132
期限 n. period; deadline; term 4865
危険性 n. danger 4413
気候 n. climate 3708

機構 n. mechanism, structure, system 4855
聞こえる v. hear; sound 738
帰国(する) n., v. going/coming back to one's own country 2925
記載(する) n. registration entry v. record, write down 1705
刻む v. cut into fine pieces; engrave; tick 3163
記事 n. article 958
生地 n. cloth, material; dough 1572
儀式 n. ceremony, ritual 4637
記者 n. journalist, reporter 3988
汽車 n. train 4940
記述(する) n. description, account v. describe 2695
技術 n. technique, skill 954
技術的 na-adj. technical, practical 4182
基準 n. standard 1600
キス(する) n. kiss v. kiss 3670
傷 n. injury; scratch; bruise; flaw; stain 2062
築く v. build, have 2791
傷つく v. be injured, be hurt 4241
傷付ける v. hurt; damage 3295
絆 n. tie, bond 4716
規制(する) n. regulation v. regulate 1885
犠牲 n. sacrifice, expense 2862
季節 n. season 1335
着せる v. put on, dress 4852
基礎 n. basis, basics, foundation 2398
規則 n. rule, regulation 3494
貴族 n. noble, nobility, aristocracy 4540
既存 n. existing 4906
北 n. north 1594
ギター n. guitar 1987
期待(する) n. expectation v. expect 701
鍛える v. train, discipline 2772
帰宅(する) n. coming home v. come home 3496
北朝鮮 n. Democratic People's Republic of Korea, North Korea 3082
汚い i-adj. dirty; unfair; vulgar 1826
吉祥寺 n. Kichijoji (place name) 4628
貴重 na-adj. precious, valuable 2302
きちんと adv. precisely, accurately, neatly 892
きつい i-adj. tight; hard, severe; strong 1786
きっかけ n. opportunity, motive 811
気付く v. notice, become aware 644
喫茶店 n. tearoom, coffee shop, café 2995
きっちり adv. tightly 3971
キッチン n. kitchen 4112
きっと adv. surely, certainly 636
切符 n. ticket 4162

規定(する) *n.* regulations, stipulations *v.* prescribe 523
起動(する) *n.* starting *v.* start 4805
記入(する) *n.* entry *v.* fill in 2821
記念(する) *n.* commemoration *v.* commemorate 3846
昨日 *n.* yesterday 758
機能(する) *n.* function, capability, feature *v.* function, work 1021
基盤 *n.* base, basis 3621
厳しい *i-adj.* strict, hard 681
気分 *n.* feeling, mood 830
規模 *n.* scale 2257
希望(する) *n.* hope, wish, request *v.* hope, wish, desire 1055
基本 *n.* foundation, basis, basic 1387
基本的 *na-adj.* basic, fundamental 655
決まり *n.* regulation; arrangement, settlement 4859
決まる *v.* be decided 613
君 *n.* you 657
奇妙 *na-adj.* strange, odd 3419
義務 *n.* duty, obligation 2607
決める *v.* decide, fix 440
気持ち *n.* feeling 231
着物 *n.* kimono 2015
疑問 *n.* question, problem, doubt 1254
客 *n.* guest, visitor; customer 505
逆 *n., na-adj.* contrary, opposite 447
虐待(する) *n.* abuse *v.* abuse 4065
客観的 *na-adj.* objective 3495
キャベツ *n.* cabbage 4511
キャラクター *n.* character 4150
キャンプ *n.* camp 2428
急 *na-adj.* urgent, sudden; steep; sharp 1056
九 *num.* nine 1243
救急車 *n.* ambulance 4085
休憩(する) *n.* rest, break *v.* take a rest 3897
急激 *na-adj.* sudden; drastic 3643
休日 *n.* holiday, day off 3325
九州 *n.* Kyushu 2681
吸収(する) *n.* absorption, assimilation *v.* absorb, assimilate 2803
急速 *na-adj.* rapid, speedy 2677
牛肉 *n.* beef 4847
牛乳 *n.* (cow's) milk 1977
九年 *n.* nine years 4484
給付(する) *n.* provision *v.* provide 4987
きゅうり *n.* cucumber 4829
給料 *n.* salary 2576
寄与(する) *n.* contribution *v.* contribute 4725
今日 *n.* today 263

教育(する) *n.* education *v.* educate 924
強化(する) *n., v.* tighten, strengthen 1877
教会 *n.* church 1998
業界 *n.* business world 2921
教科書 *n.* textbook 2552
共感(する) *n.* sympathy *v.* sympathize 4701
協議(する) *n.* consultation, discussion *v.* consult, discuss 3610
供給(する) *n.* supply *v.* supply 3009
教師 *n.* teacher 1743
行事 *n.* event 2481
教室 *n.* classroom, . . . school 1700
業者 *n.* dealer, agent, operator 2953
教授 *n.* professor 2307
業種 *n.* category of business, type of industry 4939
行政 *n.* administration, government 2504
業績 *n.* achievements 4804
競争(する) *n.* competition, contest *v.* compete 2691
兄弟 *n.* brother; sister; sibling 1750
強調(する) *n.* emphasis, stress *v.* emphasize, stress 2346
共通(する) *n., v.* common 1644
京都 *n.* Kyoto 1415
共同 *n.* cooperation; common 3587
恐怖 *n.* fear, dread, terror 2327
興味 *n.* interest 534
興味深い *i-adj.* interesting 4228
業務 *n.* business, work 1831
共有(する) *n.* share *v.* share 3114
協力(する) *n.* cooperation, collaboration *v.* cooperate, collaborate 1107
強力 *na-adj.* strong, powerful 3079
強烈 *na-adj.* strong, intense 3847
行列(する) *n.* procession, line, parade *v.* line up, queue 4491
餃子 *n.* Chinese dumpling 3980
許可(する) *n.* permission, leave *v.* permit, authorize 2268
曲 *n.* piece (music), song, tune 739
極端 *na-adj.* extreme 2839
極力 *adv.* as much as possible 4897
巨人 *n.* giant 3263
巨大 *na-adj.* huge, enormous, gigantic 2309
去年 *adv., n.* last year 1078
拒否(する) *n.* refusal *v.* refuse, reject 3310
距離 *n.* distance 1345
嫌い *na-adj.* dislike, hate 1362
嫌う *v.* hate, detest 2730
気楽 *na-adj.* comfortable, easy, easygoing 4994

きり *p.* only 1685
霧 *n.* fog 4552
切り替える *v.* switch, change 4094
ぎりぎり *adv.* barely 3275
キリスト *n.* Christ 4609
キリスト教 *n.* Christianity 3281
切り取る *v.* cut off, tear off 4971
切る *v.* cut 428
着る *v.* put on, wear 648
きれい *na-adj.* beautiful, pretty; clean 341
切れる *v.* expire, run out 1511
記録（する）*n.* record, document *v.* record, write down 1191
議論（する）*n.* argument, discussion, controversy *v.* discuss 1190
極めて *adv.* very, extremely 1200
金 *n.* gold, money 1452
銀 *n.* silver 4126
禁煙（する）*n.* no-smoking *v.* stop smoking 4841
金額 *n.* amount of money 1240
銀行 *n.* bank 1082
銀座 *n.* Ginza (place name) 2842
禁止（する）*n.* prohibition, ban *v.* prohibit, ban 2332
近所 *n.* neighborhood 916
金属 *n.* metal 4176
緊張（する）*n.* tension *v.* get tense 1491
緊張感 *n.* tension 4575
筋肉 *n.* muscle 1927
近年 *adv.* in recent years 1909
勤務（する）*n.* service, duty, work *v.* work, serve 3050
金融機関 *n.* financial institution 3255
金曜日 *n.* Friday 4187
金利 *n.* interest 4019

く

区 *n.* ward, district 3057
具 *n.* ingredient 4152
具合 *n.* condition 1502
食う *v.* eat, consume 1273
空間 *n.* space 1778
空気 *n.* air, atmosphere 1077
空港 *n.* airport 2074
偶然 *adv.* by chance *n.* chance, accident 2192
九月 *n.* September 810
草 *n.* grass, weed 2400
臭い *i-adj.* smelly 3639
腐る *v.* rot, decay, go off 4606
九時 *n.* nine o'clock 1353
苦笑 *v.* wry smile 3979

苦情 *n.* complaint 4433
崩す *v.* destroy; put into disorder; change 3402
薬 *n.* medicine 1017
崩れる *v.* crumble, collapse 2794
癖 *n.* habit, peculiarity 1899
具体的 *na-adj.* specific, concrete 791
くださる *v.* give (honorific) 1721
下す *v.* give, issue; make a decision 3572
果物 *n.* fruit 2786
下る *v.* go down 2157
口 *n.* mouth 442
唇 *n.* lip 2139
口調 *n.* tone, voice 2718
靴 *n.* shoe 1933
苦痛 *n.* pain 3265
くっ付く *v.* stick, keep close; go out 3352
国 *n.* country 224
国々 *n.* countries 3995
配る *v.* deal, distribute, deliver 2603
首 *n.* neck, head; firing, sacking (of an employee) 853
工夫（する）*n.* device, idea *v.* devise, plan 1698
区分（する）*n.* division, classification *v.* separate 4756
区別（する）*n.* distinction *v.* distinguish 2236
熊 *n.* bear 3811
組み合わせ *n.* combination, matching 3168
組み合わせる *v.* combine, put together, match 3321
組み込む *v.* build in; insert; integrate 4875
組み立てる *v.* assemble 4824
組む *v.* pair with; cross 1603
雲 *n.* cloud 2453
悔しい *i-adj.* regrettable, frustrating; feel regret 2448
くらい、ぐらい *p.* about, around 88
暗い *i-adj.* dark; depressed 1145
グラウンド *n.* ground, playground, sports field 4422
暮らし *n.* life, livelihood 2622
暮らす *v.* live 835
クラス *n.* class 1262
グラス *n.* glass 4090
クラブ *n.* club 2195
グラフ *n.* graph 4873
比べる *v.* compare, contrast 573
栗 *n.* chestnut 3447
クリア（する）*n.* clearing, clearance *na-adj.* clear *v.* clear 3888
繰り返し *n.* repetition 3613
繰り返す *v.* repeat, do over again 794
クリスマス *n.* Christmas 2580
クリック（する）*n.* click *v.* click 1225
来る *v.* come 64

狂う *v.* go mad 3608
グループ *n.* group, team 1351
ぐるぐる *adv.* round and round 4210
苦しい *i-adj.* painful, hard, difficult 1450
苦しみ *n.* suffering, agony 3689
苦しむ *v.* feel pain, suffer 2340
車 *n.* car; wheel 283
車椅子 *n.* wheelchair 4475
くれる *v.* give 1135
黒 *n.* black 1410
黒い *i-adj.* black 1352
苦労(する) *n.* hardship, difficulty, trouble *v.* have trouble, have a hard time 1168
加える *v.* add, include 568
くわえる *v.* take, hold 4730
詳しい *i-adj.* detailed, know well, in detail 755
加わる *v.* increase, add; join 2256
軍 *n.* army 3950
軍隊 *n.* army, troops 3657
群馬県 *n.* Gunma Prefecture 4871
訓練(する) *n.* training *v.* train 2235

け

け *p. disc.* QUESTION ABOUT SOMETHING SPEAKER FORGOT 1732
毛 *n.* hair; fur; wool 2972
経緯 *n.* details, process 3209
経営(する) *n.* management *v.* manage, run 1330
経営者 *n.* manager, proprietor 3149
経過(する) *n.* progress, development *v.* pass 2035
計画(する) *n.* project, schedule, plan *v.* plan 1039
計画的 *na-adj.* planned, deliberate, premeditated 4878
景気 *n.* business conditions, economy 2713
契機 *n.* momentum; opportunity, chance 4891
経験(する) *n.* experience *v.* experience 409
軽減(する) *n.* reduction *v.* reduce 4265
稽古(する) *n.* practice, exercise *v.* practice 4246
傾向 *n.* tendency, trend, inclination 1249
掲載(する) *n.* publication *v.* publish, print 2459
経済 *n.* economy; finance 1693
経済的 *na-adj.* economical; economic; financial 2200
警察 *n.* police 1133
警察官 *n.* police officer 4600
計算(する) *n.* calculation *v.* calculate, count, figure 1293
刑事 *n.* police detective 4909
形式 *n.* form 3765
掲示板 *n.* bulletin board, noticeboard 4622
芸術 *n.* art 3481

計上(する) *n.* appropriation *v.* appropriate 4492
形成(する) *n.* formation *v.* take form 1609
継続(する) *n.* continuation *v.* continue 2651
携帯(する) *n.* portable *v.* carry 1364
形態 *n.* form 3045
携帯電話 *n.* cell phone 1509
芸能人 *n.* entertainer 4445
競馬 *n.* horse racing 3403
経費 *n.* expense, cost 2976
契約(する) *n., v.* contract 1602
ケーキ *n.* cake 2686
ケース *n.* case 1248
ゲーム *n.* game 1444
けが(する) *n.* injury *v.* hurt, injure 1749
劇団 *n.* theatrical company 2883
今朝 *n.* this morning 2834
景色 *n.* scenery, view, scene 1890
化粧(する) *n.* makeup *v.* put on makeup 3938
消す *v.* put out, turn off; erase 1794
削る *v.* save; sharpen, plane 2213
月 *n.* Monday, Mon. 2095
決意(する) *n.* determination *v.* resolve 2980
血液 *n.* blood 3093
結果 *n.* result 351
結果的 *na-adj.* result 2663
血管 *n.* blood vessel 3599
結局 *adv.* after all, in the end, finally 291
結構 *adv.* quite *na-adj.* good 166
結合(する) *n.* combination *v.* combine, join 4207
結婚(する) *n.* marriage *v.* marry, get married 489
結婚式 *n.* wedding ceremony 1845
決して *adv.* never, by no means 906
決心(する) *n.* resolution *v.* decide 3660
結成(する) *n.* formation *v.* form, organize 3770
決断(する) *n.* decision *v.* decide 4052
決定(する) *n.* decision, determination *v.* decide, determine 1117
決定的 *na-adj.* definitive, absolute 4450
欠点 *n.* fault, defect; drawback, weak point 3580
月曜日 *n.* Monday 4476
結論 *n.* conclusion 1731
懸念(する) *n.* fear *v.* fear 3815
気配 *n.* indication, sign 3099
煙 *n.* smoke, fumes; fog 2496
蹴る *v.* kick 3823
けれど *conj.* though, although 31
県 *n.* prefecture 2045
件 *n.* affair, matter, issue 2672
剣 *n.* sword 3668

権威 n. authority 4237
原因 n. cause 597
けんか(する) n. fight, quarrel v. fight, quarrel 1719
見解 n. opinion, view 3102
限界 n. limit, boundary 2415
見学(する) n. studying by observation, field trip v. visit for study, go on a field trip 3358
玄関 n. entrance, front door 1950
元気 n. health, vigor na-adj. lively, vigorous, well 736
研究(する) n. research, study v. do research, study 694
研究開発 n. research and development 4970
研究者 n. researcher 3771
研究所 n. research institute, laboratory 4390
現金 n. cash 3722
権限 n. authority, power 3222
言語 n. language, tongue, speech 2512
健康 n. health 667
原稿 n. manuscript, draft 3354
検査(する) n. inspection v. inspect 1454
現在 n. present time, now 227
検索(する) n. search v. search, look up 2531
現実 n. reality, actuality 820
現実的 na-adj. realistic 3978
研修(する) n. training v. study 2942
検証(する) n. verification v. verify 4830
減少(する) n. decrease, reduction v. decline, decrease 1228
現象 n. phenomenon, happening; phase 2265
現状 n. present condition, existing state 1256
建設(する) n. construction v. build, construct 2110
健全 na-adj. healthy 3944
原則 n. principle 1651
現代 n. the present age, today 1638
現地 n. field, on-site, local 1419
建築(する) n. architecture, construction v. build 3012
顕著 na-adj. conspicuous, remarkable 4572
限定(する) n. restriction, limitation v. restrict, limit 2882
原点 n. starting point, origin 4261
検討(する) n. consideration, discussion examination v. consider, discuss 983
剣道 n. kendo 4395
現に adv. as a matter of fact, actually 3776
現場 n. field, scene, spot 1314
原爆 n. atomic bomb 4275
憲法 n. constitution 2671
権利 n. right, claim, entitlement 1291
原理 n. principle 4173

原料 n. raw material, ingredient 4405
権力 n. power, authority 3309

こ

子 n. child 268
五 n. five 436
後 n. after, later, since 565
語 n. word; language 4326
濃い i-adj. thick; strong; heavy; deep 1930
恋 n. love (romantic) 2264
こいつ pron. this fellow; this thing 2948
恋人 n. lover, boyfriend, girlfriend 2621
こう adv. so, like this 60
行為 n. action; motion; behavior 1187
合意(する) n. mutual agreement v. agree 3464
幸運 n. (good) luck, fortune na-adj. lucky, fortunate 4706
公園 n. park 1011
公演 n. performance 4394
講演 n. lecture, talk 4612
効果 n. effectiveness, effect 819
高価 na-adj. expensive 3856
豪華 na-adj. luxurious, gorgeous 4084
公開(する) n. exhibition, presentation v. release 2590
後悔(する) n. repentance, regret v. regret 2830
郊外 n. suburb 3869
合格(する) n. passing an exam v. pass an exam 2166
効果的 na-adj. effective 2458
交換(する) n. exchange v. exchange 2075
講義 n. lecture 4098
抗議(する) n. protest, objection v. object 4956
好奇心 n. curiosity 3863
公共 n. public, common 4539
工具 n. tool 4439
光景 n. sight, spectacle 2240
合計(する) n. sum total v. total 2298
攻撃(する) n. attack v. attack 1999
貢献(する) n. contribution, service v. contribute 2592
高校 n. high school 574
高校時代 n. high school days 2225
高校生 n. high school student 1521
広告(する) n. advertisement, flyer v. advertise 2344
講座 n. course, lecture 4489
考察(する) n. consideration, examination v. consider, examine 4500
講師 n. speaker, lecturer 2637
行使 n. exercise 4003
工事(する) n. construction, work v. construct 2876
後者 n. the latter 3443

交渉(する) *n.* negotiation, treaty *v.* negotiate 2549
向上(する) *n.* improvement, progress *v.* improve, advance 1565
工場 *n.* factory 1618
更新(する) *n.* renewal *v.* renew, update 2709
講ずる *v.* take 2556
構成(する) *n.* constitution, structure *v.* compose 1403
厚生省 *n.* Ministry of Welfare 4040
構造 *n.* structure 1926
高速道路 *n.* freeway 4223
交代(する) *n.* change, shift *v.* take turns 3976
広大 *na-adj.* vast, huge, extensive 4136
構築(する) *n.* construction *v.* construct 3144
紅茶 *n.* tea (black) 2598
交通 *n.* traffic; transportation 2920
交通事故 *n.* traffic accident 3456
高度 *n.* altitude *na-adj.* high, advanced 2924
行動(する) *n.* action, act *v.* act, behave 732
購入(する) *n.* buying *v.* purchase, buy 1085
後輩 *n.* one's junior 3530
後半 *n.* latter half, second half 2735
公表(する) *n.* publication *v.* make public 3383
交付(する) *n.* issue *v.* issue, grant 3927
幸福 *n.* happiness 3343
興奮(する) *n.* excitement *v.* be excited 2490
神戸 *n.* Kobe 3080
公務員 *n.* civil servant, government employee 3864
項目 *n.* item, heading 2897
紅葉(する) *n.* autumn leaves *v.* put on fall colors 3298
効率 *n.* efficiency 3887
効率的 *na-adj.* efficient 4292
合理的 *na-adj.* reasonable, rational 4550
交流(する) *n.* interchange, exchange *v.* interact 1893
考慮(する) *n.* thought *v.* think over, consider 2184
効力 *n.* effect 4714
高齢化(する) *n.* aging; increase in age 4862
高齢者 *n.* senior citizen 1613
声 *n.* voice 279
越える *v.* cross over, go over 586
コース *n.* course, route, lane 2029
コート *n.* coat; court 3171
コーナー *n.* corner 3286
コーヒー *n.* coffee 1641
氷 *n.* ice 2949
ゴール *n.* goal 4061
誤解(する) *n.* misunderstanding *v.* misunderstand 3053
五回 *n.* five times 4364
五月 *n.* May 868
顧客 *n.* customer 3653

呼吸(する) *n.* breath *v.* breathe 3285
故郷 *n.* home town 3724
ごく *adv.* very 1866
国語 *n.* Japanese language 4442
国際的 *na-adj.* international 3000
黒人 *n.* black person 3777
国鉄 *n.* national railway 4934
国道 *n.* national highway 4587
国内 *n.* domestic, home 1811
告白(する) *n.* confession *v.* confess 3367
克服(する) *n.* conquest *v.* conquer, overcome 4346
国民 *n.* nation, people (of country), public 824
国連 *n.* United Nations 3874
ここ *pron.* here 141
個々 *n.* individual, each 2787
午後 *n.* afternoon, p.m. 564
九日 *n.* ninth (date); nine days 2960
心 *n.* mind, heart; thought; feeling 246
心がける *v.* be careful, be prudent 2701
試み *n.* attempt, try 4255
試みる *v.* try 3659
五歳 *n.* five years old 4942
小さじ *n.* teaspoon 3476
ございます (<ござる) *v.* [very polite form of "de aru"] 182
腰 *n.* back, lower back, waist, hip 1140
五時 *n.* five o'clock 2000
五十 *num.* fifty 3444
五十代 *n.* fifties 4723
五十年 *n.* fifty years 3019
こしょう *n.* pepper 3230
個人 *n.* individual 1012
個人的 *na-adj.* private, personal, individual 1446
越す *v.* cross, pass 3067
コスト *n.* cost 3458
個性 *n.* personality, character 2573
午前 *n.* morning, a.m. 879
五千円 *n.* five thousand yen 4285
午前中 *n.* in the morning, throughout the morning 2926
こそ *p.* EMPHATIC 450
子育て *n.* child rearing, bringing up one's child 2112
ご存じ *n.* know, knowing (honorific) 1033
古代 *n.* ancient times 3674
答え *n.* answer, solution 1269
答える *v.* answer, respond 555
子達 *n.* children 3350
こだわり *n.* concern, obsession 4607
こだわる *v.* stick to; be particular about 2765

ごちそう（する）*n.* feast *v.* give a dinner, treat 3803
こちら *pron.* this place, here; this way; this 329
こつ *n.* knack 3059
国家 *n.* state, country, nation 1861
国会 *n.* national assembly, Diet 3174
国境 *n.* border 4078
こっそり *adv.* secretly, on the sly 4822
こっち *pron.* here; this; I; we 1969
固定（する）*n.* fixing *v.* fix 3366
事 *n.* thing 17
ごと *suffix* every 4846
ことがある *cp.* have done; there are sometimes 775
ことができる *cp.* can, be able to 300
事柄 *n.* matter, issue 3778
孤独 *na-adj.* lonely 3400
今年 *n.* this year 515
ごとし *aux.* like, as if (Classical) 1687
こととなる *aux.* it has been decided that 3365
異なる *v.* be different 873
ことにする *aux.* decide to, pretend to 1337
ことになる *cp.* it happens that..., it is decided that 326
言葉 *n.* word; language 188
ことはない *aux.* not have to, there is no need for 1445
子供 *n.* child 128
こともある *cp.* sometimes, can be 999
子供たち *n.* children 432
断る *v.* decline, refuse, reject, turn down; ask permission; give notice 2046
粉 *n.* flour, powder 3042
こなす *v.* cope with; finish 3331
五人 *n.* five people 2042
こねる *v.* knead, squeeze, work 4690
五年 *n.* five years 1537
五年間 *n.* five years 4076
この *adn.* this 46
この間 *n. adv.* a few days ago; recently, lately 3638
この方 *pron.* this person 4788
このごろ *n.* these days 2509
好み *n.* liking, taste 1903
好む *v.* like, be fond of, love, care 2339
この世 *n.* this world 3278
ご飯 *n.* rice, meal 919
コピー（する）*n.* copy *v.* copy 2212
五百円 *n.* five hundred yen 3121
五分 *n.* five minutes 2053
細かい *i-adj.* small, fine; trivial; sensitive 1138
ごまかす *v.* cheat, deceive 4563
困る *v.* have difficulty, be in trouble 569

ごみ *n.* rubbish, garbage, trash 1132
コミュニケーション（する）*n.* communication *v.* communicate 1349
混む *v.* be crowded 2790
小麦粉 *n.* flour 3098
米 *n.* rice 1963
込める *v.* put into, pour into 1992
ご免 *n.* pardon, sorry [to decline] 3228
コメント（する）*n.* comment *v.* comment 2052
ごめんなさい *interj.* I'm sorry, Excuse me 1961
籠もる *v.* shut oneself up; be full of 3345
小屋 *n.* hut, cabin, barn, shed 2571
雇用（する）*n.* employment *v.* employ 3323
ご覧 *n.* looking, seeing (honorific) 2144
凝る *v.* be absorbed, be devoted; become stiff 4048
ゴルフ *n.* golf 2164
これ *pron.* this 51
これら *pron.* these 491
頃 *n.* time, about, when 170
転がる *v.* roll 4409
殺す *v.* kill 832
転ぶ *v.* fall, slip 4578
怖い *i-adj.* frightening, scary; terrified 591
壊す *v.* break; impair; upset 2018
壊れる *v.* be broken, be damaged; be destroyed 2086
今回 *n.* this time 403
根拠 *n.* ground, evidence 2715
コンクリート *n.* concrete 4376
今月 *n.* this month 3487
今後 *adv.* in the future, from now on 582
今後とも *adv.* from now on, in the future 4547
コンサート *n.* concert 3041
今週 *n.* this week 4464
今度 *n.* this time, next time 285
コントロール（する）*n.* control *v.* control 3477
こんな *adn.* such, like that 218
困難 *n.* difficulty *na-adj.* difficult 1481
今日 *adv.* today, these days 1764
こんにちは *interj.* Hello, Good afternoon 4446
コンビニ *n.* convenience store 2421
コンピューター、コンピュータ *n.* computer 1422
根本的 *na-adj.* fundamental, basic 3687
今夜 *n.* tonight 2744
混乱（する）*n.* confusion *v.* get confused 3036

さ

さ *p. disc.* ATTRACT ATTENTION 721
差 *n.* difference, gap, margin 1271
さあ *interj.* come on, now, well 1573

サークル *n.* circle, club 2238
サービス(する) *n.* service *v.* attend, serve 1310
際 *n.* when, in case of 692
最悪 *na-adj.* worst 3274
再会(する) *n.* reunion *v.* meet again 4636
災害 *n.* disaster, calamity 2999
最近 *n.* recently, lately 215
債権者 *n.* creditor 4792
最後 *n.* last, end 282
最高 *n., na-adj* best, highest 1367
財産 *n.* property; fortune 2232
最終的 *na-adj.* final, last, ultimate 1391
最初 *n.* first 208
最新 *n.* newest, latest 4602
サイズ *n.* size 2109
再生(する) *n.* rebirth *v.* regenerate 3474
最大 *n.* biggest, largest 1472
埼玉 *n.* Saitama 4687
埼玉県 *n.* Saitama prefecture 2676
最中 *n.* in the middle of 3420
最低 *n.* minimum, lowest 2808
最低限 *n.* minimum 4240
最適 *na-adj.* best, optimum 4119
サイト *n.* website 2105
再度 *adv.* twice, again 3809
際に *p.* when 3430
才能 *n.* talent, ability 3073
栽培(する) *n.* cultivation *v.* cultivate 3732
裁判 *n.* trial; judgment; justice 2655
裁判官 *n.* judge 4372
裁判所 *n.* court, courthouse 2812
財布 *n.* wallet 3890
細胞 *n.* cell 2861
債務 *n.* debt, obligation 4724
債務者 *n.* debtor 4453
採用(する) *n.* adoption, employment *v.* employ 1583
材料 *n.* materials, ingredient 890
幸い *na-adj.* lucky, fortunate *n.* happiness *adv.* fortunately 1832
サイン(する) *n.* signature, autograph *v.* sign 3280
さえ *p.* even; besides; if only 632
坂 *n.* slope, hill 2530
境 *n.* boundary, border 4441
栄える *v.* prosper, flourish 4810
探す *v.* look for, search for, seek 532
魚 *n.* fish 660
遡る *v.* go back; be retroactive 3554
下がる *v.* fall, drop, step back 1460
盛ん *na-adj.* popular; active; prosperous 1734

先 *n.* end, front 298
先程 *n.* a short while ago 478
作業(する) *n.* operation, work *v.* work 967
咲く *v.* bloom 1386
削減(する) *n.* cut, reduction *v.* cut, slash 3652
作者 *n.* author 3711
削除(する) *n.* deletion *v.* delete 2088
作成(する) *n., v.* make, create 994
策定(する) *n.* settling on *v.* settle on 3369
昨年 *adv., n.* last year 1227
作品 *n.* work, production 541
昨夜 *n.* last night 4014
桜 *n.* cherry tree; cherry blossom 1442
探る *v.* fumble; probe 3210
酒 *n.* alcohol, sake, rice wine 596
叫ぶ *v.* shout 1604
避ける *v.* avoid, keep away from 1221
下げる *v.* lower; hang 1580
支える *v.* support, hold, sustain 1287
捧げる *v.* offer, dedicate, sacrifice 4693
ささやく *v.* whisper 4527
差し込む *v.* insert, plug in; come in, shine in 4367
差し出す *v.* hold out 3718
刺し身 *n* sashimi 4734
さす *v.* shine; pour; put 825
さすが *adv.* as might be expected, as one would expect 1048
挫折(する) *n.* setback *v.* fail 4828
誘う *v.* invite 1581
定める *v.* provide; stipulate, decide 714
撮影(する) *n.* shooting *v.* shoot, photograph 1324
作家 *n.* writer 2161
サッカー *n.* football, soccer 1617
錯覚(する) *n.* illusion, delusion, trick *v.* have the illusion/impression 4558
さっき *adv., n.* a little while ago 1865
作曲(する) *n.* musical composition *v.* compose 4945
昨今 *n.* nowadays 4383
さっさと *adv.* quickly 4469
雑誌 *n.* magazine 838
殺人 *n.* murder 4400
早速 *adv.* at once, lose no time in doing 1905
さっと *adv.* quickly 3820
さっぱり *adv.* not at all 3205
札幌 *n.* Sapporo 3448
さて *conj.* well, now 1062
里 *n.* village, countryside, one's parents' home 4858
砂糖 *n.* sugar 1510
悟る *v.* realize 4633

砂漠 *n.* desert 3972
寂しい *i-adj.* lonely, lonesome 1049
寂しさ *n.* loneliness 4154
差別(する) *n.* discrimination *v.* discriminate 2936
サポート(する) *n.* support *v.* support 4577
さほど *adv.* (not) particularly 3992
様 *n.* Mr., Mrs., Miss., Ms. 4025
様々 *na-adj.* various, all kinds of 554
覚ます *v.* wake up 4817
サミット *n.* summit 4739
寒い *i-adj.* cold 943
寒さ *n.* cold 2991
覚める *v.* wake up 3615
冷める *v.* cool, get cold 4336
左右(する) *n.* right and left *v.* determine, influence 1888
作用(する) *n.* action *v.* act 2932
皿 *n.* plate, dish 2207
さらす *v.* expose 3179
サラダ *n.* salad 4582
さらに *adv.* again, still more, moreover 254
サラリーマン *n.* salaried worker, office worker 2215
去る *v., adn.* leave, pass, be gone 2041
猿 *n.* monkey 3902
ざるを得ない *cp.* have to, cannot help doing 1921
騒ぐ *v.* make a noise, make a fuss 2567
爽やか *na-adj.* fresh, refreshing 4664
触る *v.* touch 1699
三 *num.* three 207
～さん *suffix* Mr., Mrs., Miss., Ms. 4682
参加(する) *n.* participation *v.* take part in, participate 543
三回 *n.* three times 1937
三ヶ月 *n.* three months 2060
参加者 *n.* participant 4194
三月 *n.* March 723
参加費 *n.* participation fee 4721
産業 *n.* industry 2801
残業 *n.* overtime work 4399
参考 *n.* reference 1543
三歳 *n.* three years old 3225
散々 *adv.* severely, repeatedly 4733
三時 *n.* three o'clock 2099
三時間 *n.* three hours 2829
三十歳 *n.* thirty years old 4740
三十分 *n.* thirty minutes 687
三十 *num.* thirty 2489
三十一日 *n.* thirty-first (date); thirty one days 2534
三十代 *n.* thirties 3736

三十日 *n.* thirtieth (date); thirty days 2541
三十人 *n.* thirty people 4443
三十年 *n.* thirty years 2734
参照(する) *n.* reference *v.* consult, refer 2497
賛成(する) *n.* agreement *v.* agree 3044
三千円 *n.* three thousand yen 4992
酸素 *n.* oxygen 3251
三度 *n.* three times 4307
三人 *n.* three people 633
三年 *n.* three years 948
残念 *na-adj.* disappointing, regrettable 803
三年間 *n.* three years 2520
三年生 *n.* third grade, third year 2820
三番目 *n.* third 3124
三百円 *n.* three hundred yen 4436
三分 *n.* three minutes 4718
三分の一 *n., num.* one-third 3964
散歩(する) *n., v.* walk, stroll 1350
三本 *n.* three (long/cylindrical objects) 4062

し

し *p. conj.* and, besides 96
死 *n.* death 912
市 *n.* city, town 1211
詩 *n.* poem, poetry 2034
字 *n.* letter, character; handwriting 1328
試合 *n.* match, game, bout 1018
仕上げる *v.* finish, complete 3472
幸せ *na-adj.* happy *n.* happiness; fortune, luck 897
CM *n.* commercial 1868
(お)じいさん *n.* grandfather 1406
シーズン *n.* season 4221
CD *n.* CD, compact disk 1567
シート *n.* seat; sheet 4797
強いる *v.* force 4796
シーン *n.* scene 2242
シェア(する) *n.* share *v.* share 3844
自衛隊 *n.* Self-Defense Forces 3872
JR *n.* Japan Railways (JR) 2511
支援(する) *n.* support, assistance *v.* support, assist 1725
塩 *n.* salt 1241
しか *p.* only, just, no more than 211
司会(する) *n.* host, emcee *v.* host, emcee, take the chair 4705
次回 *n.* next time 3620
資格 *n.* qualification; capacity 1703
自覚(する) *n.* consciousness, awareness *v.* realize 2833
仕掛け *n.* device, system 4657

仕掛ける *v.* begin, start; set 4820
しかし *conj.* but, however 162
しかしながら *aux.* however, but 2516
仕方 *n.* way, method 1060
仕方が無い *cp.* cannot be helped, no use 4193
しかたない *i-adj.* It can't be helped, be beyond any help, I can't help ... 2135
四月 *n.* April 656
しかない *cp.* can't but, can only, have no choice 2297
しかも *conj.* moreover, besides 456
然り *v. (Classical)* to be so 4066
叱る *v.* scold, admonish 2620
時間 *n.* time 183
時間帯 *n.* time (period), time zone 3601
式 *n.* ceremony 2373
四季 *n.* four seasons 4202
指揮(する) *n.* direction, command *v.* conduct, direct 4494
時期 *n.* time, period, season 446
敷地 *n.* site, ground 4335
支給(する) *n.* provision, payment *v.* provide, pay 2975
事業 *n.* business, enterprise, project 1181
資金 *n.* funds 2134
敷く *v.* spread, lay 2165
軸 *n.* axis; shaft; stem 4772
仕草 *n.* behavior, gesture 4517
仕組み *n.* structure, mechanism 1919
刺激(する) *n., v.* stimulate, incite, excite 1761
試験(する) *n.* exam, test, trial *v.* examine 1448
資源 *n.* resource 3977
事件 *n.* incident, event 547
事故 *n.* accident, incident, trouble 1203
自己 *n.* oneself, self 2253
施行(する) *n.* enforcement *v.* enforce 3483
思考(する) *n.* thought *v.* think 3834
事項 *n.* matter, fact, item 2039
地獄 *n.* hell 4083
仕事(する) *n.* work, job *v.* work 152
示唆(する) *n.* suggestion *v.* suggest 4991
施策 *n.* policy, measure 3219
自殺(する) *n.* suicide *v.* commit suicide 2501
資産 *n.* assets, property 2983
持参(する) *n.* bringing, taking *v.* bring, take 3941
指示(する) *n.* instruction, direction *v.* instruct, direct 1844
支持(する) *n.* support *v.* support 2959
事実 *n.* fact, actuality 702
死者 *n.* dead 4201
四十 *num.* forty 3675

支出 *n.* expenses, payment, expenditure, spending 4771
辞書 *n.* dictionary 3697
支障 *n.* obstacle 4010
市場 *n.* market 2014
事情 *n.* circumstance, situation, reason 1277
詩人 *n.* poet 4989
自信 *n.* confidence 1213
地震 *n.* earthquake 1774
自身 *n.* oneself 3551
静か *na-adj.* quiet, silent 1139
システム *n.* system 1319
沈む *v.* sink, go down 2943
資する *v.* contribute 4904
姿勢 *n.* posture, attitude 1485
施設 *n.* facility, institution, plant 1176
視線 *n.* eyes, gaze, look 1925
自然 *n.* nature *na-adj.* natural *adv.* naturally 412
事前 *n.* prior 2476
思想 *n.* thought, idea 2442
子孫 *n.* descendant; posterity 4282
下 *n.* under; below; down; low 387
舌 *n.* tongue 2828
死体 *n.* dead body 3340
次第 *adv.* depend on; as soon as *n.* order 1127
事態 *n.* situation 1839
時代 *n.* time, era 354
従う *v.* obey, follow 982
したがって *conj.* accordingly, consequently 857
支度(する) *n.* preparations *v.* prepare 4930
自宅 *n.* home, house 1426
親しい *i-adj.* close, friendly 2330
下町 *n.* Shitamachi (place name); traditional working-class neighborhood 3436
七月 *n.* July 866
七時 *n.* seven o'clock 2644
自治体 *n.* municipality 3667
七人 *n.* seven people 4294
七年 *n.* seven years 3767
市町村 *n.* municipality 2450
質 *n.* nature, quality 2422
実 *n.* truth, true, real 377
実家 *n.* one's parents' home 991
しっかり *adv.* hard, tight 650
実感(する) *n.* real feeling *v.* actually feel 1461
じっくり *adv.* without haste, deliberately 3427
しつけ *n.* tacking (sewing); discipline 4171
実験(する) *n.* experimentation *v.* experiment 2217
実現(する) *n.* realization, implementation *v.* realize, put into practice 1083

しつこい *i-adj.* persistent; over-rich (food) 4964
執行(する) *n.* execution, enforcement *v.* carry out, enforce 4920
実行(する) *n.* practice *v.* carry out 1726
実際 *n.* actually, in fact 242
実施(する) *n.* operation *v.* enforce, conduct 581
実質的 *na-adj.* substantial; essential 4418
実情 *n.* case, actual situation 3936
実績 *n.* achievement 4109
実践(する) *n.* practice *v.* practice 2927
実態 *n.* actual situation 2350
じっと(する) *adv., v.* still, fixedly, intently 1676
室内 *n.* indoor 3832
実は *adv.* actually, in fact 926
失敗(する) *n.* failure, mistake *v.* fail 1103
十分 *n.* ten minutes 1624
しっぽ *n.* tail 4064
質問(する) *n.* question *v.* question 506
実力 *n.* real ability 3269
失礼(する) *n.* rudeness, impoliteness *v.* be rude, be impolite *na-adj.* rude, impolite *interj.* Excuse me 1939
指定(する) *n.* appointment *v.* specify 1329
指摘(する) *n.* designation *v.* point out, indicate 1029
視点 *n.* viewpoint 2209
時点 *n.* point of time, as of 1160
自転車 *n.* bicycle 782
指導(する) *n.* guidance *v.* guide, coach 1325
児童 *n.* pupil 3818
指導者 *n.* leader, coach 4172
自動車 *n.* car 1753
自動的 *na-adj.* automatic 3532
品 *n.* goods, article 4222
市内 *n.* within the city 2515
品物 *n.* goods, article 3393
次男 *n.* second son 3759
死ぬ *v.* die 402
支配(する) *n.* rule, control *v.* rule, control, govern 2328
芝居 *n.* play, drama 2056
しばしば *adv.* always, often 2318
支払い *n.* payment 3127
支払う *v.* pay 1906
しばらく *adv.* for a while, a minute, for a long time 654
縛る *v.* bind, tie 3935
市販(する) *n.* on the market *v.* market 3277
渋谷 *n.* Shibuya (place name) 2291
自分 *n.* oneself 72
自分自身 *n.* oneself 1114

自分達 *n.* themselves; ourselves 754
自分なり *n.* in one's own way 2544
死亡(する) *n.* death, decease *v.* die 2860
脂肪 *n.* fat 3921
絞る *v.* squeeze 2154
資本 *n.* capital 3967
島 *n.* island 706
お仕舞い *n.* end, be all up with 3644
しまう *v.* put away 1649
始末(する) *n.* disposal, circumstances *v.* manage, deal with, dispose of 4455
自慢(する) *n.* pride, boast *v.* boast, brag 2706
地味 *na-adj.* simple 3909
しみじみ *adv.* keenly, heartily, from one's heart 4990
市民 *n.* resident (of a city), citizen 1907
自民党 *n.* Liberal Democratic Party 3142
事務 *n.* office work 3993
事務所 *n.* office 2047
氏名 *n.* name 4121
示す *v.* show 449
占める *v.* occupy, account for 984
締める *v.* tie; tighten 1673
しめる *aux.* (Classical) 3762
地面 *n.* ground, land 2591
しも *p.* EMPHASIS (Classical) 3727
地元 *n.* home area, local area 1046
視野 *n.* perspective, view 3733
じゃ *conj.* well, so, then 352
じゃ *aux.* COPULA is, are 1773
社員 *n.* employee, member of staff 2094
社会 *n.* society 583
社会人 *n.* adult; full member of society 2377
社会的 *na-adj.* social 2881
じゃが芋 *n.* potato 3783
市役所 *n.* city hall 3955
写真 *n.* picture, photo 431
ジャズ *n.* jazz 4073
社宅 *n.* company housing 4726
社長 *n.* company president 1689
シャツ *n.* shirt 3837
若干 *adv.* slightly *n.* a little, few, some 1980
借金(する) *n.* debt, loan *v.* borrow (money) 2755
しゃべる *v.* talk, chat 823
邪魔(する) *n.* obstacle, disturbance, interruption *v.* disturb, interrupt 2616
三味線 *n.* shamisen 4651
車両 *n.* car, carriage 3956
シャワー *n.* shower 3446
じゃん *p. disc.* isn't it? 3016

上海 *n.* Shanghai 4571
ジャンル *n.* genre, category 3376
種 *n.* kind, species 1670
週 *n.* week 1588
州 *n.* state 4619
十 *num.* ten 1094
銃 *n.* gun 4546
自由 *n.* freedom, liberty *na-adj.* free 671
周囲 *n.* surroundings 1527
十一 *num.* eleven 1869
十一月 *n.* November 874
十一時 *n.* eleven o'clock 2326
十一日 *n.* eleventh (date); eleven days 2807
十一年 *n.* eleven years 4595
収穫(する) *n.* harvest *v.* harvest 3597
十月 *n.* October 829
習慣 *n.* custom, habit 1991
十九 *num.* nineteen 3590
住居 *n.* house 4818
宗教 *n.* religion 1549
従業員 *n.* employee, worker 2996
十九日 *n.* nineteenth (date); nineteen days 3164
十五 *num.* fifteen 2163
十五日 *n.* fifteenth (date); fifteen days 2141
十五年 *n.* fifteen years 2843
十五分 *n.* fifteen minutes 2131
十三 *num.* thirteen 2379
十三日 *n.* thirteenth (date); thirteen days 3025
十三年 *n.* thirteen years 4149
重視(する) *n.* respect *v.* make a point of, consider important 2487
十四 *num.* fourteen 2596
十時 *n.* ten o'clock 1321
従事(する) *n.* engagement in *v.* be engaged in 3903
十七日 *n.* seventeenth (date); seventeen days 2950
充実(する) *n.* fullness *v.* enrich, fullfill 1347
収集(する) *n.* collection *v.* collect 3987
住所 *n.* address 2027
就職(する) *n.* job hunting *v.* find employment, get a job 1416
就職活動(する) *n.* job-hunting *v.* look for a job 3774
ジュース *n.* juice 4264
修正(する) *n.* revision *v.* revise 3645
渋滞(する) *n.* traffic jam, delay *v.* be delayed 4461
重大 *na-adj.* serious, important 3118
十代 *n.* teen years, teens 4843
住宅 *n.* house, residence 2183
住宅街 *n.* housing; residential area 4949
住宅地 *n.* residential area 4623

集団 *n.* group, mass 2518
集中(する) *n.* concentration *v.* concentrate 1842
十七 *num.* seventeen 3223
十七歳 *n.* seventeen years old 3628
十二 *num.* twelve 1772
十二月 *n.* December 850
十二時 *n.* twelve o'clock 3315
十二日 *n.* twelfth (date), twelve days 2916
十二年 *n.* twelve years 3970
収入 *n.* income 2012
就任(する) *n.* assumption *v.* assume 4665
十人 *n.* ten people 2609
十年 *n.* ten years, decade 1086
十年間 *n.* ten years 4086
十八 *num.* eighteen 2929
十八日 *n.* eighteenth (date); eighteen days 2918
十八歳 *n.* eighteen years old 4861
十分 *na-adj.* enough, sufficient *adv.* fully, sufficiently, adequately 480
周辺 *n.* outskirts, around 2007
週末 *n.* weekend 3154
住民 *n.* inhabitant, resident 1985
重要 *na-adj.* important 485
重要性 *n.* importance 3611
十四日 *n.* fourteenth (date); fourteen days 2847
従来 *adv., n.* up to now, conventional, traditional 1361
修理(する) *n.* repair *v.* repair 3553
終了(する) *n.* end *v.* end, be over 1798
十六 *num.* sixteen 2809
十六日 *n.* sixteenth (date); sixteen days 2788
授業 *n.* class, lesson at school 812
塾 *n.* cram school 2040
縮小(する) *n.* reduction *v.* reduce 4145
宿題 *n.* homework 4120
受験(する) *n.* examination *v.* take an examination 1857
主催(する) *n.* promotion, organizing *v.* host, promote, organize 4553
取材(する) *n.* interview, report *v.* gather information 2535
趣旨 *n.* purpose, intention, point 2826
手術(する) *n.* surgery, operation *v.* operate 1158
首相 *n.* prime minister 3428
受賞(する) *n.* winning a prize *v.* win (receive) a prize, be awarded a prize 4933
主人 *n.* shop owner; husband 567
受診(する) *n.* (medical) consultation *v.* consult, have a medical examination 4493
主人公 *n.* hero, heroine 2221

主体 *n.* main constituent; subject 3449
手段 *n.* means 1606
主張(する) *n.* argument, claim *v.* argue, insist 1175
出演(する) *n.* appearance, broadcast *v.* appear (on stage, TV) 2646
出現(する) *n.* appearance, dawn, birth, advent *v.* appear 2873
出産(する) *n.* birth *v.* give birth 2358
出場(する) *n.* participation *v.* participate 3318
出身 *n.* hometown; alma mater 3056
出席(する) *n.* attendance *v.* attend 2608
出発(する) *n.* departure *v.* leave 1741
出版(する) *n.* publication *v.* publish 3234
出品(する) *n.* exhibit *v.* submit 3122
出品者 *n.* exhibitor 3155
首都 *n.* capital city 4234
取得(する) *n.* acquisition *v.* acquire 2009
主婦 *n.* housewife 1878
手法 *n.* technique, method 3605
趣味 *n.* hobby 979
寿命 *n.* life expectancy 3686
主役 *n.* main character 3758
主要 *na-adj.* major, main 3634
需要 *n.* demand 2923
主流 *n.* mainstream 3991
種類 *n.* kind, sort, variety 881
手話 *n.* sign language 4968
順 *n.* order 2878
瞬間 *adv., n.* moment, instant, second 1142
純粋 *na-adj.* pure; genuine 3200
順調 *na-adj.* satisfactory, favorable, smooth 3007
順番 *n.* turn, order 2811
準備(する) *n.* preparation *v.* prepare 934
準用(する) *n., v.* apply mutatis mutandis, with necessary modification 3745
賞 *n.* prize, award 4533
使用(する) *n.* use *v.* use 585
仕様 *n.* style, specification, method 1471
上位 *n.* higher rank 4789
生姜 *n.* ginger 4391
紹介(する) *n.* introduction *v.* introduce 518
障害 *n.* obstacle, handicap 1655
生涯 *n.* life, lifetime; career 2887
障害者 *n.* disabled person, handicapped person 4164
小学生 *n.* elementary school pupil, primary school pupil 1500
正月 *n.* New Year 1664
小学校 *n.* elementary school, primary school 600

しょうがない, しょうがない *i-adj.* it can't be helped, nothing can be done 1429
将棋 *n.* shogi, Japanese chess 3452
上記 *n.* the above, above-mentioned 3539
状況 *n.* state of affairs, situation 353
上京(する) *n.* coming/going to Tokyo *v.* come/go to Tokyo 4673
将軍 *n.* general, shogun 4675
上下 *n.* up and down 3729
衝撃 *n.* shock, impact 3094
証言(する) *n.* evidence *v.* give testimony 3928
条件 *n.* condition 972
証拠 *n.* evidence 2233
正午 *n.* noon, midday 4233
詳細 *n.* details *na-adj.* detailed 2175
上司 *n.* boss 1730
正直 *n.* honesty *na-adj.* honest, truthful *adv.* honestly 1409
常識 *n.* common sense, general knowledge 2756
少女 *n.* girl 2251
少々 *adv.* a little, a minute 1928
症状 *n.* symptom 1708
上昇(する) *n.* rise *v.* rise 1777
生じる *v.* bring about, cause, arise 883
上手 *na-adj.* good, skillful 1659
称する *v.* call; pretend 2957
小説 *n.* novel, fiction, story 1380
招待(する) *n.* invitation *v.* invite 4593
状態 *n.* state, conditions 303
上達(する) *n.* improvement *v.* improve, progress 4001
冗談 *n.* joke 2856
承知(する) *n.* agreement *v.* agree, understand 2177
象徴(する) *n.* symbol *v.* symbolize 3355
焦点 *n.* focus 4295
商店街 *n.* shopping street 1650
譲渡(する) *n.* transfer *v.* transfer, hand over 4826
衝突(する) *n.* collision *v.* collide, clash 4315
承認(する) *n.* approval *v.* approve 3103
情熱 *n.* passion 4293
少年 *n.* boy, juvenile 1023
商売 *n.* business 2269
消費(する) *n.* consumption *v.* consume 3027
消費者 *n.* consumer 2128
商品 *n.* goods, item of merchandise 882
勝負(する) *n.* victory or defeat, match *v.* play 3115
丈夫 *na-adj.* strong; healthy 3469
情報 *n.* information 473
証明(する) *n.* proof *v.* prove 1956
照明 *n.* lighting 4592

消滅(する) n. disappearance v. disappear 4163
正面 n. front 3206
条約 n. treaty, agreement 4507
しょう油 n. soy sauce 3058
将来 n. future 780
勝利 n. victory, triumph, winning 2832
昭和 n. Showa era 464
ショー n. show 4389
初期 n. early days, initial stage 3260
食 n. meal, diet 3641
職 n. job, work 3961
職員 n. staff member 2051
職業 n. occupation, trade, profession 2414
食材 n. ingredient, foodstuff 3166
食事(する) n. meal v. have a meal 575
食生活 n. eating habits 3677
食卓 n. dining table 4297
食堂 n. cafeteria, dining room 3981
職人 n. craftsman, workman 4148
職場 n. workplace 1713
食品 n. food 2401
植物 n. plant 1601
職務 n. duty 4915
食物 n. food, dish 4773
食欲 n. appetite 4325
食料 n. food, provisions 2123
女子 n. woman, girl 2510
徐々 n. gradually 1879
初心者 n. beginner 3132
女性 n. woman, female 294
助成(する) n. subsidy v. subsidize 4807
所属(する) n. affiliation v. attach, be attached, belong 2566
食器 n. dish 4679
ショック n. shock 1486
しょっちゅう adv. often, always 2460
ショップ n. shop 4794
所得 n. income 3661
初日 n. first day 3867
処分(する) n. disposal, disposition v. dispose of 2610
庶民 n. common people, ordinary people, masses 4813
署名(する) n. signature v. sign 4988
書物 n. book 4883
所有(する) n. ownership v. own 3543
処理(する) n. management, processing v. manage, process 1480
書類 n. document 2445
調べる v. investigate; look up; examine; check 606

(お)尻 n. hips 2799
知り合い n. acquaintance 1791
知り合う v. get to know 2361
シリーズ n. series 3676
私立 n. private 4898
自立(する) n. independence v. be independent 3569
資料 n. document, material, data 1026
知る v. know 134
印 n. mark, tick, check 4463
記す v. write down; mark 1882
事例 n. case 2853
知れる v. come out, come to light, be discovered 1080
白 n. white; innocence 1456
城 n. castle 2304
白い i-adj. white 783
素人 n. amateur, beginner 3627
しわ n. wrinkle, line 4177
真 n. truth; reality 2357
進化(する) n. evolution v. evolve, develop 2584
進学(する) n. going on to the next level of education v. go on to the next level of education 4648
人格 n. character, personality 4762
シンガポール n. Singapore 4238
新幹線 n. bullet train 2587
審議(する) n. discussion, deliberation v. discuss, deliberate 4514
心境 n. state of mind 4948
神経 n. nerve 3035
真剣 na-adj. serious 1959
人権 n. human rights 4614
進行(する) n. progression v. progress 2477
信仰(する) n. religious faith v. believe 3300
信号 n. traffic light, signal 3773
人口 n. population 1300
深刻 na-adj. serious 2928
審査(する) n. examination v. examine 3740
人材 n. talent 3560
診察(する) n. medical examination, consultation v. examine 4984
真実 n. truth, reality 2874
神社 n. shrine 2524
人種 n. race 4124
新宿 n. Shinjuku (place name) 1407
進出(する) n. advance v. launch into 3544
信じる v. believe, trust 718
心身 n. mind and body 4791
申請(する) n. application, petition v. apply 2360
人生 n. life 405

親戚 *n.* relative 2274
親切 *na-adj.* kind 2675
新鮮 *na-adj.* fresh 2243
心臓 *n.* heart 2564
迅速 *na-adj.* quick, swift 4703
身体 *n.* body 1506
診断(する) *n.* diagnosis *v.* diagnose 3227
慎重 *na-adj.* careful, discreet 2984
身長 *n.* height 3043
進展(する) *n.* progress, development, evolution *v.* develop, progress, advance 2858
浸透(する) *n.* soaking, penetration *v.* soak, penetrate 4588
侵入(する) *n.* invasion *v.* break into, invade 4302
信念 *n.* belief, faith 4959
心配(する) *na-adj.* anxious, worried *n.* anxiety, worry, care *v.* worry, be anxious 560
新婦 *n.* bride 4407
人物 *n.* person, character 1344
シンプル *na-adj.* simple 3493
新聞 *n.* newspaper 643
進歩(する) *n.* progress, advance *v.* progress, advance 2797
深夜 *n.* middle of the night 3478
親友 *n.* best friend, close friend 3541
信用(する) *n.* trust, rely on 2439
信頼(する) *n., v.* trust, rely on 2096
心理 *n.* psychology 4310
森林 *n.* forest, woods 3182
人類 *n.* human race, mankind 1776
新郎 *n.* groom, bridegroom 3842

す

巣 *n.* nest 2857
酢 *n.* vinegar 3306
ず *aux.* NEGATION 56
図 *n.* drawing, figure, diagram 517
水 *n.* Wednesday, Wed. 2072
推移(する) *n.* transition, change *v.* change, shift 1806
水泳 *n.* swimming 4671
吸い込む *v.* breathe in; suck up 4321
水準 *n.* standard, level 3426
推進(する) *n.* propulsion *v.* promote, drive 965
スイス *n.* Switzerland 3655
推測(する) *n.* assumption, guess *v.* guess, presume 3747
スイッチ *n.* switch 4254
推定(する) *n.* presumption, estimation *v.* presume, estimate 3877

水道 *n.* water supply 4049
水分 *n.* water, moisture 2434
ずいぶん *adv.* very, pretty, quite 827
睡眠 *n.* sleep 4782
吸う *v.* breathe in, sip, smoke 1053
数学 *n.* mathematics 3211
数字 *n.* number, figure 1420
数日 *n.* few days 4958
数値 *n.* numerical value; score, count 3189
スーツ *n.* suit 3764
数人 *n.* several people 4250
数年 *n.* several years 1637
スーパー *n.* supermarket 1411
スープ *n.* soup 2500
末 *n.* end, last 2679
据える *v.* set, place 4803
スカート *n.* skirt 4027
姿 *n.* figure, shape, appearance 444
好き *na-adj.* favorite, like, love 196
隙 *n.* space, room, gap 4884
杉 *n.* Japanese cedar 4659
スキー *n.* ski; skiing 1432
スキー場 *n.* ski ground, ski resort 4096
隙間 *n.* crevice, opening, gap 3378
過ぎる *v.* pass, exceed 651
空く *v.* become empty, be free; get hungry 3311
すぐ *adv.* soon 221
救う *v.* save, rescue 2471
少ない *i-adj.* a little, a few 355
少なくとも *adv.* at least 1525
優れる *v.* be superior 1711
スケジュール *n.* schedule 3717
すごい *i-adj.* fantastic, wonderful; terrible 101
少し *adv.* a little, a few 190
過ごす *v.* spend, live 556
筋 *n.* tendon; line; reason 3239
涼しい *i-adj.* cool 4515
進む *v.* to go forward, make progress 497
お勧め(する) *n.* recommendation, advice *v.* recommend, advise 1222
進める *v.* advance, move forward 677
勧める *v.* encourage, recommend 1057
スタート(する) *n.* start *v.* get off, start 1473
スタイル *n.* style, body, figure 2312
スタジオ *n.* studio 4350
スタッフ *n.* staff 2026
ずつ *p.* each, ... by ... 549
すっかり *adv.* entirely, completely 1554
すっきり(する) *adv., v.* feel refreshed 2915

すっと *adv.* quickly; quietly; straight 4538
ずっと *adv.* all the time, for a long time 253
ステージ *n.* stage 3065
素敵 *na-adj.* lovely, nice, wonderful 1516
ステップ *n.* step 4565
すでに *adv.* already, before 463
捨てる *v.* throw away, abandon 896
ストーリー *n.* story 3066
ストレス *n.* stress 1148
砂 *n.* sand 2901
素直 *na-adj.* obedient, tame 2210
砂浜 *n.* beach, sand 4719
すなわち *conj.* that is (to say), namely 922
スパゲッティー *n.* spaghetti 4560
素早い *i-adj.* quick 3423
素晴らしい *i-adj.* wonderful, marvelous 712
スピーチ *n.* speech 2967
スピード *n.* speed 1975
図表 *n.* chart 3691
スペイン *n.* Spain 2654
スペース *n.* space, room 2662
すべて *n.* everything, all 266
滑る *v.* slide, slip; be slippery 2838
スポーツ *n.* sports 1044
スポーツクラブ *n.* sports club, gym 4870
ズボン *n.* pants, trousers 4702
住まい *n.* house, residence 3116
隅 *n.* corner 3734
炭 *n.* charcoal 4278
すみません *interj.* Thank you; I am sorry; Excuse me 1640
住む *v.* live 214
済む *v.* end, finish 698
スムーズ *na-adj.* smooth 3579
すら *p.* even 1665
する *v.* do; make 22
擦る *v.* rub, strike; lose 4634
すると *conj.* then, if so 1710
鋭い *i-adj.* sharp, pointed 2951
ずれる *v.* be out of step, slip 4008
座る *v.* sit 713

せ

背 *n.* stature; back 1766
ぜ *p.* EMPHASIS 2013
せい *n.* fault, cause for blame, because of 703
性 *n.* sex, gender 4516
成果 *n.* result, product 1964
正解(する) *n.* correct answer *v.* answer correctly 4632
性格 *n.* character, personality 911
正確 *na-adj.* correct, exact, accurate 1619
生活(する) *n.* life *v.* live 223
正義 *n.* justice, right 4776
請求(する) *n.* demand, request, charge *v.* demand, claim 2283
税金 *n.* tax 2625
制限(する) *n.* restriction *v.* limit, restrict 2216
成功(する) *n.* success, achievement *v.* succeed 1105
政策 *n.* policy 2424
制作(する) *n.* production *v.* produce 3441
製作(する) *n.* production *v.* manufacture 4753
生産(する) *n.* production *v.* produce 1873
政治 *n.* politics 1556
政治家 *n.* politician 2366
正式 *na-adj.* formal, official 3157
性質 *n.* nature, disposition 2392
政治的 *na-adj.* political 4483
聖書 *n.* Bible 3034
正常 *na-adj.* normal 4067
青少年 *n.* young people, juvenile 4676
精神 *n.* mind, spirit 1769
成人(する) *n.* adult *v.* come of age 4438
精神的 *na-adj.* spiritual 1532
せいぜい *adv.* at most 3513
成績 *n.* record, result, grade, mark 2343
製造(する) *n.* production *v.* produce 3096
贅沢 *n.* luxury *na-adj.* luxurious 3254
成長(する) *n.* growth *v.* grow 1019
制定(する) *n.* enactment *v.* enact 3258
生徒 *n.* student, pupil 980
制度 *n.* system, institution 1235
青年 *n.* young man 2946
性能 *n.* performance, capability 4368
整備(する) *n.* maintenance, service *v.* prepare 840
製品 *n.* product 1911
政府 *n.* government 1037
制服 *n.* uniform 4530
生物 *n.* living thing; biology 2437
成分 *n.* ingredient, constituent, component 4458
生命 *n.* life 2278
制約(する) *n.* restriction, constraint *v.* restrict, constrain 4033
西洋 *n.* the West 3945
整理(する) *n.* arrangement *v.* arrange, put in order, dispose of 2049
成立(する) *n.* completion *v.* establish, conclude, come into existence 1334
勢力 *n.* power, influence, strength 4470

政令 *n.* government ordinance 3520
背負う *v.* carry something on one's back 3618
世界 *n.* world 302
世界中 *n.* around the world, throughout the world 2032
世界的 *na-adj.* world, global 2565
席 *n.* seat 1497
責任 *n.* responsibility 951
石油 *n.* oil 4354
世間 *n.* world, public, society 2092
世帯 *n.* household, family 4754
世代 *n.* generation 1952
世田谷 *n.* Setagaya (place name) 4857
説 *n.* theory; explanation 2523
せっかく *adv.* with effort, take the trouble to 1307
積極的 *na-adj.* active, positive, aggressive 1202
セックス(する) *n.* sex *v.* have sex 3538
設計(する) *n.* plan, design *v.* plan, design 2614
接触(する) *n.* touch, contact *v.* touch 3754
接する *v.* adjoin, come in contact 1552
接続(する) *n.* connection *v.* connect 2639
絶対 *n., adv.* absolute, absolutely, whatever 424
設置(する) *n.* installation *v.* set up, place 1199
設定(する) *n.* establishment *v.* establish, set 854
セット *n.* set 2293
説得(する) *n.* persuasion *v.* persuade 3344
設備 *n.* equipment, facilities 3021
説明(する) *n.* explanation *v.* explain 370
節約(する) *n.* saving, economy *v.* save, economize on 4108
設立(する) *n.* establishment *v.* establish, set up 2152
背中 *n.* back 1679
是非 *adv.* by all means, please; definitely, certainly 631
狭い *i-adj.* narrow, small 1101
迫る *v.* approach, draw near; demand 1792
せめて *adv.* at least, at most 2994
攻める *v.* attack 3913
責める *v.* accuse, blame 4720
台詞 *n.* lines, speech, words 3170
せる *aux.* CAUSATIVE 50
ゼロ *n.* zero 2606
世話(する) *n.* care *v.* take care of, look after 1270
線 *n.* line 2111
全員 *adv., n.* all members, everyone 1341
千円 *n.* one thousand yen 2560
前回 *n.* last time, previous time 2875
千九百九十九年 *n.* 1999 (year) 4812
千九百九十年 *n.* 1990 (year) 4814
選挙 *n.* election 2708
専業主婦 *n.* housewife 4331

宣言(する) *n.* declaration *v.* declare 3510
戦後 *adv., n.* postwar, after the war 1215
前後 *n.* back and forth 2864
前項 *n.* previous page 2707
全国 *n.* nationwide, whole country, national 1268
全国的 *na-adj.* nationwide 3965
先日 *adv., n.* the other day, recently 1396
前日 *n.* eve, previous day 2802
前者 *n.* former 4249
選手 *n.* player, athlete 986
先週 *n.* last week 4440
前述(する) *n., v.* above-mentioned, mentioned above 3394
前条 *n.* preceding article 4867
全身 *n.* all over, whole body 2724
先進国 *n.* developed country 4338
センス *n.* sense 4746
先生 *n.* teacher 243
戦前 *n.* pre-war 3440
全然 *adv.* (not) at all; utterly, completely 306
戦争 *n.* war 673
センター *n.* center 4205
仙台 *n.* Sendai 3488
全体 *n.* total, whole, entire 1088
全体的 *na-adj.* whole, overall 3602
選択(する) *n.* selection, choice *v.* choose 952
洗濯(する) *n.* washing *v.* wash 3630
選択肢 *n.* choices, alternatives 4554
先端 *n.* tip, point, forefront 4666
前提 *n.* assumption, premise 1800
宣伝(する) *n.* advertisement *v.* advertise 3831
先頭 *n.* head, lead 4536
前年 *n.* previous year, year before 2539
前年度 *n.* preceding year 3841
先輩 *n.* senior, elder 1340
前半 *n.* first half 4388
全部 *adv.* all, whole, entire 338
鮮明 *na-adj.* clear, vivid 4863
専門 *n.* specialty, speciality 3008
専門家 *n.* expert, specialist 2659
専門学校 *n.* technical school, college, vocational school 4347
専門的 *na-adj.* technical, academic 4093
戦略 *n.* strategy 4373
線路 *n.* track, railroad 4749

そ

ぞ *p. disc.* EMPHASIS 641
そいつ *n.* that guy 3658

そう *adv.* so, such 39
そう *n., na-adj.* be about to 145
沿う *v.* along; in line with, according to, meet 2097
像 *n.* figure, statue 4508
象 *n.* elephant 4700
相違 *n.* difference, disagreement 4449
増加（する）*n.* increase, gain *v.* increase, grow 800
倉庫 *n.* warehouse, storehouse 4396
相互 *n.* mutual, each other 4784
そうこう *adv.* in the meantime 3985
総合的 *na-adj.* synthetic, integrated, comprehensive 2835
操作（する）*n.* operation *v.* operate 2462
捜査（する）*n.* criminal investigation *v.* investigate 3775
掃除（する）*n.* cleaning *v.* clean 1876
創設（する）*n.* foundation, creation *v.* found, create 4414
想像（する）*n.* imagination, image *v.* imagine 925
創造（する）*n.* creation *v.* create 4251
増大（する）*n.* increase, growth; increase, grow 2690
相談（する）*n.* consultation *v.* consult 844
装置（する）*n.* device, equipment *v.* be equipped with 4667
早朝 *n.* early morning 4355
想定（する）*n.* assumption, supposition *v.* assume, suppose 2684
相当（する）*na-adj.* considerable *n.* equivalence *v.* be equivalent *adv.* considerably, pretty 981
挿入（する）*n.* insertion *v.* insert 4604
双方 *n.* both sides, both parties 4274
添える *v.* attach, add 2780
ソース *n.* sauce; source 3062
即 *adv.* at once, immediately 4345
俗 *n., na-adj.* common, popular 4365
促進（する）*n.* promotion *v.* promote 1889
属する *v.* belong to, be a member of 2126
測定（する）*n.* measurement *v.* measure 3546
速度 *n.* speed 3780
側面 *n.* side; flank 3083
そこ *pron.* there; then 103
底 *n.* bottom; sole 1760
そこそこ *adv.* about; in a hurry; all right 3547
そこで *conj.* so 1629
そこらへん *n.* around there; such a matter 3424
素材 *n.* material 2151
組織（する）*n.* organization, structure *v.* organize 1298
そして *conj.* and, so 113
訴訟 *n.* suit, action 4426
注ぐ *v.* flow into; water; pour 2286
育つ *v.* grow up 903

育てる *v.* bring up, train, develop 880
措置（する）*n.* measure *v.* take measures 1922
そちら *pron.* your place; there; you 893
卒業（する）*n.* graduation *v.* graduate 1111
そっくり *na-adj.* resembling, just like *adv.* altogether 3934
そっと *adv.* softly, lightly 2568
外 *n.* outside 496
外側 *n.* outside 3636
備える *v.* get something ready, prepare 2181
その *adn.* that 30
その *interj.* uh, er, um, mm 65
そば *n.* side, beside 956
祖父 *n.* grandfather 2406
ソファー *n.* sofa 3866
ソフト *n.* software *na-adj.* soft 1862
祖母 *n.* grandmother 1787
染める *v.* dye, color 4095
そもそも *adv., n.* in the first place 1518
空 *n.* sky, air 1006
そりゃ *pron.* that is 4597
それ *pron.* that 44
それから *conj.* and then, after that, and 136
それぞれ *n.* each 367
それで *conj.* and then; so; that is why 108
それでは、それじゃ *conj.* then, well, so 1166
それでも *conj.* but, still 561
それとも *conj.* or 1492
それなり *n.* in itself, as it is, in its way 1255
それゆえ *adv.* therefore, thus 4263
それら *pron.* those, these, they 1032
ソ連 *n.* the Soviet Union 2805
揃う *v.* become complete; be equal 1579
揃える *v.* arrange, prepare 2321
そろそろ *adv.* soon; slowly 1747
損 *n.* loss, damage 4042
損害 *n.* damage, loss 4774
尊敬（する）*n.* respect *v.* respect 2986
存在（する）*n.* existence *v.* exist 423
存ずる *v.* know 3696
尊重（する）*n.* respect *v.* give something serious consideration 3624
そんな *adn.* that, such 118
そんなこんな *adv.* what with one thing and another; after many twists and turns 4816

た

た *aux.* PAST 4
他 *n.* another, other 356

だ *aux.* COPULA 6
たい *aux.* want to, like to 76
タイ *n.* Thailand 2868
台 *n.* stand, rack 4165
体育 *n.* physical education, gymnastics 4005
体育館 *n.* gym 4635
第一 *n.* first 947
第一号 *n.* first 4128
退院(する) *n.* leaving hospital *v.* be discharged from hospital 3215
ダイエット(する) *n.* diet *v.* go on a diet 2277
対応(する) *n.* correspondence, response *v.* respond to 572
大会 *n.* convention, mass meeting, tournament 2145
大概 *n.* generally 4922
大学 *n.* university, college 375
大学時代 *n.* college days, university days 3705
大学生 *n.* college student, university student 2773
大企業 *n.* big business 3997
大規模 *na-adj.* large-scale 4012
大嫌い *na-adj.* hate 4946
体験(する) *n.* experience *v.* experience, have experience of 889
対抗(する) *n.* competition, rivalry *v.* oppose, rival 4598
大根 *n.* Japanese radish, radish 2902
滞在(する) *n.* stay, visit *v.* stay, visit, stop 2749
対策 *n.* measure 1929
第三 *n.* third 2588
第三者 *n.* outsider, third party 4195
大事 *na-adj.* important, serious 393
たいした *adn.* not big, not much; great, quite 1900
体質 *n.* constitution (physical) 4191
たいして *adv.* (not) very much 3646
体重 *n.* (body) weight 1729
対処(する) *n.* handling, coping *v.* deal with 2305
対象 *n.* object, target, subject 618
大正 *n.* Taisho era 3506
大丈夫 *na-adj.* safe, all right 626
退職(する) *n.* retirement, resignation *v.* retire, resign 3159
大臣 *n.* Cabinet minister, minister of state 2595
大好き *na-adj.* love 885
対する *v.* toward, against; compare, receive 1771
体制 *n.* system, structure 3537
大切 *na-adj.* important 426
大切さ *n.* importance 4053
大体 *adv.* almost, nearly 259
大地 *n.* earth, ground 4151
体調 *n.* physical condition 2519

大抵 *adv.* usually 1789
態度 *n.* attitude, manner, behavior 1266
大統領 *n.* President 3578
台所 *n.* kitchen 2970
タイトル *n.* title 335
体内 *n.* inside the body 4235
第二 *num.* second, secondary; another 1189
大半 *n.* better part, most part 2954
代表(する) *n.* representative *v.* represent, stand for 1458
代表的 *na-adj.* representative, typical 3130
タイプ(する) *n.* type *v.* type 1027
大分 *adv.* very, a lot, much 1289
台風 *n.* typhoon 2593
大部分 *n.* majority *adv.* mostly 3439
大変 *na-adj.* serious, terrible; hard, difficult 238
逮捕(する) *n.* arrest *v.* arrest 2547
タイミング *n.* timing 3152
題名 *n.* title 4800
タイヤ *n.* tire 4649
太陽 *n.* sun 1514
平ら *na-adj.* flat 4429
対立(する) *n.* opposition, conflict *v.* be opposed to 2865
大量 *n., na-adj.* large quantity, a lot 1946
体力 *n.* physical strength 1860
対話(する) *n.* dialogue, conversation *v.* converse, discuss 4384
台湾 *n.* Taiwan 2890
耐える *v.* stand, endure, bear 2050
絶える *v.* cease, fail 2533
倒す *v.* knock down 3998
タオル *n.* towel 3801
倒れる *v.* fall (down), collapse 1707
だが *conj.* but, however 612
高い *i-adj.* high, tall; expensive 228
互い *n.* each other 647
高さ *n.* height 1513
高まる *v.* rise, heighten, grow 1955
高める *v.* raise 1781
だから *conj.* so, therefore, because 185
たがる *aux.* want to 2574
滝 *n.* waterfall 4332
たく *v.* burn 2736
類い *n.* kind, sort, type 4759
たくさん *adv.* many, much 257
タクシー *n.* taxi 1997
竹 *n.* bamboo 3523
だけ *p.* only, alone, merely 87

だけでなく *cp.* not only 1574
だけど *conj.* but, however 3889
だけれど *conj.* despite, though 933
出し *n.* soup stock 4917
確か *na-adj., adv.* sure, certain, reliable
    adv. maybe, probably; if I remember rightly, it's my understanding that 366
確かめる *v.* confirm, make sure 2219
他者 *n.* another person, others 4603
多少 *adv., n.* more or less; somewhat; a little 1098
足す *v.* add 3836
出す *v.* take out; pay; send 178
多数 *n.* many, a number of 2178
助かる *v.* survive, be saved; be helpful 2472
助け *n.* help, assistance 3712
助ける *v.* help, rescue, save 1282
携わる *v.* participate, be engaged 3167
尋ねる *v.* ask, look for 1232
訪ねる *v.* visit, go to see 2030
多々 *adv.* many 3760
ただ *conj.* just *adv.* only, just, merely 184
ただ *n.* just, mere, only 1453
ただいま *adv.* now, just now, at once; I'm back! 3024
戦い *n.* fight, battle 1633
戦う *v.* fight 1495
たたく *v.* slap, hit, knock, clap 1204
ただし *conj.* but, however, though 724
正しい *i-adj.* right, accurate, proper 1001
ただただ *adv.* all (someone) can do is, simply, nothing but 4938
直ちに *adv.* immediately, directly 3089
畳 *n.* tatami mat 3725
漂う *v.* drift, float 2844
立ち上がる *v.* stand up, rise 1804
立ち上げる *v.* boot up, start 4932
立ち止まる *v.* stop, pause 4257
立場 *n.* position, standpoint, situation 772
たちまち *adv.* in a moment, at once; suddenly 3471
立つ *v.* stand 342
経つ *v.* pass, go by 477
脱出（する）*n.* escape *v.* escape, break out 3989
達する *v.* reach 1499
達成（する）*n.* achievement, attainment *v.* achieve, attain 2359
たった *adv.* just, only 2776
たって *p.* even if 2150
だって *conj.* because, but 2193
たっぷり *adv.* full, plenty *n.* fullness 1971
縦 *n.* length; height; vertical 3377

建物 *n.* building 842
立てる *v.* stand, set up, put up 529
たとえ *adv.* even if 1544
例えば *adv.* for example, such as 168
例える *v.* compare 4974
たどり着く *v.* finally arrive at, struggle along to 3133
たどる *v.* follow, trace, search 2852
棚 *n.* shelf 4063
谷 *n.* valley; ravine, gorge 4197
他人 *n.* others, unrelated person, stranger 1075
種 *n.* seed 2444
楽しい *i-adj.* pleasant, happy, enjoyable 277
楽しさ *n.* pleasure, charm 3468
楽しみ *n.* pleasure, enjoyment 716
楽しむ *v.* enjoy, have a good time 435
頼む *v.* ask, order 888
タバコ *n.* cigarette, tobacco 870
旅 *n.* trip, journey 941
たび *n.* every time 969
度々 *adv.* often 3825
WWW *n.* World Wide Web 4343
たぶん *adv.* probably, perhaps, maybe 320
食べ物 *n.* food 931
食べる *v.* eat 160
他方 *n.* the other side 3455
玉 *n.* ball; coin 3005
卵 *n.* egg, spawn 1369
魂 *n.* soul, spirit 2748
だます *v.* cheat, trick, deceive 3319
たまたま *adv.* accidentally, by chance 719
たまに *adv.* occasionally, once in a while 961
玉ねぎ *n.* onion 2296
たまる *v.* accumulate, build up 1531
たまる *v.* bear, endure 2348
黙る *v.* hold one's tongue, become silent 1684
ため *n.* for 100
だめ *na-adj.* useless, hopeless, impossible 476
ため息 *n.* sigh 3642
試す *v.* try, attempt 1854
ために *cp.* for 344
溜める *v.* save, store, accumulate 2569
保つ *v.* keep, maintain 1752
多様 *na-adj.* various 3014
多様化（する）*n.* diversification *v.* diversify 4851
頼り *n.* support, dependence 3952
頼る *v.* depend, turn to, trust 2633
たり *p.* and 68
足りる *v.* be sufficient, be enough, be worthy 1457
足る *v.* be enough; deserve 3680

誰 *pron.* who, whose, whom 217
タレント *n.* celebrity, entertainer 4844
単位 *n.* unit, credit 3105
段階 *n.* grade, stage, step 1040
単語 *n.* word 3338
男子 *n.* boy, man 2944
単純 *na-adj.* simple 1591
男女 *n.* men and women 2482
誕生(する) *n.* birth *v.* be born, be created 1825
誕生日 *n.* birthday 3018
ダンス *n.* dancing 4122
男性 *n.* male, man 675
団体 *n.* party, group, organization 2174
だんだん *adv.* gradually, more and more, less and less 433
団地 *n.* housing development 3373
担当(する) *n.* charge *v.* be in charge of 1564
担当者 *n.* person in charge 4038
旦那 *n.* husband 1577
単なる *adn.* mere, simple 2399
単に *adv.* just, simply 1496
担任 *n.* class teacher 3526
たんぱく質 *n.* protein 3501
田んぼ *n.* rice field 2989
ダンボール *n.* cardboard 4184

ち

血 *n.* blood 1121
地 *n.* earth, ground, land, place 1267
地位 *n.* rank, position 2416
地域 *n.* region, area 508
小さい *i-adj.* small, little, tiny 314
小さな *adn.* small, little, tiny 481
チーズ *n.* cheese 3484
チーム *n.* team 1237
知恵 *n.* wisdom 2463
チェック(する) *n.* check *v.* check 1177
地下 *n.* basement; underground 3143
近い *i-adj.* near, close 488
違い *n.* difference 649
誓う *v.* vow, swear 4833
違う *v.* be different; be wrong 186
近く *n.* near, nearby 420
近頃 *n.* recently, lately 4283
近付く *v.* approach, get closer to 1143
近づける *v.* bring close 4487
地下鉄 *n.* subway, underground 2658
力 *n.* power, strength 395
力強い *i-adj.* strong, powerful 4837

地球 *n.* earth, globe 1010
地球上 *n.* on the earth 3996
地区 *n.* area 3665
蓄積(する) *n.* storage, accumulation *v.* store, accumulate 3904
地形 *n.* topography, landform 4977
チケット *n.* ticket 2716
知識 *n.* knowledge, information 1097
地上 *n.* ground 3415
知人 *n.* acquaintance 3162
地図 *n.* map 2138
父 *n.* father 365
父親 *n.* father 662
秩序 *n.* order, system 4732
ちなみに *conj.* by the way, incidentally 904
千葉 *n.* Chiba 3582
千葉県 *n.* Chiba prefecture 3165
地方 *n.* area, district, countryside 1280
地方公共団体 *n.* local public body 3015
ちまう *aux.* do something completely 3878
地名 *n.* place name 3463
茶 *n.* tea; brown 816
着実 *na-adj.* steady 4856
チャレンジ *n.* challenge 4277
チャンス *n.* chance 1870
ちゃんと *adv.* exactly, regularly, properly 533
注 *n.* note, annotation, comment 1302
注意(する) *n.* attention *v.* notice, be careful 768
注意点 *n.* important point 4583
中央 *n.* center *adj.* central 2279
中学 *n.* junior high school 1317
中学生 *n.* junior high school student 1822
中学校 *n.* junior high school 1533
中間 *n.* middle, halfway 4868
中国 *n.* China 548
中国語 *n.* Chinese (language) 3698
中国人 *n.* Chinese (person) 3032
中止(する) *n.* cancellation *v.* cancel, call off 3334
注射 *n.* injection 3959
駐車場 *n.* parking space, parking lot, car park 2371
中小企業 *n.* small and medium-sized enterprises 3292
昼食 *n.* lunch 3958
中心 *n.* center 525
中世 *n.* Middle Ages, medieval 4499
抽選(する) *n.* lottery *v.* draw lots 3604
中途半端 *na-adj.* unfinished, half-done 4925
注目(する) *n.* attention *v.* pay attention, watch 1363
注文(する) *n.* order *v.* order 2061
長官 *n.* director general 4795

長期 *n.* long term 4351
彫刻 *n.* sculpture, carving 4661
調査(する) *n.* investigation *v.* investigate, inquire, explore 989
調子 *n.* condition, tone 1599
長女 *n.* eldest daughter 4300
頂上 *n.* top, summit 4781
朝食 *n.* breakfast 3226
調整(する) *n.* adjustment *v.* adjust 1994
調節(する) *n.* adjustment *v.* adjust 4880
挑戦(する) *n.* challenge *v.* challenge, try 2010
朝鮮 *n.* Korea 4650
調達(する) *n.* supply, procurement *v.* supply, procure 4528
ちょうど *adv.* just, exactly 373
長男 *n.* eldest son 1863
調味料 *n.* seasoning, spice 4951
調理(する) *n.* cooking *v.* cook 3664
調和(する) *n.* harmony, balance *v.* harmonize, match 4236
貯金 *n.* savings, deposit 4181
直後 *n.* immediately after, just after 3511
直接 *n., adv.* directly, direct 817
直前 *n.* just before 3054
直面(する) *n.* confrontation *v.* confront, face 3892
チョコレート *n.* chocolate 4654
著者 *n.* author, writer 4036
直径 *n.* diameter 4398
ちょっと *adv.* (just) a little, a bit 85
チラシ *n.* flyer, leaflet, handout 4437
治療(する) *n.* cure, treatment, therapy *v.* treat, cure 1304
散る *v.* fall, drop 4541
賃金 *n.* salary, wage 4357
沈黙(する) *n.* silence *v.* be silent 3808

つ

つ *p.* [indicating contrasts or coordinations] 4908
ツアー *n.* tour 2037
つい *adv.* without thinking, unintentionally 1488
追加(する) *n.* addition, supplement *v.* add, supplement 2889
追及(する) *n.* pursuit *v.* pursue the question 3486
一日 *n.* first (date) 1161
ついで *n.* on one's way, along the way 2770
次いで *adv.* next, after that 4074
ついに *adv.* at last, finally 1501
通過(する) *n.* passage *v.* pass 3075

通勤(する) *n.* commute *v.* commute 3744
通常 *adv., n.* normally, ordinary, regular 1185
通じる *v.* lead; communicate, understand 1217
通信 *n.* correspondence, communication 4327
通知(する) *n.* notice, notification *v.* notify 3409
通訳 *n.* interpreter 3828
通用(する) *n.* currency *v.* accept, obtain 4009
使い方 *n.* how to use 2202
使う *v.* use, handle 119
捕まえる *v.* catch, arrest 2947
捕まる *v.* be caught, be arrested; hold 3454
つかむ *v.* catch, grasp 1672
浸かる *v.* be flooded; soak 4317
疲れ *n.* fatigue, exhaustion, tiredness 3208
疲れる *v.* get tired 1063
月 *n.* month; moon 937
次 *n.* next, following, coming 165
付き合い *n.* association, acquaintance 1437
付き合う *v.* associate with, go out with, go along with 970
次々 *adv.* one after another 1809
尽きる *v.* run out 3873
付く *v.* stick; be stained with 176
着く *v.* arrive, reach 680
突く *v.* push; prick 2747
吐く *v.* tell (a lie); sigh 4155
継ぐ *v.* succeed, take over 1401
次ぐ *v.* next to, after 4313
机 *n.* desk 2201
尽くす *v.* do one's best, devote; exhaust 2987
つくづく *adv.* thoroughly, deeply, carefully 3497
作り *n.* make, construction 3085
作り上げる *v.* make up, build up 2955
作り方 *n.* how to make 735
作り出す *v.* make, create 2426
作る *v.* make, create, cook 110
付け加える *v.* add 3994
付ける *v.* put; attach; apply 204
漬ける *v.* soak; pickle 2785
告げる *v.* tell, announce 2263
都合(する) *n.* convenience, circumstances *v.* arrange *adv.* altogether 1813
伝える *v.* tell; deliver; hand down 670
伝わる *v.* spread, descend, travel 1323
土 *n.* soil 1489
つつ *p. conj.* while doing; though 744
つつある *cp.* be in the process of doing, be doing 2143
続く *v.* continue, go on, last 361

続ける v. continue, keep up, go on 484
突っ込む v. thrust, stick; dip; shove 2491
包む v. wrap 1837
都度 n. every time 4199
勤める v. be employed, work for 1052
努める v. make efforts 1784
つながり n. connection, relation 2728
つながる v. be connected, be related 808
つなぐ v. connect, tie 1836
つなげる v. connect, tie 4523
常 n. way adv. always, usually 725
潰す v. smash; crush, squash; ruin 2479
つぶやく v. mutter, murmur 2324
潰れる v. be crushed; go bankrupt; become useless 3231
壺 n. pot, vase 4488
妻 n. wife 789
つまり adv. in short, that is to say, after all 421
詰まる v. be blocked, be packed, be clogged 1283
罪 n. crime; guilt 2172
積む v. pile up, heap up; acquire, accumulate 2270
爪 n. nail; claw 2945
冷たい i-adj. cold 1546
詰める v. plug, pack, stuff 2831
つもり n. intention 727
強い i-adj. strong, powerful 288
強さ n. strength, power 3194
強める v. strengthen, increase 4840
つらい i-adj. hard, difficult, painful 522
辛さ n. pain 4610
貫く v. persist, stick to; pierce 4629
釣り n. fishing 2140
つる v. hang 1498
連れる v. take somebody, accompany 466

て

手 n. hand 194
で p. case in; at; from; by 12
で conj. so, then 35
て p. conj. REASON 8
出会い n. encounter 1728
出会う v. meet, come across 964
てあげる cp. do something for somebody 770
手足 n. limb 4116
てある cp. [describes a state resulting from someone's action] 360
である cp. COPULA (formal) 53
提案(する) n. proposal v. propose 1830
DNA n. DNA, deoxyribonucleic acid 4584

Tシャツ n. T-shirt 3911
TV n. television 4137
DVD n. DVD 3703
定員 n. capacity (people) 2370
低下(する) n. decline, fall v. decline, fall 1555
定義 n. definition 2404
定期的 na-adj. regular 3761
提供(する) n. offer v. supply, sponsor 1076
ていく, てく cp. go and ... 92
締結(する) n. conclusion v. conclude 3983
抵抗(する) n. resistance v. resist, offer opposition 2325
停止(する) n. stop, suspension v. stop, suspend 3673
提示(する) n. presentation v. present 3434
提出(する) n. submission v. submit, hand in 1421
ていただく cp. [receive a favor (humble)] 252
定着(する) n. fixing v. fix; become established 3421
程度 n. degree, grade, level, limit 460
丁寧 na-adj. careful, polite 2443
定年(する) n. retirement v. retire 3821
ている, てる cp. CONTINUATION 13
手入れ n. repair, maintenance 4379
データ n. data 1182
デート(する) n. date v. date 3861
テープ n. tape 2702
テーブル n. table 1733
テーマ n. theme, subject 301
ておく cp. do something in advance, in preparation for something 269
ておる cp. CONTINUATION (polite) 106
でかい i-adj. big, huge 3571
手書き n. handwriting 4102
出かける v. go out, leave 798
手紙 n. letter 797
手軽 na-adj. light; simple; reasonable 3875
敵 n. enemy, opponent 1465
出来上がる v. be completed, be finished, be ready 1379
的確 na-adj. precise, exact 3804
出来事 n. event, affair, happening 1193
テキスト n. textbook 4319
適する v. suit, fit 3146
適正 na-adj. appropriate, proper, reasonable 3581
適切 na-adj. suitable, proper 1758
適度 na-adj. moderate 4943
適当 na-adj. proper, appropriate, suitable; irresponsible, whimsical 1632
適用(する) n. application v. apply 1548
できる v. be ready 80
てくださる cp. [do something as a favor (honorific)] 172

テクニック *n.* technique 4564
てくる *cp.* go and … 86
てくれる *cp.* [do something as a favor] 114
でございます *cp.* be (formal) 542
デザート *n.* dessert 4512
デザイン(する) *n.* design *v.* design 1666
弟子 *n.* pupil, disciple 4524
てしまう *cp.* end up doing … 43
手順 *n.* order, process, plan 3457
です *aux.* COPULA (polite) 14
ですが *conj.* but, however 2818
ですから *conj.* so, therefore 376
ですけれど *conj.* but 3140
テスト(する) *n.* test *v.* test 2224
鉄 *n.* iron, steel 2650
哲学 *n.* philosophy 4218
手作り *n.* handmade, homemade 3433
手伝い *n.* help 2859
手伝う *v.* help 2093
手続き *n.* procedure, formalities 1819
徹底(する) *n.* thoroughgoing, out-and-out
   v. be thorough 3137
徹底的 *na-adj.* thorough, complete 3891
鉄道 *n.* railroad, railway 3017
鉄板 *n.* hot plate, iron plate 4708
でない *cp.* COPULA (NEGATIVE) 461
テニス *n.* tennis 1982
手のひら *n.* palm of the hand 3414
ては *p., conj.* alternately do … and … 2538
では *conj.* then, well 769
では *p.* in; on; as for 3299
デパート *n.* department store 2137
ではありません、じゃありません *cp.* not, no 1130
てはいけない、ちゃいけない *cp.* must not,
   should not 1000
ではない *cp.* it is not the case that … 89
てはならない *cp.* must not, should not 2294
デビュー(する) *n.* debut *v.* make one's debut 3679
てほしい *cp.* want/ask someone to do 536
手間 *n.* labour; time 3180
て参る *cp.* begin to, come to; have been; go and
   come (humble) 1986
手前 *n.* this side 2521
てみる *cp.* try … ing 111
デメリット *n.* disadvantage 4586
ても *p. conj.* even if 131
でも *conj.* but, however 140
でもある *aux.* be … , too 4827
てもいい *cp.* (I) don't mind if 454

でもって *cp.* by, with, in 1477
手元 *n.* at hand, with one 3640
てもらう *cp.* [receive a favor] 198
てやる *cp.* do something for somebody/
   something 779
寺 *n.* temple 1756
照らす *v.* light 3786
出る *v.* go out, come out; attend 99
テレビ *n.* television, TV 408
点 *n.* point, score 411
天 *n.* sky, heaven 2895
店員 *n.* clerk, sales assistant 4731
天下 *n.* the whole world 4808
展開(する) *n.* development *v.* develop, unfold 1180
転換(する) *n.* conversion *v.* convert, change 3500
天気 *n.* weather 2160
電気 *n.* electricity; electric light 1898
転勤(する) *n.* transfer *v.* be transferred 3201
典型的 *na-adj.* typical 4879
電源 *n.* power supply 4143
天候 *n.* weather 4412
展示(する) *n.* display, exhibition
   v. display, exhibit 3224
電車 *n.* train 676
天井 *n.* ceiling 2992
転職(する) *n.* change of job *v.* change job 4758
転ずる *v.* switch, shift 4304
伝説 *n.* legend, tradition 4668
テント *n.* tent 2313
伝統 *n.* tradition 2464
伝統的 *na-adj.* traditional 3406
店内 *n.* inside a shop 4356
天皇 *n.* Emperor (of Japan) 2435
店舗 *n.* store, shop 4639
電話(する) *n.* telephone, call *v.* phone, call 324
電話番号 *n.* telephone number 2789

と

と *p. case* and; or; with; if 9
と *p. conj.* if, when; with 41
と *interj.* well, erm (abbreviation of "eeto") 304
土 *n.* Saturday 1587
ど *p.* but (Classical) 3037
ドア *n.* door 1150
問い *n.* question 3701
問い合わせ *n.* inquiry 1915
問い合わせ *n.* inquiry 4801
という、つう *cp.* called, named 16
ドイツ *n.* Germany 1257

ドイツ語 *n.* German language 4192
といった *cp.* like, such as 486
といっても *p.* even though 2720
トイレ *n.* toilet, restroom, bathroom 1219
問う *v.* ask, question; charge 1400
等 *suffix* and so on 1694
島 *n.* island 3245
塔 *n.* tower 4965
どう *adv.* how, what 95
同 *n.* same 1805
同意(する) *n.* agreement, consent *v.* agree 3241
統一(する) *n.* unity *v.* unify 3685
同一 *na-adj.* same, identical 4901
動機 *n.* motive 3566
同期 *n.* same period, same class 3943
同級生 *n.* schoolmate 3648
同居(する) *n.* coexistence, living together *v.* live together, live with 4026
東京 *n.* Tokyo 359
東京都 *n.* Tokyo, Tokyo metropolitan government, Tokyo metropolitan area 1423
道具 *n.* tool, instrument 1315
統合(する) *n.* integration *v.* integrate, combine 4402
動向 *n.* trend, movement 2898
動作(する) *n.* movement, operation *v.* operate 3040
お父さん *n.* father 777
倒産(する) *n.* bankruptcy *v.* go bankrupt 4203
投資(する) *n.* investment *v.* invest 2692
当時 *n.* then, at that time 274
同時 *n.* simultaneous, at the same time 605
当事者 *n.* parties concerned 4220
当日 *n.* that day, current day 1723
どうして *adv.* why 637
どうしても *adv.* by all means, at any cost, no matter what, after all 510
当初 *n.* beginning, original *adv.* at first 1895
登場(する) *n.* entry, appearance *v.* appear, emerge 1238
どうせ *adv.* anyway 2529
当然 *adv., n.* naturally, as a matter of course 374
どうぞ *adv.* please 1793
到達(する) *n.* arrival *v.* reach 4569
到着(する) *n.* arrival *v.* arrive 1849
到底 *adv.* (cannot) possibly, no matter how 4213
とうとう *adv.* finally 2508
堂々 *adv.* nobly, openly 4140
東南アジア *n.* Southeast Asia 4174
投入(する) *n.* investment *v.* throw, invest 4744
導入(する) *n.* introduction *v.* introduce 1336

同年 *n.* same year 4057
豆腐 *n.* tofu, bean curd 4704
動物 *n.* animal 709
答弁 *n.* answer, defense 4217
東北 *n.* Northeast, Tohoku region 4580
透明 *na-adj.* transparent, clear 4344
当面 *n.* present, current; for the time being 4180
同様 *na-adj.* similar, same 945
動揺(する) *n.* unrest *v.* be agitated 4999
同僚 *n.* colleague 3467
道路 *n.* road, way, street 1072
登録(する) *n.* registration, entry *v.* register, enroll 1701
遠い *i-adj.* far, distant 1167
十日 *n.* tenth (date); ten days 2008
遠く *adv.* far, remote *n.* distance 1316
通す *v.* pass, show ... into 898
通り *n.* street; as 406
通り過ぎる *v.* pass, go past 3763
通る *v.* pass, go along 699
とか *p.* and; or 45
都会 *n.* city 1945
溶かす *v.* dissolve; melt 4123
時 *n.* time 54
時々 *adv.* sometimes, once in a while, on occasion 1109
どきどき(する) *v.* throb, beat fast 4081
とく *aux.* [shortened form of "te oku"] 865
解く *v.* untie; solve; remove 3070
とく *n., adj.* [shortened form of "teoku"] 3296
説く *v.* explain; preach; persuade 3356
得意 *na-adj. n.* be good at, be proud; customer 1913
独自 *na-adj.* original, own 2561
読者 *n.* reader 2879
特殊 *na-adj.* special 2652
読書 *n.* reading 4006
特色 *n.* characteristic, feature 3849
独身 *n.* single, unmarried 4860
特性 *n.* character, property 3514
特徴 *n.* characteristic, feature 833
特定(する) *n.* specific *v.* specify 1780
独特 *na-adj.* peculiar, unique; personal 2743
特に *adv.* especially, particularly 216
特別 *na-adj.* special, particular 1383
独立(する) *n.* independence *v.* be independent 2011
時計 *n.* watch; clock 2452
溶ける *v.* melt, thaw; dissolve 3418
遂げる *v.* achieve 3799
どこ *pron.* where 181
所 *n.* place, point; part; aspect 71
どころ *p.* far from, on the contrary, can't even 1902

ところが *conj.* however 552
ところで *conj.* by the way, well 2155
年 *n.* year; age 470
都市 *n.* city 1569
年上 *n.* older, senior 4836
としたら *p. conj.* if so 2645
として *cp.* as 82
としても *cp.* assuming, even if 1205
図書館 *n.* library 1932
年寄り *n.* old people 3282
閉じる *v.* close, shut 2055
都心 *n.* city center, downtown area 2381
とすれば *p. conj.* if that is the case 2958
とたん *n.* as soon as 2004
土地 *n.* land, ground 745
途中 *n.* on the way; in the middle of 693
どちら *pron.* where; which; who 524
特許 *n.* patent 3489
突然 *adv.* suddenly 852
どっち *pron.* which 2543
トップ *n.* top 2354
とても, とっても *adv.* very 142
都道府県 *n.* prefectures 3052
届く *v.* reach, arrive 1146
届け出 *n.* report, notification 4252
届ける *v.* deliver; send; report 2795
整う *v.* be ready; be well-regulated 3131
整える *v.* arrange, prepare 2036
留まる *v.* stay 2465
留める *v.* hold, keep 4931
とともに *cp.* together with, with 1171
都内 *n.* in the city 2913
唱える *v.* recite; advocate 3710
どなた *pron.* who 2854
隣り *n.* next door, next 786
怒鳴る *v.* shout 4329
とにかく *adv.* anyway, regardless 381
土日 *n.* Saturday and Sunday 3242
どの *adn.* which, what 328
とはいえ *p. conj.* though, however 2982
飛ばす *v.* let fly, fly 2732
飛び込む *v.* dive, plunge 2615
飛び出す *v.* spring out; come rushing out 2367
扉 *n.* door 2407
飛ぶ *v.* fly 836
徒歩 *n.* on foot, walk 3287
乏しい *i-adj.* few, little 4935
トマト *n.* tomato 2963
戸惑う *v.* confuse, puzzle 4153

止まる *v.* stop 846
泊まる *v.* stay 1346
富む *v.* be rich (in); grow 4101
止める *v.* stop 814
共 *n.* with, together 422
とも *p.* all, both 1996
友 *n.* friend 3789
ともかく *adv.* in any case, anyway 1736
友達 *n.* friend 219
伴う *v.* accompany, involve 900
土曜日 *n.* Saturday 2384
ドライバー *n.* driver 4460
ドライブ *n.* drive 4318
捕らえる *v.* catch, grasp, seize, arrest 1226
トラック *n.* truck 2502
トラブル *n.* trouble 2402
ドラマ *n.* TV drama, drama 1611
捕われる *v.* be arrested, be captured, stick to 4640
鳥 *n.* bird; poultry 1209
取り敢えず *adv.* for the time being; at once 551
取り上げる *v.* pick up, adopt; take away 1258
取り扱い *n.* treatment, handling 4340
取り扱う *v.* handle, treat 3839
取り入れる *v.* take in; adopt; harvest 1943
取り組み *n.* match; approach 2363
取り組む *v.* tackle, deal with 1558
取り込む *v.* take in 3562
取り出す *v.* take out, extract 1714
取り付ける *v.* install, arrange 3353
取り除く *v.* remove 3588
取り引き *n.* business, dealing, trade 2554
取り巻く *v.* surround, enclose 4190
取り戻す *v.* take back, repossess 2848
努力(する) *n.* effort *v.* make an effort 799
とりわけ *adv.* especially 3097
取る *v.* take, get; have; pass 132
とる *aux.* [shortened form of "teoru"] 2513
どれ *pron.* which 663
トレーニング *n.* training 2527
取れる *v.* come off; be removed 570
とんでも *adv.* unexpected; outrageous, very offensive 2585
どんどん *adv.* rapidly, fast, soon 379
どんな *adn.* what, what kind of 322
トンネル *n.* tunnel 4642

な

な *p. disc.* PROHIBITION 55
名 *n.* name 995

ない *aux.* not 27
無い *i-adj.* There is no . . . , no . . . 47
ないし *conj.* or, otherwise 2494
ないといけない *cp.* must, have to 3002
ナイフ *n.* knife 1405
内部 *n.* inside, interior 2660
内容 *n.* contents 407
なお *adv.* more, still 639
なおかつ *adv.* besides, and yet 3479
直す *v.* fix, repair, mend 1441
直る *v.* be repaired; be corrected; get better 1590
中 *n.* inside, in; into 78
仲 *n.* relations, terms 1821
長い *i-adj.* long 325
長さ *n.* length 1702
長崎 *n.* Nagasaki 3110
流す *v.* flush; pour; drain 1054
なかなか *adv.* very, quite; (not) easily 297
長年 *adv.* long time; many years 2938
中野 *n.* Nakano (place name) 3360
半ば *n.* half, middle *adv.* partly 3307
仲間 *n.* company, fellow, mate, group 1095
中身 *n.* contents; substance 1974
眺める *v.* see, view, gaze 1197
仲良く *adv.* friendly 1534
ながら *p. conj.* with, over, while 117
流れ *n.* stream, flow, current 902
流れる *v.* flow, float, pass 674
泣く *v.* cry 795
鳴く *v.* cry, sing 3284
慰める *v.* console, comfort 4465
なくす *v.* lose 1807
亡くす *v.* lose 4581
なくてはいけない *cp.* have to, must 1853
なくてはならない *cp.* must 3342
なくなる *v.* disappear; be gone 445
亡くなる *v.* die, pass away 813
殴る *v.* hit, strike 2863
投げる *v.* throw; give up 1949
なければいけない *cp.* must, have to, need to 371
なければならない *cp.* must 495
名古屋 *n.* Nagoya 3187
情けない *i-adj.* miserable 4157
なさる *v.* do (honorific) 2019
なし *n.* without, no 1061
なじみ *n.* familiarity 4975
なじむ *v.* become accustomed 3857
成す *v.* form, constitute 859
なぜ *adv.* why 272

謎 *n.* mystery, riddle 2988
夏 *n.* summer 544
懐かしい *i-adj.* nostalgic 2196
名付ける *v.* name 3772
納豆 *n.* fermented soybeans 4139
納得(する) *n.* agreement *v.* understand, be convinced 1297
夏休み *n.* summer holiday 2017
撫でる *v.* stroke 4018
など *p.* and so on, etc. 81
七 *n.* seven 796
七十 *num.* seventy 4850
斜め *n.* diagonal 4287
何 *pron.* what; something; anything; nothing 40
何事 *n.* what 2601
何しろ *adv.* anyhow, anyway 2418
何せ *adv.* anyhow, after all, in any case 4903
何々 *pron.* such and such, this and that 1292
なにより *adv.* above all, chiefly, more than anything 2551
七日 *n.* seventh (date); seven days 2703
なので *conj.* because, as 2153
名乗る *v.* give one's name 4186
鍋 *n.* pan, pot; hot-pot 1622
生 *n.* raw; fresh; live 1767
名前 *n.* name 337
生クリーム *n.* fresh cream 4185
波 *n.* wave 1820
涙 *n.* tear 1123
なめる *v.* lick; suck 3715
悩み *n.* trouble, worry 2258
悩む *v.* be worried, be troubled, suffer 1188
習う *v.* take lessons, be taught, learn 1245
鳴らす *v.* ring 3584
ならびに *conj.* and, both . . . and 3461
並ぶ *v.* line, stand in line 863
並べる *v.* arrange; line up; enumerate 1683
なり *p.* or, whether or not 1474
成り立つ *v.* be concluded; consist of 2388
なる *v.* become, get; come to do, start to do; turn into 28
鳴る *v.* sound; ring 2259
なるべく *adv.* as . . . as possible, if possible 1264
なるほど *adv.* I see, indeed, to be sure, of course 2073
慣れる *v.* get used to 962
なんか *p.* such as, like 189
何回 *n.* how many times 1036
何時 *n.* what time 3540
何時間 *n.* how many hours 4953

何だか *adv.* somewhat; somehow 1917
なんて *p.* [expresses belittlement] 229
何でも *adv.* anything; nothing; everything 1626
何と *adv.* how, what 2419
何度 *n.* how many times, how often 710
何とか *adv.* somehow *n.* something 1210
何日 *n.* many days; how many days 2737
何人 *n.* how many people 1311
何年 *n.* what year, how many years 1507
ナンバー *n.* number 4211
なんら *adv.* nothing 1557

に

に *p. case* at; on; in; to; for 2
二 *n.* two 148
似合う *v.* suit 4107
にあたって *cp.* at the time of 1953
二位 *n.* second place 4431
新潟 *n.* Niigata 4630
兄さん *n.* elder brother 2725
ニーズ *n.* needs 3721
匂い *n.* smell, odor, scent 1081
において *cp.* at; in; on 233
における *cp.* in 362
二回 *n.* twice 1303
二階 *n.* second floor 1935
二回目 *n.* second time 3363
二ヶ月 *n.* two months 2382
二月 *n.* February 935
苦手 *na-adj.* not good at, weak point 2311
に関して *cp.* about, regarding, concerning 595
に関する *cp.* be concerned with, be related to 404
にぎやか *na-adj.* busy, bustling 3769
握る *v.* hold, grasp, clasp 1727
賑わう *v.* be crowded with 4082
肉 *n.* meat, flesh, fat 1263
肉体 *n.* body 3606
に比べて *cp.* compared to 3713
逃げ出す *v.* run away 4544
逃げる *v.* run away, escape 1126
二個 *n.* two (pieces, things) 3751
ニコニコ（する） *v.* smile *adv.* smiling 4016
煮込む *v.* stew 4556
二歳 *n.* two years old 3797
二三日 *n.* two or three days 4611
西 *n.* west 2038
二時 *n.* two o'clock 2480
二時間 *n.* two hours 1785
二十歳 *n.* twenty years old 4888

二十世紀 *n.* twentieth century 3048
二十分 *n.* twenty minutes 2115
にしても *cp.* even if, even though 1342
二十 *num.* twenty 2158
二重 *n.* double 4686
二十一 *n.* twenty-one 3088
二十一日 *n.* twenty-first (date); twenty-one days 2909
二十一年 *n.* twenty-one years 4330
二十一世紀 *n.* twenty-first century 756
二週間 *n.* two weeks 1914
二十九 *n.* twenty-nine 4976
二十九日 *n.* twenty-ninth (date); twenty-nine days 3276
二十五 *num.* twenty-five 3574
二十五日 *n.* twenty-fifth (date); twenty-five days 2714
二十三 *num.* twenty-three 3827
二十三日 *n.* twenty-third (date); twenty-three days 2974
二十四 *num.* twenty-four 3939
二十七日 *n.* twenty-seventh (date); twenty-seven days 3221
二十代 *n.* twenties 3399
二十七 *n. num.* twenty-seven 4785
二十二 *num.* twenty-two 3592
二十二日 *n.* twenty-second (date); twenty-two days 3063
二十人 *n.* twenty people 3800
二十年 *n.* twenty years 1530
二十八日 *n.* twenty-eighth (date); twenty-eight days 3117
二十四日 *n.* twenty-fourth (date); twenty-four days 2985
二十六 *num.* twenty-six 4529
二十六日 *n.* twenty-sixth (date); twenty-six days 3156
二種類 *n.* two kinds 3757
にしろ *p. conj.* even if 2899
にすぎない *aux.* just, mere 2683
二千 *num.* two thousand 4482
二千一年 *n.* 2001 (year) 3384
二千円 *n.* two thousand yen 4510
二千三年 *n.* 2003 (year) 4562
二千二年 *n.* 2002 (year) 3291
二千年 *n.* 2000 (year); two thousand years 2495
二千八年 *n.* 2008 (year) 4271
に対し *cp.* toward; against; in contrast to 1007
に対して *cp.* to, toward; for; against 270
に対する *cp.* to; for; against 348
に違いない *aux.* must be, no doubt that 2431
日時 *n.* date and time 1966
日常 *n., adv.* everyday, daily, usually 2167
日常生活 *n.* daily life 2891
日常的 *na-adj.* routine 4621
日曜 *n.* Sunday 4382
日曜日 *n.* Sunday 1748

について *cp.* about, concerning, as to 107
日記 *n.* diary 2666
日中 *n.* during the day 4944
日程 *n.* schedule, itinerary 4359
日本 *n.* Japan 120
につれて *cp.* as 3046
にて *p. case* by; in; at 1561
二度 *n.* twice 1479
にとって *cp.* for 278
二度目 *n.* second time 4835
担う *v.* cover, carry, take 2667
二年 *n.* two years 942
二年間 *n.* two years 3247
二年生 *n.* second grade, second year 3172
二年目 *n.* second year 4854
二倍 *n.* twice, double 4741
二番目 *n.* second 2148
二匹 *n.* two (animals) 4411
二本 *n.* two (long/cylindrical objects) 2300
日本一 *n.* most…in Japan 4641
日本語 *n.* Japanese language 828
日本酒 *n.* sake, Japanese rice wine 4342
日本人 *n.* Japanese (person) 425
二枚 *n.* two (sheets) 3883
にもかかわらず *p. conj.* in spite of, though, despite 2697
荷物 *n.* baggage, parcel, burden 1312
入院(する) *n.* hospitalization, admission to hospital *v.* hospitalize 1201
入学(する) *n.* (school etc.) entrance, admission *v.* enter (school etc.) 2597
入札(する) *n.* bid, tender *v.* bid, tender 3614
ニュージーランド *n.* New Zealand 4204
入社(する) *n.* entry to a company *v.* enter a company, get a job 4434
入手(する) *n.* acquisition *v.* get, obtain 3398
ニュース *n.* news 729
ニューヨーク *n.* New York 2218
入力(する) *n.* input *v.* type 1867
女房 *n.* wife 3072
によって *cp.* by, because of; depend on, depending on 154
によっては *cp.* depending on 2374
により *cp.* by; with; depending on 340
による *cp.* be due to, be based on 239
によると *cp.* according to 1348
によれば *cp.* according to,…say 2351
にらむ *v.* stare 4981
似る *v.* look like, resemble 751

煮る *v.* boil, cook 2245
庭 *n.* garden, yard 1296
にわたって *cp.* throughout, over a period of 2409
にわたる *cp.* ranging, covering 3536
鶏 *n.* chicken; baby bird 3556
認可(する) *n.* permission, approval *v.* permit, approve 4504
人気 *n.* popularity 1065
人形 *n.* doll 4050
人間 *n.* human being, man 180
人間関係 *n.* interpersonal relationship 2249
認識(する) *n.* recognition, awareness *v.* recognize, be aware 1090
妊娠(する) *n.* pregnancy *v.* get pregnant 2079
人参 *n.* carrot 2885
人数 *n.* number of people 2389
認定(する) *n.* authorization *v.* authorize 3243
にんにく *n.* garlic 2810
任務 *n.* duty, task, mission, role 4566

ぬ

縫う *v.* sew 4311
抜く *v.* pull, extract 1463
脱ぐ *v.* take off 3138
抜ける *v.* fall out; come loose; be omitted; leave 1470
主 *n.* head, master 2315
盗む *v.* steal 3192
布 *n.* cloth 2436
塗る *v.* spread; paint 1642
ぬれる *v.* get wet 3261

ね

ね *p. disc.* isn't it?, don't you? 26
根 *n.* root 2438
ねえ *interj.* hey 3512
お姉さん *n.* elder sister 2412
願い *n.* wish, hope 2113
願う *v.* wish, ask, pray 462
葱 *n.* leek 4802
猫 *n.* cat 603
ネズミ *n.* rat; mouse 3720
ねた *n.* material; ingredient 3301
値段 *n.* price, value, cost 1216
熱 *n.* fever; heat 1738
熱心 *na-adj.* eager, enthusiastic 3190
熱する *v.* heat 4923
ネット *n.* net 2267
ネットワーク *n.* network 3568
ねばならない *cp.* must, have to 2971

寝袋 *n.* sleeping bag 3326
眠い *i-adj.* sleepy 3289
眠り *n.* sleep 4662
眠る *v.* sleep 1212
狙い *n.* aim, target 4051
狙う *v.* aim at 1790
寝る *v.* sleep; lie down, go to bed 438
練る *v.* knead; polish; elaborate 4146
年 *n.* year 944
念 *n.* sense, feeling 2841
年賀状 *n.* New Year's card 3906
年間 *n.* year; annual 2611
年金 *n.* pension, annuity 2630
年代 *n.* era; generation; date 2649
年々 *adv.* year after year 4594
年配 *n.* elderly person 4520
年末 *n.* end of the year 4415
燃料 *n.* fuel 4793
年齢 *n.* age, years 1058

の

の *p.* *case* of; in; at; for; by 1
の *p.* PARTICLE 24
の *p. disc.* EMOTION/QUESTION 309
脳 *n.* brain 1745
農家 *n.* farmer 2449
農業 *n.* agriculture 2441
農民 *n.* farmer 4375
能力 *n.* ability, capacity, power; proficiency 1299
ノート *n.* notebook 2781
逃れる *v.* escape 3692
残す *v.* leave 392
残り *n.* rest, remainder 1724
残る *v.* remain, be left 281
乗せる *v.* take on, put on, pick up 781
覗き込む *v.* look into 4755
除く *v.* remove; except; get rid of 1031
のぞく *v.* look through, look down; drop in 1824
望ましい *i-adj.* desirable 3583
望む *v.* hope 1547
臨む *v.* face 3960
のだ、んだ *cp.* ASSERTION 49
後 *n., adv.* after, later 1598
ので、んで *p. conj.* as, because, since 57
のである *cp.* ASSERTION (formal) 202
のです、んです *cp.* ASSERTION (polite) 20
のではない、んではない *cp.* it is not that... 125
喉 *n.* throat; voice 2129
のに *p. conj.* although, though; in order to 511

伸ばす *v.* extend, lengthen; postpone 1149
伸び *n.* growth 2851
伸びる *v.* grow, stretch, extend 1184
述べる *v.* describe, say, state 630
のぼる *v.* go up, rise; reach 607
のみ *p.* only, merely 609
飲み込む *v.* swallow 4147
のみならず *p.* not only...but, as well as 4775
飲み物 *n.* drink 3851
飲む *v.* drink 307
飲める *v.* be able to drink 2664
乗り換える *v.* change, transfer 4215
乗り越える *v.* climb over; overcome 3324
乗り込む *v.* board, get into 3594
乗り出す *v.* venture out; embark on 4815
乗り物 *n.* vehicle; (amusement park) ride 4559
乗る *v.* ride, get on, take 232
のんびり *adv.* tranquil, leisurely, easygoing 2319

は

は *p.* TOPIC 3
歯 *n.* tooth 1503
葉 *n.* leaf 1669
ば *p. conj.* if 62
場 *n.* field; place; occasion 615
はあ *interj.* oh, Oh boy, Oh dear 2656
バー *n.* bar 4424
場合 *n.* case, occasion 115
把握(する) *n.* grasp *v.* grasp 1770
(お)ばあさん *n.* old lady; grandmother 877
パーティー *n.* party 3407
ハード *na-adj.* hard, tight 4747
パート *n.* part; part-time 3413
パートナー *n.* partner 4496
はい *interj.* yes; all right 502
倍 *n.* times 4937
俳句 *n.* haiku (Japanese poem of seventeen syllables) 3848
バイク *n.* motorcycle, motorbike 1847
背景 *n.* background, context, setting 1275
背後 *n.* back; background 3074
廃止(する) *n.* abolition *v.* repeal 2753
排除(する) *n.* removal *v.* remove 3563
配置(する) *n.* arrangement, layout *v.* arrange 2782
バイト *n.* part-time job 1623
配布(する) *n.* distribution *v.* distribute 4068
俳優 *n.* actor 4290
入り込む *v.* go into; come into 3445
配慮(する) *n.* consideration *v.* consider 2067

入る *v.* enter, come in, go in 109
這う *v.* creep, crawl 4691
生える *v.* grow, sprout, cut (teeth), 2076
墓 *n.* grave 2378
馬鹿 *na-adj.* foolish *n.* fool 1162
破壊（する）*n.* destruction, demolition *v.* destroy, demolish 2087
はがき *n.* postcard 3262
ばかり *p.* only, just, almost 271
図る *v.* attempt; plan; strive 587
測る *v.* measure; weigh 2845
履く *v.* put on, wear 1828
吐く *v.* exhale, breathe out; vomit; spit 2290
白人 *n.* white person 4534
漠然 *adv.* vague, obscure 3919
爆発（する）*n.* explosion *v.* explode 3654
幕府 *n.* shogunate 3688
激しい *i-adj.* fierce, intense, severe 1015
励ます *v.* cheer up, encourage 3695
励む *v.* work hard, make efforts 4273
派遣（する）*n., v.* dispatch, send 2089
箱 *n.* box, case 1981
運ぶ *v.* carry, transport, move 998
挟む *v.* put in, sandwich between; catch in 1634
端 *n.* end, tip, edge 2255
橋 *n.* bridge 2308
箸 *n.* chopsticks 4324
始まり *n.* beginning, origin 3069
始まる *v.* start, begin 401
初め *n.* beginning 747
始め *adv., n.* beginning, origin 1372
初めて *adv.* for the first time, first 284
始める *v.* start, begin 388
場所 *n.* place, spot 275
柱 *n.* pillar, post 2647
走り回る *v.* run around 4655
走る *v.* run 429
はず *n.* ought to, should 369
バス *n.* bus 818
パス（する）*n.* pass *v.* pass 3951
恥ずかしい *i-adj.* ashamed, embarrassed 1451
外す *v.* undo; take off, remove 1625
パスタ *n.* pasta 4366
パスポート *n.* passport 4683
外れる *v.* be off, get out of place, be dislocated 2199
パソコン *n.* personal computer 683
肌 *n.* skin 1706
バター *n.* butter 2499
パターン *n.* pattern 2241

裸 *n.* naked, nude 3984
畑 *n.* field (for fruit, vegetables); garden 1827
果たして *adv.* really; just as one thought 1912
果たす *v.* carry out, achieve, fulfil 1286
はたち *n.* twenty years old 4926
働き *n.* work 2185
働く *v.* work 418
破綻（する）*n.* bankruptcy, collapse *v.* fail, go bankrupt 4270
八 *n.* eight 930
八王子 *n.* Hachioji (place name) 3812
八月 *n.* August 864
八時 *n.* eight o'clock 2064
八年 *n.* eight years 3139
蜂蜜 *n.* honey 3824
パチンコ *n.* pachinko, Japanese pinball 3332
初 *n.* first 4459
発音（する）*n.* pronunciation *v.* pronounce 3113
二十日 *n.* twentieth (date); twenty days 2365
発揮（する）*n.* exhibition, show *v.* display, exhibit 2054
はっきり *adv.* clearly, certainly 590
バック（する）*n.* back, background *v.* reverse, back 3737
バッグ *n.* bag 3090
発見（する）*n.* discovery *v.* discover 843
発言（する）*n.* remark *v.* speak 1947
発行（する）*n.* publication, issue *v.* publish, issue 2280
発酵（する）*n.* fermentation *v.* ferment 3612
発する *v.* emit, release 2432
発生（する）*n.* occurrence *v.* occur, happen 793
発想 *n.* idea, conception 2272
発送（する）*n., v.* send, ship, dispatch 4208
発達（する）*n.* development *v.* develop 1631
発展（する）*n.* development *v.* develop, expand 914
ぱっと *adv.* suddenly 2454
葉っぱ *n.* leaf 2815
発売（する）*n.* sale *v.* sell, put on sale 2387
発表（する）*n.* announcement, publication *v.* announce, publish 992
発明（する）*n.* invention *v.* invent 3704
果て *n.* the end 4551
派手 *na-adj.* flamboyant, flashy 3702
花 *n.* flower 471
鼻 *n.* nose 1635
話 *n.* story, talk 116
話し合い *n.* discussion, meeting 2823
話し合う *v.* talk, discuss 2285
話しかける *v.* speak to 2320
話す *v.* talk, tell, speak 195
離す *v.* separate, divide; keep apart 3188

放つ v. fly, loose 2869
バナナ n. banana 4339
花火 n. firework 2896
華やか na-adj. gorgeous 3855
離れる v. separate; leave; be away from 579
羽根 n. wing; feather 3617
母 n. mother 316
幅 n. width, breadth; difference; latitude 2006
パパ n. papa, dad 3030
母親 n. mother 550
幅広い i-adj. wide, broad 3313
バブル n. bubble 3907
はまる v. fit; fall; be addicted to 1904
ハム n. ham 4983
ハムスター n. hamster 3570
羽目 n. plight, predicament 4672
場面 n. scene, sight 1654
刃物 n. cutlery, edged tool, knife 4432
早い i-adj. early, soon 310
早く n. early, soon 3779
林 n. grove, forest, wood 3814
早め n. early 2742
はやる v. be fashionable, be popular, go around 1972
腹 n. belly, stomach 1427
バラ n. rose 3598
払う v. pay; sweep away 807
バラバラ na-adj. separate 4023
バランス n. balance 1536
針 n. needle; stitch 2517
パリ n. Paris 1560
張る v. stretch, put up 918
春 n. spring 940
遥か na-adj. faraway, far 1856
晴れる v. clear up, be dispelled; be refreshed 2977
ばれる v. come out, be discovered 3593
パワー n. power 3266
ハワイ n. Hawaii 2203
晩 n. night, evening 2570
パン n. bread 1261
範囲 n. extent, range 1551
範囲内 n. in range, within the limits 4885
反映(する) n. reflection v. reflect 2159
繁栄(する) n. prosperity v. prosper, flourish 4545
番組 n. show, program 1246
判決(する) n. decision v. decide 3792
番号 n. number 3148
犯罪 n. crime, offense 1739
反する v. go against, be contrary 3508

反省(する) n. soul-searching, reflection v. reflect on 2247
反対(する) n. opposition, contrast, objection v. oppose 1074
反対側 n. opposite side 3693
判断(する) n. judgment v. judge 801
パンツ n. pants, shorts, underpants 4209
判定(する) n. decision, judgment v. decide, judge 4380
バンド n. band; belt 1859
半年 n. half a year 1924
犯人 n. criminal, culprit 1737
反応(する) n. reaction, response v. respond 1404
販売(する) n. sale v. sell 1652
反発(する) n. repulsion, resistance v. react, resist, rebel, repel 4169
パンフレット n. brochure 4532
半分 n. half 971
判明(する) n. proving v. turn out, identify 4401
反面 n. other side 3129
反論(する) n. argument, objection v. argue, object 4710

ひ

日, 陽 n. day; sun 177
火 n. fire 580
ピアノ n. piano 1186
ピーク n. peak 4838
PC n. personal computer 2763
ビートルズ n. Beatles 3202
ビール n. beer 1663
冷える v. chill, become cold, feel cold 4308
被害 n. damage, harm 1439
被害者 n. victim 2451
控える v. abstain, hold back, refrain 2599
比較(する) n. comparison v. compare 1358
比較的 na-adj. comparative, relative 1309
東 n. east 2220
光 n. light 862
光る v. shine, glitter, twinkle 2641
引き上げる v. pull up; increase, raise 2653
率いる v. head, lead, command 4248
引き受ける v. undertake 3147
引き起こす v. raise up, cause 3238
引きずる v. drag, trail 4022
引き出す v. pull out, bring out; withdraw 3328
引き継ぐ v. take over 4071
引き付ける v. attract 4680
引き続く v. continue; follow 2118
引き取る v. take back, collect; leave 3371

引く v. pull, draw, lead; subtract 576
弾く v. play (musical instrument) 1425
低い i-adj. low, short 733
髭 n. mustache 4929
悲劇 n. tragedy 4299
飛行機 n. airplane 876
日頃 n. everyday 2900
膝 n. knee, lap 1829
ビザ n. visa 4674
日差し n. sunshine 4761
久しぶり n. after a long time 2003
久々 n., adv. for the first time in a long time 4713
悲惨 na-adj. miserable 4608
肘 n. elbow 4677
ビジネス n. business 3312
美術館 n. art gallery, museum of art 3750
非常 na-adj. very, extremely 129
美人 n. beautiful woman, beauty 4352
ひそか na-adj. secret, confidential adv. secretly 3785
ひたすら adv. determinedly, earnestly 2394
ビタミン n. vitamin 4645
左 n. left 1230
左側 n. left, left side 3859
左手 n. left hand; on one's left 2774
引っ掛かる v. catch; be caught 2907
筆記用具 n. stationery, writing materials 4353
びっくり(する) n. surprise v. be surprised, be amazed 734
引っ繰り返す v. overturn, upset, turn over 4711
日付け n. date, day 4448
引っ越し(する) n. moving, removal v. move house 1938
引っ越す v. move (house) 1529
必死 na-adj. desperate 1958
羊 n. sheep 4387
筆者 n. writer, author 4031
ぴったり adv. tight; exactly 2779
ヒット n. hit 4323
引っ張る v. pull 2303
必要 na-adj. necessary n. necessity 151
必要性 n. necessity 2643
否定(する) n. denial, negative v. deny 1978
ビデオ n. video 1757
人 n. person, people, human being 58
ひどい i-adj. cruel, serious, terrible 757
人柄 n. personality 4913
一口 n. bite, sip, mouthful 3609
一言 n. one word, single word, brief comment 1233
等しい i-adj. equal 3896
人たち n. people 262

一つ n. one 127
一つ目 n. first 3498
人々 n. people 451
瞳 n. pupil; eye 3220
一目 n. glance 4777
一人 n. one person; alone 179
一人暮らし n. living alone, single life 2825
一人一人 n. one by one, each (people) 2108
非難(する) n. criticism v. criticize 3709
避難(する) n. evacuation v. evacuate 4763
ひねる v. twist 4333
批判(する) n. criticism v. criticize 1740
日々 adv. every day, daily n. days 1250
響き n. sound; echo 4419
響く v. affect 2475
皮膚 n. skin 3128
暇 na-adj., n. free, not busy 1487
秘密 n. secret, confidence 2395
微妙 na-adj. delicate, subtle 2228
悲鳴 n. scream 4267
紐 n. string; lace 3195
百 n. hundred 2798
百円 n. one hundred yen 3256
百年 n. hundred years, century 4778
百パーセント n. one hundred percent 3153
冷やす v. keep cool, cool 3752
表 n. table, chart 928
費用 n. cost 1570
病院 n. hospital, clinic 469
評価(する) n. evaluation v. evaluate 748
病気 n. sickness, illness 559
表現(する) n. expression v. express 766
表示(する) n. indication v. display, indicate 976
表情 n. expression, facial expression, look 1124
平等 n. equality na-adj. equal 3401
評判 n. reputation; popularity 2990
表明(する) n. expression, manifestation v. express, manifest 4004
表面 n. surface, outside, appearance 2211
ひょっとする v. perhaps 3049
開く v. open; bloom; hold 482
比率 n. ratio, proportion 2867
昼 n. noon; daytime 1305
ビル n. building 2230
昼間 n. daytime 1872
広い i-adj. wide, broad, large 602
拾う v. pick up, gather, pick out 2146
披露(する) n. announcement, introduction v. announce, introduce 4786

披露宴 *n.* wedding reception 3707
広がる *v.* spread, stretch 891
広げる *v.* spread, expand 1542
広さ *n.* area; width; extent 3794
広島 *n.* Hiroshima 2612
広場 *n.* square, plaza 4133
広まる *v.* spread, get around 4088
瓶 *n.* bottle 3933
敏感 *na-adj.* sensitive 3929
ピンク *n.* pink 3766
ヒント *n.* hint, clue 4097
頻繁 *na-adj.* frequent 2935

ふ

部 *n.* division, department, section; club 3853
ファイル *n.* file 2187
ファックス(する) *n.* fax *v.* fax 1592
ファッション *n.* fashion 4574
ファン *n.* fan 1596
不安 *n.* anxiety, concern *na-adj.* uneasy, insecure 686
不安定 *na-adj.* unstable, uneasy 4260
不意 *na-adj.* sudden, unexpected *n.* suddenness 4279
フィリピン *n.* Philippines 4291
フィルム *n.* film 4341
風 *na-adj.* style, type, way, like 121
風景 *n.* scenery, landscape 1686
夫婦 *n.* (married) couple 1620
ブーム *n.* boom 4103
プール *n.* pool 2618
フェリー *n.* ferry 4590
増える *v.* increase, gain 493
部下 *n.* subordinate 3047
深い *i-adj.* deep 669
不可欠 *na-adj.* indispensable 3589
深さ *n.* depth 4681
部活 *n.* club 2214
不可能 *na-adj.* impossible *n.* impossibility 2102
深める *v.* deepen 3029
武器 *n.* weapon 2912
普及(する) *n.* spread, diffusion *v.* spread 1709
不況 *n.* recession 3671
服 *n.* clothes, dress, outfit 1370
吹く *v.* blow; breathe out; play (musical instrument) 1763
拭く *v.* wipe, dry 2892
福岡 *n.* Fukuoka 3743
複雑 *na-adj.* complicated, complex 1779
副作用 *n.* side effect 4457
福祉 *n.* welfare 3728

複数 *n.* plural 2488
服装 *n.* clothes, dress 3357
含む *v.* contain, include 507
含める *v.* include, add 678
膨らむ *v.* swell, expand 2507
袋 *n.* bag, sack, pouch 2688
不幸 *na-adj.* unhappiness, misfortune 2764
ふさぐ *v.* cover; stop; block 4845
ふさわしい *i-adj.* suitable, appropriate 2719
武士 *n.* warrior, samurai 4596
無事 *adv.* safely *n.* safety *na-adj.* safe 1505
不思議 *n.* wonder *na-adj.* wonderful, strange, mysterious 815
富士山 *n.* Mt. Fuji 2642
不自由 *n.* inconvenience; disability 4266
防ぐ *v.* defend, protect; prevent, keep away 2077
不足(する) *n.* lack, shortage *v.* be insufficient 2880
蓋 *n.* lid 2375
豚 *n.* pig 3966
舞台 *n.* stage, scene 1418
再び *adv.* again, once more 1050
二つ *num.* two 434
二つ目 *n.* second 2704
豚肉 *n.* pork 4736
二人 *n.* two people 245
二人共 *adv.* both of them, two people 2338
負担(する) *n.* burden, load, charge *v.* bear 1276
普段 *n.* usually, ordinarily 787
部長 *n.* head of department, manager 4738
普通 *na-adj.* normal, regular, ordinary, common 280
二日 *n.* second (date); two days 1523
物価 *n.* prices 4117
復活(する) *n.* revival, restoration *v.* revive, restore 2754
二日目 *n.* second day 4985
ぶつかる *v.* strike, bump, collide 2536
復帰(する) *n.* return, comeback *v.* return, come back, make a comeback 4314
仏教 *n.* Buddhism 3753
ぶつける *v.* hit; throw 4506
物件 *n.* article, object; property 4866
物質 *n.* matter, material 2390
ふっと *adv.* suddenly 4447
沸騰(する) *n.* boiling *v.* boil 4819
筆 *n.* brush 4032
ふと *adv.* casually; suddenly 1815
太い *i-adj.* thick; heavy; bold 2557
不動産 *n.* real estate, property 4087
太る *v.* get fat, gain weight 1940
布団 *n.* futon, Japanese-style bedding 2130

船 *n.* ship, boat 809
部品 *n.* parts, components 4118
部分 *n.* part, section 349
不便 *n.* inconvenience *na-adj.* inconvenient 2759
踏まえる *v.* be based on 1979
不満 *n.* dissatisfaction, discontent *na-adj.* discontented 2194
踏む *v.* step on, tread on 2186
不明 *na-adj., n.* unknown, unidentified 3716
増やす *v.* increase, add 1696
冬 *n.* winter 790
不要 *na-adj.* unnecessary 3901
プライド *n.* pride 4799
フライパン *n.* frying pan 3203
ブラジル *n.* Brazil 3482
プラス(する) *n.* plus, benefit *v.* benefit, add to 1788
プラスチック *n.* plastic 4963
ふらふら(する) *adv.* aimlessly, unsteadily *na-adj.* unsteady on one's feet *v.* stagger, be dizzy 4692
プラン *n.* plan 4421
フランス *n.* France 1059
フランス語 *n.* French language 2761
ブランド *n.* brand 3585
振り *n.* pretence 3010
振り返る *v.* turn one's head, look back 746
振り向く *v.* look around, turn around 3796
振る *v.* wave, shake, swing 974
降る *v.* fall, come down 1112
古い *i-adj.* old 720
振う *v.* flourish, prosper 3509
ブルー *n.* blue 4337
フルーツ *n.* fruit 4872
震える *v.* shake, tremble 2563
古く *n.* ancient times *adv.* anciently 3385
故郷 *n.* hometown 4002
触れ合い *n.* touching, contact 4896
プレー *n.* play 2796
プレゼント *n.* present 2602
プレッシャー *n.* pressure 3946
触れる *v.* touch; experience 821
風呂 *n.* bath 1430
プロ *n.* professional, pro 1412
ブログ *n.* blog 2682
プログラム *n.* program 2413
プロジェクト *n.* project 3694
プロセス *n.* process 3868
プロ野球 *n.* professional baseball 3882
分 *adv., n.* part, share, portion 990

文 *n.* sentence 3031
雰囲気 *n.* atmosphere, ambience 771
文化 *n.* culture 929
分解(する) *n.* analysis *v.* resolve, dismantle, take apart, analyze 4525
文学 *n.* literature 3910
分割(する) *n.* division *v.* divide 4144
文献 *n.* literature 4697
文書 *n.* document; writing 3259
文章 *n.* sentence; writing, text 1274
分析(する) *n.* analysis *v.* analyze 2057
紛争 *n.* dispute, trouble, strife 4893
分布(する) *n.* distribution *v.* distribute 4230
文明 *n.* civilization 3109
分野 *n.* field, discipline 1483
分離(する) *n.* separation, detachment *v.* separate, detach 4620
分量 *n.* quantity, amount 4921
分類(する) *n.* classification *v.* classify 2542

へ

へ *p. case* DESTINATION 94
兵 *n.* soldier, troops 4737
米 *n.* meter 3086
平気 *na-adj.* insensitive, fine *n.* calmness 2028
平均(する) *n.* average *v.* average 3055
米軍 *n.* US armed forces 4585
米国 *n.* United States 1526
兵士 *n.* soldier 4444
平日 *n.* weekday 3126
平成 *n.* Heisei era 516
平和 *n.* peace *na-adj.* peaceful 1716
ページ *n.* page 2197
ベース *n.* base, basis 2266
ペース *n.* pace 3577
北京 *n.* Beijing 4477
べし *aux.* must, should 236
ベスト *n.* best; vest 3616
下手 *na-adj.* not good at, poor, bad, unskilled 2033
別 *na-adj.* separate, different 333
ベッド *n.* bed 1504
ペット *n.* pet 2100
別に *adv.* (not) particularly 2917
別々 *na-adj.* separate, individual 4115
ベトナム *n.* Vietnam 3316
蛇 *n.* snake 3550
部屋 *n.* room 372
減らす *v.* reduce, cut down 2162
ベランダ *n.* porch, balcony 3925

減る *v.* decrease, become less 957
経る *v.* pass through, experience 1578
辺 *n.* region, area around 577
変 *na-adj.* strange, unusual, funny 849
へん *aux.* NEGATION (dialectal) 4823
変化(する) *n.* change *v.* change, vary 539
変換(する) *n.* change, conversion *v.* convert 4768
勉強(する) *n.* study *v.* learn, study 385
偏見 *n.* prejudice, bias 4889
変更(する) *n.* change, modification, revision
    v. change, revise 1155
弁護士 *n.* lawyer, counsellor 2619
返済(する) *n.* repayment *v.* repay 4973
返事(する) *n.* answer, reply *v.* answer, reply 1712
編集(する) *n.* editing *v.* edit 3351
ベンチ *n.* bench 4742
変動(する) *n.* change, fluctuation, movement
    v. change, fluctuate 4320
(お)弁当 *n.* lunch box 2001
便利 *n.* convenience *na-adj.* useful, convenient 763

ほ

保育園 *n.* nursery school, day care 4044
ポイント *n.* point 1093
方 *n.* direction, way; side 91
法 *n.* law 2171
棒 *n.* stick, pole, bar 3364
法案 *n.* bill 4160
貿易 *n.* trade, commerce 4591
崩壊(する) *n.* collapse *v.* collapse 3087
放棄(する) *n.* abandonment, renunciation
    v. abandon, renounce 4757
方言 *n.* dialect 3600
方向 *n.* direction, course 1024
報告(する) *n.* report, information, account
    v. inform 1115
報告書 *n.* report 4486
防止(する) *n.* prevention *v.* prevent 2738
帽子 *n.* hat, cap 3185
方式 *n.* method 3932
放出(する) *n.* emission *v.* emit 4980
方針 *n.* course, line; policy, plan; principle 2393
法人 *n.* corporation 2837
放送(する) *n.* broadcasting, telecasting
    v. broadcast 2248
法則 *n.* law 2981
膨大 *na-adj.* enormous 3684
放置(する) *n.* leaving something as it is *v.* neglect 3347
包丁 *n.* kitchen knife 4079

報道(する) *n.* report *v.* report 1894
冒頭 *n.* beginning 4392
豊富 *na-adj.* rich, abundant 2127
方法 *n.* way, method 368
訪問(する) *n.* visit, call *v.* visit, call (on) 2966
法律 *n.* law 788
暴力 *n.* violence 3524
放る *v.* throw; leave something undone 3912
頬 *n.* cheek 3504
ぼおっと *adv.* vacantly; dimly 3061
ホーム *n.* platform 2632
ホームページ *n.* home page 2078
ボーリング *n.* bowling 4910
ホール *n.* hall 4106
ボール *n.* ball 1022
他 *n.* other, another; else 173
保管(する) *n.* keeping, storage *v.* keep 4495
僕 *pron.* I (used by male speakers) 156
僕達 *pron.* we (used by male speakers) 2408
僕ら *pron.* we 1803
ポケット *n.* pocket 2979
保険 *n.* insurance 1884
保険会社 *n.* insurance company 4652
保険料 *n.* insurance premium 2731
保護(する) *n.* protection *v.* protect 1691
保護者 *n.* protector 3557
誇り *n.* pride, honor 3084
埃 *n.* dust 4905
誇る *v.* be proud, boast 3858
星 *n.* star 1508
ほしい *i-adj.* want, desire 642
募集(する) *n.* recruitment *v.* recruit 2120
補助(する) *n.* help, aid, assistance *v.* help, aid,
    assist 4288
保証(する) *n.* guarantee *v.* guarantee 3372
保障(する) *n.* guarantee *v.* guarantee 3735
干す *v.* dry 3706
ポスター *n.* poster 4658
ポスト *n.* post, postbox, mailbox 4045
保全(する) *n.* preservation, maintenance *v.* preserve,
    maintain 4206
細い *i-adj.* thin, narrow, slender 1589
保存(する) *n.* preservation, storage *v.* preserve,
    store 1688
ボタン *n.* button 2250
北海道 *n.* Hokkaido 1402
発足(する) *n.* start *v.* start 4497
ほっとする *v.* be relieved 2693
ホテル *n.* hotel 617

ほど *p.* about; extent 161
歩道 *n.* sidewalk, pavement 4481
施す *v.* give, do, apply, add 3559
ほとんど *adv.* almost, nearly 241
骨 *n.* bone 1715
炎 *n.* flame 3926
ほぼ *adv.* about, nearly, almost 1002
微笑む *v.* smile 4059
ほめる *v.* praise, speak well of, commend 2281
保有(する) *n.* possession *v.* hold, possess 4168
ほら *interj.* Look! 2910
ボランティア *n.* volunteer 2106
掘る *v.* dig 3106
ぼろぼろ *na-adj.* ragged, worn out *adv.* in drops 4684
本 *n.* book 327
お盆 *n.* Bon Festival, Obon 3739
本格的 *na-adj.* genuine, real; full-scale 2334
本気 *n.* seriousness, earnestness *na-adj.* serious, earnest 2819
香港 *n.* Hong Kong 2870
本質 *n.* nature, essence 3954
本日 *n.* today 2345
本社 *n.* head office 4198
本書 *n.* this book 3091
本当 *n.* truth, right 97
本人 *n.* person himself/herself, person in question 959
本音 *n.* true feeling; truth 3756
ほんの *adn.* just, nothing but, only 1754
本能 *n.* instinct 4978
本番 *n.* performance 3466
本物 *n.* real (thing), genuine 2425
本屋 *n.* bookshop 2740
翻訳(する) *n.* translation *v.* translate 3060
ぼんやり(する) *adv.* vacantly, vaguely, dimly *v.* be vague, be blurred 4200
本来 *adv., n.* originally, essentially, by nature, proper 1153

ま

間 *n.* time, interval; space 774
まあ *adv.* Oh!, well, now 761
まー, まあ *interj.* Wow!, Oh my God! 23
マーク *n.* mark 3916
まあまあ *na-adj.* so-so, not bad *adv.* fairly, moderately 5000
まい *aux.* INTENTION OF NEGATION 1718
毎朝 *adv.* every morning *n.* every morning 3908
毎回 *n.* every time 2168
マイク *n.* microphone 4876
毎週 *adv.* every week 2933
毎月 *n.* every month 2322
毎年 *adv., n.* every year, annually 1004
マイナス *n.* minus 3183
毎日 *adv.* every day 343
参る *v.* go, come, visit (humble); be in trouble, be embarrassed 1073
前 *n.* forward; front; before 123
前向き *na-adj.* facing forward; positive 3390
任せる *v.* entrust, leave 2066
曲がる *v.* bend, wind; turn 2537
巻き込む *v.* involve 3214
巻く *v.* roll up, wind up; wear around 1968
撒く *v.* scatter, water 4549
負ける *v.* lose, be beaten 953
曲げる *v.* bend, twist 4091
孫 *n.* grandchild 1835
真 *n.* truth, fact 2965
まさか *adv.* surely not, cannot possibly *n.* the worst 1960
まさしく *adv.* surely, exactly 3884
まさに *adv.* exactly 985
まし *na-adj.* better *n.* increase 4579
まして *adv.* much less, much more 2905
真面目 *na-adj.* serious; steady; honest 2205
ます *aux.* POLITE (after verb) 10
増す *v.* increase 2287
まず *adv.* first; anyway 150
まずい *i-adj.* not taste good; awkward 2122
マスコミ *n.* mass media, mass communication 2577
貧しい *i-adj.* poor 3516
マスター(する) *n.* master *v.* master 4518
ますます *adv.* more and more, increasingly 1390
混ぜ合わせる *v.* mix 4227
交ぜる *v.* mix, shuffle 1377
また *adv.* additionally, moreover *conj.* again; too, and 84
まだ *n.* yet, still 193
または *conj.* or 346
まだまだ *adv.* still, still more 1244
町, 街 *n.* town, city 255
街, 町 *n.* town, city 1941
間違い *n.* mistake, error 1717
間違い無い *i-adj.* must be 2331
間違う *v.* be wrong, make a mistake 1484
間違える *v.* make a mistake 2292
町作り *n.* town development 3651
町中 *n.* downtown 4035
町並み *n.* street, row of town houses 3876

待つ *v.* wait 430
松 *n.* pine 3672
真っ赤 *na-adj.* bright red; downright 3177
真っ暗 *na-adj.* black *n.* pitch-dark 4361
真っ黒 *na-adj.* black 4537
マッサージ(する) *n.* massage *v.* massage 4834
真っ白 *na-adj.* pure white 3819
まっすぐ *n.* straight, direct *adv.* honest 2084
全く *adv.* entirely, completely; (not) at all 289
マッチ(する) *n.* match *v.* match 4509
祭り *n.* festival 1469
祭る *v.* enshrine; worship; deify 4305
まで *p.* to, till, until 66
までもない *cp.* needless 3699
窓 *n.* window 1147
窓口 *n.* window, counter 3596
まとまる *v.* be well arranged; be united; be settled 3068
まとめる *v.* summarize, settle, gather 1067
まとも *na-adj.* direct; honest; proper 3397
マナー *n.* manners 3518
学ぶ *v.* learn 851
間に合う *v.* catch, get, make it 2648
免れる *v.* escape, avoid 4996
真似(する) *n.* imitation, mimicry, impersonation *v.* imitate, copy 2624
招く *v.* invite 2364
魔法 *n.* magic 4894
まま *v.* as it is 191
ママ *n.* mom, mummy 2081
豆 *n.* bean, pea 4041
守る *v.* protect, defend; keep, obey 599
眉 *n.* eyebrow 4362
迷う *v.* get lost; cannot decide 1765
マラソン *n.* marathon 3793
丸 *n.* circle, ring 3622
まるい *i-adj.* round, circular 2173
まるで *adv.* just like, quite 997
丸める *v.* curl, wad 4601
まれ *na-adj.* rare 3782
回す *v.* turn, rotate, spin 1464
まわり *n.* circumference; surroundings, neighborhood, around 389
回る *v.* spin, turn, go around; go via 601
マンガ *n.* comics, cartoon 1610
万が一 *adv.* just in case 4521
マンション *n.* apartment, condominium, flat 1106
満足(する) *n.* satisfaction *v.* be satisfied 2226
真ん中 *n.* middle 1662

み

身 *n.* body, oneself; position 504
実 *n.* seed; berry; fruit; nut; pulp 2376
見上げる *v.* look up; respect 2822
見出だす *v.* find, discover 3081
見える *v.* see, be seen 234
見送る *v.* see off 4070
見下ろす *v.* look down, overlook 4695
磨く *v.* polish, brush; improve 3039
見かける *v.* see 1541
見方 *n.* point of view, way of looking 2341
味方(する) *n.* supporter *v.* support 3199
右 *n.* right 1087
右側 *n.* right side 3746
右手 *n.* right hand 2329
見事 *na-adj.* excellent *adv.* completely 1759
見込み *n.* hope, chance, expectation 4663
見込む *v.* expect, trust 4479
短い *i-adj.* short 1016
みじん切り *n.* minced, cut into fine pieces, chopped 4839
ミス(する) *n.* mistake *v.* make a mistake 3197
水 *n.* water 273
湖 *n.* lake 2871
自ら *n.* personally, oneself, own 966
水気 *n.* moisture 4403
店 *n.* store, shop 321
見せる *v.* show 513
みそ *n.* miso; key point 4954
みたい *na-adj.* like 139
満たす *v.* fill, satisfy, meet 2024
見た目 *n.* appearance, looks 3962
道 *n.* way, road 452
身近 *na-adj.* familiar, close 1449
導く *v.* guide, lead 3333
満ちる *v.* be full; rise 3160
三日 *n.* third (date); three days 1494
三日間 *n.* three days 4017
見付かる *v.* be found, be discovered 1172
見付ける *v.* find, look for 664
密接 *na-adj.* close 4555
三つ *num.* three 535
三つ目 *n.* third 2956
見つめる *v.* stare, gaze 1468
見通し *n.* prospect, outlook 3969
認める *v.* recognize, acknowledge, admit, approve, accept 490
緑 *n.* green; greenery 1099

緑色 *n.* green 4543
皆 *n.* everyone; everything 157
見直し *n.* review, reconsideration 3191
見直す *v.* review, look over 2699
皆様 *n.* everybody 2239
皆さん *n.* everybody, everyone 339
見なす *v.* be considered, look upon 2273
港 *n.* harbour, port 3272
南 *n.* south 1333
見逃す *v.* miss, overlook 4748
身分 *n.* position, status 4334
見守る *v.* watch, observe 2758
見回す *v.* look around, look about 4358
耳 *n.* ear 765
お土産 *n.* present, souvenir 2694
都 *n.* capital 4007
ミュージカル *n.* musical 3787
妙 *na-adj.* strange, curious 2262
未来 *n.* future 1802
魅力 *n.* charm, attraction, appeal 1313
魅力的 *na-adj.* charming, attractive 3635
見る *v.* see; look at, watch; check 67
ミルク *n.* milk 4281
見渡す *v.* look around 4832
民間 *n.* private, non government 2717
民衆 *n.* people, public 4627
民族 *n.* people, race, nation 2894
民法 *n.* civil law 4972

む

六日 *n.* sixth (date); six days 2866
無意識 *n.* unconsciousness *na-adj.* unconscious 4451
向かう *v.* face; go (toward, in the direction of 465
迎える *v.* go to meet, invite, receive 764
昔 *n.* ancient times, in the past, once 264
向き *n.* direction, aspect; suitable 4075
向く *v.* turn, face, look 1389
むく *v.* peel, pare 2674
向ける *v.* turn, point 610
向こう *n.* other side; over there 604
無言 *n.* silence, in silence, without speaking 4950
無視(する) *n., v.* neglect, ignore 1817
虫 *n.* insect, bug; worm 1846
矛盾(する) *n.* contradiction, conflict *v.* contradict 3370
むしろ *adv.* rather, if anything 993
無人 *n.* uninhabited, empty 2700
無人島 *n.* uninhabited island 483
難しい *i-adj.* difficult, hard 457
息子 *n.* son 749
結び付く *v.* join, be connected with 2793
結びつける *v.* connect, tie, bind 3880
結ぶ *v.* tie, connect, unite 1359
娘 *n.* daughter 512
無駄 *na-adj.* useless, futile *n.* waste 1614
夢中 *n., na-adj.* crazy about, obsessed with 2526
六つ *num.* six 4887
胸 *n.* chest, heart 887
旨 *n.* effect; principle 2246
村 *n.* village 1318
無理 *na-adj.* unreasonable, impossible; compulsory 666
無理矢理 *adv.* forcibly, against one's will 3120
無料 *n.* free, no charge 1436
群れ *n.* group; herd 4406
むろん *adv.* of course 3322

め

目, 眼 *n.* eye 169
芽 *n.* bud, shoot 4037
明確 *na-adj.* clear, definite 1704
明記(する) *n.* writing clearly *v.* write clearly 4899
明治 *n.* Meiji period 1608
名称 *n.* name 2771
命ずる *v.* order 2252
命令(する) *n.* order, command, direction *v.* order, command 2335
迷惑(する) *na-adj.* troublesome, annoying *n.* annoyance, nuisance, trouble *v.* be inconvenienced 1671
メイン *n.* main 2483
メーカー *n.* maker, manufacturer 1880
メール *n.* e-mail 760
眼鏡 *n.* glasses, spectacles 2721
メキシコ *n.* Mexico 4423
恵まれる *v.* be blessed 2244
巡る *v.* go around 2473
目指す *v.* aim, go toward 856
目覚める *v.* wake up 3895
飯 *n.* rice 4158
メジャー *n.* measure 4393
雌 *n.* female animal 2961
珍しい *i-adj.* rare, unusual, unique 1231
目立つ *v.* be conspicuous, stand out 1690
メッセージ *n.* message 2455
滅多 *na-adj.* rash, thoughtless; seldom 3431
メディア *n.* media 3248
メニュー *n.* menu 2016
メモ(する) *n.* memo *v.* take notes 3125

目安 *n.* standard, criterion 3894
メリット *n.* merit, advantage 1908
メロディー *n.* melody 4626
面 *n.* side; page; surface 722
麺 *n.* noodles 4259
免許 *n.* license, permit 2555
面する *v.* face 3270
面積 *n.* area, size 3505
面接（する） *n.* interview *v.* interview 1984
面倒 *na-adj.* troublesome *n.* bother, care 1646
メンバー *n.* member, participant 1278

も

も *p.* too, also 11
もう *adv.* already; soon; again 52
儲かる *v.* profit, gain 4712
設ける *v.* institute, set up 1476
儲ける *v.* profit, earn, gain 4502
申し上げる *v.* tell, say (humble) 628
申し込み *n.* application 1954
申し込む *v.* apply 3678
申し訳 *n.* excuse, apology 2814
申す *v.* say, be (humble) 949
燃える *v.* burn, flame, glow, be on fire 2678
目的 *n.* purpose 553
目標 *n.* goal, objective, target 1152
潜る *v.* dive; go underground 3386
もし *adv.* if, in case 305
文字 *n.* letter, character, writing 1005
もしくは *conj.* or, otherwise 963
もたらす *v.* bring, cause, 1398
餅 *n.* rice cake 4616
持ち上げる *v.* lift, raise 4069
用いる *v.* use, adopt 785
持ち込む *v.* bring, import 2723
持ち出す *v.* carry out, take out 4316
持ち主 *n.* owner 4212
持ち物 *n.* personal belongings 4408
もちろん *adv.* of course, needless to say 260
持つ *v.* have, take, hold 98
もったいない *i-adj.* wasteful; too good 3271
もっと *adv.* more 299
最も *adv.* most, extremely 530
もっとも *conj.* though, although 2222
もっぱら *adv.* entirely 3982
モテる *v.* be popular 1944
モデル *n.* model 2116
元 *n.* beginning; original 731
もと *n.* under 792

戻す *v.* put back, restore 1553
基づく *v.* be based 773
求める *v.* ask for, request, demand 472
元々 *adv.* from the first, originally 711
戻る *v.* return, go back 384
物 *n.* thing, object, stuff 38
者 *n.* person, people 334
もの *p.* because 1886
物語 *n.* tale, story 1965
物事 *n.* thing 2628
ものすごい *i-adj.* terrible *adv.* terribly 696
者達 *n.* people 4599
ものの *p. conj.* but, although, despite 1179
もはや *adv.* now, already; not . . . any longer 2356
燃やす *v.* burn 3816
模様 *n.* pattern, design, look 3028
もらう *v.* get, have, receive 474
漏らす *v.* betray 4000
森 *n.* forest, woods, grove 1151
盛り上がる *v.* swell, rise; liven up 2405
盛る *v.* serve, heap 4303
漏れる *v.* leak, escape; be omitted 3392
問 *n.* question number; counter for questions 2104
門 *n.* gate 2850
文句 *n.* words; complaint 2271
問題 *n.* problem, question 167
問題点 *n.* problem, point at issue 2107
文部省 *n.* Ministry of Education, Culture, Sports 3879

や

や *p.* and; or 63
や *aux.* COPULA (dialectal) 936
やがて *adv.* soon, before long, after all 1129
やがる *aux.* VERB SUFFIX (vulgarism) 4698
野球 *n.* baseball 1223
焼く *v.* roast, bake 960
役 *n.* part, role, duty 1183
役員 *n.* official, director 3020
役者 *n.* actor, actress 2640
役所 *n.* government office 4435
訳す *v.* translate 4110
約束（する） *n.* promise, appointment *v.* promise, make an appointment 1519
役立つ *v.* useful 2383
役目 *n.* duty, role 3408
役割 *n.* part, role 1009
焼ける *v.* be burned; be roasted; be sunburned 3134
野菜 *n.* vegetable 1113
優しい *i-adj.* gentle, tender, kind, friendly 869

優しさ *n.* kindness 3918
屋敷 *n.* mansion, residence, estate 4092
養う *v.* bring up, keep, support 4114
安い *i-adj.* low, cheap 520
休み *n.* holiday; rest; be closed 1385
休む *v.* take a rest, be absent from 1365
痩せる *v.* become thin, lose weight 1851
やたら *adv.* freely, thoughtlessly 3573
家賃 *n.* rent 3549
奴 *n.* guy, fellow 589
やっと *adv.* at last 741
奴ら *n.* fellow 4111
宿 *n.* inn, hotel 2380
雇う *v.* employ, hire 3302
屋根 *n.* roof 2579
やばい *i-adj.* risky, chancy 2855
やはり, やっぱり *adv.* as (one) expected, still 75
破る *v.* tear; break; beat 3176
山 *n.* mountain 459
病 *n.* illness, disease 4161
闇 *n.* darkness, dark 2757
止む *v.* stop 2198
やめる *v.* stop, give up 386
やや *adv.* a little, slightly 1656
やら *p.* and, or 1013
槍 *n.* spear 4729
やり方 *n.* way of doing, how to, approach 826
やりとり *n.* exchange, interchange 2631
やる *v.* do; make; give 77
軟らかい *i-adj.* soft, tender 2627
柔らかい *i-adj.* soft 2827

ゆ

湯 *n.* hot water 1517
唯一 *n., adv.* only 1795
URL *n.* URL, Uniform Resource Locator 4916
遊園地 *n.* amusement park 4886
夕方 *adv., n.* evening 1459
勇気 *n.* courage, bravery 2206
有効 *na-adj.* valid; effective 1808
ユーザー *n.* user 4030
融資(する) *n.* loan *v.* loan, lend 4269
優秀 *na-adj.* excellent 3217
優勝(する) *n.* championship, victory *v.* win 2124
夕食 *n.* dinner 2562
友人 *n.* friend 475
友人達 *n.* friends 4452
有する *v.* have 1462
優先(する) *n.* priority *v.* have priority 3438

郵送 *n.* mail, post 4428
夕日 *n.* evening sun, sunset 4214
郵便局 *n.* post office 3533
有名 *na-adj.* famous, well-known 453
有利 *na-adj.* profitable, advantageous 3425
有力 *na-adj.* powerful, strong, important 4656
ゆえ *n.* reason; therefore 2745
床 *n.* floor 1681
浴衣 *n.* yukata, cotton kimono 4397
雪 *n.* snow 1092
輸出(する) *n.* exportation *v.* export 2783
譲る *v.* give; sell; offer 3552
豊か *na-adj.* abundant, plentiful, rich 1281
ユダヤ人 *n.* Jew, Jewish person 2314
ゆっくり *adv.* slowly, leisurely; plenty of time 855
ゆったり *adv.* comfortably; calm; loose 3391
ゆでる *v.* boil 2617
ゆとり *n.* have something to spare 3741
輸入(する) *n.* import *v.* import 2023
指 *n.* finger 1265
指差す *v.* point 4503
夢 *n.* dream 521
由来(する) *n.* origin, history *v.* originate 3237
許す *v.* allow, permit, forgive 927
緩やか *na-adj.* gentle, soft, mild 4783
揺れる *v.* shake, wave, swing 2668

よ

よ *p. disc.* ASSERTION, REMINDING (informal) 59
世 *n.* world, public; age, reign 2101
良い, いい *i-adj.* good 70
よう *aux.* INDUCEMENT 33
要 *n.* in short 1874
用 *n.* something to do; use 3023
酔う *v.* get drunk, feel sick 4239
用意(する) *n.* preparation *v.* prepare 848
容易 *na-adj.* easy 2317
要因 *n.* factor, main cause 2189
八日 *n.* eighth (date); eight days 2778
容器 *n.* container, vessel 4576
要求(する) *n.* demand, request, claim *v.* demand, request, claim 1373
要件 *n.* important matter; requirement 3690
用事 *n.* business 3886
幼児 *n.* infant 4159
様子 *n.* state of affairs, situation; appearance 695
要する *v.* need, take 2005
要するに *conj.* in short, to sum up 578
要請 *n.* request 2411

要素 *n.* element, factor 1988
幼稚園 *n.* preschool, kindergarten 1478
用途 *n.* use 4647
洋服 *n.* clothes, suit, dress 2176
要望(する) *n.* demand *v.* make demands 3410
ようやく *adv.* at last, gradually, barely 1279
ヨーロッパ *n.* Europe 1030
予感(する) *n.* presentiment, foreboding, hunch
    v. have a presentiment/foreboding/hunch 4473
よく *adv.* good, well; often 126
翌日 *n.* next day 1648
抑制(する) *n.* control, restraint *v.* control, restrain 3862
翌年 *n.* the next year, the following year 3250
欲望 *n.* desire, passion 3949
余計 *na-adj.* additional, extra 2117
横 *n.* side, beside 899
横浜 *n.* Yokohama 1744
汚れ *n.* dirt 3730
汚れる *v.* dirty, soil 2800
良さ *n.* good point, good 2149
予算 *n.* estimate, budget 2204
良し *i-adj.* good, OK 2299
よし *interj.* All right!, Good! 3252
四時 *n.* four o'clock 2336
寄せる *v.* let come near, bring near; put;
    be dependent on 2369
よそ *n.* other, elsewhere 4054
予想(する) *n.* expectation *v.* expect 1575
予測(する) *n.* prospect *v.* predict, estimate 2726
余談 *n.* digression 4047
余地 *n.* room, space 4100
四日 *n.* fourth (date); four days 2237
四つ *num.* four 1801
予定(する) *n.* plan, schedule *v.* plan 905
夜中 *n.* middle of the night 1840
四人 *n.* four people 1343
四年 *n.* four years 1816
四年間 *n.* four years 4750
世の中 *n.* world, society 938
呼びかける *v.* call out, appeal 4046
予備校 *n.* cram school preparing for university
    entrance examinations 3683
呼び出す *v.* call, summon 3990
呼ぶ *v.* call 290
予防(する) *n.* prevention *v.* prevent 3503
よほど、よっぽど *adv.* very, greatly 2528
よみがえる *v.* revive, come back 3905
読む *v.* read 261
嫁 *n.* wife; bride; daughter-in-law 2997

予約(する) *n.* reservation *v.* reserve, book 2474
余裕 *n.* leeway 1559
より *p. case* than; from 135
より *adv.* more, better 726
夜 *n.* night, evening 332
よる *v.* be due to 545
寄る *v.* stop by; move to one side 1568
喜び *n.* pleasure, delight 1428
喜ぶ *v.* be glad, rejoice 762
よろしい *i-adj.* all right, good, may (I) (formal) 2114
よろしく *adv.* well, properly, best regards 1253
弱い *i-adj.* weak, faint, light 1066
四 *num.* four 319
四回 *n.* four times 3915
四ヶ月 *n.* four months 4454
四歳 *n.* four years old 4183
四十分 *n.* forty minutes 4480
四十代 *n.* forties 4625
四十年 *n.* forty years 3681

ら

ラーメン *n.* Chinese noodles 3184
来週 *n.* next week 4993
ライター *n.* lighter 4378
来年 *n.* next year 1967
ライブ *n.* live (music) 2751
ライン *n.* line 3748
楽 *na-adj.* comfort, ease, comfortable 1128
落札(する) *n.* successful bid *v.* make a successful
    bid 3317
落札者 *n.* successful bidder 4268
らしい *aux.* seem, look 248
ラジオ *n.* radio 1674
ラスベガス *n.* Las Vegas 4764
ラッキー *na-adj.* lucky 3362

り

リーダー *n.* leader 3663
リード(する) *n.* lead *v.* take a lead 4790
利益 *n.* profit, benefit, gain 1395
理解(する) *n.* understanding *v.* understand 546
理屈 *n.* reason, logic, theory 4890
離婚(する) *n.* divorce *v.* divorce, get divorced 2457
リサイクル(する) *n.* recycling *v.* recycle 4280
リスク *n.* risk 2906
リスト *n.* list 3795
リストラ *n.* restructuring, downsizing 4216
リズム *n.* rhythm 2746
理想 *n.* ideal, dream 2575

立派 *na-adj.* fine, splendid, great 1417
利点 *n.* advantage 3375
理念 *n.* philosophy 4371
略 *n.* omission, abbreviation 4995
理由 *n.* reason 398
留学(する) *n.* study abroad *v.* study abroad 2840
流行(する) *n.* fashion, epidemic *v.* come into fashion, be rife 3101
流通(する) *n.* circulation, distribution *v.* circulate, distribute 4427
量 *n.* quantity, volume, amount 1041
利用(する) *n.* use, utilization *v.* utilize 417
領域 *n.* territory, field 3233
両側 *n.* both sides 4615
料金 *n.* charge, fee, fare 2136
両者 *n.* both, the two 3145
利用者 *n.* user 3013
両親 *n.* (both) parents 802
両手 *n.* both hands, both arms 1843
両方 *n.* both 1680
料理(する) *n.* cooking, dish *v.* cook 634
旅館 *n.* inn, Japanese-style hotel 4296
旅行(する) *n.* journey, travel *v.* travel 661
リラックス(する) *n., v.* relax 3218
理論 *n.* theory 3100
リンク(する) *n.* link *v.* link 4751
りんご *n.* apple 2121
隣接(する) *n.* adjacent, adjoin, next to *v.* be adjacent, adjoin, be next to 4561

る

ルート *n.* route 4127
ルール *n.* rule 2261

れ

例 *n.* example 592
0 *n.* zero 1864
礼 *n.* bow; courtesy 2323
霊 *n.* spirit, soul 4472
例外 *n.* exception 3881
冷静 *na-adj.* calm 3169
冷蔵庫 *n.* refrigerator 2065
レース *n.* race 2893
歴史 *n.* history 492
歴史的 *na-adj.* historical, historic 3379
レコード *n.* record 3429
レシピ *n.* recipe 4490
レストラン *n.* restaurant 1746
列 *n.* line 3865
列車 *n.* train 2525
レッスン *n.* lesson 3346
レベル *n.* level 1252
レモン *n.* lemon 4134
れる *aux.* PASSIVE 15
恋愛(する) *n.* love (romantic) *v.* love 3051
連携(する) *n.* cooperation *v.* work together with 2750
練習(する) *n.* practice, training *v.* practice, train 584
レンズ *n.* lens 4363
連続(する) *n.* continuation, succession *v.* continue 3335
連中 *n.* company, crowd; those guys 1796
連絡(する) *n.* connection, contact *v.* contact 845

ろ

廊下 *n.* corridor 2410
老後 *n.* old age 4243
老人 *n.* old person, the old 1643
労働(する) *n.* work, labor *v.* work, labor 3491
労働者 *n.* laborer, working man 2385
ロープ *n.* rope 4568
ローマ *n.* Rome 3535
六 *num.* six 608
録音(する) *n.* record *v.* record 3807
六月 *n.* June 872
六時 *n.* six o'clock 2553
六十歳 *n.* sixty years old 4348
六十 *num.* sixty 3870
六十年 *n.* sixty years 4918
六人 *n.* six people 3359
六年 *n.* six years 2687
六年生 *n.* sixth grade, sixth year 4967
路地 *n.* alley, lane 4542
ロシア *n.* Russia 2440
六ヶ月 *n.* six months 4420
ロック *n.* rock; lock 3173
ロボット *n.* robot 2433
論ずる *v.* argue, discuss 3548
ロンドン *n.* London 2254
論文 *n.* essay, thesis, paper, dissertation 3151
論理 *n.* logic 4478

わ

わ *p. disc.* EXCLAMATION 331
輪 *n.* circle, ring; loop 3460
わー *interj.* wow! 3112
ワープロ *n.* word processor 4699
ワールドカップ *n.* World Cup 4104
ワイン *n.* wine 1520

我が *adn.* my, our, one's 509
若い *i-adj.* young 397
わがまま *na-adj.* selfish, disobedient *n.* selfishness 3475
若者 *n.* youth 1605
若者達 *n.* young people 4766
我が家 *n.* one's house, one's family, one's home 1540
分かりやすい *i-adj.* easy to understand 1910
分かる *v.* understand, see 105
別れ *n.* parting, farewell 3071
分かれる *v.* divide, split, part 1467
別れる *v.* part; divorce, break up 1871
脇 *n.* side 2722
沸く *v.* boil; be in uproar 1957
枠 *n.* frame 3817
枠組み *n.* frame, framework 4848
わくわく(する) *v.* be bubbling; be excited 4020
訳 *n.* reason, cause 93
分ける *v.* divide, distribute; classify 1038
技 *n.* skill, technique, trick 3470
わざと *adv.* intentionally 3840
わざわざ *adv.* take the trouble, especially 1667
わし *n.* I (used by old men) 2190
わずか *na-adj* a few, a little, a bit *adv.* only 1144
忘れる *v.* forget 441
話題 *n.* topic, subject 1089
私共 *pron.* we 1438
私 *pron.* I 42

私自身 *n.* myself, my own 968
私達 *pron.* we 287
渡す *v.* carry across, hand, transfer 1413
渡る *v.* cross, go across 1069
笑い *n.* laugh, laughter 563
笑う *v.* laugh; smile 658
割 *n.* cost, rate 2665
割合 *adv.* comparatively *n.* ratio, percentage 1118
割と *adv.* comparatively, rather 625
割る *v.* break; crack 2661
悪い *i-adj.* bad 230
我 *pron.* I; oneself 2234
我ら *pron.* we 4404
割れる *v.* split; break 3603
我々 *pron.* we 527

を

を *p. case* ACCUSATIVE 5
を通じて *cp.* throughout, across, through 1306
を通して *cp.* according to; through 2911
をはじめ *p.* starting with ..., including 2769
をめぐる *cp.* over, concerning 3411
をもって *cp.* by; with; as of 1799

ん

ん *interj.* oh, mm, well 73
んと *interj.* well 841

Part of speech index

> rank, **lemma**, English gloss

Noun: 3279 words

- 17 **事** thing
- 38 **物** thing, object, stuff
- 54 **時** time
- 58 **人** person, people, human being
- 69 **今** now
- 71 **所** place, point; part; aspect
- 72 **自分** oneself
- 78 **中** inside, in; into
- 83 **後** after, later
- 91 **方** direction, way; side
- 93 **訳** reason, cause
- 97 **本当** truth, right
- 100 **ため** for
- 115 **場合** case, occasion
- 116 **話** story, talk
- 120 **日本** Japan
- 123 **前** forward; front; before
- 127 **一つ** one
- 128 **子供** child
- 130 **気** mind, heart
- 133 **うち** inside; of; before
- 138 **感じ** feeling, impression; atmosphere
- 144 **一** one
- 145 **そう** be about to
- 148 **二** two
- 151 **必要** necessary; necessity
- 152 **仕事(する)** work, job; work
- 153 **余り** the rest; (not) much
- 157 **皆** everyone; everything
- 159 **方** person, man
- 165 **次** next, following, coming
- 167 **問題** problem, question
- 169 **目, 眼** eye
- 170 **頃** time, about, when
- 171 **上** top; above; up; on
- 173 **他** other, another; else
- 175 **家** house, home
- 177 **日, 陽** day; sun
- 179 **一人** one person; alone
- 180 **人間** human being, man
- 183 **時間** time
- 188 **言葉** word; language
- 193 **まだ** yet, still
- 194 **手** hand
- 201 **意味(する)** meaning, sense; mean
- 205 **形** form, shape, figure
- 207 **三** three
- 208 **最初** first
- 209 **間** distance; period
- 215 **最近** recently, lately
- 219 **友達** friend
- 222 **一緒** together, with
- 223 **生活(する)** life; live
- 224 **国** country
- 227 **現在** present time, now
- 231 **気持ち** feeling
- 240 **会社** company, firm
- 242 **実際** actually, in fact
- 243 **先生** teacher
- 245 **二人** two people
- 246 **心** mind, heart; thought; feeling
- 250 **金** money
- 251 **顔** face
- 255 **町, 街** town, city
- 262 **人たち** people
- 263 **今日** today
- 264 **昔** ancient times, in the past, once
- 266 **すべて** everything, all
- 268 **子** child
- 273 **水** water
- 274 **当時** then, at that time
- 275 **場所** place, spot
- 279 **声** voice
- 282 **最後** last, end
- 283 **車** car; wheel
- 285 **今度** this time, next time
- 286 **体** body
- 293 **男** man, male
- 294 **女性** woman, female
- 295 **学校** school
- 298 **先** end, front
- 301 **テーマ** theme, subject
- 302 **世界** world
- 303 **状態** state, conditions
- 312 **アメリカ** America
- 315 **相手** companion; partner
- 316 **母** mother
- 317 **以上** more than; mentioned above; since
- 318 **関係** relationship, connection
- 319 **四** four
- 321 **店** store, shop
- 323 **頭** head
- 324 **電話(する)** telephone, call; phone, call
- 327 **本** book
- 332 **夜** night, evening
- 334 **者** person, people
- 335 **タイトル** title
- 336 **親** parent
- 337 **名前** name
- 339 **皆さん** everybody, everyone
- 347 **家族** family
- 349 **部分** part, section
- 350 **一度** once
- 351 **結果** result
- 353 **状況** state of affairs, situation
- 354 **時代** time, era
- 356 **他** another, other
- 359 **東京** Tokyo
- 365 **父** father
- 367 **それぞれ** each
- 368 **方法** way, method
- 369 **はず** ought to, should

370	説明(する)	explanation; explain
372	部屋	room
374	当然	naturally, as a matter of course
375	大学	university, college
377	実	truth, true, real
378	朝	morning
385	勉強(する)	study; learn, study
387	下	under; below; down; low
389	まわり	circumference; surroundings, neighborhood, around
390	犬	dog
395	力	power, strength
398	理由	reason
399	女	woman, female
403	今回	this time
405	人生	life
406	通り	street; as
407	内容	contents
408	テレビ	television, TV
409	経験(する)	experience; experience
410	木	wood; tree
411	点	point, score
412	自然	nature; natural; naturally
413	音	sound, noise
414	海	sea, ocean
417	利用(する)	use, utilization; utilize
419	一杯	cup(ful), glass(ful), be full of, a lot of
420	近く	near, nearby
422	共	with, together
423	存在(する)	existence; exist
424	絶対	absolute, absolutely, whatever
425	日本人	Japanese (person)
427	足	foot; leg
431	写真	picture, photo
432	子供たち	children
434	二つ	two
436	五	five
437	多く	many, most
439	英語	English language
442	口	mouth
444	姿	figure, shape, appearance
446	時期	time, period, season
447	逆	contrary, opposite
451	人々	people
452	道	way, road
455	思い	thought, mind, heart
459	山	mountain
460	程度	degree, grade, level, limit
464	昭和	Showa era
468	影響(する)	influence; affect, influence
469	病院	hospital, clinic
470	年	year; age
471	花	flower
473	情報	information
475	友人	friend
478	先程	a short while ago
479	一回	once
483	無人島	uninhabited island
489	結婚(する)	marriage; marry, get married
492	歴史	history
494	音楽	music
496	外	outside
499	嫌	unpleasant, disagreeable
500	駅	station
503	映画	movie
504	身	body, oneself; position
505	客	guest, visitor; customer
506	質問(する)	question; question
508	地域	region, area
512	娘	daughter
514	一日	a day, the day, one day
515	今年	this year
516	平成	Heisei era
517	図	drawing, figure, diagram
518	紹介(する)	introduction; introduce
521	夢	dream
523	規定(する)	regulations, stipulations; prescribe
525	中心	center
528	(お)母さん	mother, Mom
531	色	color
534	興味	interest
535	三つ	three
539	変化(する)	change; change, vary
540	印象	impression
541	作品	work, production
543	参加(する)	participation; take part in, participate
544	夏	summer
546	理解(する)	understanding; understand
547	事件	incident, event
548	中国	China
550	母親	mother
553	目的	purpose
558	一方	one side; on the other hand
559	病気	sickness, illness
560	心配(する)	anxious, worried; anxiety, worry, care; worry, be anxious
562	イメージ(する)	image; imagine, have an impression
563	笑い	laugh, laughter
564	午後	afternoon, p.m.
565	後	after, later, since
567	主人	shop owner; husband
571	環境	environment
572	対応(する)	correspondence, response; respond to
574	高校	high school
575	食事(する)	meal; have a meal
577	辺	region, area around
580	火	fire
581	実施(する)	operation; enforce, conduct
583	社会	society
584	練習(する)	practice, training; practice, train
585	使用(する)	use; use
588	企業	company, business
589	奴	guy, fellow
592	例	example
593	絵	picture, painting
596	酒	alcohol, sake, rice wine
597	原因	cause
598	お前	you (colloquial)
600	小学校	elementary school, primary school
603	猫	cat
604	向こう	other side; over there

605	同時	simultaneous, at the same time
608	六	six
615	場	field; place; occasion
617	ホテル	hotel
618	対象	object, target, subject
620	以前	before, formerly
621	夫	husband
622	確認(する)	confirmation; confirm
623	数	number
624	意見	opinion, idea
629	可能性	possibility
633	三人	three people
634	料理(する)	cooking, dish; cook
635	一部	part
640	幾つ	how many, how old
643	新聞	newspaper
645	歌	song
647	互い	each other
649	違い	difference
652	記憶(する)	memory; memorize
653	思い出	memory, reminiscence
656	四月	April
657	君	you
660	魚	fish
661	旅行(する)	journey, travel; travel
662	父親	father
667	健康	health
668	味	flavor, taste
671	自由	freedom, liberty; free
673	戦争	war
675	男性	male, man
676	電車	train
682	女の子	girl
683	パソコン	personal computer
685	活動(する)	activity; be active
686	不安	anxiety, concern; uneasy, insecure
687	三十分	thirty minutes
688	限り	limit
692	際	when, in case of
693	途中	on the way; in the middle of
694	研究(する)	research, study; do research, study
695	様子	state of affairs, situation; appearance
700	大人	adult
701	期待(する)	expectation; expect
702	事実	fact, actuality
703	せい	fault, cause for blame, because of
704	一年	one year
705	一体	how, what, why, who
706	島	island
709	動物	animal
710	何度	how many times, how often
715	機会	opportunity
716	楽しみ	pleasure, enjoyment
717	考え	idea, thought
722	面	side; page; surface
723	三月	March
725	常	way; always, usually
727	つもり	intention
728	考え方	way of thinking, attitude
729	ニュース	news
730	意識(する)	consciousness, awareness; be conscious
731	元	beginning; original
732	行動(する)	action, act; act, behave
734	びっくり(する)	surprise; be surprised, be amazed
735	作り方	how to make
736	元気	health, vigor; lively, vigorous, well
739	曲	piece (music), song, tune
740	過去	past
745	土地	land, ground
747	初め	beginning
748	評価(する)	evaluation; evaluate
749	息子	son
753	雨	rain
754	自分達	themselves; ourselves
756	二十一世紀	twenty-first century
758	昨日	yesterday
760	メール	e-mail
763	便利	convenience; useful, convenient
765	耳	ear
766	表現(する)	expression; express
767	動き	movement, action, motion
768	注意(する)	attention; notice, be careful
771	雰囲気	atmosphere, ambience
772	立場	position, standpoint, situation
774	間	time, interval; space
777	お父さん	father
778	辺り	area around
780	将来	future
782	自転車	bicycle
784	川	river, stream
786	隣り	next door, next
787	普段	usually, ordinarily
788	法律	law
789	妻	wife
790	冬	winter
792	もと	under
793	発生(する)	occurrence; occur, happen
796	七	seven
797	手紙	letter
799	努力(する)	effort; make an effort
800	増加(する)	increase, gain; increase, grow
801	判断(する)	judgment; judge
802	両親	(both) parents
805	家庭	home, household, family
809	船	ship, boat
810	九月	September
811	きっかけ	opportunity, motive
812	授業	class, lesson at school
815	不思議	wonder; wonderful, strange, mysterious
816	茶	tea; brown
817	直接	directly, direct
818	バス	bus
819	効果	effectiveness, effect

820 現実 reality, actuality	889 体験(する) experience; experience, have experience of	947 第一 first
824 国民 nation, people (of country), public		948 三年 three years
		951 責任 responsibility
826 やり方 way of doing, how to, approach	890 材料 materials, ingredient	952 選択(する) selection, choice; choose
	895 運動(する) exercise; exercise, move	
828 日本語 Japanese language		954 技術 technique, skill
829 十月 October	897 幸せ happy; happiness; fortune, luck	956 そば side, beside
830 気分 feeling, mood		958 記事 article
831 開発(する) development; develop	899 横 side, beside	959 本人 person himself/herself, person in question
	901 命 life	
833 特徴 characteristic, feature	902 流れ stream, flow, current	965 推進(する) propulsion; promote, drive
834 神 God, deity, spirit	905 予定(する) plan, schedule; plan	
837 終わり end		966 自ら personally, oneself, own
838 雑誌 magazine	907 馬 horse	967 作業(する) operation, work; work
840 整備(する) maintenance, service; prepare	909 学生 student	
	910 風 wind	968 私自身 myself, my own
842 建物 building	911 性格 character, personality	969 たび every time
843 発見(する) discovery; discover	912 死 death	971 半分 half
	913 位置(する) position, location; be located	972 条件 condition
844 相談(する) consultation; consult		973 医者 doctor
	914 発展(する) development; develop, expand	975 関心 interest
845 連絡(する) connection, contact; contact		976 表示(する) indication; display, indicate
	916 近所 neighborhood	
848 用意(する) preparation; prepare	917 一本 one (long/cylindrical object)	977 秋 autumn, fall
		979 趣味 hobby
850 十二月 December	919 ご飯 rice, meal	980 生徒 student, pupil
853 首 neck, head; firing, sacking (of an employee)	920 危険 danger, hazard; dangerous	981 相当(する) considerable; equivalence; be equivalent; considerably, pretty;
854 設定(する) establishment; establish, set	923 海外 overseas, abroad, foreign	
	924 教育(する) education; educate	983 検討(する) consideration, discussion examination; consider, discuss
858 一月 January		
862 光 light	925 想像(する) imagination, image; imagine	
864 八月 August		986 選手 player, athlete
866 七月 July	928 表 table, chart	987 以下 below, the following
868 五月 May	929 文化 culture	988 大きさ size
870 タバコ cigarette, tobacco	930 八 eight	989 調査(する) investigation; investigate, inquire, explore
871 後ろ behind, back	931 食べ物 food	
872 六月 June	934 準備(する) preparation; prepare	
874 十一月 November		990 分 part, share, portion
876 飛行機 airplane	935 二月 February	991 実家 one's parents' home
877 お婆さん old lady; grandmother	937 月 month; moon	992 発表(する) announcement, publication; announce, publish
	938 世の中 world, society	
879 午前 morning, a.m.	939 インターネット Internet	
881 種類 kind, sort, variety	940 春 spring	994 作成(する) make, create
882 商品 goods, item of merchandise	941 旅 trip, journey	995 名 name
	942 二年 two years	996 確保(する) securement, reservation; secure, maintain, guarantee
884 イギリス United Kingdom, Britain, England	944 年 year	
	946 一般 general	
887 胸 chest, heart		

1004	毎年	every year, annually
1005	文字	letter, character, writing
1006	空	sky, air
1008	明日	tomorrow
1009	役割	part, role
1010	地球	earth, globe
1011	公園	park
1012	個人	individual
1017	薬	medicine
1018	試合	match, game, bout
1019	成長(する)	growth; grow
1020	おなか	stomach, belly
1021	機能(する)	function, capability, feature; function, work
1022	ボール	ball
1023	少年	boy, juvenile
1024	方向	direction, course
1026	資料	document, material, data
1027	タイプ(する)	type; type
1029	指摘(する)	designation; point out, indicate
1030	ヨーロッパ	Europe
1033	ご存じ	know, knowing (honorific)
1035	一週間	one week
1036	何回	how many times
1037	政府	government
1039	計画(する)	project, schedule, plan; plan
1040	段階	grade, stage, step
1041	量	quantity, volume, amount
1042	田舎	countryside; one's hometown
1043	感動(する)	deep emotion; be impressed, be moved
1044	スポーツ	sports
1045	感覚	sense; sensation, feeling
1046	地元	home area, local area
1055	希望(する)	hope, wish, request; hope, wish, desire
1058	年齢	age, years
1059	フランス	France
1060	仕方	way, method
1061	なし	without, no
1065	人気	popularity
1068	格好	appearance, shape, look
1070	患者	patient, case
1071	壁	wall, barrier
1072	道路	road, way, street
1074	反対(する)	opposition, contrast, objection; oppose
1075	他人	others, unrelated person, stranger
1076	提供(する)	offer; supply, sponsor
1077	空気	air, atmosphere
1078	去年	last year
1079	肩	shoulder
1081	匂い	smell, odor, scent
1082	銀行	bank
1083	実現(する)	realization, implementation; realize, put into practice
1085	購入(する)	buying; purchase, buy
1086	十年	ten years, decade
1087	右	right
1088	全体	total, whole, entire
1089	話題	topic, subject
1090	認識(する)	recognition, awareness; recognize, be aware
1091	安心(する)	peace of mind, relief; feel relieved
1092	雪	snow
1093	ポイント	point
1094	十	ten
1095	仲間	company, fellow, mate, group
1097	知識	knowledge, information
1098	多少	more or less; somewhat; a little
1099	緑	green; greenery
1100	解決(する)	solution, settlement; solve, settle
1102	一時間	one hour
1103	失敗(する)	failure, mistake; fail
1105	成功(する)	success, achievement; succeed
1106	マンション	apartment, condominium, flat
1107	協力(する)	cooperation, collaboration; cooperate, collaborate
1108	伯父	uncle
1111	卒業(する)	graduation; graduate
1113	野菜	vegetable
1114	自分自身	oneself
1115	報告(する)	report, information, account; inform
1117	決定(する)	decision, determination; decide, determine
1118	割合	comparatively; ratio, percentage
1119	移動(する)	movement; transfer, move, migrate
1121	血	blood
1123	涙	tear
1124	表情	expression, facial expression, look
1127	次第	order; depend on; as soon as
1132	ごみ	rubbish, garbage, trash
1133	警察	police
1134	兄	elder brother
1136	代わり	substitute, replacement, alternative
1137	外国	foreign country
1140	腰	back, lower back, waist, hip
1141	開催(する)	holding, opening; hold, open
1142	瞬間	moment, instant, second
1147	窓	window
1148	ストレス	stress
1150	ドア	door
1151	森	forest, woods, grove
1152	目標	goal, objective, target
1153	本来	originally, essentially, by nature, proper
1155	変更(する)	change, modification, revision; change, revise
1156	感謝(する)	gratitude, appreciation; thank, be grateful

#	Term	#	Term	#	Term
1157	腕 arm; skill, ability	1207	方々 people	1256	現状 present condition, existing state
1158	手術(する) surgery, operation; operate	1209	鳥 bird; poultry	1257	ドイツ Germany
1160	時点 point of time, as of	1210	何とか somehow; something	1260	伯母 aunt
1161	一日 first (date)	1211	市 city, town	1261	パン bread
1162	馬鹿 foolish; fool	1213	自信 confidence	1262	クラス class
1168	苦労(する) hardship, difficulty, trouble; have trouble, have a hard time	1215	戦後 postwar, after the war	1263	肉 meat, flesh, fat
		1216	値段 price, value, cost	1265	指 finger
		1219	トイレ toilet, restroom, bathroom	1266	態度 attitude, manner, behavior
1170	課題 subject; assignment, task	1222	お勧め(する) recommendation, advice; recommend, advise	1267	地 earth, ground, land, place
1173	うそ lie, falsehood			1268	全国 nationwide, whole country, national
1175	主張(する) argument, claim; argue, insist	1223	野球 baseball	1269	答え answer, solution
		1224	穴 hole, pit	1270	世話(する) care; take care of, look after
1176	施設 facility, institution, plant	1225	クリック(する) click; click		
1177	チェック(する) check; check	1227	昨年 last year	1271	差 difference, gap, margin
1178	一ヶ月 one month	1228	減少(する) decrease, reduction; decline, decrease	1272	一切 all, entirely, not...at all
1180	展開(する) development; develop, unfold			1274	文章 sentence; writing, text
		1230	左 left	1275	背景 background, context, setting
1181	事業 business, enterprise, project	1233	一言 one word, single word, brief comment		
				1276	負担(する) burden, load, charge; bear
1182	データ data	1234	男の子 boy, male child	1277	事情 circumstance, situation, reason
1183	役 part, role, duty	1235	制度 system, institution		
1185	通常 normally, ordinary, regular	1236	買い物(する) shopping; go shopping	1278	メンバー member, participant
1186	ピアノ piano	1237	チーム team	1280	地方 area, district, countryside
1187	行為 action; motion; behavior	1238	登場(する) entry, appearance; appear, emerge		
				1284	一個 one, piece
1189	第二 second, secondary; another	1239	期間 period, term, interval	1285	大阪 Osaka
		1240	金額 amount of money	1291	権利 right, claim, entitlement
1190	議論(する) argument, discussion, controversy; discuss	1241	塩 salt		
		1242	奥 inner part, back; bottom	1293	計算(する) calculation; calculate, count, figure
1191	記録(する) record, document; record, write down	1243	九 nine		
		1246	番組 show, program	1294	痛み pain, ache
		1247	一時 at one time, temporary, for a while	1296	庭 garden, yard
1193	出来事 event, affair, happening			1297	納得(する) agreement; understand, be convinced
		1248	ケース case		
1195	おかげ thanks, virtue	1249	傾向 tendency, trend, inclination	1298	組織(する) organization, structure; organize
1196	安全 safe; safety, security				
1199	設置(する) installation; set up, place	1250	日々 every day, daily; days	1299	能力 ability, capacity, power; proficiency
		1251	拡大(する) enlargement, expansion; enlarge, expand		
1201	入院(する) hospitalization, admission to hospital; hospitalize			1300	人口 population
		1252	レベル level	1302	注 note, annotation, comment
		1254	疑問 question, problem, doubt		
1203	事故 accident, incident, trouble			1303	二回 twice
		1255	それなり in itself, as it is, in its way	1304	治療(する) cure, treatment, therapy; treat, cure
1206	会話(する) conversation; talk, chat				

#	Japanese	English
1305	昼	noon; daytime
1310	サービス(する)	service; attend, serve
1311	何人	how many people
1312	荷物	baggage, parcel, burden
1313	魅力	charm, attraction, appeal
1314	現場	field, scene, spot
1315	道具	tool, instrument
1316	遠く	far, remote; distance
1317	中学	junior high school
1318	村	village
1319	システム	system
1321	十時	ten o'clock
1322	息	breath, respiration
1324	撮影(する)	shooting; shoot, photograph
1325	指導(する)	guidance; guide, coach
1327	韓国	Korea, South Korea, Republic of Korea
1328	字	letter, character; handwriting
1329	指定(する)	appointment; specify
1330	経営(する)	management; manage, run
1332	価値	value, worth
1333	南	south
1334	成立(する)	completion; establish, conclude, come into existence
1335	季節	season
1336	導入(する)	introduction; introduce
1338	一枚	one (sheet, slice)
1340	先輩	senior, elder
1341	全員	all members, everyone
1343	四人	four people
1344	人物	person, character
1345	距離	distance
1347	充実(する)	fullness; enrich, fullfill
1349	コミュニケーション(する)	communication; communicate
1350	散歩(する)	walk, stroll
1351	グループ	group, team
1353	九時	nine o'clock
1354	石	stone, rock
1355	エネルギー	energy, power
1356	挨拶(する)	greeting; greet
1357	愛	love, affection
1358	比較(する)	comparison; compare
1361	従来	up to now, conventional, traditional
1363	注目(する)	attention; pay attention, watch
1364	携帯(する)	portable; carry
1367	最高	best, highest
1368	弟	younger brother
1369	卵	egg, spawn
1370	服	clothes, dress, outfit
1371	赤ちゃん	baby, infant
1372	始め	beginning, origin
1373	要求(する)	demand, request, claim; demand, request, claim
1374	紙	paper
1375	妹	younger sister
1376	額	amount of money; frame
1380	小説	novel, fiction, story
1382	汗	sweat, perspiration
1384	改善(する)	improvement, reform; improve
1385	休み	holiday; rest; be closed
1387	基本	foundation, basis, basic
1392	感情	feeling, emotion
1393	我慢(する)	patience, endurance, tolerance; be patient, endure
1395	利益	profit, benefit, gain
1396	先日	the other day, recently
1397	裏	reverse, back; rear
1399	姉	elder sister
1402	北海道	Hokkaido
1403	構成(する)	constitution, structure; compose
1404	反応(する)	reaction, response; respond
1405	ナイフ	knife
1406	おじいさん	grandfather
1407	新宿	Shinjuku (place name)
1408	活用(する)	application; exploit, take advantage of
1409	正直	honesty; honest, truthful; honestly
1410	黒	black
1411	スーパー	supermarket
1412	プロ	professional, pro
1415	京都	Kyoto
1416	就職(する)	job hunting; find employment, get a job
1418	舞台	stage, scene
1419	現地	field, on-site, local
1420	数字	number, figure
1421	提出(する)	submission; submit, hand in
1422	コンピューター、コンピュータ	computer
1423	東京都	Tokyo, Tokyo metropolitan government, Tokyo metropolitan area
1426	自宅	home, house
1427	腹	belly, stomach
1428	喜び	pleasure, delight
1430	風呂	bath
1431	香り	smell, scent
1432	スキー	ski; skiing
1435	お菓子	sweets, snack food
1436	無料	free, no charge
1437	付き合い	association, acquaintance
1439	被害	damage, harm
1440	椅子	chair
1442	桜	cherry tree; cherry blossom
1443	回答(する)	answer, response, reply; answer, respond, reply
1444	ゲーム	game
1447	活躍(する)	activity, action; be active, flourish
1448	試験(する)	exam, test, trial; examine
1452	金	gold, money
1453	ただ	just, mere, only
1454	検査(する)	inspection; inspect
1455	皮、革	skin, hide, jacket
1456	白	white; innocence
1458	代表(する)	representative; represent, stand for
1459	夕方	evening
1461	実感(する)	real feeling; actually feel

1465 敵 enemy, opponent	1520 ワイン wine	1587 土 Saturday
1466 側 side	1521 高校生 high school student	1588 週 week
1469 祭り festival	1522 イベント event	1592 ファックス(する) fax; fax
1471 仕様 style, specification, method	1523 二日 second (date); two days	1593 アルバイト part-time job
	1526 米国 United States	1594 北 north
1472 最大 biggest, largest	1527 周囲 surroundings	1595 一生 life
1473 スタート(する) start; get off, start	1530 二十年 twenty years	1596 ファン fan
	1533 中学校 junior high school	1598 後 after, later
1475 沖縄 Okinawa	1535 言い方 way to say	1599 調子 condition, tone
1478 幼稚園 preschool, kindergarten	1536 バランス balance	1600 基準 standard
	1537 五年 five years	1601 植物 plant
1479 二度 twice	1538 安定(する) stability; become stable	1602 契約(する) contract
1480 処理(する) management, processing; manage, process		1605 若者 youth
	1539 完成(する) completion; complete	1606 手段 means
		1608 明治 Meiji period
1481 困難 difficulty; difficult	1540 我が家 one's house, one's family, one's home	1609 形成(する) formation; take form
1483 分野 field, discipline		
1485 姿勢 posture, attitude	1543 参考 reference	1610 マンガ comics, cartoon
1486 ショック shock	1548 適用(する) application; apply	1611 ドラマ TV drama, drama
1487 暇 free, not busy		1613 高齢者 senior citizen
1489 土 soil	1549 宗教 religion	1614 無駄 useless, futile; waste
1491 緊張(する) tension; get tense	1550 一年間 one year	1615 髪 hair
1493 帰り return	1551 範囲 extent, range	1616 管理(する) control, management; manage, control
1494 三日 third (date); three days	1555 低下(する) decline, fall; decline, fall	
1497 席 seat		
1500 小学生 elementary school pupil, primary school pupil	1556 政治 politics	1617 サッカー football, soccer
	1559 余裕 leeway	1618 工場 factory
	1560 パリ Paris	1620 夫婦 (married) couple
1502 具合 condition	1562 奥さん wife	1621 監督(する) manager, director, proctor, invigilator; supervise, direct
1503 歯 tooth	1564 担当(する) charge; be in charge of	
1504 ベッド bed		
1505 無事 safely; safety; safe	1565 向上(する) improvement, progress; improve, advance	
1506 身体 body		1622 鍋 pan, pot; hot-pot
1507 何年 what year, how many years		1623 バイト part-time job
	1566 機械 machine	1624 十分 ten minutes
1508 星 star	1567 CD compact disk	1627 階段 stairs
1509 携帯電話 cell phone	1569 都市 city	1628 オーストラリア Australia
1510 砂糖 sugar	1570 費用 cost	1630 オーケー O.K.
1512 維持(する) maintenance, preservation; keep, maintain	1571 運転(する) driving, operation; drive	1631 発達(する) development; develop
	1572 生地 cloth, material; dough	1633 戦い fight, battle
1513 高さ height	1575 予想(する) expectation; expect	1635 鼻 nose
1514 太陽 sun		1636 会 meeting, gathering
1515 会場 hall; site	1576 一層 more	1637 数年 several years
1517 湯 hot water	1577 旦那 husband	1638 現代 the present age, today
1518 そもそも in the first place	1583 採用(する) adoption, employment; employ	1639 回復(する) recovery; recover
1519 約束(する) promise, appointment; promise, make an appointment		1641 コーヒー coffee
	1584 価格 price	1643 老人 old person, the old
	1586 がん cancer	1644 共通(する) common

1645	一瞬	a moment, an instant
1646	面倒	troublesome; bother, care
1647	開始(する)	beginning, start; begin, start
1648	翌日	next day
1650	商店街	shopping street
1651	原則	principle
1652	販売(する)	sale; sell
1654	場面	scene, sight
1655	障害	obstacle, handicap
1657	一定(する)	a certain, fixed, constant
1660	関連(する)	relation, connection; be related, be connected
1661	笑顔	smile
1662	真ん中	middle
1663	ビール	beer
1664	正月	New Year
1666	デザイン(する)	design; design
1669	葉	leaf
1670	種	kind, species
1671	迷惑(する)	troublesome, annoying; annoyance, nuisance, trouble; be inconvenienced
1674	ラジオ	radio
1678	餌	feed; bait
1679	背中	back
1680	両方	both
1681	床	floor
1686	風景	scenery, landscape
1688	保存(する)	preservation, storage; preserve, store
1689	社長	company president
1691	保護(する)	protection; protect
1693	経済	economy; finance
1695	演奏(する)	(musical) performance; perform, play
1697	温泉	hot spring, spa
1698	工夫(する)	device, idea; devise, plan
1700	教室	classroom, ... school
1701	登録(する)	registration, entry; register, enroll
1702	長さ	length
1703	資格	qualification; capacity
1705	記載(する)	registration entry; record, write down
1706	肌	skin
1708	症状	symptom
1709	普及(する)	spread, diffusion; spread
1712	返事(する)	answer, reply; answer, reply
1713	職場	workplace
1715	骨	bone
1716	平和	peace; peaceful
1717	間違い	mistake, error
1719	けんか(する)	fight, quarrel; fight, quarrel
1723	当日	that day, current day
1724	残り	rest, remainder
1725	支援(する)	support, assistance; support, assist
1726	実行(する)	practice; carry out
1728	出会い	encounter
1729	体重	(body) weight
1730	上司	boss
1731	結論	conclusion
1733	テーブル	table
1737	犯人	criminal, culprit
1738	熱	fever; heat
1739	犯罪	crime, offense
1740	批判(する)	criticism; criticize
1741	出発(する)	departure; leave
1742	遊び	play, game
1743	教師	teacher
1744	横浜	Yokohama
1745	脳	brain
1746	レストラン	restaurant
1748	日曜日	Sunday
1749	けが(する)	injury; hurt, injure
1750	兄弟	brother; sister; sibling
1751	楽器	musical instrument
1753	自動車	car
1755	カメラ	camera
1756	寺	temple
1757	ビデオ	video
1760	底	bottom; sole
1761	刺激(する)	stimulate, incite, excite
1762	勢い	speed; force; vigor
1766	背	stature; back
1767	生	raw; fresh; live
1769	精神	mind, spirit
1770	把握(する)	grasp; grasp
1772	十二	twelve
1774	地震	earthquake
1775	応援(する)	support; cheer, support
1776	人類	human race, mankind
1777	上昇(する)	rise; rise
1778	空間	space
1780	特定(する)	specific; specify
1782	以外	except
1783	観点	viewpoint, standpoint
1785	二時間	two hours
1787	祖母	grandmother
1788	プラス(する)	plus, benefit; benefit, add to
1791	知り合い	acquaintance
1795	唯一	only
1796	連中	company, crowd; those guys
1798	終了(する)	end; end, be over
1800	前提	assumption, premise
1801	四つ	four
1802	未来	future
1805	同	same
1806	推移(する)	transition, change; change, shift
1811	国内	domestic, home
1813	都合(する)	convenience, circumstances; arrange; altogether
1816	四年	four years
1817	無視(する)	neglect, ignore
1818	一気	at a stretch, in one gulp
1819	手続き	procedure, formalities
1820	波	wave
1821	仲	relations, terms
1822	中学生	junior high school student
1823	イタリア	Italy
1825	誕生(する)	birth; be born, be created
1827	畑	field (for fruit, vegetables); garden

1829	膝	knee, lap
1830	提案（する）	proposal; propose
1831	業務	business, work
1832	幸い	lucky, fortunate; happiness; fortunately
1834	画像	picture, image
1835	孫	grandchild
1839	事態	situation
1840	夜中	middle of the night
1842	集中（する）	concentration; concentrate
1843	両手	both hands, both arms
1844	指示（する）	instruction, direction; instruct, direct
1845	結婚式	wedding ceremony
1846	虫	insect, bug; worm
1847	バイク	motorcycle, motorbike
1848	確立（する）	establishment; establish
1849	到着（する）	arrival; arrive
1852	親父	father; old man; boss
1857	受験（する）	examination; take an examination
1858	医師	doctor
1859	バンド	band; belt
1860	体力	physical strength
1861	国家	state, country, nation
1862	ソフト	software; soft
1863	長男	eldest son
1864	0	zero
1865	さっき	a little while ago
1867	入力（する）	input; type
1868	CM	commercial
1869	十一	eleven
1870	チャンス	chance
1872	昼間	daytime
1873	生産（する）	production; produce
1874	要	in short
1876	掃除（する）	cleaning; clean
1877	強化（する）	tighten, strengthen
1878	主婦	housewife
1879	徐々	gradually
1880	メーカー	maker, manufacturer
1883	うわさ（する）	gossip, rumor; talk about
1884	保険	insurance
1885	規制（する）	regulation; regulate
1887	感想	feeling, impression
1888	左右（する）	right and left; determine, influence
1889	促進（する）	promotion; promote
1890	景色	scenery, view, scene
1892	アジア	Asia
1893	交流（する）	interchange, exchange; interact
1894	報道（する）	report; report
1895	当初	beginning, original; at first
1896	インド	India
1897	観察（する）	observation; observe
1898	電気	electricity; electric light
1899	癖	habit, peculiarity
1901	あり方	way something ought to be, state of things
1903	好み	liking, taste
1907	市民	resident (of a city), citizen
1908	メリット	merit, advantage
1911	製品	product
1913	得意	be good at, be proud; customer
1914	二週間	two weeks
1915	問い合わせ	inquiry
1918	過程	process
1919	仕組み	structure, mechanism
1922	措置（する）	measure; take measures
1923	油	oil
1924	半年	half a year
1925	視線	eyes, gaze, look
1926	構造	structure
1927	筋肉	muscle
1929	対策	measure
1931	異常	abnormal; disorder
1932	図書館	library
1933	靴	shoe
1934	おそれ	fear, danger
1935	二階	second floor
1937	三回	three times
1938	引っ越し（する）	moving, removal; move house
1939	失礼（する）	rudeness, impoliteness; be rude, be impolite; rude, impolite; Excuse me
1941	街, 町	town, city
1945	都会	city
1946	大量	large quantity, a lot
1947	発言（する）	remark; speak
1950	玄関	entrance, front door
1951	一種	kind, sort, species
1952	世代	generation
1954	申し込み	application
1956	証明（する）	proof; prove
1960	まさか	surely not, cannot possibly; the worst
1962	画面	screen
1963	米	rice
1964	成果	result, product
1965	物語	tale, story
1966	日時	date and time
1967	来年	next year
1971	たっぷり	full, plenty; fullness
1974	中身	contents; substance
1975	スピード	speed
1976	一歩	step
1977	牛乳	(cow's) milk
1978	否定（する）	denial, negative; deny
1980	若干	slightly; a little, few, some
1981	箱	box, case
1982	テニス	tennis
1983	アパート	apartment
1984	面接（する）	interview; interview
1985	住民	inhabitant, resident
1987	ギター	guitar
1988	要素	element, factor
1990	大勢	a large number of, many
1991	習慣	custom, habit
1993	風邪	cold
1994	調整（する）	adjustment; adjust
1997	タクシー	taxi
1998	教会	church
1999	攻撃（する）	attack; attack

2000	五時	five o'clock
2001	(お)弁当	lunch box
2002	方達	people (honorific)
2003	久しぶり	after a long time
2004	とたん	as soon as
2006	幅	width, breadth; difference; latitude
2007	周辺	outskirts, around
2008	十日	tenth (date); ten days
2009	取得(する)	acquisition; acquire
2010	挑戦(する)	challenge; challenge, try
2011	独立(する)	independence; be independent
2012	収入	income
2014	市場	market
2015	着物	kimono
2016	メニュー	menu
2017	夏休み	summer holiday
2020	仮	temporary, provisional; assumed
2023	輸入(する)	import; import
2026	スタッフ	staff
2027	住所	address
2028	平気	insensitive, fine; calmness
2029	コース	course, route, lane
2031	鍵	key
2032	世界中	around the world, throughout the world
2034	詩	poem, poetry
2035	経過(する)	progress, development; pass
2037	ツアー	tour
2038	西	west
2039	事項	matter, fact, item
2040	塾	cram school
2042	五人	five people
2043	入り口	entrance
2045	県	prefecture
2047	事務所	office
2048	大さじ	tablespoon
2049	整理(する)	arrangement; arrange, put in order, dispose of
2051	職員	staff member
2052	コメント(する)	comment; comment
2053	五分	five minutes
2054	発揮(する)	exhibition, show; display, exhibit
2056	芝居	play, drama
2057	分析(する)	analysis; analyze
2058	解釈(する)	interpretation; interpret
2060	三ヶ月	three months
2061	注文(する)	order; order
2062	傷	injury; scratch; bruise; flaw; stain
2063	外国人	foreigner
2064	八時	eight o'clock
2065	冷蔵庫	refrigerator
2067	配慮(する)	consideration; consider
2068	赤	red
2070	海外旅行	travel abroad, foreign trip
2071	営業(する)	business, sales; do business
2072	水	Wednesday, Wed.
2074	空港	airport
2075	交換(する)	exchange; exchange
2078	ホームページ	home page
2079	妊娠(する)	pregnancy; get pregnant
2081	ママ	mom, mummy
2084	まっすぐ	straight, direct; honest
2085	映像	picture, image, video
2087	破壊(する)	destruction, demolition; destroy, demolish
2088	削除(する)	deletion; delete
2089	派遣(する)	dispatch, send
2090	カード	card
2091	改正(する)	amendment; amend
2092	世間	world, public, society
2094	社員	employee, member of staff
2095	月	Monday, Mon.
2096	信頼(する)	trust, rely on
2099	三時	three o'clock
2100	ペット	pet
2101	世	world, public; age, reign
2102	不可能	impossible; impossibility
2104	問	question number; counter for questions
2105	サイト	website
2106	ボランティア	volunteer
2107	問題点	problem, point at issue
2108	一人一人	one by one, each (people)
2109	サイズ	size
2110	建設(する)	construction; build, construct
2111	線	line
2112	子育て	child rearing, bringing up one's child
2113	願い	wish, hope
2115	二十分	twenty minutes
2116	モデル	model
2120	募集(する)	recruitment; recruit
2121	りんご	apple
2123	食料	food, provisions
2124	優勝(する)	championship, victory; win
2125	間	during; between
2128	消費者	consumer
2129	喉	throat; voice
2130	布団	futon, Japanese-style bedding
2131	十五分	fifteen minutes
2132	宇宙	universe, space
2134	資金	funds
2136	料金	charge, fee, fare
2137	デパート	department store
2138	地図	map
2139	唇	lip
2140	釣り	fishing
2141	十五日	fifteenth (date); fifteen days
2142	駅前	in front of the station
2144	ご覧	looking, seeing (honorific)
2145	大会	convention, mass meeting, tournament
2148	二番目	second
2149	良さ	good point, good
2151	素材	material

#	Japanese	English
2152	設立(する)	establishment; establish, set up
2156	江戸	Edo
2158	二十	twenty
2159	反映(する)	reflection; reflect
2160	天気	weather
2161	作家	writer
2163	十五	fifteen
2164	ゴルフ	golf
2166	合格(する)	passing an exam; pass an exam
2167	日常	everyday, daily, usually
2168	毎回	every time
2169	影	shadow
2171	法	law
2172	罪	crime; guilt
2174	団体	party, group, organization
2175	詳細	details; detailed
2176	洋服	clothes, suit, dress
2177	承知(する)	agreement; agree, understand
2178	多数	many, a number of
2179	運営(する)	management; manage, run
2180	生き方	way of life
2183	住宅	house, residence
2184	考慮(する)	thought; think over, consider
2185	働き	work
2187	ファイル	file
2188	有り	exist; live
2189	要因	factor, main cause
2190	わし	I (used by old men)
2191	火	fire; Tuesday, Tue.
2192	偶然	by chance; chance, accident
2194	不満	dissatisfaction, discontent; discontented
2195	クラブ	club
2197	ページ	page
2201	机	desk
2202	使い方	how to use
2203	ハワイ	Hawaii
2204	予算	estimate, budget
2206	勇気	courage, bravery
2207	皿	plate, dish
2209	視点	viewpoint
2211	表面	surface, outside, appearance
2212	コピー(する)	copy; copy
2214	部活	club
2215	サラリーマン	salaried worker, office worker
2216	制限(する)	restriction; limit, restrict
2217	実験(する)	experimentation; experiment
2218	ニューヨーク	New York
2220	東	east
2221	主人公	hero, heroine
2223	アメリカ人	American (person)
2224	テスト(する)	test; test
2225	高校時代	high school days
2226	満足(する)	satisfaction; be satisfied
2227	愛情	love, affection
2230	ビル	building
2232	財産	property; fortune
2233	証拠	evidence
2235	訓練(する)	training; train
2236	区別(する)	distinction; distinguish
2237	四日	fourth (date); four days
2238	サークル	circle, club
2239	皆様	everybody
2240	光景	sight, spectacle
2241	パターン	pattern
2242	シーン	scene
2246	旨	effect; principle
2247	反省(する)	soul-searching, reflection; reflect on
2248	放送(する)	broadcasting, telecasting; broadcast
2249	人間関係	interpersonal relationship
2250	ボタン	button
2251	少女	girl
2253	自己	oneself, self
2254	ロンドン	London
2255	端	end, tip, edge
2257	規模	scale
2258	悩み	trouble, worry
2260	運	luck, fortune
2261	ルール	rule
2264	恋	love (romantic)
2265	現象	phenomenon, happening; phase
2266	ベース	base, basis
2267	ネット	net
2268	許可(する)	permission, leave; permit, authorize
2269	商売	business
2271	文句	words; complaint
2272	発想	idea, conception
2274	親戚	relative
2276	アドバイス	advice
2277	ダイエット(する)	diet; go on a diet
2278	生命	life
2279	中央	center; central
2280	発行(する)	publication, issue; publish, issue
2282	カナダ	Canada
2283	請求(する)	demand, request, charge; demand, claim
2284	企画(する)	planning; plan
2289	縁	chance, fate, destiny
2291	渋谷	Shibuya (place name)
2293	セット	set
2295	明かり	light
2296	玉ねぎ	onion
2298	合計(する)	sum total; total
2300	二本	two (long/cylindrical objects)
2304	城	castle
2305	対処(する)	handling, coping; deal with
2307	教授	professor
2308	橋	bridge
2312	スタイル	style, body, figure
2313	テント	tent
2314	ユダヤ人	Jewish person
2315	主	head, master
2316	意志	will, willpower
2322	毎月	every month
2323	礼	bow; courtesy
2325	抵抗(する)	resistance; resist, offer opposition
2326	十一時	eleven o'clock
2327	恐怖	fear, dread, terror
2328	支配(する)	rule, control; rule, control, govern
2329	右手	right hand

2332	禁止(する)	prohibition, ban; prohibit, ban
2333	怒り	anger, rage, fury
2335	命令(する)	order, command, direction; order, command
2336	四時	four o'clock
2337	援助(する)	assistance, aid, support; help, support, assist
2341	見方	point of view, way of looking
2342	介護(する)	nursing, care; nurse, look after
2343	成績	record, result, grade, mark
2344	広告(する)	advertisement, flyer; advertise
2345	本日	today
2346	強調(する)	emphasis, stress; emphasize, stress
2349	お子さん	(someone else's) child
2350	実態	actual situation
2354	トップ	top
2355	依頼(する)	request; request, ask
2357	真	truth; reality
2358	出産(する)	birth; give birth
2359	達成(する)	achievement, attainment; achieve, attain
2360	申請(する)	application, petition; apply
2362	親子	parent and child, parents and children
2363	取り組み	match; approach
2365	二十日	twentieth (date); twenty days
2366	政治家	politician
2370	定員	capacity (people)
2371	駐車場	parking space, parking lot, car park
2372	彼氏	boyfriend
2373	式	ceremony
2375	蓋	lid
2376	実	seed; berry; fruit; nut; pulp
2377	社会人	adult; full member of society
2378	墓	grave
2379	十三	thirteen
2380	宿	inn, hotel
2381	都心	city center, downtown area
2382	二ヶ月	two months
2384	土曜日	Saturday
2385	労働者	laborer, working man
2386	五日	fifth (date); five days
2387	発売(する)	sale; sell, put on sale
2389	人数	number of people
2390	物質	matter, material
2391	温度	temperature; heat
2392	性質	nature, disposition
2393	方針	course, line; policy, plan; principle
2395	秘密	secret, confidence
2396	該当(する)	fall under, be applicable, correspond
2397	案内	guidance; guide, sign
2398	基礎	basis, basics, foundation
2400	草	grass, weed
2401	食品	food
2402	トラブル	trouble
2404	定義	definition
2406	祖父	grandfather
2407	扉	door
2410	廊下	corridor
2411	要請	request
2412	お姉さん	elder sister
2413	プログラム	program
2414	職業	occupation, trade, profession
2415	限界	limit, boundary
2416	地位	rank, position
2420	エンジン	engine
2421	コンビニ	convenience store
2422	質	nature, quality
2423	漢字	kanji, Chinese character
2424	政策	policy
2425	本物	real (thing), genuine
2427	解消(する)	cancellation, annulment; cancel, dissolve
2428	キャンプ	camp
2429	アルバム	album
2430	運命	destiny, fate
2433	ロボット	robot
2434	水分	water, moisture
2435	天皇	Emperor
2436	布	cloth
2437	生物	living thing; biology
2438	根	root
2439	信用(する)	trust, rely on
2440	ロシア	Russia
2441	農業	agriculture
2442	思想	thought, idea
2444	種	seed
2445	書類	document
2447	神様	god, God
2449	農家	farmer
2450	市町村	municipality
2451	被害者	victim
2452	時計	watch; clock
2453	雲	cloud
2455	メッセージ	message
2456	いじめ	bullying
2457	離婚(する)	divorce; divorce, get divorced
2459	掲載(する)	publication; publish, print
2461	オリンピック	Olympics
2462	操作(する)	operation; operate
2463	知恵	wisdom
2464	伝統	tradition
2469	カレー	curry
2470	ウインドウズ	Windows
2474	予約(する)	reservation; reserve, book
2476	事前	prior
2477	進行(する)	progression; progress
2478	解説(する)	explanation, comment, description; explain
2480	二時	two o'clock
2481	行事	event
2482	男女	men and women
2483	メイン	main
2486	概念	notion, idea, concept
2487	重視(する)	respect; make a point of, consider important
2488	複数	plural

- 2489 三十 thirty
- 2490 興奮(する) excitement; be excited
- 2492 牛 cattle, cow, ox
- 2493 鏡 mirror
- 2495 二千年 2000 (year); two thousand years
- 2496 煙 smoke, fumes; fog
- 2497 参照(する) reference; consult, refer
- 2498 価値観 sense of values
- 2499 バター butter
- 2500 スープ soup
- 2501 自殺(する) suicide; commit suicide
- 2502 トラック truck
- 2503 委員 committee member; councillor
- 2504 行政 administration, government
- 2505 一年生 first grade, first year
- 2509 このごろ these days
- 2510 女子 woman, girl
- 2511 JR Japan Railways (JR)
- 2512 言語 language, tongue, speech
- 2514 以来 since
- 2515 市内 within the city
- 2517 針 needle; stitch
- 2518 集団 group, mass
- 2519 体調 physical condition
- 2520 三年間 three years
- 2521 手前 this side
- 2523 説 theory; explanation
- 2524 神社 shrine
- 2525 列車 train
- 2526 夢中 crazy about, obsessed with
- 2527 トレーニング training
- 2530 坂 slope, hill
- 2531 検索(する) search; search, look up
- 2532 アップ(する) raise; go up
- 2534 三十一日 thirty-first (date); thirty one days
- 2535 取材(する) interview, report; gather information
- 2539 前年 previous year, year before
- 2541 三十日 thirtieth (date); thirty days
- 2542 分類(する) classification; classify
- 2544 自分なり in one's own way
- 2545 覚悟(する) readiness, preparedness; be ready
- 2546 糸 thread, string
- 2547 逮捕(する) arrest; arrest
- 2549 交渉(する) negotiation, treaty; negotiate
- 2550 枝 branch, twig, bough
- 2552 教科書 textbook
- 2553 六時 six o'clock
- 2554 取り引き business, dealing, trade
- 2555 免許 license, permit
- 2560 千円 one thousand yen
- 2562 夕食 dinner
- 2564 心臓 heart
- 2566 所属(する) affiliation; attach, be attached, belong
- 2570 晩 night, evening
- 2571 小屋 hut, cabin, barn, shed
- 2572 会議 meeting
- 2573 個性 personality, character
- 2575 理想 ideal, dream
- 2576 給料 salary
- 2577 マスコミ mass media, mass communication
- 2579 屋根 roof
- 2580 クリスマス Christmas
- 2582 各地 each place
- 2584 進化(する) evolution; evolve, develop
- 2587 新幹線 bullet train
- 2588 第三 third
- 2590 公開(する) exhibition, presentation; release
- 2591 地面 ground, land
- 2592 貢献(する) contribution, service; contribute
- 2593 台風 typhoon
- 2595 大臣 Cabinet minister, minister of state
- 2596 十四 fourteen
- 2597 入学(する) (school etc.) entrance, admission; enter (school etc.)
- 2598 紅茶 tea (black)
- 2601 何事 what
- 2602 プレゼント present
- 2604 改革(する) reform; make reforms
- 2605 一致(する) agreement, accord; consent, agree
- 2606 ゼロ zero
- 2607 義務 duty, obligation
- 2608 出席(する) attendance; attend
- 2609 十人 ten people
- 2610 処分(する) disposal, disposition; dispose of
- 2611 年間 year; annual
- 2612 広島 Hiroshima
- 2613 NHK Nihon Hoso Kyokai (Japan Broadcasting Corporation)
- 2614 設計(する) plan, design; plan, design
- 2616 邪魔(する) obstacle, disturbance, interruption; disturb, interrupt
- 2618 プール pool
- 2619 弁護士 lawyer, counsellor
- 2621 恋人 lover, boyfriend, girlfriend
- 2622 暮らし life, livelihood
- 2623 王 king, monarch
- 2624 真似(する) imitation, mimicry, impersonation; imitate, copy
- 2625 税金 tax
- 2628 物事 thing
- 2630 年金 pension, annuity
- 2631 やりとり exchange, interchange
- 2632 ホーム platform
- 2634 学生時代 student days, university days
- 2635 憧れ admiration
- 2636 内側 inside, interior, inner
- 2637 講師 speaker, lecturer
- 2638 池 pond
- 2639 接続(する) connection; connect
- 2640 役者 actor, actress
- 2642 富士山 Mt.Fuji

2643 必要性 necessity
2644 七時 seven o'clock
2646 出演(する) appearance, broadcast; appear (on stage, TV)
2647 柱 pillar, post
2649 年代 era; generation; date
2650 鉄 iron, steel
2651 継続(する) continuation; continue
2654 スペイン Spain
2655 裁判 trial; judgment; justice
2658 地下鉄 subway, underground
2659 専門家 expert, specialist
2660 内部 inside, interior
2662 スペース space, room
2665 割 cost, rate
2666 日記 diary
2670 一匹 one (animal)
2671 憲法 constitution
2672 件 affair, matter, issue
2673 江戸時代 Edo era
2676 埼玉県 Saitama prefecture
2679 末 end, last
2680 胃 stomach, belly
2681 九州 Kyushu
2682 ブログ blog
2684 想定(する) assumption, supposition; assume, suppose
2685 学習(する) learning, study; learn, study
2686 ケーキ cake
2687 六年 six years
2688 袋 bag, sack, pouch
2689 医療 medical care, medical treatment
2690 増大(する) increase, growth; increase, grow
2691 競争(する) competition, contest; compete
2692 投資(する) investment; invest
2694 お土産 present, souvenir
2695 記述(する) description, account; describe
2698 獲得(する) acquisition; get, gain
2700 無人 uninhabited, empty
2702 テープ tape
2703 七日 seventh (date); seven days
2704 二つ目 second
2705 板 board, plate
2706 自慢(する) pride, boast; boast, brag
2707 前項 previous page
2708 選挙 election
2709 更新(する) renewal; renew, update
2710 IT IT
2713 景気 business conditions, economy
2714 二十五日 twenty-fifth (date); twenty-five days
2715 根拠 ground, evidence
2716 チケット ticket
2717 民間 private, non government
2718 口調 tone, voice
2721 眼鏡 glasses, spectacles
2722 脇 side
2724 全身 all over, whole body
2725 兄さん elder brother
2726 予測(する) prospect; predict, estimate
2728 つながり connection, relation
2731 保険料 insurance premium
2734 三十年 thirty years
2735 後半 latter half, second half
2737 何日 many days; how many days
2738 防止(する) prevention; prevent
2739 遺伝子 gene
2740 本屋 bookshop
2741 明日 tomorrow
2742 早め early
2744 今夜 tonight
2745 ゆえ reason; therefore
2746 リズム rhythm
2748 魂 soul, spirit
2749 滞在(する) stay, visit; stay, visit, stop
2750 連携(する) cooperation; work together with
2751 ライブ live (music)
2753 廃止(する) abolition; repeal
2754 復活(する) revival, restoration; revive, restore
2755 借金(する) debt, loan; borrow (money)
2756 常識 common sense, general knowledge
2757 闇 darkness, dark
2759 不便 inconvenience; inconvenient
2760 栄養 nutrition
2761 フランス語 French language
2762 アクセス access
2763 PC personal computer
2766 カット cut
2768 おまけ addition, free gift
2770 ついで on one's way, along the way
2771 名称 name
2773 大学生 college student, university student
2774 左手 left hand; on one's left
2775 乾燥(する) dryness; dry
2778 八日 eighth (date); eight days
2781 ノート notebook
2782 配置(する) arrangement, layout; arrange
2783 輸出(する) exportation; export
2784 陰 shade, shadow; behind someone's back
2786 果物 fruit
2787 個々 individual, each
2788 十六日 sixteenth (date); sixteen days
2789 電話番号 telephone number
2796 プレー play
2797 進歩(する) progress, advance; progress, advance
2798 百 hundred
2799 お尻 hips
2801 産業 industry
2802 前日 eve, previous day
2803 吸収(する) absorption, assimilation; absorb, assimilate
2804 驚き surprise, amazement
2805 ソ連 Soviet Union

2806	悲しみ	sadness, grief
2807	十一日	eleventh (date); eleven days
2808	最低	minimum, lowest
2809	十六	sixteen
2810	にんにく	garlic
2811	順番	turn, order
2812	裁判所	court, courthouse
2813	観光(する)	sightseeing; go sightseeing
2814	申し訳	excuse, apology
2815	葉っぱ	leaf
2816	生き物	creature, life
2817	演出(する)	direction, direct
2819	本気	seriousness, earnestness; serious, earnest
2820	三年生	third grade, third year
2821	記入(する)	entry; fill in
2823	話し合い	discussion, meeting
2824	値	price
2825	一人暮らし	living alone, single life
2826	趣旨	purpose, intention, point
2828	舌	tongue
2829	三時間	three hours
2830	後悔(する)	repentance, regret; regret
2832	勝利	victory, triumph, winning
2833	自覚(する)	consciousness, awareness; realize
2834	今朝	this morning
2836	美しさ	beauty
2837	法人	corporation
2840	留学(する)	study abroad; study abroad
2841	念	sense, feeling
2842	銀座	Ginza (place name)
2843	十五年	fifteen years
2846	永遠	eternity, permanence
2847	十四日	fourteenth (date); fourteen days
2849	いっぺん	at the same time; altogether
2850	門	gate
2851	伸び	growth
2853	事例	case
2856	冗談	joke
2857	巣	nest
2858	進展(する)	progress, development, evolution; develop, progress, advance
2859	手伝い	help
2860	死亡(する)	death, decease; die
2861	細胞	cell
2862	犠牲	sacrifice, expense
2864	前後	back and forth
2865	対立(する)	opposition, conflict; be opposed to
2866	六日	sixth (date); six days
2867	比率	ratio, proportion
2868	タイ	Thailand
2870	香港	Hong Kong
2871	湖	lake
2873	出現(する)	appearance, dawn, birth, advent; appear
2874	真実	truth, reality
2875	前回	last time, previous time
2876	工事(する)	construction, work; construct
2877	科学	science
2878	順	order
2879	読者	reader
2880	不足(する)	lack, shortage; be insufficient
2882	限定(する)	restriction, limitation; restrict, limit
2883	劇団	theatrical company
2884	看護婦	nurse (female)
2885	人参	carrot
2886	一面	side, facet
2887	生涯	life, lifetime; career
2888	意思	will, intention
2889	追加(する)	addition, supplement; add, supplement
2890	台湾	Taiwan
2891	日常生活	daily life
2893	レース	race
2894	民族	people, race, nation
2895	天	sky, heaven
2896	花火	firework
2897	項目	item, heading
2898	動向	trend, movement
2900	日頃	everyday
2901	砂	sand
2902	大根	Japanese radish, radish
2903	感激(する)	deep emotion; be impressed
2906	リスク	risk
2908	オークション	auction
2909	二十一日	twenty-first (date); twenty-one days
2912	武器	weapon
2913	都内	in the city
2914	違反(する)	violation; violate
2916	十二日	twelfth (date), twelve days
2918	十八日	eighteenth (date); eighteen days
2919	お宅	your house
2920	交通	traffic; transportation
2921	業界	business world
2922	解放(する)	liberation; liberate
2923	需要	demand
2924	高度	altitude; high, advanced
2925	帰国(する)	going/coming back to one's own country
2926	午前中	in the morning, throughout the morning
2927	実践(する)	practice; practice
2929	十八	eighteen
2930	関係者	person concerned
2932	作用(する)	action; act
2934	五つ	five
2936	差別(する)	discrimination; discriminate
2937	大声	loud voice
2939	固まり	mass, lump
2942	研修(する)	training; study
2944	男子	boy, man
2945	爪	nail; claw
2946	青年	young man
2949	氷	ice
2950	十七日	seventeenth (date); seventeen days
2953	業者	dealer, agent, operator

2954	大半	better part, most part
2956	三つ目	third
2959	支持(する)	support; support
2960	九日	ninth (date); nine days
2961	雌	female animal
2962	跡	track, trail; mark, sign
2963	トマト	tomato
2964	エピソード	episode, anecdote
2965	真	truth, fact
2966	訪問(する)	visit, call; visit, call (on)
2967	スピーチ	speech
2969	足元	at one's feet; step
2970	台所	kitchen
2972	毛	hair; fur; wool
2973	一点	point, single point
2974	二十三日	twenty-third (date); twenty-three days
2975	支給(する)	provision, payment; provide, pay
2976	経費	expense, cost
2978	感心(する)	admiration; admire
2979	ポケット	pocket
2980	決意(する)	determination; resolve
2981	法則	law
2983	資産	assets, property
2985	二十四日	twenty-fourth (date); twenty-four days
2986	尊敬(する)	respect; respect
2988	謎	mystery, riddle
2989	田んぼ	rice field
2990	評判	reputation; popularity
2991	寒さ	cold
2992	天井	ceiling
2993	池袋	Ikebukuro (place name)
2995	喫茶店	tearoom, coffee shop, café
2996	従業員	employee, worker
2997	嫁	wife; bride; daughter-in-law
2999	災害	disaster, calamity
3001	髪の毛	hair
3003	加入(する)	admission, joining; join
3004	受け付け	acceptance, information desk, reception (desk)
3005	玉	ball; coin
3006	型	model, pattern, type
3008	専門	specialty, speciality
3009	供給(する)	supply; supply
3010	振り	pretence
3011	売り上げ	sales
3012	建築(する)	architecture, construction; build
3013	利用者	user
3015	地方公共団体	local public body
3017	鉄道	railroad, railway
3018	誕生日	birthday
3019	五十年	fifty years
3020	役員	official, director
3021	設備	equipment, facilities
3022	悪化(する)	change for the worse; worsen
3023	用	something to do; use
3025	十三日	thirteenth (date); thirteen days
3026	遺跡	ruins, remains
3027	消費(する)	consumption; consume
3028	模様	pattern, design, look
3030	パパ	papa, dad
3031	文	sentence
3032	中国人	Chinese (person)
3033	活性化(する)	revitalization; revitalize
3034	聖書	Bible
3035	神経	nerve
3036	混乱(する)	confusion; get confused
3040	動作(する)	movement, operation; operate
3041	コンサート	concert
3042	粉	flour, powder
3043	身長	height
3044	賛成(する)	agreement; agree
3045	形態	form
3047	部下	subordinate
3048	二十世紀	twentieth century
3050	勤務(する)	service, duty, work; work, serve
3051	恋愛(する)	love (romantic); love
3052	都道府県	prefectures
3053	誤解(する)	misunderstanding; misunderstand
3054	直前	just before
3055	平均(する)	average; average
3056	出身	hometown; alma mater
3057	区	ward, district
3058	しょう油	soy sauce
3059	こつ	knack
3060	翻訳(する)	translation; translate
3062	ソース	sauce; source
3063	二十二日	twenty-second (date); twenty-two days
3065	ステージ	stage
3066	ストーリー	story
3069	始まり	beginning, origin
3071	別れ	parting, farewell
3072	女房	wife
3073	才能	talent, ability
3074	背後	back; background
3075	通過(する)	passage; pass
3076	確信(する)	conviction; be convinced
3077	株	stump; stock, share
3080	神戸	Kobe
3082	北朝鮮	Democratic People's Republic of Korea, North Korea
3083	側面	side; flank
3084	誇り	pride, honor
3085	作り	make, construction
3086	米	meter
3087	崩壊(する)	collapse; collapse
3088	二十一	twenty-one
3090	バッグ	bag
3091	本書	this book
3092	器	container
3093	血液	blood
3094	衝撃	shock, impact
3096	製造(する)	production; produce
3098	小麦粉	flour
3099	気配	indication, sign
3100	理論	theory
3101	流行(する)	fashion, epidemic; come into fashion, be rife

#	Term	Meaning
3102	見解	opinion, view
3103	承認 (する)	approval; approve
3105	単位	unit, credit
3107	歌詞	song lyrics
3109	文明	civilization
3110	長崎	Nagasaki
3113	発音 (する)	pronunciation; pronounce
3114	共有 (する)	share; share
3115	勝負 (する)	victory or defeat, match; play
3116	住まい	house, residence
3117	二十八日	twenty-eighth (date); twenty-eight days
3119	各国	each country, various countries
3121	五百円	five hundred yen
3122	出品 (する)	exhibit; submit
3124	三番目	third
3125	メモ (する)	memo; take notes
3126	平日	weekday
3127	支払い	payment
3128	皮膚	skin
3129	反面	other side
3132	初心者	beginner
3135	合併 (する)	combination, merger; combine, merge
3136	ウサギ	rabbit
3137	徹底 (する)	thoroughgoing, out-and-out; be thorough
3139	八年	eight years
3141	意	mind; will; sense
3142	自民党	Liberal Democratic Party
3143	地下	basement; underground
3144	構築 (する)	construction; construct
3145	両者	both, the two
3148	番号	number
3149	経営者	manager, proprietor
3151	論文	essay, thesis, paper, dissertation
3152	タイミング	timing
3153	百パーセント	one hundred percent
3154	週末	weekend
3155	出品者	exhibitor
3156	二十六日	twenty-sixth (date); twenty-six days
3158	カラオケ	karaoke
3159	退職 (する)	retirement, resignation; retire, resign
3162	知人	acquaintance
3164	十九日	nineteenth (date); nineteen days
3165	千葉県	Chiba prefecture
3166	食材	ingredient, foodstuff
3168	組み合わせ	combination, matching
3170	台詞	lines, speech, words
3171	コート	coat; court
3172	二年生	second grade, second year
3173	ロック	rock; lock
3174	国会	national assembly, Diet
3178	意図	intention
3180	手間	labour; time
3182	森林	forest, woods
3183	マイナス	minus
3184	ラーメン	Chinese noodles
3185	帽子	hat, cap
3186	オープン (する)	open
3187	名古屋	Nagoya
3189	数値	numerical value; score, count
3191	見直し	review, reconsideration
3193	一冊	one (book)
3194	強さ	strength, power
3195	紐	string; lace
3196	岩	rock
3197	ミス (する)	mistake; make a mistake
3198	移行 (する)	shift; shift
3199	味方 (する)	supporter; support
3201	転勤 (する)	transfer; be transferred
3202	ビートルズ	Beatles
3203	フライパン	frying pan
3204	一階	first floor, ground floor
3206	正面	front
3207	演劇	drama, play
3208	疲れ	fatigue, exhaustion, tiredness
3209	経緯	details, process
3211	数学	mathematics
3212	関わり	relation, connection
3213	英国	United Kingdom, Britain
3215	退院 (する)	leaving hospital; be discharged from hospital
3216	覚え	memory
3218	リラックス (する)	relax
3219	施策	policy, measure
3220	瞳	pupil; eye
3221	二十七日	twenty-seventh (date); twenty-seven days
3222	権限	authority, power
3223	十七	seventeen
3224	展示 (する)	display, exhibition; display, exhibit
3225	三歳	three years old
3226	朝食	breakfast
3227	診断 (する)	diagnosis; diagnose
3228	ご免	pardon, sorry, [to decline]
3229	缶詰	canned food
3230	こしょう	pepper
3232	海岸	seashore, seaside
3233	領域	territory, field
3234	出版 (する)	publication; publish
3235	映画館	movie theater, cinema
3236	気温	temperature
3237	由来 (する)	origin, history; originate
3239	筋	tendon; line; reason
3240	ガラス	glass
3241	同意 (する)	agreement, consent; agree
3242	土日	Saturday and Sunday
3243	認定 (する)	authorization; authorize
3244	おもちゃ	toy
3245	島	island
3246	丘	hill
3247	二年間	two years
3248	メディア	media
3249	一台	one (machine/vehicle)
3250	翌年	the next year, the following year

#	Word	Meaning
3251	酸素	oxygen
3254	贅沢	luxury; luxurious
3255	金融機関	financial institution
3256	百円	one hundred yen
3257	黄色	yellow
3258	制定(する)	enactment; enact
3259	文書	document; writing
3260	初期	early days, initial stage
3262	はがき	postcard
3263	巨人	giant
3264	俺達	we (used by male speakers)
3265	苦痛	pain
3266	パワー	power
3269	実力	real ability
3272	港	harbour, port
3273	片方	one side; the other one
3276	二十九日	twenty-ninth (date); twenty-nine days
3277	市販(する)	on the market; market
3278	この世	this world
3279	片手	one hand
3280	サイン(する)	signature, autograph; sign
3281	キリスト教	Christianity
3282	年寄り	old people
3285	呼吸(する)	breath; breathe
3286	コーナー	corner
3287	徒歩	on foot, walk
3288	延長(する)	extension; extend
3291	二千二年	2002 (year)
3292	中小企業	small and medium-sized enterprises
3293	浅草	Asakusa (place name)
3296	とく	[shortened form of "teoku"]
3297	あご	jaw, chin
3298	紅葉(する)	autumn leaves; put on fall colors
3300	信仰(する)	religious faith; believe
3301	ねた	material; ingredient
3303	雄	male animal
3304	欧米	Europe and America
3305	運用(する)	making use of; manage
3306	酢	vinegar
3307	半ば	half, middle; partly
3309	権力	power, authority
3310	拒否(する)	refusal; refuse, reject
3312	ビジネス	business
3314	アイデア	idea
3315	十二時	twelve o'clock
3316	ベトナム	Vietnam
3317	落札(する)	successful bid; make a successful bid
3318	出場(する)	participation; participate
3323	雇用(する)	employment; employ
3325	休日	holiday, day off
3326	寝袋	sleeping bag
3327	疑い	doubt, suspicion
3329	折	occasion, opportunity
3330	印刷(する)	printing; print
3332	パチンコ	pachinko, Japanese pinball
3334	中止(する)	cancellation; cancel, call off
3335	連続(する)	continuation, succession; continue
3337	関西	Kansai region
3338	単語	word
3340	死体	dead body
3341	アフリカ	Africa
3343	幸福	happiness
3344	説得(する)	persuasion; persuade
3346	レッスン	lesson
3347	放置(する)	leaving something as it is; neglect
3348	危機	crisis, critical moment
3349	アーティスト	artist
3350	子達	children
3351	編集(する)	editing; edit
3354	原稿	manuscript, draft
3355	象徴(する)	symbol; symbolize
3357	服装	clothes, dress
3358	見学(する)	studying by observation, field trip; visit for study, go on a field trip
3359	六人	six people
3360	中野	Nakano (place name)
3361	応募(する)	application; apply for
3363	二回目	second time
3364	棒	stick, pole, bar
3366	固定(する)	fixing; fix
3367	告白(する)	confession; confess
3369	策定(する)	settling on; settle on
3370	矛盾(する)	contradiction, conflict; contradict
3372	保証(する)	guarantee; guarantee
3373	団地	housing development
3374	会長	president, chairperson
3375	利点	advantage
3376	ジャンル	genre, category
3377	縦	length; height; vertical
3378	隙間	crevice, opening, gap
3381	ガス	gas
3382	ウイルス	virus
3383	公表(する)	publication; make public
3384	二千一年	2001 (year)
3385	古く	ancient times; anciently
3387	一万円	ten thousand yen
3388	意義	meaning, significance
3393	品物	goods, article
3394	前述(する)	above-mentioned, mentioned above
3396	OS	operating system
3398	入手(する)	acquisition; get, obtain
3399	二十代	twenties
3403	競馬	horse racing
3407	パーティー	party
3408	役目	duty, role
3409	通知(する)	notice, notification; notify
3410	要望(する)	demand; make demands
3413	パート	part; part-time

#		#		#	
3414	手のひら palm of the hand	3465	大手 major companies	3514	特性 character, property
3415	地上 ground	3466	本番 performance	3515	解散(する) dissolution; dissolve, break up
3416	踊り dance	3467	同僚 colleague	3517	回転(する) revolution; revolve, turn round, spin
3420	最中 in the middle of	3468	楽しさ pleasure, charm		
3421	定着(する) fixing; fix; become established	3470	技 skill, technique, trick	3518	マナー manners
		3473	回収(する) collection; collect	3520	政令 government ordinance
3424	そこらへん around there; such a matter	3474	再生(する) rebirth; regenerate	3521	王様 king
		3475	わがまま selfish, disobedient; selfishness	3523	竹 bamboo
3426	水準 standard, level			3524	暴力 violence
3428	首相 prime minister	3476	小さじ teaspoon	3525	えび prawn, shrimp
3429	レコード record	3477	コントロール(する) control; control	3526	担任 class teacher
3432	機関 engine; organization; facilities			3527	角度 angle
		3478	深夜 middle of the night	3528	革命 revolution
3433	手作り handmade, homemade	3481	芸術 art	3529	合宿(する) training camp; stay together in a camp
		3482	ブラジル Brazil		
3434	提示(する) presentation; present	3483	施行(する) enforcement; enforce	3530	後輩 one's junior
				3531	一連 course of, series of
3435	エジプト Egypt	3484	チーズ cheese	3533	郵便局 post office
3436	下町 Shitamachi (place name); traditional working-class neighborhood	3485	教え teaching, lesson, doctrine	3534	概要 outline, summary
		3486	追及(する) pursuit; pursue the question	3535	ローマ Rome
				3537	体制 system, structure
3438	優先(する) priority; have priority	3487	今月 this month	3538	セックス(する) sex; have sex
		3488	仙台 Sendai	3539	上記 the above, above-mentioned
3439	大部分 majority; mostly	3489	特許 patent		
3440	戦前 pre-war	3490	株式 stock, shares	3540	何時 what time
3441	制作(する) production; produce	3491	労働(する) work, labor; work, labor	3541	親友 best friend, close friend
				3542	お袋 mother
3443	後者 the latter	3492	カフェ café	3543	所有(する) ownership; own
3444	五十 fifty	3494	規則 rule, regulation	3544	進出(する) advance; launch into
3446	シャワー shower	3496	帰宅(する) coming home; come home		
3447	栗 chestnut			3546	測定(する) measurement; measure
3448	札幌 Sapporo	3498	一つ目 first		
3449	主体 main constituent; subject	3499	汚染(する) pollution; pollute	3549	家賃 rent
				3550	蛇 snake
3450	家内 one's family; my wife	3500	転換(する) conversion; convert, change	3551	自身 oneself
3451	看板 signboard, billboard; attraction			3553	修理(する) repair; repair
		3501	たんぱく質 protein	3555	加工(する) processing; process
3452	将棋 shogi, Japanese chess	3502	Eメール e-mail		
3453	家事 housework	3503	予防(する) prevention; prevent	3556	鶏 chicken; baby bird
3455	他方 the other side			3557	保護者 protector
3456	交通事故 traffic accident	3504	頬 cheek	3560	人材 talent
3457	手順 order, process, plan	3505	面積 area, size	3563	排除(する) removal; remove
3458	コスト cost	3506	大正 Taisho era	3564	育成(する) cultivation; bring up, cultivate, mold
3460	輪 circle, ring; loop	3510	宣言(する) declaration; declare		
3462	男達 men			3565	移転(する) move; move
3463	地名 place name	3511	直後 immediately after, just after	3566	動機 motive
3464	合意(する) mutual agreement; agree			3568	ネットワーク network

#	Word	Meaning
3569	自立（する）	independence; be independent
3570	ハムスター	hamster
3574	二十五	twenty-five
3576	確率	probability
3577	ペース	pace
3578	大統領	President
3580	欠点	fault, defect; drawback, weak point
3582	千葉	Chiba
3585	ブランド	brand
3586	学問	study, learning
3587	共同	cooperation; common
3590	十九	nineteen
3591	神奈川県	Kanagawa Prefecture
3592	二十二	twenty-two
3596	窓口	window, counter
3597	収穫（する）	harvest; harvest
3598	バラ	rose
3599	血管	blood vessel
3600	方言	dialect
3601	時間帯	time (period), time zone
3604	抽選（する）	lottery; draw lots
3605	手法	technique, method
3606	肉体	body
3609	一口	bite, sip, mouthful
3610	協議（する）	consultation, discussion; consult, discuss
3611	重要性	importance
3612	発酵（する）	fermentation; ferment
3613	繰り返し	repetition
3614	入札（する）	bid, tender; bid, tender
3616	ベスト	best; vest
3617	羽根	wing; feather
3620	次回	next time
3621	基盤	base, basis
3622	丸	circle, ring
3623	感染（する）	infection; contract, catch, be infected
3624	尊重（する）	respect; give something serious consideration
3625	オフィス	office
3626	否	no
3627	素人	amateur, beginner
3628	十七歳	seventeen years old
3629	一環	part of
3630	洗濯（する）	washing; wash
3633	観光客	tourist
3636	外側	outside
3638	この間	a few days ago; recently, lately
3640	手元	at hand, with one
3641	食	meal, diet
3642	ため息	sigh
3644	お仕舞い	end, be all up with
3645	修正（する）	revision; revise
3647	インタビュー（する）	interview; interview
3648	同級生	schoolmate
3650	重さ	weight
3651	町作り	town development
3652	削減（する）	cut, reduction; cut, slash
3653	顧客	customer
3654	爆発（する）	explosion; explode
3655	スイス	Switzerland
3657	軍隊	army, troops
3658	そいつ	that guy
3660	決心（する）	resolution; decide
3661	所得	income
3663	リーダー	leader
3664	調理（する）	cooking; cook
3665	地区	area
3666	家具	furniture
3667	自治体	municipality
3668	剣	sword
3669	介護保険	nursing care insurance
3670	キス（する）	kiss; kiss
3671	不況	recession
3672	松	pine
3673	停止（する）	stop, suspension; stop, suspend
3674	古代	ancient times
3675	四十	forty
3676	シリーズ	series
3677	食生活	eating habits
3679	デビュー（する）	debut; make one's debut
3681	四十年	forty years
3683	予備校	cram school preparing for university entrance examinations
3685	統一（する）	unity; unify
3686	寿命	life expectancy
3688	幕府	shogunate
3689	苦しみ	suffering, agony
3690	要件	important matter; requirement
3691	図表	chart
3693	反対側	opposite side
3694	プロジェクト	project
3697	辞書	dictionary
3698	中国語	Chinese language
3700	カラス	crow
3701	問い	question
3703	DVD	DVD
3704	発明（する）	invention; invent
3705	大学時代	college days, university days
3707	披露宴	wedding reception
3708	気候	climate
3709	非難（する）	criticism; criticize
3711	作者	author
3712	助け	help, assistance
3714	関東	Kanto region
3717	スケジュール	schedule
3719	外部	outside
3720	ネズミ	rat; mouse
3721	ニーズ	needs
3722	現金	cash
3723	彼女達	they (female)
3724	故郷	home town
3725	畳	tatami mat
3728	福祉	welfare
3729	上下	up and down
3730	汚れ	dirt
3732	栽培（する）	cultivation; cultivate
3733	視野	perspective, view
3734	隅	corner
3735	保障（する）	guarantee; guarantee
3736	三十代	thirties
3737	バック（する）	back, background; reverse, back
3738	一斉	all at once

#	Word	Meaning
3739	お盆	Bon Festival, Obon
3740	審査(する)	examination; examine
3741	ゆとり	have something to spare
3743	福岡	Fukuoka
3744	通勤(する)	commute; commute
3745	準用(する)	apply mutatis mutandis, with necessary modification
3746	右側	right side
3747	推測(する)	assumption, guess; guess, presume
3748	ライン	line
3750	美術館	art gallery, museum of art
3751	二個	two (pieces, things)
3753	仏教	Buddhism
3754	接触(する)	touch, contact; touch
3755	意欲	will, motivation
3756	本音	true feeling; truth
3757	二種類	two kinds
3758	主役	main character
3759	次男	second son
3764	スーツ	suit
3765	形式	form
3766	ピンク	pink
3767	七年	seven years
3768	生きがい	pupose in life, something to live for
3770	結成(する)	formation; form, organize
3771	研究者	researcher
3773	信号	traffic light, signal
3774	就職活動(する)	job-hunting; look for a job
3775	捜査(する)	criminal investigation; investigate
3777	黒人	black person
3778	事柄	matter, issue
3779	早く	early, soon
3780	速度	speed
3781	奥様	wife (honorific)
3783	じゃが芋	potato
3787	ミュージカル	musical
3789	友	friend
3791	鉛筆	pencil
3792	判決(する)	decision; decide
3793	マラソン	marathon
3794	広さ	area; width; extent
3795	リスト	list
3797	二歳	two years old
3798	関与(する)	participation; participate
3800	二十人	twenty people
3801	タオル	towel
3802	一泊	one night stay
3803	ごちそう(する)	feast; give a dinner, treat
3805	運転手	driver
3806	各種	various, all sorts of
3807	録音(する)	record; record
3808	沈黙(する)	silence; be silent
3811	熊	bear
3812	八王子	Hachioji (place name)
3814	林	grove, forest, wood
3815	懸念(する)	fear; fear
3817	枠	frame
3818	児童	pupil
3821	定年(する)	retirement; retire
3822	育児(する)	childcare; take care of a child
3824	蜂蜜	honey
3826	完了(する)	complete; complete
3827	二十三	twenty-three
3828	通訳	interpreter
3829	飼い主	pet owner
3830	傍ら	side, besides
3831	宣伝(する)	advertisement; advertise
3832	室内	indoor
3833	会員	member
3834	思考(する)	thought; think
3835	衣装	costume
3837	シャツ	shirt
3838	イラク	Iraq
3841	前年度	preceding year
3842	新郎	groom, bridegroom
3843	幹部	executive
3844	シェア(する)	share; share
3845	ガソリン	gasoline, petrol
3846	記念(する)	commemoration; commemorate
3848	俳句	haiku (Japanese poem of seventeen syllables)
3849	特色	characteristic, feature
3850	引退(する)	retirement; retire
3851	飲み物	drink
3853	部	division, department, section; club
3854	オランダ	Netherlands
3859	左側	left, left side
3860	浮気	affair
3861	デート(する)	date; date
3862	抑制(する)	control, restraint; control, restrain
3863	好奇心	curiosity
3864	公務員	civil servant, government employee
3865	列	line
3866	ソファー	sofa
3867	初日	first day
3868	プロセス	process
3869	郊外	suburb
3870	六十	sixty
3872	自衛隊	Self-Defense Forces
3874	国連	United Nations
3876	町並み	street, row of town houses
3877	推定(する)	presumption, estimation; presume, estimate
3879	文部省	Ministry of Education, Culture, Sports
3881	例外	exception
3882	プロ野球	professional baseball
3883	二枚	two (sheets)
3885	変わり	change
3886	用事	business
3887	効率	efficiency
3888	クリア(する)	clearing, clearance; clear; clear
3890	財布	wallet
3892	直面(する)	confrontation; confront, face
3893	己	oneself (first person pronoun)
3894	目安	standard, criterion
3897	休憩(する)	rest, break; take a rest
3898	一日中	all day
3899	有無	existence, presence

#	Word	Meaning
3900	HP	home page
3902	猿	monkey
3903	従事(する)	engagement in; be engaged in
3904	蓄積(する)	storage, accumulation; store, accumulate
3906	年賀状	New Year's card
3907	バブル	bubble
3908	毎朝	every morning; every morning
3910	文学	literature
3911	Tシャツ	T-shirt
3915	四回	four times
3916	マーク	mark
3917	アルコール	alcohol
3918	優しさ	kindness
3921	脂肪	fat
3923	青	blue
3924	キーワード	keyword
3925	ベランダ	porch, balcony
3926	炎	flame
3927	交付(する)	issue; issue, grant
3928	証言(する)	evidence; give testimony
3931	解明(する)	clarification; solve
3932	方式	method
3933	瓶	bottle
3936	実情	case, actual situation
3937	円	yen; circle
3938	化粧(する)	makeup; put on makeup
3939	二十四	twenty-four
3940	数々	many, numerous
3941	持参(する)	bringing, taking; bring, take
3942	引用(する)	quotation; quote
3943	同期	same period, same class
3945	西洋	the West
3946	プレッシャー	pressure
3947	赤ん坊	baby
3948	打ち合わせ	meeting
3949	欲望	desire, passion
3950	軍	army
3951	パス(する)	pass; pass
3952	頼り	support, dependence
3953	扱い	treatment
3954	本質	nature, essence
3955	市役所	city hall
3956	車両	car, carriage
3957	株価	stock prices
3958	昼食	lunch
3959	注射	injection
3961	職	job, work
3962	見た目	appearance, looks
3963	アピール(する)	appeal; appeal
3964	三分の一	one-third
3966	豚	pig
3967	資本	capital
3968	思いやり	consideration
3969	見通し	prospect, outlook
3970	十二年	twelve years
3972	砂漠	desert
3973	エレベーター	elevator
3975	カバー	cover
3976	交代(する)	change, shift; take turns
3977	資源	resource
3980	餃子	Chinese dumpling
3981	食堂	cafeteria, dining room
3983	締結(する)	conclusion; conclude
3984	裸	naked, nude
3987	収集(する)	collection; collect
3988	記者	journalist, reporter
3989	脱出(する)	escape; escape, break out
3991	主流	mainstream
3993	事務	office work
3995	国々	countries
3996	地球上	on the earth
3997	大企業	big business
4001	上達(する)	improvement; improve, progress
4002	故郷	hometown
4003	行使	exercise
4004	表明(する)	expression, manifestation; express, manifest
4005	体育	physical education, gymnastics
4006	読書	reading
4007	都	capital
4009	通用(する)	currency; accept, obtain
4010	支障	obstacle
4011	カウンター	counter
4013	大家さん	landlord, owner
4014	昨夜	last night
4015	角	corner
4017	三日間	three days
4019	金利	interest
4021	仮定(する)	assumption, supposition; assume, suppose
4024	依存(する)	dependence, reliance; depend, rely
4025	様	Mr., Mrs., Miss., Ms.
4026	同居(する)	coexistence, living together; live together, live with
4027	スカート	skirt
4028	柄	pattern, character
4029	回数	frequency
4030	ユーザー	user
4031	筆者	writer, author
4032	筆	brush
4033	制約(する)	restriction, constraint; restrict, constrain
4034	絵本	picture book
4035	町中	downtown
4036	著者	author, writer
4037	芽	bud, shoot
4038	担当者	person in charge
4039	嵐	storm
4040	厚生省	Ministry of Welfare
4041	豆	bean, pea
4042	損	loss, damage
4044	保育園	nursery school, day care
4045	ポスト	post, postbox, mailbox
4047	余談	digression
4049	水道	water supply
4050	人形	doll
4051	狙い	aim, target
3401	平等	equality; equal
4052	決断(する)	decision; decide
4053	大切さ	importance
4054	よそ	other, elsewhere
4055	蚊	mosquito

#	Japanese	English
4056	監視(する)	observation; watch
4057	同年	same year
4061	ゴール	goal
4062	三本	three (long/cylindrical objects)
4063	棚	shelf
4064	しっぽ	tail
4065	虐待(する)	abuse; abuse
4068	配布(する)	distribution; distribute
4072	違和感	uncomfortable feeling
4073	ジャズ	jazz
4075	向き	direction, aspect; suitable
4076	五年間	five years
4077	安全性	safety, security
4078	国境	border
4079	包丁	kitchen knife
4080	キー	key
4083	地獄	hell
4085	救急車	ambulance
4086	十年間	ten years
4087	不動産	real estate, property
4089	外出(する)	going out, outing; go out
4090	グラス	glass
4092	屋敷	mansion, residence, estate
4096	スキー場	ski ground, ski resort
4097	ヒント	hint, clue
4098	講義	lecture
4100	余地	room, space
4102	手書き	handwriting
4103	ブーム	boom
4104	ワールドカップ	World Cup
4105	鬼	ogre, devil, demon
4106	ホール	hall
4108	節約(する)	saving, economy; save, economize on
4109	実績	achievement
4111	奴ら	fellow
4112	キッチン	kitchen
4116	手足	limb
4117	物価	prices
4118	部品	parts, components
4120	宿題	homework
4121	氏名	name
4122	ダンス	dancing
4124	人種	race
4125	歌手	singer
4126	銀	silver
4127	ルート	route
4128	第一号	first
4129	従兄弟	cousin
4131	往復	round trip
4132	起源	origin
4133	広場	square, plaza
4134	レモン	lemon
4137	TV	television
4138	カップル	couple
4139	納豆	fermented soybeans
4141	肝臓	liver
4143	電源	power supply
4144	分割(する)	division; divide
4145	縮小(する)	reduction; reduce
4148	職人	craftsman, workman
4149	十三年	thirteen years
4150	キャラクター	character
4151	大地	earth, ground
4152	具	ingredient
4154	寂しさ	loneliness
4156	カーテン	curtain
4158	飯	rice
4159	幼児	infant
4160	法案	bill
4161	病	illness, disease
4162	切符	ticket
4163	消滅(する)	disappearance; disappear
4164	障害者	disabled person, handicapped person
4165	台	stand, rack
4166	面白さ	interest, fun
4167	生まれ	birth; birthplace
4168	保有(する)	possession; hold, possess
4169	反発(する)	repulsion, resistance; react, resist, rebel, repel
4170	アレンジ(する)	arrangement; arrange
4171	しつけ	tacking (sewing); discipline
4172	指導者	leader, coach
4173	原理	principle
4174	東南アジア	Southeast Asia
4175	ID	identification, ID
4176	金属	metal
4177	しわ	wrinkle, line
4179	一分	one minute
4180	当面	present, current; for the time being
4181	貯金	savings, deposit
4183	四歳	four years old
4184	ダンボール	cardboard
4185	生クリーム	fresh cream
4187	金曜日	Friday
4189	演技	performance
4191	体質	constitution (physical)
4192	ドイツ語	German language
4194	参加者	participant
4195	第三者	outsider, third party
4196	感性	sensitivity, sensibility
4197	谷	valley; ravine, gorge
4198	本社	head office
4199	都度	every time
4201	死者	dead
4202	四季	four seasons
4203	倒産(する)	bankruptcy; go bankrupt
4204	ニュージーランド	New Zealand
4205	センター	center
4206	保全(する)	preservation, maintenance; preserve, maintain
4207	結合(する)	combination; combine, join
4208	発送(する)	send, ship, dispatch
4209	パンツ	pants, shorts, underpants
4211	ナンバー	number
4212	持ち主	owner
4214	夕日	evening sun, sunset
4216	リストラ	restructuring, downsizing
4217	答弁	answer, defense
4218	哲学	philosophy
4220	当事者	parties concerned
4221	シーズン	season
4222	品	goods, article
4223	高速道路	freeway

#	Word	Meaning
4224	一員	member
4225	確定(する)	determination, decision; determine, decide
4226	委員会	committee
4230	分布(する)	distribution; distribute
4231	観客	audience
4232	鮎	sweetfish, ayu
4233	正午	noon, midday
4234	首都	capital city
4235	体内	inside the body
4236	調和(する)	harmony, balance; harmonize, match
4237	権威	authority
4238	シンガポール	Singapore
4240	最低限	minimum
4242	カボチャ	pumpkin
4243	老後	old age
4245	害	harm, damage
4246	稽古(する)	practice, exercise; practice
4247	一位	first prize
4249	前者	former
4250	数人	several people
4251	創造(する)	creation; create
4252	届け出	report, notification
4253	荻窪	Ogikubo (place name)
4254	スイッチ	switch
4255	試み	attempt, try
4259	麺	noodles
4261	原点	starting point, origin
4264	ジュース	juice
4265	軽減(する)	reduction; reduce
4266	不自由	inconvenience; disability
4267	悲鳴	scream
4268	落札者	successful bidder
4269	融資(する)	loan; loan, lend
4270	破綻(する)	bankruptcy, collapse; fail, go bankrupt
4271	二千八年	2008 (year)
4272	アドレス	address
4274	双方	both sides, both parties
4275	原爆	atomic bomb
4276	傘	umbrella
4277	チャレンジ	challenge
4278	炭	charcoal
4279	不意	sudden, unexpected; suddenness
4280	リサイクル(する)	recycling; recycle
4281	ミルク	milk
4282	子孫	descendant; posterity
4283	近頃	recently, lately
4284	鞄	bag
4285	五千円	five thousand yen
4286	圧力	pressure, stress
4287	斜め	diagonal
4288	補助(する)	help, aid, assistance; help, aid, assist
4289	改良	improvement
4290	俳優	actor
4291	フィリピン	Philippines
4293	情熱	passion
4294	七人	seven people
4295	焦点	focus
4296	旅館	inn, Japanese-style hotel
4297	食卓	dining table
4299	悲劇	tragedy
4300	長女	eldest daughter
4301	議会	Diet, Parliament, Congress
4302	侵入(する)	invasion; break into, invade
4306	笑み	smile
4307	三度	three times
4309	案	plan, proposal, idea
4310	心理	psychology
4312	おしゃべり(する)	chat, talk; chat, talk
4314	復帰(する)	return, comeback; return, come back, make a comeback
4315	衝突(する)	collision; collide, clash
4318	ドライブ	drive
4319	テキスト	textbook
4320	変動(する)	change, fluctuation, movement; change, fluctuate
4322	木々	trees
4323	ヒット	hit
4324	箸	chopsticks
4325	食欲	appetite
4326	語	word; language
4327	通信	correspondence, communication
4328	一家	family, house, household
4330	二十一年	twenty-one years
4331	専業主婦	housewife
4332	滝	waterfall
4334	身分	position, status
4335	敷地	site, ground
4337	ブルー	blue
4338	先進国	developed country
4339	バナナ	banana
4340	取り扱い	treatment, handling
4341	フィルム	film
4342	日本酒	sake, Japanese rice wine
4343	WWW	World Wide Web
4346	克服(する)	conquest; conquer, overcome
4347	専門学校	technical school, college, vocational school
4348	六十歳	sixty years old
4349	朝日	rising sun, morning sun
4350	スタジオ	studio
4351	長期	long term
4352	美人	beautiful woman, beauty
4353	筆記用具	stationery, writing materials
4354	石油	oil
4355	早朝	early morning
4356	店内	inside a shop
4357	賃金	salary, wage
4359	日程	schedule, itinerary
4360	応用(する)	application; apply
4361	真っ暗	black; pitch-dark
4362	眉	eyebrow
4363	レンズ	lens
4364	五回	five times
4365	俗	common, popular
4366	パスタ	pasta
4368	性能	performance, capability
4369	絵画	painting, picture
4370	刀	sword

#	Japanese	English
4371	理念	philosophy
4372	裁判官	judge
4373	戦略	strategy
4374	核	nucleus, core
4375	農民	farmer
4376	コンクリート	concrete
4377	環境問題	environmental problem
4378	ライター	lighter
4379	手入れ	repair, maintenance
4380	判定（する）	decision, judgment; decide, judge
4382	日曜	Sunday
4383	昨今	nowadays
4384	対話（する）	dialogue, conversation; converse, discuss
4385	帯	kimono sash, belt
4386	お好み焼き	okonomiyaki (Japanese-style savoury pancake with vegetables, meat, seafood etc.)
4387	羊	sheep
4388	前半	first half
4389	ショー	show
4390	研究所	research institute, laboratory
4391	生姜	ginger
4392	冒頭	beginning
4393	メジャー	measure
4394	公演	performance
4395	剣道	kendo
4396	倉庫	warehouse, storehouse
4397	浴衣	yukata, cotton kimono
4398	直径	diameter
4399	残業	overtime work
4400	殺人	murder
4401	判明（する）	proving; turn out, identify
4402	統合（する）	integration; integrate, combine
4403	水気	moisture
4405	原料	raw material, ingredient
4406	群れ	group; herd
4407	新婦	bride
4408	持ち物	personal belongings
4411	二匹	two (animals)
4412	天候	weather
4413	危険性	danger
4414	創設（する）	foundation, creation; found, create
4415	年末	end of the year
4416	感	feeling, emotion
4417	イコール	equal
4419	響き	sound; echo
4420	六ヶ月	six months
4421	プラン	plan
4422	グラウンド	ground, playground, sports field
4423	メキシコ	Mexico
4424	バー	bar
4425	カップ	cup
4426	訴訟	suit, action
4427	流通（する）	circulation, distribution; circulate, distribute
4428	郵送	mail, post
3716	不明	unknown, unidentified
4430	赤字	deficit, loss, the red
4431	二位	second place
4432	刃物	cutlery, edged tool, knife
4433	苦情	complaint
4434	入社（する）	entry to a company; enter a company, get a job
4435	役所	government office
4436	三百円	three hundred yen
4437	チラシ	flyer, leaflet, handout
4438	成人（する）	adult; come of age
4439	工具	tool
4440	先週	last week
4441	境	boundary, border
4442	国語	Japanese language
4443	三十人	thirty people
4444	兵士	soldier
4445	芸能人	entertainer
4448	日付け	date, day
4449	相違	difference, disagreement
4451	無意識	unconsciousness; unconscious
4452	友人達	friends
4453	債務者	debtor
4454	四ヶ月	four months
4455	始末（する）	disposal, circumstances; manage, deal with, dispose of
4456	合間	interval, pause, spare moment
4457	副作用	side effect
4458	成分	ingredient, constituent, component
4459	初	first
4460	ドライバー	driver
4461	渋滞（する）	traffic jam, delay; be delayed
4462	遠慮（する）	reserve; hesitate
4463	印	mark, tick, check
4464	今週	this week
4467	開設（する）	establishment; establish, set up
4468	アニメ	animation
4470	勢力	power, influence, strength
4471	梅	plum, Japanese apricot
4472	霊	spirit, soul
4473	予感（する）	presentiment, foreboding, hunch; have a presentiment/ foreboding/hunch
4474	学者	scholar
4475	車椅子	wheelchair
4476	月曜日	Monday
4477	北京	Beijing
4478	論理	logic
4480	四十分	forty minutes
4481	歩道	sidewalk, pavement
4482	二千	two thousand
4484	九年	nine years
4486	報告書	report
4488	壺	pot, vase
4489	講座	course, lecture
4490	レシピ	recipe
4491	行列（する）	procession, line, parade; line up, queue
4492	計上（する）	appropriation; appropriate
4493	受診（する）	(medical) consultation; consult, have a medical examination
4494	指揮（する）	direction, command; conduct, direct

#	Word	Meaning
4495	保管(する)	keeping, storage; keep
4496	パートナー	partner
4497	発足(する)	start; start
4498	火事	fire
4499	中世	Middle Ages, medieval
4500	考察(する)	consideration, examination; consider, examine
4501	祝い	celebration
4504	認可(する)	permission, approval; permit, approve
4507	条約	treaty, agreement
4508	像	figure, statue
4509	マッチ(する)	match; match
4510	二千円	two thousand yen
4511	キャベツ	cabbage
4512	デザート	dessert
4513	議員	member of Diet/Congress/Parliament
4514	審議(する)	discussion, deliberation; discuss, deliberate
4516	性	sex, gender
4517	仕草	behavior, gesture
4518	マスター(する)	master; master
4519	泡	bubble, foam
4520	年配	elderly person
4522	挙げ句	in the end, finally
4524	弟子	pupil, disciple
4525	分解(する)	analysis; resolve, dismantle, take apart, analyze
4526	一発	shot, punch
4528	調達(する)	supply, procurement; supply, procure
4529	二十六	twenty-six
4530	制服	uniform
4531	オーブン	oven
4532	パンフレット	brochure
4533	賞	prize, award
4534	白人	white person
4536	先頭	head, lead
4539	公共	public, common
4540	貴族	noble, nobility, aristocracy
4542	路地	alley, lane
4543	緑色	green
4545	繁栄(する)	prosperity; prosper, flourish
4546	銃	gun
4551	果て	the end
4552	霧	fog
4553	主催(する)	promotion, organizing; host, promote, organize
4554	選択肢	choices, alternatives
4557	表	front; outside, surface
4558	錯覚(する)	illusion, delusion, trick; have the illusion/impression
4559	乗り物	vehicle; (amusement park) ride
4560	スパゲッティー	spaghetti
4561	隣接(する)	adjacent, adjoin, next to; be adjacent, adjoin, be next to
4562	二千三年	2003 (year)
4564	テクニック	technique
4565	ステップ	step
4566	任務	duty, task, mission, role
4567	小川	stream
4568	ロープ	rope
4569	到達(する)	arrival; reach
4570	イエス	yes; Jesus (Christ)
4571	上海	Shanghai
4574	ファッション	fashion
4575	緊張感	tension
4576	容器	container, vessel
4577	サポート(する)	support; support
4580	東北	Northeast, Tohoku region
4582	サラダ	salad
4583	注意点	important point
4584	DNA	DNA, deoxyribonucleic acid
4585	米軍	US armed forces
4586	デメリット	disadvantage
4587	国道	national highway
4588	浸透(する)	soaking, penetration; soak, penetrate
4589	合図(する)	signal, sign; signal, sign
4590	フェリー	ferry
4591	貿易	trade, commerce
4592	照明	lighting
4593	招待(する)	invitation; invite
4595	十一年	eleven years
4596	武士	warrior, samurai
4598	対抗(する)	competition, rivalry; oppose, rival
4599	者達	people
4600	警察官	police officer
4602	最新	newest, latest
4603	他者	another person, others
4604	挿入(する)	insertion; insert
4607	こだわり	concern, obsession
4579	まし	better; increase
4609	キリスト	Christ
4610	辛さ	pain
4611	二三日	two or three days
4612	講演	lecture, talk
4614	人権	human rights
4615	両側	both sides
4616	餅	rice cake
4617	鎌倉	Kamakura
4618	運動会	sports meeting
4619	州	state
4620	分離(する)	separation, detachment; separate, detach
4622	掲示板	bulletin board, noticeboard
4623	住宅地	residential area
4624	亀	turtle, tortoise
4625	四十代	forties
4626	メロディー	melody
4627	民衆	people, public
4628	吉祥寺	Kichijoji (place name)
4630	新潟	Niigata
4631	箇所	place, point, part
4632	正解(する)	correct answer; answer correctly
4635	体育館	gym
4636	再会(する)	reunion; meet again
4637	儀式	ceremony, ritual
4639	店舗	store, shop
4641	日本一	most ... in Japan
4642	トンネル	tunnel
4643	一歳	one year old
4644	暑さ	heat

#	Word	Meaning
4645	ビタミン	vitamin
4647	用途	use
4648	進学(する)	going on to the next level of education; go on to the next level of education
4649	タイヤ	tire
4650	朝鮮	Korea
4651	三味線	shamisen
4652	保険会社	insurance company
4654	チョコレート	chocolate
4657	仕掛け	device, system
4658	ポスター	poster
4659	杉	Japanese cedar
4661	彫刻	sculpture, carving
4662	眠り	sleep
4663	見込み	hope, chance, expectation
4665	就任(する)	assumption; assume
4666	先端	tip, point, forefront
4667	装置(する)	device, equipment; be equipped with
4668	伝説	legend, tradition
4669	今頃	this time
4670	学部	faculty, department
4671	水泳	swimming
4672	羽目	plight, predicament
4673	上京(する)	coming/going to Tokyo; come/go to Tokyo
4674	ビザ	visa
4675	将軍	general, shogun
4676	青少年	young people, juvenile
4677	肘	elbow
4679	食器	dish
4681	深さ	depth
4683	パスポート	passport
4685	いつ頃	around what time
4686	二重	double
4687	埼玉	Saitama
4688	いたずら(する)	mischief, trick, joke; be mischievous, play a trick
4694	居酒屋	(Japanese style) bar, tavern
4696	一貫	consistent
4697	文献	literature
4699	ワープロ	word processor
4700	象	elephant
4701	共感(する)	sympathy; sympathize
4702	ズボン	pants, trousers
4704	豆腐	tofu, bean curd
4705	司会(する)	host, emcee; host, emcee, take the chair
4706	幸運	(good) luck, fortune; lucky, fortunate
4707	緩和(する)	relaxation, relief; relieve
4708	鉄板	hot plate, iron plate
4710	反論(する)	argument, objection; argue, object
4713	久々	for the first time in a long time
4714	効力	effect
4716	絆	tie, bond
4717	相性	compatibility
4718	三分	three minutes
4719	砂浜	beach, sand
4721	参加費	participation fee
4722	井戸	well
4723	五十代	fifties
4724	債務	debt, obligation
4725	寄与(する)	contribution; contribute
4726	社宅	company housing
4727	下記	the following, mentioned below
4728	委員長	chairperson
4729	槍	spear
4731	店員	clerk, sales assistant
4732	秩序	order, system
4734	刺し身	sashimi
4735	おかず	food, side dish
4736	豚肉	pork
4737	兵	soldier, troops
4738	部長	head of department, manager
4739	サミット	summit
4740	三十歳	thirty years old
4741	二倍	twice, double
4742	ベンチ	bench
4744	投入(する)	investment; throw, invest
4745	争い	fight, struggle, competition
4746	センス	sense
4749	線路	track, railroad
4750	四年間	four years
4751	リンク(する)	link; link
4752	大蔵省	Ministry of Finance
4753	製作(する)	production; manufacture
4754	世帯	household, family
4756	区分(する)	division, classification; separate
4757	放棄(する)	abandonment, renunciation; abandon, renounce
4758	転職(する)	change of job; change job
4759	類い	kind, sort, type
4760	活気	vigor, energy, liveliness
4761	日差し	sunshine
4762	人格	character, personality
4763	避難(する)	evacuation; evacuate
4764	ラスベガス	Las Vegas
4765	鐘	bell, chime
4766	若者達	young people
4767	集まり	meeting, gathering, group
4768	変換(する)	change, conversion; convert
4769	歓迎(する)	reception, welcome; welcome
4770	川崎	Kawasaki
4771	支出	expenses, payment, expenditure, spending
4772	軸	axis; shaft; stem
4773	食物	food, dish
4774	損害	damage, loss
4776	正義	justice, right
4777	一目	glance
4778	百年	hundred years, century
4779	ガイド(する)	guide, conductor; guide
4780	大型	big, large
4781	頂上	top, summit
4782	睡眠	sleep
4784	相互	mutual, each other
4785	二十七	twenty-seven

4786	披露(する) announcement, introduction; announce, introduce	4844	タレント celebrity, entertainer	4891	契機 momentum; opportunity, chance
4787	OB OB (old boy), alumnus	4847	牛肉 beef	4892	一軒 one building
4789	上位 higher rank	4848	枠組み frame, framework	4893	紛争 dispute, trouble, strife
4790	リード(する) lead; take a lead	4850	七十 seventy	4894	魔法 magic
4791	心身 mind and body	4851	多様化(する) diversification; diversify	4895	影響力 influence, impact
4792	債権者 creditor	4853	インストール(する) installation; install	4896	触れ合い touching, contact
4793	燃料 fuel	4854	二年目 second year	4898	私立 private
4794	ショップ shop	4855	機構 mechanism, structure, system	4899	明記(する) writing clearly; write clearly
4795	長官 director general	4857	世田谷 Setagaya (place name)	4900	塩分 salt
4797	シート seat; sheet	4858	里 village, countryside, one's parents' home	4902	顔色 complexion
4799	プライド pride	4859	決まり regulation; arrangement, settlement	4905	埃 dust
4800	題名 title	4860	独身 single, unmarried	4906	既存 existing
4801	問い合わせ inquiry	4861	十八歳 eighteen years old	4907	網 net
4802	葱 leek	4862	高齢化(する) aging; increase in age	4909	刑事 police detective
4804	業績 achievements	4864	エアコン air-conditioning, air conditioner	4910	ボーリング bowling
4805	起動(する) starting; start	4865	期限 period; deadline; term	4911	感触 feel, touch
4806	学年 grade, year	4866	物件 article, object; property	4913	人柄 personality
4807	助成(する) subsidy; subsidize	4867	前条 preceding article	4914	各々 each
4808	天下 the whole world	4868	中間 middle, halfway	4915	職務 duty
4812	千九百九十九年 1999 (year)	4869	カラー color	4916	URL URL, Uniform Resource Locator
4813	庶民 common people, ordinary people, masses	4870	スポーツクラブ sports club, gym	4917	出し soup stock
4814	千九百九十年 1990 (year)	4871	群馬県 Gunma Prefecture	4918	六十年 sixty years
4818	住居 house	4872	フルーツ fruit	4920	執行(する) execution, enforcement; carry out, enforce
4819	沸騰(する) boiling; boil	4873	グラフ graph	4921	分量 quantity, amount
4821	一年半 one year and a half	4874	画家 artist, painter	4922	大概 generally
4826	譲渡(する) transfer; transfer, hand over	4876	マイク microphone	4924	味わい profound, thought-provoking
4828	挫折(する) setback; fail	4880	調節(する) adjustment; adjust	4926	はたち twenty years old
4829	きゅうり cucumber	4881	回避(する) avoidance; avoid	4927	一周 one round
4830	検証(する) verification; verify	4883	書物 book	4929	髭 mustache
4831	株主 stockholder, shareholder	4884	隙 space, room, gap	4930	支度(する) preparations; prepare
4834	マッサージ(する) massage; massage	4885	範囲内 in range, within the limits	4933	受賞(する) winning a prize; win (receive) a prize, be awarded a prize
4835	二度目 second time	4886	遊園地 amusement park	4934	国鉄 national railway
4836	年上 older, senior	4887	六つ six	4937	倍 times
4838	ピーク peak	4888	二十歳 twenty years old	4939	業種 category of business, type of industry
4839	みじん切り minced, cut into fine pieces, chopped	4889	偏見 prejudice, bias	4940	汽車 train
4841	禁煙(する) no-smoking; stop smoking	4890	理屈 reason, logic, theory	4941	うどん udon, thick white noodles
4842	厚さ thickness			4942	五歳 five years old
4843	十代 teen years, teens			4944	日中 during the day

4945 作曲(する) musical composition; compose	4992 三千円 three thousand yen	2711 あちら that way; that place, there; that
4947 居間 living room	4993 来週 next week	2854 どなた who
4948 心境 state of mind	4995 略 omission, abbreviation	2941 あいつ that fellow; that thing
4949 住宅街 housing; residential area	4998 一段 one step	2948 こいつ this fellow; this thing
4950 無言 silence, in silence, without speaking	4999 動揺(する) unrest; be agitated	3268 あちこち here and there, everywhere
4951 調味料 seasoning, spice	**Pronoun: 43 words**	4404 我ら we
4952 一回目 first time	40 何 what; something; anything; nothing	4597 そりゃ that is
4953 何時間 how many hours	42 私 I	4788 この方 this person
4954 みそ miso; key point	44 それ that	
4955 花粉 pollen	51 これ this	**Verbs: 1489 words**
4956 抗議(する) protest, objection; object	103 そこ there; then	19 言う say, speak, talk
4958 数日 few days	141 ここ here	22 する do; make
4959 信念 belief, faith	156 僕 I (used by male speakers)	25 ある be (existence), have (possession), happen, occur
4960 イスラエル Israel	158 彼 he	28 なる become, get; come to do, start to do; turn into
4961 遅く late	174 いつ when	
4963 プラスチック plastic	181 どこ where	34 思う think, believe; feel; expect
4965 塔 tower	217 誰 who, whose, whom	
4966 家 house, home	226 あなた, あんた you	48 行く go; come
4967 六年生 sixth grade, sixth year	244 彼女 she; girlfriend	64 来る come
4968 手話 sign language	287 私達 we	67 見る see; look at, watch; check
4970 研究開発 research and development	313 あれ that	
	329 こちら this place, here; this way; this	77 やる do; make; give
4972 民法 civil law		79 いる be, exist; stay
4973 返済(する) repayment; repay	363 俺 I (used by male speakers)	80 できる be ready
4975 なじみ familiarity	458 彼ら they	98 持つ have, take, hold
4976 二十九 twenty-nine	491 これら these	99 出る go out, come out; attend
4977 地形 topography, landform	524 どちら where; which; who	
4978 本能 instinct	527 我々 we	102 考える think
4979 解除(する) cancellation; cancel, lift	616 いずれ anyway, sooner or later; either	105 分かる understand, see
		109 入る enter, come in, go in
4980 放出(する) emission; emit	663 どれ which	110 作る make, create, cook
4982 悪魔 devil, demon	893 そちら your place; there; you	112 聞く, 聴く hear; listen; listen to, obey
4983 ハム ham		
4984 診察(する) medical examination, consultation; examine	1032 それら those, these, they	119 使う use, handle
	1292 何々 such and such, this and that	132 取る take, get; have; pass
	1320 あそこ there, over there	134 知る know
4985 二日目 second day	1438 私共 we	146 行なう do, carry out, hold
4986 柿 persimmon	1803 僕ら we	152 仕事(する) work, job; work
4987 給付(する) provision; provide	1969 こっち here; this; I; we	160 食べる eat
	2234 我 I; oneself	163 書く write
4988 署名(する) signature; sign	2310 あちらこちら here and there	164 入れる put in; include
4989 詩人 poet	2408 僕達 we (used by male speakers)	176 付く stick; be stained with
4991 示唆(する) suggestion; suggest	2543 どっち which	178 出す take out; pay; send
	2669 彼 he	182 ございます (くござる) [very polite form of "de aru"]

#	Word	Meaning
186	違う	be different; be wrong
187	受ける	get, receive, take
191	まま	as it is
195	話す	talk, tell, speak
197	返る	return
199	掛ける	hang; take; cost
200	終わる	end, finish
201	意味(する)	meaning, sense; mean
204	付ける	put; attach; apply
210	感じる	feel
212	かかる	hang; take; cost
214	住む	live
223	生活(する)	life; live
225	あげる	raise, lift
232	乗る	ride, get on, take
234	見える	see, be seen
235	変わる	change
261	読む	read
267	教える	teach, tell
276	置く	put, place; leave
281	残る	remain, be left
290	呼ぶ	call
292	歩く	walk
296	生きる	live
307	飲む	drink
311	会う	meet, see
324	電話(する)	telephone, call; phone, call
342	立つ	stand
358	覚える	learn, remember, memorize
361	続く	continue, go on, last
364	生まれる	be born
370	説明(する)	explanation; explain
380	得る	get, obtain
382	選ぶ	choose, select
384	戻る	return, go back
385	勉強(する)	study; learn, study
386	やめる	stop, give up
388	始める	start, begin
392	残す	leave
396	遊ぶ	play
401	始まる	start, begin
402	死ぬ	die
409	経験(する)	experience; experience
416	与える	give, present
417	利用(する)	use, utilization; utilize
418	働く	work
423	存在(する)	existence; exist
428	切る	cut
429	走る	run
430	待つ	wait
435	楽しむ	enjoy, have a good time
438	寝る	sleep; lie down, go to bed
440	決める	decide, fix
441	忘れる	forget
443	送る	send; spend (time)
445	なくなる	disappear; be gone
448	頑張る	do one's best
449	示す	show
462	願う	wish, ask, pray
465	向かう	face; go (toward, in the direction of)
466	連れる	take somebody, accompany
467	変える	change
468	影響(する)	influence; affect, influence
472	求める	ask for, request, demand
474	もらう	get, have, receive
477	経つ	pass, go by
482	開く	open; bloom; hold
484	続ける	continue, keep up, go on
487	当たる	hit, bump, touch; guess right, win
489	結婚(する)	marriage; marry, get married
490	認める	recognize, acknowledge, admit, approve, accept
493	増える	increase, gain
497	進む	to go forward, make progress
498	起きる	get up; wake; happen
506	質問(する)	question; question
507	含む	contain, include
513	見せる	show
518	紹介(する)	introduction; introduce
519	合わせる	join, add up; adjust
523	規定(する)	regulations, stipulations; prescribe
526	起こる	happen, occur, take place
529	立てる	stand, set up, put up
532	探す	look for, search for, seek
537	いただく	get, receive (humble)
538	売る	sell
539	変化(する)	change; change, vary
543	参加(する)	participation; take part in, participate
545	よる	be due to
546	理解(する)	understanding; understand
555	答える	answer, respond
556	過ごす	spend, live
557	上がる	go up, rise; end; get nervous
560	心配(する)	anxious, worried; anxiety, worry, care; worry, be anxious
562	イメージ(する)	image; imagine, have an impression
566	動く	move; work (machine)
568	加える	add, include
569	困る	have difficulty, be in trouble
570	取れる	come off; be removed
572	対応(する)	correspondence, response; respond to
573	比べる	compare, contrast
575	食事(する)	meal; have a meal
576	引く	pull, draw, lead; subtract
579	離れる	separate; leave; be away from
581	実施(する)	operation; enforce, conduct
584	練習(する)	practice, training; practice, train
585	使用(する)	use; use
586	越える	cross over, go over
587	図る	attempt; plan; strive
594	思い出す	remember

599	守る protect, defend; keep, obey	698	済む end, finish	807	払う pay; sweep away
601	回る spin, turn, go around; go via	699	通る pass, go along	808	つながる be connected, be related
606	調べる investigate; look up; examine; check	701	期待(する) expectation; expect	813	亡くなる die, pass away
607	のぼる go up, rise; reach	707	描く draw; describe	814	止める stop
610	向ける turn, point	708	驚く be surprised	821	触れる touch; experience
611	落ちる fall, drop	713	座る sit	822	飼う keep, have, breed
613	決まる be decided	714	定める provide; stipulate, decide	823	しゃべる talk, chat
614	起こす wake; raise; cause	718	信じる believe, trust	825	さす shine; pour; put
619	打つ hit, strike, beat	730	意識(する) consciousness, awareness; be conscious	831	開発(する) development; develop
622	確認(する) confirmation; confirm	732	行動(する) action, act; act, behave	832	殺す kill
627	通う attend, go to, commute	734	びっくり(する) surprise; be surprised, be amazed	835	暮らす live
628	申し上げる tell, say (humble)	737	現われる appear, come into sight	836	飛ぶ fly
630	述べる describe, say, state	738	聞こえる hear; sound	839	怒る get angry
634	料理(する) cooking, dish; cook	742	思える it seems that	840	整備(する) maintenance, service; prepare
638	歌う sing	746	振り返る turn one's head, look back	843	発見(する) discovery; discover
644	気付く notice, become aware	748	評価(する) evaluation; evaluate	844	相談(する) consultation; consult
646	開ける open	750	限る limit, restrict	845	連絡(する) connection, contact; contact
648	着る put on, wear	751	似る look like, resemble	846	止まる stop
651	過ぎる pass, exceed	759	下りる go down; come down	848	用意(する) preparation; prepare
652	記憶(する) memory; memorize	762	喜ぶ be glad, rejoice	851	学ぶ learn
658	笑う laugh; smile	764	迎える go to meet, invite, receive	854	設定(する) establishment; establish, set
661	旅行(する) journey, travel; travel	766	表現(する) expression; express	856	目指す aim, go toward
664	見付ける find, look for	768	注意(する) attention; notice, be careful	859	成す form, constitute
665	関わる concern, affect, be involved	773	基づく be based	860	集める gather, collect
670	伝える tell; deliver; hand down	781	乗せる take on, put on, pick up	861	失う lose
672	集まる gather, crowd	785	用いる use, adopt	863	並ぶ line, stand in line
674	流れる flow, float, pass	793	発生(する) occurrence; occur, happen	873	異なる be different
677	進める advance, move forward	794	繰り返す repeat, do over again	878	至る lead to, get
678	含める include, add	795	泣く cry	880	育てる bring up, train, develop
679	致す do (humble)	798	出かける go out, leave	883	生じる bring about, cause, arise
680	着く arrive, reach	799	努力(する) effort; make an effort	886	語る talk, tell
684	おる be, exist (humble)	800	増加(する) increase, gain; increase, grow	888	頼む ask, order
685	活動(する) activity; be active	801	判断(する) judgment; judge	889	体験(する) experience; experience, have experience of
689	いらっしゃる come, go (honorific); be (honorific)			891	広がる spread, stretch
694	研究(する) research, study; do research, study			894	勝つ win, defeat
697	合う fit, suit, agree			895	運動(する) exercise; exercise, move

896	捨てる throw away, abandon	
898	通す pass, show ... into	
900	伴う accompany, involve	
903	育つ grow up	
905	予定(する) plan, schedule; plan	
913	位置(する) position, location; be located	
914	発展(する) development; develop, expand	
918	張る stretch, put up	
924	教育(する) education; educate	
925	想像(する) imagination, image; imagine	
927	許す allow, permit, forgive	
932	借りる borrow, rent	
934	準備(する) preparation; prepare	
949	申す say, be (humble)	
950	押す push, press	
952	選択(する) selection, choice; choose	
953	負ける lose, be beaten	
957	減る decrease, become less	
960	焼く roast, bake	
962	慣れる get used to	
964	出会う meet, come across	
965	推進(する) propulsion; promote, drive	
967	作業(する) operation, work; work	
970	付き合う associate with, go out with, go along with	
974	振る wave, shake, swing	
976	表示(する) indication; display, indicate	
981	相当(する) considerable; equivalence; be equivalent; considerably, pretty;	
982	従う obey, follow	
983	検討(する) consideration, discussion examination; consider, discuss	
984	占める occupy, account for	
989	調査(する) investigation; investigate, inquire, explore	
992	発表(する) announcement, publication; announce, publish	
994	作成(する) make, create	
996	確保(する) securement, reservation; secure, maintain, guarantee	
998	運ぶ carry, transport, move	
1003	表わす show, express, symbolize	
1014	消える go off; disappear	
1019	成長(する) growth; grow	
1021	機能(する) function, capability, feature; function, work	
1027	タイプ(する) type; type	
1028	扱う deal with, handle, treat	
1029	指摘(する) designation; point out, indicate	
1031	除く remove; except; get rid of	
1038	分ける divide, distribute; classify	
1039	計画(する) project, schedule, plan; plan	
1043	感動(する) deep emotion; be impressed, be moved	
1051	利く act, work	
1052	勤める be employed, work for	
1053	吸う breathe in, sip, smoke	
1054	流す flush; pour; drain	
1055	希望(する) hope, wish, request; hope, wish, desire	
1057	勧める encourage, recommend	
1063	疲れる get tired	
1064	落とす drop, lose, turn down	
1067	まとめる summarize, settle, gather	
1069	渡る cross, go across	
1073	参る go, come, visit (humble); be in trouble, be embarrassed	
1074	反対(する) opposition, contrast, objection; oppose	
1076	提供(する) offer; supply, sponsor	
1080	知れる come out, come to light, be discovered	
1083	実現(する) realization, implementation; realize, put into practice	
1085	購入(する) buying; purchase, buy	
1090	認識(する) recognition, awareness; recognize, be aware	
1091	安心(する) peace of mind, relief; feel relieved	
1100	解決(する) solution, settlement; solve, settle	
1103	失敗(する) failure, mistake; fail	
1105	成功(する) success, achievement; succeed	
1107	協力(する) cooperation, collaboration; cooperate, collaborate	
1110	産む, 生む give birth; produce	
1111	卒業(する) graduation; graduate	
1112	降る fall, come down	
1115	報告(する) report, information, account; inform	
1116	落ち着く settle, calm down	
1117	決定(する) decision, determination; decide, determine	
1119	移動(する) movement; transfer, move, migrate	
1122	応ずる、応じる answer, respond, accept	
1126	逃げる run away, escape	
1135	くれる give	
1141	開催(する) holding, opening; hold, open	
1143	近付く approach, get closer to	
1146	届く reach, arrive	
1149	伸ばす extend, lengthen; postpone	
1155	変更(する) change, modification, revision; change, revise	

#	Word	Meaning
1156	感謝(する)	gratitude, appreciation; thank, be grateful
1158	手術(する)	surgery, operation; operate
1164	おく	at; in; on
1165	愛(する)	love, care
1168	苦労(する)	hardship, difficulty, trouble; have trouble, have a hard time
1169	押さえる	press down, hold
1172	見付かる	be found, be discovered
1174	仰る	say, tell, speak (honorific)
1175	主張(する)	argument, claim; argue, insist
1177	チェック(する)	check; check
1180	展開(する)	development; develop, unfold
1184	伸びる	grow, stretch, extend
1188	悩む	be worried, be troubled, suffer
1190	議論(する)	argument, discussion, controversy; discuss
1191	記録(する)	record, document; record, write down
1192	当てる	hit, put, expose, guess
1197	眺める	see, view, gaze
1199	設置(する)	installation; set up, place
1201	入院(する)	hospitalization, admission to hospital; hospitalize
1204	たたく	slap, hit, knock, clap
1206	会話(する)	conversation; talk, chat
1208	要る	need, want
1212	眠る	sleep
1217	通じる	lead; communicate, understand
1218	動かす	move, shift, operate
1221	避ける	avoid, keep away from
1222	お勧め(する)	recommendation, advice; recommend, advise
1225	クリック(する)	click; click
1226	捕らえる	catch, grasp, seize, arrest
1228	減少(する)	decrease, reduction; decline, decrease
1229	洗う	wash
1232	尋ねる	ask, look for
1236	買い物(する)	shopping; go shopping
1238	登場(する)	entry, appearance; appear, emerge
1245	習う	take lessons, be taught, learn
1251	拡大(する)	enlargement, expansion; enlarge, expand
1258	取り上げる	pick up, adopt; take away
1270	世話(する)	care; take care of, look after
1273	食う	eat, consume
1276	負担(する)	burden, load, charge; bear
1282	助ける	help, rescue, save
1283	詰まる	be blocked, be packed, be clogged
1286	果たす	carry out, achieve, fulfil
1287	支える	support, hold, sustain
1288	抱える	hold, carry, employ
1290	追う	follow, chase, pursue
1293	計算(する)	calculation; calculate, count, figure
1295	返す	return; repay; turn over
1297	納得(する)	agreement; understand, be convinced
1298	組織(する)	organization, structure; organize
1304	治療(する)	cure, treatment, therapy; treat, cure
1310	サービス(する)	service; attend, serve
1323	伝わる	spread, descend, travel
1324	撮影(する)	shooting; shoot, photograph
1325	指導(する)	guidance; guide, coach
1326	生かす	keep alive; make use of
1329	指定(する)	appointment; specify
1330	経営(する)	management; manage, run
1334	成立(する)	completion; establish, conclude, come into existence
1336	導入(する)	introduction; introduce
1346	泊まる	stay
1347	充実(する)	fullness; enrich, fullfill
1349	コミュニケーション(する)	communication; communicate
1350	散歩(する)	walk, stroll
1356	挨拶(する)	greeting; greet
1358	比較(する)	comparison; compare
1359	結ぶ	tie, connect, unite
1360	移る	move, transfer, shift
1363	注目(する)	attention; pay attention, watch
1364	携帯(する)	portable; carry
1365	休む	take a rest, be absent from
1373	要求(する)	demand, request, claim; demand, request, claim
1377	交ぜる	mix, shuffle
1378	抱く	have, hold, embrace
1379	出来上がる	be completed, be finished, be ready
1381	訪れる	visit, call on, arrive
1384	改善(する)	improvement, reform; improve
1386	咲く	bloom
1389	向く	turn, face, look
1393	我慢(する)	patience, endurance, tolerance; be patient, endure
1394	浮かぶ	float, rise
1398	もたらす	bring, cause
1400	問う	ask, question; charge
1401	継ぐ	succeed, take over
1403	構成(する)	constitution, structure; compose

#	Word	Meaning
1404	反応(する)	reaction, response; respond
1408	活用(する)	application; exploit, take advantage of
1413	渡す	carry across, hand, transfer
1414	掲げる	hang out, hold up
1416	就職(する)	job hunting; find employment, get a job
1421	提出(する)	submission; submit, hand in
1425	弾く	play (musical instrument)
1433	構う	mind, care about
1434	受け入れる	receive, accept, agree
1441	直す	fix, repair, mend
1443	回答(する)	answer, response, reply; answer, respond, reply
1447	活躍(する)	activity, action; be active, flourish
1448	試験(する)	exam, test, trial; examine
1454	検査(する)	inspection; inspect
1457	足りる	be sufficient, be enough, be worthy
1458	代表(する)	representative; represent, stand for
1460	下がる	fall, drop, step back
1461	実感(する)	real feeling; actually feel
1462	有する	have
1463	抜く	pull, extract
1464	回す	turn, rotate, spin
1467	分かれる	divide, split, part
1468	見つめる	stare, gaze
1470	抜ける	fall out; come loose; be omitted; leave
1473	スタート(する)	start; get off, start
1476	設ける	institute, set up
1480	処理(する)	management, processing; manage, process
1484	間違う	be wrong, make a mistake
1490	隠す	hide, conceal
1491	緊張(する)	tension; get tense
1495	戦う	fight
1498	つる	hang
1499	達する	reach
1511	切れる	expire, run out
1512	維持(する)	maintenance, preservation; keep, maintain
1519	約束(する)	promise, appointment; promise, make an appointment
1524	売れる	sell
1528	伺う	ask, inquire
1529	引っ越す	move (house)
1531	たまる	accumulate, build up
1538	安定(する)	stability; become stable
1539	完成(する)	completion; complete
1541	見かける	see
1542	広げる	spread, expand
1545	受け取る	get, accept
1547	望む	hope
1548	適用(する)	application; apply
1552	接する	adjoin, come in contact
1553	戻す	put back, restore
1555	低下(する)	decline, fall; decline, fall
1558	取り組む	tackle, deal with
1563	遅れる	be late, be delayed
1564	担当(する)	charge; be in charge of
1565	向上(する)	improvement, progress; improve, advance
1568	寄る	stop by; move to one side
1571	運転(する)	driving, operation; drive
1575	予想(する)	expectation; expect
1578	経る	pass through, experience
1579	揃う	become complete; be equal
1580	下げる	lower; hang
1581	誘う	invite
1582	重ねる	stack; repeat
1583	採用(する)	adoption, employment; employ
1585	飾る	decorate
1590	直る	be repaired; be corrected; get better
1592	ファックス(する)	fax; fax
1597	及ぶ	reach
1602	契約(する)	contract
1603	組む	pair with; cross
1604	叫ぶ	shout
1607	下ろす	take down; unload; withdraw; fillet (fish); grate
1609	形成(する)	formation; take form
1616	管理(する)	control, management; manage, control
1621	監督(する)	manager, director, proctor, invigilator; supervise, direct
1625	外す	undo; take off, remove
1631	発達(する)	development; develop
1634	挟む	put in, sandwich between; catch in
1639	回復(する)	recovery; recover
1642	塗る	spread; paint
1644	共通(する)	common
1647	開始(する)	beginning, start; begin, start
1649	しまう	put away
1652	販売(する)	sale; sell
1653	諦める	give up, quit
1657	一定(する)	a certain, fixed, constant
1660	関連(する)	relation, connection; be related, be connected
1666	デザイン(する)	design; design
1668	あふれる	overflow, be filled with
1671	迷惑(する)	troublesome, annoying; annoyance, nuisance, trouble; be inconvenienced

#	Word	Meaning		#	Word	Meaning		#	Word	Meaning
1672	つかむ	catch, grasp		1763	吹く	blow; breathe out; play (musical instrument)		1854	試す	try, attempt
1673	締める	tie; tighten		1765	迷う	get lost; cannot decide		1855	終える	finish, end
1675	入る	come in, enter; join		1768	訴える	sue; complain; appeal		1857	受験（する）	examination; take an examination
1677	うなずく	nod		1770	把握（する）	grasp; grasp		1867	入力（する）	input; type
1682	囲む	surround		1771	対する	toward, against; compare, receive		1871	別れる	part; divorce, break up
1683	並べる	arrange; line up; enumerate		1775	応援（する）	support; cheer, support		1873	生産（する）	production; produce
1684	黙る	hold one's tongue, become silent		1777	上昇（する）	rise; rise		1875	収める	obtain, gain; put; keep
1688	保存（する）	preservation, storage; preserve, store		1780	特定（する）	specific; specify		1876	掃除（する）	cleaning; clean
1690	目立つ	be conspicuous, stand out		1781	高める	raise		1877	強化（する）	tighten, strengthen
1691	保護（する）	protection; protect		1784	努める	make efforts		1881	あり得る	be possible, be likely, be probable
1695	演奏（する）	(musical) performance; perform, play		1788	プラス（する）	plus, benefit; benefit, add to		1882	記す	write down; mark
1696	増やす	increase, add		1790	狙う	aim at		1883	うわさ（する）	gossip, rumor; talk about
1698	工夫（する）	device, idea; devise, plan		1792	迫る	approach, draw near; demand		1885	規制（する）	regulation; regulate
1699	触る	touch		1794	消す	put out, turn off; erase		1888	左右（する）	right and left; determine, influence
1701	登録（する）	registration, entry; register, enroll		1798	終了（する）	end; end, be over		1889	促進（する）	promotion; promote
1705	記載（する）	registration entry; record, write down		1804	立ち上がる	stand up, rise		1891	味わう	taste, savor
1707	倒れる	fall (down), collapse		1806	推移（する）	transition, change; change, shift		1893	交流（する）	interchange, exchange; interact
1709	普及（する）	spread, diffusion; spread		1807	なくす	lose		1894	報道（する）	report; report
1711	優れる	be superior		1813	都合（する）	convenience, circumstances; arrange; altogether		1897	観察（する）	observation; observe
1712	返事（する）	answer, reply; answer, reply		1817	無視（する）	neglect, ignore		1904	はまる	fit; fall; be addicted to
1714	取り出す	take out, extract		1824	のぞく	look through, look down; drop in		1906	支払う	pay
1719	けんか（する）	fight, quarrel; fight, quarrel		1825	誕生（する）	birth; be born, be created		1920	慌てる	be flustered, be in a hurry
1721	くださる	give (honorific)		1828	履く	put on, wear		1922	措置（する）	measure; take measures
1725	支援（する）	support, assistance; support, assist		1830	提案（する）	proposal; propose		1938	引っ越し（する）	moving, removal; move house
1726	実行（する）	practice; carry out		1836	つなぐ	connect, tie		1939	失礼（する）	rudeness, impoliteness; be rude, be impolite; rude, impolite; Excuse me
1727	握る	hold, grasp, clasp		1837	包む	wrap		1940	太る	get fat, gain weight
1735	急ぐ	hurry		1838	思い切る	give up; venture		1943	取り入れる	take in; adopt; harvest
1740	批判（する）	criticism; criticize		1841	改める	change; reform		1944	モテる	be popular
1741	出発（する）	departure; leave		1842	集中（する）	concentration; concentrate		1947	発言（する）	remark; speak
1749	けが（する）	injury; hurt, injure		1844	指示（する）	instruction, direction; instruct, direct				
1752	保つ	keep, maintain		1848	確立（する）	establishment; establish				
1761	刺激（する）	stimulate, incite, excite		1849	到着（する）	arrival; arrive				
				1850	かく	scratch; paddle; shovel				
				1851	痩せる	become thin, lose weight				

#	Japanese	English
1948	炒める	fry, stir-fry
1949	投げる	throw; give up
1955	高まる	rise, heighten, grow
1956	証明(する)	proof; prove
1957	沸く	boil; be in uproar
1968	巻く	roll up, wind up; wear around
1972	はやる	be fashionable, be popular, go around
1978	否定(する)	denial, negative; deny
1979	踏まえる	be based on
1984	面接(する)	interview; interview
1989	泳ぐ	swim
1992	込める	put into, pour into
1994	調整(する)	adjustment; adjust
1995	踊る	dance
1999	攻撃(する)	attack; attack
2005	要する	need, take
2009	取得(する)	acquisition; acquire
2010	挑戦(する)	challenge; challenge, try
2011	独立(する)	independence; be independent
2018	壊す	break; impair; upset
2019	なさる	do (honorific)
2022	関する	be related to, be concerned with
2023	輸入(する)	import; import
2024	満たす	fill, satisfy, meet
2030	訪ねる	visit, go to see
2035	経過(する)	progress, development; pass
2036	整える	arrange, prepare
2041	去る	leave, pass, be gone
2046	断る	decline, refuse, reject, turn down; ask permission; give notice
2049	整理(する)	arrangement; arrange, put in order, dispose of
2050	耐える	stand, endure, bear
2052	コメント(する)	comment; comment
2054	発揮(する)	exhibition, show; display, exhibit
2055	閉じる	close, shut
2057	分析(する)	analysis; analyze
2058	解釈(する)	interpretation; interpret
2059	奪う	rob, take by force; fascinate
2061	注文(する)	order; order
2066	任せる	entrust, leave
2067	配慮(する)	consideration; consider
2069	かぶる	put on, cover
2071	営業(する)	business, sales; do business
2075	交換(する)	exchange; exchange
2076	生える	grow, sprout, cut (teeth),
2077	防ぐ	defend, protect; prevent, keep away
2079	妊娠(する)	pregnancy; get pregnant
2080	貸す	lend, rent
2082	空く	become vacant, be free
2086	壊れる	be broken, be damaged; be destroyed
2087	破壊(する)	destruction, demolition; destroy, demolish
2088	削除(する)	deletion; delete
2089	派遣(する)	dispatch, send
2091	改正(する)	amendment; amend
2093	手伝う	help
2096	信頼(する)	trust, rely on
2097	沿う	along; in line with, according to, meet
2098	輝く	shine, glitter, twinkle, glow
2103	襲う	attack, hit; seize
2110	建設(する)	construction; build, construct
2118	引き続く	continue; follow
2119	移す	move, transfer, shift
2120	募集(する)	recruitment; recruit
2124	優勝(する)	championship, victory; win
2126	属する	belong to, be a member of
2146	拾う	pick up, gather, pick out
2152	設立(する)	establishment; establish, set up
2154	絞る	squeeze
2157	下る	go down
2159	反映(する)	reflection; reflect
2162	減らす	reduce, cut down
2165	敷く	spread, lay
2166	合格(する)	passing an exam; pass an exam
2177	承知(する)	agreement; agree, understand
2179	運営(する)	management; manage, run
2181	備える	get something ready, prepare
2184	考慮(する)	thought; think over, consider
2186	踏む	step on, tread on
2188	有り	exist; live
2198	止む	stop
2199	外れる	be off, get out of place, be dislocated
2212	コピー(する)	copy; copy
2213	削る	save; sharpen, plane
2216	制限(する)	restriction; limit, restrict
2217	実験(する)	experimentation; experiment
2219	確かめる	confirm, make sure
2224	テスト(する)	test; test
2226	満足(する)	satisfaction; be satisfied
2229	生み出す	create, invent
2235	訓練(する)	training; train
2236	区別(する)	distinction; distinguish
2244	恵まれる	be blessed
2245	煮る	boil, cook
2247	反省(する)	soul-searching, reflection; reflect on
2248	放送(する)	broadcasting, telecasting; broadcast
2252	命ずる	order
2256	加わる	increase, add; join
2259	鳴る	sound; ring
2263	告げる	tell, announce
2268	許可(する)	permission, leave; permit, authorize

#		#		#	
2270	積む pile up, heap up; acquire, accumulate	2352	隠れる be hidden, hide	2479	潰す smash; crush, squash; ruin
2273	見なす be considered, look upon	2353	埋める cover, bury	2484	かむ bite; chew
2277	ダイエット(する) diet; go on a diet	2355	依頼(する) request; request, ask	2485	温める warm, heat
2280	発行(する) publication, issue; publish, issue	2358	出産(する) birth; give birth	2487	重視(する) respect; make a point of, consider important
2281	ほめる praise, speak well, commend	2359	達成(する) achievement, attainment; achieve, attain	2490	興奮(する) excitement; be excited
2283	請求(する) demand, request, charge; demand, claim	2360	申請(する) application, petition; apply	2491	突っ込む thrust, stick; dip; shove
2284	企画(する) planning; plan	2361	知り合う get to know	2497	参照(する) reference; consult, refer
2285	話し合う talk, discuss	2364	招く invite	2501	自殺(する) suicide; commit suicide
2286	注ぐ flow into; water; pour	2367	飛び出す spring out; come rushing out	2506	犯す commit, offend; break
2287	増す increase	2368	陥る fall into	2507	膨らむ swell, expand
2288	浴びる bathe; pour	2369	寄せる let come near, bring near; put; be dependent on	2531	検索(する) search; search, look up
2290	吐く exhale, breathe out; vomit; spit	2383	役立つ useful	2532	アップ(する) raise; go up
2292	間違える make a mistake	2387	発売(する) sale; sell, put on sale	2533	絶える cease, fail
2298	合計(する) sum total; total	2388	成り立つ be concluded; consist of	2535	取材(する) interview, report; gather information
2303	引っ張る pull	2403	植える plant	2536	ぶつかる strike, bump, collide
2305	対処(する) handling, coping; deal with	2405	盛り上がる swell, rise; liven up	2537	曲がる bend, wind; turn
2306	覆う cover	2417	負う take, assume	2540	飽きる tire, weary, be tired of, get bored
2320	話しかける speak to	2426	作り出す make, create	2542	分類(する) classification; classify
2321	揃える arrange, prepare	2432	発する emit, release	2545	覚悟(する) readiness, preparedness; be ready
2324	つぶやく mutter, murmur	2446	疑う suspect, doubt	2547	逮捕(する) arrest; arrest
2325	抵抗(する) resistance; resist, offer opposition	2457	離婚(する) divorce; divorce, get divorced	2548	収まる hold, pack
2328	支配(する) rule, control; rule, control, govern	2459	掲載(する) publication; publish, print	2549	交渉(する) negotiation, treaty; negotiate
2332	禁止(する) prohibition, ban; prohibit, ban	2462	操作(する) operation; operate	2556	講ずる take
2335	命令(する) order, command, direction; order, command	2465	留まる stay	2558	開く open
2337	援助(する) assistance, aid, support; help, support, assist	2466	受かる pass	2559	及ぼす influence, affect
2339	好む like, be fond of, love, care	2467	恐れる fear, be afraid	2563	震える shake, tremble
2340	苦しむ feel pain, suffer	2471	救う save, rescue	2566	所属(する) affiliation; attach, be attached, belong
2342	介護(する) nursing, care; nurse, look after	2472	助かる survive, be saved; be helpful	2567	騒ぐ make a noise, make a fuss
2344	広告(する) advertisement, flyer; advertise	2473	巡る go around	2569	溜める save, store, accumulate
2346	強調(する) emphasis, stress; emphasize, stress	2474	予約(する) reservation; reserve, book	2581	重なる pile up; conspire
2348	たまる bear, endure	2475	響く affect	2583	落ち込む sink, go down; be depressed
		2477	進行(する) progression; progress		
		2478	解説(する) explanation, comment, description; explain		

#	Word	Meaning
2584	進化(する)	evolution; evolve, develop
2586	思い付く	think of, guess, conceive
2589	数える	count, number
2590	公開(する)	exhibition, presentation; release
2592	貢献(する)	contribution, service; contribute
2594	映る	reflect
2597	入学(する)	(school etc.) entrance, admission; enter (school etc.)
2599	控える	abstain, hold back, refrain
2600	促す	urge
2603	配る	deal, distribute, deliver
2604	改革(する)	reform; make reforms
2605	一致(する)	agreement, accord; consent, agree
2608	出席(する)	attendance; attend
2610	処分(する)	disposal, disposition; dispose of
2614	設計(する)	plan, design; plan, design
2615	飛び込む	dive, plunge
2616	邪魔(する)	obstacle, disturbance, interruption; disturb, interrupt
2617	ゆでる	boil
2620	叱る	scold, admonish
2624	真似(する)	imitation, mimicry, impersonation; imitate, copy
2626	預ける	leave, check, deposit
2633	頼る	depend, turn to, trust
2639	接続(する)	connection; connect
2641	光る	shine, glitter, twinkle
2646	出演(する)	appearance, broadcast; appear (on stage, TV)
2648	間に合う	catch, get, make it
2651	継続(する)	continuation; continue
2653	引き上げる	pull up; increase, raise
2657	上回る	exceed, surpass
2661	割る	break; crack
2664	飲める	be able to drink
2667	担う	cover, carry, take
2668	揺れる	shake, wave, swing
2674	むく	peel, pare
2678	燃える	burn, flame, glow, be on fire
2684	想定(する)	assumption, supposition; assume, suppose
2685	学習(する)	learning, study; learn, study
2691	競争(する)	competition, contest; compete
2692	投資(する)	investment; invest
2693	ほっとする	be relieved
2695	記述(する)	description, account; describe
2696	謝る	apologize
2698	獲得(する)	acquisition; get, gain
2699	見直す	review, look over
2701	心がける	be careful, be prudent
2706	自慢(する)	pride, boast; boast, brag
2709	更新(する)	renewal; renew, update
2712	受け止める	take, catch
2723	持ち込む	bring, import
2726	予測(する)	prospect; predict, estimate
2729	欠ける	lack; chip
2730	嫌う	hate, detest
2732	飛ばす	let fly, fly
2733	教わる	learn
2736	たく	burn
2738	防止(する)	prevention; prevent
2747	突く	push; prick
2749	滞在(する)	stay, visit; stay, visit, stop
2750	連携(する)	cooperation; work together with
2752	演ずる	play, perform
2753	廃止(する)	abolition; repeal
2754	復活(する)	revival, restoration; revive, restore
2755	借金(する)	debt, loan; borrow (money)
2758	見守る	watch, observe
2765	こだわる	stick to; be particular about
2767	乾く	dry
2772	鍛える	train, discipline
2775	乾燥(する)	dryness; dry
2780	添える	attach, add
2782	配置(する)	arrangement, layout; arrange
2783	輸出(する)	exportation; export
2785	漬ける	soak; pickle
2790	混む	be crowded
2791	築く	build, have
2793	結び付く	join, be connected with
2794	崩れる	crumble, collapse
2795	届ける	deliver; send; report
2797	進歩(する)	progress, advance; progress, advance
2800	汚れる	dirty, soil
2803	吸収(する)	absorption, assimilation; absorb, assimilate
2813	観光(する)	sightseeing; go sightseeing
2817	演出(する)	direction, direct
2821	記入(する)	entry; fill in
2822	見上げる	look up; respect
2830	後悔(する)	repentance, regret; regret
2831	詰める	plug, pack, stuff
2833	自覚(する)	consciousness, awareness; realize
2838	滑る	slide, slip; be slippery
2840	留学(する)	study abroad; study abroad
2844	漂う	drift, float
2845	測る	measure; weigh
2848	取り戻す	take back, repossess
2852	たどる	follow, trace, search
2858	進展(する)	progress, development, evolution; develop, progress, advance

#	Term	Meaning
2860	死亡(する)	death, decease; die
2863	殴る	hit, strike
2865	対立(する)	opposition, conflict; be opposed to
2869	放つ	fly, loose
2872	稼ぐ	earn
2873	出現(する)	appearance, dawn, birth, advent; appear
2876	工事(する)	construction, work; construct
2880	不足(する)	lack, shortage; be insufficient
2882	限定(する)	restriction, limitation; restrict, limit
2889	追加(する)	addition, supplement; add, supplement
2892	拭く	wipe, dry
2903	感激(する)	deep emotion; be impressed
2904	浮く	float, suspend
2907	引っ掛かる	catch; be caught
2914	違反(する)	violation; violate
2915	すっきり(する)	feel refreshed
2922	解放(する)	liberation; liberate
2925	帰国(する)	going/coming back to one's own country
2927	実践(する)	practice; practice
2931	追いかける	run after, chase
2932	作用(する)	action; act
2936	差別(する)	discrimination; discriminate
2942	研修(する)	training; study
2943	沈む	sink, go down
2947	捕まえる	catch, arrest
2952	いじめる	torment, bully, tease
2955	作り上げる	make up, build up
2957	称する	call; pretend
2959	支持(する)	support; support
2966	訪問(する)	visit, call; visit, call (on)
2975	支給(する)	provision, payment; provide, pay
2977	晴れる	clear up, be dispelled; be refreshed
2978	感心(する)	admiration; admire
2980	決意(する)	determination; resolve
2986	尊敬(する)	respect; respect
2987	尽くす	do one's best, devote; exhaust
2998	浮かべる	float; show; imagine
3003	加入(する)	admission, joining; join
3009	供給(する)	supply; supply
3012	建築(する)	architecture, construction; build
3022	悪化(する)	change for the worse; worsen
3027	消費(する)	consumption; consume
3029	深める	deepen
3033	活性化(する)	revitalization; revitalize
3036	混乱(する)	confusion; get confused
3038	癒す	heal, cure, recover from
3039	磨く	polish, brush; improve
3040	動作(する)	movement, operation; operate
3044	賛成(する)	agreement; agree
3049	ひょっとする	perhaps
3050	勤務(する)	service, duty, work; work, serve
3051	恋愛(する)	love (romantic); love
3053	誤解(する)	misunderstanding; misunderstand
3055	平均(する)	average; average
3060	翻訳(する)	translation; translate
3064	固まる	harden; become certain
3067	越す	cross, pass
3068	まとまる	be well arranged; be united; be settled
3070	解く	untie; solve; remove
3075	通過(する)	passage; pass
3076	確信(する)	conviction; be convinced
3081	見出だす	find, discover
3087	崩壊(する)	collapse; collapse
3095	嫌がる	be reluctant; hate
3096	製造(する)	production; produce
3101	流行(する)	fashion, epidemic; come into fashion, be rife
3103	承認(する)	approval; approve
3106	掘る	dig
3108	絡む	get entangled, involve; pick a quarrel
3111	構える	get set, get ready; set up
3113	発音(する)	pronunciation; pronounce
3114	共有(する)	share; share
3115	勝負(する)	victory or defeat, match; play
3122	出品(する)	exhibit; submit
3123	祈る	pray, wish
3125	メモ(する)	memo; take notes
3131	整う	be ready; be well-regulated
3133	たどり着く	finally arrive at, struggle along to
3134	焼ける	be burned; be roasted; be sunburned
3135	合併(する)	combination, merger; combine, merge
3137	徹底(する)	thoroughgoing, out-and-out; be thorough
3138	脱ぐ	take off
3144	構築(する)	construction; construct
3146	適する	suit, fit
3147	引き受ける	undertake
3150	焦る	be in a hurry; be impatient; be eager
3159	退職(する)	retirement, resignation; retire, resign
3160	満ちる	be full; rise
3163	刻む	cut into fine pieces; engrave; tick
3167	携わる	participate, be engaged
3175	編む	knit, braid

#	Word	Meaning
3176	破る	tear; break; beat
3179	さらす	expose
3181	可愛がる	love, treat with affection
3186	オープン(する)	open
3188	離す	separate, divide; keep apart
3192	盗む	steal
3197	ミス(する)	mistake; make a mistake
3198	移行(する)	shift; shift
3199	味方(する)	supporter; support
3201	転勤(する)	transfer; be transferred
3210	探る	fumble; probe
3214	巻き込む	involve
3215	退院(する)	leaving hospital; be discharged from hospital
3218	リラックス(する)	relax
3224	展示(する)	display, exhibition; display, exhibit
3227	診断(する)	diagnosis; diagnose
3231	潰れる	be crushed; go bankrupt; become useless
3234	出版(する)	publication; publish
3237	由来(する)	origin, history; originate
3238	引き起こす	raise up, cause
3241	同意(する)	agreement, consent; agree
3243	認定(する)	authorization; authorize
3258	制定(する)	enactment; enact
3261	ぬれる	get wet
3270	面する	face
3277	市販(する)	on the market; market
3280	サイン(する)	signature, autograph; sign
3284	鳴く	cry, sing
3285	呼吸(する)	breath; breathe
3288	延長(する)	extension; extend
3295	傷付ける	hurt; damage
3298	紅葉(する)	autumn leaves; put on fall colors
3300	信仰(する)	religious faith; believe
3302	雇う	employ, hire
3305	運用(する)	making use of; manage
3310	拒否(する)	refusal; refuse, reject
3311	空く	become empty, be free; get hungry
3317	落札(する)	successful bid; make a successful bid
3318	出場(する)	participation; participate
3319	だます	cheat, trick, deceive
3320	片付ける	put in order, tidy; clear away; finish
3321	組み合わせる	combine, put together, match
3323	雇用(する)	employment; employ
3324	乗り越える	climb over; overcome
3328	引き出す	pull out, bring out; withdraw
3330	印刷(する)	printing; print
3331	こなす	cope with; finish
3333	導く	guide, lead
3334	中止(する)	cancellation; cancel, call off
3335	連続(する)	continuation, succession; continue
3336	折る	break; fold; bend
3344	説得(する)	persuasion; persuade
3345	籠もる	shut oneself up; be full of
3347	放置(する)	leaving something as it is; neglect
3351	編集(する)	editing; edit
3352	くっ付く	stick, keep close; go out
3353	取り付ける	install, arrange
3355	象徴(する)	symbol; symbolize
3356	説く	explain; preach; persuade
3358	見学(する)	studying by observation, field trip; visit for study, go on a field trip
3361	応募(する)	application; apply for
3366	固定(する)	fixing; fix
3367	告白(する)	confession; confess
3369	策定(する)	settling on; settle on
3370	矛盾(する)	contradiction, conflict; contradict
3371	引き取る	take back, collect; leave
3372	保証(する)	guarantee; guarantee
3383	公表(する)	publication; make public
3386	潜る	dive; go underground
3389	憧れる	long for; admire
3392	漏れる	leak, escape; be omitted
3394	前述(する)	above-mentioned, mentioned above
3398	入手(する)	acquisition; get, obtain
3402	崩す	destroy; put into disorder; change
3405	交わす	exchange
3409	通知(する)	notice, notification; notify
3410	要望(する)	demand; make demands
3412	営む	run a business; engage in; hold a ceremony
3417	押し付ける	press against, force
3418	溶ける	melt, thaw; dissolve
3421	定着(する)	fixing; fix; become established
3434	提示(する)	presentation; present
3438	優先(する)	priority; have priority
3441	制作(する)	production; produce
3445	入り込む	go into; come into

#	Word	Meaning
3454	捕まる	be caught, be arrested; hold
3459	余る	be left over; be too many
3464	合意(する)	mutual agreement; agree
3472	仕上げる	finish, complete
3473	回収(する)	collection; collect
3474	再生(する)	rebirth; regenerate
3477	コントロール(する)	control; control
3483	施行(する)	enforcement; enforce
3486	追及(する)	pursuit; pursue the question
3491	労働(する)	work, labor; work, labor
3496	帰宅(する)	coming home; come home
3499	汚染(する)	pollution; pollute
3500	転換(する)	conversion; convert, change
3503	予防(する)	prevention; prevent
3507	固める	make something hard, strengthen
3508	反する	go against, be contrary
3509	振るう	flourish, prosper
3510	宣言(する)	declaration; declare
3515	解散(する)	dissolution; dissolve, break up
3517	回転(する)	revolution; revolve, turn round, spin
3522	折れる	break
3529	合宿(する)	training camp; stay together in a camp
3538	セックス(する)	sex; have sex
3543	所有(する)	ownership; own
3544	進出(する)	advance; launch into
3546	測定(する)	measurement; measure
3548	論ずる	argue, discuss
3552	譲る	give; sell; offer
3553	修理(する)	repair; repair
3554	遡る	go back; be retroactive
3555	加工(する)	processing; process
3559	施す	give, do, apply, add
3562	取り込む	take in
3563	排除(する)	removal; remove
3564	育成(する)	cultivation; bring up, cultivate, mold
3565	移転(する)	move; move
3567	兼ねる	combine; serve both
3569	自立(する)	independence; be independent
3572	下す	give, issue; make a decision
3584	鳴らす	ring
3588	取り除く	remove
3593	ばれる	come out, be discovered
3594	乗り込む	board, get into
3595	欠かせる	cause to lack
3597	収穫(する)	harvest; harvest
3603	割れる	split; break
3604	抽選(する)	lottery; draw lots
3608	狂う	go mad
3610	協議(する)	consultation, discussion; consult, discuss
3612	発酵(する)	fermentation; ferment
3614	入札(する)	bid, tender; bid, tender
3615	覚める	wake up
3618	背負う	carry something on one's back
3623	感染(する)	infection; contract, catch, be infected
3624	尊重(する)	respect; give something serious consideration
3630	洗濯(する)	washing; wash
3631	争う	compete
3637	勘違い(する)	misunderstand, mistake
3645	修正(する)	revision; revise
3647	インタビュー(する)	interview; interview
3649	受け継ぐ	inherit
3652	削減(する)	cut, reduction; cut, slash
3654	爆発(する)	explosion; explode
3656	うかがう	peep, peer; watch for (the chance)
3659	試みる	try
3660	決心(する)	resolution; decide
3664	調理(する)	cooking; cook
3670	キス(する)	kiss; kiss
3673	停止(する)	stop, suspension; stop, suspend
3678	申し込む	apply
3679	デビュー(する)	debut; make one's debut
3680	足る	be enough; deserve
3682	思い込む	be obsessed with the idea
3685	統一(する)	unity; unify
3692	逃れる	escape
3695	励ます	cheer up, encourage
3696	存ずる	know
3704	発明(する)	invention; invent
3706	干す	dry
3709	非難(する)	criticism; criticize
3710	唱える	recite; advocate
3715	なめる	lick; suck
3718	差し出す	hold out
3726	がっかり(する)	be disappointed
3731	書き込む	write in, jot down
3732	栽培(する)	cultivation; cultivate
3735	保障(する)	guarantee; guarantee
3737	バック(する)	back, background; reverse, back
3740	審査(する)	examination; examine
3742	打ち込む	devote oneself
3744	通勤(する)	commute; commute
3745	準用(する)	apply mutatis mutandis, with necessary modification
3747	推測(する)	assumption, guess; guess, presume

#	Word	Meaning
3749	預かる	keep, look after
3752	冷やす	keep cool, cool
3754	接触(する)	touch, contact; touch
3763	通り過ぎる	pass, go past
3770	結成(する)	formation; form, organize
3772	名付ける	name
3774	就職活動(する)	job-hunting; look for a job
3775	捜査(する)	criminal investigation; investigate
3786	照らす	light
3790	傾ける	tilt, incline
3792	判決(する)	decision; decide
3796	振り向く	look around, turn around
3798	関与(する)	participation; participate
3799	遂げる	achieve
3803	ごちそう(する)	feast; give a dinner, treat
3807	録音(する)	record; record
3808	沈黙(する)	silence; be silent
3813	贈る	give (as a present), send
3815	懸念(する)	fear; fear
3816	燃やす	burn
3821	定年(する)	retirement; retire
3822	育児(する)	childcare; take care of a child
3823	蹴る	kick
3826	完了(する)	complete; complete
3831	宣伝(する)	advertisement; advertise
3834	思考(する)	thought; think
3836	足す	add
3839	取り扱う	handle, treat
3844	シェア(する)	share; share
3846	記念(する)	commemoration; commemorate
3850	引退(する)	retirement; retire
3857	なじむ	become accustomed
3858	誇る	be proud, boast
3861	デート(する)	date; date
3862	抑制(する)	control, restraint; control, restrain
3871	痛む	ache, hurt, pain
3873	尽きる	run out
3877	推定(する)	presumption, estimation; presume, estimate
3880	結びつける	connect, tie, bind
3888	クリア(する)	clearing, clearance; clear; clear
3892	直面(する)	confrontation; confront, face
3895	目覚める	wake up
3897	休憩(する)	rest, break; take a rest
3903	従事(する)	engagement in; be engaged in
3904	蓄積(する)	storage, accumulation; store, accumulate
3905	よみがえる	revive, come back
3912	放る	throw; leave something undone
3913	攻める	attack
3914	位置付ける	rank; evaluate
3922	言い出す	propose, suggest
3927	交付(する)	issue; issue, grant
3928	証言(する)	evidence; give testimony
3931	解明(する)	clarification; solve
3935	縛る	bind, tie
3938	化粧(する)	makeup; put on makeup
3941	持参(する)	bringing, taking; bring, take
3942	引用(する)	quotation; quote
3951	パス(する)	pass; pass
3960	臨む	face
3963	アピール(する)	appeal; appeal
3976	交代(する)	change, shift; take turns
3979	苦笑	wry smile
3983	締結(する)	conclusion; conclude
3986	いらいら(する)	be annoyed, be irritated, be impatient
3987	収集(する)	collection; collect
3989	脱出(する)	escape; escape, break out
3990	呼び出す	call, summon
3994	付け加える	add
3998	倒す	knock down
3999	写す	photograph
4000	漏らす	betray
4001	上達(する)	improvement; improve, progress
4004	表明(する)	expression, manifestation; express, manifest
4008	ずれる	be out of step, slip
4009	通用(する)	currency; accept, obtain
4016	ニコニコ(する)	smile; smiling
4018	撫でる	stroke
4020	わくわく(する)	be bubbling; be excited
4021	仮定(する)	assumption, supposition; assume, suppose
4022	引きずる	drag, trail
4024	依存(する)	dependence, reliance; depend, rely
4026	同居(する)	coexistence, living together; live together, live with
4033	制約(する)	restriction, constraint; restrict, constrain
4046	呼びかける	call out, appeal
4048	凝る	be absorbed, be devoted; become stiff
4052	決断(する)	decision; decide
4056	監視(する)	observation; watch
4059	微笑む	smile
4060	駆け付ける	run, rush
4065	虐待(する)	abuse; abuse
4066	然り	to be so
4068	配布(する)	distribution; distribute
4069	持ち上げる	lift, raise
4070	見送る	see off
4071	引き継ぐ	take over
4081	どきどき(する)	throb, beat fast
4082	賑わう	be crowded with

4088	広まる spread, get around	4208	発送(する) send, ship, dispatch	4316	持ち出す carry out, take out
4089	外出(する) going out, outing; go out	4215	乗り換える change, transfer	4317	浸かる be flooded; soak
4091	曲げる bend, twist	4225	確定(する) determination, decision; determine, decide	4320	変動(する) change, fluctuation, movement; change, fluctuate
4094	切り替える switch, change			4321	吸い込む breathe in; suck up
4095	染める dye, color	4227	混ぜ合わせる mix		
4099	裏切る betray	4230	分布(する) distribution; distribute	4329	怒鳴る shout
4101	富む be rich (in); grow			4333	ひねる twist
4107	似合う suit	4236	調和(する) harmony, balance; harmonize, match	4336	冷める cool, get cold
4108	節約(する) saving, economy; save, economize on			4346	克服(する) conquest; conquer, overcome
4110	訳す translate	4239	酔う get drunk, feel sick	4358	見回す look around, look about
4113	課する assign, charge, impose	4241	傷つく be injured, be hurt		
		4244	当てはまる apply	4360	応用(する) application; apply
4114	養う bring up, keep, support	4246	稽古(する) practice, exercise; practice		
4123	溶かす dissolve; melt			4367	差し込む insert, plug in; come in, shine in
4142	味わえる can taste, can enjoy	4248	率いる head, lead, command		
		4251	創造(する) creation; create	4380	判定(する) decision, judgment; decide, judge
4144	分割(する) division; divide	4256	歩む walk, go through		
4145	縮小(する) reduction; reduce	4257	立ち止まる stop, pause	4381	帯びる have a trace of, be tinged with
		4265	軽減(する) reduction; reduce		
4146	練る knead; polish; elaborate			4384	対話(する) dialogue, conversation; converse, discuss
4147	飲み込む swallow	4269	融資(する) loan; loan, lend		
4153	戸惑う confuse, puzzle	4270	破綻(する) bankruptcy, collapse; fail, go bankrupt		
4155	吐く tell (a lie); sigh			4401	判明(する) proving; turn out, identify
4163	消滅(する) disappearance; disappear	4273	励む work hard, make efforts		
				4402	統合(する) integration; integrate, combine
4168	保有(する) possession; hold, possess	4280	リサイクル(する) recycling; recycle		
				4409	転がる roll
4169	反発(する) repulsion, resistance; react, resist, rebel, repel	4288	補助(する) help, aid, assistance; help, aid, assist	4414	創設(する) foundation, creation; found, create
		4298	歩き回る walk about	4427	流通(する) circulation, distribution; circulate, distribute
4170	アレンジ(する) arrangement; arrange	4302	侵入(する) invasion; break into, invade		
				4434	入社(する) entry to a company; enter a company, get a job
4178	思い浮かべる recall, remember	4303	盛る serve, heap		
		4304	転ずる switch, shift		
4186	名乗る give one's name	4305	祭る enshrine; worship; deify	4438	成人(する) adult; come of age
4188	生き残る survive				
4190	取り巻く surround, enclose	4308	冷える chill, become cold, feel cold	4455	始末(する) disposal, circumstances; manage, deal with, dispose of
4200	ぼんやり(する) vacantly, vaguely, dimly; be vague, be blurred	4311	縫う sew		
		4312	おしゃべり(する) chat, talk; chat, talk	4461	渋滞(する) traffic jam, delay; be delayed
4203	倒産(する) bankruptcy; go bankrupt	4313	次ぐ next to, after	4462	遠慮(する) reserve; hesitate
		4314	復帰(する) return, comeback; return, come back, make a comeback	4465	慰める console, comfort
4206	保全(する) preservation, maintenance; preserve, maintain			4467	開設(する) establishment; establish, set up
4207	結合(する) combination; combine, join	4315	衝突(する) collision; collide, clash		

4473	予感(する) presentiment, foreboding, hunch; have a presentiment/foreboding/hunch
4479	見込む expect, trust
4485	欠く lack; chip
4487	近づける bring close
4491	行列(する) procession, line, parade; line up, queue
4492	計上(する) appropriation; appropriate
4493	受診(する) (medical) consultation; consult, have a medical examination
4494	指揮(する) direction, command; conduct, direct
4495	保管(する) keeping, storage; keep
4497	発足(する) start; start
4500	考察(する) consideration, examination; consider, examine
4502	儲ける profit, earn, gain
4503	指差す point
4504	認可(する) permission, approval; permit, approve
4505	劣る be inferior
4506	ぶつける hit; throw
4509	マッチ(する) match; match
4514	審議(する) discussion, deliberation; discuss, deliberate
4518	マスター(する) master; master
4523	つなげる connect, tie
4525	分解(する) analysis; resolve, dismantle, take apart, analyze
4527	ささやく whisper
4528	調達(する) supply, procurement; supply, procure
4541	散る fall, drop
4544	逃げ出す run away
4545	繁栄(する) prosperity; prosper, flourish
4548	担ぐ carry, shoulder
4549	撒く scatter, water
4553	主催(する) promotion, organizing; host, promote, organize
4556	煮込む stew
4558	錯覚(する) illusion, delusion, trick; have the illusion/impression
4561	隣接(する) adjacent, adjoin, next to; be adjacent, adjoin, be next to
4563	ごまかす cheat, deceive
4569	到達(する) arrival; reach
4573	生まれ育つ be born and raised
4577	サポート(する) support; support
4578	転ぶ fall, slip
4581	亡くす lose
4588	浸透(する) soaking, penetration; soak, penetrate
4589	合図(する) signal, sign; signal, sign
4593	招待(する) invitation; invite
4598	対抗(する) competition, rivalry; oppose, rival
4601	丸める curl, wad
4604	挿入(する) insertion; insert
4606	腐る rot, decay, go off
4613	誤る make a mistake, be wrong
4620	分離(する) separation, detachment; separate, detach
4629	貫く persist, stick to; pierce
4632	正解(する) correct answer; answer correctly
4633	悟る realize
4634	擦る rub, strike; lose
4636	再会(する) reunion; meet again
4640	捕らわれる be arrested, be captured, stick to
4648	進学(する) going on to the next level of education; go on to the next level of education
4653	写す copy, trace
4655	走り回る run around
4665	就任(する) assumption; assume
4667	装置(する) device, equipment; be equipped with
4673	上京(する) coming/going to Tokyo; come/go to Tokyo
4680	引き付ける attract
4688	いたずら(する) mischief, trick, joke; be mischievous, play a trick
4689	受け付ける accept
4690	こねる knead, squeeze, work
4691	這う creep, crawl
4692	ふらふら(する) aimlessly, unsteadily; unsteady on one's feet; stagger, be dizzy
4693	捧げる offer, dedicate, sacrifice
4695	見下ろす look down, overlook
4701	共感(する) sympathy; sympathize
4705	司会(する) host, emcee; host, emcee, take the chair
4707	緩和(する) relaxation, relief; relieve
4709	明ける begin, dawn, break
4710	反論(する) argument, objection; argue, object
4711	引っ繰り返す overturn, upset, turn over
4712	儲かる profit, gain
4715	枯れる wither, die
4720	責める accuse, blame
4725	寄与(する) contribution; contribute
4730	くわえる take, hold
4743	補う supplement, compensate
4744	投入(する) investment; throw, invest
4748	見逃す miss, overlook
4751	リンク(する) link; link
4753	製作(する) production; manufacture
4755	覗き込む look into

4756	区分(する) division, classification; separate	
4757	放棄(する) abandonment, renunciation; abandon, renounce	
4758	転職(する) change of job; change job	
4763	避難(する) evacuation; evacuate	
4768	変換(する) change, conversion; convert	
4769	歓迎(する) reception, welcome; welcome	
4779	ガイド(する) guide, conductor; guide	
4786	披露(する) announcement, introduction; announce, introduce	
4790	リード(する) lead; take a lead	
4796	強いる force	
4798	追い込む drive into	
4803	据える set, place	
4805	起動(する) starting; start	
4807	助成(する) subsidy; subsidize	
4809	打ち出す work out, come up with; announce	
4810	栄える prosper, flourish	
4815	乗り出す venture out; embark on	
4817	覚ます wake up	
4819	沸騰(する) boiling; boil	
4820	仕掛ける begin, start; set	
4824	組み立てる assemble	
4826	譲渡(する) transfer; transfer, hand over	
4828	挫折(する) setback; fail	
4830	検証(する) verification; verify	
4832	見渡す look around	
4833	誓う vow, swear	
4834	マッサージ(する) massage; massage	
4840	強める strengthen, increase	
4841	禁煙(する) no-smoking; stop smoking	
4845	ふさぐ cover; stop; block	
4851	多様化(する) diversification; diversify	
4852	着せる put on, dress	
4853	インストール(する) installation; install	
4875	組み込む build in; insert; integrate	
4877	着替える change clothes; get dressed	
4880	調節(する) adjustment; adjust	
4881	回避(する) avoidance; avoid	
4882	打ち明ける speak one's mind; confess	
4899	明記(する) writing clearly; write clearly	
4904	資する contribute	
4912	明く open	
4919	薄れる become dim	
4920	執行(する) execution, enforcement; carry out, enforce	
4923	熱する heat	
4930	支度(する) preparations; prepare	
4931	留める hold, keep	
4932	立ち上げる boot up, start	
4933	受賞(する) winning a prize; win (receive) a prize, be awarded a prize	
4936	祝う celebrate	
4945	作曲(する) musical composition; compose	
4956	抗議(する) protest, objection; object	
4957	あきれる be amazed, be disgusted	
4962	追い詰める run down, corner	
4969	痛める hurt	
4971	切り取る cut off, tear off	
4973	返済(する) repayment; repay	
4974	例える compare	
4979	解除(する) cancellation; cancel, lift	
4980	放出(する) emission; emit	
4981	にらむ stare	
4984	診察(する) medical examination, consultation; examine	
4987	給付(する) provision; provide	
4988	署名(する) signature; sign	
4991	示唆(する) suggestion; suggest	
4996	免れる escape, avoid	
4997	相次ぐ happen one after another	
4999	動揺(する) unrest; be agitated	

i-adjectives: 122 words

47	無い There is no …, no …	
70	良い、いい good	
101	すごい fantastic, wonderful; terrible	
124	多い many, much, a lot of	
220	大きい big, large, great	
228	高い high, tall; expensive	
230	悪い bad	
277	楽しい pleasant, happy, enjoyable	
288	強い strong, powerful	
308	新しい new, fresh	
310	早い early, soon	
314	小さい small, little, tiny	
325	長い long	
345	おいしい delicious, tasty	
355	少ない a little, a few	
357	うまい delicious, tasty; good at	
383	面白い interesting; fun; funny	
394	嬉しい glad, happy	
397	若い young	
457	難しい difficult, hard	
488	近い near, close	
520	安い low, cheap	
522	つらい hard, difficult, painful	
591	怖い frightening, scary; terrified	
602	広い wide, broad, large	
642	ほしい want, desire	
669	深い deep	
681	厳しい strict, hard	
691	可愛い cute, nice, lovely	
696	ものすごい terrible; terribly	
712	素晴らしい wonderful, marvelous	

#	Word	Meaning
720	古い	old
733	低い	low, short
752	悲しい	sad, unhappy
755	詳しい	detailed, know well, in detail
757	ひどい	cruel, serious, terrible
776	痛い	painful, hurt
783	白い	white
806	軽い	light, slight
867	美しい	beautiful
869	優しい	gentle, tender, kind, friendly
915	おかしい	funny, amusing
943	寒い	cold
978	明るい	bright, light; cheerful
1001	正しい	right, accurate, proper
1015	激しい	fierce, intense, severe
1016	短い	short
1025	遅い	late; slow
1049	寂しい	lonely, lonesome
1066	弱い	weak, faint, light
1101	狭い	narrow, small
1138	細かい	small, fine; trivial; sensitive
1145	暗い	dark; depressed
1154	重い	heavy, important
1163	忙しい	busy, occupied
1167	遠い	far, distant
1194	温かい	warm, genial
1214	固い	hard, solid, stiff
1231	珍しい	rare, unusual, unique
1301	薄い	thin, light, weak
1308	赤い	red
1352	黒い	black
1366	甘い	sweet; soft
1388	暑い	hot, warm
1429	しょうがない, しょうがない	it can't be helped, nothing can be done
1450	苦しい	painful, hard, difficult
1451	恥ずかしい	ashamed, embarrassed
1546	冷たい	cold
1589	細い	thin, narrow, slender
1720	偉い	great, big
1722	熱い	hot, heated
1786	きつい	tight; hard, severe; strong
1797	青い	blue; pale; unripe
1826	汚い	dirty; unfair; vulgar
1910	分かりやすい	easy to understand
1930	濃い	thick; strong; heavy; deep
1973	恐ろしい	terrible, frightful, amazing, awful
2083	危ない	dangerous, risky; questionable
2114	よろしい	all right, good, may (I) (formal)
2122	まずい	not taste good; awkward
2135	しかたない	It can't be helped, be beyond any help, I can't help …
2170	うるさい	noisy; annoying
2173	まるい	round, circular
2196	懐かしい	nostalgic
2208	ありがたい	kind, welcome
2299	良し	good, OK
2330	親しい	close, friendly
2331	間違い無い	must be
2448	悔しい	regrettable, frustrating; feel regret
2468	著しい	significant
2522	幼い	young, immature, childish
2557	太い	thick; heavy; bold
2627	軟らかい	soft, tender
2719	ふさわしい	suitable, appropriate
2827	柔らかい	soft
2855	やばい	risky, chancy
2951	鋭い	sharp, pointed
3161	おとなしい	gentle, well-behaved, quiet
3271	もったいない	wasteful; too good
3289	眠い	sleepy
3290	厚い	thick; kind; abundant
3313	幅広い	wide, broad
3380	羨ましい	envious; enviable
3404	格好良い	cool, good-looking
3423	素早い	quick
3516	貧しい	poor
3571	でかい	big, huge
3575	黄色い	yellow
3583	望ましい	desirable
3639	臭い	smelly
3788	怪しい	eerie; doubtful
3896	等しい	equal
3974	浅い	shallow
4157	情けない	miserable
4228	興味深い	interesting
4515	涼しい	cool
4605	賢い	wise, clever
4660	可愛らしい	lovely
4837	力強い	strong, powerful
4849	かゆい	itchy
4935	乏しい	few, little
4964	しつこい	persistent; over-rich (food)

na-adjectives: 261 words

#	Word	Meaning
121	風	style, type, way, like
129	非常	very, extremely
139	みたい	like
143	いろいろ	various
145	そう	be about to
151	必要	necessary; necessity
166	結構	quite; good
196	好き	favorite, like, love
238	大変	serious, terrible; hard, difficult
280	普通	normal, regular, ordinary, common
333	別	separate, different
341	きれい	beautiful, pretty; clean
366	確か	sure, certain, reliable; maybe, probably; if I remember rightly, it's my understanding that
393	大事	important, serious
400	簡単	easy
412	自然	nature; natural; naturally
426	大切	important
447	逆	contrary, opposite
453	有名	famous, well-known
476	だめ	useless, hopeless, impossible
480	十分	enough, sufficient; fully, sufficiently, adequately
485	重要	important

#	Japanese	English
499	嫌	unpleasant, disagreeable
554	様々	various, all kinds of
560	心配(する)	anxious, worried; anxiety, worry, care; worry, be anxious
626	大丈夫	safe, all right
655	基本的	basic, fundamental
666	無理	unreasonable, impossible; compulsory
671	自由	freedom, liberty; free
686	不安	anxiety, concern; uneasy, insecure
690	可能	possible
736	元気	health, vigor; lively, vigorous, well
743	明らか	clear, obvious
763	便利	convenience; useful, convenient
791	具体的	specific, concrete
803	残念	disappointing, regrettable
815	不思議	wonder; wonderful, strange, mysterious
847	一生懸命	hard, as hard as one can
849	変	strange, unusual, funny
875	新た	another
885	大好き	love
897	幸せ	happy; happiness; fortune, luck
908	完全	perfect, complete
920	危険	danger, hazard; dangerous
945	同様	similar, same
955	一般的	general, common, ordinary
981	相当(する)	considerable; equivalence; be equivalent; considerably, pretty;
1034	意外	unexpected, surprising
1047	勝手	on one's own, at one's convenience
1056	急	urgent, sudden; steep; sharp
1128	楽	comfort, ease, comfortable
1139	静か	quiet, silent
1144	わずか	a few, a little, a bit; only
1159	当たり前	natural, usual, common, ordinary
1162	馬鹿	foolish; fool
1196	安全	safe; safety, security
1202	積極的	active, positive, aggressive
1281	豊か	abundant, plentiful, rich
1309	比較的	comparative, relative
1362	嫌い	dislike, hate
1367	最高	best, highest
1383	特別	special, particular
1391	最終的	final, last, ultimate
1409	正直	honesty; honest, truthful; honestly
1417	立派	fine, splendid, great
1446	個人的	private, personal, individual
1449	身近	familiar, close
1481	困難	difficulty; difficult
1487	暇	free, not busy
1505	無事	safely; safety; safe
1516	素敵	lovely, nice, wonderful
1532	精神的	spiritual
1591	単純	simple
1614	無駄	useless, futile; waste
1619	正確	correct, exact, accurate
1632	適当	proper, appropriate, suitable; irresponsible, whimsical
1646	面倒	troublesome; bother, care
1658	いかが	how
1659	上手	good, skillful
1671	迷惑(する)	troublesome, annoying; annoyance, nuisance, trouble; be inconvenienced
1692	確実	certain, sure
1704	明確	clear, definite
1716	平和	peace; peaceful
1734	盛ん	popular; active; prosperous
1758	適切	suitable, proper
1759	見事	excellent; completely
1779	複雑	complicated, complex
1808	有効	valid; effective
1832	幸い	lucky, fortunate; happiness; fortunately
1833	かわいそう	pitiful, miserable
1856	遥か	faraway, far
1862	ソフト	software; soft
1913	得意	be good at, be proud; customer
1931	異常	abnormal; disorder
1939	失礼(する)	rudeness, impoliteness; be rude, be impolite; rude, impolite; Excuse me
1946	大量	large quantity, a lot
1958	必死	desperate
1959	真剣	serious
2028	平気	insensitive, fine; calmness
2033	下手	not good at, poor, bad, unskilled
2102	不可能	impossible; impossibility
2117	余計	additional, extra
2127	豊富	rich, abundant
2175	詳細	details; detailed
2182	おしゃれ	fashionable, smart
2194	不満	dissatisfaction, discontent; discontented
2200	経済的	economical; economic; financial
2205	真面目	serious; steady; honest
2210	素直	obedient, tame
2228	微妙	delicate, subtle
2243	新鮮	fresh
2262	妙	strange, curious
2275	大幅	steep, big, sharp
2302	貴重	precious, valuable
2309	巨大	huge, enormous, gigantic
2311	苦手	not good at, weak point
2317	容易	easy
2334	本格的	genuine, real; full-scale
2443	丁寧	careful, polite
2458	効果的	effective
2526	夢中	crazy about, obsessed with
2561	独自	original, own
2565	世界的	world, global
2652	特殊	special

#	Word	Meaning
2663	結果的	result
2675	親切	kind
2677	急速	rapid, speedy
2743	独特	peculiar, unique; personal
2759	不便	inconvenience; inconvenient
2764	不幸	unhappiness, misfortune
2792	穏やか	mild; calm, peaceful
2819	本気	seriousness, earnestness; serious, earnest
2835	総合的	synthetic, integrated, comprehensive
2839	極端	extreme
2881	社会的	social
2924	高度	altitude; high, advanced
2928	深刻	serious
2935	頻繁	frequent
2940	快適	comfortable
2984	慎重	careful, discreet
3000	国際的	international
3007	順調	satisfactory, favorable, smooth
3014	多様	various
3079	強力	strong, powerful
3118	重大	serious, important
3130	代表的	representative, typical
3157	正式	formal, official
3169	冷静	calm
3177	真っ赤	bright red; downright
3190	熱心	eager, enthusiastic
3200	純粋	pure; genuine
3217	優秀	excellent
3254	贅沢	luxury; luxurious
3274	最悪	worst
3283	気軽	light-hearted, feel free
3294	完璧	perfect
3308	印象的	impressive
3339	曖昧	vague, ambiguous
3362	ラッキー	lucky
3368	圧倒的	overwhelming
3379	歴史的	historical, historic
3390	前向き	facing forward; positive
3397	まとも	direct; honest; proper
3400	孤独	lonely
3406	伝統的	traditional
3419	奇妙	strange, odd
3425	有利	profitable, advantageous
3431	滅多	rash, thoughtless; seldom
3442	いい加減	irresponsible, groundless
3469	丈夫	strong; healthy
3475	わがまま	selfish, disobedient; selfishness
3480	活発	lively, active; brisk
3493	シンプル	simple
3495	客観的	objective
3532	自動的	automatic
3545	大げさ	exaggerated
3561	かすか	a few, a little
3579	スムーズ	smooth
3581	適正	appropriate, proper, reasonable
3589	不可欠	indispensable
3602	全体的	whole, overall
3632	一時的	temporary
3634	主要	major, main
3635	魅力的	charming, attractive
3643	急激	sudden; drastic
3684	膨大	enormous
3687	根本的	fundamental, basic
3702	派手	flamboyant, flashy
3761	定期的	regular
3769	にぎやか	busy, bustling
3782	まれ	rare
3785	ひそか	secret, confidential; secretly
3804	的確	precise, exact
3819	真っ白	pure white
3847	強烈	strong, intense
3855	華やか	gorgeous
3856	高価	expensive
3875	手軽	light; simple; reasonable
3888	クリア(する)	clearing, clearance; clear; clear
3891	徹底的	thorough, complete
3901	不要	unnecessary
3909	地味	simple
3920	偉大	great, grand
3929	敏感	sensitive
3930	鮮やか	vivid, lively; skillful
3944	健全	healthy
3965	全国的	nationwide
3978	現実的	realistic
4012	大規模	large-scale
4023	バラバラ	separate
4043	肝心	main, essential, important
3401	平等	equality; equal
4067	正常	normal
4084	豪華	luxurious, gorgeous
4093	専門的	technical, academic
4115	別々	separate, individual
4119	最適	best, optimum
4135	円滑	smooth
4136	広大	vast, huge, extensive
4182	技術的	technical, practical
4260	不安定	unstable, uneasy
4279	不意	sudden, unexpected; suddenness
4292	効率的	efficient
4344	透明	transparent, clear
4361	真っ暗	black; pitch-dark
4365	俗	common, popular
4418	実質的	substantial; essential
3716	不明	unknown, unidentified
4429	平ら	flat
4450	決定的	definitive, absolute
4451	無意識	unconsciousness; unconscious
4466	一方的	unilateral, one-sided
4483	政治的	political
4537	真っ黒	black
4550	合理的	reasonable, rational
4555	密接	close
3934	そっくり	resembling, just like; altogether
4572	顕著	conspicuous, remarkable
4579	まし	better; increase
4608	悲惨	miserable
4621	日常的	routine
4656	有力	powerful, strong, important
4664	爽やか	fresh, refreshing
4684	ぼろぼろ	ragged, worn out; in drops
4703	迅速	quick, swift

4706	幸運 (good) luck, fortune; lucky, fortunate	
4747	ハード hard, tight	
4783	緩やか gentle, soft, mild	
4811	科学的 scientific	
4856	着実 steady	
4863	鮮明 clear, vivid	
4878	計画的 planned, deliberate, premeditated	
4879	典型的 typical	
4901	同一 same, identical	
4925	中途半端 unfinished, half-done	
4928	異様 strange	
4943	適度 moderate	
4946	大嫌い hate	
4994	気楽 comfortable, easy, easygoing	
5000	まあまあ so-so, not bad; fairly, moderately	
4692	ふらふら(する) aimlessly, unsteadily; unsteady on one's feet; stagger, be dizzy	

Adnominals: 23 words

30	その that
46	この this
118	そんな that, such
149	同じ same
203	いろんな various
213	大きな big, large, great
218	こんな such, like that
247	あの that, those
249	ある one, a, some, a certain
322	どんな what, what kind of
328	どの which, what
330	いわゆる what is called, what you call, so-called
481	小さな small, little, tiny
509	我が my, our, one's
1220	あんな such, like that
1331	あらゆる every, all, any
1754	ほんの just, nothing but, only
1814	主な main, chief
1900	たいした not big, not much; great, quite
2041	去る leave, pass, be gone
2399	単なる mere, simple
3267	いかなる what kind of, any
4219	おかしな funny, ridiculous

Adverbs: 290 words

39	そう so, such
52	もう already; soon; again
60	こう so, like this
75	やはり、やっぱり as (one) expected, still
84	また additionally, moreover; again; too, and
85	ちょっと (just) a little, a bit
95	どう how, what
126	よく good, well; often
142	とても、とっても very
143	いろいろ various
147	一番 number one, first, most
150	まず first; anyway
153	余り the rest; (not) much
166	結構 quite; good
168	例えば for example, such as
184	ただ just; only, just, merely
190	少し a little, a few
192	買う buy
206	かなり considerably, rather
216	特に especially, particularly
221	すぐ soon
241	ほとんど almost, nearly
253	ずっと all the time, for a long time
254	さらに again, still more, moreover
257	たくさん many, much
259	大体 almost, nearly
260	もちろん of course, needless to say
272	なぜ why
284	初めて for the first time, first
289	全く entirely, completely; (not) at all
291	結局 after all, in the end, finally
297	なかなか very, quite; (not) easily
299	もっと more
305	もし if, in case
306	全然 (not) at all; utterly, completely
320	たぶん probably, perhaps, maybe
338	全部 all, whole, entire
343	毎日 every day
366	確か sure, certain, reliable; maybe, probably; if I remember rightly, it's my understanding that
373	ちょうど just, exactly
374	当然 naturally, as a matter of course
379	どんどん rapidly, fast, soon
381	とにかく anyway, regardless
391	必ず always, certainly, surely
412	自然 nature; natural; naturally
415	一応 at first glance; at least, just
419	一杯 cup(ful), glass(ful), be full of, a lot of
421	つまり in short, that is to say, after all
424	絶対 absolute, absolutely, whatever
433	だんだん gradually, more and more, less and less
463	すでに already, before
480	十分 enough, sufficient; fully, sufficiently, adequately
510	どうしても by all means, at any cost, no matter what, after all
530	最も most, extremely
533	ちゃんと exactly, regularly, properly
551	取り敢えず for the time being; at once
582	今後 in the future, from now on
590	はっきり clearly, certainly
616	いずれ anyway, sooner or later; either
625	割と comparatively, rather
631	是非 by all means, please; definitely, certainly
636	きっと surely, certainly

#	Word	Meaning
637	どうして	why
639	なお	more, still
650	しっかり	hard, tight
654	しばらく	for a while, a minute, for a long time
659	いくら	how much, however
696	ものすごい	terrible; terribly
705	一体	how, what, why, who
711	元々	from the first, originally
719	たまたま	accidentally, by chance
725	常	way; always, usually
726	より	more, better
741	やっと	at last
761	まあ	Oh!, well, now
804	おそらく	probably, likely
817	直接	directly, direct
827	ずいぶん	very, pretty, quite
852	突然	suddenly
855	ゆっくり	slowly, leisurely; plenty of time
892	きちんと	precisely, accurately, neatly
906	決して	never, by no means
926	実は	actually, in fact
961	たまに	occasionally, once in a while
981	相当(する)	considerable; equivalence; be equivalent; considerably, pretty;
985	まさに	exactly
990	分	part, share, portion
993	むしろ	rather, if anything
997	まるで	just like, quite
1002	ほぼ	about, nearly, almost
1004	毎年	every year, annually
1008	明日	tomorrow
1048	さすが	as might be expected, as one would expect
1050	再び	again, once more
1078	去年	last year
1098	多少	more or less; somewhat; a little
1104	いきなり	suddenly, without notice
1109	時々	sometimes, once in a while, on occasion
1118	割合	comparatively; ratio, percentage
1120	いまだ	still, yet, so far
1125	ああ	like that
1127	次第	order; depend on; as soon as
1129	やがて	soon, before long, after all
1131	かつて	once, before, ever, former
1142	瞬間	moment, instant, second
1144	わずか	a few, a little, a bit; only
1153	本来	originally, essentially, by nature, proper
1185	通常	normally, ordinary, regular
1198	いかに	how, in what way
1200	極めて	very, extremely
1210	何とか	somehow; something
1215	戦後	postwar, after the war
1227	昨年	last year
1244	まだまだ	still, still more
1247	一時	at one time, temporary, for a while
1250	日々	every day, daily; days
1253	よろしく	well, properly, best regards
1259	主に	mainly, for the most part, chiefly
1264	なるべく	as ... as possible, if possible
1272	一切	all, entirely, not ... at all
1279	ようやく	at last, gradually, barely
1289	大分	very, a lot, much
1307	せっかく	with effort, take the trouble to
1316	遠く	far, remote; distance
1341	全員	all members, everyone
1361	従来	up to now, conventional, traditional
1372	始め	beginning, origin
1390	ますます	more and more, increasingly
1396	先日	the other day, recently
1409	正直	honesty; honest, truthful; honestly
1459	夕方	evening
1482	あくまで	only, to the last
1488	つい	without thinking, unintentionally
1496	単に	just, simply
1501	ついに	at last, finally
1505	無事	safely; safety; safe
1518	そもそも	in the first place
1525	少なくとも	at least
1534	仲良く	friendly
1544	たとえ	even if
1554	すっかり	entirely, completely
1557	なんら	nothing
1576	一層	more
1598	後	after, later
1612	いよいよ	finally, at last
1626	何でも	anything; nothing; everything
1645	一瞬	a moment, an instant
1656	やや	a little, slightly
1667	わざわざ	take the trouble, especially
1736	ともかく	in any case, anyway
1747	そろそろ	soon; slowly
1759	見事	excellent; completely
1764	今日	today, these days
1789	大抵	usually
1793	どうぞ	please
1795	唯一	only
1809	次々	one after another
1813	都合(する)	convenience, circumstances; arrange; altogether
1818	一気	at a stretch, in one gulp
1832	幸い	lucky, fortunate; happiness; fortunately
1865	さっき	a little while ago
1866	ごく	very
1895	当初	beginning, original; at first
1905	早速	at once, lose no time in doing
1909	近年	in recent years
1912	果たして	really; just as one thought
1815	ふと	casually; suddenly
1917	何だか	somewhat; somehow
1928	少々	a little, a minute

#	Word	Meaning
1936	あえて	dare
1942	いったん	once; for a moment
1960	まさか	surely not, cannot possibly; the worst
1970	必ずしも	not necessarily, not always
1971	たっぷり	full, plenty; fullness
1980	若干	slightly; a little, few, some
2021	かえって	on the contrary, rather
2025	いわば	so to speak, as it were
2044	改めて	over again; some other time
1676	じっと(する)	still, fixedly, intently
2073	なるほど	I see, indeed, to be sure, of course
2084	まっすぐ	straight, direct; honest
2133	同じく	likewise, like, as
2147	いざ	when one comes to, if compelled
2167	日常	everyday, daily, usually
2192	偶然	by chance; chance, accident
2231	あらかじめ	beforehand, in advance
2318	しばしば	always, often
2338	二人共	both of them, two people
2319	のんびり	tranquil, leisurely, easygoing
2347	大いに	very, greatly
2356	もはや	now, already; not ... any longer
2394	ひたすら	determinedly, earnestly
2418	何しろ	anyhow, anyway
2419	何と	how, what
2460	しょっちゅう	often, always
2508	とうとう	finally
2529	どうせ	anyway
2454	ぱっと	suddenly
2551	なにより	above all, chiefly, more than anything
2585	とんでも	unexpected; outrageous, very offensive
2629	相変わらず	as ever, as usual, the same, as before [always]
2776	たった	just, only
2777	およそ	around, about
2779	ぴったり	tight; exactly
2568	そっと	softly, lightly
2905	まして	much less, much more
2917	別に	(not) particularly
2933	毎週	every week
2938	長年	long time; many years
2528	よほど、よっぽど	very, greatly
2968	一見	at a glance
2994	せめて	at least, at most
3024	ただいま	now, just now, at once; I'm back!
3061	ぼおっと	vacantly; dimly
3078	いまさら	now (after such a long time)
3089	直ちに	immediately, directly
3097	とりわけ	especially
3104	いかにも	indeed, really, just
3120	無理矢理	forcibly, against one's will
3205	さっぱり	not at all
3253	いまや	now
3275	ぎりぎり	barely
3307	半ば	half, middle; partly
3322	むろん	of course
3385	古く	ancient times; anciently
3391	ゆったり	comfortably; calm; loose
3422	依然	still, as before
3439	大部分	majority; mostly
3427	じっくり	without haste, deliberately
3471	たちまち	in a moment, at once; suddenly
3479	なおかつ	besides, and yet
3497	つくづく	thoroughly, deeply, carefully
3513	せいぜい	at most
3519	いちいち	one by one; everything
3547	そこそこ	about; in a hurry; all right
3573	やたら	freely, thoughtlessly
3619	いつか	someday
3638	この間	a few days ago; recently, lately
3646	たいして	(not) very much
3760	多々	many
3776	現に	as a matter of fact, actually
3784	数多く	many, a number of
3785	ひそか	secret, confidential; secretly
3809	再度	twice, again
3810	以後	after this, since then
3820	さっと	quickly
3825	度々	often
3840	わざと	intentionally
3884	まさしく	surely, exactly
3908	毎朝	every morning; every morning
3919	漠然	vague, obscure
3971	きっちり	tightly
3982	もっぱら	entirely
3985	そうこう	in the meantime
3992	さほど	(not) particularly
4058	あっさり	easily, flatly, simple, plain
4074	次いで	next, after that
4016	ニコニコ(する)	smile; smiling
4130	概ね	mostly, mainly, generally
4140	堂々	nobly, openly
4200	ぼんやり(する)	vacantly, vaguely, dimly; be vague, be blurred
4213	到底	(cannot) possibly, no matter how
4210	ぐるぐる	round and round
4229	あれこれ	this and that
4258	いまいち	not quite, not really
4262	一向	(not) at all; completely
4263	それゆえ	therefore, thus
4345	即	at once, immediately
4469	さっさと	quickly
4447	ふっと	suddenly
4521	万が一	just in case
4535	いささか	a little, slightly, rather
4547	今後とも	from now on, in the future
4538	すっと	quickly; quietly; straight

3607	生き生き lively, fresh	456	しかも moreover, besides	137	うー Woo, Oooh
3934	そっくり resembling, just like; altogether	552	ところが however	258	いー good, great
		558	一方 one side; on the other hand	265	うん yes, yeah
4594	年々 year after year			304	と well, erm (abbreviation of "eeto")
4678	延々 on and on, dragging on	561	それでも but, still		
4684	ぼろぼろ ragged, worn out; in drops	578	要するに in short, to sum up	501	いや No
		612	だが but, however	502	はい yes; all right
4713	久々 for the first time in a long time	724	ただし but, however, though	841	んと well
		769	では then, well	1084	ありがとう thank you
4733	散々 severely, repeatedly	857	したがって accordingly, consequently	1573	さあ come on, now, well
4816	そんなこんな what with one thing and another; after many twists and turns			1640	すみません Thank you; I am sorry; Excuse me
		904	ちなみに by the way, incidentally	1916	あっ Ah!, Oh!, Hey!
4825	案外 unexpectedly	922	すなわち that is (to say), namely	1939	失礼(する) rudeness, impoliteness; be rude, be impolite; rude, impolite; Excuse me
4822	こっそり secretly, on the sly				
4897	極力 as much as possible	933	だけれど despite, though		
4903	何せ anyhow, after all, in any case	963	もしくは or, otherwise		
		1062	さて well, now	1961	ごめんなさい I'm sorry, Excuse me
4938	ただただ all (someone) can do is, simply, nothing but	1096	かつ besides, also, as well		
		1166	それでは, それじゃ then, well, so	2578	おい hey
5000	まあまあ so-so, not bad; fairly, moderately			2656	はあ oh, Oh boy, Oh dear
		1424	から because	2727	あれ Oh
4692	ふらふら(する) aimlessly, unsteadily; unsteady on one's feet; stagger, be dizzy	1492	それとも or	2910	ほら Look!
		1629	そこで so	3112	わー wow!
		1710	すると then, if so	3252	よし All right!, Good!
		1812	が but	3395	あら Oh! (used by female speakers)
4990	しみじみ keenly, heartily, from one's heart	2153	なので because, as		
		2155	ところで by the way, well	3437	ううん no; well
Conjunctions: 45 words		2193	だって because, but	3512	ねえ hey
31	けれど though, although	2222	もっとも though, although	3558	いえ no
35	で so, then	2494	ないし or, otherwise	3852	いいえ no
84	また additionally, moreover; again; too, and	2818	ですが but, however	4410	おはよう good morning
		3140	ですけれど but	4446	こんにちは Hello, Good afternoon
108	それで and then; so; that is why	3461	ならびに and, both . . . and		
		3889	だけど but, however	4638	いやあ Well, sorry
113	そして and, so			4646	おめでとう congratulations
136	それから and then, after that, and	**Interjections: 36 words**			
		18	えー, ええ eh?, what?; well, yes	**Case-marking particles: 10 words**	
140	でも but, however				
162	しかし but, however	21	あの, あのう, あのー Excuse me; uh, eh, um, ah, er	1	の of; in; at; for; by
184	ただ just; only, just, merely			2	に at; on; in; to; for
185	だから so, therefore, because	23	まー, まあ Wow!, Oh my God!	5	を ACCUSATIVE
237	あるいは or; perhaps, probably, maybe			7	が NOMINATIVE
		65	その uh, er, um, mm	9	と and; or; with; if
		73	ん oh, mm, well	12	で in; at; from; by
256	及び and, as well as	74	あー er, uh, um, hmm, ah, oh	32	から from
346	または or			94	へ DESTINATION
352	じゃ well, so, then	90	えーと well, let me see	135	より than; from
376	ですから so, therefore	122	おー Oh, Wow!	1561	にて by; in; at

Binding particles & Adverbial paticles: 37 words

- 3 は TOPIC
- 11 も too, also
- 24 の POSSESSIVE
- 36 か if; or
- 45 とか and; or
- 63 や and; or
- 66 まで to, till, until
- 68 たり and
- 81 など and so on, etc.
- 87 だけ only, alone, merely
- 88 くらい, ぐらい about, around
- 161 ほど about; extent
- 189 なんか such as, like
- 211 しか only, just, no more than
- 229 なんて [expresses belittlement]
- 271 ばかり only, just, almost
- 450 こそ EMPHATIC
- 549 ずつ each, ...by...
- 609 のみ only, merely
- 632 さえ even; besides; if only
- 1013 やら and, or
- 1474 なり or, whether or not
- 1665 すら even
- 1685 きり only
- 1886 もの because
- 1902 どころ far from, on the contrary, can't even
- 1996 とも all, both
- 2013 ぜ EMPHASIS
- 2150 たって even if
- 2720 といっても even though
- 2769 をはじめ starting with..., including
- 3037 ど but (Classical)
- 3299 では in; on; as for
- 3430 際に when
- 3727 しも EMPHASIS (Classical)
- 4775 のみならず not only ... but, as well as
- 4908 つ [indicating contrasts or coordinations]

Conjunctive particles: 18 words

- 8 て REASON
- 37 が ADVERSATIVE
- 41 と if, when; with
- 57 ので, んで as, because, since
- 61 から because, since
- 62 ば if
- 96 し and, besides
- 117 ながら with, over, while
- 131 ても even if
- 511 のに although, though; in order to
- 744 つつ while doing; though
- 1179 ものの but, although, despite
- 2538 ては alternately do ... and ...
- 2645 としたら if so
- 2697 にもかかわらず in spite of, though, despite
- 2899 にしろ even if
- 2958 とすれば if that is the case
- 2982 とはいえ though, however

Sentence-ending particles: 12 words

- 26 ね isn't it?, don't you?
- 29 か QUESTION
- 55 な PROHIBITION
- 59 よ ASSERTION, REMINDING (informal)
- 309 の EMOTION/QUESTION
- 331 わ EXCLAMATION
- 641 ぞ EMPHASIS
- 721 さ ATTRACT ATTENTION
- 921 かしら I wonder
- 1339 い QUESTION
- 1732 け QUESTION ABOUT SOMETHING SPEAKER FORGOT
- 3016 じゃん isn't it

Auxiliaries: 31 words

- 4 た PAST
- 6 だ COPULA
- 10 ます POLITE (after verb)
- 14 です COPULA (polite)
- 15 れる PASSIVE
- 27 ない not
- 33 よう INDUCEMENT
- 50 せる CAUSATIVE
- 56 ず NEGATION
- 76 たい want to, like to
- 104 う SOLICITATION
- 236 べし must, should
- 248 らしい seem, look
- 865 とく [shortened form of "te oku"]
- 936 や COPULA (dialectal)
- 1337 ことにする decide to, pretend to
- 1445 ことはない not have to, there is no need for
- 1687 ごとし like, as if (Classical)
- 1718 まい INTENTION OF NEGATION
- 1773 じゃ (COPULA) is, are
- 2431 に違いない must be, no doubt that
- 2513 とる [shortened form of "teoru"]
- 2516 しかしながら however, but
- 2574 たがる want to
- 2683 にすぎない just, mere
- 3365 こととなる it has been decided that
- 3762 しめる (Classical)
- 3878 ちまう do something completely
- 4698 やがる VERB SUFFIX (vulgarism)
- 4823 へん NEGATION (dialectal)
- 4827 でもある be ..., too

Compound particles: 78 words

- 13 ている, てる CONTINUATION
- 16 という, つう called, named
- 20 のです, んです ASSERTION (polite)
- 43 てしまう end up doing ...
- 49 のだ, んだ ASSERTION
- 53 である COPULA (formal)
- 82 として as
- 86 てくる go and ...
- 89 ではない it is not the case that ...
- 92 ていく, てく go and ...
- 106 ておる CONTINUATION (polite)
- 107 について about, concerning, as to

#	Word	Meaning
111	てみる	try ...ing
114	てくれる	[do something as a favor]
125	のではない, んではない	it is not that ...
154	によって	by, because of; depend on, depending on
155	かもしれない	perhaps, maybe
172	てくださる	[do something as a favor (honorific)]
198	てもらう	[receive a favor]
202	のである	ASSERTION (formal)
233	において	at; in; on
239	による	be due to, be based on
252	ていただく	[receive a favor (humble)]
269	ておく	do something in advance, in preparation for something
270	に対して	to, toward; for; against
278	にとって	for
300	ことができる	can, be able to
326	ことになる	it happens that ..., it is decided that
340	により	by; with; depending on
344	ために	for
348	に対する	to; for; against
360	てある	[describes a state resulting from someone's action]
362	における	in
371	なければいけない	must, have to, need to
404	に関する	be concerned with, be related to
454	てもいい	(I) don't mind if
461	でない	COPULA (NEGATIVE)
486	といった	like, such as
495	なければならない	must
536	てほしい	want/ask someone to do
542	でございます	be (formal)
595	に関して	about, regarding, concerning
770	てあげる	do something for somebody
775	ことがある	have done; there are sometimes
779	てやる	do something for somebody/something
999	こともある	sometimes, can be
1000	てはいけない, ちゃいけない	must not, should not
1007	に対し	toward; against; in contrast to
1130	ではありません, じゃありません	not, no
1171	とともに	together with, with
1205	としても	assuming, even if
1306	を通じて	throughout, across, through
1342	にしても	even if, even though
1348	によると	according to
1477	でもって	by, with, in
1574	だけでなく	not only
1799	をもって	by; with; as of
1810	上で	after; in the context of
1853	なくてはいけない	have to, must
1921	ざるを得ない	have to, cannot help doing
1953	にあたって	at the time of
1986	て参る	begin to, come to; have been; go and come (humble)
2143	つつある	be in the process of doing, be doing
2294	てはならない	must not, should not
2297	しかない	can't but, can only, have no choice
2351	によれば	according to, ...say
2374	によっては	depending on
2409	にわたって	throughout, over a period of
2911	を通して	according to; through
2971	ねばならない	must, have to
3002	ないといけない	must, have to
3046	につれて	as
3342	なくてはならない	must
3411	をめぐる	over, concerning
3536	にわたる	ranging, covering
3699	までもない	needless
3713	に比べて	compared to
4193	仕方が無い	cannot be helped, no use

Prefix: 1 word

2301	御	POLITENESS PREFIX

Suffixes: 4 words

1694	等	and so on
3662	難い	hard to ...
4682	～さん	Mr., Mrs., Miss., Ms.
4846	ごと	every

Word types (origins)

Definition of word types
1和 *wago* (Japanese origin)
2漢 *kango* (Chinese origin)
3外 *gairaigo* (foreign loan word)
4混 *konseigo* (hybrid: *wago* + *kango*)
5固 proper name

1和 *wago* (Japanese origin)
1. の no *p. case* of; in; at; for; by
2. に ni *p. case* at; on; in; to; for
3. は wa *p.* TOPIC
4. た ta *aux.* PAST
5. を o *p. case* ACCUSATIVE
6. だ da *aux.* COPULA
7. が ga *p. case* NOMINATIVE
8. て te *p. conj.* REASON
9. と to *p. case* and; or; with; if
10. ます masu *aux.* POLITE (after verb)
11. も mo *p.* too, also
12. で de *p. case* in; at; from; by
13. ている, てる te iru, te ru *cp.* CONTINUATION
14. です desu *aux.* COPULA (polite)
15. れる reru *aux.* PASSIVE
16. という, つう to iu, to yuu, tsuu *cp.* called, named
17. 事 koto *n.* thing
18. えー, ええ ee *interj.* eh?, what?; well, yes
19. 言う iu, yuu *v.* say, speak, talk
20. のです, んです no desu, n desu *cp.* ASSERTION (polite)
21. あの, あのう, あのー ano, anoo *interj.* Excuse me; uh, eh, um, ah, er
22. する suru *v.* do; make
23. まー, まあ maa *interj.* Wow!, Oh my God!
24. の no *p.* POSSESSIVE
25. ある aru *v.* be (existence), have (possession), happen, occur
26. ね ne *p. disc.* isn't it?, don't you?
27. ない nai *aux.* not
28. なる naru *v.* become, get; come to do, start to do; turn into
29. か ka *p. disc.* QUESTION
30. その sono *adn.* that
31. けれど keredo *conj.* though, although
32. から kara *p. case* from
34. 思う omou *v.* think, believe; feel; expect
35. で de *conj.* so, then
36. か ka *p.* if; or
37. が ga *p. conj.* ADVERSATIVE
38. 物 mono *n.* thing, object, stuff
39. そう soo *adv.* so, such
40. 何 nani *pron.* what; something; anything; nothing
41. と to *p. conj.* if, when; with
42. 私 watashi, watakushi, atashi *pron.* I
43. てしまう te shimau *cp.* end up doing . . .
44. それ sore *pron.* that
45. とか toka *p.* and; or
46. この kono *adn.* this
47. 無い nai *i-adj.* There is no . . . , no . . .
48. 行く iku, yuku *v.* go; come
49. のだ, んだ no da, n da *cp.* ASSERTION
50. せる seru *aux.* CAUSATIVE
51. これ kore *pron.* this
52. もう moo *adv.* already; soon; again
53. である de aru *cp.* COPULA (formal)
54. 時 toki *n.* time
55. な na *p. disc.* PROHIBITION
56. ず zu *aux.* NEGATION
57. ので, んで no de, n de *p. conj.* as, because, since
58. 人 hito *n.* person, people, human being
59. よ yo *p. disc.* ASSERTION, REMINDING (informal)
60. こう koo *adv.* so, like this
61. から kara *p. conj.* because, since
62. ば ba *p. conj.* if
63. や ya *p.* and; or
64. 来る kuru *v.* come
65. その sono *interj.* uh, er, um, mm
66. まで made *p.* to, till, until

67 見る miru *v.* see; look at, watch; check
68 たり tari *p.* and
69 今 ima *n.* now
70 良い, いい yoi, ii *i-adj.* good
71 所 tokoro *n.* place, point; part; aspect
73 ん n *interj.* oh, mm, well
74 あー aa *interj.* er, uh, um, hmm, ah, oh
75 やはり, やっぱり yahari, yappari *adv.* as (one) expected, still
76 たい tai *aux.* want to, like to
77 やる yaru *v.* do; make; give
78 中 naka *n.* inside, in; into
79 いる iru *v.* be, exist; stay
80 できる dekiru *v.* be ready
81 など nado *p.* and so on, etc.
82 として to shite *cp.* as
83 後 ato *n.* after, later
84 また mata *adv.* additionally, moreover *conj.* again; too, and
85 ちょっと chotto *adv.* (just) a little, a bit
86 てくる te kuru *cp.* go and . . .
87 だけ dake *p.* only, alone, merely
88 くらい, ぐらい kurai, gurai *p.* about, around
89 ではない de wa nai *cp.* it is not the case that . . .
90 えーと eeto *interj.* well, let me see
92 ていく, てく te iku, te ku *cp.* go and . . .
93 訳 wake *n.* reason, cause
94 へ e *p. case* DESTINATION
95 どう dou *adv.* how, what
96 し shi *p. conj.* and, besides
98 持つ motsu *v.* have, take, hold
99 出る deru *v.* go out, come out; attend
100 ため tame *n.* for
101 すごい sugoi *i-adj.* fantastic, wonderful; terrible
102 考える kangaeru *v.* think
103 そこ soko *pron.* there; then
104 う u *aux.* SOLICITATION
105 分かる wakaru *v.* understand, see
106 ておる te oru *cp.* CONTINUATION (polite)
107 について ni tsui te *cp.* about, concerning, as to
108 それで sorede *conj.* and then; so; that is why
109 入る hairu *v.* enter, come in, go in
110 作る tsukuru *v.* make, create, cook
111 てみる te miru *cp.* try . . . ing
112 聞く, 聴く kiku *v.* hear; listen; listen to, obey
113 そして soshite *conj.* and, so
114 てくれる te kureru *cp.* [do something as a favor]
115 場合 baai *n.* case, occasion
116 話 hanashi *n.* story, talk
117 ながら nagara *p. conj.* with, over, while
118 そんな sonna *adn.* that, such
119 使う tsukau *v.* use, handle
122 おー oo *interj.* Oh, Wow!
123 前 mae *n.* forward; front; before
124 多い ooi *i-adj.* many, much, a lot of
125 のではない, んではない no de wa nai, n de wa nai *cp.* it is not that . . .
126 よく yoku *adv.* good, well; often
127 一つ hito-tsu *n.* one
128 子供 kodomo *n.* child
131 ても temo *p. conj.* even if
132 取る toru *v.* take, get; have; pass
133 うち uchi *n.* inside; of; before
134 知る shiru *v.* know
135 より yori *p. case* than; from
136 それから sorekara *conj.* and then, after that, and
137 うー uu *interj.* Woo, Oooh
139 みたい mitai *na-adj.* like
140 でも demo *conj.* but, however
141 ここ koko *pron.* here
142 とても, とっても totemo, tottemo *adv.* very
143 いろいろ iroiro *adv., na-adj.* various
145 そう sou *n., na-adj.* be about to
146 行なう okonau *v.* do, carry out, hold
149 同じ onaji *adn.* same
150 まず mazu *adv.* first; anyway
152 仕事(する) shigoto(suru) *n.* work, job *v.* work
153 余り amari *adv.* the rest *n.* (not) much
154 によって ni yotte *cp.* by, because of; depend on, depending on
155 かもしれない kamo shirenai *cp.* perhaps, maybe
157 皆 mina, minna *n.* everyone; everything
158 彼 kare *pron.* he
159 方 kata *n.* person, man
160 食べる taberu *v.* eat
161 ほど hodo *p.* about; extent
162 しかし shikashi *conj.* but, however
163 書く kaku *v.* write
164 入れる ireru *v.* put in; include
165 次 tsugi *n.* next, following, coming
168 例えば tatoeba *adv.* for example, such as

169 目, 眼 me *n.* eye
170 頃 koro *n.* time, about, when
171 上 ue *n.* top; above; up; on
172 てくださる te kudasaru *cp.* [do something as a favor (honorific)]
173 他 hoka *n.* other, another; else
174 いつ itsu *pron.* when
175 家 ie *n.* house, home
176 付く tsuku *v.* stick; be stained with
177 日, 陽 hi *n.* day; sun
178 出す dasu *v.* take out; pay; send
179 一人 hito-ri *n.* one person; alone
181 どこ doko *pron.* where
184 ただ tada *conj.* just *adv.* only, just, merely
185 だから dakara *conj.* so, therefore, because
186 違う chigau *v.* be different; be wrong
187 受ける ukeru *v.* get, receive, take
188 言葉 kotoba *n.* word; language
189 なんか nanka *p.* such as, like
190 少し sukoshi *adv.* a little, a few
191 まま mama *adv.* as it is
192 買う kau *v.* buy
193 まだ mada *n.* yet, still
194 手 te *n.* hand
195 話す hanasu *v.* talk, tell, speak
196 好き suki *na-adj.* favorite, like, love
197 返る kaeru *v.* return
198 てもらう te morau *cp.* [receive a favor]
199 掛ける kakeru *v.* hang; take; cost
200 終わる owaru *v.* end, finish
202 のである no de aru *cp.* ASSERTION (formal)
203 いろんな ironna *adn.* various
204 付ける tsukeru *v.* put; attach; apply
205 形 katachi *n.* form, shape, figure
209 間 aida *n.* distance; period
211 しか shika *p.* only, just, no more than
212 かかる kakaru *v.* hang; take; cost
213 大きな ookina *adn.* big, large, great
214 住む sumu *v.* live
217 誰 dare *pron.* who, whose, whom
218 こんな konna *adn.* such, like that
219 友達 tomodachi *n.* friend
220 大きい ookii *i-adj.* big, large, great
221 すぐ sugu *adv.* soon
224 国 kuni *n.* country
225 あげる ageru *v.* raise, lift
226 あなた, あんた anata, anta *pron.* you
228 高い takai *i-adj.* high, tall; expensive
229 なんて nante *p.* [expresses belittlement]

230 悪い warui *i-adj.* bad
232 乗る noru *v.* ride, get on, take
233 において ni oite *cp.* at; in; on
234 見える mieru *v.* see, be seen
235 変わる kawaru *v.* change
236 べし beshi *aux.* must, should
237 あるいは aruiwa *conj.* or; perhaps, probably, maybe
239 による ni yoru *cp.* be due to, be based on
241 ほとんど hotondo *adv.* almost, nearly
245 二人 futa-ri *n.* two people
246 心 kokoro *n.* mind, heart; thought; feeling
247 あの ano *adn.* that, those
248 らしい rashii *aux.* seem, look
249 ある aru *adn.* one, a, some, a certain
250 金 kane *n.* money
251 顔 kao *n.* face
252 ていただく te itadaku *cp.* [receive a favor (humble)]
253 ずっと zutto *adv.* all the time, for a long time
254 さらに sarani *adv.* again, still more, moreover
255 町, 街 machi *n.* town, city
256 及び oyobi *conj.* and, as well as
258 いー ii *interj.* good, great
261 読む yomu *v.* read
262 人たち hito-tachi *n.* people
263 今日 kyou *n.* today
264 昔 mukashi *n.* ancient times, in the past, once
265 うん un *interj.* yes, yeah
266 すべて subete *n.* everything, all
267 教える oshieru *v.* teach, tell
268 子 ko *n.* child
269 ておく te oku *cp.* do something in advance, in preparation for something
271 ばかり bakari *p.* only, just, almost
272 なぜ naze *adv.* why
273 水 mizu *n.* water
276 置く oku *v.* put, place; leave
277 楽しい tanoshii *i-adj.* pleasant, happy, enjoyable
278 にとって ni totte *cp.* for
279 声 koe *n.* voice
281 残る nokoru *v.* remain, be left
283 車 kuruma *n.* car; wheel
284 初めて hajimete *adv.* for the first time, first
286 体 karada *n.* body
287 私達 watashi-tachi, watakushi-tachi *pron.* we
288 強い tsuyoi *i-adj.* strong, powerful

- **289** 全く mattaku *adv.* entirely, completely; (not) at all
- **290** 呼ぶ yobu *v.* call
- **292** 歩く aruku *v.* walk
- **293** 男 otoko *n.* man, male
- **296** 生きる ikiru *v.* live
- **297** なかなか nakanaka *adv.* very, quite; (not) easily
- **298** 先 saki *n.* end, front
- **299** もっと motto *adv.* more
- **300** ことができる koto ga dekiru *cp.* can, be able to
- **304** と to *interj.* well, erm (abbreviation of "eeto")
- **305** もし moshi *adv.* if, in case
- **307** 飲む nomu *v.* drink
- **308** 新しい atarashii *i-adj.* new, fresh
- **309** の no *p. disc.* EMOTION/QUESTION
- **310** 早い hayai *i-adj.* early, soon
- **311** 会う au *v.* meet, see
- **313** あれ are *pron.* that
- **314** 小さい chiisai *i-adj.* small, little, tiny
- **315** 相手 aite *n.* companion; partner
- **316** 母 haha *n.* mother
- **319** 四 yon, shi *n.* four
- **321** 店 mise *n.* store, shop
- **322** どんな donna *adn.* what, what kind of
- **323** 頭 atama *n.* head
- **325** 長い nagai *i-adj.* long
- **326** ことになる koto ni naru *cp.* it happens that…, it is decided that
- **328** どの dono *adn.* which, what
- **329** こちら kochira *pron.* this place, here; this way; this
- **330** いわゆる iwayuru *adn.* what is called, what you call, so-called
- **331** わ wa *p. disc.* EXCLAMATION
- **332** 夜 yoru *n.* night, evening
- **334** 者 mono *n.* person, people
- **336** 親 oya *n.* parent
- **337** 名前 namae *n.* name
- **339** 皆さん mina-san *n.* everybody, everyone
- **340** により ni yori *cp.* by; with; depending on
- **342** 立つ tatsu *v.* stand
- **344** ために tameni *cp.* for
- **345** おいしい oishii *i-adj.* delicious, tasty
- **346** または matawa *conj.* or
- **352** じゃ ja *conj.* well, so, then
- **355** 少ない sukunai *i-adj.* a little, a few
- **357** うまい umai *i-adj.* delicious, tasty; good at
- **358** 覚える oboeru *v.* learn, remember, memorize
- **360** てある te aru *cp.* [describes a state resulting from someone's action]
- **361** 続く tsuzuku *v.* continue, go on, last
- **362** における ni okeru *cp.* in
- **363** 俺 ore *pron.* I (used by male speakers)
- **364** 生まれる umareru *v.* be born
- **365** 父 chichi *n.* father
- **366** 確か tashika *na-adj., adv.* sure, certain, reliable *adv.* maybe, probably; if I remember rightly, it's my understanding that
- **367** それぞれ sorezore *n.* each
- **369** はず hazu *n.* ought to, should
- **371** なければいけない nakereba ikenai *cp.* must, have to, need to
- **372** 部屋 heya *n.* room
- **376** ですから desukara *conj.* so, therefore
- **378** 朝 asa *n.* morning
- **379** どんどん dondon *adv.* rapidly, fast, soon
- **380** 得る eru, uru *v.* get, obtain
- **381** とにかく tonikaku *adv.* anyway, regardless
- **382** 選ぶ erabu *v.* choose, select
- **383** 面白い omoshiroi *i-adj.* interesting; fun; funny
- **384** 戻る modoru *v.* return, go back
- **386** やめる yameru *v.* stop, give up
- **387** 下 shita *n.* under; below; down; low
- **388** 始める hajimeru *v.* start, begin
- **389** まわり mawari *n.* circumference; surroundings, neighborhood, around
- **390** 犬 inu *n.* dog
- **391** 必ず kanarazu *adv.* always, certainly, surely
- **392** 残す nokosu *v.* leave
- **394** 嬉しい ureshii *i-adj.* glad, happy
- **395** 力 chikara *n.* power, strength
- **396** 遊ぶ asobu *v.* play
- **397** 若い wakai *i-adj.* young
- **399** 女 onna *n.* woman, female
- **401** 始まる hajimaru *v.* start, begin
- **402** 死ぬ shinu *v.* die
- **406** 通り touri *n.* street; as
- **410** 木 ki *n.* wood; tree
- **413** 音 oto *n.* sound, noise
- **414** 海 umi *n.* sea, ocean
- **416** 与える ataeru *v.* give, present
- **418** 働く hataraku *v.* work
- **420** 近く chikaku *n.* near, nearby
- **421** つまり tsumari *adv.* in short, that is to say, after all

422 共 tomo *n.* with, together
427 足 ashi *n.* foot; leg
428 切る kiru *v.* cut
429 走る hashiru *v.* run
430 待つ matsu *v.* wait
432 子供たち kodomo-tachi *n.* children
434 二つ futa-tsu *n.* two
435 楽しむ tanoshimu *v.* enjoy, have a good time
437 多く ooku *n.* many, most
438 寝る neru *v.* sleep; lie down, go to bed
440 決める kimeru *v.* decide, fix
441 忘れる wasureru *v.* forget
442 口 kuchi *n.* mouth
443 送る okuru *v.* send; spend (time)
444 姿 sugata *n.* figure, shape, appearance
445 なくなる nakunaru *v.* disappear; be gone
449 示す shimesu *v.* show
450 こそ koso *p.* EMPHATIC
451 人々 hitobito *n.* people
452 道 michi *n.* way, road
454 てもいい te mo ii *cp.* (I) don't mind if
455 思い omoi *n.* thought, mind, heart
456 しかも shikamo *conj.* moreover, besides
457 難しい muzukashii, mutsukashii *i-adj.* difficult, hard
458 彼ら kare-ra *pron.* they
459 山 yama *n.* mountain
461 でない de nai *cp.* COPULA (NEGATIVE)
462 願う negau *v.* wish, ask, pray
463 すでに sudeni *adv.* already, before
465 向かう mukau *v.* face; go (toward, in the direction of)
466 連れる tsureru *v.* take somebody, accompany
467 変える kaeru *v.* change
470 年 toshi *n.* year; age
471 花 hana *n.* flower
472 求める motomeru *v.* ask for, request, demand
474 もらう morau *v.* get, have, receive
477 経つ tatsu *v.* pass, go by
478 先程 sakihodo *n.* a short while ago
481 小さな chiisana *adn.* small, little, tiny
482 開く hiraku *v.* open; bloom; hold
484 続ける tsuzukeru *v.* continue, keep up, go on
486 といった to itta *cp.* like, such as
487 当たる ataru *v.* hit, bump, touch; guess right, win
488 近い chikai *i-adj.* near, close
490 認める mitomeru *v.* recognize, acknowledge, admit, approve, accept
491 これら kore-ra *pron.* these
493 増える fueru *v.* increase, gain
495 なければならない nakere ba naranai *cp.* must
496 外 soto *n.* outside
497 進む susumu *v.* to go forward, make progress
498 起きる okiru *v.* get up; wake; happen
499 嫌 iya, ya *n., na-adj.* unpleasant, disagreeable
501 いや iya *interj.* No
502 はい hai *interj.* yes; all right
504 身 mi *n.* body, oneself; position
507 含む fukumu *v.* contain, include
509 我が waga *adn.* my, our, one's
510 どうしても doushitemo *adv.* by all means, at any cost, no matter what, after all
511 のに noni *p. conj.* although, though; in order to
512 娘 musume *n.* daughter
513 見せる miseru *v.* show
515 今年 kotoshi *n.* this year
519 合わせる awaseru *v.* join, add up; adjust
520 安い yasui *i-adj.* low, cheap
521 夢 yume *n.* dream
522 つらい tsurai *i-adj.* hard, difficult, painful
524 どちら dochira *pron.* where; which; who
526 起こる okoru *v.* happen, occur, take place
527 我々 wareware *pron.* we
528 (お)母さん (o)-kaa-san *n.* mother, Mom
529 立てる tateru *v.* stand, set up, put up
530 最も mottomo *adv.* most, extremely
531 色 iro *n.* color
532 探す sagasu *v.* look for, search for, seek
533 ちゃんと chanto *adv.* exactly, regularly, properly
535 三つ mit-tsu *n.* three
536 てほしい te hoshii *cp.* want/ask someone to do
537 いただく itadaku *v.* get, receive (humble)
538 売る uru *v.* sell
542 でございます de gozai masu *cp.* be (formal)
544 夏 natsu *n.* summer
545 よる yoru *v.* be due to
549 ずつ ...zutsu *p.* each, ... by ...
550 母親 hahaoya *n.* mother
551 取り敢えず toriaezu *adv.* for the time being; at once
552 ところが tokoroga *conj.* however
554 様々 samazama *na-adj.* various, all kinds of
555 答える kotaeru *v.* answer, respond
556 過ごす sugosu *v.* spend, live

557 上がる agaru v. go up, rise; end; get nervous
561 それでも soredemo conj. but, still
563 笑い warai n. laugh, laughter
566 動く ugoku v. move; work (machine)
568 加える kuwaeru v. add, include
569 困る komaru v. have difficulty, be in trouble
570 取れる toreru v. come off; be removed
573 比べる kuraberu v. compare, contrast
576 引く hiku v. pull, draw, lead; subtract
579 離れる hanareru v. separate; leave; be away from
580 火 hi n. fire
586 越える koeru v. cross over, go over
587 図る hakaru v. attempt; plan; strive
589 奴 yatsu n. guy, fellow
590 はっきり hakkiri adv. clearly, certainly
591 怖い kowai i-adj. frightening, scary; terrified
594 思い出す omoidasu v. remember
596 酒 sake n. alcohol, sake, rice wine
598 お前 omae n. you (colloquial)
599 守る mamoru v. protect, defend; keep, obey
601 回る mawaru v. spin, turn, go around; go via
602 広い hiroi i-adj. wide, broad, large
603 猫 neko n. cat
604 向こう mukou n. other side; over there
606 調べる shiraberu v. investigate; look up; examine; check
607 のぼる noboru v. go up, rise; reach
609 のみ nomi p. only, merely
610 向ける mukeru v. turn, point
611 落ちる ochiru v. fall, drop
612 だが daga conj. but, however
613 決まる kimaru v. be decided
614 起こす okosu v. wake; raise; cause
615 場 ba n. field; place; occasion
616 いずれ izure adv. anyway, sooner or later pron. either
619 打つ utsu v. hit, strike, beat
621 夫 otto n. husband
623 数 kazu n. number
625 割と wari to adv. comparatively, rather
627 通う kayou v. attend, go to, commute
628 申し上げる moushiageru v. tell, say (humble)
630 述べる noberu v. describe, say, state
632 さえ sae p. even; besides; if only
636 きっと kitto adv. surely, certainly
637 どうして doushite adv. why
638 歌う utau v. sing
639 なお nao adv. more, still

640 幾つ ikutsu n. how many, how old
641 ぞ zo p. disc. EMPHASIS
642 ほしい hoshii i-adj. want, desire
645 歌 uta n. song
646 開ける akeru v. open
647 互い tagai n. each other
648 着る kiru v. put on, wear
649 違い chigai n. difference
650 しっかり shikkari adv. hard, tight
651 過ぎる sugiru v. pass, exceed
653 思い出 omoide n. memory, reminiscence
654 しばらく shibaraku adv. for a while, a minute, for a long time
657 君 kimi n. you
658 笑う warau v. laugh; smile
659 いくら ikura adv. how much, however
660 魚 sakana n. fish
662 父親 chichioya n. father
663 どれ dore pron. which
664 見付ける mitsukeru v. find, look for
665 関わる kakawaru v. concern, affect, be involved
668 味 aji n. flavor, taste
669 深い fukai i-adj. deep
670 伝える tsutaeru v. tell; deliver; hand down
672 集まる atsumaru v. gather, crowd
674 流れる nagareru v. flow, float, pass
677 進める susumeru v. advance, move forward
678 含める fukumeru v. include, add
679 致す itasu v. do (humble)
680 着く tsuku v. arrive, reach
681 厳しい kibishii i-adj. strict, hard
682 女の子 onna no ko n. girl
684 おる oru v. be, exist (humble)
688 限り kagiri n. limit
689 いらっしゃる irassharu v. come, go (honorific); be (honorific)
691 可愛い kawaii i-adj. cute, nice, lovely
696 ものすごい monosugoi i-adj. terrible adv. terribly
697 合う au v. fit, suit, agree
698 済む sumu v. end, finish
699 通る tooru v. pass, go along
700 大人 otona n. adult
706 島 shima n. island
708 驚く odoroku v. be surprised
711 元々 motomoto adv. from the first, originally
712 素晴らしい subarashii i-adj. wonderful, marvelous

713 座る suwaru *v.* sit
714 定める sadameru *v.* provide; stipulate, decide
716 楽しみ tanoshimi *n.* pleasure, enjoyment
717 考え kangae *n.* idea, thought
719 たまたま tamatama *adv.* accidentally, by chance
720 古い furui *i-adj.* old
721 さ sa *p. disc.* ATTRACT ATTENTION
724 ただし tadashi *conj.* but, however, though
725 常 tsune *n.* way *adv.* always, usually
726 より yori *adv.* more, better
727 つもり tsumori *n.* intention
728 考え方 kangaekata *n.* way of thinking, attitude
731 元 moto *n.* beginning; original
733 低い hikui *i-adj.* low, short
734 びっくり(する) bikkuri(suru) *n.* surprise *v.* be surprised, be amazed
735 作り方 tsukurikata *n.* how to make
737 現われる arawareru *v.* appear, come into sight
738 聞こえる kikoeru *v.* hear; sound
741 やっと yatto *adv.* at last
742 思える omoeru *v.* it seems that
743 明らか akiraka *na-adj.* clear, obvious
744 つつ tsutsu *p. conj.* while doing; though
746 振り返る furikaeru *v.* turn one's head, look back
747 初め hajime *n.* beginning
749 息子 musuko *n.* son
750 限る kagiru *v.* limit, restrict
751 似る niru *v.* look like, resemble
752 悲しい kanashii *i-adj.* sad, unhappy
753 雨 ame *n.* rain
755 詳しい kuwashii *i-adj.* detailed, know well, in detail
757 ひどい hidoi *i-adj.* cruel, serious, terrible
758 昨日 kinou *n.* yesterday
759 下りる oriru *v.* go down; come down
761 まあ maa *adv.* Oh!, Well, Now
762 喜ぶ yorokobu *v.* be glad, rejoice
764 迎える mukaeru *v.* go to meet, invite, receive
765 耳 mimi *n.* ear
767 動き ugoki *n.* movement, action, motion
769 では dewa *conj.* then, well
770 てあげる te ageru *cp.* do something for somebody
772 立場 tachiba *n.* position, standpoint, situation
773 基づく motozuku *v.* be based
774 間 ma *n.* time, interval; space
775 ことがある koto ga aru *cp.* have done; there are sometimes
776 痛い itai *i-adj.* painful, hurt
777 お父さん o-tou-san *n.* father
778 辺り atari *n.* area around
779 てやる te yaru *cp.* do something for somebody/something
781 乗せる noseru *v.* take on, put on, pick up
783 白い shiroi *i-adj.* white
784 川 kawa *n.* river, stream
785 用いる mochiiru *v.* use, adopt
786 隣り tonari *n.* next door, next
789 妻 tsuma *n.* wife
790 冬 fuyu *n.* winter
792 もと moto *n.* under
794 繰り返す kurikaesu *v.* repeat, do over again
795 泣く naku *v.* cry
796 七 nana *num.* seven
797 手紙 tegami *n.* letter
798 出かける dekakeru *v.* go out, leave
804 おそらく osoraku *adv.* probably, likely
806 軽い karui *i-adj.* light, slight
807 払う harau *v.* pay; sweep away
808 つながる tsunagaru *v.* be connected, be related
809 船 fune *n.* ship, boat
811 きっかけ kikkake *n.* opportunity, motive
813 亡くなる nakunaru *v.* die, pass away
814 止める tomeru *v.* stop
821 触れる fureru *v.* touch; experience
822 飼う kau *v.* keep, have, breed
823 しゃべる shaberu *v.* talk, chat
825 さす sasu *v.* shine; pour; put
826 やり方 yarikata *n.* way of doing, how to, approach
832 殺す korosu *v.* kill
834 神 kami *n.* God, deity, spirit
835 暮らす kurasu *v.* live
836 飛ぶ tobu *v.* fly
837 終わり owari *n.* end
839 怒る okoru *v.* get angry
841 んと nto *interj.* well
842 建物 tatemono *n.* building
846 止まる tomaru *v.* stop
851 学ぶ manabu *v.* learn
853 首 kubi *n.* neck, head; firing, sacking (of an employee)
855 ゆっくり yukkuri *adv.* slowly, leisurely; plenty of time

856 目指す mezasu *v.* aim, go toward
857 したがって shitagatte *conj.* accordingly, consequently
859 成す nasu *v.* form, constitute
860 集める atsumeru *v.* gather, collect
861 失う ushinau *v.* lose
862 光 hikari *n.* light
863 並ぶ narabu *v.* line, stand in line
865 とく toku *aux.* [shortened form of "te oku"]
867 美しい utsukushii *i-adj.* beautiful
869 優しい yasashii *i-adj.* gentle, tender, kind, friendly
871 後ろ ushiro *n.* behind, back
873 異なる kotonaru *v.* be different
875 新た arata *na-adj.* another
877 お婆さん o-baa-san *n.* old lady; grandmother
878 至る itaru *v.* lead to, get
880 育てる sodateru *v.* bring up, train, develop
886 語る kataru *v.* talk, tell
887 胸 mune *n.* chest, heart
888 頼む tanomu *v.* ask, order
891 広がる hirogaru *v.* spread, stretch
892 きちんと kichin to *adv.* precisely, accurately, neatly
893 そちら sochira *pron.* your place; there; you
894 勝つ katsu *v.* win, defeat
896 捨てる suteru *v.* throw away, abandon
897 幸せ shiawase *na-adj.* happy *n.* happiness; fortune, luck
898 通す tousu *v.* pass, show ... into
899 横 yoko *n.* side, beside
900 伴う tomonau *v.* accompany, involve
901 命 inochi *n.* life
902 流れ nagare *n.* stream, flow, current
903 育つ sodatsu *v.* grow up
904 ちなみに chinamini *conj.* by the way, incidentally
907 馬 uma *n.* horse
910 風 kaze *n.* wind
915 おかしい okashii *i-adj.* funny, amusing
918 張る haru *v.* stretch, put up
921 かしら kashira *p. disc.* I wonder
922 すなわち sunawachi *conj.* that is (to say), namely
927 許す yurusu *v.* allow, permit, forgive
931 食べ物 tabemono *n.* food
932 借りる kariru *v.* borrow, rent
933 だけれど dakeredo *conj.* despite, though
936 や ya *aux.* COPULA (dialectal)
937 月 tsuki *n.* month; moon
938 世の中 yo no naka *n.* world, society
940 春 haru *n.* spring
941 旅 tabi *n.* trip, journey
943 寒い samui *i-adj.* cold
949 申す mousu *v.* say, be (humble)
950 押す osu *v.* push, press
953 負ける makeru *v.* lose, be beaten
956 そば soba *n.* side, beside
957 減る heru *v.* decrease, become less
960 焼く yaku *v.* roast, bake
961 たまに tama ni *adv.* occasionally, once in a while
962 慣れる nareru *v.* get used to
963 もしくは moshikuwa *conj.* or, otherwise
964 出会う deau *v.* meet, come across
966 自ら mizukara *n.* personally, oneself, own
969 たび tabi *n.* every time
970 付き合う tsukiau *v.* associate with, go out with, go along with
974 振る furu *v.* wave, shake, swing
977 秋 aki *n.* autumn, fall
978 明るい akarui *i-adj.* bright, light; cheerful
982 従う shitagau *v.* obey, follow
984 占める shimeru *v.* occupy, account for
985 まさに masani *adv.* exactly
988 大きさ ooki-sa *n.* size
993 むしろ mushiro *adv.* rather, if anything
995 名 na *n.* name
997 まるで marude *adv.* just like, quite
998 運ぶ hakobu *v.* carry, transport, move
999 こともある koto mo aru *cp.* sometimes, can be
1000 てはいけない、ちゃいけない te wa ikenai, cha ikenai *cp.* must not, should not

2漢 *kango* (Chinese origin)

33 よう you *aux.* INDUCEMENT
72 自分 jibun *n.* oneself
91 方 hou *n.* direction, way; side
97 本当 hontou *n.* truth, right
121 風 fuu *na-adj.* style, type, way, like
129 非常 hijou *na-adj.* very, extremely
130 気 ki *n.* mind, heart
144 一 ichi *num.* one
147 一番 ichi-ban *adv.* number one, first, most
148 二 ni *num.* two
151 必要 hitsuyou *na-adj.* necessary *n* necessity
156 僕 boku *pron.* I (used by male speakers)

166 結構 kekkou *adv.* quite *na-adj.* good
167 問題 mondai *n.* problem, question
180 人間 ningen *n.* human being, man
183 時間 jikan *n.* time
201 意味(する) imi(suru) *n.* meaning, sense *v.* mean
207 三 san *num.* three
208 最初 saisho *n.* first
215 最近 saikin *n.* recently, lately
222 一緒 issho *n.* together, with
223 生活(する) seikatsu(suru) *n.* life *v.* live
227 現在 genzai *n.* present time, now
238 大変 taihen *na-adj.* serious, terrible; hard, difficult
240 会社 kaisha *n.* company, firm
242 実際 jissai *n.* actually, in fact
243 先生 sensei *n.* teacher
257 たくさん takusan *adv.* many, much
259 大体 daitai *adv.* almost, nearly
260 もちろん mochiron *adv.* of course, needless to say
274 当時 touji *n.* then, at that time
280 普通 futsuu *na-adj.* normal, regular, ordinary, common
282 最後 saigo *n.* last, end
285 今度 kondo *n.* this time, next time
291 結局 kekkyoku *adv.* after all, in the end, finally
294 女性 josei *n.* woman, female
295 学校 gakkou *n.* school
302 世界 sekai *n.* world
303 状態 joutai *n.* state, conditions
306 全然 zenzen *adv.* (not) at all; utterly, completely
317 以上 ijou *n.* more than; mentioned above; since
318 関係 kankei *n.* relationship, connection
320 たぶん tabun *adv.* probably, perhaps, maybe
324 電話(する) denwa(suru) *n.* telephone, call *v.* phone, call
327 本 hon *n.* book
333 別 betsu *na-adj.* separate, different
338 全部 zenbu *adv.* all, whole, entire
341 きれい kirei *na-adj.* beautiful, pretty; clean
343 毎日 mainichi *adv.* every day
347 家族 kazoku *n.* family
349 部分 bubun *n.* part, section
350 一度 ichi-do *n.* once
351 結果 kekka *n.* result

353 状況 joukyou *n.* state of affairs, situation
354 時代 jidai *n.* time, era
356 他 hoka *n.* another, other
368 方法 houhou *n.* way, method
370 説明(する) setsumei(suru) *n.* explanation *v.* explain
373 ちょうど choudo *adv.* just, exactly
374 当然 touzen *adv., n.* naturally, as a matter of course
375 大学 daigaku *n.* university, college
377 実 jitsu *n.* truth, true, real
385 勉強(する) benkyou(suru) *n.* study *v.* learn, study
393 大事 daiji *na-adj.* important, serious
398 理由 riyuu *n.* reason
400 簡単 kantan *na-adj.* easy
403 今回 konkai *n.* this time
405 人生 jinsei *n.* life
407 内容 naiyou *n.* contents
409 経験(する) keiken(suru) *n.* experience *v.* experience
411 点 ten *n.* point, score
412 自然 shizen *n.* nature *na-adj.* natural *adv.* naturally
415 一応 ichiou *adv.* at first glance; at least, just
417 利用(する) riyou(suru) *n.* use, utilization *v.* utilize
419 一杯 ip-pai *n., adv.* cup(ful), glass(ful), be full of, a lot of
423 存在(する) sonzai(suru) *n.* existence *v.* exist
424 絶対 zettai *n., adv.* absolute, absolutely, whatever
425 日本人 nihon-jin, nippon-jin *n.* Japanese (person)
426 大切 taisetsu *na-adj.* important
431 写真 shashin *n.* picture, photo
433 だんだん dandan *adv.* gradually, more and more, less and less
436 五 go *num.* five
439 英語 eigo *n.* English (language)
446 時期 jiki *n.* time, period, season
447 逆 gyaku *n., na-adj.* contrary, opposite
453 有名 yuumei *na-adj.* famous, well-known
460 程度 teido *n.* degree, grade, level, limit
468 影響(する) eikyou(suru) *n.* influence *v.* affect, influence
469 病院 byouin *n.* hospital, clinic
473 情報 jouhou *n.* information
475 友人 yuujin *n.* friend

479 一回 ik-kai *n.* once
480 十分 juubun *na-adj.* enough, sufficient *adv.* fully, sufficiently, adequately
483 無人島 mujin-tou *n.* uninhabited island
485 重要 juuyoo *na-adj.* important
489 結婚(する) kekkon(suru) *n.* marriage *v.* marry, get married
492 歴史 rekishi *n.* history
494 音楽 ongaku *n.* music
500 駅 eki *n.* station
503 映画 eiga *n.* movie
505 客 kyaku *n.* guest, visitor; customer
506 質問(する) shitsumon(suru) *n.* question *v.* question
508 地域 chiiki *n.* region, area
514 一日 ichi-nichi *n.* a day, the day, one day
517 図 zu *n.* drawing, figure, diagram
518 紹介(する) shoukai(suru) *n.* introduction *v.* introduce
523 規定(する) kitei(suru) *n.* regulations, stipulations *v.* prescribe
525 中心 chuushin *n.* center
534 興味 kyoumi *n.* interest
539 変化(する) henka(suru) *n.* change *v.* change, vary
540 印象 inshou *n.* impression
541 作品 sakuhin *n.* work, production
543 参加(する) sanka(suru) *n.* participation *v.* take part in, participate
546 理解(する) rikai(suru) *n.* understanding *v.* understand
547 事件 jiken *n.* incident, event
553 目的 mokuteki *n.* purpose
558 一方 ippou *n.* one side *conj.* on the other hand
559 病気 byouki *n.* sickness, illness
560 心配(する) shinpai(suru) *na-adj.* anxious, worried *n.* anxiety, worry, care *v.* worry, be anxious
564 午後 gogo *n.* afternoon, p.m.
565 後 go *n.* after, later, since
567 主人 shujin *n.* shop owner; husband
571 環境 kankyou *n.* environment
572 対応(する) taiou(suru) *n.* correspondence, response *v.* respond to
574 高校 koukou *n.* high school
575 食事(する) shokuji(suru) *n.* meal *v.* have a meal
577 辺 hen *n.* region, area around

581 実施(する) jisshi(suru) *n.* operation *v.* enforce, conduct
582 今後 kongo *adv.* in the future, from now on
583 社会 shakai *n.* society
584 練習(する) renshuu(suru) *n.* practice, training *v.* practice, train
585 使用(する) shiyou(suru) *n.* use *v.* use
588 企業 kigyou *n.* company, business
592 例 rei *n.* example
593 絵 e *n.* picture, painting
597 原因 gen'in *n.* cause
600 小学校 shou-gakkou *n.* elementary school, primary school
605 同時 douji *n.* simultaneous, at the same time
608 六 roku *num.* six
618 対象 taishou *n.* object, target, subject
620 以前 izen *n.* before, formerly
622 確認(する) kakunin(suru) *n.* confirmation *v.* confirm
624 意見 iken *n.* opinion, idea
626 大丈夫 daijoubu *na-adj.* safe, all right
629 可能性 kanousei *n.* possibility
631 是非 zehi *adv.* by all means, please; definitely, certainly
633 三人 san-nin *n.* three people
634 料理(する) ryouri(suru) *n.* cooking, dish *v.* cook
635 一部 ichibu *n.* part
643 新聞 shinbun *n.* newspaper
652 記憶(する) kioku(suru) *n.* memory *v.* memorize
655 基本的 kihon-teki *na-adj.* basic, fundamental
656 四月 shi-gatsu *n.* April
661 旅行(する) ryokou(suru) *n.* journey, travel *v.* travel
666 無理 muri *na-adj.* unreasonable, impossible; compulsory
667 健康 kenkou *n.* health
671 自由 jiyuu *n.* freedom, liberty *na-adj.* free
673 戦争 sensou *n.* war
675 男性 dansei *n.* male, man
676 電車 densha *n.* train
685 活動(する) katsudou(suru) *n.* activity *v.* be active
686 不安 fuan *n.* anxiety, concern *na-adj.* uneasy, insecure
687 三十分 sanjup-pun, sanjip-pun *n.* thirty minutes
690 可能 kanou *na-adj.* possible

692 際 sai *n.* when, in case of
693 途中 tochuu *n.* on the way; in the middle of
694 研究(する) kenkyuu(suru) *n.* research, study *v.* do research, study
695 様子 yousu *n.* state of affairs, situation; appearance
701 期待(する) kitai(suru) *n.* expectation *v.* expect
702 事実 jijitsu *n.* fact, actuality
703 せい sei *n.* fault, cause for blame, because of
704 一年 ichi-nen *n.* one year
705 一体 ittai *n., adv.* how, what, why, who
709 動物 doubutsu *n.* animal
715 機会 kikai *n.* opportunity
722 面 men *n.* side; page; surface
723 三月 san-gatsu *n.* March
730 意識(する) ishiki(suru) *n.* consciousness, awareness *v.* be conscious
732 行動(する) koudou(suru) *n.* action, act *v.* act, behave
736 元気 genki *n.* health, vigor *na-adj.* lively, vigorous, well
739 曲 kyoku *n.* piece (music), song, tune
740 過去 kako *n.* past
745 土地 tochi *n.* land, ground
748 評価(する) hyouka(suru) *n.* evaluation *v.* evaluate
756 二十一世紀 nijuuisseiki *n.* twenty-first century
763 便利 benri *n.* convenience *na-adj.* useful, convenient
766 表現(する) hyougen(suru) *n.* expression *v.* express
768 注意(する) chuui(suru) *n.* attention *v.* notice, be careful
771 雰囲気 fun'iki *n.* atmosphere, ambience
780 将来 shourai *n.* future
782 自転車 jitensha *n.* bicycle
787 普段 fudan *n.* usually, ordinarily
788 法律 houritsu *n.* law
791 具体的 gutai-teki *na-adj.* specific, concrete
793 発生(する) hassei(suru) *n.* occurrence *v.* occur, happen
799 努力(する) doryoku(suru) *n.* effort *v.* make an effort
800 増加(する) zouka(suru) *n.* increase, gain *v.* increase, grow
801 判断(する) handan(suru) *n.* judgment *v.* judge
802 両親 ryoushin *n.* (both) parents
803 残念 zannen *na-adj.* disappointing, regrettable
805 家庭 katei *n.* home, household, family
810 九月 ku-gatsu *n.* September
812 授業 jugyou *n.* class, lesson at school
815 不思議 fushigi *n.* wonder *na-adj.* wonderful, strange, mysterious
816 茶 cha *n.* tea; brown
817 直接 chokusetsu *n., adv.* directly, direct
819 効果 kouka *n.* effectiveness, effect
820 現実 genjitsu *n.* reality, actuality
824 国民 kokumin *n.* nation, people (of country), public
827 ずいぶん zuibun *adv.* very, pretty, quite
829 十月 juu-gatsu *n.* October
830 気分 kibun *n.* feeling, mood
831 開発(する) kaihatsu(suru) *n.* development *v.* develop
833 特徴 tokuchou *n.* characteristic, feature
838 雑誌 zasshi *n.* magazine
840 整備(する) seibi(suru) *n.* maintenance, service *v.* prepare
843 発見(する) hakken(suru) *n.* discovery *v.* discover
844 相談(する) soudan(suru) *n.* consultation *v.* consult
845 連絡(する) renraku(suru) *n.* connection, contact *v.* contact
847 一生懸命 isshoukenmei *na-adj.* hard, as hard as one can
848 用意(する) youi(suru) *n.* preparation *v.* prepare
849 変 hen *na-adj.* strange, unusual, funny
850 十二月 juuni-gatsu *n.* December
852 突然 totsuzen *adv.* suddenly
854 設定(する) settei(suru) *n.* establishment *v.* establish, set
858 一月 ichi-gatsu *n.* January
864 八月 hachi-gatsu *n.* August
866 七月 shichi-gatsu *n.* July
868 五月 go-gatsu *n.* May
872 六月 roku-gatsu *n.* June
874 十一月 juuichi-gatsu *n.* November
876 飛行機 hikouki *n.* airplane
879 午前 gozen *n.* morning, a.m.
881 種類 shurui *n.* kind, sort, variety
882 商品 shouhin *n.* goods, item of merchandise
889 体験(する) taiken(suru) *n.* experience *v.* experience, have experience of

890 材料 zairyou *n.* materials, ingredient
895 運動（する） undou(suru) *n.* exercise *v.* exercise, move
905 予定（する） yotei(suru) *n.* plan, schedule *v.* plan
908 完全 kanzen *na-adj.* perfect, complete
909 学生 gakusei *n.* student
911 性格 seikaku *n.* character, personality
912 死 shi *n.* death
913 位置（する） ichi(suru) *n.* position, location *v.* be located
914 発展（する） hatten(suru) *n.* development *v.* develop, expand
916 近所 kinjo *n.* neighborhood
917 一本 ip-pon *n.* one (long/cylindrical object}
919 ご飯 gohan *n.* rice, meal
920 危険 kiken *n.* danger, hazard *na-adj.* dangerous
923 海外 kaigai *n.* overseas, abroad, foreign
924 教育（する） kyouiku(suru) *n.* education *v.* educate
925 想像（する） souzou(suru) *n.* imagination, image *v.* imagine
928 表 hyou *n.* table, chart
929 文化 bunka *n.* culture
930 八 hachi *num.* eight
934 準備（する） junbi(suru) *n.* preparation *v.* prepare
935 二月 ni-gatsu *n.* February
942 二年 ni-nen *n.* two years
944 年 nen *n.* year
945 同様 douyou *na-adj.* similar, same
946 一般 ippan *n.* general
947 第一 dai-ichi *n.* first
948 三年 san-nen *n.* three years
951 責任 sekinin *n.* responsibility
952 選択（する） sentaku(suru) *n.* selection, choice *v.* choose
954 技術 gijutsu, gijitsu *n.* technique, skill
955 一般的 ippan-teki *na-adj.* general, common, ordinary
958 記事 kiji *n.* article
959 本人 honnin *n.* person himself/herself, person in question
965 推進（する） suishin(suru) *n.* propulsion *v.* promote, drive
967 作業（する） sagyou(suru) *n.* operation, work *v.* work

971 半分 hanbun *n.* half
972 条件 jouken *n.* condition
973 医者 isha *n.* doctor
975 関心 kanshin *n.* interest
976 表示（する） hyouji(suru) *n.* indication *v.* display, indicate
979 趣味 shumi *n.* hobby
980 生徒 seito *n.* student, pupil
981 相当（する） soutou(suru) *na-adj.* considerable *n.* equivalence *v.* be equivalent *adv.* considerably, pretty
983 検討（する） kentou(suru) *n.* consideration, discussion examination *v.* consider, discuss
986 選手 senshu *n.* player, athlete
987 以下 ika *n.* below, the following
989 調査（する） chousa(suru) *n.* investigation *v.* investigate, inquire, explore
990 分 bun *adv., n.* part, share, portion
991 実家 jikka *n.* one's parents' home
992 発表（する） happyou(suru) *n.* announcement, publication *v.* announce, publish
994 作成（する） sakusei(suru) *n., v.* make, create
996 確保（する） kakuho(suru) *n.* securement, reservation *v.* secure, maintain, guarantee

3 外 *gairaigo* (foreign loan word)

301 テーマ teema *n.* theme, subject
335 タイトル taitoru *n.* title
408 テレビ terebi *n.* television, TV
562 イメージ（する） imeeji(suru) *n.* image *v.* imagine, have an impression
617 ホテル hoteru *n.* hotel
683 パソコン pasokon *n.* personal computer
729 ニュース nyuusu *n.* news
760 メール meeru *n.* e-mail
818 バス basu *n.* bus
870 タバコ tabako *n.* cigarette, tobacco
939 インターネット intaanetto *n.* Internet

4 混 *konseigo* (hybrid: *wago* + *kango*)

138 感じ kanji *n.* feeling, impression; atmosphere
182 ございます (＜ござる) gozai masu *v.* [very polite form of "de aru"]
206 かなり kanari *adv.* considerably, rather
210 感じる kanjiru *v.* feel
216 特に tokuni *adv.* especially, particularly
231 気持ち kimochi *n.* feeling
244 彼女 kanojo *pron.* she; girlfriend

270 に対して ni taishite *cp.* to, toward; for; against
275 場所 basho *n.* place, spot
348 に対する ni taisuru *cp.* to; for; against
404 に関する ni kansuru *cp.* be concerned with, be related to
448 頑張る ganbaru *v.* do one's best
476 だめ dame *na-adj.* useless, hopeless, impossible
578 要するに yousuru ni *conj.* in short, to sum up
595 に関して ni kanshite *cp.* about, regarding, concerning
644 気付く kizuku *v.* notice, become aware
707 描く egaku *v.* draw; describe
710 何度 nando *n.* how many times, how often
718 信じる shinjiru *v.* believe, trust
754 自分達 jibun-tachi *n.* themselves; ourselves
828 日本語 nihon-go, nippon-go *n.* Japanese language
883 生じる shoujiru, shouzuru *v.* bring about, cause, arise
885 大好き daisuki *na-adj.* love
906 決して kesshite *adv.* never, by no means
926 実は jitsu wa *adv.* actually, in fact
968 私自身 watashi-jishin *n.* myself, my own

5固 Proper names
120 日本 nihon, nippon *n.* Japan
312 アメリカ amerika *n.* America
359 東京 toukyou *n.* Tokyo
464 昭和 shouwa *n.* Showa era
516 平成 heisei *n.* Heisei era
548 中国 chuugoku *n.* China
884 イギリス igirisu *n.* United Kingdom, Britain, England